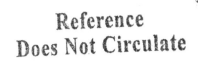

Social Trends & Indicators USA

Volume 4:
Crime & Justice

Social Trends & Indicators USA

Volume 4:
Crime & Justice

Arsen J. Darnay, Managing Editor

Robert Lazich, Editor

Helen S. Fisher, Monique D. Magee,
Joyce Piwowarski, and Linda Schmittroth,
Assistant Editors

GALE®

THOMSON
————★————™
GALE

Detroit • New York • San Diego • San Francisco • Cleveland • New Haven, Conn. • Waterville, Maine • London • Munich

Social Trends & Indicators USA
Crime & Justice

Robert Lazich, Editor

Project Editor
Amanda C. Quick

Editorial
Arsen J. Darnay, Helen S. Fisher, Monique D. Magee, Joyce Piwowarski, Linda Schmittroth

Product Design
Pamela A. E. Galbreath

Manufacturing
NeKita McKee

ISBN 0-7876-5906-1 (set)
ISBN 0-7876-5907-X (v.1)
ISBN 0-7876-5908-8 (v.2)
ISBN 0-7876-5909-6 (v.3)
ISBN 0-7876-5910-X (v.4)
Library of Congress Control Number: 2002117074

Printed in the United States of America
10 9 8 7 6 5 4 3 2 1

TABLE OF CONTENTS

Introduction

Upon this gifted age, in its dark hour,
Rains from the sky a meteoric shower
Of facts ... they lie unquestioned, uncombined.
Wisdom enough to leech us of our ill
Is daily spun; but there exists no loom
To weave it into fabric.
                                        Edna St. Vincent Millay

Social Trends & Indicators – The Concept

The idea for this series, *Social Trends & Indicators USA*, arose because we are inundated by statistics, but the meaning of the numbers is often elusive. We are getting outrageously obese, for instance, yet we are living longer. Layoffs are devastating sectors, yet the economy seems to be booming. We are the most educated society on earth, yet Johnny can't read. The crime rate is dropping, but we do not feel safe. The workweek is shrinking, yet we never have time.

The Federal Government's many statistical agencies produce a great wealth of superb data. We are undoubtedly the best documented and most measured society that has ever existed. Newspapers attractively box factoids to amaze or to alarm us. Competing interests marshal their data to make their cases, often omitting numbers that do not bolster the argument. Statistics become catch-phrases. The rich fabric of our national experience is thinned by the speed and noise of the mass media attempting to "infotain" us.

But statistics out of context — and without historical background — are often less than informative. They can be confusing and lead to wrong conclusions. Whereas a properly developed presentation on an issue, using what numbers are available, is often very revealing, at times sobering, and frequently reassuring. A balanced presentation of facts within context can serve the public by illuminating hidden facets of an issue and, as often happens, show that beneath the hoopla and the hype is a deeper-lying demographic movement.

This series was born from such considerations, and from our long experience in dealing with, and publishing, statistics. The idea, simply, was to present statistics in context, with as much historical background as possible, in order to answer questions and to pinpoint trends.

Organization of the Series

Work & Leisure deals with the whole economic realm — work, productivity, employment, unemployment, income, and fringe benefits — and with how we organize our leisure time. *Community & Education* covers who we are, where we live, all kinds of family structures, race and ethnicity, politics, religion, and the vast subject of education and the many issues it encompasses. *Crime & Justice*, the current volume in the series, attempts to shine a statistical light into the darker woods of our nature — victimization, crime, law enforcement, the drug war, terrorism, the justice system, and how all these matters affect us. *Health & Sickness* takes on the body and the mind and what can go wrong with us — our state of health and illness, old and emerging diseases, risky behaviors, prevention and treatment, our preoccupation with drugs, disability, sexuality, and the people and institutions that deal with us when we are ailing.

Each volume, of course, is divided into chapters. In their totality, the chapters present a fairly complete picture of the subject in each volume. But the objective is not to create a compendium on health and sickness, for instance, but to deal with issues of current concern. Dealing with the issues of today, of course, often causes us to look backwards — all the way back to the 19th century sometimes. But the focus is on current trends and on indicators of what is likely to happen tomorrow.

Each chapter is divided into several so-called "panels" (see below). Panels tend to come in two flavors: those that provide background information on a subject, including general trends, and those aimed specifically at answering a question: "Is government really growing? Which parts? Why?" "Will future jobs all require an advanced degree? No? Why not?" "Why are today's children suddenly so frequently 'learning disabled'?"

The Mode of Presentation: The Panel and the Tables

Each volume in the series presents statistical information in two forms. In Part I of the book, data are presented in graphic format followed by explanations and commentaries.

The principal unit of presentation in Part I is thus a "panel" — one topic, one main graphic, and a commentary of usually no more than two pages. Panels sometimes also feature additional graphics and statistics laid out in tabular format. The text is a discussion of the topic. It may feature footnotes for additional comment. A source note concludes each panel citing the sources used. In most instances, web addresses are provided pointing to sites where the user can obtain additional information.

Sometimes a single panel is not sufficient to develop a subject. In that case, the discussion continues with another panel, with its own graphic. Groups of panels form chapters, and each chapter has a brief introduction.

Users of such works as *Social Trends & Indicators USA* find graphics a vivid way to show data, but they want to see the actual numbers as well. For this reason, *Crime & Justice* produces all of the data graphed in Part II, the Data Presentation. Here, statistical data are presented in tabular format. Frequently only the data used to create the graphics are shown. Sometimes, however, additional time series are provided as well for a more comprehensive documentation of the subject. Tables in Part II are organized by chapters for rapid access. These chapters are organized to correspond to panels in Part I. The tables are also fully indexed.

Accessing Information

Each volume of *Social Trends & Indicators USA* provides a Table of Contents and an Index. The Table of Contents will guide the user to appropriate chapters. The Index lists important concepts, names, institutions, and issues. Page numbers cited refer to the pages where text or data can be found under the topic listed.

Sources of Information

Data presented in *Crime & Justice*, and in the other volumes, come predominantly, but not exclusively, from Federal or State statistical agencies. Data from not-for-profit organizations and from commercial sources are also sometimes shown. Sources of data are always referenced in footnotes or source notes. Where such data are copyrighted, the copyright notice is provided.

An important feature of this series is that data from different sources are analytically combined and presented together. A typical example might be to show birth data in combination with population data on women of child-bearing age. Another might be to show a flow of expenditures but rendered in constant dollars (for comparability year to year) — for which purpose index data from the Consumer Price Index (or the Gross Domestic Product deflator) may have been used to transform the dollar quantities. Data on alcohol, tobacco, and illegal drug consumption — derived from three sources — might be shown together.

Data were obtained using the Internet or from print sources. Web-based data are "sourced" showing the web site from which they were obtained. The links shown, however, are not guaranteed to be functioning at some later date. Most will be accessible because they are predominantly governmental sites. Historical data were obtained from the *Historical Statistics of the United States, Colonial Times to 1970*, published by the Bureau of the Census.

Authorship and Presentation

Crime & Justice was prepared by five individuals (three women, two men), each responsible for chapter-length segments of the book. The authors are all skilled statistical analysts but none is an expert on the subject presented. All members of the editorial group reviewed and discussed every panel contained in this work. Changes, revisions, and augmentation of the material took place as a consequence of these reviews. Finally, all materials were reviewed and edited by the senior editor in charge. However, no attempts were made — or thought to be desirable — to conform the presentational style of the authors to produce a uniform (and possibly bureaucratic-sounding) voice.

Our aim is to present often complicated and difficult subjects — as these are seen by the educated layperson — the view of the proverbial "man on the street." To the extent that expert opinion was required, it was obtained from the literature and is quoted in the panels. We made a serious effort to present as balanced a view as possible, resisting both the temptation to be politically correct and the temptation to range far off the reservation. No doubt people of all persuasions will find fault with something in these panels, all will find something to applaud.

How to Use this Book

Although *Crime & Justice* is, above all, a reference work, it is best approached by actually *reading* a chapter. Within a chapter, the different panels are closely related to develop the subject. The panels are relatively short. It is not difficult to peruse a chapter from beginning to end.

Use of a panel should begin with a close study of the graphic presented (only very few panels lack a graphic). Each graphic has a title. The meaning of the curves and bars is indicated in legends (or shown in the graph itself). Sometimes both the left and the right scale of the graphic is used to measure data sets that would not otherwise be visible. Please note that some of the graphics are in logarithmic scale. The log scale is used when the lowest value charted would be all but invisible — or in cases where the slope of curves is important to show how one set of data is growing more or less than the other. Some graphics are quite "busy," but a little study will well repay the effort. The general message is usually contained in the chart, although, in a few instances, the graphic is just a way of enticing the user to read the text.

Once the graphic is understood, the text will be more accessible. The objective of the text is to make clear what is depicted and then to add other information to put the subject into perspective. Sometimes parts of the information charted are also shown in tabular form in the text itself. This is done in those cases where the numerical values — not merely the pattern that they form — is of great importance. Sometimes additional, smaller graphics are shown to highlight additional aspects of the data or to present new information.

The user who wishes to look at the numbers charted can immediately refer to Part II, which presents data in tabular format.

The source note at the end of the panel may list one or more web sites for more information. The user might wish to be "distracted" into checking out those web sites — or continue on to the next panel until the entire subject is fully developed.

Introduction to this Volume – *Crime & Justice*

At the outset we may as well tell you what *Crime & Justice* doesn't cover. We do not deal even in a cursory manner with driving above the speed limit or parking in a no-parking zone. A large part of the day-to-day activity of our police forces and, to a lesser extent, the administrative organs of our lowest courts, concern themselves with traffic violations. We don't give them any ink at all. We make contact with traffic only in the case of drunken driving violations. We are similarly silent about civil law. The reader will not hear in this book about the massive lawsuits of states against the tobacco industry, labor litigation, patent infringements, contract law, bankruptcy, civil rights litigation, and many other subjects of that nature.

Crime & Justice is narrowly focused on serious crimes and lesser offenses. The most serious crime we cover is homicide, the least serious offense is loitering. We also cover special forms of lawlessness like drug law violations and terrorism. The focus may be narrow, but the subject is actually vast. At the individual level, we deal with victims of crime using statistics from the U.S. Department of Justice on "victimization." Similarly we use FBI statistics to look at offenses committed, taken from the *Uniform Crime Reports*. In fact the book kicks off with a look at these two different but related lenses through which the whole phenomenon of crime is viewed in the United States.

At the institutional level we deal with the big three organs of law enforcement: Police, the Law, and finally Corrections. Each of these specializations works closely together and each is present at all levels of government: municipal and county (the local level), state, and federal. The local cop has his counterpart in the state trooper, the trooper in the FBI agent at the federal level. The municipal court at one end of the spectrum has its counterpart in the Supreme Court. The local jail has its more serious counterpart in the state prison; at the peak of corrections is the federal penitentiary in Leavenworth, Kansas.

Crime itself is hierarchically arranged. At the top is violent crime, at the very top murder. A larger but lower level represents property crime. Lower yet, and most numerous, are other offenses variously categorized. A subset of crimes, the most serious, are grouped together as the indexed crimes — which, together, produce the crime rate that the media sometimes turn into stories. Most crimes (80% of all arrests) are not highlighted by the official crime reporting mechanisms. Most crimes, in fact, are not reported to the police at all (more than half). During the roughly 30-year period on which we report in this book, the crime rate rose sharply and then declined, with secondary peaks in the middle. Graphics in this book keep forming what look like mountains. Analogies to mountains have had a tendency to creep into our commentary.

Several broad themes have emerged from this research and its analysis. **Crime is down**. Crime is down by all measures and rather decisively, but this is from a peak never before reached in our history. Those interviewed for the Justice Department's victimization survey report experiencing less violence and much less property loss. Arrest reports collected by law enforcement agencies and fed to the FBI mirror this public perception, although at a reduced intensity. **Incarcerations rates are up**. In graphical depictions, they form a steeply rising slope. We have the distinction, in the U.S., of having the highest rates of incarceration of any country in the world. We imprison one quarter of all people behind bars in the world. We have introduced for-profit, privately run jails, and they are a booming industry. Ten percent of all non-Hispanic black males between 25 and 29 are currently in prison. **Our court systems are under pressure**. They have a difficult time in keeping up with the high rates of arrest we have experienced in recent years, with mandatory sentencing provisions, and with the tracking of people on probation and parole. Some courts have been forced to institute night courts. It is taking longer and longer to bring people to justice.

What has been going on? Those with mature experience in this field are very reluctant to provide definitive answers. Crime is a complex phenomenon arising from many factors. Some of the correlations are rather obvious, of course. Poor economic times and high rates of unemployment produce spikes in property crime. The 1990s have been boom times, and property crime rates inversely mirror that. Demographics and social factors — not least family stability, education, poverty — have a strong influence on violent crime rates. During the period covered, the Baby Boom generation passed through those years during which people, especially males, are most prone to commit violent crimes. But that does not explain things.

Although it may not be obvious to the majority of people living ordinary lives, we have been going through a period very much like Prohibition. We call it **the war on drugs**. Throughout this book, drugs keep surfacing as a major issue, possibly *the* issue of crime and justice in the 1970-2002 period. Many facets of the crime situation can be traced back to this war, not least spiking rates of homicide — echoing those during Prohibition — which reflect gang violence associated with the manufacture and distribution of crack cocaine. As crack lost its popularity, the murder rate also dropped. Use and distribution of drugs is centered in inner-city ghettos; drug consumption is a more wide-spread phenomenon. Prosecution of the war on drugs has fallen disproportionately on the black population. Prisons have filled with drug offenders, so much so that, today, one in five prisoners is behind bars for drugs, most for trafficking, the minority for possession. We try to shine as many floodlights on this phenomenon as possible.

The book is conventionally organized. We begin with an overview of crime and then take closer looks at violent and property crimes and then at lesser crimes and offenses. One chapter is dedicated to juveniles, safety in schools, child abuse, and related subjects. One chapter is devoted entirely to drugs, but drugs are also covered in a variety of other contexts. The index will guide the reader to all mentions of the subject. Next we look at the special subject of terrorism. The last three chapters deal with policing, prisons, and the legal system.

Much of the content of *Crime & Justice* leaves one with a sense of unease. Matters that particularly stand out include the heavy impact of crime on African Americans, both as victims and offenders. Another is the faddish nature of legislation, moving in waves, in reaction to specific events. The public is perhaps whiplashed by media panics to which the political structure responds or, conversely, elected officials respond to news gauging the impact of the news on the public. Data on drug use suggest massive public disobedience confronted by a grim law enforcement response, uneven sentencing requirements, and racially uneven outcomes. The massive incarceration rates remind us that more and more people will be pouring *out* of prisons as well as in, in coming years, in an era when rehabilitation, as we show, has lost its credibility.

Crime is down. But one has the uneasy feeling that it will soon be back up again. No final victories.

Comments and Suggestions

Those of us who have labored on *Crime & Justice* — and those who have suffered us while we did so — welcome your comments and suggestions. We have made every effort to be accurate, fair, and complete. No doubt we succeeded only in trying. Should errors have occurred, despite best efforts, they will be corrected in future editions. We shall be pleased to incorporate users' suggestions to the extent possible. To reach authors directly, please call Editorial Code and Data, Inc. at (248) 356-6990.

Please address other communications to:

Editor
Social Trends & Indicators USA
Crime & Justice
Gale
27500 Drake Road
Farmington Hills, MI 48331-3535
248-699-GALE
BusinessProducts@gale.com

Chapter 1

Crime Overview

Picture crime as the upper portion of a gradually rising mountain of lawlessness. The low foothills of this mountain are traffic violations too numerous to count — no one in fact does so at the national level. Next come offenses serious enough to merit arrest. The bulk of all arrests, however — for some 20 broad categories — are not serious enough to make it into the crime rate reported by the FBI — or the National Criminal Victimization Survey, another major tool of measurement. The upper reaches of this mountain — and at this height the number of incidents is lower but the seriousness of the crimes has soared — are the so-called "index crimes" that law enforcement agencies use to see whether or not "crime is up," as they say, or "the crime rate is dropping." The blood-red tip of this mountain is the most violent of crimes, homicide. The numbers are tiny, but the impact ultimate.

So much for measurement. But this mountain also has a shadowy companion, difficult to see. We can't measure it properly. A very large percentage of all crimes, except homicide, go unreported — but the government collects data to give us some indistinct idea of that other mountain hidden in the fog of people's fears, shame (in the case of rape), or indifference to smaller losses.

We begin this chapter by trying to give dimension to these mountains. We look at how crime is reported. Two major series are available. Both show that the crime rate is trending down. We deal first with violent crime — which is down since 1973 as measured by reported victimizations and up slightly as measured by police statistics. Next we look at property crime — which is down by both measures. In these introductory panels, we also characterize the components that make up the official, "indexed" crimes that yield the crime rate.

Next we turn to the much broader range of lesser offenses, measured by arrests. They make up more than 80% of all arrests. Drug-related crimes fall into this non-indexed category. Too bad. The dynamism in this field (arrests, budgets, incarcerations) owes much to the war on drugs. We note, in passing, that alcohol-related offenses are still substantially higher than drug offenses.

Because drugs are so much in the news, we take a look at trends in drug-related arrests and note that most arrests are for possession but most incarcerations are for sale or manufacture of illegal substances. We wind up with a look back 40 years and see the crime rate rising, then flattening, then dropping — as incarceration rates begin to climb and then to soar.

In the next two panels, we take a look at the offenders and notice that women are participating more in crime and that blacks are a disproportionate component of the so-called correctional population — people on probation or parole, in prison or in jail.

The last two panels attempt to portray the Justice System and its three major components — Police Protection, Judicial and Legal institutions, and Corrections. These exist at every level of government and get more or less emphasis depending on the level. We use employment and expenditures as two measures.

To summarize this chapter in a word or two, we might say that (1) lawlessness has increased sharply in the last two decades, by any measure, but that (2) the crime rate has been falling in recent years — because (3) substantial amounts of money have been spent and large numbers of people now work at preventing or punishing crime. As a consequence (4) the correctional population is at unprecedented levels — especially among blacks. These efforts have led to (5) spiraling expenditures on all aspects of criminal justice, but mostly on its tail end — legal institutions and corrections, not so much police. Finally, (6) women are showing their liberation by going into all kinds of activities outside the home — including crime.

Indexes of Crime

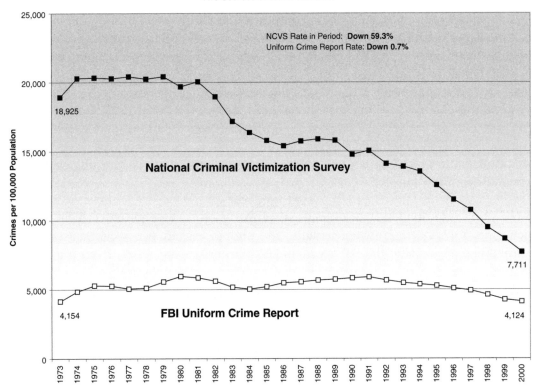

Two Sources of Crime Statistics

NCVS Rate in Period: **Down 59.3%**
Uniform Crime Report Rate: **Down 0.7%**

National Criminal Victimization Survey

FBI Uniform Crime Report

You would think that a nation able to land a man on the moon could measure the rate of crime in the nation. As a "can do" sort of nation, the difficult we do immediately. The impossible will take a bit of time.

We're not altogether sure how much crime actually takes place. Two ways are used to measure the crime rate, both under the aegis of the U.S. Department of Justice. The better known measure is that produced by the FBI and published annually as the **Uniform Crime Report**. It features an Index of Crime which is known as the crime rate. It is collected from law enforcement agencies in a uniform format and covers nearly 100% of all jurisdictions. The index measures murder and non-negligent manslaughter, forcible rape, robbery and aggravated assault, burglary, larceny/theft, vehicular theft, and arson. The measure is expressed as crime events per 100,000 population. Thus it is an index that can be compared one year to the next. This measure is also known as "reported crime" — because not all crimes are reported.

The Uniform Crime Report began its life in 1929. It was further refined in 1958 and is available from 1957 forward in the same general format.

The FBI collects data on many other crimes not included in the Crime Index — but, generally, when people or the media speak of the "crime rate" dropping or increasing, what is meant is the UCR and its index, broken into two components, violent and property crime. Other crime categories are offenses such as the sale or possession of drugs, prostitution and gambling, and offenses against the public order like drunkenness, vagrancy, driving while intoxicated, and so on. These are not used as a general index of crime.

To get a better feel for *actual* crime occurrence in the U.S. — including unreported crime — the Justice Department conducts the **National Crime Victimization Survey**. It has been under way since 1973. The graphic on the previous page displays both rates side by side. A glance reveals that there is much more crime than is reported. The NCVS series is sometimes spoken of as the "actual" or as the "estimated" crime rate.

To do this survey, Justice interviews 49,000 households twice a year, speaking to all members of the household aged 12 or older. A household participates for three years running and is then replaced by another. The sample of households is carefully drawn to be representative of the nation.

The NCVS is also divided into violent and property crime categories. Violent crime includes rape, robbery, aggravated assault, and simple assault (no weapon is involved). When publishing its data, the NCVS includes the murder rate, taken from the FBI's series. In the data shown in this panel, we have eliminated simple assault — which is not included in the FBI's index and would therefore exaggerate the gap between "actual" and "reported" crime as shown above.

Property crimes under NCVS are personal theft, burglary, theft, and car/truck theft. The NCVS, however, excludes commercial property crime whereas the FBI index includes it.

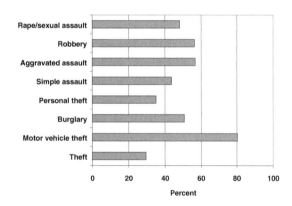

The percent of crimes reported to the police varies from a low of 29.4% for theft of objects from a car or a home to 80.4% for car theft. The data are from 2000. Reporting rates have improved over time, but only very slightly. Not including homicide, which is almost always reported, less than half of violent crime is reported (including simple assault, which is the largest category), and about 35% of household-level property crime. This suggests that the nation's experience of criminal loss and violence exists on two levels, a large and shadowy part of which is not officially recognized. The entire justice system exists to handle the smaller portion.

Both the estimated and official crime rates have been trending down. We shall explore that subject in detail in many ways throughout this book.

Sources: U.S. Department of Justice, Federal Bureau of Investigation, Uniform Crime Reports, and National Criminal Victimization Survey, both accessible from http://www.ojp.usdoj.gov/bjs/welcome.html.

Violent Crime

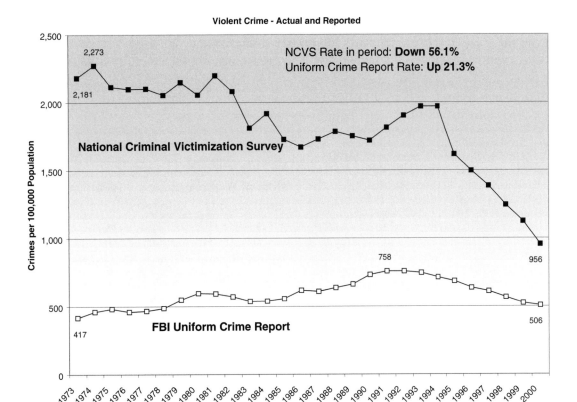

Violent Crime - Actual and Reported

NCVS Rate in period: **Down 56.1%**
Uniform Crime Report Rate: **Up 21.3%**

National Criminal Victimization Survey

2,273

2,181

FBI Uniform Crime Report

758

956

417

506

Crimes per 100,000 Population

In this graphic we are looking at about 12% of crimes — excluding, for the moment, lesser offenses; we shall deal with those later. In 2000, an estimated 956 people out of every 100,000 had some experience with serious violent crime — aggravated assault, robbery, and rape — or they were victims of murder or manslaughter. In this graphic, simple assault is excluded; if it were showing, the NCVS rate for violent crime for 2000 would be 2,736 — because 1,780 simple assaults where reported in the survey per 100,000 people.

Of the 956 reported serious violent crimes, 506 per 100,000 made it into the FBI's Uniform Crime Report. As shown in the previous panel, many crimes are not reported. The NCVS and FBI categories here are the same.

In the period shown, the NCVS rate peaked in 1974 and has been generally on the down-trend since. The FBI's peak came in 1991. Since then the rate has been steadily dropping, although preliminary data for 2001 indicate an up-tick. The estimated (NCVS) violent crime rate has been dropping uniformly and steeply since 1994.

When normalized as shown here — meaning that the values are expressed per 100,000 people — an increase in the violent crime means absolutely more violence not merely a greater number of crimes because the population is increasing. Similarly, a drop in violent crime is an absolute decrease in the "social war." Why does violent crime increase or decrease?

The explanation of crime is a hazardous and complex business. Much effort will be devoted to presenting speculations, correlations, and explanations in coming panels. To over-simplify, violent crime appears to be the consequence of economic stress and is associated more with poverty than wealth. It increases as social structures weaken or as mob wars break out over substances or rackets — prohibition of alcohol, the drug wars, gambling, prostitution. There is a demographic aspect to violent crime in that younger males are more prone to violent behavior; their numbers, as a percentile of the total population, change over time. Law enforcement actions (and consequences for the offenders) also have an influence of course.

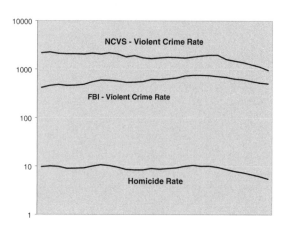

Murder is the ultimate violent crime. The homicide rate — along with the two violent crime rates, on logarithmic scale, are shown to the left. Homicides are included in the data of the other curves. The murder rate resembles the FBI's violent crime rate in its shape and fluctuations. Murder and manslaughter represented 1.1% of reported violent crimes and 0.1% of *all* reported crimes in the FBI Crime Index. It has been declining annually since 1991 and at a more rapid rate than total violent crime.

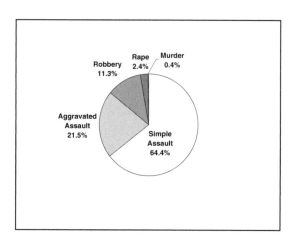

Murder is an even smaller percentage of violent crime if we use the National Crime Victimization Survey data, include simple assault (which is not included in the curves) and use 2000 numbers to avoid the distortions created by the terrorist attack on 9/11/2001. The pie-chart to the left shows the results. The more serious the crime, the smaller its share of the total — thank heaven! The "robbery" included in this chart is of the armed variety — which, when failing, can result in murder.

We now complete this overview of the two different crime rates by looking at property crime in the next panel.

Sources: U.S. Department of Justice, Federal Bureau of Investigation, Uniform Crime Reports, and National Criminal Victimization Survey, both accessible from http://www.ojp.usdoj.gov/bjs/welcome.html.

Property Crime

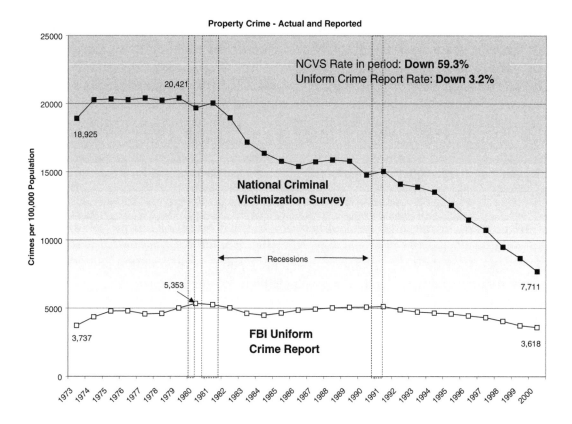

Property Crime - Actual and Reported

NCVS Rate in period: **Down 59.3%**
Uniform Crime Report Rate: **Down 3.2%**

National Criminal
Victimization Survey

FBI Uniform
Crime Report

Recessions

20,421

18,925

5,353

3,737

7,711

3,618

Crimes per 100,000 Population

Property crime rates have been dropping since the end of the 1990-1991 recession — both as measured by the National Criminal Victimization Survey ("estimated" crime rate) and the FBI's Uniform Crime Report ("reported" crime rate). The NCVS rate was down 59.3% in this period, the UCR rate 3.2%.

Property crime represents around 88% of all crime, not counting offenses of a public order nature — meaning violations of drug laws, gambling laws, traffic laws, prostitution statutes, vagrancy, and so on. Property crime incidence is so large that it dwarfs all other crimes in reporting, and when property crime is down, the overall crime rate follows.

The components of the NCVS and UCR rates are identical: burglary, larceny/theft, and motor vehicle theft. The chief difference is that the FBI includes and the NCVS (a household survey) excludes crimes involving commercial property. The FBI's Index officially includes arson as well, but the data — which are not as uniformly collected as for the other crimes — are not included in the total index by the FBI. The table shows which category of crime contributes what percentage to the Uniform Crime Report and the National Criminal Victimization Index. The largest category in each case is larceny/theft, the smallest is motor vehicle theft.

	UCR	NCVS
Burglary	20.1	17.9
Larceny/Theft	68.4	77.3
Motor Vehicle Theft	11.4	4.8

Burglary involves the unlawful entry of a structure in order to commit a felony or a theft. Burglary has a three-fold classification as (1) forcible entry, (2) unlawful entry where no force is employed, and (3) attempted forcible entry. **Larceny/theft** is all kinds of stealing without the use of force — excluding theft during burglary or motor vehicle theft. But otherwise it covers anything from picking a pocket to stealing a car radio to taking off with a bike left unattended. Interestingly enough, the FBI's definition excludes the more clever means of acquiring wealth illegally — including embezzlement, confidence games, forgery, and the writing of big bad checks. The FBI's definition is silent about the big-boy crimes of people who walk off with the pension funds of thousands.

Property crime rates appear to act as a kind of indicator of economic cycles. The NCVS index peaked the year before the two recessions of the early 1980s and rose again as the 1990-1991 recession ended — dropping steadily thereafter as the good times of the 1990s began to roll.

The FBI property crime index peaked between the two recessions in the 1980s and immediately after the 1990-1991 recession. After that it too headed down — as we all embraced the world-wide-web. The index ticked up 2 points between 2000 and 2001 as the economy stuttered a little — with motor vehicle theft leading the charge.

Property crime is thus a reflection of our economic lives and moves in step with unemployment, with the fluctuations in the poverty level, and vaguely reflects changes in income maintenance programs. It would be nice to see these rates combined with measures of white-collar crime — some of which seem to *increase* in times of economic exuberance whereas the crimes of ordinary Johns and Janes thin out with high rates of employment and lots of overtime.

Still, even at the very height of the good times, in 2000, 7,711 people out of every 100,000 experienced some kind of property loss: 1,380 of these experienced a burglary, 5,960 had something stolen, and 370 lost a car to thieves.

Another way to look at the matter — in crime statistics there is always another way — is to use the FBI's "crime clock," which is based on *reported* crimes.

In 2000, there was a property crime every 3.1 seconds, a larceny every 4.5 seconds, a burglary every 15.4 seconds, a car stolen every 27.1 seconds. Hadn't you better glance out the window? Now?

Sources: U.S. Department of Justice, Federal Bureau of Investigation, Uniform Crime Reports, and National Criminal Victimization Survey, both accessible from http://www.ojp.usdoj.gov/bjs/welcome.html.

Other Crimes and Offenses

Arrests for Indexed and Other Offenses in 2000

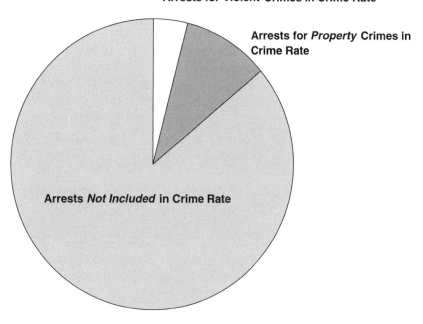

Arrests for *Violent* Crimes in Crime Rate

Arrests for *Property* Crimes in Crime Rate

Arrests *Not Included* in Crime Rate

Arrests shown exclude arrests for traffic violations.

The FBI's crime index (the "crime rate") is built around serious offenses reported to law-enforcement authorities. We've had occasion to look at these closer in the last three panels. These so-called indexed crimes have a large unreported shadow captured, to some extent, by the National Crime Victimization Survey. According to that survey, the FBI's data collection captured only 48% of violent crime and 35% of the property crime incidents. The rest went unreported. But the crimes covered by these two surveys excluded a whole battalion of other offenses, many of them felonies. We want to look more closely at these non-indexed breaches of the law. To do this, we look at the FBI's Uniform Crime Report, which also captures arrests. Clearly not all arrests result in convictions — but some kind of crime or offense gave rise to the arrest. Therefore arrests can serve as an indirect measure of lawlessness.

One glance at the pie chart tells the whole story. The vast majority of arrests in the U.S. (83.9% in 2000, excluding traffic violations), do not make it into the crime rate. These crimes and offenses produced 11.7 million arrests out of 13.89 million in 2000. Corresponding values for 1995 were higher: 12.2 million arrests out of 15.1 million total; the proportion was 80.7%, suggesting that in 2000 the relative share in crime of this "all other" category has risen by about three points.

All crime appeared to be dropping in the 1990s. If we assume that each of the arrests excluded from the crime index represented one crime/offense, and express these in terms of arrests per 100,000 population in 1995 and 2000, we see that the non-index crime rate was 4,640 in 1995 and 4,251 in 2000, a drop of 389 arrests per 100,000 population. The drop in reported, indexed, serious crimes in the same period was 1,151 crimes. Thus the "all other" category, while dropping, has not been dropping as rapidly as serious crime.

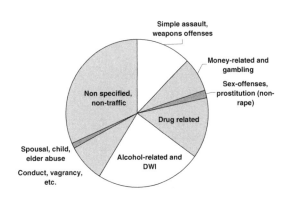

What is the nature of this mix. The FBI divides these crimes/ offenses into 20 categories. Data in Part II of this volume lists them all specifically. For purposes of display, we have grouped them under eight categories for overview. The largest category is the miscellaneous. Next in order are offenses associated with alcohol, the biggest component being drunken driving; drunkenness, and offenses related to liquor laws are included. Note that the alcohol-related category is larger than drug offenses — and would be larger still if disorderly conduct were included, which is often associated with alcohol consumption. After drugs, the next largest category is simple assault — which is well tracked by the National Crime Victimization Survey. Offenses associated with the possession and carrying of weapons are included under the category. Disorderly conduct, vagrancy, loitering, and similar offenses come next. Money-related crimes/offenses include fraud, embezzlement, and buying and selling stolen property. We have included gambling offenses there. Sexual offenses and arrests for abuse are relatively small.

The non-specified ("miscellaneous") category records arrests for violations of state or local laws/ordinances not included in the other categories. These arrests exclude all traffic violations. Fraud and embezzlement are the only categories likely to capture what is known as white collar crime.

We turn next to look more closely at drug-related offenses.

Source: U.S. Department of Justice, Federal Bureau of Investigation, *Uniform Crime Reports*, 1995 and 2000, accessible at http://www.fbi.gov/ucr/00cius.htm.

Drug War Trends: Arrests

Drug Arrests

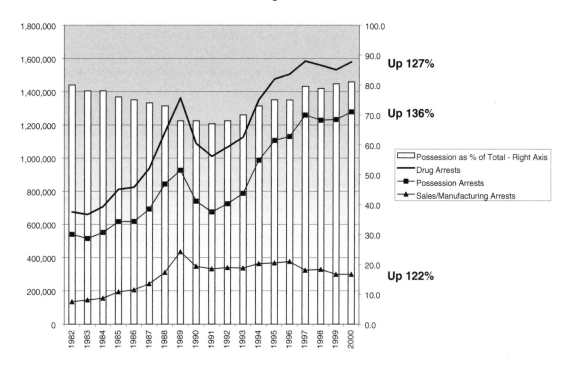

Between 1982 and 2000, the population in the United States increased 19.2%. Arrests for drug-related charges were up 127% during the same period. Arrests for the "possession" — of marijuana, cocaine powder, crack cocaine, methamphetamine, heroin and other opiates, and other drugs (barbiturates, stimulants, and hallucinogens) — were up most, 136%; arrests for sale and manufacturing of illegal substances were up 122%.

The majority of arrests were for the possession of illegal substances, although the ratios shifted over time. In the 1982 to 2000 period, just under three-quarters of arrests were for possession on average, although in the middle of this period (1989-1992), rates dropped into the high 60% range.

It may be well to put these steeply rising curves into some kind of perspective. The table on the beginning on the following page does the job.

It is clear from the table that the "war on drugs," which began officially in 1971, had started well before that date. Since then 13 major legislative actions at the national level have tried to bring drugs — and drug users — under control. Before that time, to the start of the 20th century, 12 other significant events took place. Not shown is the biggest single legislative effort *ever* to try to change our consumption of "substances" — the prohibition of alcohol (1920-1933). It required a constitutional amendment to establish (the 19th, also known as the Volstead Act of 1919) and to remove (the 20th Amendment, passed in 1933).

Key Events in the "War on Drugs"

Year	Event	Year	Event
1914	Harrison Act. Outlaws opiates, cocaine.	1972	Drug Abuse Office and Treatment Act — introduces Federal prevention, treatment programs.
1915	First anti-marijuana law passed in Utah by the state legislature dominated by Mormons.	1973	Methadone Control Act, Heroin Trafficking Act. Alcohol, Drug Abuse, and Mental Health Administration (ADAMHA) established.
1922	Narcotic Drug Import and Export Act – intended to eliminate narcotics except in medicine.	1974	Drug Abuse Treatment and Control Amendments.
1924	Heroin Act – Prohibits manufacture of heroin.	1978	Alcohol and Drug Abuse Education Amendments. Department of Education gets a role. CDACA amendments allow authorities to seize drug traffickers' assets.
1937	Marihuana Tax Act. The legislation extends controls over marijuana modeled on the control of other narcotics.	1980	Drug Abuse Prevention, Treatment, and Rehabilitation Amendments — expands education and treatment programs.
1942	Opium Poppy Control Act – licenses growing the poppy.	1984	Drug Offenders Act — authorizes special offender treatment programs.
1951	Harrison Act Amendment – imposes mandatory sentences for narcotics violations.	1986	Analogue (Designer Drug) Act — makes illegal substances that mimic in effect or function natural drugs.
1956	Narcotics Control Act — increases penalties for violation of narcotics laws.	1988	Anti-Drug Abuse Act — establishes an oversight policy for the National Drug Control Policy.
1965	Drug Abuse Control Amendments (DACDA) — bring LSD, barbiturates, amphetamines under control.	1989	America's first Drug Czar is William Bennett under the first Bush administration.
1966	Narcotic Addict Rehabilitation Act — treatment permitted as alternative to incarceration.	1992	ADAMHA Reorganization. New organization is Substance Abuse and Mental Health Services Administration (SAMHSA). From Uncle Adam to Uncle Sam?
1968	DACDA Amendments. Liberalizes punishments for non-repeaters.	1995	Congress overrides U.S. Sentencing Commission recommendation to correct racial imbalances in white/black sentencing for cocaine, crack.
1970	Comprehensive Drug Abuse and Control Act (CDACA)— includes Controlled Substances Act. "No-knock" searches authorized.	1996	General Barry McCaffrey as new drug czar under the Clinton administration.
1971	Nixon declares "War on Drugs," creates the Special Action Office for Drug Abuse Prevention (SAODAP).		

Also omitted are laws and regulations attempting to curb Americans' consumption of tobacco. Tobacco and alcohol are unquestionably two "drugs" that cause more premature deaths in the nation than all other "substances" combined. The war against tobacco is still in its warm-up stages (cigarette "speak-easies" haven't appeared yet). The war on drugs is in full cry. We capitulated to alcohol 70 years ago.

To some extent a tongue-in-cheek characterization is justified: as a nation we seem adamantly determined to hang on to our chemical crutches — and our drugs of choice appear to pass, over the decades, from permissible enjoyments into criminal consumption then back into legality again. Meanwhile, in every instance, crime waves arise and then only subside again after legalization.

In the next panel we look at the consequences of these arrests — how they turn into incarcerations.

Sources: Arrest statistics from U.S. Department of Justice, Federal Bureau of Investigation, *Crime in the United States*, accessible at http://www.fbi.gov/ucr/00cius.htm. Timelines from Schaffer Library of Drug Policy, "Drug Law Timeline," http://www/druglibrary.org and Public Broadcasting System, "Thirty Years of America's Drug War," www.pbs.org.

Drug Wars: Incarcerations

State Correctional Population
(Number per 100,000 U.S. Population)

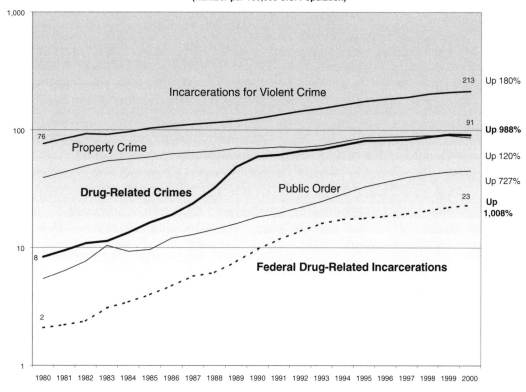

Between 1980 and 2000, the U.S. population increased 21.5%. Prisoners in state institutions incarcerated for drug-related crimes increased 988% when measured as inmates per 100,000 population. Inmates in Federal prison were up even more steeply on the same basis: 1,008%. All incarcerations had increased in this period as well, but nowhere near the level of drug-related confinements. In 1980, at the state level, 6.5% of prisoners were behind bars for drug-related offenses (19,000 people). In 2000, these prisoners, 251,100 in number, were 20.9% of all state prisoners. The data are graphed on logarithmic scale to show growth rates most accurately. The steepest curves have the greatest rates of growth.

Growth rates in actual prisoners, of course, are even higher — but expressing the data in prisoners per 100,000 population normalizes the series for year-to-year comparison. The data indicate that our society has grown much more lawless since 1980 — or, at any rate, we're putting more people in jails and prisons.

More people are **arrested** for possession of drugs than for trafficking, but more people are **imprisoned** for trafficking. Of those sentenced to do time in 1998 for drug offenses at the state level, 36% were sentenced for possession, the rest for trafficking. In the Federal system, the overwhelming majority were sentenced to prison terms for trafficking. Sentences for possession were typically shorter, of course.

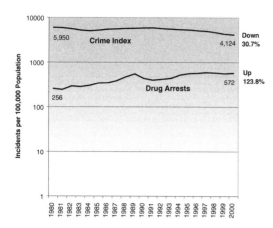

The graphic to the left charts the official crime rate, the FBI's Crime Index, produced from the agency's Uniform Crime Reports. Against that index, which is built up from violent and property crime rates, we have charted drug arrests. All incidents (crimes or arrests) are expressed as a ratio per 100,000 of U.S. population in each year shown. The graphic indicates that the official crime rate is trending down. It dropped nearly 31% in the 1980 to 2000 period. Drug arrests increased in the same period by nearly 124%. Note here that drug offenses are *not* included in the official Crime Index except that violent crimes (murder, assault, armed robbery) committed in connection with drug-related events *are* included — as are property crimes (thefts, larcenies, burglaries) committed to obtain funds to support a drug habit. The influence of the drug culture on these types of crimes will be explored elsewhere. Here the point we make is that drug-related offenses are rising sharply in an environment where the index that tracks "serious" crime is dropping.

The drug war is certainly having an impact on the nation's correctional system. In 2000, nearly 272,700 people were imprisoned for drug offenses (8% in Federal facilities, the rest in state facilities), up from 25,500 in 1980. That's rather a large number of people being housed and fed at public expense — bigger than the population of Amarillo, TX or Binghamton, NY or Duluth, MN — and nearly as large as Savannah, GA.

To complete our overview of the extent of crime — and some of the major components within that phenomenon — we look next at the crime rate and the incarceration rate over some period of time.

Sources: State data: U.S. Department of Justice, *Correctional Populations in the United States, 1997* and *Prisoners in 2000*, available from http://www.ojp.usdoj.gov/bjs/welcome.html. Federal data from: *Federal Drug Offenders, 1999*, with trends 1984-99 (NCJ 187285), from the same agency. Crime rate from Federal Bureau of Investigation, *Uniform Crime Reports*, various years, available from http://www.fbi.gov/ucr/00cius.htm.

Crime and Punishment: The Longer View

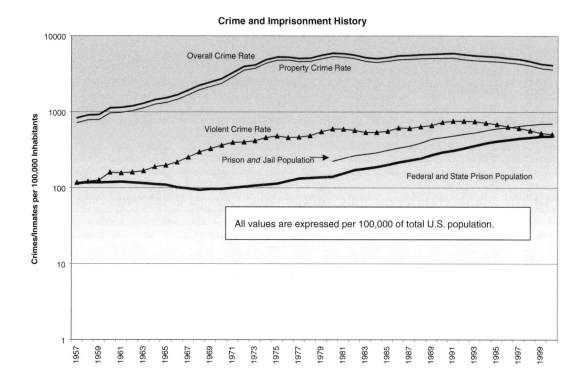

Crime and Imprisonment History

In this panel we extend our view of the crime rate back to 1957 using the *Historical Statistics of the United States*. The crime rate combines rates for property and for violent crime, both expressed as events/occurrences per 100,000 inhabitants in a given year. This interesting tabulation shows us how the crime rate and the incarceration rate may influence each other.

Note that the data are normalized so that both reported crime events and inmates in state and federal detention are expressed as ratios — per 100,000 population. This brings home the fact that our property and our persons are significantly less safe today than they were four decades ago — and that a larger percentage of the population lives behind bars.

Note next that the data are charted on a logarithmic scale. This means that the growth and/or decline rates of values — the slope of the curves — can be compared without scale distortions. Note next that the crime rate — both property and violent crime, increased at a brisk rate to about the mid 1970s. The number of individuals in state and federal prisons declined until 1970 and then began a slow growth — even as the crime rate continued to climb.

Beginning in the mid-1970s, the incarceration rate began to climb and the crime rate began to flatten out. Toward the end of this period, when incarceration was rising sharply, the crime rate began to drop. It has been falling steadily, year by year, since 1991. The relationships are presented in the table on the next page.

Before we look at the table, note that the decline in violent crime has been sharper than the downturn in property crime. Along with prison population ratios, data for both prisons and jails are graphed from 1980 forward. Persons in prison are incarcerated for periods of more than one year. Persons in jail typically serve one year or less.

Percent Change in Selected Period

Period	Crime Rate	Prisoner Population
1957-1967	130.7	-14.0
1967-1977	162.5	35.0
1977-1987	9.9	73.0
1987-1997	-11.3	94.3
1997-2000	-16.3	7.2

The table shows percent change in the official crime rate and in the rate of the prisoner population for four decades and for the final three year period graphed. Thus in the 1957 to 1967 period, the crime rate shot up nearly 131% while people in prison dropped by 14% (per 100,000 inhabitants). In the 1987 to 1997 period, the crime rate dropped more than 11% and the prisoner population shot up nearly 100%.

The table appears to show a societal "reaction lag." Energetic measures to counter the rising crime wave took some time to develop. Eventually it took hold. Statistics are simply photographs of a situation. They do not logically force the conclusion that locking up the bad guys reduces crime — but an inference may be permissible, perhaps. The lag is illustrated by the fact that the 94.3% increase in incarcerations in the '87 to '97 period seems to have "spilled over" into the next period. In the three years between 1997 and 2000, the crime rate dropped more rapidly than in the entire decade before.

We look next at some of the demographics of crime.

Sources: U.S. Bureau of the Census, *Historical Statistics of the United States,* September 1995 and *Statistical Abstract of the United States*, 1980, 1990, 1995, 2001. The primary data source cited by these sources are data from the FBI's Uniform Crime Reports (for crime rate) and the U.S. Bureau of Justice Statistic's *Prisoners in State and Federal Institutions* and *Correctional Populations in the United States*.

Offenders: Women Reaching for Equality

Correctional Population

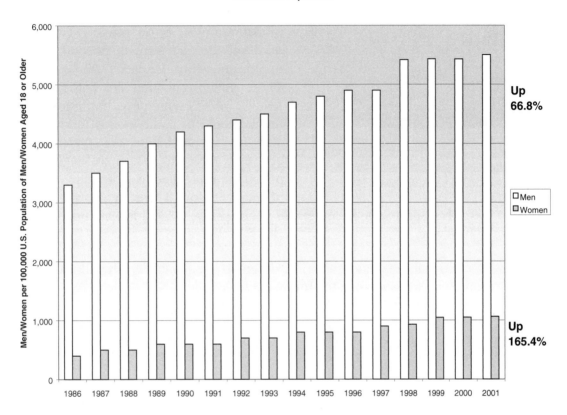

In 2001, nearly 6.6 million individuals were under the supervision of parts of the correctional system of the United States — under Federal, State, or local jurisdictions. The most pronounced trend in recent years has been the growth in the number of women under correctional supervision. In 1986, 13 of 100 people under correctional supervision were women; by 2001, the ratio had increased to 17 women per 100 people on probation, parole, in jail, or in prison.

In 2001, 5,500 men out of 100,000 men aged 18 or older were under some kind of correctional supervision. The matching number for women was 1,060 per 100,000 women (same age group). In 1986, the numbers were 3,300 for men, 400 for women. In this 15-year period, women under supervision grew 165.4%, men by 66.8% — while the population of the 18 and older age group increased 17.7% — women less than men (16 vs. 19.5%).

Why are women striving for parity with men — in crime, of all places? Enough equality already! But the reasons for this increase may well have to do with the much more enabled role of women in society as a whole. Women are proportionately more present in the worlds of business, government, and the not-for-profit sector as well. During this period, women's participation in the labor force (those aged 20 and over) increased from 55.6% in 1986 to 61% in 2000, up 5 points (male participation actually dropped, from

78.4 to 76.5%). Women's increasing involvement in the sphere beyond the home and hearth goes far in explaining their growing presence among offenders.

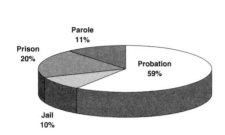

The vast majority of people under correctional supervision in 2001 were either on probation (59%) or on parole (11%). Two thirds of the rest were in prison (20% of total), one third in jail (10% of total). Those under probation are convicted offenders in the community, but living under the oversight of some kind of correctional authority. Probationers are typically required to adhere to specific rules. Those in prison are sentenced to more than one year of incarceration. Those in jail are serving one year or less. Those on parole have been in jail or prison as well but are now out and about for good behavior.

In 2001, the correctional population was 17.2% female, 82.8% male. The allocation between males and females is shown in the following table:

Correctional Supervision	Men - %	Women - %
Total Correctional Population	83	17
Probation	78	22
Parole	88	12
Jail or Prison	93	7

It is evident from this table that women are less subject (in proportion to their presence) to being incarcerated and more likely to get a probationary sentence. The participation of the sexes in various crimes will be explored in more detail in other panels, but, in general, women commit fewer violent crimes than men.

We look next at the racial composition of offenders.

Sources: U.S. Department of Justice, Correctional Populations in the United States, annual, Prisoners in 2001, and Probation and Parole in the United States, 2001. These publications and data can be reached at http://www.ojp.usdoj.gov/bjs/welcome.html.

Offenders: Blacks at High Rates

Correctional Population by Race

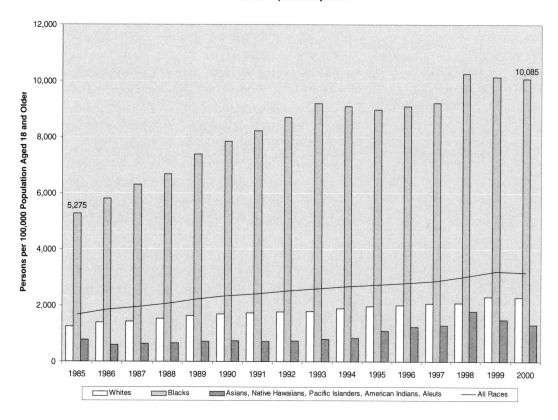

During the 15 year period charted above, more of the black population aged 18 years and older was under correctional supervision that either the white or the other races, or both of those combined. To illustrate how this chart works, consider the year 2000. In that year 10,085 blacks, out of 100,000 blacks aged 18 and over, were under correctional supervision. The corresponding value for whites was 2,275 and for the other races combined 1,305 per 100,000 (of the respective race) aged 18 and over. Another way to put this is to say that 10% of the black adult population, 2.3% of the white, and 1.3% of the other races were under probation, in jail, in prison, or on parole.

In raw numbers, of course, whites are the majority of this population. Whites are the majority racial groups. Whites were 83% of the 18+ population but only 60% of the correctional population, blacks were 12% of this age group but 38% of corrections — this is a pattern that repeats in many different contexts. The other races were 4.7% of population,1.9% of corrections and thus had the best ratio — they had the fewest people in corrections. As shown on the chart, the "all other" category includes Asians, Native Hawaiians, other Pacific Islanders, American Indian, and Aleuts.

The correctional population has grown within each group — least among other races, where 2000 values are 1.7 times 1985 values. Among whites, this multiple is 1.8, among blacks 1.9 — in other words, nearly twice as many people are under correctional supervision in 2000 than were in 1985. The many possible reasons for this will be explored in the remainder of this volume.

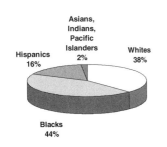

Blacks and whites shown are non-Hispanics. The majority of Hispanics are of Caucasian origin.

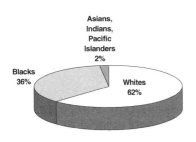

All races shown include those of Hispanic origin. The probation and parole population was 17% Hispanic in 2000.

The pie chart to the left shows the racial breakdown of those who were either in jail or in prison in 2000. The majority of those confined (67.9% of some 1.9 million people) were in prison (1.3 million), incarcerated for more than one year. The pie chart is somewhat misleading because it segregates Hispanics as if they were a racial group. Alas, the data come that way. If the Hispanic portion were reported by race, whites would have the largest share of the incarcerated population because Hispanics are predominantly of Caucasian race. The black slice would be a slight bit larger, the "other races" by a sliver.[1]

The correctional population on probation and parole, which is shown on the next pie chart, is reported by race alone, Hispanics being folded into the respective racial categories — but they comprise 17% of this population, slightly higher than in prisons and jails. Note the effect that has on the population of white probationers and parolees. Whites have a higher share of the probation and parole population than blacks. In 2000, 3.8 million people were on probation and 725,500 on parole.

Sources: U.S. Department of Justice, *Correctional Populations in the United States*, multiple years, *Prison and Jail Inmates at Midyear*, multiple years, and *Prisoners in 1998, 1999,* and *2000*. Data are available from http://www.ojp.usdoj.gov/bjs/pubalp2.htm.

---

[1] Just at the moment, the Federal Government is apparently intent on creating a new racio-ethnic category, Hispanics. Numerous agencies are doing this by reporting whites and blacks as non-Hispanic but not dividing Hispanics by race. Reports from series to series and year to year are not consistent — and make the life of analysts "interesting."

Trends in the Justice System

**Justice System Employment —
and Crime Rate and Correctional Population**

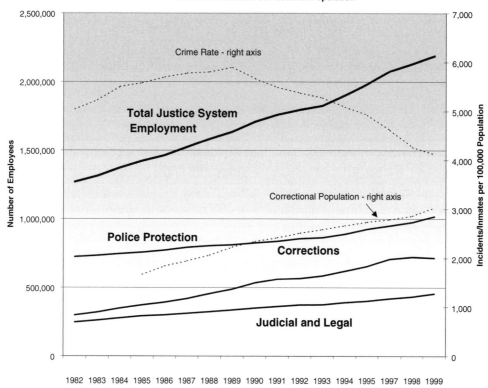

In 1999, the Justice System as a whole — society's response to crime — employed nearly 2.2 million people, divided into the categories of police protection (47%), corrections (33%), and judicial and legal (20%). In this period, the "downstream" elements of this system have grown fastest — corrections 140% from 1982 to 1999, judicial and legal 84%, and police protection 41%.

The crime rate, shown as a dotted line on top — and calibrated to the right axis — shows a decline from 1982 to 1999 of 18% and the correctional population (probate, parole, prison, and jail) shows an increase of 82% measured form 1985.

If employment in the justice system has a direct impact on crime — and if the correctional population's increase is in part a reflection of success against offenders — then the justice system seems to be working. How cost effective it is is another question we shall explore later on. In this panel the object is to show some contrasting trends, the "us against them." Society has clearly poured human resources into combating the incidence of crime — which was rising until 1989 but has been dropping rapidly since.

The burdens between four levels of government — each of which fields its own forces of deterrence, prosecution, and correction — are roughly equal as shown in the table on the following page. The federal role is the smallest, representing 8.7%, the local role is largest (59.1%) — if counties and municipalities are combined — and the state role falls in the middle (32.2%). State justice employment is just slightly more than that of municipalities.

1999 Allocation of Justice System Employment

	Total Employment	Percent of Total	Percent of Sector		
			Police	Legal	Corrections
Federal	191,169	8.7	54.5	29.3	16.2
State	704,902	32.2	14.1	21.1	**64.8**
County	606,645	27.7	36.8	**31.4**	31.8
Municipality	686,761	31.4	**86.0**	8.7	5.2

Note that the different roles of different levels of government are indicated by the distribution of employment by category. Police protection plays the greatest role at the municipal level, judicial and legal activity at the county level — where, normally, the probates are located — the states maintain the prisons. Within the Federal Government, the policing function absorbs the largest number of people.

It is well to keep in mind that the Justice System in the United States is highly layered. Data are collected in different ways at different levels, and piecing together the "national" picture is therefore no simple business.

Source: U.S. Department of Justice, *Sourcebook of Criminal Justice Statistics, 2000*, downloaded from http://www.albany.edu/sourcebook/.

The Cost of Crime Control

Justice System Costs

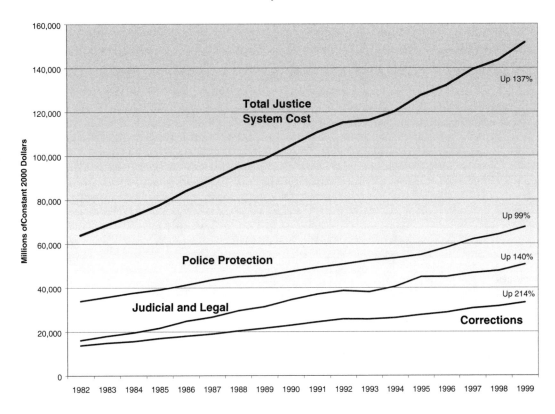

If you believe that crime — heaven be thanked — doesn't affect you much, think again. You're paying for police and for police cars; for lawyers, judges, judges' gowns; for prisons, food, and prison guards — and the bills are going up. In 1982, the nation expended $35.8 billion in *actual* dollars, in 1999 $146.6 billion — that's a 309% increase in actual dollars. In constant dollars the 1982 expenditure was $64.0 billion and rose to $151.5 billion by 1999, a growth rate of 137%. Either way, the national response to a rising crime rate has brought rising costs. And the period shown does not yet reflect the events of 9/11/2001. After that date, expenditures on domestic security will spike even higher — but the data to chart those expenditures are not yet available.

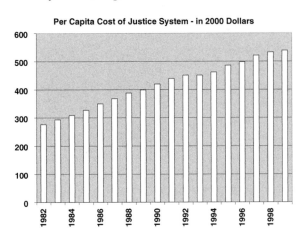

Just the *increase*, in constant dollars, between 1982 and 1999, was $262 for every man, woman, and child. A family of four is paying somewhat over $1,000 a year for the *increase* in crime-control expenditures. And those increases have not purchased a greater sense of security. On the day that this was written (October 7, 2002), a sniper was killing people at random in the Maryland suburbs of Washington, D.C. A 13-year-old boy had just been hit. It's not surprising that there is little public resistance to steeply climbing expenditures on safety and all that it entails. The rise in per capita spending, in constant dollars, is shown in the small chart on the previous page.

The distribution of expenditures by major category — police protection, judicial and legal, and corrections — closely parallel the allocation of employment in the Justice System — suggesting that this is a people-intensive activity. The municipalities again expend the bulk of their money on policing. When looking at the judicial and legal system, the Federal Government edges out counties as the having the leading share. And the states, again, expend most of their resources on prisons.

Percent Distribution of Expenditures by Level of Government and Activity, 1999

	Percent of Total	Percent of Sector		
		Police Protection	Judicial and Legal	Corrections
Federal	17.2	54.0	**31.1**	14.9
States	36.0	16.8	22.5	**60.6**
Counties	22.1	35.5	30.0	34.5
Municipalities	24.7	**84.3**	8.6	7.2
Total	100.0	44.0	22.2	33.8

Nearly 47% of all justice dollars are spent at the local level (counties and municipalities combined). The states participate principally in maintaining prisons, although they have a policing functions as well (State Police, Texas constables) and operate their own level of the judiciary. Each level is mirrored by the Federal Government. Its police forces are the FBI; the armed agents of the Bureau of Alcohol, Tobacco, and Firearms; the Border Patrol; the Coast Guard Law Enforcement Detachments (LEDETS); Treasury Agents; and assorted other marshals — not least airport security forces, of late. The Federal Government's judicial branch includes, most prominently, the Supreme Court. And the prison of prisons in this country is the Federal Penitentiary in Leavenworth, Kansas.

The armed forces of the United States are *not* engaged in law enforcement activity, indeed are prohibited from doing so by the Posse Comitatus Act of 1878 (and its amendments) which expressly prohibits the military from "executing the law."

Each of the major parts of the Justice System will be covered, in more detail, later.

Source: U.S. Department of Justice, *Sourcebook of Criminal Justice Statistics, 2000*, downloaded from http://www.albany.edu/sourcebook/.

Chapter 2

Violent Crime

This chapter focuses on violent crimes. These are the ones that send a chill down the spine. Violent crimes include murder, rape, robbery, aggravated assault and simple assault. After two and a half decades of high rates of violent crime, trends in all violent crimes during the late 1990s have been down. Fewer of such crimes are being committed.

The first panels in this chapter provide an overview of the subject, covering all violent crimes by type over a twenty seven year period and murder over the entire 20th century. What becomes clear is that crime is the male domain. Many more men than women commit crimes of all types and far more men are victimized by crime than are women. Even among male infants this fact holds. Violent crime is also a youthful activity. The rate at which young people age 18 to 24 years commit homicide, for example, is five times the rate seen in the population over age of 35.

Striking differentials in violent crime rates between the races, between our poorest and our most affluent, and among residential area types (urban, suburban and rural) are discussed in three different panels.

The 1980s and 1990s witnessed an explosion in youth gang violence which coincided with the rise of crack cocaine. The fuzzy official data on youth gang membership tells an unsettling story of steadily increasing numbers. Although membership in youth gangs has continued to increase through the end of the century, gang related crime dropped. The possible reasons for this are discussed in a series of panels.

Approximately 40% of all American households count among their belongings at least one gun. We take a look at data on violent crimes committed with a firearm and review the history of gun control legislation in America.

Next, we try to uncover data on the sad and often silent subject of domestic violence, focusing primarily on violence between intimate partners. Here, women take the brunt. Rape and sexual assault, the least reported violent crimes, are also covered in a separate panel.

Finally, a look at the most dangerous jobs in terms of violence on the job is presented. The most dangerous jobs in this regard are; law enforcement officers, mental health workers, and retail store clerks. Nonetheless, in a study of the locations in which violent acts occur, the home is still the number one spot. One third of all violent acts occur at or neat the victims home.

Violent Crimes are Down

Number of Violent Crimes per 1,000 Population Aged 12 and Over, 1973-2000

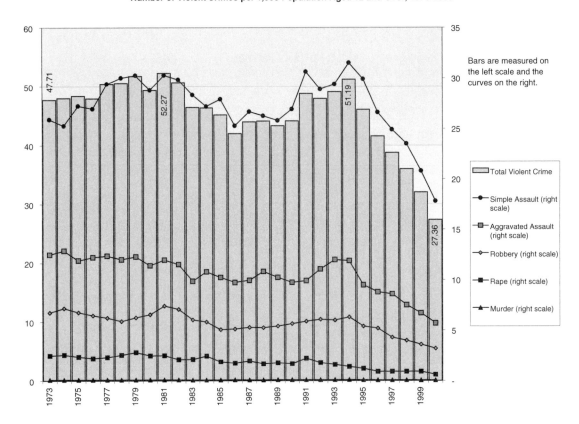

Bars are measured on the left scale and the curves on the right.

Total Violent Crime

Simple Assault (right scale)

Aggravated Assault (right scale)

Robbery (right scale)

Rape (right scale)

Murder (right scale)

Violent crime? It's the stuff we watch on our TVs, it's the suspense that keeps us turning the pages of our mysteries. The reality of violent crime is quite something else, of course. It is a brutal act that shatters lives, a jarring deed in perpetrating which the offender inflicts serious harm or death on others. Starting from the "top," violent crimes include murder, rape, armed robbery, aggravated assault, and simple assault. The aggravated kind involves a weapon — gun, knife, crowbar. Simple assault is with the body — fists, fingernails, elbows, knees, and feet.

The graph shows the rates at which each of these crimes is committed every year. The measure used is incidents per 1,000 people of the population, aged 12 years or older. Tracking crime as a rate is useful because it eliminates the influence of demographic factors — and of population growth — on the measurement of crime. Rates are comparable over periods of time. The chart also shows the rate for all violent crimes combined as reported by the Justice Department's *National Crime Victimization Survey* (NCVS).

Violent crime is down and down decisively. For the period 1973 to 2000 all violent crime is down by 43%. Individual categories are also down, simple assault by 31%, aggravated assault by 54%, armed robbery by 53%, rape by 76%, and murder by 42%. Over this span of time there were two periods in which the rates rose, between 1977 and 1982 and again between 1990 and 1994. After 1994 the rates have dropped sharply and across all violent crime categories.

Why this downward trend? There are numerous theories. Three of the most prominent are based on demographics, law enforcement, and the good economy.

1. Changing demographics have favored a decline. The age cohorts trailing the aging Baby Boom are smaller. Those most involved in criminal activity, the 18 to 34 age group, are less numerous. Hence violent crime is down.

2. We have become much harder on the criminal. Unprecedented numbers are now behind bars. Stricter gun control laws, tougher mandatory sentencing laws, and the intensified war on drugs have been succeeding in disarming criminals or getting them out of circulation. We have put more officers on the street. We have spent the necessary money.

3. The vibrant economy of the middle to late 1990s has increased economic opportunity for everyone, including the criminal classes. Property crime is down and hence also violent crime.

Research into each of these explanations continues at a healthy pace. The issue is, of course, far from decided. In late 2001, while we were consumed with our concerns about terrorism in the aftermath of 9/11, early signs showed that the decline in crime might be over. Violent crime might even but up slightly[1]. As usually, vast social phenomena, like the crime rate, are not subject to simplistic explanations — not by three theories or even by thirty. Too many social, political, economic, and psychological forces impinge on behavior.

Next, we turn to a review of homicide rates over the last century.

Source: U.S. Bureau of Justice Statistics, *National Criminal Victimization Survey*, "Violent Crime Trends, 1973-2001," August 2002, available online at http://www/ojp/usdoj.gov/glance/tables/viortrdtab.htm. Oliver, Willard M. *Review of The Crime Drop*, published online without a date and available at http://www.scja.net/oliver2.html.

---

[1] This book is being completed in October 2002. Final data on crime rates for 2001 are due to be published later in 2002.

A Century of Murder

Homicide Rates in the 20th Century

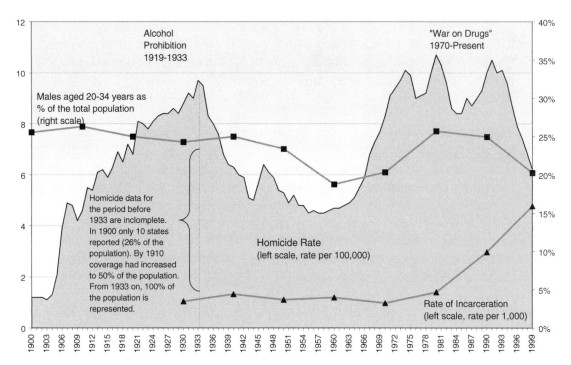

Murders are tracked well and have been for more than a century. National data on other crimes, covering long periods of time, are much harder to find. In part this is because murder is murder is murder. Differences of type exist — first-degree murder, second degree murder, involuntary manslaughter — but these are simply modifiers of the ultimate crime, murder. It may be, as Shakespeare's ghost in *Hamlet* suggests, that murder is most foul, unnatural, and strange, but it is also easily recognizable.

Over the 20th century the homicide rate in the United States fluctuated greatly. Please note that the homicide rates presented for the period 1900 to 1932 are incomplete. The sudden jump between 1905 to 1906 is more a factor of data inconsistency than an epidemic rise in the homicide rate. After rising in the early years of the century, as urbanization increased, a peak was reached in 1933. Thereafter the rate fell pretty steadily for 30 years, with one up surge as U.S. service men returned from World War II. The middle of the century busied itself with having babies and raising the boom generation. Then, in the middle of the1960s, the Baby Boomers started reaching their teens, and the homicide rate began to grow, quickly. By 1973 a rate of 9.7 murders per 100,000 population was reached equaling the previous century peak hit in 1933. The rate than dipped and grew hitting two more peaks in the late 20th century before heading down sharply from 1994 through 2000.

The graph charts the homicide rate as well as the rate of incarceration in state and federal prisons. A curve showing the percentage of the population made up of males between the ages of 20 and 34 years is also provided. This is the age group that is responsible for the greatest number of crimes and it is therefore of interest to see how their relative position in the demographic landscape relates to the homicide rate.

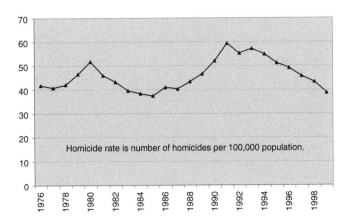

Homicide Offender Rates of those Aged 18-34 Years, 1976-1999

Homicide rate is number of homicides per 100,000 population.

For a closer look at the age distribution we can chart the rate of homicides committed by those age 18 through 34[2]. This age group is consistently responsible for close to half of all murders. The decline in the percentage of murders carried out by people in this age group in the middle to end of the 1990s corresponds with their decline as a percentage of the population as a whole. It also corresponds with the decline in the overall homicide rate.

Another factor to consider when viewing the homicide rate over the 20th century is the interesting rise of homicides during periods of prohibition and crackdowns on illicit substances generally. During the period of alcohol prohibition, a black market in alcohol grew and, as is often the case with markets for illicit goods, it was a system in which force ruled. The market for illegal drugs is much the same. As drug lords battle over territories and markets, levels of violence in society increase.

Illegal drugs are consumed disproportionately by the young. The period 1965 to 1994 saw the Baby Boom reach and pass through its "prime" drug consuming age, 15 to 34 years.

Baby Boomers by Age between 1945 and 1995

1945	Born			
1950	5	Born		
1955	10	5	Born	
1960	**15**	10	5	Born
1965	**20**	**15**	10	5
1970	**25**	**20**	**15**	10
1975	**30**	**25**	**20**	**15**
1980	**35**	**30**	**25**	**20**
1985	40	**35**	**30**	**25**
1990	45	40	**35**	**30**
1995	50	45	40	**35**

In 1995 the last of the "official" Baby Boom (born in 1960) reached 35 years of age. Not surprisingly, the years 1965 to 1995 were years of high demand for illegal drugs. And where there is a demand for a product there is supply. In the case of illicit drugs, the supply comes accompanied by an increase in violence.

[2] Because the primary graph in this panel covers the entire century and population data were not available for the age breakdown 18 through 34 for this entire period, the age range 20-34 was used instead.

To this strong demographic trend is added the impact of law enforcement trends in the latter part of the century. In 1970, President Nixon declared a war on drugs. Although not remembered for his progressive attitudes, Nixon's war on drugs was actually very much focused on treatment for hard-core users, according to Michael Massing, a journalist who, in 2000, published a book called *The Fix* about America's war on drugs. The policies that have followed under every administration since Nixon's have been increasingly Draconian. Enforcement increased, incarceration rates began to rise, and while the consumer market was strong, rates of violence rose as well. The homicide rate did not begin to fall, despite the vigorous war on drugs, until two things occurred in the middle of the 1990s. Incarceration rates began to reach unprecedented highs and the Baby Boom passed out of its "prime" criminal and drug consuming age (teens to 34)[3].

At the close of the 20th century the homicide rate was down sharply from the various peaks it had reached during the century. In 2001, however, it stopped declining.

The next panel will look more closely at the income distribution of criminal victimization.

Source: U.S. Centers for Disease Control, National Center for Health Statistics, *Vital Statistics*, "Homicide rate per 100,000 population, 1900-1999," October 2001, available online at http://www.cdc.gov/. Leibovich, Lori. "Fixin' Under Nixon," *Salon.com*, May 1999, available online at http://www.salon.com/news/feature/1999/05/11/nixon/print.html.

---

[3] For more on the subject of the "war on drugs" see Chapter 6 in this volume.

The Poorer You Are, The More Vulnerable to Violent Crime

Violent Crime Victimization Rates by Household Income, 1993 and 2001

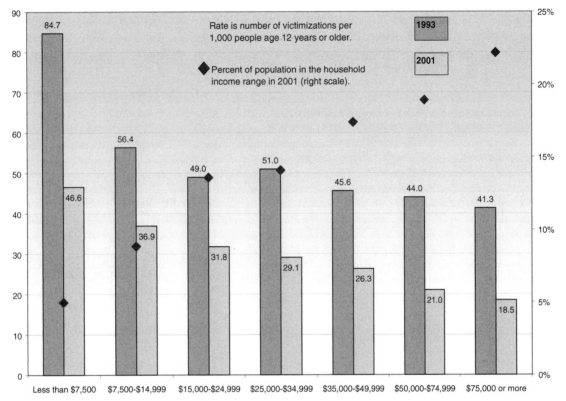

If, in 2001, your Mercedes was your favorite vehicle (of several), if you lived on the large estate your dearly-departed-husband of 30 years had left you, if that place was in the rural northeast somewhere, then you probably were *not* the victim of a violent crime. In fact, your likelihood of having been victimized was about as low as it gets.

Those with a "widowed" marital status have lower victimization rates than married couples who, in turn, have much lower rates than those who have never been married or those divorced or separated. Women are victimized less often than men. Victimization rates decrease with age, the younger you are, the more at risk.

In 2001, the northeast beat out the south in terms of violent victimization rates by region. The west had the highest rates followed by the midwest, south, and northeast. Rural areas beat out suburban areas and suburbs saw lower rates of crime than urban centers. Finally, those with high household incomes were victimized at a lesser rate than those with low household incomes.

The victimization rates presented in the graph are for the crimes of rape, robbery, and assault, both simple and aggravated. They come from the U.S. Department of Justice's *National Crime Victimization Survey*. Rates are given for seven categories of annual household income and for two years, 1993 and 2001. The rates are the number of victimizations per 1,000 people age 12 or older in the income range listed. The pattern is clear. There is an inverse correlation between household income and likelihood of violent criminal victimization.

The overall rate of crime rises and falls over time for a variety of reasons. The relatively higher rates at which the poor are victimized (and offend) as compared to the more affluent changes very little. During the period shown in the graph, 1993 to 2001, the rate of victimization for the most affluent group dropped by 55% and for the poorest group by 45%. Consequently, the *difference* in their rates actually grew over this period despite the fact that rates fell for all income groups.

Percentage Rate difference between Victimization Rates for the Lowest Income Group and the Highest Income Group, 1993-2001

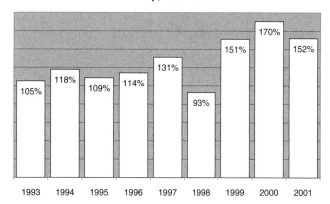

In 1993, those with an income of $7,500 or less were more than twice as likely to have been violently victimized than those with incomes of $75,000 or more — 105% more. The difference between these groups was least in 1998 and then rose again to end the period at 152% — more than two and a half times higher rates for poor than rich.

The same pattern is not seen for property crimes, which are suffered disproportionately by the more affluent. However, for property crimes as for violent crimes, rates dropped more over this period for those with higher incomes than for those with lower incomes. It would appear that the minimum levels of victimization is more persistent for the poor than for the wealthy.

The next panel will address differences in criminal activity by age group.

Source: U.S. Bureau of Justice Statistics, National Crime Victimization Survey, "Criminal Victimization 2001, Changes 2000-2001 with Trends 1993-2001," September 2002, p. 15.

Murder, Youth, and Growing Up

Homicide Offenders by Age Group, Annually, 1976-1999

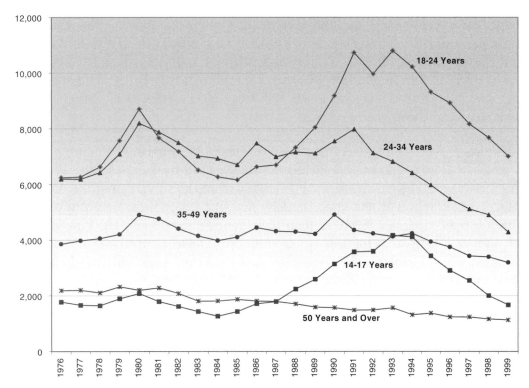

The strong correlation between age and likelihood of being involved in a violent crime, as a perpetrator or a victim, makes the subject worth of a closer look. Our teenage years are a time in our lives when we begin the transition from childhood to adulthood. It is a time when energy is high and the ability to control emotions not highly developed. In our teens and twenties we feel invincible, we take risks, we take drugs, we die in accidents at higher rates than later in life, we commit suicide at high rates, and we commit violent criminal acts at higher rate than at any other time in our lives.

The graph presents data on homicide offenders by age group from 1976 to 1999. The curve at the top of the chart shows all homicide offenders aged 18 to 24 years. Their homicide rates exceed that of all other age groups except for the period 1981-89 during which the next oldest age group (24-34) surpassed its younger peers in the dubious distinction of being the most violent age group. If we combine these groups and look at all people aged 18 to 34, we are looking at the group responsible for well over half of all homicides in the United States. Between 1976 and 1999, they represented an average 66.5% of all homicide offenders annually.

Among young teens, those aged 14 to 17 years, this period was one of great volatility. We see a sharp rise in the number of murders committed by these young offenders starting in 1989 and extending through 1994. This dramatic rise, from a rate per 100,000 people in the age group of 8.5 in 1984 to a rate of 30.2 in 1993, caused much concern in society as a whole. There were fearful predictions of what were then termed "juvenile su-

---

perpreditors." As juvenile crime rates soared in the early 1990s, state legislatures began to lower the age at which juveniles could be tried as adults. What was happening to cause the rise in juvenile rates of violent crime? And why, after 1993-1994 did the rate drop so precipitously?

Many believe that youth gangs and the cocaine trade are at the heart of the matter. Michael J. Sniffen presents a consensus theory in his article about the *decline* in youth violence that started in 1994. "Police executives, academics, and politicians have attributed the decrease to a decline in demand for crack cocaine, truces between remaining crack gangs that provided guns to juveniles in the 1980s, police crackdowns on illegal guns and stiffer sentencing of repeat violent offenders."

There was also a move to try juveniles as adults. Part of the impetus behind trying children as adults was an attempt to counteract a strategy used by gangs. In the late 1980s and early 1990s gangs began to use their youngest members to carry out the most dangerous and visible tasks with the understanding that, if caught, these youthful offenders would be subjected to lesser penalties than their gang "elders." Did cracking down on youthful offenders help stem the tide of juvenile crime? Or, as many argue, did these harsher sentencing guidelines come about after juvenile crime rates had already begun to fall? These questions are hotly debated in judicial and law enforcement circles.

Although the homicide rate fell during the period 1994-1999 across all age groups, the greatest decline was for the youngest age group, those aged 14 to 17.

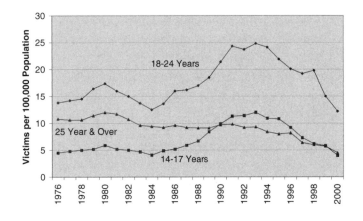

Homicide Victimization Rates by Age, 1976-2000

Statistics on the age of homicide *victims* parallel very closely the statistics on offenders. More people in the age group 18-24 are murdered than are people in any other age group. During the early 1990s those 14-17 saw their rates of victimization rise sharply, paralleling their offender rates. As the offender rates fell in the late 1990s, so to did their rates of victimization.

When it comes to gender differences in both offender rates and victimization rates, the story is pretty clear. Men offend and are victimized at higher rates than are women. The next panel will look into these differences.

Source: U.S. Federal Bureau of Investigation, Supplementary Homicide Reports, 1976-99, available at http://www.fbi.gov/. Victimization rates are from and FBI report, *Crime in the United States 2000*, October 2001, available online at http://www.fbi.gov/ucr/00cius.htm.

Gender Differences in Violent Crime Offenders

Homicide Offender Rates by Gender, 1976-1999

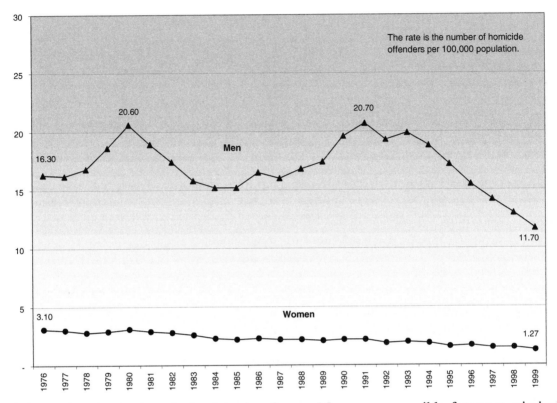

Violent crime is very much the domain of men. Men are responsible for most criminal acts and they are the victims more often than women. This is true even in the acutely tragic cases of the murder of a child. Of murder victims aged 5 years or under, most are males and most are killed by a man.

The graph presents homicide offender rates for men and women. Rates charted are the number of homicide offenders, by gender and year, for every 100,000 people in the population. Men murder on average 8 times for every murder perpetrated by a woman. The homicide rate "gender gap" hasn't closed over the years. In fact it has increased, and this despite a decline in number of homicides. In 1976 the ratio of male murderers to female was 5 to 1. By 1999 it was 9 to 1 and at its peak, in 1995, it reached a surprisingly high 11 to 1 ratio.

Homicides can be broken into four categories by gender of offender and victim. Here is the breakdown for murders committed in 1999:

Male offender / Male victim	65.1%
Male offender / Female victim	22.4%
Female offender / Male victim	10.1%
Female offender / Female victim	2.4%

Murder is, of course, the most extreme of violent crimes. Is the gender gap for all violent crimes as large as it is for homicide? No. Based on the average annual number of offenders reported by victims during the five-year period 1993-97, the following gender breakdown by type of violent crime was found.

Average Number of Violent Crimes Committed Annually, 1993-1997

Offenses	Female Offenders	Male Offenders	Women as % of Violent Offenders
Homicide	1,468	14,196	9
Sexual Assault	10,000	442,000	2
Armed Robbery	157,000	2,051,000	7
Aggravated Assault	435,000	3,419,000	11
Simple Assault	1,533,000	7,187,000	18
Total	**2,136,468**	**13,113,196**	**14**

With more than 2.1 million violent offenses committed annually by women, one must not confuse a lower rate of violent activity with no violent criminal activity. However, women do commit violent acts at a substantially lower rate than their male counterparts, once for every 7.15 times that a man commits a violent act.

Female offenders differ from male offenders in a number of ways. Women are less likely than men to use a weapon such as a blunt object, knife, or firearm in the commission of a crime: 15% of women do while 28% of men do. Women are more likely than men to have had a prior relationship with their victims, 62% versus 36%.

In the case of murder, the offender gender difference is even greater. Of the 59,996 murders committed by women between 1976 and 1997 just over 60% of the victims were intimates or family members of the murderess. Among the 395,446 victims murdered by men during this period, only 20% were family members or intimates. Of course, that means that about 36,000 people lost their lives at the hands of a female family member and about 80,000 were killed by a male family member.

In conclusion, women are less violent than men. When they do act violently, they lash out against those they know and either love or once loved.

Victimization rates by gender is our next subject.

Source: U.S. Bureau of Justice Statistics, "Homicide Trends in the U.S.," a series of statistical tables and graphs published online, January 2001, available at http://www.ojp.usdoj.gov/bjs/homicide/gender.htm. Greenfeld, Lawrence A. and Tracy L. Snell, Women Offenders, December 1999, pp. 1, 2, 4.

Victims of Violent Crimes — Most Are Men

Violent Victimization Rates by Gender, 1973-2001

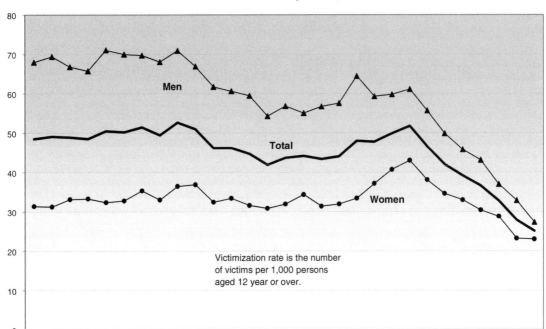

Victimization rate is the number of victims per 1,000 persons aged 12 year or over.

Men are responsible for most violent crimes. They are also victimized most by violent crimes. The graph charts violent[4] victimization rates for men, women and all persons age 12 years and over.

Overall, rates are down across the board. The rate has dropped most precipitously for men, declining 60% between 1973 and 2001. Women too saw a decline in their rate, although a lesser one, it fell by 27%.

Men started the period with a rate of violent victimization (victims per 1,000 adults) of 68 while women had a rate of 31, less than half the men's rate. The rate for men then fluctuated quite a bit over the intervening years. By 2001 the rate for both men and women had dropped, for men it was down to 27 and for women 23 bringing the gender gap in victimization rates to its smallest number for the entire period. Only 4 more men than women (per 1,000 adults) were the victims of a violent crime in 2001. More encouraging still is the fact that the rates of victimization experienced by both men and women in 2001[5] were the lowest ever recorded since the *National Crime Victimization Survey* began in 1973.

---

[4] Violent crimes included are homicide, rape, robbery, and both forms of assault, simple and aggravated.

[5] The victims killed or harmed as a direct result of the terrorist acts of September 11, 2001 are not included.

Men and women suffer different crimes at different rates. The following table shows breakdowns of victimization rates (number per 1,000 people age 12 years or older) by type of crime excluding homicide.

Victimization Rates by Gender for Violent Crimes Committed in 2000

Violent Crime	Male		Female	
	Rate	% of Total	Rate	% of Total
Rape/Sexual Assault	0.1	0.03	2.10	9.10
Armed Robbery	4.5	13.70	2.00	8.60
Aggravated Assault	8.3	25.20	3.20	13.80
Simple Assault	19.9	60.50	15.80	68.10

Men are victims of all forms of violent crime other than rape and sexual assault at higher rates than are women. Murder is no exception. Men account for three-quarters of all murder victims.

Apart from the kinds of crimes they suffer, men and women's rates of victimization differ in another way. Women are victimized by people they know far more often than are men (and women victimize people they know at a higher rate, as we saw in the previous panel). In the 1992-93 period, women experienced 7 times as many incidents of non-fatal violence by an intimate (husband, ex-husband, boyfriend or ex-boyfriend) as did men. On average, woman experience 1 million violent victimizations by an intimate every year compared to about 143,000 incidents that men experience. In general, when it comes to non-fatal violence by a lone offender, women report knowing their assailants in 78% of the cases while men know their assailants in only half (51%).

The year 1994 was a peak crime year. For women it was a particularly bad year. The rate of female victimization hit a high of 43 per 1,000 adult women. The men's rate jumped that year as well but was far short of its high rate for the period experienced in 1977. Nobody knows for sure why women took the brunt of the increased violence during the years 1992 to 1994. Since then, their numbers have again dropped.

Source: U.S. Bureau of Justice Statistics, *Key Facts at a Glance*, "Violent Victimization Rates by Gender, 1973-2001, September 2002, available online at http://www.ojp.usdoj.gov/bjs/glance/tables.

Guns and Gangs

Homicide Arrest Rates by Age and Use of Guns, 1976-1999

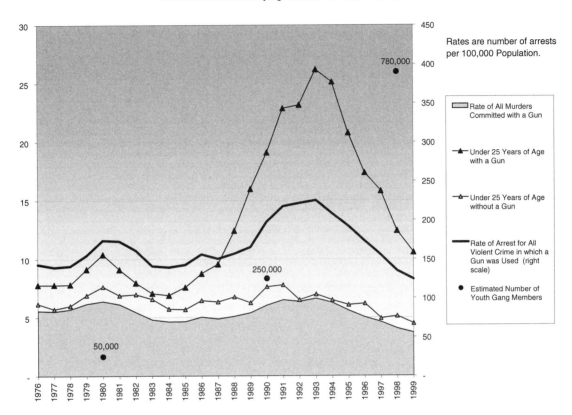

Rates are number of arrests per 100,000 Population.

Rate of All Murders Committed with a Gun

Under 25 Years of Age with a Gun

Under 25 Years of Age without a Gun

Rate of Arrest for All Violent Crime in which a Gun was Used (right scale)

● Estimated Number of Youth Gang Members

Firearm injuries are among the top ten causes of death for anyone under the age of 45 in the United States. In additional, for every fatal shooting, there are roughly three nonfatal shootings. In 2000, 28,663 people died as a result of a firearm injury. Of these, 16,586 were suicides and 1,898 were the result of either accidental discharges or legal interventions. The remainder, 36% or 10,179, were homicides. Of all homicides committed in 2000, 65% involved a firearm, down from 70% in 1994.

One of the leading factors in the dramatic increase in murders experienced in the late 1980s and early 1990s was the increase in gun crimes among juvenile and young adult offenders. The graph charts homicide arrest rates per 100,000 population for crimes committed with and without guns by those under 25 years of age.

The rates for murders committed with guns and without guns were very close together for the 12 years 1976-1987. Then, starting in 1988 the rates for murders committed with and without a gun began to diverge sharply. The arrest rate of young people for murders committed with a gun rose 174% in a matter of seven years, from 9.6 per 100,000 in 1987 to 26.2 in 1993. The rate for murders committed without a gun stayed relatively flat, 6.3 in 1987 and 7.0 in 1993, the peak year. The entire rise in murders that occurred between 1987 and 1993 was the result of higher numbers of murders committed with guns.

Handguns were the firearms of choice during the late 1980 and early 1990s. It is generally believed that the liberal distribution of handguns to juveniles in youth gangs was behind the rise in youth violence and particularly the growth in gun violence. Youth gangs grew throughout the 1980s and 90s. The graph presents Department of Justice estimates of youth gang membership in three select years. The growth is remarkable and it should be noted that the number of gang members continued to grow well after the rate of arrest of young people for homicide began to decline sharply in 1994 and 1995.

For many reasons, beginning in the mid 1980s, juveniles were recruited into gangs, many of which were heavily involved in the new crack cocaine trade. Although these juveniles were initially recruited as low-level drug carriers they tended to advance quickly. These youths could be paid less than older gang members, fewer of them had developed a drug addition, making them more trustworthy, and they faced more lenient penalties in the legal system if caught. They were provided guns. The crack cocaine market flourished. The gun-related murder rate rose, as did violent crime generally.

The reasons for the decline in gun violence, starting in 1994, are somewhat less well understood. The crack cocaine market began to decline in the mid 1990s. Some believe that this occurred when young people came to understand the devastating effects that crack addiction has on its users. There were also increased policing efforts, harsher sentences for those found guilty of drug crimes and for those found to be members of gangs, and the number of gun tracing programs in large cities grew during the mid 1990s. All of this raised the price of participation in gangs, particularly for those at the lower levels of the organizations.

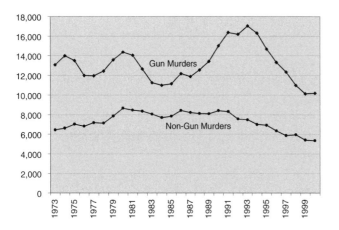

Murders Committed With and Without Guns, 1973-2000

One additional factor may have contributed to the decline in gun homicides. In 1992 a large gang in southern California, known as the Mexican Mafia, orchestrated a gang truce. The truce was commonly known as the "Eme Edict" after the nickname for the gang, La Eme. The extent to which this truce was effective in California and beyond is not known. It did, however, coincide with a decline in youth violence and murder rates and a striking decline in drive-by shooting incidents during the summer of 1993 in Los Angeles.

Unfortunately, there is reason in 2002 to be worried that the decline experienced in the last years of the 1990s may be coming to an end. Los Angeles is one of the cities with the greatest number of gangs. Young gang members may no longer feel bound by truces reached in the early 1990s. In an interview for the L.A. *Times*, one young gang member put it this way; "Yeah, I remember hearing about the truce. I remember hearing about JFK getting killed too." According to the Associated Press, there were 158 murders in

Los Angeles between January and May of 2002. Police fear that if the pace set in the early months of the year is kept up, as many as 370 people will be murdered in 2002. That is a figure higher than was reached in the peak year of 1993 when 346 people were murdered. A disquieting development to say the least.

Another disquieting development is the proliferation of youth gangs in non-urban areas, their traditional stronghold. We will use one more panel to try and assess trends in youth gang numbers and membership.

Source: U.S. Bureau of Justice Statistics, "Total Arrests by Age, 1970-1999," based on data from the Federal Bureau of Investigations annual Uniform Crime Reports for each year reported. Travis, Jeremy and Michelle Waul, The Urban Institute Justice Policy Center, *Reflections on the Crime Decline, Lessons for the Future?* August 2002, p. 42. U.S. Centers for Disease Control and Prevention, *National Vital Statistics Report*, "Number of Deaths from Injury by Firearm by Age, Race, and Sex: United States, 2000," September 16, 2002, p. 69. U.S. Bureau of Justice Statistics, *Key Facts at a Glance*, "Crimes Committed with Firearms, 1973-2000," table available online at http://www.ojp.usdoj.gov/glance/tables/guncrime tab.htm. *Young L.A. Gang Members Send Murder Rate Soaring*, an article without attribution posted on the Internet on July 22, 2002, and available at http://www.bet.com/article/1,,c1gb3381-4049,00.html.

The Diversification of Gangs

Presence of Gangs in Schools by Residential Area, 1989 and 1995

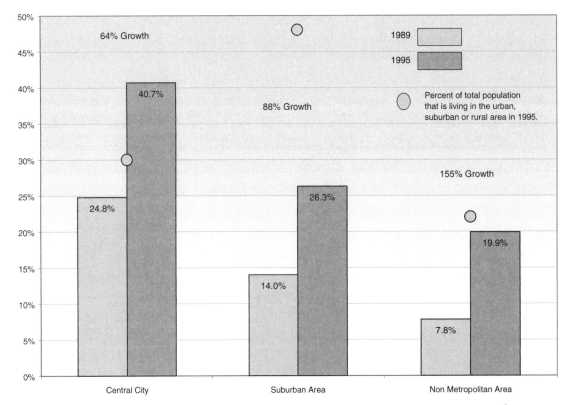

Finding reliable data that measures and quantifies organizations that live outside of the normal bounds of society is a tricky matter. Youth gangs, often called street gangs, are no exception. Estimates about membership in youth gangs vary widely. The U.S. Bureau of Justice Statistics estimates that in 1998 there were 28,700 youth gangs with 780,000 members across the nation.

Not all gangs are involved in criminal activities and membership in them rises and falls over time. Nonetheless, many gangs are involved in drug trafficking, car theft rings, loan sharking, larceny, or extortion. Even gangs not directly involved in such undertakings are usually governed by norms that support the explicit use of violence to settle disputes.

The graph presents data from a special supplement to the annual survey conducted by the U.S. Justice Department, the *National Crime Victimization Survey*. In both 1989 and 1995, special questions were added to the survey by way of assessing youth gang prevalence nation wide. Students between the ages of 12 and 19 were asked whether they were aware of a street gang presence in their schools. The responses for both years and by residential area are charted. For example, 14% of suburban children in 1989 claimed a gang presence in their schools. By 1995 that figure had increased by 88% to 26.3%.

Youth gangs have traditionally been racially and ethnically segregated, located in large urban centers, and associated with violent activity. This profile is changing.

In all three residential settings presented in the graph — central cities, suburbs and non-metropolitan areas — the presence of gang members in schools increased sharply over the period 1989 to 1995. Not surprisingly gang presence in city centers grew at the slowest pace, although a growth rate of 64% can hardly be considered slow. Gangs were already present in great numbers in urban centers when the first survey results were collected. Their presence in suburban and non metropolitan areas was much smaller and thus offered greater growth "opportunities" for new gangs and for expansion of existing gangs into new territories.

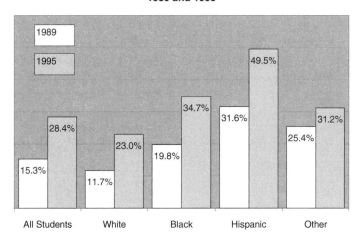

Presence of Gangs in Schools by Race and Ethnicity, 1989 and 1995

As youth gangs spread beyond their traditional settings, their demographic make-up is also changing. Gang presence in schools differs by race and ethnicity. As can be seen in the small graph, Hispanics have the highest rates of gang participation and have for some time now. This follows a pattern seen throughout U.S. history. New immigrant groups that enter the United States often flock to the same area and in short order form gang like organizations. Some of the early ones include the Irish gangs of the mid-1800s with names like Whyos, Dead Rabbits, and Plug Uglies. In New York City the Monk Eastman Gang, made up primarily of Jewish immigrants, terrorized the streets during the late 1800s. Among the Monk Eastman Gang's rivals were the newly forming Italian gangs, like the Five Point Gang. This group roamed the streets of New York before expanding to Chicago where one of its most infamous members ended up running the show. That was Al "Scarface" Capone.

By the 1940s and 50s the Hispanic gangs began to grow in number and strength. They tended to be centered in the west and in Chicago. As these gangs grew to control large areas of Los Angeles and Chicago, black gangs began to form. This brings us to the 1970s, to a thriving drug market supported by the large Baby Boom generation, and to the war on drugs.

As we saw in the previous panel, the 1980s and 1990s saw an enormous proliferation of youth gangs. It also saw the development of what are now called "Super Gangs." These are gangs that have expanded into multiple cities and states. They tend to have extensive drug networks, and their large membership rolls are far more multiethnic than was ever the case in the past. Gangs that fit this profile include the Crips, Gangster Disciples, Bloods, and Latin Kings.

The racial and ethnic desegregation of gangs was documented in a Justice Department study published in June 2002. The report was based on data collected in a survey of police departments across the nation, 3,000 enforcement jurisdictions in all. It found that jurisdictions that had gang problems starting before 1981 reported that 18% of those gangs were racially or ethnically mixed. In jurisdictions that did not see gang problems until after 1990 the percentage of gangs with a mixed racial or ethnic make-up exceeded 50%. This suggests that the gangs established prior to 1980 were more homogeneous than gangs established (or moving into a new territories) after 1990. A single race or single ethnicity are no longer a standard characteristic of youth gangs.

Primary Racial/Ethnic Make Up of Gangs Established before 1981 and after 1990

Establishment Date	Percent by Predominant Racial/Ethnic Membership					% With a significant mixture
	Hispanic	African American	Asian	White, Non-Hispanic	Other	
Before 1981	59	21	7	10	3	18
After 1990	20	33	5	39	3	50

Gangs no longer match the stereotypes that used to describe them. They have diversified both geographically and demographically. They are younger; many of their older members have been killed or are "doing time," having succumbed to increased law enforcement efforts and higher minimum sentences. Some gangs now include women among their numbers, although this is still unusual. Girl gangs exist, but little in the way of data is available to track their numbers. In general, during the 1990s, gangs have become less Hispanic and more suburban. Many of the newer gangs are less involved in violent crime and drug trafficking than their predecessors. At least so far they have been less involved.

Law enforcement professionals are monitoring youth gang activities closely. There is concern because the number of gangs has risen steadily throughout a period of declining crime rates. People incarcerated during the late 1980s and early 1990s will be released in ever greater numbers during the early 2000s. For example, in 2001, approximately 635,000 former prisoners (about 1,700 a day) were released back into their communities from state and federal correctional facilities. Many of these ex-convicts are gang members; many became gang members while in prison. How will communities handle this influx of former prisoners many of whom need assistance in making the transition from prison life to civilian life? Will they return to the gang life they once knew? Or will they mentor younger gang members on the potential downside to the lifestyle?

It is no wonder that professionals in law enforcement and within the justice system generally are keeping an eye on this potentially volatile situation.

Next we turn to a review of recent gun control efforts.

Source: U.S. Bureau of Justice Statistics and the National Center for Education Statistics, *Students' Reports of School Crime: 1989 and 1995*, March 1998, p. 8, available online at http://www.ojp.usdoj.gov/bjs/abstract/srsc.htm. U. S. Bureau of Justice Statistics, *Juvenile Justice Bulletin*, "Modern-Day Youth Gangs," June 2002, p. 4. Savelli, Sergeant Lou. Introduction to East Coast Gangs, November 2002, available online at http://www.nagia.org/east_coast_gangs.htm. Travis, Jeremy and Michelle Waul, The Urban Institute Justice Policy Center, *Reflections on the Crime Decline, Lessons for the Future?* August 2002, p. 21.

Guns A-Plenty

Percent of Selected Violent Crimes Committed with a Firearm, 1973-2000

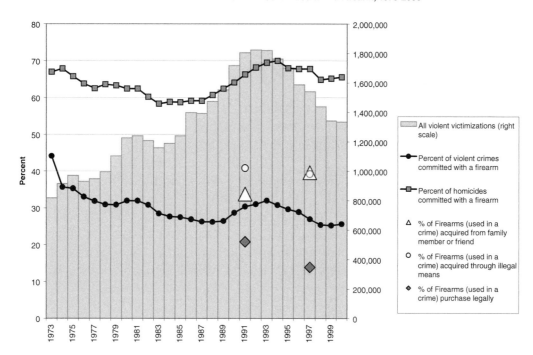

The second amendment of the United States Bill of Rights states that "A well regulated militia, being necessary to the security of a free state, the right of the people to keep and bear arms, shall not be infringed."

According to the U.S. Department of Justice, there were approximately 44 million gun owners in the United States in 1997. That is equivalent to a quarter of all adults and means that 40% of all households contain one or more firearms. Approximately 37,500 guns are sold within the United States every day; 17,800 are handguns. Our right to keep and bear arms is very much alive and well.

Considering the number of guns present in the society at large, it is almost surprising that more crimes are not committed with the aid of a gun. In 1994 alone, close to 600,000 guns were reported stolen during burglaries. In the following year, 503,600 violent crimes were committed in which a firearm was used.

About half of all violent crimes are committed with the use of a firearm, including homicides. Of all those arrested under suspicion of having committed a violent crime in 1999, 53% were for crimes committed with a gun. This was down from a high of 77% in 1993. When segregated by type of crime, the percentages vary. Sixty-six percent of murders in 2000 were committed with a firearm, as were 41% of robberies and 18% of aggravated assaults. The use of a firearm was involved in fewer than 18% of all other violent crimes.

The prevalence of firepower in our midst, combined with high rates of crime during the 1970s and 1980s, caused a rejuvenation of the debate about the merits of gun control. When debating this controversial subject, many are motivated by a belief that stricter gun regulations are a reasonable means of saving lives by reducing violent crime as well as other firearm-related deaths. Many others are fearful that gun regulations will slowly whittle away the right to have firearms and, in so doing, make the citizens of the nation vulnerable to tyranny. Underlying these views are strong philosophical positions. Events tend to influence the mood of the nation on this subject.

In 1934 congress passed the **National Firearms Act**, the nation's first federal gun control law. The law imposed a tax on the manufacture, sale, and transfer of sawed-off shotguns, sawed-off rifles, machine guns, and silencers. It also required buyers to fill out paperwork subject to Treasury Department approval. The mood of the nation was one of concern about the lawlessness and gangster culture that had evolved during the prohibition era. This law was intended to combat these forces.

The **Federal Firearms Act** followed in 1938. This act targeted sellers and shippers of arms and required that they obtain a federal firearms license. Sellers were also required to start keeping records of the names and addresses of all purchasers of firearms. Sales to known criminals were prohibited.

From 1938 through the mid-1960s, crime rates were down. No new gun control legislation passed.

Between 1960 and 1970, the homicide rate grew 77%. In 1963, John F. Kennedy was assassinated with a gun. In 1965 Malcolm X was assassinated with a gun. In 1968 Martin Luther King, Jr. and Robert F. Kennedy were assassinated with guns. In 1968 the **Gun Control Act** was passed.

The Gun Control Act of 1968 increased the number of categories of people who are prohibited from purchasing *or* owning guns. It also established a serial number requirement on all guns, prohibited the import of a variety of types of firearms, and authorized federal officials to inspect arms dealers' records and inventories. It greatly expanded the law established in the two earlier firearms acts. In 1970 Nixon declared a "war on drugs."

In 1981 there was an attempted assassination of President Reagan who was injured in the gun attack but not as severely as his Press Secretary, James Brady. As Mr. Brady recovered, he and his wife became active in the organization Handgun Control, Inc. In the mid-1980s they spearheaded a gun control initiative that bears the Brady name.

Between 1985 and 1993, the number of violent crimes committed in the United States increased 47% and the percentage of these that were committed with a gun rose 16%. In 1994 the **Brady Handgun Violence Protection Act** became law.

This law is best known as the Brady Bill or the Brady Law. Its primary features are the establishment of a five-day waiting period during which a background check must be run on anyone buying a gun. The law also authorized the development of a National Instant

Criminal Background Check System to be run by the Federal Bureau of Investigations. This system was put into service in 1998.

The 1990s were a period of much legislative activity in the area of gun control. The first law passed was the Brady Bill, followed shortly thereafter by the **Violent Crime Control and Law Enforcement Act.** It is generally referred to as the assault weapons ban. This act increased the number of categories of semi-automatic weapons that are illegal to manufacture, sell, or to possess.

In 1996 the **Domestic Violence Offender Gun Ban** became law. This law increases the list of those for whom gun ownership is prohibited to include anyone who has ever been convicted of a misdemeanor domestic violence offense or is currently subject to a restraining order regarding an intimate partner or the child of such a partner.

The late 1990s saw a decline in all types of crime. Between 1993 and 2000, violent crime dropped 27% and the portion of violent crimes committed with a gun dropped 20%. The economy was strong and people felt secure. There was no loud push for new gun control legislation. The mood was shifting away from concern for more gun control legislation as the crime rate dropped.

In September of 2001 the nation was stunned by a series of terrorist acts which took place on Tuesday the 11th. The mood became one of uncertainty and concern. Early and anecdotal reports from gun dealers suggest that gun sales soared in the second half of 2001. According to an article in the *Christian Science Monitor*, "…since September 11, it appears that Americans nationwide are finding comfort, increasingly, in a warm gun… And a Gallup poll taken a month after the attacks found American's desire for stricter firearm laws had dropped, with only 53% in support of such measures — the number had not been below 60% for nearly a decade."

The debate about gun control is one that will, no doubt, rage on. Is the drop in crime experienced in the late 1990s due in part to the Brady Handgun Violence Protection Act of 1993? Are most guns used in criminal actions purchased through legal means? We really don't know. We do know that fewer guns used in the commission of crimes by felons behind bars in 1997 were purchased legally than had been by those incarcerated in 1991, 14% in 1997 versus 21% in 1991.

If history is any guide in this matter we will likely see more support for gun control regulation if and when the crime rate begins to rise. In the meantime, existing laws will be enforced and the debate will continue.

Source: U.S. Bureau of Justice Statistics, *Estimated Firearm Crime*, "Murders, Robberies, and Aggravated Assaults in which a Firearm were Used, 1973-2000," available online at http://www.ojp.usdoj.gov/bjs/glance/tables/guncrimetab.htm. *Firearm Use by Offenders*, November 2001, p. 1. U.S. Department of Justice, *Promising Strategies to Reduce Gun Violence*, section 1, available online at http://www.ojp.usdoj.gov/bjs/pub/pdf/fuo.pdf. Chinni, Dante and Tim Vanderpool, "More in US Carry Guns; Restrictions Lose Support," *The Christian Science Monitor*, December 2001, p.1, section 3.

Extreme Domestic Violence

Murder Rate of Females by Their Intimate Partner, 1976-1999

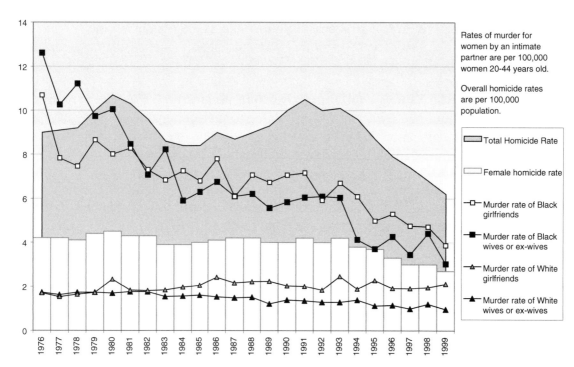

Rates of murder for women by an intimate partner are per 100,000 women 20-44 years old.

Overall homicide rates are per 100,000 population.

Legend:
- Total Homicide Rate
- Female homicide rate
- Murder rate of Black girlfriends
- Murder rate of Black wives or ex-wives
- Murder rate of White girlfriends
- Murder rate of White wives or ex-wives

Home safe and sound, a familiar phrase that conjures up all the warmth that one should feel about one's home. Home: a place of comfort and safety, a place of refuge from the wider world, somewhere to relax and rest. Domestic violence destroys the refuge.

American women have more to fear from the men they know and once loved than from any stranger. During 1999, females experienced 671,110 violent victimizations at the hand of an intimate partner[6]. The number of males victimized by a partner that year was 120,100[7].

Domestic violence lives in the shadows. Victims are often reluctant to seek help or admit that a problem exists for fear of making the situation worse. Collecting reliable data with which to quantify and measure the problem is therefore difficult. A much easier task, sadly, is to count the number of people killed by a domestic partner. The graph presents

---

[6] Some caution must be used when assessing these figures that come from the National Crime Victimization Survey. The survey is a survey of households, it does not cover those living in institutional settings, like shelters for battered women. In 2000 there were 2,000 federally recognized shelters for battered women throughout the United States.

[7] Of male victims in 1999, 10% were victimized by a same sex partner. Two percent of female victims suffered their injuries at the hands of a lesbian partner.

homicide rates for women who were killed by a partner (husband, ex-husband, boyfriend or ex-boyfriend) in 1976 through 1999. The total homicide rate and the homicide rate for all females are also provided by way of comparison.

Happily, the trend is downward. Rates for white and black women are very different. Black women have on average a rate 4.5 times higher than white women. In 1999 for women of both races, wives and ex-wives were killed by a partner at the lowest rates for the entire period 1976-1999. The rate for white wives and ex-wives declined by 45% over the period and for black wives and ex-wives by 76% thus reducing slightly the wide difference between them.

The rate at which black girlfriends are killed is also down substantially over the period, from a high of 10.7 per 100,000 in 1976 to a low of 3.9 in 1999. The data on white girlfriends paints a somewhat less rosy picture. They started out the period with a rate of homicide by intimate partner of 1.7. Over the next 24 years their rate fluctuated on its upward trajectory ending in 1999 at 2.1 per 100,000. Of the four categories of woman charted, white girlfriends were the only ones who saw their rate rise over the period.

For both white and black women, the rates at which wives and ex-wives are killed by a partner has been surpassed by the rates at which girlfriends are killed. In 1999 there were many more women who had never married than there were in 1976, primarily the result of later average entry into marriage. However, since we are looking at rates per 100,000 in the defined category, changes in population size don't explain changes in rates.

We do know that many more unmarried couples cohabited in 1999 than did so in 1976[8]. The relationship pressures on a couple who is dating versus a couple who is living together are different and may account for some small part of the rise in the rate of girlfriend homicide. So too might the added pressure on an unmarried couple caused when one of them is raising children for whom the other is not officially a parent. This does not, however, explain why black woman, who are single mothers at a higher rate than women in any other racial group, have seen a decline in their rate of intimate homicide while white girlfriends have seen their rate increase. The idea that added pressure in the relationship may be one factor in the rates of homicides among intimate unmarried couples is only a theory and one that is impossible to prove with the data available today.

Although many fewer men are murdered by their mates than are women, we should at least look briefly at trends in their rates of intimate homicide. That is what we turn to in the next panel.

Source: U.S. Department of Justice, Bureau of Justice Statistics, *Homicide Trends in the United States*, "Intimate Homicides," January 4, 2001, available online at http://www.ojp.usdoj.gov/bjs/homicide/intimates.htm. Bureau of Justice Statistics Special Report, *Intimate Partner Violence and Age of Victim, 1993-1999*, October 2001, p. 1. U.S. Centers for Disease Control, National Center for Health Statistics, *Vital Statistics*, "Homicide rate per 100,000 population, 1900-2000," October 2002, available online at http://www.ojp.usdoj.gov/bjs/glance/hmrt.htm.

---

[8] The number of unmarried, heterosexual couples cohabiting in 1980 was 1.6 million, according to U.S. Census Bureau estimates. By 2000 that number had risen to 5.3 million.

Victims of a Black Widow?

Rate for Husbands and Ex-Husbands Killed by Their Wives or Ex-Wives, 1976-1999

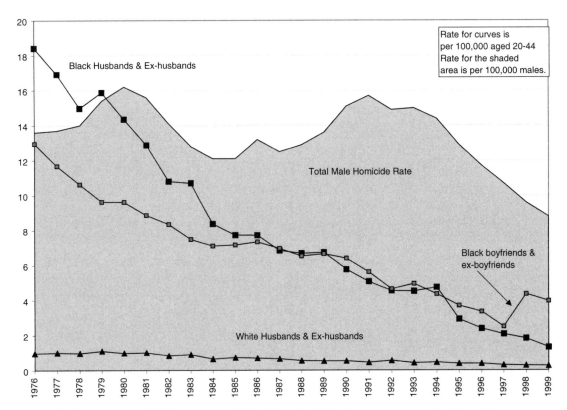

Trends in the rate at which men are killed by their intimate partners follow the same patterns seen for women. In short, the trend is down, and dramatically so for black men.

The graph charts homicide rates for men by race and marital status. The dark shaded area is the overall male homicide rate. Rates for white boyfriends are so close to the rates for white husbands that they were left off the graph to avoid a cluttered presentation.

For all men, rates are down. Black husbands and ex-husbands have experienced the most dramatic decline in victimization. Their rate of murder by a mate fell from a high in 1976 of 18.42 per 100,000 men age 20 to 44, to a low in 1999 of 1.33. This decline approaches an astonishing decrease of 1,300%. The question that strikes one looking at these data is: What was happening in the late 1970s and early 1980s with black married couples? A black husband or ex-husband was, in 1976, almost half as likely to be killed by his wife/ex-wife as by anyone else. Happily, black women no longer kill their husbands at such a high rate. In fact, black husbands and ex-husbands now have one of the lower rates of intimate homicide of all gender/race groupings.

Between 1976 and 1999, on average, 5.6% of all men who were murdered annually died at the hands of an intimate partner. For women, that number was 30%.

In this panel we see again that blacks have higher rates of victimization than whites, this time as males. The graphic below summarizes the pattern for both races and both genders. The bars represent victims. Thus, in 1999, 3.97 black boyfriends (of 100,000 black males aged 20 to 44) died at the hands of their girlfriends. The victimization rate of this group decreased 226% in the 1976 to 1999 period.

Intimate Homicide Rate by Victim's Relationship, 1999

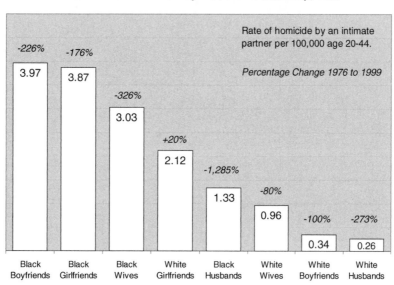

Blacks dominate the left-hand side of the graph where the rates are highest. Of the top four, three are black categories and three are female categories. Of the four lowest ranked categories, three are white and three are male.

We mustn't forget children as we conclude this discussion of domestic violence. Children are often caught in the middle of the violence carried on by the adults in a household and are sometime the direct victims of violent outbursts. Please see Chapter 5 for a discussion of child abuse.

We will look next at violent crime rates by race.

Source: U.S. Department of Justice, Bureau of Justice Statistics, *Homicide Trends in the United States*, "Intimate Homicides," January 4, 2001, available online at http://www.ojp.usdoj.gov/bjs/homicide/intimates.htm. Bureau of Justice Statistics Special Report, *Intimate Partner Violence and Age of Victim, 1993-1999*, October 2001, p. 1. U.S. Centers for Disease Control, National Center for Health Statistics, *Vital Statistics*, "Homicide rate per 100,000 population, 1900-2000," October 2002, available online at http://www.ojp.usdoj.gov/bjs/glance/hmrt.htm.

Racial Differences in Murder

Rates of Violent Victimization by Race, 1973-2001

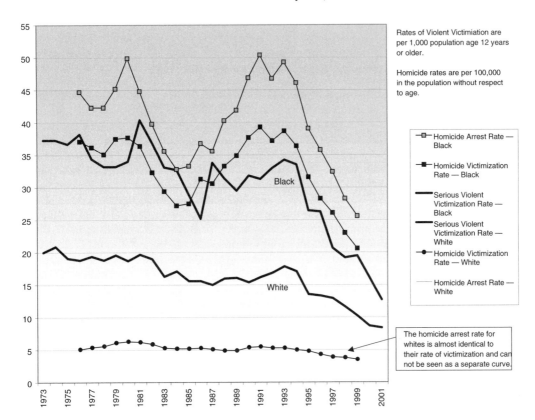

Rates of Violent Victimiation are per 1,000 population age 12 years or older.

Homicide rates are per 100,000 in the population without respect to age.

Legend:
- Homicide Arrest Rate — Black
- Homicide Victimization Rate — Black
- Serious Violent Victimization Rate — Black
- Serious Violent Victimization Rate — White
- Homicide Victimization Rate — White
- Homicide Arrest Rate — White

The homicide arrest rate for whites is almost identical to their rate of victimization and can not be seen as a separate curve.

"A central problem — perhaps *the* central problem — in improving the relationship between white and black America is the difference in racial crime rates." So begins a thorough and sobering paper by Dr. James Q. Wilson on the existence of large crime rate differentials in the white and black populations of the United States[9].

The graph charts violent crime victimization[10] rates (per 1,000 age 12 or older) for whites and blacks. Also shown are homicide offender and victimization rates (per 100,000 population). Rates for the two races differ greatly. Over the period 1973 through 2001, blacks were almost twice as likely as whites of being the victims of a violent crime.

When the specific crime of murder is segregated from all violent crimes, the picture becomes even more disparate. On average, over the period presented, blacks were 6.3 times more likely to be murdered than whites and they were 7.7 times as likely to be arrested

---

[9] The quote is from a book by the Hoover Institution Press. See the source note for a full citation.

[10] Violent crimes included are homicide, rape, robbery, and both simple and aggravated assault.

for murder. These figures represent a tremendous disparity. According to Dr. Wilson it is this difference that has done more to impeded racial amity than any other one factor.

The reasons for the higher rates of criminal activity in the African American community are complex — as are so many subjects that rest on an analysis of social structures. Throughout history, poor enclaves have tended to be areas in which the social structures that support a community are weaker than in other areas. There are many indicators of a weakened social structure. The presence of any one indicator does not necessarily signify weakness. The presence of several such indicators does, however, suggest that a community is in trouble. The following table lists a few such indicators and provides related data on the white and black populations in the United States.

Selected Social Indicators of a Weakened Social Structure

Social Indicator	Data from:	White Population	Black Population
High death rates from preventable conditions	1998	Maternal mortality rate of 5.5 per 100,000 live births. New cases of lung cancer per 100,000 population of 63.7.	Maternal mortality rate of 23.3 per 100,000 live births. New cases of lung cancer, same basis as white, 100.5.
Low levels of educational attainment	1990 / 2000	78% of those age 25 or older had a high school diploma. High school drop out rate was 6.9%.	63% of those age 25 or older had a high school diploma. High school drop out rate was 13.1%.
High levels of unemployment	2002 / 3rd Quarter	7.7% of men aged 20-24 were unemployed and 4.9% of all men age 16 or older.	20.4% of men aged 20-24 were unemployed and 10.1% of all men age 16 or older.
Low levels of family cohesion	2000	26% of families with children are single parent households.	61% of families with children are single parent households.
High levels of poverty	1998	8.4% of families and 11.0% of individuals were below the poverty rate.	23.6% of families and 26.5% of individuals were below the poverty rate.
High rates of substance abuse	1999-2000 average	5.7% of individuals 12 and older had used illegal substances in the month just past.	6.3% of individuals, same age group, had used illegal substances in the month just past.

The term "rough neighborhood" does not refer to a rich enclave with a rocky terrain. It means a rough, tough neighborhood where it is hard to make ends meet. These places are usually crowded, densely settled, and frictions ignite into conflict easier. Such neighborhoods, historically, have had high rates of crime. Large proportions of African Americans live in such neighborhoods. Therefore, the black crime rate reflects this reality. The crime rate is not a black phenomenon so much as a broad indicator of social distress.

The white population has "rough" neighborhoods as well, with equally high crime rates, but detailed statistics to track these are not available. The much better-off white majority's statistics absorb such data and hide them.

Nonetheless, the disparity between black arrest rates and victimization and the white rates tends to focus the discussion on *race* when more may be gained by viewing the crime rates as an indicator of a community's overall wellbeing. Policies designed to combat the poor health of a community may have just as salutary an impact on crime rates as policies designed to increase aggressive law enforcement measures.

The late 1990s saw a time of economic expansion great enough to reach the lowest levels of society. Unemployment rates dropped to 20-year lows. Crime rates dropped sharply, especially among blacks. The mid-1990s also saw a rising awareness within black leadership circles of the social cost associated with the deterioration of the family structure. In the 1990s, research came out showing that failed marriages and poor single-parent families produce extremely high social costs, one of these being higher rates of crime, especially crime perpetrated by youths.

There may be reason for optimism. The declining crime rate has already reduced the differential between the black crime rate and the white crime rate and if the underlying ills of the communities involved can be addressed, this may establish a new trend. Such a trend would be helpful in improving relations between white and black Americans.

Source: U.S. Bureau of Justice Statistics, *Homicide Trends in the United States*, based on data from the *National Crime Victimization Survey* and the *Uniform Crime Reports* series, March 2001, available online at http://www.ojp.usdoj.gov/bjs/homicide/homtrnd.htm. The quote from Dr. James Q. Wilson is from Thernstrom, Abigail and Stephen Thernstrom, *Beyond the Color Line: New Perspectives on Race and Ethnicity in America*, Hoover Institution Press, January 2002, p. 115. Educational attainment figures are from the U.S. Department of Education, National Center for Education Statistics, *Digest of Education Statistics, 2001*, "Educational Attainment of Persons 25 Years Old and Over, by State and Race/Ethnicity: April 1990," available online at http://nces.ed.gov/pubs2002/digest2001/tables/ dt012.asp. Figures on maternal mortality are from the U.S. Department of Health and Human Services, *Health, United States, 2001*, available online at http://www.cdc.gov/nchs/products/pubs/pubd/hus/tables/2001/01hus044.pdf. Data on high school dropout rates are from the U.S. Department of Education, National Center for Education Statistics, *Dropout Rates in the United States: 2000*, available online at http://nces.ed.gov/pubs2002/pubs2002/droppub_2001/. Unemployment rates are from the U.S. Bureau of Labor Statistics, *Household Data Not Seasonally Adjusted, Quarterly Averages*, "Unemployment Rates by Age, Sex, Race, and Hispanic Origin," available online at http://ftp.bls.gov/pub/suppl/empsit.cpseed17.txt.

Suffered in Silence

Rape and Sexual Assault, Annual Averages, 1992-2000

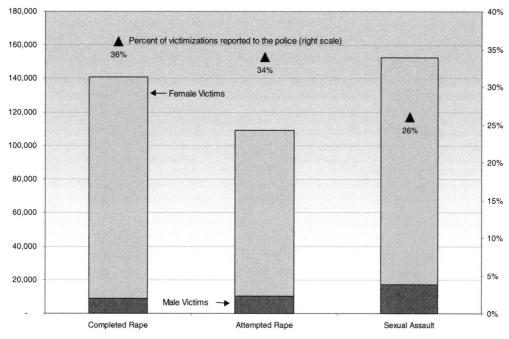

Altho ugh 386 people are raped every day in the United States it is one of the least reported of the violent crimes. Rape, attempted rape, and sexual assault are crimes suffered in silence.

The graph presents data on the number of rapes, attempted rapes, and instances of sexual assault perpetrated on average every year between 1992 and 2000. Although primarily a crime against women, men too suffer these attacks. The percent of violations reported in the *National Survey of Criminal Victimization* that were also reported to the police is presented on the graph with a triangle-shaped marker.

Rape is defined as forced intercourse with the attacker using a weapon, threat, coercion, violence or the threat of violence on the victim. Sexual assault has a broader definition: any unwanted sexual contact.

Most victims of these crimes are women. Most victims are attacked by a person whom they know. A stranger is the perpetrator in only one out of five instances. Most victims are young. The poor have higher rates of victimization than the more affluent. In 2000, those with an annual income under $7,500 suffered 5.2 rapes or sexual assaults per 1,000 people age 12 or older, those with income under $15,000 the rate was 3 rapes or sexual assaults. The rate dropped to 2 per 100 for those with $15,000 in income or higher.

During the 1990s, trends in rape and sexual assault followed the overall trends in crime: they were down 52% between 1993 and 2000. Nonetheless, one trend during this period is worth noting. Drug-induced rapes came to the attention of lawmakers during the 1990s.

Rohypnol, GHB, "ActiveSeX", and Roche are all names describing date rape drugs. These drugs are odorless, usually tasteless, and difficult to detect when in drinks or mixed with other drugs or food. The use of these drugs motivated the passage in 1996 of the Drug-Induced Rape Prevention and Punishment Act. This law provides criminal penalties of up to 20 years imprisonment for any person who distributes a controlled substance to another with the intent to commit a crime of violence, including rape. How effective this act is likely to be in reducing drug-inducted rapes will depend on whether or not victims of the crime come forward and press charges at rates greater than has been the case in the past. The deterrent effect of such legislation is also doubtful. Those who use rape-drugs are not likely to weight issues with a cold rationality.

In a review of rape and sexual assault trends, it is worth mentioning the crisis that gripped the Catholic Church during the 1990s. In the first six months of 2002 alone 225 Catholic priests left the church or were suspended due to allegations of sexual misconduct, primarily with adolescent boys. The abuses by a small number of priests and the seemingly willful ignorance of the matter by those higher up in church hierarchies is what appears to be most damaging to the Catholic Church.

It is worthwhile to note that 225 priests in a total of 45,000 Catholic priests is equal to 0.5% of all Catholic priests. This is *not* a higher percentage of pedophiles than is estimated for the society at large[11]. Nonetheless, it is the unique relationship that exists between a priest and a parishioner, particularly a young one, that makes these crimes so tragic and sensational. It is also what brings media attention to the subject and why this reasonably small percentage of all sexual abuse cases gains so much more attention than do all the rest combined.

An interesting fact that distinguishes rape and sexual assault from all other violent crimes is the fact that the rate at which it is perpetrated in urban, suburban, and rural areas does not differ greatly. All other violent crimes are committed at much higher rates in urban areas than in suburban areas and at higher rates in suburbs than in rural areas. Not so for rape and sexual assault.

The next panel will look at urban, suburban, and rural crime rate differentials.

Source: U.S. Department of Justice, Bureau of Justice Statistics, *Rape and Sexual Assault: Reporting to Police and Medical Attention, 1992-2000*, August 2002, p. 1 and Crime Victimization 2000, June 2001, p. 11 and *Violence Against Women: Estimates for the Redesigned Survey*, August 1995, p. 1. National Institute for the Renewal of the Priesthood, "Interesting Statistics Affecting the Priesthood," available online at http://www.jknirp.com/stats.html.

---

[11] For an overview of child abuse and the victimization of children please see Chapter 5.

The Pressures of Density

Violent Victimization and Homicide Rates by Population Density, 1993-1998

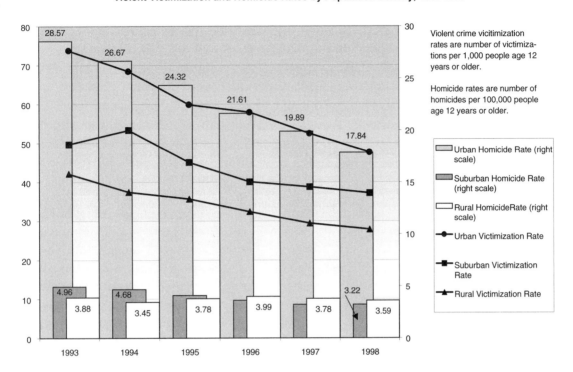

The likelihood of being the victim of a violent crime is lowest if you live in a rural area, followed by the more populous areas, suburbs. It is highest in our most densely populated areas, urban centers. The same pattern is visible when it comes to the likelihood of being murdered.

The graph presents data on both violent victimization rates (curves) and homicide rates (bars) for urban centers, suburbs and rural areas. The six-year period presented, 1993-1998, was one of declining crime rates as we have seen throughout this chapter and is again visible here in all six rates charted. All the rates are down by between 25% and 37% except for one, the rural homicide rate which, although down, is only down 7.5%.

The observable pattern in the graph is one of overwhelmingly higher rates of victimization in urban areas versus suburban and rural areas. This is nothing new. It is the pattern observed in all industrialized countries and to some extent in human societies throughout history. Where people congregate in large numbers they interact more often in both positive and negative ways. Crime is, of course, one of the negative ways.

The graph depicts trends that are, for the most part, very positive. Violent victimizations are on the decline, as are murders. Of particular interest is the fact that homicide rates in rural areas have declined far *less* than in either of the other geographic categories presented. The percent at which each rate of violent victimization declined over the period 1993-1998 is shown in the table on the next page.

Percentage Declines in Violent Victimization Rates, 1993-98

Crimes	Urban Centers	Suburbs	Rural Areas
Violent Victimizations	35.4	25.2	33.9
Homicides	37.5	35.1	**7.5**

There are several possible reasons for why the homicide rate in rural America dropped least over this time period. The rural homicide rate started off at the lowest rate of the three, 3.88 per 100,000 people age 12 years or older, compared with 28.97 and 4.95 for urban areas and suburbs respectively. Some criminologists believe that there is a sort of irreducible minimum level of crime, although it is never specifically quantified. Perhaps the homicide rate in rural areas is near that minimum level and has very little downward flexibility.

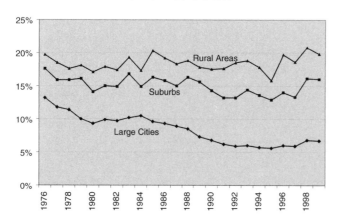

Intimate Murders as Percent of All Murders by Type of Residential Area, 1976-1999

The percentage of rural homicides that are committed by those with an intimate connection to the victim is much higher than in urban and suburban areas. This fact may support the minimum level of crime theory and suggest that rural areas are nearer the theoretical minimum.

One other trend affecting rural communities is worth noting. During the 1990s illicit drug manufacturing (primarily the manufacture of methamphetamines) began to spread into rural areas and youth gangs began to appear in small rural towns. Both of these newcomers to the rural landscape bring with them increased criminal activity. This fact very likely contributed to the more modest drop in homicide rates seen in rural areas as compared with suburbs and urban centers during the late 1990s. For more on the prevalence of methamphetamines in rural America, see Chapter Six, Drugs.

In the last panel we mentioned rape pointing out that it is equally prevalent in all regions of density. This is true at a summary level. Violent crime overall is twice as common in central cities than it is in the country. Assaults of both kinds, simple and aggravated, are twice as likely to occur in the city. Robbery is three times more prevalent. But rape is equivalent. Small differences do appear. In central cities the rate was 1.8 per 1,000 population, 1.4 in suburbs, 1.3 in rural areas. This category, however, showed the smallest differences between geographies of increasing population density.

The pattern of higher rates of crime in more populated areas has not changed. Crime is down across all types of communities. The greatest declines were experienced in those areas that had the highest rates during recent periods of peak crime, urban centers. This has caused a slight reduction in the differential rates of crime experienced in urban, suburban, and rural areas. Nonetheless, where more people live together in densely packed areas there is more crime, a situation that is unlikely to change anytime soon.

Source: U.S. Bureau of Justice Statistics, *Urban, Suburban, and Rural Victimization*, 1993-1998, October 2000, pp. 3 and 11. Homicide Trends in the U.S., "Homicides by Location Types," January 2001, available online at http://www.ojp.usdoj.gov/bjs/homicide/tables/urbantab.htm and "Percent Intimate Homicide Victims by Location," available online at http:// www.ojp.usdoj.gov/bjs/homicide/tables/int_urbtab.htm.

Violence in the Workplace

In What Occupations Are You at Most Risk?

Decline in the Rate of Violent Victimizations per 1,000 Workers between 1993 and 1999

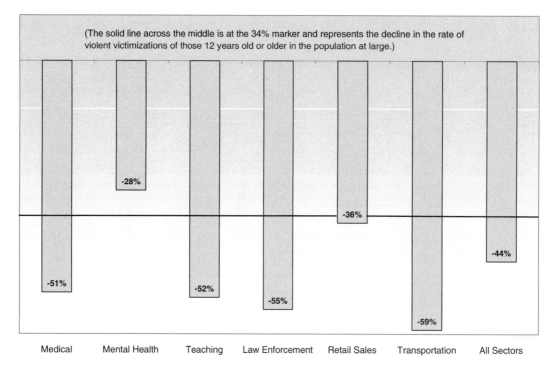

(The solid line across the middle is at the 34% marker and represents the decline in the rate of violent victimizations of those 12 years old or older in the population at large.)

-28%

-36%

-44%

-51%

-52%

-55%

-59%

Medical   Mental Health   Teaching   Law Enforcement   Retail Sales   Transportation   All Sectors

Finally, a brief look at violence in the workplace. It shows that the same trends seen in violent victimization rates generally are mirrored in the workplace.

This graph presents data on the decline in the number of violent incidents in the workplace between 1993 and 1999. The six individual employment categories presented have the dubious distinction of being the categories with the highest rates of violent criminal victimization. Policemen, nurses, psychiatrists, cabbies, and cashiers, all are at high risk of being assaulted on-the-job. A total workplace figure is provided under the heading "All Sectors."

The trend is clear. Violent acts in the workplace have declined sharply. For the workplace as a whole, the decline between 1993 and 1999 was 44%, a full 10 percentage points greater than the decline experienced by the society as a whole. Violent crime in the general population fell 34% during this period. A line has been drawn across the graph at the 34% mark by way of highlighting the decline in violent crime in society generally.

In all but one of the most vulnerable employment categories, the rates of violent crime dropped by more than the rate dropped in the society at large. The one exception was for those people who work with the mentally ill. They saw saw the most modest decline in their rates of violent victimization. But even in this category the decline in violent acts on-the-job was significant, 28%.

Because the chart shows changes in percentage and does not provide a sense of how vulnerable to violent assault one group is relative to another, the following table is provided. Here one can see how frequently those employed in the six categories presented are victimized. Here, again, we see that with the exception of those working in law enforcement or with the mentally ill, one is safer at work than in the public square.

Rates of Violent Victimization per 1,000 Workers

Category / Industry	1993	1999
All Private Employment	16.0	9.0
Law Enforcement	163.1	74.1
Mental Health	64.4	46.1
Teaching	25.8	12.4
Retail Sales	21.9	14.1
Transportation	20.6	8.4
Medical Fields	20.3	10.0
Society at Large *	50.0	33.0

*In the case of the "society at large," rates are per 1,000 people aged 12 years or older.

For every 1,000 people age 12 years or older, 33 were the victims of a violent act at some time during 1999, down by 34% from the rate of 50 in 1993.

Violent acts are down, both in the workplace and in the society at large. It is, in fact, more likely that one will be assaulted off-the-job than on-the-job. In an analysis of the location in which violent acts occur, the victim's home is the leading location accounting for 15% of all violent victimizations (not including murder). A somewhat less than reassuring fact.

Source: U.S. Department of Justice, Bureau of Justice Statistics, Violent Crime Victimization Survey 2000, table entitled *Violence in the Workplace*, 1993-99, available online at http:// www.ojp.usdoj.gov/bjs/abstract/cvusst.htm. For data on the rates of violent crime generally; U.S. Department of Justice, Bureau of Justice Statistics, National Crime Victimization Survey, *Criminal Victimization 1999, Changes 1998-99 with Trends 1993-99*, page 1. Data on the location of in which violent victimizations occur is from the Bureau of Justice Statistics, "Urban, Suburban, and Rural Victimization, 1993-1998," October 2000, p. 8.

Chapter 3

Property Crime

You suddenly realize your purse is missing. You come home from work and the television is gone. As you walk though the mall parking lot, searching for your vehicle, you realize someone actually *has* stolen it. These are called property crimes: larcenies, burglaries and motor vehicle thefts. By one very conservative estimate, annual losses are thought to exceed at least $15 billion.

Such crimes have been largely on the decline since the 1970s. Some writers have theorized that changes in American lifestyle and culture have played a significant role in this trend. Many of us spend our evenings at home; indeed, many of us work *from* our homes. Does this foil the plans of the typical burglar? More homes have two car garages; 64% to be exact, up from 48% of homes in 1973, according to the National Home Builders Association. Cars are now kept inside as opposed to parked on the street where they may be stolen or vandalized. Not just automobiles either, of course: lawn tools, bicycles, and other home necessities are now tucked away from a thief's appraising eye. We now lock our doors and windows. Some of us have bars on our windows. Some of us set our burglar alarms; the average system is now fairly affordable, having fallen about 34% in the 1990s. An estimated 20,000 gated communities exist in the nation, housing more than 8 million people. According to one study, 97% of them have electronic keypads (a far smaller percentage have guards for the property).

There will always be thieves, of course. The number of them is influenced to no small degree by the state of the economy. When times are tough, there is going to be some segment of the population that will just take what they can't afford.

The first panels in the chapter will provide an introduction to property offenses: the rate of those victimized and those arrested for such deeds. Other panels will look at each segment of property crime: larcenies, burglaries, and car theft. What are the major trends around these crimes? The level of some crimes has remained curiously consistent; purse snatching, for example, has made up 1% of all larcenies during the last 30 years. Other crimes have changed in subtle ways. In the late 1990s, law enforcement saw an increase in burglaries committed during the day. As parked cars became more difficult to steal, the crime of carjackings began to increase.

This chapter will also look at arson. It was first indexed as a property crime in October 1978. This crime doesn't have the same basic motivations that property crime does. The panel includes details on who commits this crime and why.

The final panels in this chapter will look at a different kind of theft — fraud. Hopefully the reader will see the slightly twisted logic in grouping property crime and fraud together: if I can't steal it, one might argue, then I'll cheat you out of it. The first panel will look at common types of fraud. Later panels will examine some of these crimes in closer detail. Identity theft is a fast-growing crime; a few vital pieces of information and a crook can cause you a great deal of grief. A case of corporate wrongdoing seems to make headlines regularly in recent years, from the fall of Enron to insider trading accusations against Martha Stewart. How many businesses cook their books to meet their bottom lines? We'll see how Corporate America handles their finances.

The fraud section also includes several panels on copyright infringement — another issue important to big businesses. Should original ideas be protected? What about great works of art and music? Do they belong to the public to use as it sees fit? We'll also see how the old crime of counterfeiting has changed in the computer age. Another panel will address health care fraud, and examine just who the real offenders are. The last panel in the chapter takes a light-hearted look at one of the oldest cons in the book to show that people do indeed "still fall for that stuff."

An Introduction to Property Crime

Falling Rates for Property Crime

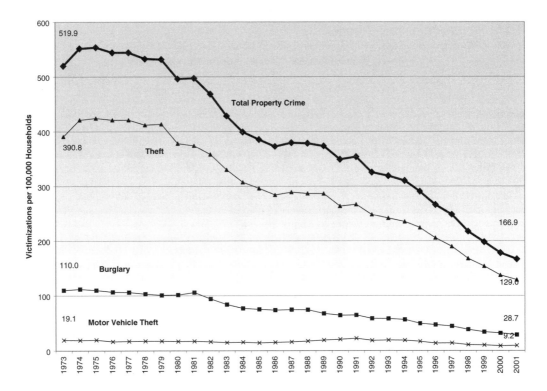

From 1973 to 2001, the rate of thefts and burglaries decreased in the United States.

Data are based on the Justice Department's National Crime Victimization Survey (NCVS). The level of property crime is measured in "victimizations" — or the number of people who experience a burglary or some theft of personal property (see the panel *Indexes of Crime* in Chapter 1 for more on the measurement of this and other crimes).

All forms of property crime decreased significantly over the period. Total property crime fell 67.8% from 1973 to 2001. Burglaries fell 74%, theft 67%, and motor vehicle thefts fell 51.8%.

Who is most affected by property crimes? The table on the next page looks at selected demographics. Blacks still are victimized more often than whites.[1] Hispanics are victimized more often than non-Hispanics. Is income a factor? One might imagine a high income would translate into a home in a safe neighborhood. But those with an income above $50,000 saw the highest levels of victimization through most of the 1990s. In 2000, property crime was spread fairly evenly over the income classes. Those making

---

[1] The Department of Justice does not collect Hispanics data in a way to make it comparable to the data for blacks and whites.

between $15,000 and $24,999 were nearly as likely to experience this sort of crime as those making $75,000 or more.

How have things changed? From 1993 to 2000, rates dropped 44% for both blacks and whites. For the lowest income class, property crime dropped 27.8%. For those making over $75,000, the crime rate dropped 50.7%.

Property Crime Rates Per 100,000 Households, 1993-2000

	1993	1994	1995	1996	1997	1998	1999	2000	Change, 93-00 - %
By Race/Ethnicity									
Whites	309.7	304.8	283.4	259.9	242.3	212.6	190.0	173.3	-44.0
Blacks	376.6	347.8	328.8	310.0	292.0	248.0	249.9	212.3	-43.6
Hispanics	429.7	435.9	385.3	328.1	329.4	267.6	232.5	227.0	-47.2
Non-Hispanics	311.0	300.3	282.8	261.2	240.8	212.5	194.6	173.4	-44.2
By Income Level									
Less than $7,500	305.9	299.6	304.3	282.7	258.8	209.0	220.8	220.9	-27.8
$7,500-$14,999	285.9	299.1	267.1	247.5	236.3	229.8	200.1	167.1	-41.6
$15,000-$24,999	307.0	308.1	289.8	273.1	242.4	211.0	214.9	193.1	-37.1
$25,000-$34,999	336.7	305.2	294.8	285.1	260.3	233.8	199.1	192.2	-42.9
$35,000-$49,999	342.7	326.9	301.5	287.6	271.7	221.7	207.6	192.9	-43.7
$50,000-$74,999	374.4	364.1	333.2	284.0	270.9	248.6	213.6	181.9	-51.1
$75,000 or more	400.3	356.0	350.4	304.6	292.8	248.6	220.4	197.2	-50.7

What are some reasons for the improved rates? Americans seem more conscious of the need to protecting themselves and their property — and those with the most income can best afford it. Spending on security systems for homes and businesses has jumped from $14.9 billion in 1998 to $17.5 billion in 2000, according to STAT Resources Inc. *SDT Magazine*, a publication of the security systems market, offers a similar estimate of the industry: $18 billion. Cost is becoming less of an issue as well, with an average home security system costing about $200 to install. The economic health of the country during this period is probably the major factor: good times have generally translated into lower incidents of property crime.

Other panels in this chapter will look at these crimes in greater detail. A question that probably needs to be asked here: If most property crimes are down, have thieves simply turned to other more lucrative areas? Credit card fraud and identity thefts have become hot topics in the media in recent years. Is it now easier to steal a person's identity than his or her car or a television set? We shall see.

Source: Chart data comes from U.S. Department of Justice, retrieved from http://www.ojp.usdoj.gov/bjs/glance/tables/proptrdtab.htm. Bureau of Justice Statistics, National Crime Victimization Survey, *Criminal Victimization 2000*; data from STAT-Resources comes from http://www.e-burglar-alarm-systems-home-security.com; "The Markets to Watch." *Catalog Age*, June 1, 2002.

Introduction to Property Crime: The Arrests

Property Crime Arrests per 100,000 People, 1971-2000

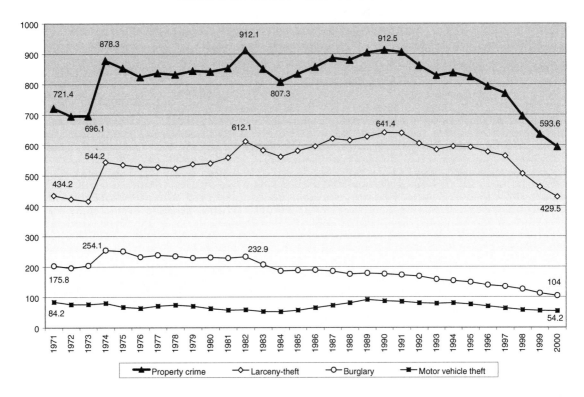

The last panel showed those who reported in surveys that they had been victimized by property crimes. This panel examines trends in arrests. Arrest rates are typically lower than victimization rates — people do not report crimes, and offenders are frequently not caught.

Property crime arrests are down 17.7% from 1973 to 2000, from 721.4 to 593.6 per 100,000 people. There have been several noticeable spikes in the arrest rate that need to be addressed. In one year, 1973 to 1974, arrests jumped 26% from 696.1 to 878.3 per 100,000 people. The rate fell 11.4% from 1982 (its peak) to 1984. Property crime spikes as the economy tanks. The arrest rate jumped during the recessions of 1974, 1980, 1981-1983, and in the wake of the 1990 recession. The rate fell during the rest of the 1990s as the economy boomed. The most frequently committed crime, larceny, gives the property crime rate its shape.

Arrests for burglaries fell 48.7% and for motor vehicle theft fell 35.6%. Burglary arrests have been on the decline since hitting a peak of 232.9 arrests in 1982. Are burglars switching to other crimes? Or is there something about the American lifestyle — people now lock their doors and more homes have security features — that makes burglary a more unattractive crime? (A future panel will look burglary in detail.) Motor vehicle arrests, by contrast, have fluctuated over the 30 year period. There were 84.2 per 100,000 arrests in 1971. By 1975, the rate had fallen to 67.1 arrests. It rose and fell in the 1980s,

---

climbed to its peak of 91.4 people in 1991 before it began a steady decline. We shall look at car thefts in more detail as well.

Arrests for larcenies and thefts fell only 1% in the period, the decline coming late in the 1990s. Theft is here to stay. People will probably always shoplift or steal a bike or snatch a cellular phone out of someone's unlocked car. Property crime dropped significantly in the prosperous 1990s: From 1997 to 2000, larcenies fell 24%, burglaries fell 23% and motor vehicle thefts fell 15%.

Arson Arrests per 100,000 People, 1979-2000

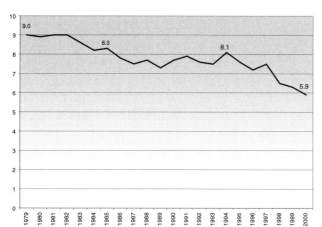

Arrests are down for arson, as well, which was not included as an index property crime until October 1978. The rate of arrest has fallen 30% from 1979 to 2000. The motivations for this type of crime are often more complex than for other forms of property crime. Arsons hide boredom, cover up crime, or express psychosocial problems. This crime will be examined more closely in an upcoming panel.

Arrests represent only a fraction of offenses — less than a fifth in the case of property crime. In 1999, 11.7 million property crimes, excluding arson, were reported to police. Of that total, 17.5% were "cleared" by an arrest. The clearance rate has fallen in recent years from 18.1% in 1996. The low point came in 1980, when only 16.5% of property crimes resulted in an arrest. During the 1980s and 1990s, the rate hovered between 17.5 and 18%. The number of reported cases fluctuated from a low of 9.9 million to a high of 11.7 million. But reported crimes are not total crimes. Many go unreported. We take up that subject in another segment.

The next panels will look at each type of property crime.

Source:, U.S. Department of Justice, Bureau of Justice Statistics, *Sourcebook of Criminal Justice Statistics, 2000*, Washington D.C., USGPO, 2001, p. 353.

Thou Shalt Not Steal

Sticky Fingers: Crimes of Larceny, 1973-2000

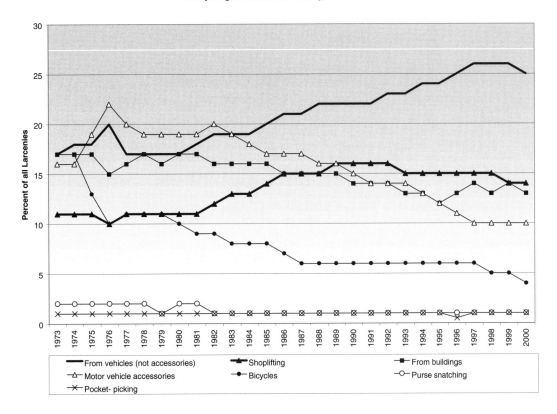

Larceny is the theft of personal property. In some states, larceny in which the property equals or exceeds a specified amount is considered grand larceny. Larceny involving lesser amounts is known as petty larceny. Many larcenies are crimes of opportunity: a car door is left unlocked, a woman is not watching her purse, an aisle in a store stands deserted.

There were 7.1 million larcenies in 1973, increasing steadily in the 1980s to 8.1 million in 1991. Then they fell slightly, began another increase, and then began to fall again in 1996. They currently stand at 6.9 million.

The two leading types of larcenies are thefts from motor vehicles and shoplifting (they're highlighted in the panel). Thefts from motor vehicles made up 25% of all reported larcenies in 2000. It's easy to see why cars draw thieves like magnets. A laptop may be lying on a backseat, a cellular phone on the front, a stack of CDs may be inviting, a purse, a gym bag with potential valuables inside it — cash, an ID card. Or the car door may be open with shopping bags from the last mall inside — while the owner is shopping some more in this new mall.

Shoplifting accounts for 14% of reported larcenies. There is no typical shoplifter, but he or she is usually young. Men and women shoplift at roughly equal rates. In one recent report, shoplifters claim they are caught once for every 49 times they steal. For some people, such crime is a lifestyle. One professional shoplifter caught by Target Corp. claimed he made $120,000 to $150,000 cash per year. He never "worked" weekends and took vacation from Thanksgiving to Christmas. (Instead of asking him "What do you do for a living," should he be asked "What do you *take* for a living?")

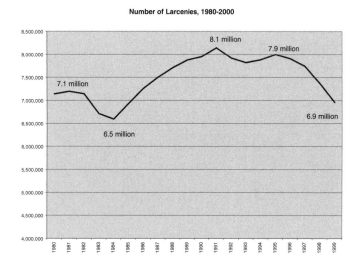

Number of Larcenies, 1980-2000

Bicycle theft fell in the mid-1970s and then again in the early 1980s. Now no one parks a bike without a lock. Thefts from buildings saw some brief increases in the 1990s. (Disgruntled employees?) Some crimes have remained constants. After 1982, both purse snatching and pocket picking have each made up 1% of the total reported larcenies.

The decline in thefts may be influenced by simple population issues. Many of these crimes are committed by and against juveniles. Their population fell steadily over the period. There were 20.5 million teenagers between 15 and 19 in 1981, 18.9 million in 1984 and 17.1 million by 1992. The pool of potential victims shrank as well. Those between 12 and 24 years of age see the highest rates of property theft. Their numbers fell from about 40 million in 1981 to 39 million in 1984 to 36.7 million in 1992.

But the population of these age groups are forecast to grow in the late 1990s. Will larcenies begin to swell?

Source: Chart: data comes from the Federal Bureau of Investigations at http://www.albany.edu/sourcebook. Note: the category coin operated machines was not included on the panel. It was 1% from 1973-2000. "Shoplifting Facts and Figures." *Virginian-Pilot,* July 14, 2002. Population figures come from the U.S. Bureau of the Census.

Auto Theft

Automobile Theft in the United States, 1980-2000

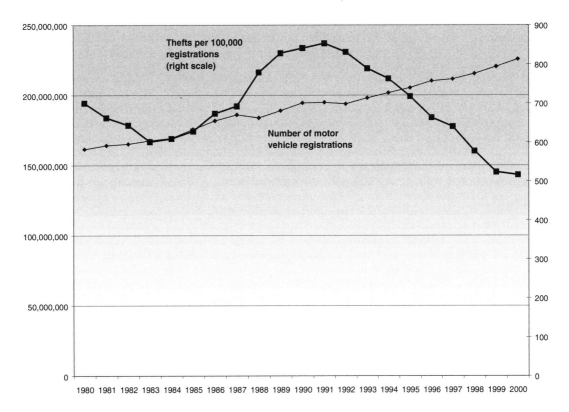

Cars valued at $7.5 billion are stolen every year. According to the National Insurance Crime Bureau, a vehicle is stolen every 30 seconds.

The number of stolen cars increased 54% from 1.0 million in 1981 to 1.66 million in 1991. The number of registered vehicles on the road increased 20%. Car thefts declined, partly because cars became more difficult to steal. Consumers spent $400 million on auto security devices in 1996, from "kill" switches to sophisticated alarm systems. LoJack Corporation provides an electronic tracking system for stolen vehicles and credits its system with the recovery of more than 50,000 vehicles valued at $1 billion.

During the early 1990s, there was evidence that stealing cars is related to offenses such as robbery and drug trafficking. The Anti-Car Theft Act, passed in 1992, is an effort to strengthen laws against auto theft, and related crimes.

The Honda Accord and Toyota Camry rank as both the top selling and most stolen vehicles in the U.S. Robert Bryant, president of the National Insurance Crime Bureau observed: "Vehicle thieves follow market trends and target the most popular vehicles because they provide the best market for stolen vehicle parts and illegal export to other countries." Pickups, mini-vans, and sport utility vehicles made up about one-third of the list of the top 50 stolen vehicles in the country.

More than 30% of stolen vehicles are never recovered. Many of the stolen vehicles are shipped overseas or driven across the border. Roughly 200,000 vehicles are illegally exported each year. The top communities for auto theft are all near borders or ports: Phoenix, AZ, Miami, FL, Fresno, CA, Detroit, MI, and Sacramento, CA.

As cars became more difficult to steal, a new type of crime arose. In carjacking a thief takes the car with actual or implied force force. A driver can be victimized anywhere at any time.

Statistics show that between 1987 and 1992, there was an average of 35,000 attempted and completed carjackings *each year* in the U.S. (Department of Justice). Between 1992 and 1996, there were 48,787 such incidents annually, an increase of 39%. The split between attempted and completed carjackings is about 50-50 for each period. Men were victimized more than women; blacks more than whites; city residents more than those in the suburbs.[2]

Annual Average Rates of Attempted or

Completed Carjackings, 1992-1996

Characteristic	Rate (per 100,000 people)
12-24 years old	2.5
25-49 years old	3.6
50 or older	0.9
Males	3.1
Females	1.9
Whites	2.0
All Hispanics	6.1
All Non-Hispanics	2.2
Urban	4.0
Suburban	2.4

The number of stolen cars increased nearly 2% from 1999 to 2000, from 1.152 million to 1.165 million vehicles. Every step we take to prevent crime helps, of course. But some of us are making theft too easy. The National Insurance Crime Bureau says that more than 21% of all car owners do not lock their doors.

Sources: "Car Theft Fact Sheet." Online. Available: http://www.carsdirect.com. "National Motor Vehicle Title Information System." Online. Available: http://www.aamva.org; "Lojack Company Overview." Retrieved from http://www.lojack.com; "Top Theft Areas." Online. Available: http://www.nicb.org/services; Bureau of Justice Statistics, *Carjacking: National Crime Victimization Survey* and *Carjackings in the United States, 1992-96.*

---

[2] In a sign that carjackings are perhaps here to stay, the word was accepted into the Shorter Oxford English Dictionary in September 2002. Other words which made their debut in the new edition include Klingons, line dancing, lap dancing, road rage, and shock jocks.

Burglaries

Percent of All Burglaries, 1976-2000

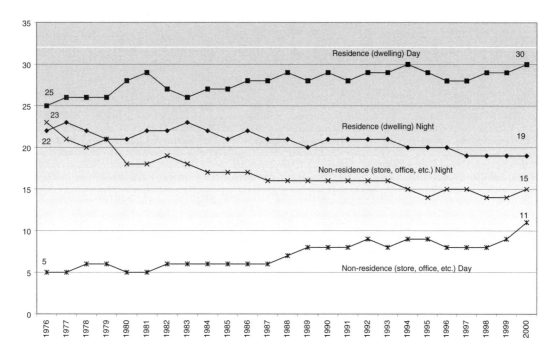

The number of burglaries in the nation increased from 2.9 million in 1976 to 3.5 million in 1980 and then declined to 1.2 million in 1999. According to FBI statistics, roughly half of all residences and businesses are robbed during the day.

Nearly 30% of all burglaries occurred at a residence during the day, a figure that has been on the increase in recent years. Eleven percent of all burglaries of offices and stores took place during the day also. About a quarter of all robberies happened at an unknown time of day, but it is reasonable to think a significant portion of them happened during the day (those robberies which occurred at an known time of day were not included in the panel.)

George Rengart, a professor in the Department of Criminology at Temple University, argues that there is more than one type of burglar. There is the "first opportunity" burglar, also known as "the smash and grab." Urban drug addicts are of this type. They need money quickly. There is also the "marriage model" burglar. He will scout homes until he finds one that he likes. The "homebuyer model" burglar develops a short list of potential houses to rob.

It is not uncommon for thieves to study houses to determine which may be empty. According to the National Burglar and Fire Alarm Association, a typical burglar may spend only minutes to break into a house, but he may spend 30 to 40 minutes choosing the dwelling. Are newspapers piled up by the door? Have garbage cans been left at curbside? Are there no lights on in the house in the evenings? All of these are potential tipoffs. Some thieves have been known to call houses to see if anyone answers. In Rengart's study, he found thieves would watch women's coming and goings to learn their schedules. As "guardians of the home" women's routines were less predictable than those of men and children (who leave every day to go to work and school at the same time). He discovered women left the home just as the typical burglar started his day. Stay-at-home mothers are one thing. What of the millions of families where both women and men are off at work all day? "Suburban two-income couples are easy marks for burglars," according to Rengart. "The only thing that protects them is the distance between the burglar and their home."

Highest growth has been associated with non-residence properties burgled by day. The share of thefts from offices and buildings grew 37.5% from 1998 to 2000. From 1976 to 2000, the category grew 120%. In a study conducted by Dr. Simon Hakim and Mary Ann Gaffney, office suites accounted for 47% of commercial burglaries, almost 2.5 times more than single office buildings. Office suites are attractive targets for crooks, especially newer buildings where tenants will have newer office equipment — equipment easier to fence. Similarly, office parks make good targets because they tend to be secluded, poorly lit, and deserted after business hours.

Businesses have, of course, taken steps to protect their property. Private security spending has increased 900% from 1975 to 1998, according to one study. The percentage of retail businesses with closed-circuit television systems has soared to 73% since the devices were first employed in the 1980s.

According to the FBI, the total dollar loss to victims was $4.3 billion in 1995, $3.1 billion in 1999. The average losses increased slightly: $1,305 to $1,441 for residences and $1,391 to $1,490 for non-residences. The greatest losses came from the theft of televisions, radios, stereos, jewelry, and currency.

In roughly half of all burglaries, thieves gain entrance through the front door. Really? Amazing…

Source: U.S. Department of Justice, Bureau of Justice Statistics, *Sourcebook of Criminal Justice Statistics*, Washington D.C., USGPO, 2001, p. 323; Calem, Robert E. "Protecting Your Turf." *Meetings & Conventions*, May 1996, p. 42; Brad Edmonson. "Time for Crime." *American Demographics*, April 1991, p. 14; Lisa Arbetter. "Understanding Commercial Burglaries." *Security Management*, June 1994, p. 13.

What Do Thieves Like to Steal?

Property Stolen from Teenagers, 1996-97

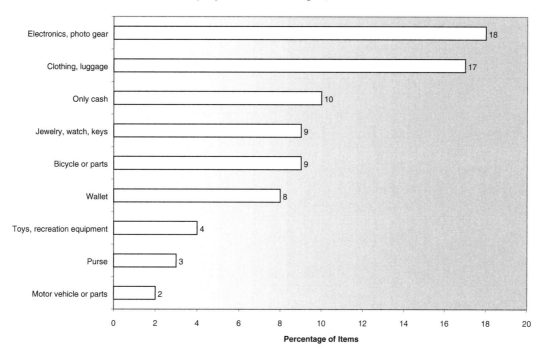

The graphic shows the types of property taken from those between the ages of 12 and 17 years of age. Data come from all property crime (larceny, robbery, burglary).

Juveniles see the highest rates of personal theft. For robbery, those 16 to 19 years of age saw a rate of 7.3 per 100,000 people. Those 12 to 15 years of age saw the second highest rates. Those 16 to 19 years of age also saw the highest rates of personal theft, with 3.0 victimizations per 100,000 people.

Victimizations per 100,000 People by Age, 2000

Age	Robbery	Personal theft
12-15	4.2	1.8
16-19	7.3	3.0
20-24	6.2	1.1
25-34	3.9	1.5
35-49	2.7	0.9
50-64	2.1	0.5
65 or older	0.7	1.2

What sort of items were reported taken? Teenagers typically lost personal electronics or camera equipment. Such objects comprised 19% of all thefts involving juveniles. Clothing and luggage was involved in 17% of all cases. 10% of cases involved just cash. A slightly smaller percentage of all thefts among young people involved bicycles, jewelry, or watches.

What about adults? As shown in the table, those in their 20s saw significant rates of theft as well. Of those 20 to 24 years old, 6.2 per 100,000 reported being the victim of a robbery. Those 25 to 34 years of age saw significant rates in both the robbery and personal theft categories.

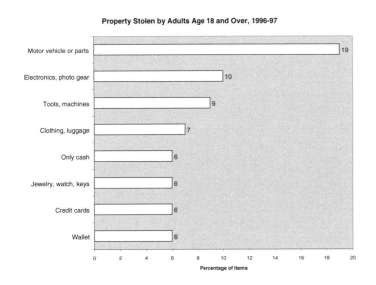

Property Stolen by Adults Age 18 and Over, 1996-97

Not too surprisingly, adults saw more expensive property taken. Motor vehicles or parts comprised 19% of all property stolen. Electronics and photo equipment was the second highest category. The third was tools and machines, 9% of all thefts among adults. A significant percentage of all thefts involved cash, clothing, luggage, jewelry, wallets, and credit cards. Such items have always been — and will probably always be — the target of thieves. The value of cash and credit cards is obvious; jewelry and watches can be quickly pawned for cash.

Another point to make here: many of these items cost only a few hundred dollars. Is it easier just to replace the item than to report it missing? Could these items affect how much property crime is reported?

Sources: "The Property Taken." Retrieved October 7, 2002 from http://www.ncjrs.org/html/ojjdp/jjbul2000_12_2/page3.html; Data are for 1996-97. Age data comes from Bureau of Justice Statistics, National Crime Victimization Survey, *Criminal Victimization, 2000,* June 2001, p. 6.

Do We Report Property Crimes?

Percent of Property Crimes Reported to the Police, 1993-2000

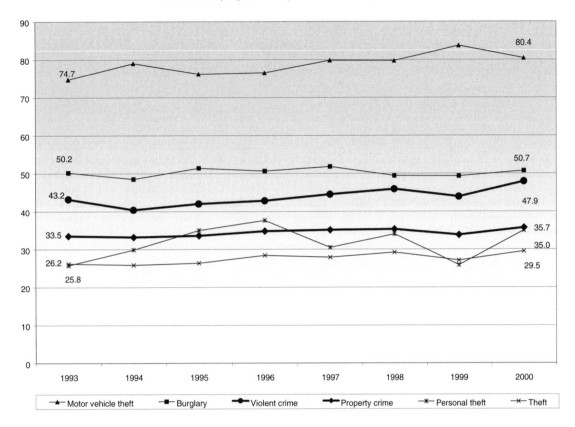

From 1993 to 2000, only about a third of property crimes were reported to the police. The property crime that is most reported is motor vehicle theft — hardly surprising considering the value of an automobile. But this means a quarter of such robberies are not brought to the attention of law enforcement. Why?

Roughly half of burglaries and a quarter of thefts were reported during the period. Reports of personal theft, which includes things such as purse snatching and pocket-picketing, have fluctuated the most, from 25.8% in 1993 to a peak of 37.6% in 1996 to 35% in 2000. The reporting rates for violent crimes (rape, sexual assault, aggravated and simple assault) have been included for comparison purposes. The main reason people report property crimes, says the Justice Department, is to collect insurance. But the second most cited reason was, simply, that victims "knew it was a crime."

Who reports property crimes to the police? In 2000, 35.6% of men and 35.9% of women did. White men reported more than black men (35.7% and 35.5%). Black women reported more property crimes than white women (35.4% and 37.6%).

Why do so many property crimes go unreported? The major reason, according to Department of Justice statistics, is that the item is often recovered without help of the police. People cite lack of proof as the second most common reason. Also, with many thefts valued at less than $250, the victim may deem reporting the crime simply not worth the bother. When analyzing reasons by specific crime (theft, motor vehicle, or burglary) other, more troubling, reasons surface. Many of those victimized think that the police don't care. Smaller shares of victims think that law enforcement is inefficient, ineffective, or biased.

Top Reasons for Not Reporting Property Crimes, (Percent Citing)[3]				
	Total prop- erty crime	Burglary	Motor vehicle theft	Theft
Object recovered/offender unsuccessful	25.7	20.5	21.3	26.5
Lack of proof	12.1	16.5	12.0	11.4
Reported to another official	10.8	6.8	5.6	11.4
Police would not want to be bothered	8.2	8.0	7.8	8.3
Unable to recover property – no ID number	7.3	7.2	NA	7.4
Not aware of crime until later	5.5	7.3	8.1	5.2
Private or personal matter	4.5	4.9	3.2	4.4
Not important enough	3.6	3.8	2.4	3.6
Police inefficient, ineffective or biased	2.7	4.1	6.8	2.5

One must wonder about some of the attitudes about the police. Are these simply stereotypes? Have victims reported crimes and been met with indifference? Also, how do we decide that a theft is "not important enough" to be reported to law enforcement? Should every crime be reported?

Source: *Sourcebook of Criminal Justice Statistics*, U.S. Department of Justice, Bureau of Justice Statistics, Washington D.C., USGPO, 2001, p. 209.

---

[3] Data are for 1999 and based on 16.8 million unreported incidents. NA = estimate is based on 10 or fewer cases.

Arson

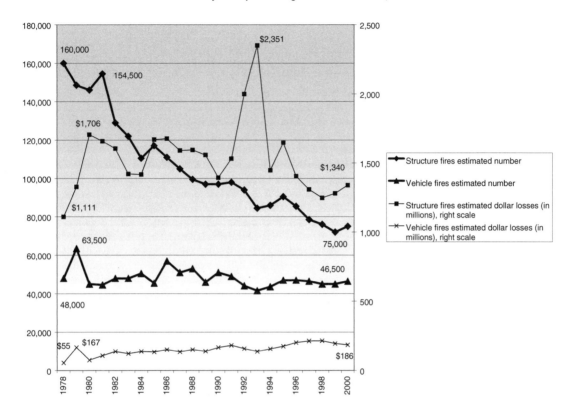

Arson is the act of "deliberately setting fire to a building, car or other property for fraudulent or malicious purposes," according to the Insurance Information Institute. The FBI first indexed arson as a property crime in October 1978. The number of structural fires purposely set or of suspicious origin fell 53% from 1978 to 2000.[4]

There were an estimated 160,000 fires of suspicious origin in 1978; they damaged $1.1 billion in property and took the lives of 930 civilians. After several years of decline, the number of fires rose to 154,500 in 1981. The number of fires increased again slightly in 1985 and 1993. In 2000, there were 75,000 fires of criminal or suspicious origin, which resulted in an estimated $1.3 billion in property damage and the deaths of 505 civilians. As the number of structural fires generally declined, the value of the property damaged often was on the increase, particularly from 1990 to 1993.

The number of vehicle fires has not shown the same level of decline. The number of fires fell only 3% in the period shown, from 48,000 incidents in 1978 to 46,500 incidents in 2000. Does torching cars "pay"? Is this some segment of crime that has and always will

---

[4] Data show only fires of incendiary or suspicious origin. It does not include fires with cause unknown or unreported. The dollar losses for fires in 1991 do not include the Oakland fire storm.

---

be with us? In many of these fires, a type of insurance fraud known as "owner give-ups" is thought to be at work. In owner give-ups, the owner reaches an agreement with an accomplice to leave a vehicle at a certain location so it can be stolen. The partner strips the car for parts and sets it on fire; the owner collects the insurance. Some areas have taken steps to combat the torching of vehicles. In 1987, officials in Boston passed the Burned Motor Vehicle Law; it requires the owner of a burned car or truck to fill out a form at the local fire station. This added step in the insurance claim appears to have been an effective deterrent. Motor vehicle arson in the area then fell 80% from 5,500 incidents in 1986 to 1,093 in 1995.

What motivates a person to set fires? Property crimes often seem to be driven by the health of the economy. Some of that is apparent here. The number of vehicle fires increased just before the recession of 1980 and during the recession of 1982. But the number of arson fires overall fell during the period. The motives behind arson are often more complex than simply financial gain.

The National Center for the Analysis of Violent Crime (NCAVC) located at the FBI Academy in Quantico, Virginia has identified six major classifications of motives for arson:

- **Vandalism**   **Revenge**

- **Profit**   **Extremist Action**

- **Crime Concealment**   **Thrill, Excitement Seeking**

Vandalism is perhaps the most easily understood motive. The offender intends to do damage. The most common targets are schools or their related property. The **Profit** motive arises when the arsonist destroys property or inventory to collect insurance. He may set a fire as a means to gain employment. Or he may get Mom to do it: Recently, the mother of a North County, California firefighter was convicted of setting five fires in the Shasta-Trinity National Forests so her son could get more overtime and hazardous-duty pay. There are also cases of private contractors of water tankers, bulldozers, and delivery trucks setting fires to boost the need for their services.

Another common reason for a fire is to conceal the evidence of **crime** — be that a burglary or homicide. Or the arson may be concealing wrongdoing by burning his business records.

Some fires are set from a wish to extract **revenge**. Fires are directed at a particular person: the fired worker angry at his boss, an evicted tenant striking at a landlord, a spurned lover evening the score. An arsonist may have some grievance with the government, a church, the academic world, the military, or a group of people. These fires are considered to be set for **extremist** reasons. A National Church Arson Task Force has opened 945 investigations on attacks on houses of worship between January 1995 and September 1998 (church arson became a federal crime in 1996). In 1998, a group called the Earth Liberation Front set fires to a ski lodge in Vail, Colorado because the lodge was encroaching on the habitat of lynxes (they did $12 million in damage).

Some fires are set from a thirst for **excitement**. This category includes bored teenagers seeking thrills or loners recognition. This latter reason is an example of something often called the "Hero Syndrome." The offender becomes a local hero for spotting a fire no one else sees — a fire *he* has set. An offender may also set fires out of sexual excitement, but such a motivation, according to the FBI, is rather rare.

Arsonists are usually young. According to the FBI, juveniles were involved in 45% of arson incidents cleared by law enforcement in 2000. About 85% of arsonists are male and 80% are white. In a 1988 Department of Justice study, 31% of prison inmates whose most serious offense was arson were under the influence of illegal drugs when they committed their crimes; 39% of inmates had used drugs in the month before their offense.

Arson is not just damaged property — scarred forests or damaged buildings. Over 15,000 civilians have lost their lives in arson fires from 1978-2000. Only 17% of these cases were solved in 2000.

Source: Chart data comes from Sourcebook of Criminal Justice Statistics Online, located at http://www.albany.edu/source book/1995/pdf/t3195.pdf; also John R. Hall, Jr. U.S. Arson Trends and Patterns (Quincy, MA; National Fire Protection Association, 2001), pp. 12-14, 16-17; and Michael J. Karter Jr., Fire Loss in the United States During 2000 (Quincy, MA; National Fire Protection Association, 2001); John R. Hall Jr. "The Truth about arson." and "classifications of motivations of arsonists." Retrieved from http://www.interfire.org; "Fire deaths down 35% in state; car arson dips." Retrieved from http://www.s-t.com/daily/10-96/10-15-96/a03sr016.htm; "Money burns." From http://www.motherjones.com; Jo Moreland, "Arson." Retrieved from http://iii.org. "Arson Case Serves as Warning, Fire Officials Say." *North Country Times*, April 15, 2002. Data retrieved October 10, 2002.

Scamming the Consumer

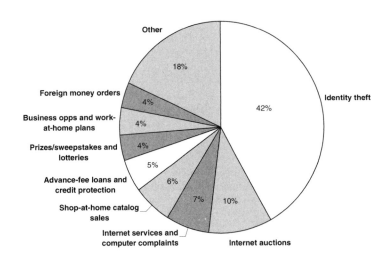

The pie chart shows the types of consumer complaints tracked by the Federal Trade Commission's ConsumerSentinel, a database of cases of fraud. The public registered 204,334 complaints in 2001.

The major category of complaints was identity theft, 42% of all complaints. Identity theft occurs when someone appropriates identifying information in order to commit fraud or theft (credit card or Social Security number). This is a growing crime; we shall focus on it in a later panel.

Many schemes to defraud the public are committed on the Internet, often using "spammed" e-mails — unsolicited e-letters purporting to offer some business or sales opportunity. The receiver is invited to visit a web site or to call a number for more information. Misbehaving Internet auctioneers triggered 10% of all complaints — for failing to deliver goods, sending goods less valuable than those advertised, or shipping late. Internet services, with 7% of total complaints, were cited for such things are charging undisclosed Web fees.

There are thought to be 14,000 telemarketing firms in the country; roughly 10% of them are thought to be fraudulent, according to the government. Congress estimates that Americans lose about $40 billion each year due to the sale of phony goods and services over the telephone (some of these plots are done through the mail as well). What are some of the schemes launched by unscrupulous people? They offer advance-fee loans, tell the caller he has won a prize in a lottery (that he must pay for first), or offer him the chance to "invest" in foreign lottery tickets. They extol the virtues of worthless credit card protection plans, promote magazine subscriptions that never arrive, and sell time-share and vacation opportunities with hidden financial catches. They also claim to offer services to help cheated people get their money back — all, of course, for a price (these "recovery services" are part of the original con).

Anyone can fall victim to one of these schemes, but the elderly often find themselves victimized repeatedly. The American Association of Retired Persons found that 56% of the names on "mooch lists" (fraudulent telemarketers' lists of most likely victims) were age 50 or over. Seniors make up 60% of the callers to the National Consumers League's National Fraud Information Center. There are numerous tragic stories: the Ohio widow who lost her life savings of $240,000 to more than 50 fraudulent telemarketers. A 92 year old California woman lost $180,000 and then another $5,250 more in supposed recovery fees to man who said he could get some of her money back. Seniors are targeted by thieves for at least three reasons. They have significant disposable income. Consumer protection literature suggests that seniors are often lonely and will stay on the phone with a telemarketer to have someone to talk to. Some seniors may be just "too nice" and too polite and trusting just to say no and hang up the phone.

Law enforcement is helping to resolve this issue. In two major undercover operations, Operation Disconnect and Operation Senior Sentinel, the Department of Justice brought federal criminal charges against more than 1,300 fraudulent telemarketers. In a statute enacted in 1994 as part of the Senior Citizens Against Marketing Scams Act, courts can impose an additional five years imprisonment where the mail, wire, or bank fraud offense was committed in connection with the conduct of telemarketing. An additional ten years may be added if the offense targeted those 55 years or older.

Source: Chart figures from the ConsumerSentinel database come from http://www.ftc.gov; "What's the Department of Justice Doing About Telemarketing Fraud?" Retrieved from http://www.usdoj.gov/crimianl/fraud/telemarketing/doj.htm; "Facts about Fraudulent Telemarketing." Retrieved from http://www.aarp.org/fraud/1fraud.htm; "Seniors as Predominant Telemarketing Fraud Victims." Retrieved from http://www.crimes-of-persuasion.com. Data retrieved October 9, 2002.

Corporate America Rechecks Its Books

Number of Financial Restatements by Companies

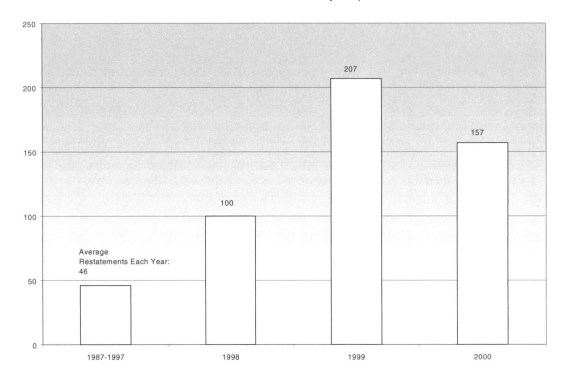

According to a study by Financial Executives International, a total of 464 companies issued restatements of their earnings in the 1998 to 2000 period. This figure is higher than in the previous ten years combined. The study argues that there was heightened pressure on corporate executives to have their companies perform (that is, to meet investor's expectations) during the bull market of the 1990s. The main reason for the restatements came from revenue errors (which accounted for 20% of the restatements, according to one study). Other reasons were improperly accounting for accounts receivable, reserves, accruals and other forms of liability.

As the graphic shows, a number of companies file restatements of their earnings every year; an average of 46 firms did so from 1987 to 1997. What touched off the push for accurate accounting in 1998? In that year, Waste Management Inc., Sunbeam Corp., and Cendant Corp. all filed large restatements of their earnings. In his speech, "The Numbers Game," Securities and Exchange Commission Chairman Arthur Levitt lamented that too many corporate managers and auditors let the desire to meet earnings expectations override their sense of good business practices. His fear was that "Managing might give way to manipulation; integrity may be losing out to illusion" (Magrath, Weld).

It is important to note that there are forms of earnings management that all companies can and should practice — reducing production schedules with excessive inventory, for example. Some, as Magrath and Weld note, are more subtle, such as pressuring sales and marketing staff to "meet the numbers" that the company has set for itself. This is accept-

---

able, but what about hazier situations — say, the sale is recorded before deliveries are completed? Carol Loomis cites the example of a corporate chief, under pressure to meet numbers, making an off-price deal at the end of a quarter that simply steals from full-priced business down the road. Something which she notes is "dumb but legal." Too often an executive may be tempted to sidestep the rules publicly owned companies are required to abide by, Generally Accepted Accounting Principles (also known by the eyebrow raising acronym GAAP).

The SEC seemed to mobilize after Levitt's speech. Financial fraud and managed earnings were noted by the commission as a top enforcement priority. The SEC even christened 1999 as "The Year of the Accountant." One must wonder how this announcement played in the hallways of Arthur Andersen and energy giant Enron Corp. In August 2000, Jeffrey Skilling quit as Chief Executive of Enron, an event generally regarded as a sign all was not well within the company. Vice Chairman Clifford Baxter resigned over the firm's "inappropriate partnerships" in May 2001. On October 16, 2001, the company was forced to admit a $1.2 billion decrease in its value from its fraudulent bookkeeping methods. Less than two months later it filed for bankruptcy. Investors in the firm lost more than $60 billion. Arthur Andersen, the firm's accountant, was convicted of obstruction of justice in destroying documents related to the Enron case while on notice of a federal investigation. It received five years of probation and a $500,000 fine. The future of the firm, which is but a shadow of its former self, remains uncertain.

A few months later came the collapse of WorldCom. In March 2002, just months after the fall of Enron, the SEC filed a request with the company for information relating to its accounting procedures. On June 26, 2002, the company admitted to inflating earnings by $3.8 billion. A handful of months later, the firm filed for bankruptcy after it admitted the total misstated earnings were in excess of $7 billion. As of August 2002, it is the largest U.S. bankruptcy on record.

There have been several other well publicized cases of fraud after the WorldCom case, most notably the arrest of executives of cable system Adelphia on fraud charges. The SEC recently informed the chief executives of 947 of the largest corporations to submit certified, accurate statements by August 14, 2002. Nearly 700 companies turned in their paperwork, eager to comply with the SEC and, presumably, to certify their numbers and to give a boost to nervous investors on the jittery stock market. A number of other companies were given later due dates because they do not report on a calendar basis.

Source: "Market Shrugs Off Certification Day." And "Restatements Rise on SEC Initiative." Retrieved from http://www.cfo.com/print articles; Hill, Patrice. "Stock Hopes Rise on SEC Order." *Washington Times*, July 29, 2002; Magrath, Lorraine and Leonard G. Weld. "Managed Earnings or Fraud: Where Do We Draw the Line." Retrieved from http://www.spectrum.troyst.edu/~symposium/2002_ papers/Magrath%2020%.weld.doc; "Why so many earnings restatements?" Retrieved from http://www.j-bradford-delong.net; "Managed Earnings" and "The Year of the Accountant." Retrieved from http://www.sec.gov; Cathy Booth. "Called to Account." *Time*, June 18, 2002. "Andersen Guilty." Retrieved from http://www.cnnmoney.com. Carol Loomis. "Lies, damned lies and managed earnings" from http://www.fortune.com; Jeanne Lang Jones. "Washington Ranks Relatively High in Financial Restatements. Puget Sound Business Journal, August 12, 2002, p. 4; Brian Morrisey. "WorldCom's Day of Reckoning." Retrieved from http://www.intenetnews.com/isp-news/article.php/1430361.

The Nigerian Letter Fraud Scheme

Request for Urgent Business Relationship

First, I must solicit your strictest confidence in this transaction. This is by virtue of its nature being utterly confidential and "Top Secret". You have been recommended by an associate who assured me in confidence of your ability and reliability to prosecute a pending business transaction of great magnitude, requiring maximum confidence.

We are top officials of the Federal Government Contracts Review panel who are interested in the importation of goods into our country with funds which are presently confined in Nigeria. In order to commence this business, we solicit your assistance to enable us to transfer into your account, the said trapped funds.

The following represents the source of the funds. During the last regime her in Nigeria, the Government officials set up companies and awarded themselves contracts which were grossly over invoiced in various ministries which informed the setting up of the Contract Review Panel by the present Military Government to advice on the aforementioned. We have identified a lot of inflated contract sums which are presently floating in the Central Bank of Nigeria ready for payment, amongst which is the said sum of US$31,200,000 (Thirty One Million, Three-Hundred and Twenty Thousand United States Dollars) that we solicit with your assistance for the transfer. As we are unable to manage the transfer by ourselves by virtue of our position as civil servants and members of its Panel, I have there fore been delegated as a matter of trust by my colleagues on the Panel to solicit for an overseas partner whose account we could transfer the said sum.

We have agreed to share the money thus:

1. 25% for the Account Owner (you) 2. 65% for us (The Officials) 3. 10% to be used in settling all expenses (our end and your end) Incidental to the realization of this transaction

It is from the 65% that we wish to commence the importation business. Please note that this transaction is 100% safe and we hope to conclude the transaction in at most 10 banking days.

(The above is an excerpt from a frequently used version in 419 fraud. Typographical errors are intended.)

Nigerian letter fraud is thought to have started in the early 1980s. It is often referred to as "Advance Fee Fraud" or "419 Fraud" after the section of the Criminal Code of Nigeria that refers to this kind of crime.

How does this scam work? The target receives an unsolicited fax, e-mail, or letter from a businessman in Nigeria. The letters have several variations. One of the most frequently used versions is seen above. It describes "overinvoiced" or "doubleinvoiced" oil or commodity contracts, and how "The Officials" want to get these funds out of Nigeria. The target is promised a handsome reward for his efforts, 25% of the $31 million sum. The target must hand over some personal information in the process, such as the name of his bank and his account number for the transfer. But in order to facilitate the transfer of funds, the target must pay an "Advance Fee" of some sort, in order to cover transfer taxes, extend credit, grant COD privileges, or some other reason. The fee can be sizeable, but small compared to the millions the target has been promised. If the target pays this fee, there are endless complications which require more money up front until the target quits or runs out of money (or both).

The letters have numerous variations, but the same basic formula. If the target receives a letter, it's easy to see how he might get taken in. The letter is printed on quality paper, with an official looking seal and personal names. The letter immediately appeals to the target's sense of adventure, with its admonitions that this deal is "top secret" and "confidential." Indeed, Douglas Cruickshank has commented on the literary merits of these letters, noting the rhythm of the language and the pictures painted of unstable governments and desperate men. The exotic names in these letters are straight out of a spy novel, in which the target is now a player: Barrister Momoh Sanni Momoh or Dr. Akeem Biobaky Ph.D. (who, incidentally, sent the letter reprinted above) or, as Cruikshank notes, the "jazzy-sounding Susan Lateef, who claims to be doing business from within the peaceful walls of La Paix Hotel in Abidjan."

The scheme also appeals to something else: greed. A reader's eyes must certainly widen at the $31 million quoted in the letter. Indeed, the writer even spells the figure out in parentheses to underscore the amount. The hope that potential riches lies before him overwhelms the impulse to view the situation with the skepticism it deserves. One interesting side note: the letter above and its $31 million figure is rather old. In recent letters, the con men have wisely adjusted for inflation and offer to transfer between $60-80 million.

Does this letter scheme still snag victims? Absolutely. The scheme has moved online, with e-mail filling millions of people's mailboxes (one study shows that e-mails by 419 scammers grew 900% between 2000 and 2001). Of the 10,000 Americans who reported being the victims of all type of online fraud, 16 fell victim to this 419 scheme. The 16 people lost $345,000 collectively, including two people who lost $78,000 and $74,000, respectively. One must wonder how many never report being victimized out of embarrassment.

The scheme is thought to have netted $5 billion worldwide by 1996. Americans lost $100 million to West African advance-fee scams (of all kinds) from 1999 to 2002. Such cons are, by some estimates, the second largest industry in Nigeria.

Sources: The letter comes from Loss Prevention Concepts retrieved from http://www.lpconline.com; Cruikshank, Douglas. "How Americans Lose Billions to Crime Syndicates Via Internet." *Africa News Service*, September 26, 2002; Pat Carbonara. "The Scam that Will Not Die." *Money*, July 1, 2002, p. 106; "Nigerian Letter Fraud Gets New Life Online." *USA Today*, April 11, 2002; "Nigeria – the 419 Coalition Website." Retrieved from http://www.home.rica/net/alphae/419coal. Data retrieved October 9, 2002.

The Inkjet Printer: A New Tool for Counterfeiters

Percent of Counterfeit Money Produced on Inkjet Printers

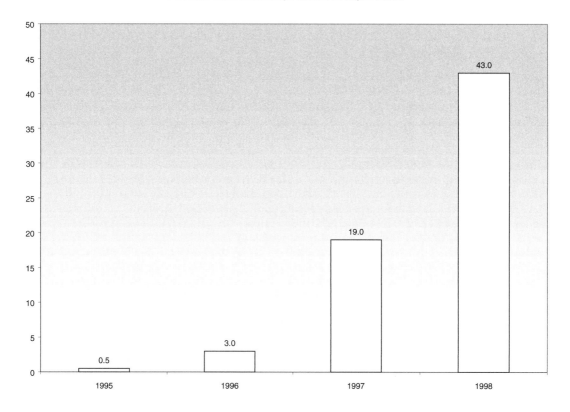

After a brief decline in the 1990s, counterfeiting has begun to increase, aided by new technology — the computer printer.

The computer printer produced just 0.5% of the counterfeit money put into circulation in 1995. By 1998, 43% of the currency was produced on inkjet printers — an increase of 8500%. Said one Secret Service agent in a hearing of the House Banking Committee: "Counterfeiting U.S. currency is as easy as a click of a mouse with computer equipment found in many homes." The Secret Service has coined a new term for this currency: P-Notes (printer notes).

How does it work? Dennis Lynch of the Secret Service offers this explanation: A scanner copies the image of a bill (the $20 bill is most popular). A computer enhances the picture's quality, and the image is then enhanced electronically and printed on a printer. The quality is, of course, affected by the quality of the equipment used. The prices of computers and printers has dropped over the years; good quality machines can be purchased for as little as $1,500.

The currency looks real enough to get accepted routinely at retail establishments. Until two years ago, counterfeit money was more likely to be seized at its source than passed into circulation. Now money counterfeited domestically is three times more likely to be passed than to be seized. In 1995, the Secret Service seized about 70% of all domestic counterfeits. By 2000, that figure had fallen to about 26%.

Production of phony money is on the increase. Agent Patrick J. Sullivan of the San Diego office of the Secret Service claims their office sees between $10,000 and $15,000 in counterfeit currency each week. Roughly half is computer-generated. Another sign of the sudden growth of this type of counterfeiting is the jump in arrests. There were 37 people arrested for P-note counterfeiting in 1995. 4,500 people were arrested in 2001.

Counterfeit currency seized by the government
June 1875-June 1876: $232,000
June 1941-June 1942: $48,000
1950s: (average annual seizure) $1,000,000
1997: $40,000,000
2001: $47,500,000

The government has continually made changes to currency to make it more difficult to replicate. ID threads have been embedded into the bills. New dyes have been used in production. A total of 16 changes were made in 1996 — such as a watermark portrait of a U.S. leader that is only visible when bills are held up to the light. Another idea has been proposed by The Bureau of Engraving and Printing: colored money. Why not $100 bills with a gold background? We have copper Lincoln pennies, as Richard Powelson points out, so why not copper Lincoln $5 bills? If the Treasury Department approves the plan, our multi-colored money might go into circulation as early as mid-2003.

The Secret Service was created in 1865 to combat counterfeit money. By 1930, an estimated $750,000 in currency was thought to be in circulation. Counterfeiting increased during the Depression. In the 1930s, it was believed that if the government published information about how to identify phony money, that would somehow encourage counterfeiting. When Frank Wilson in 1937 took over the Secret Service, he reversed these policies. The Service educated the public about how counterfeiters worked and how to spot fake money. In the early 1940s, the amount of fake money seized was only $48,000 — meaning more fake money was getting circulated than seized. During the 1950s, law enforcement was seizing more money — the government routinely making $1 million seizures. Less than 10% of counterfeit money went into circulation in the 1950s.

Less than 1% of the money in circulation is thought to be fake. $450 billion worth of genuine currency is in circulation worldwide.

Sources: United States Treasury Department, *The Use and Counterfeiting of United States Currency Abroad*, p. 63; "Tougher Counterfeiting Laws Sought." Retrieved from http://www.wired.com; Powelson, Richard. "Bluebacks or Amber Andys: A New Color of Money." From http://www.redding.com; "A Brief Counterfeiting History in U.S." Retrieved from http://www.csibusiness center.com; Kalisha Brown. "Keeping Currency Current." *Denver Business Journal*, July 7, 2000, p. 17A; "Computer-Generated Counterfeit Currency Production Is On the Rise." *Research Alert*, August 18, 2000, p. 7; Rita Fennelly. "Phony Bills Cost Merchants tons of Money." *San Diego Business Journal*, February 14, 2000, p. 2A. "New Ways to Fake Cash." Retrieved from http://www.abc news. com; "Better Technology Makes Counterfeiting Easy." Retrieved from http://www.techweb.com. Data retrieved October 1, 2002.

Stealing Your Identity

Reported Cases of Identity Theft (and Forecasts), 1998-2004

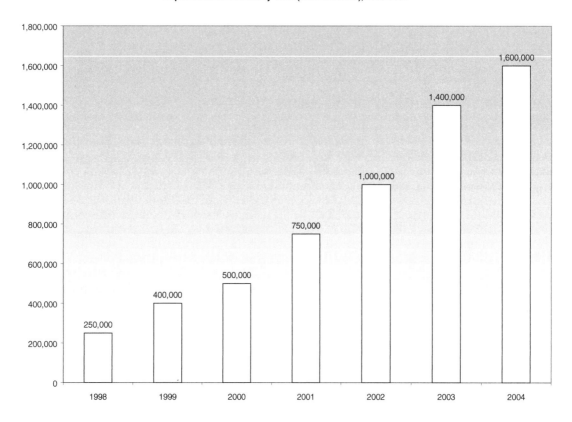

Identity theft occurs when someone steals a consumer's personal identifying information, such as name, address, credit card or Social Security number. The thief then uses the information to open new charge accounts, order merchandise or to apply for loans. The crime is on the rise. According to the Federal Trade Commission, there were 250,000 reported cases of identity theft in 1998, with the figure growing 200% to 750,000 by 2001. A study by the Celent Corp. forecasts the figure to increase from 1 million cases in 2002 1.6 million in 2004.

The information explosion of the 1990s has given crooks access all sorts of personal information about potential victims. A driver's license number, credit card number, or Social Security number truly are our "identity" — numbers that define us and are they keys to various doors in the world. A credit card account reveals all of our charges and, more importantly, the types and frequencies of our purchases. A driver's license, once intended as nothing other than a permit to get behind the wheel of a car, has become, Margaret Mannix points out, "the nation's de facto ID card." A Social Security number can be an ID number in a medical file, a financial account or a student ID. Swipe this number and a few other key pieces of information, and a thief can set up a whole new life (and credit history).

"It's too easy to commit identity fraud," says Allan Trosclair, executive director of the Coalition for the Prevention of Economic Crime. Personal information can come from many places. The Federal Trade Commission estimates that more than half of all identity thefts result from compromised business records. An employee, employer, janitor, or temp worker will steal information from a personnel file, a doctor's record, retailer database, or job application. In 1997, a woman who sometimes worked for Ericsson, the electronics company, and Perrier, passed personal data on coworkers to an accomplice. He siphoned $700,000 from victims' E*Trade stock accounts and took cash advances of $800,000 on 60 credit cards. A minimum-wage hospital worker passed on Social Security numbers for newborns to an accomplice (hospitals now help new parents get Social Security numbers for babies). In December 2000, a hacker stole 60,000 credit card numbers from Creditcards.com and tried to extort $100,000 from the company. When the company refused, the hacker posted the card numbers on the Internet. Some fraudulent activity was later reported on the cards. In one well publicized case in 2001, a New York busboy was caught with the Social Security numbers and birth dates of 217 of Forbes 400 Richest Americans.

Estimated losses from identity theft, according to the Secret Service:

1995: $442 million

1997: $745 million

1998: $851 million

2001: $1.4 billion

Connie Crowther of Coral Gables, Florida, who was robbed and then had her identity assumed by crooks, expresses the sentiments of many victims of identity fraud: "A snot nosed hooligan mugged me and robbed me in front of my own house. Now someone out there pretends they are me. They are masquerading as me and having a go at trying to be me. They want expensive stuff and expect me to pay for it."

In a Federal Trade Commission report, 19% of all victims of identity theft had some relationship with the thief: neighbor, employer or employee, roommate or family member. Six percent of identity thefts were by family members in 2001, up from 4.4% in 2000. While it appears to be growing segment of identity theft, it is difficult to measure for one obvious reason: people are often unwilling to turn a family member in to the authorities. The growth is also fueled by the ease with which a person can access personal information about a family member. Curiously, those who commit identity theft against family members rack up larger charges than those acting against strangers, according to Mr. Vonder Heide of Technology Briefing Centers. "It's usually in the $10,000 to $50,000 range. With a family member, they are going to get as much as they can."

In many cases, information is rather thoughtlessly handed out. In April 2001, the city of Biloxi, Mississippi sent out nearly 25,000 voter-identification cards imprinted with Social Security numbers, birth dates, and addresses — a wealth of personal information waiting to be seized by a thief. The IRS stopped printing Social Security numbers on mailing labels in1999 "over privacy concerns" according to IRS spokeswoman Emma Moore. The numbers are still printed on tax-return checks, however. Some have argued more safeguards should be in place in important computer systems. In April 2002, hackers broke into government computers in California and gained access to nearly every one of the Social Security numbers of the 265,000 people on the payroll. The accounts did not have addresses or credit card numbers to match with the names. But there are roughly a dozen sites on the Internet where one can use a Social Security number to search for addresses, maiden names, aliases, and other information. Setting up a new identity would take some work, but it could be done.

The average identity thief steals $17,000 from his victim and serves a minor jail sentence. John Foley, director of consumer/victim services at Identity Theft Resources, points out that the average armed robbery netted $3,500 with a 7 to 10 year sentence. "Judges still look at identity fraud as a white collar crime" (Gillin).

Identity theft did not really become a crime until 1998. Pre-1998 law prohibited the use of false identification documents, but it was not a crime to simply uses someone else's name, Social Security number, date of birth, or other identifying information. "Law enforcement must wait for an overt fraudulent act or creation of a fraudulent document before it can intercede in a case solely involving identity fraud," said James Bauer, deputy assistant director of the Secret Service told Congress in 1998 (Davis). The new legislation is called the Identity Theft and Assumption Deterrence Act and makes identity theft a federal crime punishable by up to 15 years in prison.

Sources: Mannix, Margaret. "Stolen Names, Stolen Lives." *U.S. News & World Report*, November 12, 2001, p. 40; Lim, Paul J. "Sounding an Identity Theft Alarm." *U.S. News & World Report*, April 23, 2001, p. 74; "Identity Theft Nightmare Grows." *South Florida Business Journal*, April 27, 2001, A1; "Identity Theft by Family Members Rises, Creates Greater Financial Problems."; "On-line Hackers, Insecure Government Data Open Door to Identity Theft," and "Identity Theft Growing Quickly, Many Push for More Privacy." all from *Knight-Ridder/Tribune Business News*; Gillin, Eric. "Protecting Yourself Against Identity Theft." Retrieved from http://www.thestreet.com; Federal Trade Commission. Identity Theft Clearinghouse, *Identity Theft Complaint Data: Figures and Trends on Identity Theft January 2000 through December 2000*.

Health Care Fraud

Who Commits Health Care Fraud?

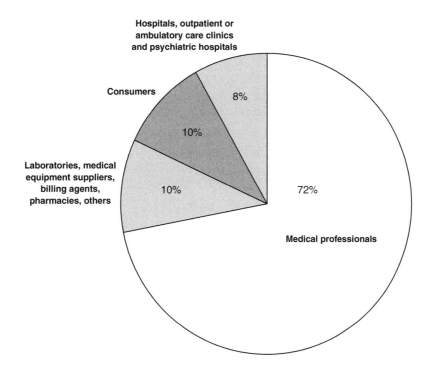

Hospitals, outpatient or ambulatory care clinics and psychiatric hospitals — 8%

Consumers — 10%

Laboratories, medical equipment suppliers, billing agents, pharmacies, others — 10%

Medical professionals — 72%

Health care spending is placed at roughly $1.2 trillion annually in the United States. What percentage of this is devoted to waste and fraudulent claims? The National Health Care Anti-Fraud Association estimates that fraud accounts for 3 to 5% of the total health care tab, or $33 to $55 billion. A report by the Government Accounting Office places the percentage even higher: closer to 10%, or $94 billion.

More than 4 billion claims are filed every year. Who is most responsible for most fraud? Some of it does come from consumers filing false claims or misrepresenting information on insurance forms. But this is only about 10%, as seen in the graphic above. According to a 1999 study by the Health Insurance Association of America, nearly three quarters of health care fraud cases come from medical professionals: doctors, dentists, and chiropractors. The most common types of fraud involved billing for services that were never provided and something known as "upcoding" — when providers submit bills for procedures that are more expensive than those actually performed.

Some examples? In October 2001, a federal grand jury returned a 407-count indictment against 19 defendants in Arizona who allegedly set up fraudulent store fronts for durable medical equipment suppliers. In May 2002, a Colorado chiropractor was sentenced for submitting approximately $219,000 in false claims to Medicare. In October 2002, a

Florida dental surgeon was charged with false billings to Medicaid of $163,000. She submitted claims for treatments she never performed, overbilled for others, and filed claims for medication her patients never received. One patient described it as "an assembly line" with oral surgeries performed on a steady line of low-income patients — often without anesthesia.

There have been some encouraging signs in the fight against health care fraud. According to a study by the Coalition Against Insurance Fraud, which examined the fraud bureaus of 41 states, fraud convictions increased from 961 in 1995 to 2,123 in 2000. Two-thirds of the bureaus also reported budget increases. The U.S. Attorney Office's largest recovery in 2000 came from National Medical Care, Fresnius' kidney dialysis subsidiary, which paid $379 million in criminal fines and civil payments in fraud charges against Medicare. Where does the nation's Medicare program stand on the fraud issue? In 1996, Medicare overpayments accounted for 14 cents out of every dollar spent, or $23 billion. In 1998, about seven cents of every dollar spent was on fraud, waste, and mistakes, or $12.6 billion. Some good news, although that figure jumped to $13.5 billion in 1999. Reportedly, the percentage of bills Medicare claims that are audited increased from 5% to 14%.

What of other types of insurance fraud? The Coalition Against Insurance Fraud estimated that in 1996 fraud hit $14.3 billion in auto insurance, $10.6 billion in business and commercial insurance, $2.1 billion in home owners insurance, and $2.1 billion in workers compensation. The figures, the organization readily admits, are guesswork. But it makes one wonder…

Sources: Chart data comes from the Health Insurance Association of America, based on a 1999 survey conducted with the assistance of the Blue Cross and Blue Shield Association and the National Health Care Anti-Fraud Association. Bender, J.P. "Waste, Fraud Cost Medicare $13.5B Last Year." *Denver Business Journal*, May 5, 2000, p. 18A; "Federal Campaign enlists seniors as Medicare fraud busters." Retrieved from http://www.cnn.com; "United States Attorney's Office recovers record-breaking $379 million in fiscal year 2000." Retrieved from http://www.prnewswire.com, January 8, 2001; Curtis M. Wong. "Growing Complexity of Scams a Challenge for Investigators." *Business Insurance*, September 17, 2001, p. 12B; Michael Prince. "High-Tech Tools Aid Insurers in Fighting Health Care Fraud." *Business Insurance*, September 17, 2001, p. 12E; "Dental patients hardly smiling about treatments." Retrieved from http://www.insurancefraud.org; "Denver chiropractor sentenced for health care fraud." Retrieved from http://du.edu/usaoco/052302Frame1Source1.htm; Daniel Hays. "Claim Fraud Slowing, But Some Raise Doubts." *National Underwriter*, January 4, 1999, p. 6.

Copyrighted Material: Can't Touch This!

In December 1997, President Clinton signed the No Electronic Theft (NET) Act into law. The law was intended to combat the growing threat of Internet copyright piracy. The NET Act makes it illegal to distribute copyrighted works even if the defendant is not acting out of financial gain. A little over a year later, the law had its first test: a 22-year-old University of Oregon senior pled guilty to a felony count of criminal infringement of copyright for making thousands of musical recordings, movies, and computer software programs available on his Web site. (He received probation.)

Copyright, according to Intellectual Property law firm Smith & Hopen, is a form of protection provided to the authors of original works of authorship including literary, dramatic, musical, and certain other intellectual works, both published and unpublished. Such industries generate billions annually.

In July 1992, a U.S. District judge ruled that a Texaco scientist violated the U.S. Copyright Law when he copied articles without providing the appropriate fee to publishers. Texaco argued that the copying fell within fair use. Publishers across the country looked to the case of American Geophysical Union v. Texaco Inc. (which lasted roughly a decade) to see what "fair use" really means. In other words, how much of a writer's work can be cited and in what way?

The Internet — which provides unfettered access to a wealth of ideas, images, and material — is turning out to be a thorny issue for those who believe an artist's work should not be easily disseminated. Photographs, writings, and commercial images are traded among Web users or posted on Web sites without the knowledge or consent of the producer. The music industry in particular has faced some tough challenges. In 1999, Shawn Fanning, a freshman at Northwestern University, founded Napster, an online music service in May 1999. The service, known as peer-to-peer file sharing, allowed users to trade and download their favorite songs … for free. Music lovers no longer had to go to the store and buy a compact disc to hear their favorite song. It was at their fingertips. After a series of court challenges by music distributors, in February 2001, the 9th U.S. Court of Appeals ruled that Napster knew its users were violating copyright laws through its file service. Napster still exists, as do similar services, but users now pay a small fee to download songs.

Where does the law stand on the copyright issue? The 1976 Copyright Act gives the owner the exclusive right to reproduce the work, perform the copyrighted work, or display it publicly. Copyright extended from the life of the author plus 50 years. In 1998, the legislation was amended, increasing the term of copyright to 70 years. Work produced for hire or anonymously was shielded by copyright for a term of 95 years. The move was immediately challenged by publishers who depend on work in the public domain (work not protected by copyright). "Congress made a choice about who would have the right to develop and exploit 75 years of American culture," said Stanford University law professor Lawrence Lessig in his legal challenge.

It's the copyright protecting well known items that often receives the most attention — such as the songs of pop music stars. But what of the copyright extended to lesser known but important works? Arnold Lutzker, a lawyer for the American Association of Law Libraries, has pointed out that there "are millions of pieces of work created by ordinary people that will be delayed decades." Protected work can not be included in, for example, university Web sites or distributed in college course packs. Some authors have copyrighted their personal correspondence and other writings, preventing from them from being excerpted in academic writing.

The challenge to the 1998 copyright extension moved to the Supreme Court in October 2002. Will the justices agree with the claim that too much work has been kept away from public use? Justice Sandra Day O'Connor has already claimed to find fault with what Congress did in 1998. But — and this is probably the key question for the justices — did the extension violate the Constitution? At stake in this debate are access to some of the treasures of American culture that were produced in the 1920s and 1930s: songs by George Gershwin, poems by Robert Frost, *The Wizard of Oz*, and Disney's Mickey Mouse.

Sources: "Oregon Student Convicted Under new Internet Copyright Theft Law." Available online at http://www.cnn.com; "American Geophysical Union V. Texaco Inc." Available online from http://www.arl.org/info/frn/copy/texaco.html; Biskupic, Joan. "Court Finds Copyright Case a Tough One." *USA Today*, October 10, 2002, p. 5A; Joan Biskupic, "Copyright Case to Determine Use of Classic Culture." *USA Today*, October 5, 2002, p. 5A. Online data retrieved October 20, 2002.

Stealing Books, Movies, and Software

U.S. Trade Losses Due to Copyright Piracy, 1997-2001

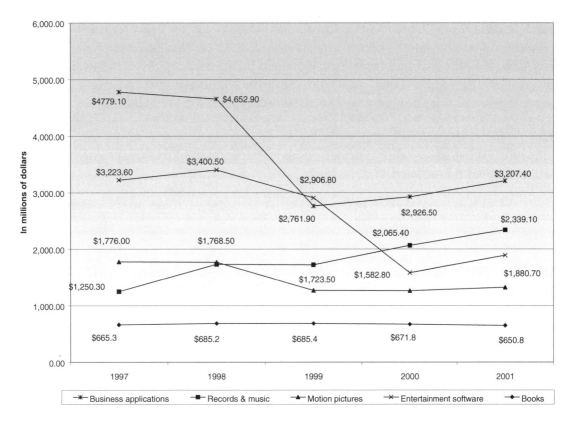

Intellectual property (IP) is a generic term that refers to patents, trademarks, copyrights, trade secrets, and other tangible personal property is created through someone's intellectual efforts.

The International Intellectual Property Association (IIPA) considers the core copyrighted industries to be the motion picture industry, the music recording industry (records, tapes, CDs), broadcasting (cable, television, and radio), the publishing industry (music, books, newspapers, and magazines), theater, and advertising. In 2001, the IIPA reports, copyrighted industries contributed $535.1 billion to the nation's GDP, growing by more than $75 billion since 1999. The Bureau of Labor Statistics reports that between 1977 and 1996 the growth in the IP segment of the economy was nearly twice that of the U.S. economy as a whole.

What kind of losses do U.S. companies in these industries see? Total estimated trade losses fell 19% from a total of $11.6 billion in 1997 to $9.4 billion in 2001. Business software losses have been on the increase since 1999, although they are down from 1997. After several years of decline, the illegal distribution of entertainment software increased from 2000 to 2001. Some countries see extremely high rates of software piracy. According to the report, 92% of the business application software in China is thought to be pirated. Ninety-nine percent of entertainment software is thought to be pirated in Brazil and the Philippines.

The world clearly hungers for Hollywood's blockbuster films; piracy losses involving motion pictures increased 37% from 1999 to 2001. Poor quality videos of *Star Wars II: Attack of the Clones*, *Titanic*, *Spider-Man,* and other American films routinely turn up on the streets of Asian countries costing several dollars. It can happen anywhere, of course; Colombia, Bolivia, and Indonesia all have video piracy rates of 90%. Some films can be downloaded from the Internet. The book publishing industry saw consistent losses over the period, with losses hovering around $650 to $680 million annually.

The graphic addresses only the trade losses around book, software, movie, and music publishing. What about other types of goods? The next panel examines losses in the apparel and general merchandise industries.

Sources: Chart data comes from http://www.iipa.org; Biskupic, Joan. Intellectual property definition comes from Smith & Hopen, p.a., located at http://www.baypatents.com; "Copyright Case to Determine Use of Classic Culture." *USA Today*, October 9, 2002, P. 5A. "IIPA Submits Special 301 Copyright Piracy recommendations to Trade Rep." Retrieved from http://www.techlawjournal.com.

Counterfeit Goods

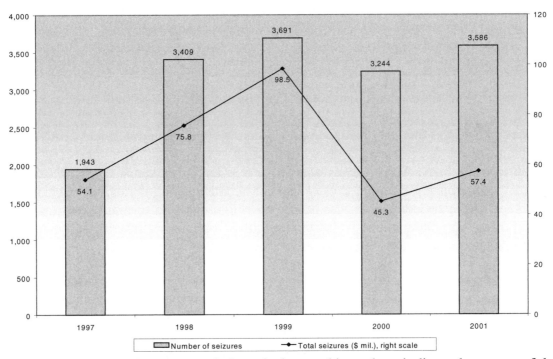

A trademark is a word, name, symbol, or device used in trade to indicate the source of the goods and to distinguish these from goods produced by others. Popular trademarks include Coca-Cola, Xerox, and Sony. The counterfeiting of brand name apparel, designer accessories, home furnishings, and even medication and auto equipment is estimated to be a $100 billion annual industry.

The Customs Service seized a total of $331.2 million in fake merchandise during the five year period shown. The value of seizures increased steadily to 1999 when several large seizures (including one valued at $29 million) drove the figure to $98.5 million. The value of seizures fell 42% to $57.4 million in 2001. The number of seizures, after the drop between 1999 and 2000, did increase to 3,586.

About 45% of fake merchandise comes from China. The country is a large producer of counterfeit goods (and is a consumer of them as well). Multinational firms and the U.S. government have routinely lobbied Beijing to protect intellectual property in the country. The Chinese government made numerous promises to launch reforms before it became a member of the World Trade Organization in December 2001. The country has made some progress, but much work remains to be done.

What types of goods are nabbed by the Customs Service? Apparel accounted for 14% of all seizures of counterfeit goods in 2001: everything from fake Nike sneakers to designer jeans with fraudulent labels sewn inside. Tim Behean, head of the Intellectual Property unit at Adidas, estimates that 10 to 12% of global sportswear sales are fakes. Sports companies have poured considerable effort into fighting counterfeiters. Adidas devotes 17

---

employees to the pursuit of the criminals who peddle goods under the Adidas name. In 2001, they uncovered 6 million counterfeit products and recovered $44 million in damages.

The next highest category was for tapes, DVDs, software, and similar media products. This segment represented 13% of all seizures. Watches and parts made up 10% of all seizures. Other items are uncovered on a regular basis: batteries, cigarettes, sunglasses, and computer hardware.

Some people purchase counterfeit goods thinking that they're getting a "steal." Some fake merchandise ends up in high-end stores where the authenticity won't be questioned. Some people realize that they are buying fakes and don't care; in our global marketplace, the "brand" is the thing. Where do many of these sales take place? The Internet — or online auction site Ebay. A sale takes place between seller and buyer — a discrete transaction taking place away from the eyes of law enforcement. The International Chamber of Commerce estimates companies lose $25 to $30 billion a year to brand and trademark abuse online. The International Anti-Counterfeiting Coalition estimates that a quarter of all branded items sold online are counterfeit.

Counterfeit merchandise affects every country, and often in profound ways: 30% of all products on mainland China are thought to be fakes, by one estimate. The quality of these goods varies greatly. Some copies of Rolex watches must be studied quite closely to determine that they are forgeries. Bootlegged vodka is often as good as the real thing in Russia (a country in which the counterfeited goods industry has been placed at between $1 to $2 billion annually). In some cases, cheap counterfeits may be deadly ones: The Pharmaceutical Society of South Africa recently complained about the dangers posed by the counterfeit medications in the country; they have cost some people their lives.

Some counterfeit products might just leave one scratching one's head. A hot seller in China is the book *Harry Potter and Leopard Walk Up to Dragon* — a book claiming to be the long awaited fifth volume in the immensely popular series. In this anonymously written book, Harry Potter is not a boy wizard but a fat, hairy dwarf. The book begins like this: "Harry doesn't know how long it will take to wash the sticky cream cake off his face. For a civilized young man it is disgusting to have dirt on any part of his body. He lies in the high-quality china bathtub, keeps wiping his face, and thinks about Dudley's face, which is as fat as the bottom of Aunt Penny."

Sources: Chart data (and trademark definition) comes from the U.S. Customs Service, located at http://www.customs.ustreas.gov; "Counterfeit Billions Waging a Sham Struggle Against Sham Products." Retrieved from the Coalition for Intellectual Property Rights, located at http://www.cipr.org; "China's Pirates." *Business Week*, June 5, 2000, p. 26; "The Counterfeiting Problem" and "Eye on Sports." Retrieved from http://www.investigation.com...cles/library/2001articles/articles25.htm; "Adidas Relishes World Cup Branding, As Do Counterfeiters." Retrieved from the World Federation of the Sporting Goods Industry located at http://www.wfsgi.org; "Customs can be a valuable ally against counterfeiting." Retrieved from http://becker-polikoff.com; "South Africa's Illegal Pharma Sector Booms." *Marketletter*, September 30, 2002. "Bogus Harry Potter Hits China; Illegal Version Portrays the Boy Wizard as a Fat, Hairy Dwarf." *School Library Journal*, August 2002, p. 20.

Chapter 4

Lesser Crimes & Offenses

Roughly 80% of crime never makes it into the crime rate. Such offenses include fraud, prostitution, sex offenses, weapons, drugs, gambling, drunk driving, and vagrancy. Many of these offenses have been addressed in other chapters. Gun possession is covered in Chapter 2 with violent crime. Fraud has been included with property crime in Chapter 3. Juvenile crimes — truancy and runaways, for example — are included in Chapter 5. Chapter 6 deals with drugs. The reader may also wish to study Chapter 8: it describes the demands that these crimes have made on law enforcement.

This chapter will focus on crimes of public order. These crimes are not about profit or revenge, which characterize many property or violent offenses. These crimes are largely about behavior that is destructive to — as the term public order suggests — a civil, smoothly flowing society. Indeed, many of these offenses, particularly prostitution, are referred to as victimless crimes.

The first panels in this chapter will provide an overview of arrests and trends in sentencing. Before examining particular offenses, the chapter will briefly examine the role alcohol plays in crime. Over 2 million alcohol-related crimes — such as drunk driving, liquor law violations, and disorderly conduct — are committed each year. This figure does not even include the violent and property crimes influenced by alcohol. Two panels follow on drinking and driving. Arrests for drunk driving have fallen since the 1980s, as have the number of fatalities in alcohol-related crashes. But there are those who still get behind the wheel when they have had too much to drink. There are still those who pay the price for this recklessness. Nearly 16,000 people die annually in alcohol-related crashes.

After a brief look at Internet gambling, the chapter will focus on sex-related crimes. Over the last decade, increased attention has been paid to stalking. What happens when an ex-spouse or boyfriend, or, indeed, a virtual stranger, starts showing up at your work or home? Is he or she a danger, even if no threats have been made? The next panel deals with sex offender registries. Current legislation demands that the public be notified when a sexual predator moves into their neighborhood.

The last panel will look at prostitution. Some communities have been overwhelmed by prostitutes and the men who go in search of them. How are local law enforcement and communities handling this issue? As the world's oldest profession, can we expect ever to rid ourselves of prostitution? What about this perennial question: Should prostitution be legalized?

Lesser Offenses in Perspective

Arrests by Categories

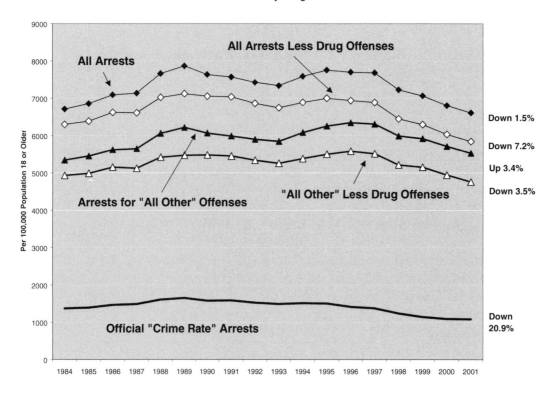

We begin our look at lesser crimes and offenses with another overview. Up to this point we have dealt with crimes included in the FBI's official crime rate; it is divided into the violent and property crime components. In Chapter 1, in the panel entitled *Other Crimes and Offenses*, we saw that the official crime rate covers but a fraction of all offenses. There we saw data for 2000. We extend that view here to the time period 1984 to 2001. Crimes and offenses are measured by arrests. In order to make the data comparable from one year to the next, arrests are expressed per 100,000 population of those aged 18 and older. This convention controls for an increase in the overall population.

We see first, again, that the official crime rate is a fraction of total crimes and offenses. Those are measured by the top curve, showing "all arrests." Note, please, that traffic violations are excluded. "All arrests" represents the sum of the official "crime rate" arrests and arrests for "other crimes and offenses." We are showing curves with solid symbols and with open ones. Those with open ones represent data that exclude all arrests for drug law violations — be it for possession or for trafficking. This allows us to see the impact of the "war on drugs" on the overall rate of "lawlessness" in the country over this period of time.

What are the important trends here? We see that serious, "official" crime is down sharply in this period, by 20.9%. We see that all crimes and offenses are down a little (1.5%). A closer look shows that if drug-related arrests are excluded, total arrests are down significantly, by 7.2%. If we examine the "all other" category, the lesser crimes and offenses covered in this chapter, we see a 3.4% increase in arrests between 1984 and 2001, but, again, if drug arrests are excluded, this "lesser" category is also down by 3.5%.

The conclusion is that in our recent history crimes and offenses are down decisively, especially the crimes labeled "serious." Whatever increase we are seeing is due to the nation's war on drugs. This alone leads us to devote a chapter to that subject. Here we shall not be discussing drugs; they will be covered in some depth in Chapter 6.

In using phrasing like "lesser" crimes and offenses, we don't intend to minimize the crimes/offenses committed. They include victimless crimes, like gambling, but also offenses such as spousal and child abuse, simple assault, and property crimes like fraud that can strip helpless old people of all of their means. The terminology is merely intended to signal that the government does not view these crimes as severe enough to track in its official index.

The graphic also shows up another pattern — the wave-like shape of the arrest statistics. In 2001 we were reaching downward to a level reached in 1984 or below. In 1984, total arrests stood at 6,714 per 100,000 of adult population; in 2001 that value was 6,612. In between, total arrests peaked in 1989 at 7,869 and again in 1995 at 7,761. *Lawlessness is a cyclical phenomenon.* It reflects, in a kind of boiled-down essence, many factors of a cultural and economic nature, including changes in the age-groups that make up the population, but demographics do not explain it all. Many factors are at work.

Next, let's take a closer look at lesser crimes and offenses and see what is behind the generally down-trending curves shown here. Aggregates hide interesting details.

Source: U.S. Department of Justice, Federal Bureau of Investigation, *Uniform Crime Reports*, 1984 through 2001. Most recent issues are accessible at http://www.fbi.gov/ucr/00cius.htm.

Lesser Offenses: The Big Five

Selected Lesser Offenses

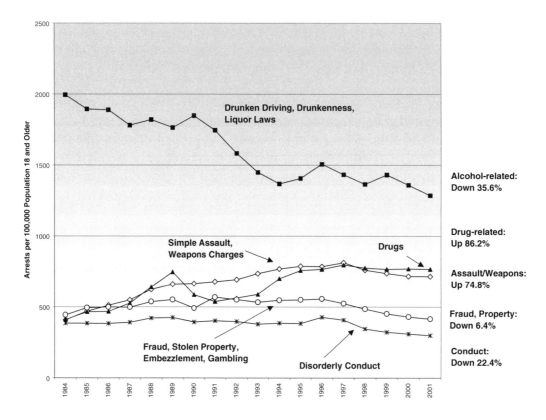

In 2001, crimes and offenses excluded from the official crime rate produced 11.45 million arrests. Of these, 3.6 million were offenses against state laws and local ordinances not specified but also not included into other categories; these excluded traffic violations. In what follows, we shall not deal further with this category (some 31.5% of non-indexed violations); instead we shall focus on those that have some recognizable designation.

In this graphic we display the Big Five of the "all other" category, again in normalized format, i.e., as arrests per 100,000 population aged 18 and older. Two of these have been trending down, two up.

The biggest category is alcohol-related crime, lead by driving while under the influence of alcohol. You might call this a "presidential" offense since the current (2002) holder of the office was once accused of DWI. Alcohol-related offenses are down in the 1984 to 2001 period: 35.6%. As we will show in Chapter 6, this period coincides with a dropping per capita consumption of the harder kinds of alcoholic beverages. Countering this trend is a sharp rise in arrests for drug violations; more than 80% of these are typically for possession of drugs, most often marijuana. This kind of violation also has a presidential aspect because our last president confessed to smoking a little pot, even if he did not inhale. Drug violations were up 86.2%. One has the sensation, looking at these data, that we are witnessing, through the blurred lens of arrest statistics, a shift in the recreational choice of drugs. Drug consumption, especially marijuana, has been up in this period.

Almost paralleling the increase in drug arrests, arrests for simple assault and weapons violations (illegal possession of firearms, carrying firearms) has been increasing, up 74.8%. Weapons are frequently associated with the drug trade, but the connection here is not evident. Arrests for weapons violations were down whereas simple assault was sharply up. It is noteworthy, however, that low-level violence — which is what simple assault actually is — has increased. It suggests rising stresses and strains mirrored in domestic abuse/problems, as we shall see in the next panel.

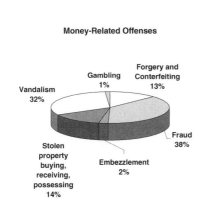

Money-Related Offenses

Gambling 1%

Forgery and Conterfeiting 13%

Vandalism 32%

Fraud 38%

Stolen property buying, receiving, possessing 14%

Embezzlement 2%

Also down, in this period, are arrests for property-related crimes not included in the more serious property crime categories. These include fraud; vandalism; forgery and counterfeiting; the buying, receiving, and possession of stolen property; embezzlement; and gambling violations. The relative shares of these offences of the total category are shown in the pie chart to the left. Within this category, embezzlement, forgery, and counterfeiting have grown. The other categories have all decreased, as measured by arrests, gambling at the highest rate. Forgery has been undergoing a radical change thanks to improvements in small computers and printers. The high-flying economy of the 1990s no doubt encouraged embezzlement.

Disorderly conduct, which may be a shadow of drunkenness, is down, along with alcohol-related crime, a meaningful 22.4%.

We turn next to four other categories of lesser crimes and offenses.

Source: U.S. Department of Justice, Federal Bureau of Investigation, *Uniform Crime Reports*, 1984 through 2001. Most recent issues are accessible at http://www.fbi.gov/ucr/00cius.htm.

Lesser Offenses: Abuse is Up

Selected Lesser Offenses

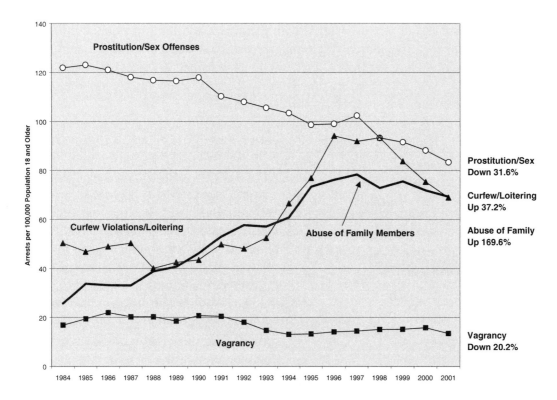

Four other broad categories encompass the balance of "lesser crimes and offenses": prostitution and non-rape sexual offenses, curfew violations and loitering, offenses against the family and children, and vagrancy. Not included, as already mentioned, is the largest category, "all other offenses"; these are violations of all manner of state laws and local ordinances that do not fit one of the other categories. We have also excluded the category of "runaways," teens who have run away from home and whose apprehensions are measured as arrests.

Data presented here are once more ratios. Thus in 2001, 83 people out of each population cluster of 100,000 people, aged 18 or older, were arrested for prostitution or some sexual offense excluding rape. The same ratio for 1984 was 122 people. Over this period, arrests were down 31.6% based on the ratio. Actual arrests in 1984 were 210,000 and in 2001 172,682, a decline of 17.1%, but population grew between those years; the normalized decline is thus significantly greater. Using ratios accounts for changes in population between 1984 and 2001 (and years in between) so that data can be compared without distortion one year to the next.

In 2001, the category of prostitution and sex offenses (not including rape) was made up 47% of prostitution and 53% of sex offenses, the exact reverse of the data in 1984. Women are predominantly arrested for prostitution, men for sex offenses. Both categories are down, based on population ratio, prostitution down 40%, sex offenses 22%. We were *not* reaching new lows in 2001. Data from 1975 indicate a rate, per 100,000, of 80 arrests for these offenses and 99 for the year 1979. In these matters no permanent victories are won. We are just catching the bottom of a wave again — this particular trough possibly caused by some combination of loosening sexual mores and consequent easier access to casual sex and/or the specter of HIV/AIDS, which is making the public cautious.

Curfew violations and loitering are not further divided in the FBI data. If these offenses are mostly loitering, those who do so must clearly have visible means of support — because arrests for vagrancy are down. Does homelessness have something to do with these two curves? Or more teenagers out on the streets? The subject deserves deeper analysis, but the means for doing so are not readily at hand. We shall defer until, perhaps, a future edition of this work.

The other data series that draws the eye is the sharp rise in arrests for what the FBI labels "offenses against the family and children." These offenses include quite a range of problems — from neglect or the abuse of children and elders to spousal abuse. As we noted in Chapter 2, homicide of intimates is sharply down. Here we see the incidence of lesser offenses within the family rising rather dramatically, especially in an environment of generally declining rates of arrests.

The phenomenon may well be due to the more frequent reporting of crimes/offenses that the police, in the past, did not hear about. The subject of abuse has been in the news for years now. Adult and child protection agencies have come into being as a consequence of law. The Child Abuse Prevention and Treatment Act (CAPTA), was originally enacted in 1974 and amended in 1996. In 1984, Congress reauthorized the Older Americans Act and strengthened the role of state and area agencies. Extensive studies have been conducted by the U.S. Department of Health and Human Services. One of these, the *Third National Incidence Study of Child Abuse and Neglect*[1], reports rising incidence of cases much in line with arrest statistics.

Some aspects of these subjects have been covered in other chapters. For instance, intimate homicide was covered in Chapter 2, Violent Crime; fraud has been discussed in Chapter 3, Property Crime; we shall deal with drugs in Chapter 6. In what follows in this chapter, other aspects of "lesser offenses" — especially those that point at trends — will be explored in a little more detail.

Source: U.S. Department of Justice, Federal Bureau of Investigation, *Uniform Crime Reports*, 1984 through 2001. Most recent issues are accessible at http://www.fbi.gov/ucr/00cius.htm.

---

[1] For a summary see www.calib.com/nccanch/pubs/statinfo/nis3.cfm.

Sentencing: Drugs and Public Order Crimes

Not in the Crime Rate but Still in the Jails

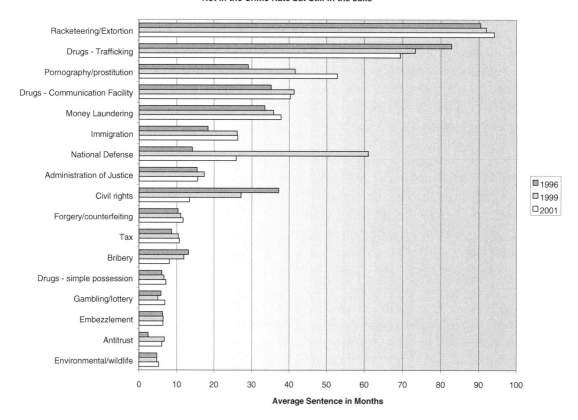

Average Sentence in Months

As stated in the panel *Other Crimes and Offenses* (Chapter 1), more than 80% of crimes do not get included in the crime rate. The panel shows the major types of offenses, and the length of the sentence offenders typically receive. Does the punishment fit the crime?

The average sentence has fluctuated for some of these crimes (the figures for 1996 to 2001 are provided in the table in the back of this book). According to these figures, provided by the U.S. Sentencing Commission, for many crimes an offender is likely to be sentenced to more jail time today then he would have been in 1996.

Let's examine some of these offenses. Average sentences for racketeering and money laundering are up for the period shown. Racketeering is now a 94.1 month (8 year) sentence, money laundering a 37.8 month (3 year) sentence. These crimes often warrant sizeable fines and restitution orders. Total payments for money laundering exceeded $394.1 million. For racketeering the total exceeded $176 million.

Crimes such as bribery, tax evasion, and fraud fall under the rubric of "white collar crime." Feel like sidestepping the tax code? That'll be roughly 11 months in jail (up from 9 in 1996). Feel like bribing someone to get what you want? You'll serve 8 months in the slammer, down from the 14 months you would have served in 1996. Itching to commit some garden variety fraud? 14 months, up from 13.2 in 1996.

White collar crime seemed to fall beneath law enforcement's radar for many years. Philip Feigin, who spent 20 years as a state securities regulator in Colorado and Wisconsin, made this analysis of going after corporate wrongdoing pre-1980: "They were too complicated, they took too long, and judges never sentenced white-collar crooks to jail even if you convicted them." This attitude did reverse itself slightly after the successful prosecutions of Wall Streeters Michael Milliken and Ivan Boesky.[2]

But the numbers show that CEOs who cook the books have little to fear. From 1992 to 2001, only 14% of the 609 tagged by the Securities and Exchange Commission for criminal prosecution wound up behind bars. In the 1990s, Greg Smith notes, a bank executive convicted in the savings and loan scandal in excess of 36 months in prison did less time than a burglar (55.6 months) or a car thief (38 months). As Smith says in his citing of this data: "If you're going to steal, make sure to steal from company coffers — not a Dodge minivan off the street." Nationally, 60% of those convicted of fraud (of any kind) received probation.

Some cases of corporate fraud cost billions. The cost of the bailout of the savings & loans in the 1980s has cost somewhere between $200 billion and $1.4 trillion by some estimates. The collapse of Enron cost $60 billion, by an early estimate. The fraud at Waste Management Inc. in the early 1990s, one of the first cases to invigorate the public debate on corporate fraud, cost investors $6 billion. In these cases, should the firms simply be fined for their behavior or should individuals be held responsible?

How about drugs? Those arrested on drug-related charges represented 20.9% of those incarcerated at the state level, up from just 6.5% in 1980. More people are arrested for possession of drugs than for trafficking, but more are imprisoned for trafficking. A drug trafficker received an average sentence of 69 months in 2001, just under 6 years, and down from the 83 months (7 years) he served in 1996. A sentence for drug possession has increased from a 6 month to a 7 month sentence. But not all drugs are equal under the law. Legislation passed by Congress in 1986 takes a harsher approach to crack over powder cocaine. Simple possession for powder cocaine is a misdemeanor; simple possession for crack cocaine is a felony. The average sentence length for powder cocaine is 77 months, compared to 119.5 for crack cocaine. That's nearly as long as the current sentences for murder (203.4 months), kidnapping/hostage taking (181.5 months), robbery (93.5 months), and arson (82.1 months). In May 2001, legislation increased sentencing around the drug Ecstasy. Possession of 800 Ecstasy pills is now a 61 month sentence, up from 18 months before the law. An Ecstasy related crime now receives a 60 month sentence, up from 25 months. (Ecstasy and other club drugs are examined in Chapter 6).

The average sentence for civil rights violations has fallen from 37.2 to 13.3 months, a drop of 64%. Cases that fall under this category include hate crimes, laws that ensure unrestricted access to abortion clinics, church arson, and official misconduct. They also include employment rights, voting rights, and housing and welfare violations. Complaints

---

[2] Milliken and Boesky both only served a fraction of their sentences. Boesky, in fact, took half of the $100 million in restitution he had to pay back and used it as a tax write off.

around these four issues filed in district courts fell slightly from 1996 to 2000, from 42,007 to 40,908. And exception: the number of civil rights complaints have increased from 18,914 in 1990 to 40,908 in 2000, an increase of 116%. Could declining complaints translate into lighter sentences? Maybe. In many cases offenders must pay a fine and perform community service (a more fitting punishment, one might argue). Still, the shorter sentences are a curious development, considering the dialogue that has taken in this country about hate crimes, tolerance, and the liberties of all. The jails are full. The courts are over-burdened.

The average sentence for prostitution and pornography charges has increased from 29.1 months in 1996 to 52.8 months in 2001. The public in general and law enforcement in particular are increasingly adopting a zero tolerance attitude to such crimes. Regulatory offenses — those involving antitrust, environmental, food and drug, and administration of justice programs — tend to warrant million dollar fines rather than jail time. But it is important to note that sentences are generally longer than they were in 1996. Is the government trying to establish more control of its branches as national security became an increasingly hot issue? Quite possibly. Offenses involving the defense program received the longest sentences, 25.8 months.

Overall, the average sentence has fallen from 50.7 months in 1996 to 46.8 months in 2001, or 4 years in jail. How much time the offender typically serves, is a different question.

Sources: Chart data comes from U.S. Sentencing Commission. Other data from the Human Rights Watch, available at http://www.hrw.org; U.S. Department of Justice, Bureau of Justice Statistics, "Civil Rights Complaints in U.S. District Courts, 2000, *Civil Justice Data Brief*, July 2002; "Stiffer Penalties Result from Graham Legislation." available from http://graham.senate.gov; "Crack vs. Powder Cocaine Sentencing." available from Families Against Mandatory Minimums from http://www.famm.org; "Enough is Enough." *Fortune*, March 18, 2002, p. 60; Reason, Tim. "Jailhouse Shock." *CFO*, September 1, 2000; Greg Smith. "Audit of Sentences Shows: Bad Execs Do Little Time." *Knight-Ridder/Tribune News Service*, August 20, 2002. "Evildoers Inc." available from http://www.chicagomediawatch.org/02_1_enron.html; Linden, Laura and Leslie Weiss, "Tim Anderson: Raising S&L Hell." *Mother Jones*, November 8, 1996.

Alcohol and Crime

The Role of Alcohol in Crime, 1996

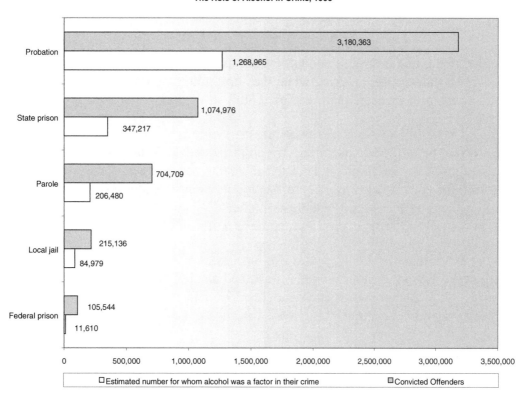

On an average day in 1996, an estimated 5.3 million convicted offenders were under the supervision of criminal justice authorities. Nearly 40% of these offenders, about 2 million, had been using alcohol at the time of the offense for which they were convicted. For those on probation 39.9% were using alcohol at the time of the offense, compared to 39.5% in local jails, 32.3% in state prisons, 29.3% on parole, and 11% of those in federal prison.

Roughly 56% of offenders in local jails were drinking at the time of the offense, as were 43% of those in state prisons and 75.1% of those who were sentenced to probation. Many of those who received probation are those who commit public order crimes such as driving under the influence, liquor law violations, drunkenness, disorderly conduct, and vagrancy. These alcohol-related crimes represented about 24% of all arrests in 2000. The actual number of arrests are shown in the table below.

Number of Alcohol-Related Arrests, 2000

Offense	Number
Driving under the influence	983,669
Liquor law violations	607,194
Disorderly conduct	504,742
Drunkenness	469,124
Vagrancy	28,335

Alcohol plays a significant role in violent crimes as well. For those in state or local jails, over 40% of offenders were drinking when they committed murder, over 30% when they committed a rape or a sexual assault, and over 30% when they committed a robbery.

According to government statistics, two-thirds of victims who suffered violence by an intimate (current or former spouse or boyfriend/girlfriend) reported that alcohol had been a factor. Roughly 7 out of 10 alcohol-related incidents occur at a residence, and the most frequent time for occurrence was 11 p.m. Such data paints a picture of how alcohol can potentially affect some crime. A couple is home, it's late, alcohol is introduced into a troubled, potentially volatile relationship, and one party (or both) become violent.

Alcohol use is an issue in property and drug crimes as well. Roughly 33% and 32% respectively of those in local and state jails consumed alcohol before committing a property crime (burglary saw the highest level). Roughly 29% and 18% respectively of those convicted of drug possession or trafficking were drinking at the time of their arrest.

The role of alcohol in crime is an obvious one: it removes inhibitions and our ability to make sound judgments. We think we can drive home just fine. We confront the spouse or lover who has hurt us. We vandalize property to make us feel better. It also tends to inflame our emotional states: someone who is depressed or angry may decide now is the time to strike back.

Source: U.S. Department of Justice, Bureau of Justice Statistics, *Alcohol and Crime*, April 1998.

Driving Under the Influence

Arrests for Driving Under the Influence (DUI), 1986-1997

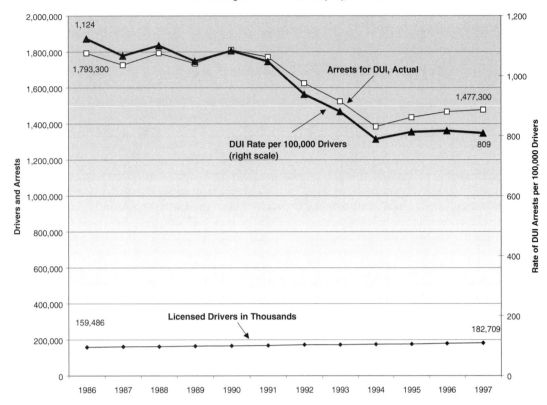

The number of drunk driving arrests fell 17.6% from 1986 to 1997. The rate of arrests per 100,000 people fell 28% over the same period: arrests were down, drivers had increased.

Several thoughts come to mind when looking at such results. One thinks about MADD, for instance. In 1980, Candy Lightner founded Mothers Against Drunk Driving after a drunk driver killed her daughter. She became an activist and set out to educate the public on alcohol behind the wheel. Similar organizations, such as Students Against Drunk Driving, soon followed. We were told to have designated drivers when going out to party — and that "Friends Don't Let Friends Drive Drunk." One of MADD's greatest triumphs was getting the drinking age raised to 21 in 1994, a factor that certainly helped to keep alcohol out of the hands of young people and in the process saved lives.

Those most likely to drink and drive are in their twenties, an age-group that has seen demographic contraction. Those in their 20s were 41.9 million of the population in 1987 and 36.3 million in 1997. Hard liquor consumption has declined per capita in this period, which may have had an influence as well. And though such a speculation is not a positive, alcohol has had some competition from other drugs of choice, like marijuana.

The table below examines DUI arrest rates by age. In 1986, those 21 to 24 years had the highest rate of arrests, 2,384 per 100,000 people. Those 19-20 had a rate of 2,006 and those 25-29 had a rate of 1,924. As drivers, they were over-represented in arrests. Those 21-24 were 9.3% of drivers, but they were 19.7% of arrests. Those 25-29 were 12.9% of drivers and 22% of all arrests. In 1997, rates dropped among all age groups. However, the basic trend in 1986 remained true. Drivers in their twenties and thirties made up the lion's share of arrests. These arrests were out of proportion to their age group. Those 45 years of age and older represented a smaller portion of arrests, particularly in comparison to their share of drivers: those 45-49 were 9.7% of drivers and 7.4% of arrests, those 65 and older were 14.3% drivers and 1.4% of DUI arrests.

Licensed Drivers and DUI Arrests by Age Group, 1986 and 1997

Age	1986			1997		
	% of Drivers	% of Arrests	Arrests per 100,000	% of Drivers	% of Arrests	Arrests per 100,000
Total	100	100	1,124	100	100	809
16-18	4.3	3.8	990	3.7	3.2	696
19-20	3.8	6.8	2,006	3.2	5.3	1,353
21-24	9.3	19.7	2,384	6.7	14.1	1,695
25-29	12.9	22.0	1,924	10.0	16.9	1,372
30-34	12.3	15.8	1,445	10.8	16.3	1,227
35-39	11.1	11.1	1,122	11.5	15.8	1,105
40-44	7.2	7.2	921	11.0	11.5	849
45-49	4.9	4.9	783	9.7	7.4	620
50-54	3.4	3.4	613	8.0	4.3	438
55-59	2.4	2.4	446	6.1	2.3	309
60-64	1.5	1.5	299	5.0	1.3	213
65 and over	1.2	1.2	114	14.3	1.4	78

In 1997, an estimated 513,200 offenders were on probation or in jail or prison for driving while intoxicated: 454,000 on probation, 41,100 in jail, and 17,600 in State prison. DWI offenders presented 14% of probationers, 7% of jail inmates, and 2% of State prisoners. Who are these people? 94.2% were men (up from 83% just in 1995). Half were in their thirties, with the average age between 36 and 38. 68% were White, 17.3% were Hispanic, and 9.8% were Blacks. They were better educated than other offenders. 37% of DWI offenders on probation, 18% of those in jail and 16% of those in prison had some college. 40% have never been married, while 15.4% were married (the rest were divorced, widowed or separated).

Down-trending rates of DUI are nice to see, but we may just be seeing a part of a wave-like cycle, caught in the trough, rather than permanent "progress." Alcohol has been with us for a long time, and these rates may turn up again.

Sources: U.S. Department of Justice, Bureau of Justice Statistics, Bureau of Justice Statistics, *DWI Offenders Under Correctional Supervision*, June 1999. Population figures from the U.S. Bureau of the Census.

Dying While Driving and Drunk

Alcohol Related Traffic Fatalities

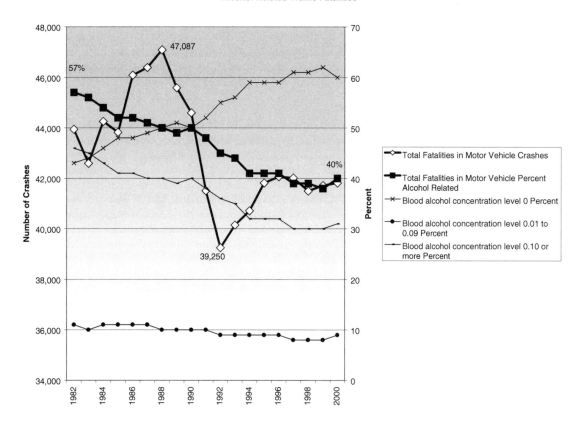

In 1999, 15,786 people died in alcohol-related crashes, one every 33 minutes. Roughly 40% of traffic fatalities were alcohol-related, down from 57% in 1982. An estimated 308,000 people were injured in accidents involving alcohol based on data from the National Highway Traffic Safety Administration.

Drunk driving is often referred to as driving while intoxicated (DWI) or driving under the influence (DUI). Drunk driving refers to driving with a blood alcohol level over the state's permissible blood alcohol concentration (BAC) level — usually 0.10%. As of October 2000, 19 states (including the District of Columbia) use 0.08% to define drunken or impaired driving. More states probably will adopt the 0.08% level; Congress recently passed legislation requiring states to adopt the 0.08% standard if they wished to avoid losing critical highway funds.

There has been a growing debate about where the cutoff for legally defined intoxication should be. How quickly one reaches a 0.08% or 0.10% BAC varies by gender and weight, although the average man reaches the limit after three or four drinks consumed in an hour. Below a BAC level of 0.10%, a driver can experience problems with vision and depth perception, and coordination and judgment are affected. But it is those with a BAC over 0.10% who cause most of the accidents. According to the National Highway Traffic Safety Administration, the average level of intoxication in fatal alcohol-related accidents is 0.17. Fatally injured drivers with BAC levels over 0.10% were six times more likely to have a prior conviction for DWI than fatally injured sober drivers.

Martin Morse Webster cites research by University of New Mexico sociologist Lawrence Ross that the 0.08 level will result in a 60% increase in DWI arrests but no significant decrease in fatalities. Webster's article repeats an intriguing question Mr. Ross poses in his book, *Confronting Drunk Driving:* "Should we put out a net so wide and so tightly woven as to sweep up huge numbers of people, or should we concentrate on those most likely to create carnage on the streets?"

The percentage of crashes involving a BAC of 0.10 or higher has been on the decline — 46.3% of all crashes in 1982, 31% in 2000. Optimism comes just when news reports are filled with reports of increased binge drinking on college campuses. In a 2000 Gallup Poll, 42% of those 18 to 29 reported drinking more than they should, while 29% of those 30 to 49 did. From 1999 to 2000, there was a slight increase in those with a BAC between 0.01 and 0.09%.

The number of traffic fatalities hit its peak in 1988 (47,087 deaths). The lowest number of deaths (39,250) occurred in 1992. Alcohol is playing a decreasing role in these deaths. Why are there fewer deaths, even as the number of licensed drivers increases? In part, things are better because there are fewer young drivers out there. The population of those in their twenties has fallen, although they are more likely to drink and drive as shown in this table.

Respondents Who Reported Driving

Under the Influence in 1998

Age Group	Percent
16-17	8.9
18-20	21.1
21-25	22.1
26-34	14.3
35 and older	8.0

Additional reasons include improvements in vehicle design and the inclusion of safety features such as airbags. Seat belt use is up, from 62% in May 1998 to 71% in September 2000 (Department of Transportation). Alcohol education programs of the 1980s and 1990s worked. The slogan "Buckle Up — It's the Law" appears to be saving lives.

The next battle will be over cellular phones. As of April 2001, 10 local communities have banned phone use while driving. Forty more states are considering similar restrictions. What about chatting on a cell-phone with a BAC level of 0.10?

Sources: Bureau of Justice Statistics. *Sourcebook of Criminal Justice Statistics, 2000*, p. 75; "Seat Belt Use Reaches All-Time High." Online. Available: http://www.nsc.org/news/n090700.htm; "What is drunk driving?" available from http://www.drunk drivingoffenses.com; National Highway Administration, *Traffic Safety Facts, 1999*; Scherer, Ron. "A Revolt Against Driving." *Christian Science Monitor*, April 18, 2001; Morse Webster, Martin. "Mothers against Drunk Driving: Has its Vision Become Blurred?" available from http://www.capitalresearch.org; online data retrieved November 20, 2002.

Illegal Gambling

Estimated Profits for Online Gambling

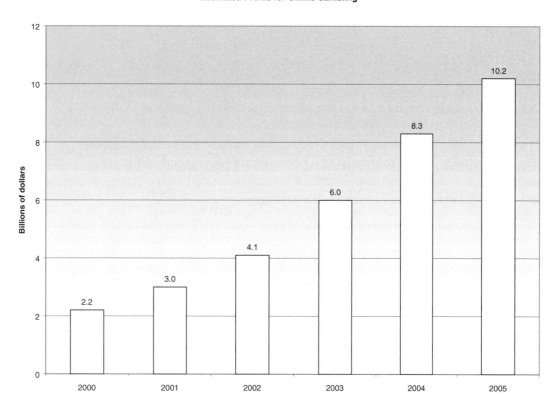

The revenues generated by legal gambling (casinos, racetracks, etc.) grew to more than $60 billion in 2000. Revenues have increased over 1,000% since 1976. There are now lotteries in 37 states; 28 states have authorized casino gambling and 43 have pari-mutuel betting. According to the National Gambling Impact Study Commission (NGISC), a legal wager may be placed in every state but Utah, Tennessee, and Hawaii.

Internet gambling, although illegal, goes on under the noses of authorities. The activity seemed to blossom with the rise of the Internet 1995. In May of 1998, according to the study, there were approximately 90 on-line casinos, 39 lotteries, 8 bingo games, and 53 sports books. One year later, there were over 250 on-line casinos, 64 lotteries, 20 bingo games, and 139 sportsbooks.

The industry is profitable, although just how much is the source of speculation. Christiansen/Cummings Associates, gaming industry analysts, has estimated profits, shown in the graphic above. They estimated that revenues for Internet gambling more than doubled from 1998 to 1999. A second study, conducted by analysts Frost & Sullivan (from NGISC), confirmed that revenues had doubled in a one-year period, from $445.4 million in 1997 to $919.1 million in 1998.

Most of these Internet sites are based outside of the U.S. This means that they are beyond the reach of the authorities. The 1961 Federal Wire Act, prohibiting the use of interstate phone lines to place wagers on sporting events, aids law enforcement in cracking down on illegal gambling. In recognition of the problem, the House of Representatives passed legislation to make Internet gambling a federal crime (the bill has not yet reached the Senate).

The real issues are control and accountability. There's no way to keep children out of these sites. Also, because so many of these online casinos are based in places like Antigua there's no legal recourse when a player is potentially cheated. You risk losing your shirt, of course, the minute you sit down at a blackjack table in Las Vegas, but the large, legal casinos have rules they must enforce. They also "know their customers." On the Internet, of course, anonymity rules. Just how many players are out there? By one count, an estimated 2 million players try their luck at more than 1,000 virtual casinos. An estimated $3.5 billion in bets will be lost this year.

There are many stories in the media of uncontrollable addictions. Debi Baptiste, a 40-year-old executive secretary, lost thousands of dollars playing video poker at a bar near the family home. The family moved to California for a fresh start and purchased a computer. Debi lost $50,000 gambling on illegal offshore sites. Her husband John changed the password on the computer. Debi started staying late at work to use her office computer to gamble. The family snapped under the pressures and Debi committed suicide. In an article in *Business Week* her husband said: "When I brought a computer into my house I had no idea I also brought a slot machine into my house."

Sports wagering is another form of illegal gambling. Betting on sporting events was banned in 1992 under the Professional and Amateur Sports Protection Act. It is legal only in Nevada. The potential size of the shadow industry is astonishing: NGISC estimates that a minimum of $80 billion in illegal wagers is placed each year. $10 billion is thought to be placed during March Madness. During Congressional testimony, William Saum of the NCAA warned that online betting could usher in a new generation of point shaving scandals that affected the basketball programs at Northwestern University and Arizona State University.

Not everyone disapproves. *USA Today* reports that the Antigua-based World Sports Exchange has 30,000 regular bettors (all from the U.S.). There have been few problems reported with this organization. Mike, a Virginia insurance agent, regularly bets on basketball and football games, claiming "I like it because you can just go online — it's 24/7."

Hmm…

Sources: McCoy, Kevin. "Online Gamble Pays Off for Internet Sports Books." *USA Today*, March 29, 2002, p. B1; "The Underground Web." *BusinessWeek*, September 2, 2002, p. 67; National Gambling Impact Study Commission Report, Gambling in the United States, p. 14-16; Horn, John. "Point and Bet." *Newsweek*, October 28, 2002, p. 50; Brian Knowles. "Should the Federal Government Prohibit Internet Gambling?" Available online at http://www.speakout.com; some gambling figures come from the American Gaming Association, found at http://www.americangaming.org.

Stalking

Victims by Sex and Relationship Between Victim and Offender

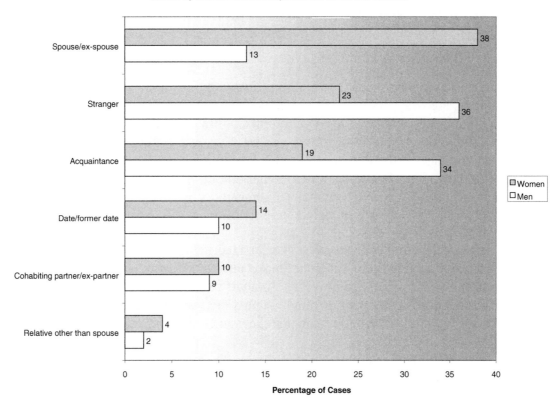

The National Institute of Justice and the Centers for Disease Control and Prevention estimate that one out of every 12 women and one out of every 45 men has been stalked in his or her lifetime.[3] Four-tenths of one percent of men and 1.0% of women had been stalked in the 12 months previous to the survey.

In the survey, 78% of stalking victims were identified as female. Eighty-seven percent of stalkers were identified as men (with a sharp split by gender: men comprised 94% of women's stalkers and 60% of men's stalkers). Just over half of victims were between 18 and 29 years of age. The study also confirmed another common belief about stalking: most victims know the perpetrators.

The graphic above examines the relationship between stalker and victim. Thirty-eight percent of women were stalked by a current or former spouse, 23% by a stranger, 19% by

---

[3] The organization defines stalking as "harassing or threatening behavior that an individual engages in repeatedly, such as following a person, appearing at a person's home or place of business, making harassing phone calls, leaving written messages or objects or vandalizing a person's property. These actions may or may not be accompanies by a credible threat of serious harm, and they may not be precursors to an assault or murder."

an acquaintance, 14% by a current or former date, and 10% by someone they currently or formerly lived with. For women, stalking seems to occur in some intimate context: the husband or boyfriend who will not accept that the relationship is over. But sometimes the stalking occurs even before the breakup. Forty-three percent of women reported that stalking occurred after the relationship ended. However, 21% claimed it started before the relationship ended; the remainder (36%) claimed stalking began before the relationship ended and continued on afterwards.

What of men? They have less intimate relationships with their stalkers. Thirty-six percent of men's stalkers are strangers to them (far higher than the category for women); 34% of them are acquaintances; 10% involved a current or former date. Only 13% of men reported being stalked by a current or former spouse. Curiously, 90% of the acquaintances and strangers are male. Why do men stalk other men? In some cases, these are erotic attachments. (Stalking prevalence was much higher among those men who had lived with another man compared to those who had not.) Some cases involved the stalker's hatred of homosexuals. Some stalker cases involved gang rivalries.

What sort of activities does the typical stalker engage in? Stalkers follow their victims, spy on them, stand outside their residence, make unwanted phone calls, send unwanted gifts or other items, and vandalize property. A small but significant percentage of cases (about 10%) involve the murder of or threat against the family pet. Such threats need to be treated seriously for the obvious reason that the stalker is turning violent.

All states have some sort of anti-stalker legislation. In 1996, the Federal Interstate Anti-Stalking Law extended federal protection to stalking victims. It expanded the definition of stalking to include mail and other forms of electronic communication (online harassment, known as cyberstalking, is a growing crime). It also requires courts to issue protection orders for victims and requires stiffer penalties for stalkers who have a history of this behavior. Some states are refining their definition of stalking: often a stalker must make an overt threat of violence for the behavior to be classified as "stalking."

The average case of stalking lasts 21 months.

Source: Tjaden, Patricia and Nancy Thoennes. U.S. Department of Justice, National Institute of Justice and the Centers for Disease Control and Prevention Research in Brief, *Stalking in America: Findings from the National Violence Against Women Survey*, April 1998.

Sex Offender Registries

Number of Registered Sex Offenders in New York State

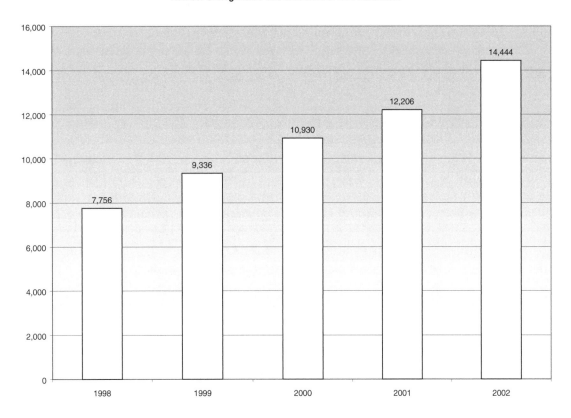

In 1990, as part of its Community Protection Act, Washington state enacted the first legislation under which authorities notify the public of the release of a dangerous sex offender. The 1994 Jacob Wetterling Act requires the states to register individuals convicted of committing sex crimes against children. Megan's Law, passed in 1996, refines the Jacob Wetterling Act and not only requires that all sex offenders be registered but that the community be notified when an offender moves into one of its neighborhoods. The law allows states to establish criteria for disclosure. Some states include the names of those considered a high-risk to commit another crime; some include those considered low-risk (most sex offenders). But all require that the names and addresses be made available to the public. Thirty-two states post such information on the Internet.

The great strength of Megan's Law, according to law enforcement people and child activists, is its requirement that offenders must register. An offender is typically given about a week to do so. The state verifies the address annually; in the case of the most dangerous offenders, the address is verified every 90 days. The offender will stay on the list for a decade or for life. Some of these lists have grown to nearly unmanageable size. Massachusetts has 18,000 names, Michigan 26,715, Arizona 11,000, Florida more than

25,000.[4] The size of the sex offender registry in New York is shown in the graphic. From 1998 to 2002, the list grew 86%, from 7,756 to 14,444 names.

California has had a number of problems with the nearly 90,000 sex offenders it must track. The state produces a CD-ROM version of its registry, but officials recently admitted that 30% of those on the list are living somewhere other than at addresses in the database. Other errors also surfaced. The system is inaccessible; users must visit a police agency to consult the list or must spend money on a 900 telephone call. Many states allow people to get off of the registry after some time. In California, one registers as a sex offender for life (the state has required sex offenders to register with them since 1947). Even the Justice Department has called California's policy "extreme" (Landon).

Other states also have problems managing their lists. About 2,900 sex offenders in Wisconsin, or 29% of the state registry's 9,900, have moved and either have not notified the state or are ignoring letters attempting to confirm their addresses. Lawsuits in Alaska and California have been filed, claiming that the registries violate privacy and due process. Texas has seen some unconventional sentences. A handful of judges there have ordered sex offenders to place signs in front of their house saying: "Danger Convicted Sex Offender Lives Here"; offenders must also place similar stickers on their vehicles.

The purpose of these registries is to inform the public. Of course, some people look up names in the registry and take the law into their own hands. "People have been run out of town because of these registries," reports Ed Barocos of the Legal Director of New Jersey American Civil Liberties Union. People drive by offenders' residences and shout insults; in some cases they vandalize property or attack the offender. The issue has been further complicated by cases of mistaken identity. One example: a Texas man was attacked when he moved into a home previously occupied by a sex offender who had left the area and hadn't notified authorities of his new address.

Do such lists violate privacy? Is there a conflict of rights here? Are the rights of children more important than those of a sex offender? There is a widespread belief that sex offenders will lapse again. Should the registries contain the names of all sex offenders or just those deemed a "high risk"? The vast majority (98% in California) are deemed to be low risk. The law also occasionally picks up a case of what one anti-registry activist called young "Romeos and Juliets".[5] Mary Coffee, the manager of Florida's Sex Offender and Predator Unit, rather colorfully sums up the real intent of sex offender registries: "Knowing where a toxic spill is won't keep you perfectly safe, but it will keep you from going there" (Sommerfeld).

---

[4] Massachusetts figure is current as of October 2001, Michigan's figure as of May 2001, Arizona's figure as of January 2001 and Florida's figure as August 2002.

[5] High school sweethearts. Many states have revised their legislation to permit judges to exempt from registration people who had consensual sex with a 13-15 year old partner when they themselves were under 19 years of age but two or more years older than the partner. Connecticut, for example, made this revision to its registration policy in 1999, just one year after its sex offender legislation was first enacted. Consensual sex between two people, both between 13-15 years of age is not a crime and does not require registration.

Lawsuits filed in Arizona and California have sent the issue to the Supreme Court. As of November 2002, the court had not yet ruled.

Sources: Chart data comes from Mahoney, Joe. "Pervert List Growing," available from http://www.nydailynews.com; Jeremy Schwartz. "Sign Postings Not First for Texas." *Caller-Times*, May 27, 2001; Lisa Sink. "State Loses Track of 2,900 Sex Offenders." *Milwaukee Journal Sentinel*, October 8, 2002; "State Sex Offender Law Filled with Flaws, Paper reports." *Sacramento Bee*, July 22, 2001; Julia Sommerfeld. "Are Online Registries Fair," available online at http://www.msnbc.com; Some information taken from KlassKids Foundation at http://www.klasskids.org.

Prostitution

Prostitution and Commercial Vice

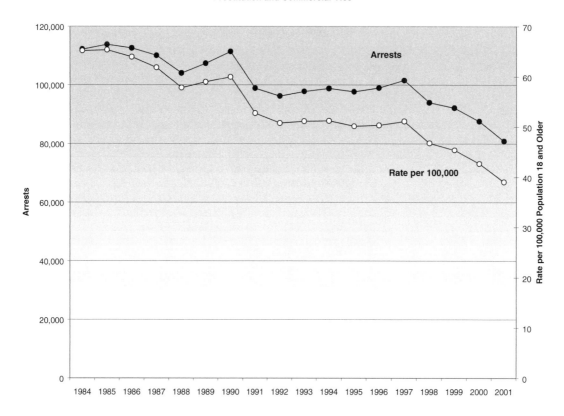

Nearly 88,000 prostitution arrests were made in 2000. About 60% of those arrested are women, 40% are men. The Prostitute Education Network believes that 90% of arrests involve prostitutes, 10% customers.

Many communities have been making concerted efforts to suppress prostitution. In the early 1990s, law enforcement started to crack down on prostitution as a way to bring down the crime rates overall. What are some cities doing? One recent trend is that men soliciting prostitutes (often undercover policewomen) will have their vehicle seized. Such programs are in effect in Detroit, Portland, Oregon, Washington D.C., and New York City. Police in some areas of Washington D.C. have even taken to handing out tickets to drivers making right turns to suppress drive-by traffic. Police in San Francisco instituted their First Offender Prostitution Program — referred to as "John school" in some circles — where men receive lectures about the evils of streetwalking and venereal diseases by police, business owners, and residents of neighborhoods plagued by prostitutes. Those who attend the program will have their records wiped clean. The program lasts only a day (a very long, humiliating day, one should think) but it has proven to be initially effective. Of the 2,181 men who have passed through the program in four years, only 18 have been rearrested. Police have offered drug dealers and prostitutes in Las Vegas a deal: stay out of the designated high crime areas for six months to a year and get suspended sentences. If they refuse and are caught in these areas again, they will be arrested on the spot. According to police and residents, it has been cleaning up downtown Las Vegas, but one can't help but wonder under what rug the dirt has been swept.

Some residents of troubled neighborhoods, fed up with prostitutes and customers conducting business on street corners, have taken matters into their own hands. They have grabbed their video cameras and filmed men with prostitutes; it's not uncommon for the amateur filmmakers to approach a parked car and interrupt the couple midway through the sex act. Brian Bates of Oklahoma first started filming in 1996 as a way to combat prostitution in his hometown. Since 1996, the "Video Vigilante" (as he calls himself on his website) has reportedly caught more than 200 hookers in the act. Bates has also photographed license plates and sent his sex tapes to the wives and these Johns. He has even alerted employers when the men were being serviced in a company car. (There goes *his* Christmas bonus.)

Should prostitution be legal? Would that reduce the trafficking in women and children across the globe, and the violence that often accompanies this activity? Prostitution is legal (or permitted with some restrictions) in such countries as Canada, England, France, and Denmark. Should certain "red light districts" be set up where customers and prostitutes can meet, with the police ensuring the safety of all parties? Few areas would welcome such a district in their neighborhood. Should we have brothels as they do in some European countries, with guidelines imposed to make sure they are run fairly? To keep their licenses, the women would have to submit to scheduled medical examinations (as they do in Nevada, where prostitution is legal). Could it also save cities money? According to a 1987 study, the average cost to bust a hooker was almost $2,000.

Occasionally, a sex worker will step forward to say how pleased she is with her profession. "Eileen K" says she chose to work for an escort service. She feels that "we are being discriminated against, having our free choices taken away and our human rights also taken away." She also stated: "Beats flipping burgers." Again, Eileen does not work on the street. The women and men who do are more likely to face violence. They will be more likely to suffer from drug addiction. Surprisingly, according to the Department of Health, only 3 to 5% of sexually transmitted disease is thought to be related to prostitution.

The Catholic Family and Human Right Institute reports that "there is universal agreement that the trafficking of women and children for prostitution is a growing menace, for the people involved and for the governments. Though most prevalent in the developing world, even in the United States women are lured into positions of sexual slavery from which they can rarely escape."

Sources: Bovard, Jerry. "The Legalization of Prostitution." available from http://www.fff.org; "Prostitution in the United States." available from http://www.bayswan.org; "Decriminalize Prostitution Now Coalition." available from http://www.sexwork.com; "Why Street Prostitution is Such a Serious Problem." available from http://www.sexwork.com; Matt Bean. "Girls on Film." available from http://www.courttv.com; "US Pushing UN to 'Legalize' Prostitution." *Catholic World News*, January 17, 2000; Andrew Kiraly. "Bad People, Go Away." *Las Vegas Mercury*, January 26, 2001; Evelyn Nieves. "Cities Study New Answer to Prostitution." *San Francisco Times*, March 21, 1999.

Chapter 5

Kids

Our children are our future. Can we keep them safe? Are we safe from them?

This chapter explores the topics of children as victims, as aggressors, and as consumers of pop culture in the form of violent video games. We begin with a look at school safety to determine how realistic are our fears for our children. Back in the 1950s we built bomb shelters to protect them against alien attacks. Somewhere between then and now, the ranks of the enemies of our children grew. Today it seems we must protect our children against threats from abroad and against enemies much closer to home — other children, family members, so-called friends. To keep our children safe at school, we have installed police officers. When surveyed in 2002, 95% of school-based police officers reported that their schools are vulnerable to a terrorist attack and 79% reported that their schools were not adequately prepared to respond to a terrorism attack.[1] If these threats are real, are we endangering our children if we fail to install metal detectors in every school in the land?

We've heard it again and again: Ours is a violent society. Our children are not immune. Our second group of panels looks at trends in the number of children who have been arrested for violent crimes. We then look at the issues of abused and missing children to try and answer these questions: Are abuse rates up? Are there more missing children? Does media coverage help to find missing children?

We close the chapter with a look at violent video games. Technological advances have made the experience of video games a lot like real life. Does playing violent video games make children more prone to acts of violence?

---

[1] 2002 NASRO School Resource Officer Survey, "Final Report on the 2nd Annual National Survey of School-Based Police Officers," September 25, 2002, http://www.nasro.org.

How Safe Are Our Schools?

Non-fatal crimes occurring at school or on the way to or from school, per 1,000 students aged 12-18

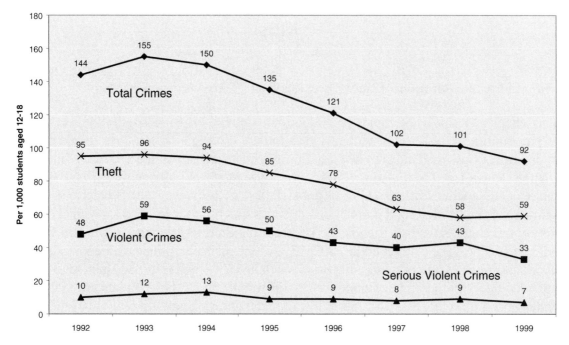

"The best data on the very specific threat of school-associated violent death reveals that children face a one in a million chance of being killed at school." — Justice Policy Institute (JPI; a Washington, D. C. research group)

Who wants to take that one in a million chance? The idea of placing one's child in harm's way by sending her to school must make the blood run cold. How safe are our schools, anyway? That question has been debated for decades. A rash of highly publicized school shootings in the 1990s and the events of September 11, 2001, lend an urgency to the debate. What do the data show about violence in our schools?

There is no national system for reporting injuries or violence in schools. The chart above shows data presented in three annual reports prepared at the request of President Clinton in 1998 in response to the extreme school violence of the late 1980s and early 1990s.

In 1999, about 52 million children were enrolled in grades K-12. That year, students aged 12 to 18 were victims of 186,000 non-fatal serious violent crimes and 880,000 non-fatal violent crimes at school.[2] The chart shows that between 1992 and 1999, schools got safer. The non-fatal victimization rate fell from 144 incidents per 1,000 students to 92. The chart shows that most school crimes involve theft.

---

[2] Serious violent crimes include murder, rape, sexual assault, suicide, robbery, and aggravated assault. Violent crimes are serious violent crimes plus simple assault.

The table shows the number of school-shooting deaths over six school years.[3] The figures
include suicides and killings of adults in schools, some of
which occurred at the hands of other adults. The most
widely publicized events of the 1990s took place in
small-town America: Springfield, Oregon (2 students
killed); Jonesboro, Arkansas (4 students killed); Pearl,
Mississippi (2 students killed); West Paducah, Kentucky
(3 students killed); Littleton, Colorado (14 students
killed, including the killers). The Justice Policy Institute
points out that 11 children die every two days from fam-
ily violence (child abuse or neglect, at the hands of their parents or guardians), indicating
that children are safer at school than at home. JPI calls school shootings "extremely idio-
syncratic events and not part of any discernible trend."

School Year	Shooting Deaths
1992-93	55
1993-94	51
1994-95	20
1995-96	35
1996-97	25
1997-98	40

Of course, school safety is not all about shootings. The University of Michigan's annual
violence survey shows that 12th graders were about as likely to report being injured with
or without a weapon in school in 1976 as in 1996. Apparently responding to "get tough
on crime" sentiments, though, Congress passed legislation to curb an alleged rising tide
of school violence, starting with the 1986 Drug Free Schools and Communities Act. The
1994 Gun-Free Schools Act requires that each state receiving federal funds under the
Elementary and Secondary Education Act have a state law requiring all local educational
agencies in the state to expel from school for at least one year any student found bringing
a firearm to school. In school year 1998-99, there were 3,371 expulsions, down 41% from
the 5,724 expulsions reported for 1996-97 (the first year totals were reported).[4] Critics of
the reporting system contend there are far more guns in the hands of schoolchildren than
have been reported by school principals.

Attempts to legislate school safety continue. One of the mandates of the 2001 No Child
Left Behind Act calls on states to identify "persistently dangerous" public schools (Unsafe School Choice Option). Students in those schools or any student who is the victim of
a violent crime at any public school will be allowed to transfer to a "safe" school within
the district or to a charter school, and the home district must pay transportation costs.

Do security devices make schools safer? We look at that issue next.

Sources: U.S. Departments of Education and Justice, *Indicators of School Crime and Safety, 2001*, http://nces.ed.gov/pubs2002/
crime2001/. Primary Source: Bureau of Justice Statistics, National Crime Victimization Survey, 1992 to 1999. Mathews, Joe, "In the
Classroom: Metal Detectors and a Search for Peace of Mind," *Los Angeles Times*, May 30, 2001, pB-2. Hayward, Ed, "Police official:
Kids want school metal detectors," *The Boston Herald*, April 3, 2001 p014. Boston Deputy Superintendent's Memorandum, School
Year 2002-2003, boston.k12.ma.us/dept/docs/oss_safety7.doc. Elizabeth Donohue, Vincent Schiraldi, and Jason Ziedenberg, *School
House Hype: School shootings and the real risks kids face in America*, Justice Policy Institute, http://www.cjcj.org/ jpi/school
house.html. Information retrieved October 8, 2002.

---

[3] JPI says there is no reliable, scientific count but says the best data source is the National School Safety
Center, which has compiled data annually since the 1992-93 school year.

[4] The most recent figures available. The Department of Education has developed a new School Survey on
Crime & Safety. A final report is to be released in 2003.

School Safety: Metal Detectors in Every School?

Serious Violent Crimes Reported, by Location of Public School: 1996-97

Population size is 78,000 public schools, of which 10.1% reported serious violent crimes.

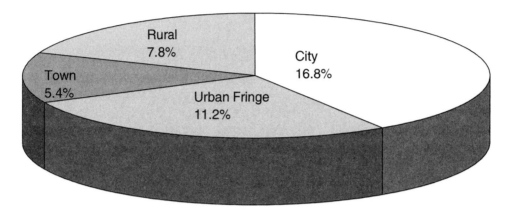

"People were saying, 'I can't believe it happened here' .... People in Boston, New York, or Los Angeles would never say it can't happen here. Folks in the big cities have responded" [to the threat of school violence represented by the Littleton, Colorado, shootings] — Northeastern University Prof. Jack Levin to reporter Angie Cannon

Are we failing our children by not installing metal detectors in every school in America?[5] We saw in the preceding panel that school crime actually declined in the 1990s. In the wake of school shootings and the events of September 11, 2001, however, school officials find themselves trying to allay rising public fears of school violence and terrorist threats, and lawmakers have given us the Gun-Free Schools Act.

Percentage of Public Schools Reporting Serious Violent Crimes (N = 78,000)

Characteristic	Total	City	Urban Fringe	Town	Rural
Total	10.1	16.8	11.2	5.4	7.8
Enrollment 300-999	9.3	12.5	9.0	3.2	13.9
Enrollment 1,000+	32.9	44.2	29.8	15.9	NA
Minority Enrollment					
5-19%	10.9	14.5	11.3	10.6	6.8
20-49%	11.1	19.1	10.1	5.0	8.0
50% or more	14.7	17.6	17.8	4.4	11.6

[5] The U.S. Department of Education reported that in school-year 1996-97, 1% of public schools required daily metal detector checks and 4% used random metal detector checks.

Serious violent crimes do take place in schools. A little over 10% of schools reported such crimes to police in 1996-97, as the table shows. Note too (chart and table) that it is big-city schools with large enrollments of minority students that are more likely to report serious violent crimes. It might be instructive to look at how some of our largest school districts approach school security.

California: In 1998-99 California ranked second in the number of students expelled from school for violations of the Gun-Free Schools Act with 290 expulsions. As of May 30, 2001, two school districts — the 710,000-student Los Angeles Unified (LAU) and Inglewood Unified — used metal detectors on a regular basis. After installing the devices in 1993, LAU used them daily on at least one class of students at each high school. Between 1993 and 2001, no guns were detected, although guns have been found concealed on school grounds. At Inglewood, one knife and one gun were detected over a five-year period. Bill Ybarra, director of the Los Angeles County Board of Education safe schools center, told Joe Mathews of the *Los Angeles Times* that the most effective crime-deterring strategies have been "maintaining phone hotlines or anonymous tip boxes to report threats, or beefing up security and patrols." He said of metal detectors: "That's a time-consuming type of search that doesn't yield much."

Boston: Massachusetts expelled 43 students in 1998-99 for violations of the Gun-Free Schools Act. In Boston, the 63,000-student school district faces pressure from parents and law enforcement personnel to install metal detectors in every school. Thomas Payzant, Deputy Superintendent of Boston Public Schools, stated his position in a September 2002 memorandum: "The decision to use metal detection devices should be based on incidents of weapons in the school or one serious incident."

States with the most students expelled for violations of the GFSA: 1998-1999

State	Expulsions
1. Texas	294
2. California	290
3. Georgia	208
4. New York	206
5. Alabama	174
6. Missouri	171
7. Tennessee	152
8. Pennsylvania	145
9. North Carolina	141
10. Virginia	115

New York: According to a 1997 New York State Education Department report, one in 10 students in New York has carried a weapon to school at least once. In 1998-99, New York ranked fourth in the number of students expelled from school for violations of the Gun-Free Schools Act with 206 expulsions. That same year, the NYPD took over security in the city's public schools. According to November 2000 news reports, after the NYPD takeover, overall school crimes decreased by 14% while sexual offenses (excluding rape) increased nearly 200%. The increase was attributed to better reporting. Metal detectors have been installed in schools in high-crime areas (about 70 schools out of 1,100). Gregory Thomas, executive director of the student and safety prevention services division, says, "Personally, I've been asked how I feel about them. After Columbine, everyone wanted them in their schools. My counterpoint was, 'No you don't.' Once you get it in your environment you're stuck with it."

Washington, D.C.: This troubled 70,000-student school district, the first to turn to an outside security service, had the third-highest ratio of students per 1,000 expelled in 1998-99 for violations of the Gun-Free Schools Act (0.181). The district uses a combination of patrols, metal detectors, alarms, closed circuit television, and surveillance cameras. It has also found a Youth Gang Intervention Unit to be effective in resolving disputes. It also has adopted a system to track violence data better.

The decision to allow metal detectors and other surveillance devices involves legal, psychological, financial, and practical issues. Superintendent Payzant says: "When you run 12-year-old kids through metal detectors, it has an impact on what their views are about the school and its climate." As a practical matter, in a world of finite school dollars, how many dollars should be devoted to security? Should those dollars be siphoned away from the school orchestra? The football team? School-based after-hours programs, even though experts say that these programs reduce crime?

The National Institute of Justice suggests: "One approach that may help some schools is to establish a policy that allows the school to do a weapon detection scan of any student who arrives at school late in the morning. This may provide the school with a lot of leverage. There could be some excellent deterrence created if students knew they would definitely be scanned when they are running late, if only to convince them to not be late."

Do surveillance devices make schools safer? "Once you put in cameras and metal detectors, you rely on them as a solution and ease up on the harder work — that is, creating a climate that teaches peaceful resolution," says Vincent Schiraldi, director of the Justice Policy Institute. According to Dale Yeager, security consultant and former criminal profiler for the Department of Justice, the education establishment would be wise to indulge in some profiling on school grounds. He contends that bullying, stalking, and harassment are the real security problems in school. Contradicting the thinking that underpins the No Child Left Behind Act, Yeager believes some children should be left behind: "Violent kids must be extracted from the school environment before their behavior escalates," he says (the next panel looks at child offenders).

At school, "zero tolerance" is the buzz-phrase of our times. Students are being suspended or expelled for infractions both great and small. What happens to the students who are therefore denied an education? What will happen if all of our schools become just like prisons?

Sources: National Center for Education Statistics, Indicators of School Crime and Safety, 2000, Table 8.1; Fast Response Survey System, Principal/School, http://nces.ed.gov/pubs2001/crime2000/. Cannon, Angie, "The Lessons of Littleton: Why?" *U.S. News & World Report*, 3 May 1999, p. 16. Daryl Gale, "Kiddie Profiling," Philadelphia citypaper.net, February 21-28, 2002, http://www.citypaper.net. Dale Yeager, "Unsafe Schools: The Problems with Current School Safety Programs," http://www.fightforchildren.com/dev/unsafe.htm. "School security in the real world," Access Control & Security Systems Integration, Feb 2001. Angela Pascopella, "Safety in the Big Apple," *School Administrator*, April 2001 v37 i4 p46. U.S. Department of Education, *Violence and Discipline Problems in U.S. Public Schools: 1996-97*, http://nces.ed.gov/pubs98/violence/index.html. Data retrieved October 8, 2002.

The Bad Seed

Juvenile Arrests for Violent Crimes: 1970 to 1999

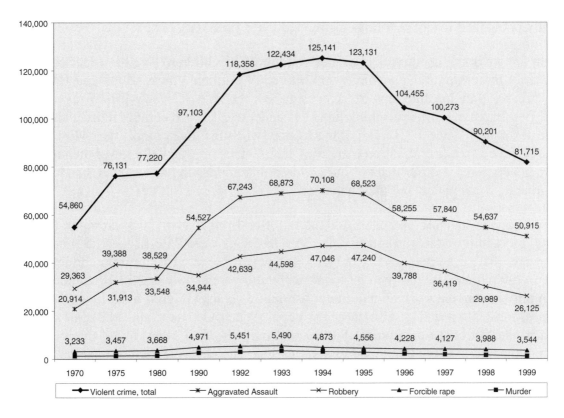

"By the early 1990's, rates of criminal violence, including youth violence, reached unparalleled levels in American society.... It might be helpful to conceptualize violence as an infectious disease spreading among the Nation's youth." — Kelley et al.

Are the young more violent now than they were 30 years ago? Apparently so, if we can go by the number of arrests of juveniles for violent crimes. The data on the graphed above and the table below are reported by law enforcement agencies to the FBI for the annual Uniform Crime Report (see *Indexes of Crime* and *Violent Crime* in Chapter 1). While we can be thankful that arrests for all types of violent crimes began to decline after peaking in 1994, over the nearly 30-year period shown, arrests for all violent crimes were up 49% (table). Aggravated assault showed the most dramatic increase (143%). Forcible rape was up 10%, and murder and robbery were down, 16% and 11% respectively.

Juvenile Arrests for Violent Crimes

	1970	1975	1980	1990	1994	1998	1999	Percent
Violent crime, total	54,860	76,131	77,220	97,103	125,141	90,201	81,715	+49%
Murder	1,350	1,373	1,475	2,661	3,114	1,587	1,131	-16%
Forcible rape	3,233	3,457	3,668	4,971	4,873	3,988	3,544	+10%
Robbery	29,363	39,388	38,529	34,944	47,046	29,989	26,125	-11%
Aggravated assault	20,914	31,913	33,548	54,527	70,108	54,637	50,915	+143%

When a child commits a violent act, it's headline news. According to Howell: "What brought the problem of violent juvenile offenders to the forefront of national attention was a doubling of the relatively small number of juvenile homicides from the mid-1980s to the mid-1990s (due largely to the availability of firearms)." These homicides include highly publicized school shootings mentioned in the preceding panels.

What are we doing about violent crimes committed by children? We have reacted (over-reacted?) by turning our juvenile courts into adult criminal courts. Butts and Harrell of the Urban Policy Institute report: "According to a recent *NBC News-Wall Street Journal* poll, two-thirds of Americans think juveniles under age 13 who commit murder should be tried as adults." Vincent Schiraldi of the Justice Policy Institute complains: "Most Americans believe juvenile crime is an increasing threat, when it is actually lower than it's been for a generation.[6] It is our fears of our children that are driving us to expel, handcuff and incarcerate a generation, not their behavior."

How does the juvenile population of today differ from that of 30 years ago? For one thing, more children live in poverty. In 1997 juveniles were 26% of the U.S. population but were 40% of all persons living below the poverty level (14.1 million children). Today's children are less likely to be living with both parents (about 3 in 10 children lived with only one parent in 1997, and more than half of black children lived in single-parent homes, most often with a woman at the head). When Comanor and Phillips examined data in the National Longitudinal Survey of Youth (NLSY),[7] they found that of all the factors that increase the likelihood of a young man encountering the criminal justice system, the most important is having *no father present* in the home. The absence of a father outweighs even family income.

Juvenile crime rates may have declined in the 1990s, but concern is voiced that rates increased in rural areas, and offenders are getting younger. More girls are taking to violent crime as well. Our next panel looks at girls' contributions to violent crime arrests.

Sources: Chart: U.S. Bureau of the Census, *Statistical Abstract of the United States: 1995*, Table 323, and *Statistical Abstract of the United States: 2001*, Table 309. Primary source: U.S. Federal Bureau of Investigation, *Crime in the United States*, annual. Kelley, Barbara Tatem et al., "Epidemiology of Serious Violence," *Juvenile Justice Bulletin*, June 1997. Howell, James, "A New Approach to Juvenile Crime," *Corrections Compendium*, September 1998. Vincent Schiraldi, "Fear of teen crime based in ignorance, and vilifying kids doesn't help matters," Justice Policy Institute, http://www.appa-net.org/TeenCrime.html. Jeffrey A. Butts and Adele V. Harrell, "Delinquents or Criminals: Policy Options for Young Offenders," The Urban Institute, www.urban.org/crime/delinq.html. William S. Comanor and Llad Phillips, *The Impact of Income and Family Structure on Delinquency*, University of California, Santa Barbara February 10, 1998, www.econ.ucsb.edu/papers/FATHERHD.pdf. Information retrieved October 9, 2002.

[6] In 1999 violent crime arrests were 6% above the 1980 level (table).

[7] The NLSY is collected annually by the Center for Human Resource Research at Ohio State University.

Violent Juveniles: Girls Reaching for Equality

Violent Crime Arrest Rates: Girls

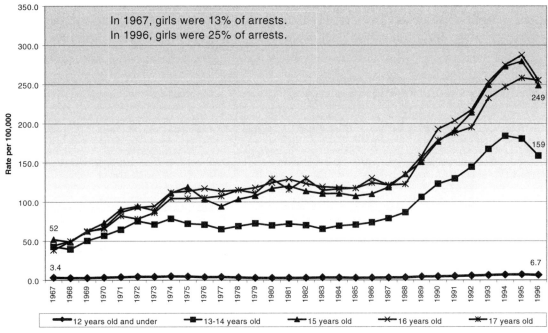

In 1967, girls were 13% of arrests.
In 1996, girls were 25% of arrests.

Legend: —◆—12 years old and under —■—13-14 years old —▲—15 years old —✕—16 years old —✱—17 years old

"'Female gangsters' or 'eight ball chicks' are buzzwords used by the media to describe the instigators of and participants in the perceived rise in adolescent female violence." — Peters and Peters (see Source Notes).

The charted data are from a special study of juvenile female crime prepared by the FBI in response to growing national attention to juvenile crime. Notice the dramatic upturn in juvenile female arrests that started in 1987. It peaked in the mid-1990s, then declined (for girls as for boys). The FBI report reveals that over the charted period (1967 to 1996), the violent crime arrest rate for all juveniles increased 143%. The increase for juvenile males was 124%; the increase for juvenile females was 345%, nearly triple.

Violent Crime Arrest Trends

Offense Charged	Males		Females		
	Total arrests, 1995	Percent change, 1986-1995	Total arrests, 1995	Percent change, 1986-1995	Percent change, 1997-1998
Violent crime total	90,687	+60.4	15,503	+86.2	-8.0
Murder/nonnegligent manslaughter	2,245	+91.9	138	+62.4	-12.0
Forcible rape	3,769	-4.0	84	+27.3	0.0
Robbery	37,978	+59.3	3,863	+119.6	-17.0
Aggravated assault	46,695	+69.2	11,418	+128.1	-3.0

The table shows total violent crime arrests in 1995 and the percent change in arrests of both boys and girls over the period 1986-1995. While girls showed a higher percentage change in arrests, in 1995 the number of arrests of girls stood at 15,503, far below the 90,687 figure for boys. Not shown are property crimes, which make up the largest percentage of arrests for both sexes. The FBI report notes that the nature of juvenile crimes has changed since the 1960s. In 1967 9% of all juvenile male arrests and 5% of female arrests were for violent crimes. By 1996 the proportions had doubled to 18% for boys and 10% for girls.

The FBI special study suggests some differences between boys and girls when it comes to violent crimes. Girls tend to discontinue involvement at a somewhat younger age than

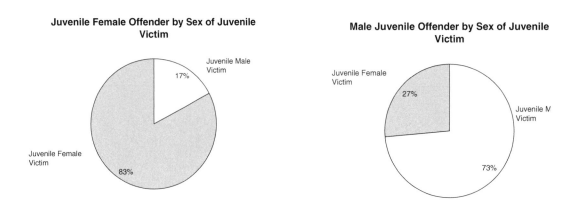

boys. Both boys and girls tend to victimize other juveniles (71.1% of female victims, 64.7% of male victims). Girls are more likely to prey on other girls (pie charts) and are twice as likely to become victims themselves in the process than are boys.

Juvenile arrest estimates for 1998, prepared by the National Center for Juvenile Justice, show that girls were arrested in numbers equal to or greater than boys for the following offenses only: prostitution and commercialized vice (50%) and running away from home (58%). Girls approached boys as a percentage of total arrests for embezzlement (42%) offenses against the family and children (37%), larceny-theft (35%), and liquor law and curfew and loitering violations (30%).

What kinds of children commit violent crimes? The National Longitudinal Study on Adolescent Health identified some of the living conditions and circumstances that increase a child's chances of violent behavior. It must come as no surprise that kids with low grade-point averages, access to guns in the home, high-risk friends, a history of illegal substance use, and experience with violence are more likely to resort to violence against others or themselves. Most serious offenders have a history of childhood misbehavior, including "antisocial behaviors such as physical aggression, conduct disorders, and disruptive, covert, oppositional, and defiant behaviors" (U.S. Department of Justice, Office of Juvenile Justice and Delinquency Prevention). Is this true of girl children? Dr. Persephanie Silverthorn, a psychologist who has done studies on violence and aggression in girls ages 12 to 18, was asked why she chose this age range. She responded that "it is very difficult to find girls who are severely anti-social in childhood" (White).

Sources: Charts: FBI, *Crime in the United States: 1997*, Section V: Juvenile Female Crime: A Special Study, Table 5.1, http://www.fbi.gov/. *Crime in the United States: 1998*. Sheila R. Peters and Sharon D. Peters, "Violent Adolescent Females," *Corrections Today*, June 1998. Joseph White, "Violence and Aggression," *Quest* (New Orleans) Winter 2001.

Violent Juveniles: Blacks at High Rates

Arrests for Violent Crimes by Race

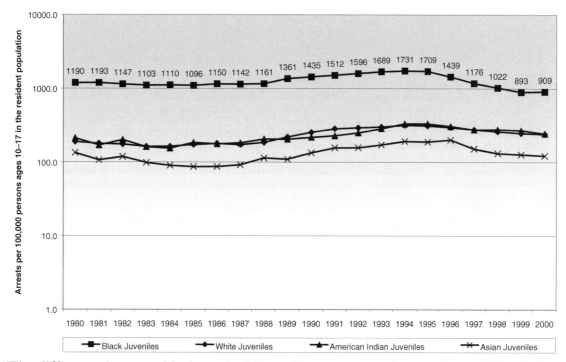

"The difference between blacks and whites with respect to crime, and especially violent crime, has, I think, done more to impede racial amity than any other factor." — James Q. Wilson, Ph.D., criminologist, economist, political analyst, author

African Americans are overrepresented at every level of the judicial system, including juvenile arrests for the violent crimes represented on the above chart (murder, forcible rape, robbery, and aggravated assault). This has been so since at least 1980 (the complete data from 1980 through 2000 appear at the back of this book). The chart shows that in 2000, 909.4 young blacks per 100,000 blacks aged 10-17 were arrested for a violent crime. That year, the number for white juveniles was 239.2 per 100,000 young whites; for American Indian juveniles, 243.5 per 100,000 young American Indians; and for Asian juveniles, 122.1 per 100,000 young Asians.

While arrests of white juveniles make up the majority of juvenile arrests (in 1999, 71% of arrests for all types of crimes), black juveniles account for a very high percentage of the arrests for violent crimes (42% in 1999). In 1980, the black-to-white ratio of juvenile arrests for murder stood at about 5 to 1. By 1993, it had jumped to 9 to 1. Thankfully, rates for both groups then fell so that, by 1999, the black-to-white arrest rate ratio was once again 5 to 1 and both rates were at their lowest levels in 20 years. Arrests of young blacks for violent crimes increased 45% between 1980 and the peak year of 1994.

Much of this violent activity can be attributed to youth gangs. In a special report prepared by the U.S. Department of Justice, researchers noted that 19 states reported gang problems in the early 1970s when the study began. By the late 1990s, all 50 states and the District of Columbia reported gang problems. In 1998, the states with the largest number of gang-problem cities were California (363), Illinois (261), Texas (156), Florida (125), and Ohio (86). The report lists seven reasons for the "striking increase in the number of gang-problem localities: drugs, immigration, gang names and alliances, migration, government policies, female-headed households, and gang subculture and the media."

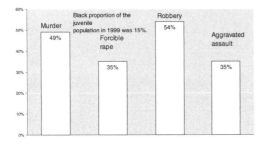

Black Proportion of Juvenile Arrests in 1999 by the Most Serious Offense Charged

The small chart brings us back to the topic of black overrepresentation in the justice system. It shows the black proportion of juvenile arrests in 1999 by the most serious offense charged. Of course, not every person arrested for a crime is guilty. The law enforcement establishment has been accused of overzealousness when it comes to arresting African Americans. James Q. Wilson notes, however, that when comparing arrest data to data obtained by interviewing victims of crimes (the National Crime Victimization Survey; see Chapter 1), researchers have found no significant difference between police arrests and victim reports. He concludes: "This suggests that, though racism may exist in policing (as in all other aspects of American life), racism cannot explain the overall black arrest rate. The arrest rate, thus, is a reasonably good proxy for the crime rate."

Sources: Chart: Office of Juvenile Justice and Delinquency Prevention, http://ojjdp.ncjrs.org/ojstatbb/asp/. Small chart: Howard N. Snyder, "Juvenile Arrests 1999," *Juvenile Justice Bulletin*, December 2000, http://www.ncjrs.org/html/. James Q. Wilson, "Crime," in *Beyond the Color Line: New Perspectives on Race and Ethnicity in America*, Thernstrom, Abigail, and Stephan Thernstrom, eds., http://www-hoover.stanford.edu/homepage/books/fulltext/colorline/default.htm. "The era of extraordinary rates of juvenile murder arrests appears to have ended," http://www.ncjrs.org/html/ojjdp/nrs_bulletin/nrs_2001_12_1/page7.html. U.S. Department of Justice, *The Growth of Youth Gang Problems in the United States: 1970-1998*, www.ncjrs.org/html/ojjdp/ojjdprpt_yth_gng_prob_2001/.

Young Victims of Abuse

Victimization of Children: 1990-2000

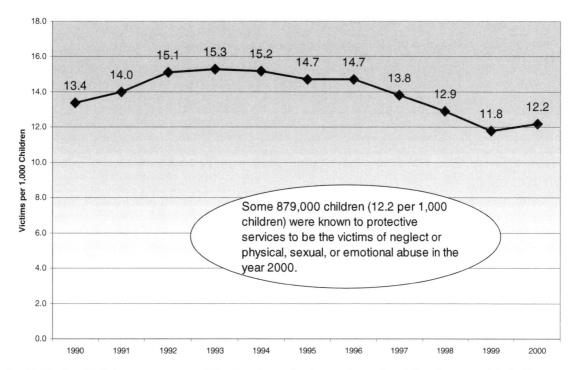

In 1999 the U.S. Department of Justice launched a series of publications entitled *Crimes Against Children.* The first issue conceded that the victimization of children is a hidden and underreported problem for which data are lacking. In fact, it is believed that the majority of victimizations of children are not reported to the police, for reasons that include "adolescent concerns about personal autonomy and fears of being blamed or not taken seriously, family concerns about the negative impact of the justice system on children, and the general perception that nonsexual assaults against youth are something other than real crimes."

Unreported crimes against children are not part of the FBI's Uniform Crime Report. The other major source of crime victimization data, the National Crime Victimization Survey (NCVS), does not survey children under the age of 12. Furthermore, the NCVS does not inquire about certain important types of child victimization, including statutory rape and incest. The authors conclude: "Juvenile justice professionals and service providers need to adopt practices that make it easier for juvenile victims to receive the benefits of the justice system."

What do we know, then, about incidence of child abuse? Is child abuse on the rise? We have data (chart) from the National Child Abuse and Neglect Data System (NCANDS), the primary source of national information on abused and neglected children known to state child protective services agencies. The chart shows a year 2000 victimization rate of 12.2 cases per 1,000 children, up slightly over the 1999 rate of 11.8 but still the second-lowest rate overall.

Maltreatment encompasses neglect (including medical neglect), physical or sexual abuse, and emotional or psychological maltreatment. The table below shows the breakdown of child victimizations by type of maltreatment from 1996 through 2000. Neglect is the most prevalent way of abusing children. "Other" abuse can include abuses such as abandonment, threats of harm, or congenital drug addiction.

Child Victimization Rates by Type of Maltreatment: 1996-2000

Type of abuse	1996	1997	1998	1999	2000
Physical abuse	3.5	3.3	2.9	2.5	2.3
Neglect	7.6	7.5	6.9	6.5	7.3
Medical neglect	0.5	0.4	0.4	0.4	0.5
Sexual abuse	1.8	1.7	1.5	1.3	1.2
Psychological abuse	0.9	0.9	0.8	0.9	1.0
Other abuse	2.9	1.8	4.1	4.4	2.7

The data shown above have been collected only since 1989 and they measure only cases of child maltreatment known to child protective services. We can assume that many more cases of maltreatment of the most vulnerable of our citizens occur behind closed doors.

Sources: Chart: U.S. Department of Health and Human Services, Administration on Children, Youth and Families, *Child Maltreatment 2000* (Washington, DC: U.S. Government Printing Office, 2002). David Finkelhor and Richard Ormrod, "Reporting Crimes Against Juveniles," U.S. Department of Justice, November 1999, http://www.ncjrs.org/pdffiles1/ojjdp/178887.pdf. Information retrieved October 11, 2002.

Children Go Missing

Reasons Children Went Missing: 1999 (Estimated Total: 1,315,600)

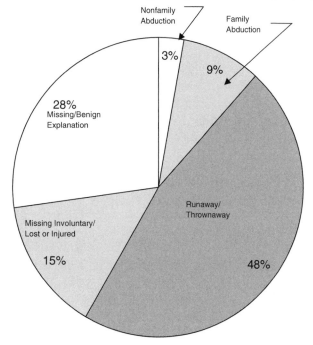

Nonfamily Abduction
3%

Family Abduction
9%

28% Missing/Benign Explanation

Runaway/ Thrownaway
48%

Missing Involuntary/ Lost or Injured
15%

"I'm a father and I'm angry.... My kids eat Cheerios in the morning and see the face of a missing child on the milk carton. They see a billboard about missing children on the way to school. At school, they get fingerprinted, footprinted and ID'd. A children's TV show is interrupted with news of missing children." — Eugene Kraybill (see Source notes)

The above quote suggests at least two questions: At what point does prudent concern for a child's safety cross over into paranoia? And does media coverage help find missing children? The first question is debatable. According to the National Center for Missing and Exploited Children (NCMEC), the answer to the second question is "Absolutely. One in six of the missing kids featured on [cards you receive in the mail] and through the efforts of other NCMEC photo partners are recovered as a direct result of the photograph."[8] And as we shall see below, other forms of media coverage and the work of child advocates have been instrumental in coordinating national efforts to count and rescue missing children.

---

[8] NCMEC does not place photos of missing children on milk cartons, and the practice is dying out. It was the innovation of members of the dairy industry and apparently started around the time 6-year-old Etan Patz disappeared (May 25, 1979). Beginning in 2003, May 25, the anniversary of the little boy's disappearance will be observed as National Missing Children's Day.

Until recently, there were no reliable estimates of the number of children who went missing each year. The data on the chart come from a study conducted by the Office of Juvenile Justice and Delinquency Prevention.[9] There were an estimated 1.3 million missing children reports filed in 1999.[10] Those missing children were far more likely to be gone of their own volition or as a result of being "thrown away" than for any other reason. A thrownaway child is one who has been forced out of the home or refused permission to return.

Kidnappings by nonfamily members are rare (3% of cases in 1999, or about 400 children). Nine percent of missing children were abducted by a family member in 1999, a phenomenon that some attribute to the divorce rate. According to *Time* magazine, based on OJJDP data, in 2001 there were about 700,000 missing children reports filed, and officials expected that the number of those children who were kidnapped and murdered would be about 100. On average, an estimated 200 to 300 children are abducted by nonfamily members each year and between 50 and 150 are held for ransom or murdered. Thankfully, about 94% of ransomed children are returned to their parents.

Highly publicized kidnappings breed legislation. The nation was riveted by the abduction of the Lindbergh baby in 1932, and the 1932 Lindbergh Law made it a federal offense to send a kidnap/ransom note across state lines. After the 1981 abduction/murder of 6-year-old Adam Walsh, his father was instrumental in getting Congress to order law enforcement personnel to enter missing children in the FBI's National Crime Information Center database. Walsh testified before Congress that "50,000 children disappear annually and are abducted by strangers for reasons of foul play" (the 50,000 figure has been challenged). Walsh later became host of the television program "America's Most Wanted."

In 1984 Congress launched NCMEC and passed the Missing Children Act to address the nation's inability to coordinate resources to locate and recover missing children.[11] After the 1993 kidnapping/murder of 12-year-old Polly Klaas, Congress passed the International Parental Kidnapping Crime Act. Before all of this happened, says NCMEC head Ernest Allen: "If you were the parents of a missing child, you were on your own."

A recent innovation, Amber, arose out of the 1996 kidnapping of 9-year-old Amber Hagerman. Amber (America's Missing: Broadcast Emergency Response) is a voluntary abduction-notification system that uses the Emergency Alert System created during the Cold War to distribute information about missing children to television and radio stations. Some states notify the public of an abduction via road signs. Between 1996 and 2002, at least 22 children are believed to have been saved with the help of an Amber

---

[9] Part of the U.S. Department of Justice. Two such studies have been conducted, but the results are not comparable. According to NCMEC, OJJDP produces the best national estimates of the number of missing children. The data are based on household surveys conducted by telephone.

[10] OJJDP reported that there were about 700,000 missing children reports filed in 2001.

[11] Coordination is important because time is of the essence in resolving missing children cases. In 1996 President Clinton noted that in 6 out of 10 recent cases, the FBI learned of an abduction from the television.

alert. In October 2002 Congress was moving toward mandating the Amber system nationwide.

The Internet plays a role in the missing children drama, for good and ill. Amber alerts are broadcast on the Internet. Some Web sites maintain databases with profiles of missing children. After a 5-year-old girl disappeared from foster care in Florida and authorities failed to notice, protective service agencies across the nation were goaded into action. Michigan was the first state to post the names and photos of missing foster children on the Internet (September 2002); other states followed. Meanwhile, bogus e-mails purporting to be from the anguished parents of kidnapped children now circulate, and pedophiles make use of the Internet to ensnare children.

Sources: Chart: U.S. Department of Justice, National Incidence Studies of Missing, Abducted, Runaway, and Thrownaway Children, ojjdp.ncjrs.org. Eugene Kraybill, "Scaring Our Kids," *U.S. News & World Report*, February 10, 1986, v100 p81(1). Chitra Ragavan et al, "Lost and Found," *U.S. News & World Report*, August 13, 2001, v131 i6 p12. "Statement on signing the memorandum on missing persons and missing children," *Weekly Compilation of Presidential Documents*, January 22, 1996, v32 n3 p78(2). Glen Hodges, "When Good Guys Lie," *The Washington Monthly*, Jan/Feb 1997. Information retrieved October 16, 2002. Jessica Reaves, "Amber Alert: Does It Work?" Time.com, August 21, 2002, and "How to Keep Your Child Safe," Time.com, July 18, 2002.

Blame the Violence on Video Games?

Some Statistics About Video Games and Violence

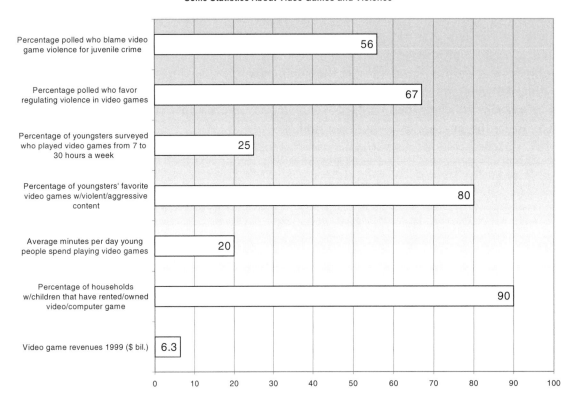

"On December 1, 1997 a fourteen-year-old boy took his thoughts and feelings, the sum total of the influences in his life, and five guns into Heath High School [in Paducah, Kentucky]. After watching students pray, he opened fire on them. Kayce, Jessica, and Nicole died that day…. We believe the Heath High School shooter was influenced by the movies he watched, the video games he played, and the Internet sites he accessed. With his easy access to guns, his violent urges were allowed to take on a life outside his own troubled mind." — From testimony before Congress of Sabrina Steger, mother of victim Kayce Steger, seeking to ban the sale of violent video games to minors

The graphic shows some statistics about video games. It's a $6.3 billion industry. Kids like to play video games — 90% of households with children have rented or owned one. Kids especially like violent video games — 80% of the games kids like best contain violent or aggressive content. We saw in an earlier panel that more kids are arrested nowadays for violent crimes than were arrested in 1970. Does playing violent video games make them more likely to commit an act of violence? Fifty-six percent of people polled thought so, and there are plenty of credible experts who agree.

Kansas State University's Professor John Murray has studied the effects of media violence for more than 30 years. He told Paul Keegan of *Mother Jones* magazine that while there is no direct proof of a cause and effect relationship and there may never be such proof, "At some point, you have to say that if exposure to violence is related to aggressive attitudes and values, and if [the latter] are related to shooting classmates or acting aggressively — all of which we know to be true — then it stands to reason that there is probably a link between exposure to violence and aggressive actions."

Keegan offered more statistics: "DUKE NUKEM is one of the bad-boy 'first-person shooter' games that have brought such disrepute to the industry. Though shooters represent less than seven percent of overall sales, a recent TIME/CNN poll showed that 50 percent of teenagers between 13 and 17 who have played video games have played them. Ten percent say they play regularly. A breakthrough game will fly off the shelves: Best-selling shooters DOOM and QUAKE have had combined sales of 4.2 million."[12] Today's video games take the notion of "you are there" to new heights. Keegan compared the experience of playing them to an "acid trip" in the way they alter one's sense of perception.

Critics often mention the desensitization to violence that comes from overexposure to it. Harvard's Sissela Bok, ethicist/philosopher, asks in her book *Mayhem: Violence as Public Entertainment*: "Is it alarmist or merely sensible to ask what happens to the souls of children nurtured, as in no past society, on images of rape, torture, bombings and massacre that are channeled into their homes from infancy?"

The armed forces use video games to train soldiers to kill by making shooting at humans seem routine. According to Lt. Colonel David Grossman (*On Killing: The Psychological Cost of Learning to Kill in War and Society*): "One of the most effective and widely used simulators developed by the United States Army in recent years, MACS (Multipurpose Arcade Combat Simulator) is nothing more than a modified Super Nintendo game."

A 1998 FBI report provided a checklist for educators to use when assessing the potential for violence when a student has uttered threats. One of the many warning signs was a "fascination with violence-filled entertainment." The report offers the reassurance that "a great many adolescents who will never commit violent acts will show some of the behaviors or personality traits included on the list." Indeed it is true that most young people do not commit violent acts. Speaking in defense of video games to *Time* magazine's Joshua Quittner is Henry Jenkins, director of comparative media studies at the Massachusetts Institute of Technology: "We can't make social policy based on the statistical aberrations of a handful of abnormal kids … moderately violent video games might even be beneficial, helping girls learn how to compete in an aggressive world."

Sources: Chart: "Video Game Violence," Mediascope Issue Briefs, http://www.mediascope.org; Arlene Moscovitch, "Electronic Media and the Family," http://www.vifamily.ca/cft/media/media.htm.; USA Weekend's Third Annual America's Poll, http://www.usaweekend.com/; "Media Violence: Its Effect on Children," www.marymount.k12.ny.us. Michele Steinberg, "Programmed to Kill: Video Games, Drugs, and the 'New Violence,'" *21st Century Science & Technology*, Fall 2000. Testimony of Sabrina Steger, Presented to the Senate Commerce Committee, March 21, 2000, http://www.lionlamb.org/steger.htm. Paul Keegan, "Culture Quake," *Mother Jones*, Nov/Dec 1999. Joshua Quittner, "Are Video Games Really So Bad?," *Time*, May 10, 1999. National Center for the Analysis of Violent Crime (NCAVC), "The School Shooter: A Threat Assessment Perspective," www.fbi.gov/publications/school/school2.pdf. "The Influence of Violent Entertainment Material on Kids: What is to be Done?" http://www.ftc.gov/speeches/pitofsky/naag99.htm. Information retrieved October 17, 2002.

---

[12] Eric Harris and Dylan Klebold, the school shooters in Littleton, Colorado, were avid players of DOOM and QUAKE.

Chapter 6

Drugs

Much as the post-war Baby Boom has had an indelible impact on the demographics, economics, and mores of the 20th century, so also the War on Drugs has had, and continues to have, a significantly uneven influence on "crime and justice," the subject of this volume. Attempts at controlling the trade in illegal substances, and to prevent people from using drugs, is accounting for about a fifth of all correctional activities and a tenth of all non-traffic police activities if measured by arrests. Very substantial budgets are associated with this war. Victory appears at least as far away as the conquest of poverty — in large part because significant parts of the public are engaged in massive disobedience of law. In this chapter, we try to hit some of the highlights of this very complicated subject.

The first panel shows the rise of what we dub "drug mountain," meaning the pattern of rising arrest rates, measured over time, and indicating what an important part of the criminal justice system drugs have become since Nixon declared war on drugs.

We follow this with a drug primer in which we try to sort out the "big actors" without neglecting the significant bit players in this drama. The big actors are, of course, marijuana, cocaine, heroin, and methamphetamine. We take a closer look at "meth" next. Those tracking the drug scene, the "critics," as it were, give these drugs the most reviews. Methamphetamine is a recent arrival and making a big run in rural America, while Miss Ecstasy is starring in clubs. Some of the main characters, however, have had a long run and will be around for decades to come.

The first panel, which showed rising drug arrests, tempted us to answer the question: "Has the energetic activity of the police caused use of drugs to drop?" We answer this question next using data from one of the institutes of the U.S. Department of Health and Human Services which routinely surveys people on their drug-use/abuse habits.

Are drugs predominantly an African American phenomenon? Are blacks using drugs much more than whites and other racial groups? We try to answer these and other race-related questions in the next three panels. We look at users of drugs by race, arrests by race, and what happens to those arrested — again by race. In this context we go deeper into the distinctions between "possession" and "trafficking" as the two chief offenses for which people are led away.

In the following two panels, we look at the "market" from two points of view: the supply and the demand side of the picture. We note that tonnages of drugs shipped have remained level, but the kinds of drugs sold have been fluctuating. Prices have been coming down. Next, we look at users of the drugs, this time in the aggregate, and look at what they like to buy.

We spent $63 billion on illegal drugs in 2000. What did we spend to control of the drug trade and drug consumption? We answer this question next using a time series on federal expenditures and a single year of state-level expenditures; state data are not routinely collected.

Now, reaching the end, we present data on alcohol and tobacco, the "legal" drugs, and try to see which category produces the most harm — and the most activity on the part of the Justice System. In the last panel, we try to summarize the role that illegal drugs play in the context of the total crime-control system of the U.S.

Drug Mountain

Drug Arrests

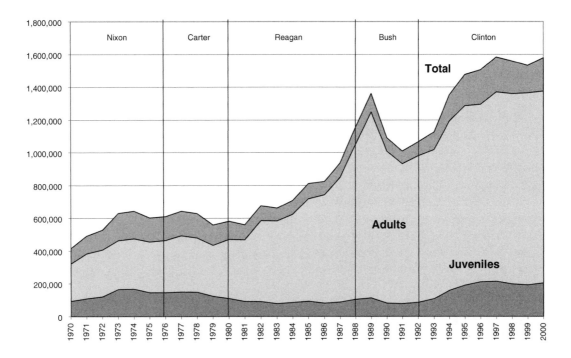

In 1970, the year when Congress passed the Comprehensive Drug Abuse and Control Act — but the year before President Nixon declared his War on Drugs — 415,000 people were arrested for drug offenses. Thirty years later, total arrests had increased to 1,579,600, up 280%. The population, in this period, increased by less than 35%. The war on drugs created "drug mountain," shown in the chart above. It has its peaks and valleys — but at ever higher elevations. Most of the increase has been among adults. Adult arrests have grown three times as fast as juvenile.

Drug arrests, of course, are just one measure of this phenomenon — but the one most expressive of governmental resolve. Note that arrests have both declined and grown under administrations of both major parties. They grew under Nixon, Reagan, and Clinton — most dramatically under the last two. They declined under Carter and they both rose and fell under the elder President Bush.

Drug violations are *not* included in the official crime rate. If they were included, the crime rate would be rising. Therefore when you hear authorities bragging that they are bringing the crime rate down, they don't mean drug offenses. Indeed, drug-related law enforcement and corrections have become an important driving force in the total justice system. Among the top seven arrest categories, drug abuse violations lead all the rest, followed by driving under the influence. More than 20% of all state prisoners are in prison for drug offenses, 60% of Federal prisoners, and more than 20% of those in local jails. To be sure, those imprisoned are a tiny fraction of those arrested, but all of those arrested must be handled: they are finger-printed, tested (blood tests, urine analysis), processed (paperwork, notices, record keeping), sometimes held, charged, tried, and administratively managed until disposition — either by release, probation, or by trial, and later, possibly by incarceration — with all the costs associated with the housing, feeding, clothing, and guarding of prisoners, including their medical care.

And the arrests, while a very high number in 2000 (at least compared with the number for 1970) represent but a small fraction of potential offenders. In 2000, an estimated 24.5 million people had used drugs in the year just past (at the time of survey). Possession of drugs is against the law. Therefore, with about 1.6 million people arrested, less than 7% of offenders were actually caught. Obviously the war on drugs has unusual aspects. We shall try to present those in the panels in this chapter.

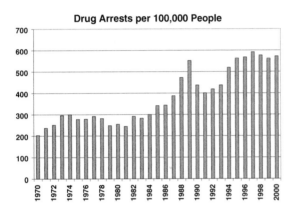

Before we do so, we present in the chart to the left the same arrest data shown above, but this time normalized by demographics. The data show drug arrests per 100,000 population for the same period, 1970 to 2000. As can be seen from this graphic, the rise in drug arrests has not been due to the mere increase in population. In 1970 we arrested 203 people per 100,000, in 2000 the number was 572. The peak was reached in 1997, when we arrested 591 out of a hundred thousand. As we shall see in coming panels, the drug-using population has been declining. Those arrested for possession are 81% of arrests, those charged with sale or manufacture are 19% of total. Blacks are disproportionately represented among those arrested — and even more among those incarcerated.

Source: U.S. Department of Justice, Federal Bureau of Investigation, *Crime in the United States*, annual, Uniform Crime Reports, downloaded from http://www.ojp.usdoj.gov/bjs/dcf/enforce.htm.

Drug Primer

Ever Used Drug in Lifetime (2000)

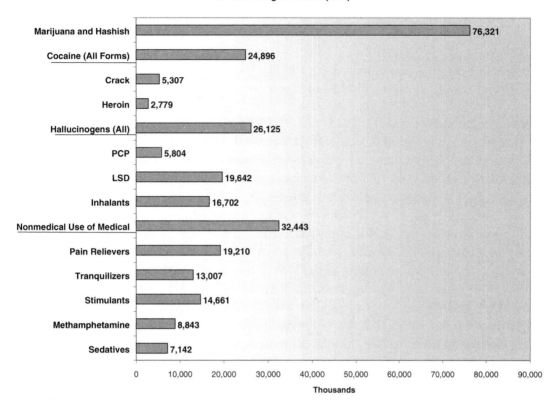

Marijuana and Hashish	76,321
Cocaine (All Forms)	24,896
Crack	5,307
Heroin	2,779
Hallucinogens (All)	26,125
PCP	5,804
LSD	19,642
Inhalants	16,702
Nonmedical Use of Medical	32,443
Pain Relievers	19,210
Tranquilizers	13,007
Stimulants	14,661
Methamphetamine	8,843
Sedatives	7,142

Thousands

Marijuana. The drug of choice is marijuana — of which hashish is a derivative. The chart above shows the number of people, of all ages, who reported using drugs in the categories shown above in 2000. 76.3 million have used marijuana. The Office of the National Drug Control Policy estimates 11.7 million active users in 2000.

Marijuana comes from the hemp plant, *Cannabis sativa*, and contains delta-9-tetrahydrocannabinol, THC, which produces the marijuana high. "Marijuana" is technically the flowery part of the hemp plant. Hashish is a pasty, dried extract of the plant which is smoked; hashish oil is a solvent-extracted part of the plant. A drop or two on a cigarette turns the cigarette as potent as a joint. Marijuana's other names are blunt, pot, grass, reefer, ganja, weed, Mary Jane, sinsemilla, roach, Thai sticks, smoke, and dope. The stuff costs about $400 to $1,000 a pound near the Southwestern U.S. border, more as you go north.

Marijuana produces a euphoric feeling. In can mitigate the nausea caused by chemotherapy, hence pressures exist for the legalization of pot for medical purposes. Controversy over marijuana's legalization continues. As far back as 1970, when Nixon launched his war on drugs, Lyndon Johnson's outgoing attorney general, William Ramsey Clark, advocated its legalization. William Buckley, conservative author, leans that way today.

Heroin comes from the poppy, *Papaver somniferum*. The poppy yields opium. These days it is made by extracting the drug from poppy straw. From opium comes morphine and from morphine heroin. The body converts the drug back into morphine, an opiate, which interacts with opiate receptors in the brain. The user feels a "rush." Heroin acts extremely fast and has a potent effect; hence it is highly addictive. It is called smack, thunder, hell dust, big H, nose drops, skag, and junk. South American heroin will fetch $50,000 to $200,000 per kilogram (2.2 lbs.) — a trunkfull is a fortune. Heroin is one of the least-used of drugs because the risks are high — and it produces some of the worst effects on its victims — hence the interest in its control.

Cocaine. Cocaine is obtained from the coca bush, *Erythroxylon*, a native of Peru and Bolivia. The natives still chew the coca leaf. It's from the coca bush that Coca-Cola got its name. Early on the drink contained a tiny bit of cocaine — but so did a number of other tonics and elixirs of the 19th century. Cocaine is extracted from the leaf by a multi-stage (and messy) chemical process. The drug affects one of the key pleasure-producing centers of the brain, the *nucleus accumbens*, which is what makes cocaine so irresistible. Crack cocaine is produced from the powdered form. Cocaine is normally snorted — it enters the body through the mucous membrane of the nose. Crack can be produced relatively easily using ammonia, baking soda, water, and heat — all readily available. This crystalline from of cocaine can be smoked. It crackles as it's smoked, hence the name. Smoking crack greatly increases the speed with which the cocaine reaches the pleasure centers of the brain — 10 seconds. Instant gratification makes crack attractive to the user. Cocaine sells for $12,000 to $35,000 per kilogram. The drug is classified as a narcotic, although, technically, it is a stimulant. Street names? They are blow, nose candy, snowball, tornado, and wicky stick among others.

Methamphetamine. This synthetic drug (similar to amphetamine but with more kick) is an addictive stimulant. It releases large amounts of dopamine, a neurotransmitter, and stimulates the brain and body movements. It is manufactured illegally and sold like any other naturally-occurring drug. Meth has a legitimate medical use (obesity control). It has destructive effects on the brain. It is called speed, meth, and chalk. A crystalline form, suitable for smoking, goes by the names ice, crystal, and glass.

The following table summarizes data on these big four — drugs the government tends to track in some detail. We go on to other drugs afterwards.

Profile of Major Drugs

Drug	Regular Users (000)	Median Weekly Expenditure (Per User - $)	Annual National Expenditures (million 1998 $)	Price per Pure Gram - $
Marijuana	11,700	75	10,400	10
Heroin	977	209	11,900	1,029
Cocaine	3,325	186	36,100	149
Methamphetamine	356	87	2,200	140

Hallucinogens. Nature produced the original hallucinogens — although these have been crowded out by synthetic competitors. The best known is the peyote cactus, *Lophophora williamsii*, also known as mesc, buttons, and cactus. Its active ingredient is **mescaline**. All hallucinogens affect the brain's functioning, produce vivid visions and distortions of reality. Another hallucinogenic plant is the mushroom *Psilocybe mexicana* "purple passion," on the street. **Psilocybe** is chemically related to the synthetic substance, **LSD**, lysergic acid diethylamide, by far the most potent hallucinogen known to science. It is called acid, microdot, cubes, blotter, and boomers. Some of the names refer to methods of ingestion (sugar cubes) or distribution (impregnated in blotters). Tiny amounts produce enormous interior "trips." LSD is now the dominant hallucinogen. Recipes for its production are available on the web, but it takes a sophisticated chemist to produce it. In 2000, an estimated 3.6 million people used hallucinogens.

Other Drugs. An estimated 8.6 million people used other drugs classified as inhalants, stimulants, sedatives, tranquilizers, and analgesics. These other drugs, including hallucinogens in the figure, produced expenditures of $2.3 billion (expressed as 1998 dollars) in 2000. All told, given these data, Americans spent $62.9 billion on illegal drugs. Not small change, that.

Variant Classifications. Different agencies classify drugs in different ways, and the results can be confusing. The usual classification is into the categories of Narcotics, Cannabis Products, Depressants, Stimulants, Hallucinogens, and as Anabolic Steroids. These classifications are based on the effect of the drug on the body. Particular kinds may be "cross dressers." And example is **ecstasy**, a potent synthetic which is both a stimulant and a hallucinogen (nicknamed XTC, go, X, Adam, and hug drug).

Under the Controlled Substances Act (CSA), drugs are classified as Schedule I through V — based on the severity of penalties imposed. Most drugs that play a role in crime statistics are Schedule I. The CSA includes cocaine under narcotics although it is technically a stimulant (it does not act on the opiate receptors).

Another category that sometimes shows up with the others already cited is "Club Drugs." This category refers to the *occasion* of use — in clubs or at parties. Club drugs include LSD (a hallucinogen), Ecstasy (stimulant/hallucinogen), and methamphetamine (a stimulant). Another category, Inhalants, defines drugs by method of ingestion. The substances inhaled are generally not prohibited per se (glue, volatile solvents).

Narcotics include opium, its derivates, and synthetic act-alikes. By the government's classification, cocaine is classified as a narcotic. **Cannabis** is marijuana and its derivatives. **Depressants** include, most prominently, barbiturates used in non-medical contexts. Alcohol is a depressant, but its use is legal. **Stimulants** include the legal caffeine and nicotine, also the very popular methamphetamine, amphetamine (which is less potent but barely distinguishable), ecstasy, an amphetamine-like European import (without any medical use), cocaine (by its function), and even that favorite of unruly children (or of frustrated teachers), ritalin. **Hallucinogens** include LSD, mescaline, PCP ("angel dust"), and the mushroom psilocybe. **Anabolic steroids**, finally, include testosterone, nandrolone, oxymetholone and their derivatives; there are a number of brand names. Abuse of steroids can produce serious health problems and irreversible damage.

Some drugs, usually classified as hallucinogens, are classified by others as "dissociative drugs" (by the National Institute on Drug Abuse, for instance) because they produce confusion, amnesia, and/or detachment. Three of the Club Drugs in this category are PCP, ketamine, and rohypnol — the latter two known as "date rape drugs." They produce dissociation — a disconnect from the environment, internal and external, uncaring detachment. Ketamine produces amnesia — she won't remember what happened...

How to find a path through this rather overwhelming chemical jungle — of which only parts have even been touched upon? Law enforcement authorities focus on the major drugs — and also on those drugs where use, distribution, or manufacture is relatively easy to detect and to interdict. Drug use by the white upper-middle ranges of society gets less attention than the small crack dealers in the ghetto. Marijuana is everywhere — and thus leads all arrests. LSD labs are very difficult to find and tiny amounts of the stuff go a long ways. Rock concerts are favorite venues of distribution. Not many arrests. And kids sniffing paint-thinner in the garage fall beneath the radar.

In the next panel, we take a closer look at methamphetamine. It illustrates, generally, the nature of man-made drugs on the one hand; on the other, it points up a new trend in the drug field: the spread of drugs from the big city out into the country.

Sources: Charted data from U.S. Department of Health and Human Services, SAMHSA, accessible at http://www.samhsa.gov/oas/ WebOnly.htm. Source of the table is Office Of National Drug Control Policy, *What America's Users Spend on Illegal Drugs, 1988-1998,* http://www.whitehousedrugpolicy.gov/publications/pdf/spending_drugs_1988_1998.pdf. *Other facts from* National Institute on Drug Abuse, http://www.drugabuse.gov/NIDAHome.html and U.S. Department of Justice, Drug Enforcement Administration, http:// www.usdoj.gov/dea/directory.htm.

Meth in America: Not in Our Town

Methamphetamine Labs

CT: NR
DE: NR
MA: 1
MD: 1
NH: 2
NJ: NR
RI: 1
VT: NR
DC: NR

Missouri? The heart of America? Leading in illegal methamphetamine labs? With more of them operating than in California? — Have we got the right chart here? Does it have the right label? Check again. Yes. It's the right data. Yes, it's true. — Disconcerting though it might seem, meth crystals are being manufactured in all but four states and the District of Columbia. Lithium from batteries, acetone from paint thinner, lye and ephedrine bought at the pharmacy (the ephedrine comes in cold medicines), and you're on your way to making "ice." It's best to find some sheltered, hidden area. Making meth is dangerous. Fires and explosions are quite common; producers often die of them. For every pound of stuff you make, you get 10 pounds of toxic residues best dumped someplace in secret. And the smell is horrendous. Those in a hurry can steal some anhydrous ammonia, used as fertilizer. The ammonia speeds up the drying of the drug, cutting 10 hours from the process. The pressurized containers of anhydrous sometimes blow up, of course. More casualties. But enterprise never dies — and folly, madness, greed march on.

Meth is big business in rural America. It's distributed by motorcycle gangs and transported into the smaller metros with the produce. It reaches the cities in bulk.

This phenomenon first reached the notice of Big City media in 2000 when the National Center on Addiction and Substance Abuse, at Columbia University (CASA), published its report, *No Place to Hide*, a study commissioned by the United States Conference of Mayors and funded by Drug Enforcement Administration (DEA) with support from the National Institute on Drug Abuse. One of the study's findings was that, in 1999, 8th graders and high school students in rural areas and small cities used meth much more than children in large metro areas. Use rates in rural areas are climbing — declining everywhere else.

The phenomenon surprised the public but was not unknown to drug enforcement agencies in the several states. Awareness of the problem led the DEA to launch its Meth Tour in America to publicize the problem. The slogan of the tour is used as the title of this panel.

Most people living in our major cities hear such news with some disquiet. We like to think that innocence survives down on the farm. Not so. Rural areas are not exempt from the troubles that beset the rest of the nation. Out in the country demoralization takes various forms. Small farmers are up against corporate farming. The population is still draining away toward the cities, actually the suburbs. It's difficult to make ends meet.

Meth is a potent drug. It induces euphoria. Users feel energetic, have no appetite, do not need sleep. The drug acts more slowly on the body than cocaine but the effect can last from eight to 12 hours. Cocaine's effect fades in one or two. Habitual users can become severely disoriented, violent, paranoid, psychotic. Sometimes they do dreadful things. Here is a brief capsule from the CASA report:

> In Fargo, North Dakota a man who claimed to be hallucinating while on meth burned his house down, killing his mother. An Arizona man high on meth for 24-hours stabbed his 14-year old son 29 times and then cut off his head, telling police he thought the boy was possessed.[1]

Psychotic symptoms can last months, sometimes years. Methamphetamine is a hard drug. Its effects are very serious. Educational efforts no doubt help — like the DEA's meth tour. The fundamental problems that induce people to reach for "ice" are systemic and societal. Education, upbringing, family cohesion — all these things play a role.

The great majority of the meth labs shown on the map, which records reports from 46 states made in 2001, have low capacity, being able to manufacture only about 8 ounces of meth a day. These labs account for only about 20% of all production. Most meth is produced in so-called "superlabs." Superlabs are principally run by Mexican drug rings of some sophistication on U.S. soil. Their typical output is 10 pounds a day.

The troubling social trend meth represents is that human-made (not merely human-grown) substances are manufactured everywhere. The many labs, all over the country, make it difficult to think of drug lords are being strange aliens living abroad. They are ourselves.

Source: Map. U.S. Drug Enforcement Administration, National Clandestine Laboratory Database, accessible at http://www.usdoj.gov/dea/pubs/pressrel/methmap.html. Background: *No Place to Hide*, Columbia University, National Center on Addiction and Substance Abuse, http://www.casacolumbia.org/.

---

[1] *No Place to Hide*, p. 14. See Source notes.

Drug Arrests Do Not Deter Use

Drug Use, Drug Arrests

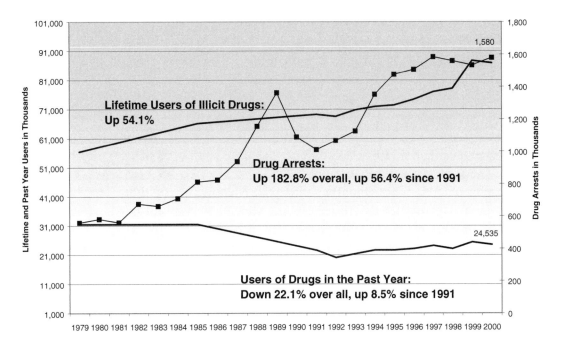

In 2000, an estimated 24.5 million people used illegal drugs in the year just past. These data are based on the National Survey on Drug Abuse conducted by the Substance Abuse and Mental Health Services Administration (SAMHSA), an agency of the U.S. Department of Health and Human Services. The survey questionnaire is quite extensive and determines the most recent use, but summaries published by SAMHSA report use of a drug, by type, within the last year and also within the respondent's lifetime. This survey is our best gauge of the prevalence of drug consumption in our society.

Since 1979, when 31.5 million people were regularly using drugs, drug use has declined some 22%. Since 1991, however, it has been rising again (8.5% from 1991 to 2000) despite a much more sharply rising wave of drug arrests (up 56.4% between 1991 and 2000). People who have "ever used" drugs has been climbing steadily, without a falter, despite heroic law enforcement efforts against drugs.

Law enforcement activity is not, seemingly putting much of a dent in the use of drugs. With 24.5 million users (technically lawbreakers), and 1.58 million arrests in 2000, only 6.4% of users are arrested. Law enforcement is thus not really affecting *use*. Indeed, law enforcement efforts are much more directed at *trafficking*, rather than at use — although some of those caught with drugs also end up as felons.

A look at 1998 data, from a special study conducted by the Bureau of Justice Statistics, gives some insight into the nature of the drug war — and why the high number of arrests do not appear to affect drug consumption much. Take a look at the table on the next page.

Drug Sentences and Arrests in 1998

	Felons Sentenced			Arrests	
	Total	State	Federal	Total	Sentenced as % of Arrested
Drugs	335,493	314,628	20,867	1,559,100	21.5
Possession	120,893	119,443	1,450	1,228,600	9.8
Trafficking	214,600	195,183	19,417	330,500	64.9
Percentiles					
Drugs	100.0	100.0	100.0	100.0	
Possession	36.0	38.0	6.9	78.8	
Trafficking	64.0	62.0	93.1	21.2	

The table shows us that, in 1998, 335,493 people were sentenced of 1.56 million arrested, or 21.5%. The vast majority of those arrested were arrested for possession (78.8%). Of those, just shy of 10% were actually sentenced. Meanwhile, of those arrested for trafficking (over a fifth of those arrested), somewhat over two-thirds (64.9%) were sentenced. Thus the war on drugs is clearly aimed at trafficking, not at possession. The assumption clearly is that if the supplies are dried up, people will stop wanting the stuff. Is that reasonable?

State-level activity dominates the war on drugs. A small number of people are sentenced at the Federal level (6.2%). But of those, nearly all (93.1%) are sentenced for trafficking.

Viewed in this manner, it is clear that law enforcement activity is heavily skewed towards arresting people who are in the possession of drugs, but the legal and correctional machineries principally deal with traffickers. The users largely get away with it.

Using 1998 data, here is how things stack up. Of an estimated 23,115,000 users breaking the law (100%), 1,228,600 were arrested (5.3%), and 120,893 (0.5%) were sentenced. In 1998, the drug-using population was equal to 8.5% of the population or 11.5% of those 18 years and over — and an even higher proportion if we use young adults as the base for calculation. Drug use clearly represents a massive social phenomenon, a form of mass disobedience. This graphically illustrates the dilemma inherent in our policy to stamp out drug use and produces not-so-faint echoes of the Prohibition. We shall compare the damage done by drugs to the damage assignable to alcohol in a later panel in this series.

Sources: U.S. Department of Health and Human Services, SAMHSA, Office of Applied Studies, *National Household Survey on Drug Abuse, 1998-2000* and earlier years. U.S. Department of Justice, Federal Bureau of Investigation, *Crime in the United States*, annual, Uniform Crime Reports, downloaded from http://www.ojp.usdoj.gov/bjs/dcf/enforce.htm and *Felony Sentences in State Courts, 1998*, Bureau of Justice Statistics.

Drug Users By Race and Ethnicity

Percentage of Population (12 and Older) Reporting Having Ever Used Drugs

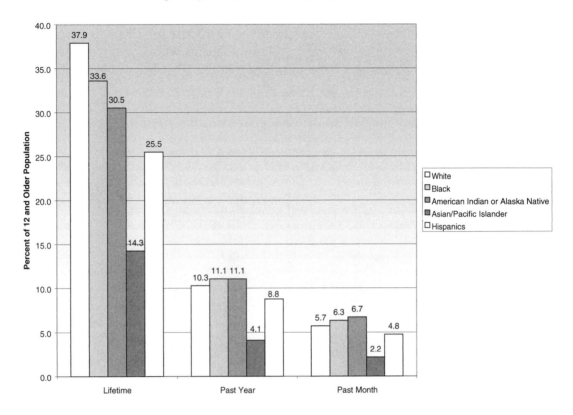

"Most drug users are white." If you submit that phrase to the Google search engine on the Internet, you will get four pages of hits. In most cases, the phrase is prefaced by the words "Although" or "While" or "Even though" — and the phrase is then followed by words stating that blacks are more frequently arrested or imprisoned.

Most drug users *are* white. But then, also, most *people* in the United States are white. Therefore it is more pertinent to ask what proportion of each racial/ethnic group uses drugs — which is what the graphic of this panel shows. The data are from the Substance Abuse and Mental Health Services Administration (SAMHSA) as normalized using 2000 Census data from the Bureau of the Census. The underlying numbers, shown in the table below, are an annualized average for the years 1999 and 2000.

In this view, proportionally more whites used drugs "ever in their lifetime," but blacks used drugs more than whites when the occasion was stated as "in the past year" or "in the past month." During recent occasions (past year, last month), the differences between whites, blacks, and American Indians/Native Alaskans are fairly small when expressed as a percentage of the population aged 12 years old or older. Asians and Pacific Islanders are least involved with drugs. People of Hispanic origin trail whites, blacks, and American Indians.

These numbers show the prevalence of drugs in our society. Nearly 4 of 10 whites, fully a third of all blacks, 3 in 10 American Indians, and a quarter of all Hispanics have used drugs sometime in their lives. Use of illegal drugs is predominantly a youth/young adult phenomenon the two largest age groups are, in this order, 18 to 25 and 12 to 17. There-fore recent users are a smaller proportion of the 12-and-older group. Nonetheless, more than 1 of 10 among whites and blacks and nearly 1 of 10 among Hispanics reached for some kind of illegal drug in the last year. Asians, some of whose ancestors first intro-duced Americans to the pleasures of the opium den in the 19th century, seemed to have learned their lesson better. They are not using drugs at the same rates.

Actual numbers reported by SAMHSA are shown in the table:

Drug Use in Thousands, 12 and Older, 1999-2000 Annualized Average

Race/Ethnicity	Used Any Illicit Drug		
	In Lifetime	In Past Year	In Past Month
White	67,807	18,411	10,231
Black	9,186	3,028	1,734
American Indian or Alaska Native	587	213	129
Asian/Pacific Islander	1,273	366	192
Hispanic Origin	6,791	2,335	1,266
Total	85,644	24,353	13,552

The table displays very large numbers: 13.6 million people in the age group used drugs in the months past (4.8% of this population), 24.4 million in the last year (8.8%), and 85.6 million in their lifetime (25.5%). This is not a small market.

We turn next to the second part of the allegation often seen in the papers and on activist web sites — namely that blacks are disproportionately punished for their indulgence in drugs.

Source: U.S. Department of Health and Human Services, SAMHSA, Office of Applied Studies, National Household Survey on Drug Abuse, 1999 and 2000.

Drugs Arrests by Race

Drug Arrests by Race

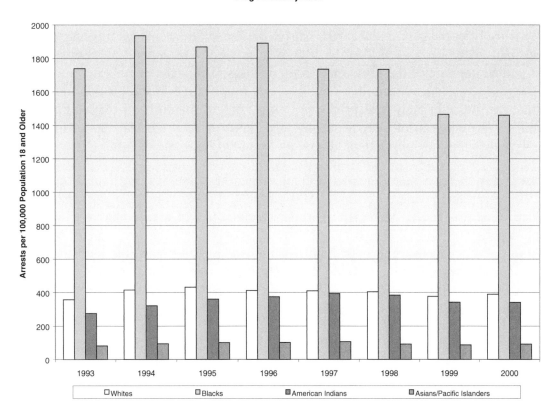

Arrest data reported by race do not clearly match total arrests — because race is not always (or unambiguously) reported. But in 2000, of a total of 1.28 million arrests where race was unambiguously stated, 64.2% of arrest were white, 34.5% were black, 0.7% were Asians/Pacific Islanders (APIs), and 0.5% were American Indians/Native Alaskans. A better way to look at such data is normalized by population — which is what we show in the graphic. The chart shows arrest rate translated into arrests per 100,000 population of each racial group. Immediately one fact leaps from the graph: proportionally many more blacks are arrested than members of the other races. The rates for whites, API's, and Indians have not changed greatly. The rates for blacks are down from a peak, in this chart, of 1,935 per 100,000 to 1,460. The actual peak was reached in 1989, when it was reported by the FBI to have been 2,464 arrests per 100,000 blacks 18 and over.

We saw in the last panel that the blacks' use of drugs is only fractionally higher than white or American Indian use. Why are the arrest rates for blacks so high? The answer provided by scholars and advocacy group — and echoed in the nation's large urban papers — is that (as one observer put it), "racial discrimination and stereotyping infect decision-making [in the criminal justice system] and skew the outcomes."[2]

Racial discrimination, while it undoubtedly exists, is not a sufficient explanation. The commerce in drugs has come to be centered in the ghettos, which are predominantly black, densely populated, and heavily patrolled. The black crime victimization rate is higher than the white rate, 37.2 for blacks, 28.2 for whites, both per 100,000 population. Most perpetrators are of the same race as the victims. The black crime rate is higher — and the justice system reflects that fact. There is more crime in the ghetto, and the deployment of police in such areas produces a higher payoff than in well-off suburbs where "narcs" would waste a lot of time staring at parked car and minimal "street life." The stereotyping is thus, to some extent, driven by an underlying state of fact.

Blacks prefer crack cocaine; 5 grams of crack constitute possession with intent to distribute. Whites prefer powdered cocaine; 500 grams (1.1 lbs.) constitute possession. It is easier to find drug users (or dealers) with small quantities of crack than people lugging around a pound or more of drugs. The ghettos are economically deprived areas. Many users in the ghetto support their habits with a little trading. Not least, the objective of the war on drugs is to break up trafficking rings. The big bosses (of whatever color) are difficult to nab. Law enforcement can thus achieve results easier in areas that tend to be poor, dense, and black.

It is almost axiomatic to say that, in this context, race is but an incidental aspects of the ghetto setting. If the ghettos were filled with Asians or whites, police practices would be the same but the racial categories would be different. Racial discrimination may not be the best explanation for patterns in drug arrests. The economically underdeveloped nature of central cities — and the social disruption that goes along with it — causes it, is caused by it — is probably a more neutral and accurate explanation.

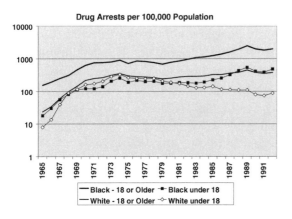

Drug Arrests per 100,000 Population

— Black - 18 or Older -■- Black under 18
— White - 18 or Older -◇- White under 18

For a somewhat deeper look into the past, the chart to the left provides a look at arrests rates back to 1965 — the year when the War on Poverty was born, the Voting Rights Act passed, the Immigration Act opened our doors to Latin America, the Vietnam War was in full swing, the Beatles were all the rage, and Watts erupted into a riot; 1965 also saw the passage of the Drug Abuse Control Amendments. It brought LSD, barbiturates, and amphetamines un-

---

[2] Sterling, Eric E., Criminal Justice Foundation, "Racially Disproportionate Outcomes in Processing Drug Cases," September 16, 1998, accessible at http://www.druglibrary.org/think/~jur/outcomes.htm.

der control. Between 1965 and 1971 (the year of the War on Drugs), arrests rates sky-rocketed — especially among whites. The arrest rate among white youths under 18 increased 22-fold, among white adults 11-fold, among black youths 7-fold, among black adults 5-fold. The black arrest rate in 1965, however, was already the highest. It increased least. And we were off.

Having looked at arrests, we turn next to what happens after the arrests. What about convictions?

Sources: U.S. Department of Justice, Federal Bureau of Investigation, *Uniform Crime Reports*, various years, as collected in *Sourcebook of Criminal Justice Statistics, 1994-2000*, downloaded from http://www.albany.edu/ sourcebook/ or obtained from the Sourcebook CD-ROM.

Drugs: Convictions and Sentencing Trends

Percent of Those Arrested, Percent of Those Convicted

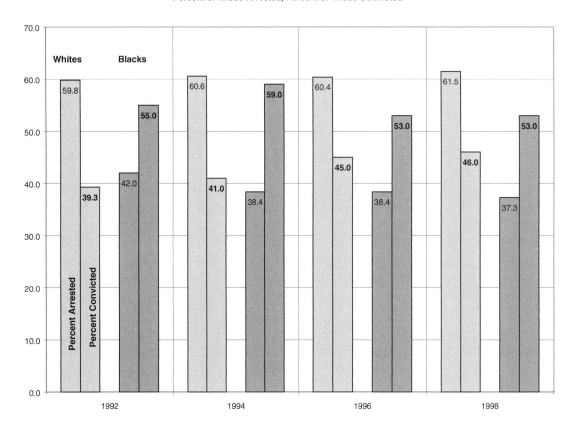

Data shown in the graphic are total arrests for drug offenses and conviction rates in state courts for four years. Only data for whites and blacks are shown. Arrest and conviction rates of other races are in the 1 to 2% range. The main point of this chart is to show that while whites are a consistently higher percentage of those arrested, they are also consistently the lower percentage of those convicted in state courts (where the overwhelming majority of cases are adjudicated). Conviction rates for whites have been trending up and rates for blacks have been trending down — possibly because these discrepancies in sentencing have produced a lot of pressure on the Justice System. But the gaps remain and — and they give rise to charges of unequal treatment of the majority and of the minority populations.

Most arrests are for possession — but most sentences are for selling or manufacturing drugs. Could this be an explanation of the uneven treatment of whites and blacks? The table on the following page provides a negative answer. It does not appear to matter what the charge is. Whether it is possession or trafficking, more blacks are convicted of the crime than whites.

Percentage Break-Down by Race of Individuals Sentenced

In State Courts for Drug Offenses

	All Drug Offenses			Possession			Trafficking		
	White	Black	Other	White	Black	Other	White	Black	Other
1992	44	55	1	44	55	1	44	55	1
1994	41	59	0	46	53	1	37	63	0
1996	45	53	2	49	49	2	43	56	1
1998	46	53	1	55	44	1	42	57	1

These numbers are startling because the black population is around 13% and the white around 75% of the population. At the front of the system, where the drug are consumed, the two major races of the nation are quite equivalent. At the tail of the system — where people are sentenced and sent to prison, the black involvement is very much out of proportion to the black's use of drugs and to the proportion of black arrests. In 1998, blacks were 37% of those arrested, but 53% of those sentenced in state courts.

It would be informative to track trends in imprisonment of whites versus blacks, — and other forms of disposition of those convicted. The table below shows that outcomes are equally unequal.

Felony Sentences Imposed by State Courts in 1992 and 1998 in Percent

	Total	Incarceration						Nonincarceration					
		Total		Prison		Jail		Total		Probation		Other	
Whites		1992	1998	1992	1998	1992	1998	1992	1998	1992	1998	1992	1998
Drug Offenses	100	75	65	34	33	41	32	25	35	24	32	1	3
Possession	100	69	67	29	31	40	36	31	33	30	30	1	3
Trafficking	100	80	64	37	35	42	29	20	36	20	33	1	3
Blacks													3
Drug Offenses	100	**74**	73	54	51	**20**	**23**	26	**27**	26	**24**	1	**2**
Possession	100	**66**	72	44	47	**23**	**25**	34	**28**	33	**25**	1	**2**
Trafficking	100	**79**	74	60	52	**18**	**21**	21	**26**	21	**24**	*	**2**

*Less than 0.5 percent.

This table shows that a smaller percentage of blacks than whites were incarcerated in 1992, a larger percentage in 1998. In both years, blacks were a substantially higher percentage of prisoners (serving more than a year). Smaller percentages of blacks received nonincarceration sentences in 1998. Blacks, in other words, received, on average, harsher sentences than whites, and the sentences have also grown harsher in the six years separating 1992 and 1998.

Lengths of sentences show a more even pattern in 1998. Using average maximum sentences imposed, we note that whites got 34 months for possession, blacks 33, whites got 54 months for trafficking, blacks 52. More blacks went to prison, but sentences were marginally lighter. Whites in jail for possession got 4 months, blacks 5, for trafficking whites got 5 month when sentence to jail, blacks 7. Whites on probation for possession got 32 months, blacks 37. The only absolute equality was in the case of probation sentences for trafficking — 36 months for both races.

Sentencing results are an improvement over 1992. That year, blacks received sentences 23.4% longer than whites for possession and 15.3% more for trafficking.

Other than assigning all the blame to plain, old-fashioned racism, which no doubt plays a role, how do we explain these differences? Two issues might suggest part of the answer: crack cocaine versus powdered cocaine and differential recidivism rates.

Crack. Blacks were 84% of crack cocaine offenders and 30% of powder cocaine offenders in 2000. A person convicted of possessing 500 grams of powdered cocaine with intent to distribute (a little over a pound) will get a mandatory 5 year sentence. For crack, the triggering quantity is 5 grams of crack (there are 28 grams to an ounce). Crack possessors are thus subject to much higher sentences, and most such people are black.

Crack is smoked and produces a rapid, intense "high." Powder is snorted. Its effect is slower, the high is less intense. Crack has developed a reputation as violence-inducing and highly addictive. The death of Len Bias in 1986, the University of Maryland Basketball player (bound for the Boston Celtics, but he never got there) was initially blamed on crack — although later it turned out that he had been using powdered cocaine on the night of his death. That event played a major role in the formation of crack's reputation.

Congress has resisted revising the quantity-ratio triggering mandatory sentencing and, in 1995, rejected a recommendation by the U.S. Sentencing Commission to equalize the ratios. "Devil Crack" remains enthroned up there with "Demon Drink."

Recidivism. Blacks are much more likely to be rearrested (72.9% versus 62.7% for whites in 1994), to be reconvicted (51.1% vs. 43.3%), and returned to prison with a new sentence (28.5% vs. 22.6% for whites). This is for all crimes. Those with prior convictions get harsher sentences. More black drug offenders may appear before the courts as repeat offenders and hence may harvest harsher sentences.

Lawyers? What about appointed versus privately-hired lawyers? Blacks were more likely to be represented by public defenders — 76.6% versus 69.0% for whites in 1997 in state courts. But publicly defended drug offenders did better than privately defended persons. They got lower sentences (97 versus 140 months) and were expected to serve less time before release (46 months versus 58 for those with the expensive lawyers).

Many other factors, of course, play a role, including the perceptions of judges and juries of the potential danger individuals pose to society. Profiling is inherent in our perceptions. Yes, it exists. As does racial bias.

Sources: *Sourcebook of Criminal Justice Statistics, 1994-2000*, downloaded from http://www.albany.edu/ sourcebook/ or obtained from the Sourcebook CD-ROM. The Sentencing Project, "Crack Cocaine Sentencing Policy: Unjustified and Unreasonable," undated, downloaded October 17, 2002 from http://www.sentencingproject.org/pubs/tsppubs/1090bs.htm. U.S. Department of Justice, *Recidivism of Prisoners Released in 1994*, June 2002.

The Traffic in Drugs

Metric Tons of Illegal Drugs Consumed, Billions of Dollars Spent (Total)

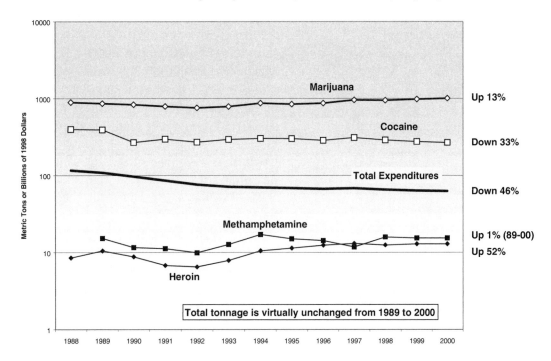

In 2000, an estimated 1,306 metric tons of drugs were sold.[3] The tonnage may not appear overwhelming (about the weight of 600 smaller automobiles), but keep in mind that a "snort" of cocaine holds only about 100 milligrams of cocaine and a joint has less than half a gram of marijuana.

In 2000 Americans spent $60.6 billion on these drugs (in 1998 constant dollars). If "other drugs" are included, the size of this market in 2000 was $62.9 billion.

Weight of marijuana, methamphetamine, and heroin was up over this period, the weight of cocaine was down. Overall tonnage was more or less flat (1.5% increase). Expenditures were down 46%, indicating that prices had declined in the 1989 to 2000 period, possibly as a consequence of softening demand. The number of users had declined, as we shall see in the next panel.

Note please that tonnage data do not in any way reflect the steeply rising arrests rates we have noted earlier. One of the interesting social trends shown by statistics on the war on drugs is that the drug trade marches on, driven by its own imperatives — and so does the

---

[3] The tonnage excludes the weight of "other drugs" not specified in the graphic; the weight of "other drugs," including hallucinogens, inhalants, uppers, downers, etc., was not available.

---

war on drugs. If the two are in any way related, it is difficult to discern that by looking at statistics.

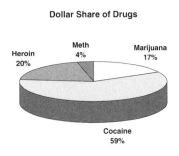

Dollar Share of Drugs

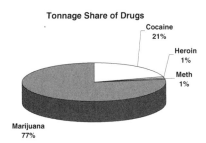

Tonnage Share of Drugs

The physical quantities represented by the major drugs, and the dollars they fetch in the retail market, are in sharp contrast as shown by the two pie charts to the left. Marijuana is a relatively small part of the dollar trade, 17%, but accounts for the bulk of the tonnage flow, the largest number of users, and the largest share of all arrests.

Cocaine is a shade over a fifth of the physical quantities distributed but accounts for 59% of dollar sales. Heroin is the most potent of the major drugs. A little goes a long ways. Heroin accounts for 1% of the tonnage but expands into 20% of the dollar value of drugs traded in 2000. Heroin also has the distinction of being the most addictive of the drugs and of causing most of the deaths from drugs — in part by its very nature, in part because, in sharing needles, users often contract HIV/AIDS. Methamphetamine, one of the modern, synthetic competitors of heroin, behaves in a similar manner; it expands from about 1% of the physical quantity sold to 17% of the dollar market.

The data shown here are at best educated guesses based on the analysis of data gathered from all available sources by Abt Associates under contract to the National Office of Drug Policy, an element of the White House. Part of the problem in assessing the war on drugs is that those who engage in the drug trade do not fill out forms when the data collectors of the Economic Census, conducted by the Bureau of the Census, call in years ending in 2 and in 7. But one gets a bit of an idea nonetheless.

Source: Office Of National Drug Control Policy, the White House, *What America's Users Spend on Illegal Drugs, 1988-1998*, Abt Associates, available at http://www.whitehousedrugpolicy.gov/publications/pdf/spending_drugs_1988_1998.pdf.

Trends in Drug Users

Users of Drugs

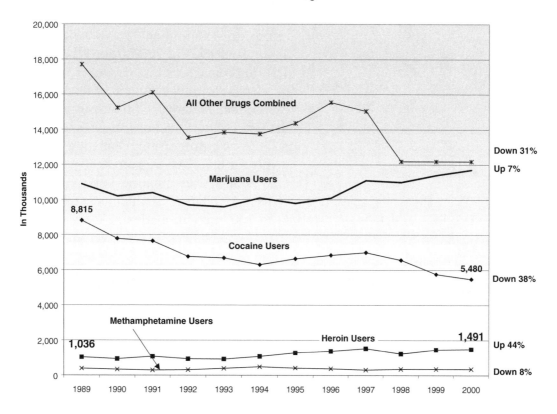

In 2000, an estimated 31.2 million people were using drugs of one kind or another. This total is built up out of household surveys and interviews of people arrested. Individuals who use more than one drug are counted for each drug they use; the total number of individuals is therefore a smaller number. The data used here are derived principally from the National Household Survey on Drug Abuse (NHSDA), conducted by the Substance Abuse and Mental Health Services Administration (SAMHSA), an element of the U.S. Department of Health and Human Services. But data have been modified and augmented by information from the Drug Use Forecasting (DUF) program of the U.S. Department of Justice to track hardcore users. Hardcore users are not well covered by the household survey.

The total estimated number of drug users was down 19% from 1989, from 38.8 to 31.2 million. Most of the decline came from a decrease in users of "all other drugs" — inhalants, hallucinogens, stimulants, sedatives, tranquilizers, and analgesics.

Among the major drugs, cocaine users decreased from 8.8 million to 5.5 million users. Declines were registered both among hardcore and casual users. Methamphetamine users dropped by 30,000 in this 11-year period. Marijuana users increased by 800,000 people, heroin users by 455,000. Among heroin users, hardcore users declined, but casual users increased, somewhat paralleling the decline in needle use and the increase in heroin snorting. Drug users are under the (false) impression that snorting heroin will not get them addicted to the drug.

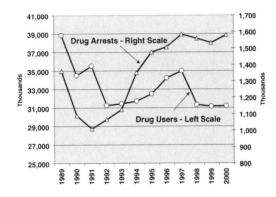

How to explain such patterns? Arrest rates declined from 1989 to 1991 from 1.3 million arrests to 1.0 million. Then they climbed again from 1991 to 2000 from 1.0 million to 1.58 million. The arrest rate and the number of users seem more to parallel than to affect each other, as shown in the inset graphic to the left. It charts total drug users and drug arrests. As the drug-using population drops, so do drug arrests. As drug arrest begin to climb (1991) drug user numbers begin to climb a year after (1992). Again, as the arrest rate softens in 1997, drug user numbers take a dive. More striking is a look at details. In the 1989 to 2000 period, marijuana users increased by 7.3%, marijuana arrests increased by 86.0%. Combined cocaine and heroin users decreased 29.2%, combined cocaine and heroin arrests decreased 28.0%. Is there a connection between these two phenomena?

Data on arrests are fairly solid. Data on the user community are based more on guesswork and on surveys. But if these numbers are to be believed, might it turn out that easing up on law enforcement efforts would cause drug use to drop?

We turn next to expenditures on drug control in light of expenditures on drugs.

Sources: Office Of National Drug Control Policy, the White House, *What America's Users Spend on Illegal Drugs, 1988-1998*, Abt Associates, available at http://www.whitehousedrugpolicy.gov/publications/pdf/spending_drugs_1988_1998.pdf. Arrest data from U.S. Department of Justice, Federal Bureau of Investigation, *Crime in the United States*, annual, Uniform Crime Reports, downloaded from http://www.ojp.usdoj.gov/bjs/dcf/enforce.htm.

Expenditures on Drug Control

Users' Expenditures on Illegal Drugs and Federal Budget For Drugs

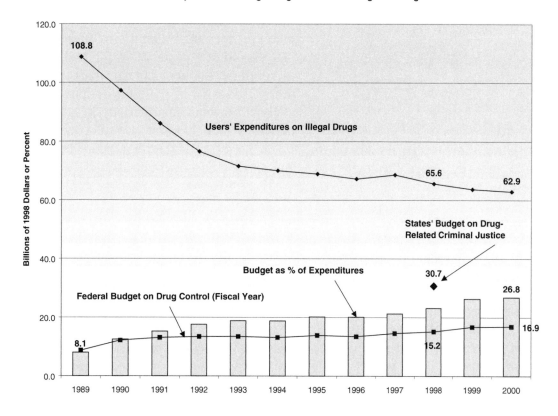

How much will it take to control the drug trade? How much public spending will it take? This panel is an attempt to give that question some shape and form. Shown in the graphic are two time series and a point. The top curve shows what people have been spending on illegal drugs. The bottom curve shows federal expenditures on drug control. Both curves are in constant 1998 dollars. For 1998, the diamond shows the total expended by all states on the criminal justice portion of drug control, $30.7 billion. The bars show the federal drug budget as a percentage of public spending on illegal drugs.

Let's focus on the year 1998. In that year the Federal government expended $15.2 billion on drug-related programs. Domestic law enforcement was $9.5 billion or 63% of that. The only data for the several states' budgets we have is for 1998. In that year the states spent $30.7 billion on the "justice" side of the subject. This means that, all told, some $45.9 billion in public money was spent in 1998 to try to prevent the public from spending $65.6 billion on drugs.

In the 1989 to 2000 period, spending on drugs declined 42%, principally because prices for drugs dropped; tonnage of drugs actually increased. The federal budget increased nearly 93%. It had no effect on the amount of drugs consumed although, indirectly perhaps, it might have caused the number of drug users to drop. No clear case is visible, however.

2001 Federal Budget

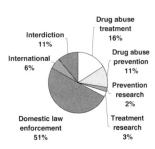

Interdiction 11%

Drug abuse treatment 16%

International 6%

Drug abuse prevention 11%

Prevention research 2%

Domestic law enforcement 51%

Treatment research 3%

A closer look at the Federal budget for drug control shows how at least a third of the money spent on this activity is subdivided into categories. One may assume that the states are continuing to spent twice again as much as does the Federal Government. The data shown are for the 2001 FY budget. Domestic law enforcement in that year had dropped to 51% of the total. If International expenditures and Interdiction are added, the budget is strongly tilted toward stemming the supply. These three categories add up to 78% of the total. Of the remainder, the largest portion is for Drug Abuse Treatment (16%) and Drug Abuse Prevention (11%). The rest is for research.

It is well to note that this war has been going on since about 1900 (the reaction against opium) or since 1970 (Nixon's "war on drugs."). In between, the nation lashed out against alcohol, but that initiative collapsed. Despite all efforts, millions of people spent billions on illegal drugs. How to explain this?

One can point at four horsemen of this particular apocalypse. The first is the misery, anomie, and the helplessness of the slums, barrios, and ghettos of our major cities — where drugs offer an escape and a source of income. The second is the recklessness of an ever more pampered youth, always testing boundaries in irresponsible ways (pill-popping and marijuana). A third is the recurrence of periods of "irrational exuberance" during which "masters of the universe" reward themselves at parties with a line of coke. And the fourth is third-world countries that have found cash crops to sell, at relatively modest profits, to the richest nation of the world.

Sources: Office Of National Drug Control Policy, the White House, *What America's Users Spend on Illegal Drugs, 1988-1998*, Abt Associates, available at http://www.whitehousedrugpolicy.gov/publications/pdf/spending_drugs_1988_1998.pdf. Budget data from U.S. Department of Justice, posted at http://www.ojp.usdoj.gov/bjs/dcf/dcb.htm.

Legal Drugs: Smoke and Booze

Alcohol and Tobacco

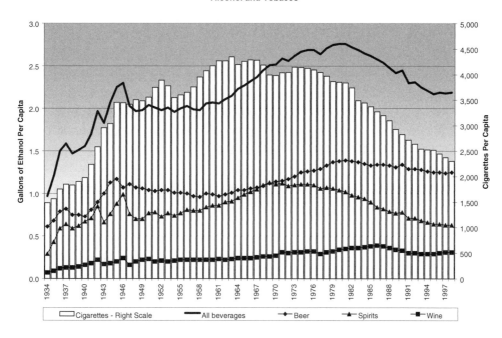

Let us take a brief respite from coke and meth and heroin and look at the nation's consumption of *legal* drugs briefly. In 1998, consumption of all alcoholic beverages was 2.2 gallons per person aged 14 years or older. In that year, also, cigarette consumption was 2,300 cigarettes per capita (population 18 and older). In 2000, 47.5 million people in that age group smoked cigarettes (most far more than just 2,300). Cigarette smokers outnumbered the nation's 11/7 million marijuana smokers four to one. In 2000, 96 million people (still 18 and older) reported being *regular* drinkers, a number more than three times that of all drug users in the same year (31.2 million). The number of people addicted to alcohol, alcoholics, is difficult to ascertain, but various sources cite numbers ranging between 15 and 18 million; 26,500 people die of cirrhosis of the liver every year. What does this tell us?

At least at present, society applies different standards to some drugs — based on tradition and long-standing practice. In fact it feels strange to talk about beer, liquor, and cigarettes as if they were drugs. But we consume these things not because we need the nutrients that they provide.

Consensus on tobacco is now fraying. Most people disapprove of smoking, including cigarette smokers, but the latter find it difficult to quit. Public opinion on alcohol is at present quiescent, perhaps because the Prohibition era is not yet entirely forgotten. Yet cigarettes may well be causing more deaths than all other drugs combined, and alcohol plays much more of a role in criminal affairs than do illegal drugs. Just to keep matters in perspective, a quick look at legal drugs is at least warranted.

Estimates of annual deaths caused directly by three classes of drugs — tobacco, alcohol, and illegal drugs — show that alcohol deaths are around 110,000 (of which about 16,000 are traffic fatalities involving alcohol); tobacco kills around 365,000 people. And drugs kill around 16,000 people (1997, Office of National Drug Control Policy), about as many as alcohol kills on the highways. The legal drugs cause as much harm as do the illegals.

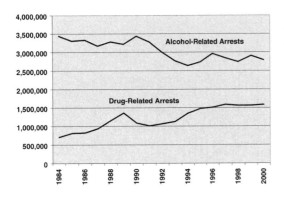

Arrest records maintained by the FBI provide a quick look at the roles drugs and alcohol play in the criminal justice system. In 2000, 2.8 million arrests took place related to alcohol — for driving under the influence, drunkenness, and violation of liquor laws. Not included are arrests for disorderly conduct, which match arrests for drunkenness. In 2000, 1.6 million people were booked for violating drug laws, the majority for possession, and half of those for possession of marijuana, 646,000 people. That number is roughly equivalent to those arrested for violating liquor laws, 683,000 in 2000.

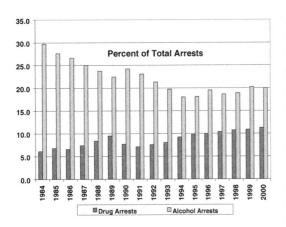

Arrests for alcohol are trending down, somewhat paralleling the decline in hard-liquor consumption. But arrests for drugs are up. In percentage terms, shown by the small inset graphic, drug arrests were 6.1% of all arrests in 1984 but 11.3% of all arrests in 2000. Alcohol arrests are down as a percentage of all arrests from 29.7% in 1984 to 20.0% in 2000, but still nearly twice as high as drug arrests. A substance need not be illegal to generate a high arrest rate. In 2000, 40.9% of drug arrests were for the possession of marijuana and 52.7% of alcohol arrests were for driving under the influence. In fact, 81% of all drug arrests were for possession. It would appear, from this, that the danger to society from alcohol was greater than from drugs.

In these matters — where massive public disobedience supports the consumption of illegal substances — conclusions must be left to individuals. Would arrests related to alcohol be vastly higher if alcohol were prohibited again? Unfortunately, data don't exist to answer the question. Would arrests related to drugs be vastly lower if marijuana were legalized or simply tolerated ("benign neglect")? Undoubtedly. Is there a compromise? Should we smoke — but not inhale?

Sources: Chart: National Institute on Alcohol Abuse and Alcoholism, U.S. Department of Health and Human Services, *Apparent Per Capita Alcohol Consumption*, December 2000; U.S. Department of Agriculture (tobacco figures). Arrest data: U.S. Department of Justice, Federal Bureau of Investigation, *Crime in the United States*, annual, Uniform Crime Reports, downloaded from http://www. ojp.usdoj.gov/bjs/dcf/enforce.htm.

Drugs in Context of Crime

Crime Rate and Drug Arrests

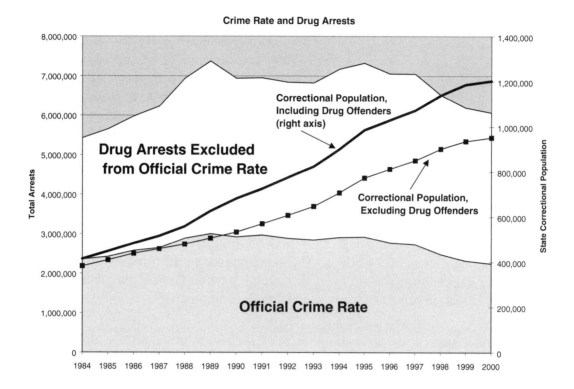

Let's conclude this chapter by trying to see the impact of drugs — and the effort to control their consumption and distribution — on the criminal justice system. We will use just a few measurements: crime rates measured as arrests, incarcerations at the state level, and the costs associated with state drug corrections.

The graphic shows the official crime rate at the bottom of the chart; this the measure used by the nation to measure the intensity of crime. As shown in Chapter 1, only selected violent and property crimes are included in the "crime rate." The crime rate, overall, has been going down (a decrease of 4.8% 1984 to 2000). But if we add drug-related arrests to the official crime arrests and chart them, we more than double the number of arrests — as shown by the snow-capped peaks in the graphic. The official and the drug crime rates, in combination, have increased 24.7%. Thus the much publicized "dropping crime rate" is accompanied by a rather sizeable shadow of rising drug-related lawlessness. Drug arrests, taken by themselves, have increased 123% in this same time period.

We are, of course, somewhat comparing apples and oranges here. The official crime rate includes the most severe crimes, not least homicides that took place in wars between drug gangs and robberies and burglaries committed by addicts trying to get money for the next injection of heroin. The drug arrests, by contrast, are predominantly for the possession of illegal substances, usually small quantities of marijuana. The commonality is that both the official crimes and the drug offenses are — against the law. They require justice system employees to handle and tax dollars to resolve. The principal disconnect is that literally millions of people are scoffing the drug laws. Meanwhile only a small minority is involved in the official, indexed crimes. The drug component of crime, therefore, shows up a social conflict — and an *intensifying* social conflict as the next graphic shows.

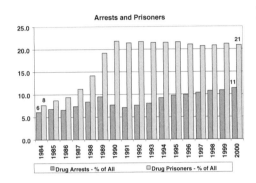

Arrests and Prisoners

☐ Drug Arrests - % of All ☐ Drug Prisoners - % of All

In 1984, drug arrests were 6.1% of all arrests. By 2000, drug arrests were 11.3% of all arrests and thus significantly more important. Similarly, in 1984, 7.7% of all individuals in state-run correctional systems (were most prisoners are sentenced) were institutionalized because of drug offenses. In 2000, this rate had increased to 20.9%. More than a fifth of state corrections existed to service drug offenders in 2000. During this period, the number of drug users actually declined.

To put some dollar figures against this, consider that in 1984, states expended about $1.25 billion on drug offenders in their correctional systems; in 1999 they spent $6.74 billion. The expenditures are in constant, 2000 dollars. The increase in expenditure was 439%. Correctional expenditures at the state level, of course, are but a fraction of what society spends on the war on drugs.

Sources: Arrest data: U.S. Department of Justice, Federal Bureau of Investigation, *Crime in the United States*, annual, Uniform Crime Reports, downloaded from http://www.ojp.usdoj.gov/bjs/dcf/enforce.htm. Expenditures: *Trends in Justice Expenditure and Employment*, NCJ 178277, Table 10 [Online]. Available: http://www.ojp.usdoj.gov/ bjs/data/eetrnd10.wk1 [Mar. 27, 2002].

Chapter 7

Terrorism

No one definition of terrorism has gained universal acceptance. Title 22 of the United States Code, Section 2656f(d) offers one definition: "The premeditated, politically motivated violence perpetrated against noncombatant targets by subnational groups or clandestine agents, usually intended to influence an audience." (Noncombatants are generally defined as civilians and unarmed military personnel.) Certainly, no terrorist attacks have had more profound impact than those conducted on September 11, 2001.

The key words in that definition are "politically motivated" and "audience." In other words, what has been the goal of those who turn to violence? In the opening panel, we'll see that their goals fall across the spectrum. Some have fought for the independence of their country. Some have turned to violence to call attention to the plight of their home land. Some have fought to protest governmental policies on the environment or civil liberties. Any change in government or society will give birth to a group of dissenters. As dire predictions were made about the depletions of natural resources, groups such as Earth First surfaced as protectors of the environment. Patriot groups and militias gained notoriety in the late 1990s out of a combination of factors: changes in gun laws and other legislation, the growth of government, an increasingly global marketplace, and the paranoia produced by the approaching Millennium.

But one person's terrorist is another's "freedom fighter." The line between terrorism and other crimes seems to becoming increasingly murky. Are all bombings terrorist acts? What about vandalism? Where does a "hate crime" — assuming such things exist — fit into the picture?

The rest of the chapter will focus exclusively on September 11, 2001. Several panels will address issues related to fighting terrorism. Billions are now being spent on securing our nation. Where are we making the improvements? Will they be successful? As the government continues its war on terrorism, some wonder if civil liberties will be among the casualties. How much privacy should be sacrificed for the greater good?

A History of Terrorism, 1961-2001

1961 - May 1: The first U.S. aircraft was hijacked. Puerto Rican born Antuilo Ramierez Ortiz forced at gunpoint a National Airlines plane to fly to Havana, Cuba where he was given asylum.

1972 - July 21: "Bloody Friday" occurred. An Irish Republican Army (IRA) bomb attack killed 11 people and injured 130 in Belfast, Northern Ireland. Ten days later, three IRA placed three car bombs in the village of Claudy. The exploding cars left six dead.

1972 - September 5: Eight Palestinian "Black September" terrorists seized 11 Israeli athletes in the Olympic Village in Munich, West Germany. In a bungled rescue by West German authorities, nine of the hostages and five terrorists were killed.

1973 - January 5: All passengers and carry-on luggage were required by law to be screened. X-ray machines and metal detectors began to be installed in airports.

1974 - February 5: Patty Hearst was kidnapped by the Symbionese Liberation Army.

1975 - January 27-29: Puerto Rican nationalists bombed a Wall Street bar killing four and injuring 60. Two days later a bomb exploded in bathroom at the U.S. State Department. The Weather Underground, a dissident group, claimed responsibility.

1976 - June 27: The People's Front for the Liberation of Palestine seized an Air France airliner and its 258 passengers. They forced the plane to land in Uganda. On July 3, Israeli commandos rescued the passengers.

1979 - November 20: Iranian radicals seized the U.S. Embassy in Tehran and took 66 American diplomats hostage. Thirteen were eventually released. The remaining 53 were held until their release in January 20, 1981.

1980 - May: The first FBI joint terrorism task force was established in New York City.

1981 - October 6: Egyptian President Anwar Sadat was assassinated.

1982 - January: The FBI's hostage rescue team was established.

1983 - February 13: The first recorded attack of right-wing anti-government group, the Sheriff's Possee Comitatus, took place.

1983 - April 18: The U.S. embassy in Lebanon was bombed with 63 dead.

1983 - October 23: A 12,000-pound truck bomb destroyed military compounds in Beirut, Lebanon; 242 Americans and 58 French troops were killed. Islamic Jihad claimed responsibility.

1984 - October 31: Prime Minister Gandhi of India was assassinated by members of her security force.

1985 - June 14: TWA flight 847 flying from Rome to Athens was hijacked by Two Lebanese Hizballah terrorists. The eight crew members and 145 passengers were held for 17 days. A Navy diver was killed.

1985 - October 7: Four PLO terrorists seized the Italian cruise liner Achille Lauro in the Mediterranean Sea.

1986 - April 5: A Berlin disco was bombed. Two soldiers were killed and 79 servicemen injured.

1988 - December 21: Pan American Airlines Flight 103 was blown up over Lockerbie, Scotland; 259 were killed.

1989 - October 13: The terrorist threat warning system was established.

1993 - February 26: The World Trade Center was damaged when a car bomb planted by Islamic terrorists exploded in a parking garage. More than 1,000 people injured.

1995 - March 20: Shinri-kyu cult members released Sarin nerve gas in an attack on subway stations in Japan.

1995 - April 19: Timothy McVeigh and Terry Nichols detonated a truck bomb that destroyed the Federal Building in Oklahoma City; 166 were killed and 642 injured.

1996 - June 25: A fuel truck carrying a bomb exploded outside the U.S. military's Khobar Towers housing facility in Dhahran, killing 19 and injuring 515.

1996 - July 27: The Centennial Olympic Park was bombed: 2 killed, 112 injured.

1998 - August 7: Bombs exploded nearly simultaneously at U.S. embassies in Kenya and Tanzania.

1998 - October 16: National Domestic Preparedness Office was established.

1999 - December 14: Ahmed Ressam was arrested trying to enter the U.S. from Canada with explosives for a Millennium bombing of LAX airport.

2000 - October 12: a small raft loaded with explosives rammed the U.S.S. Cole in Yemen. 17 sailors were killed and 39 injured.

2001 - September 11: The Attack on America. Two hijacked airliners crashed into the World Trade Center. Another crashed into the Pentagon. A fourth plane, targeted for the Capital, crashed in southern Pennsylvania. More than 3,000 people were killed.

Domestic Terrorism Before September 11, 2001

Number of Terrorist
Incidents in the United States, 1980-99

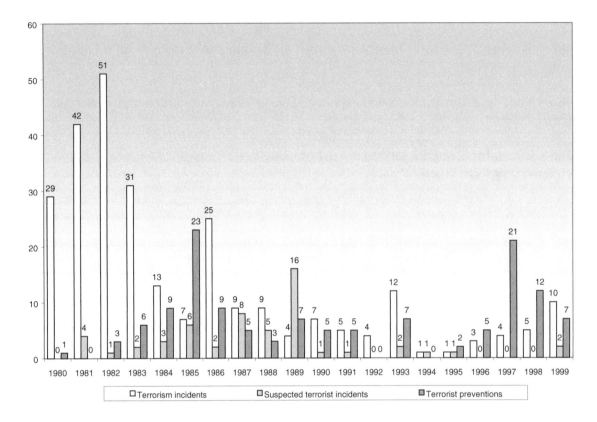

What is terrorism? Who is a terrorist? Have the methods and goals of terrorists changed over recent years?

The Federal Bureau of Investigation is the lead investigator of all terrorist acts in the United States. The FBI divides terrorist activity into three main categories:

- A terrorist incident is "a violent act or an act dangerous to human life, in violation of the criminal laws of the United States, or of any state, to intimidate or coerce a government, the civilian population, or any segment thereof, in furtherance of political or social objectives."

- A suspected terrorist incident is a "potential act of terrorism for which responsibility cannot be attributed to a known group or suspected group. Assessment of the circumstances surrounding the act determines its inclusion in this category."

- A terrorist prevention is "a documented instance in which a violent act by a known or suspected terrorist group or individual with the means and a proven propensity for violence is successfully interdicted through investigative activity."

A total of 457 incidents took place in the United States from 1980 to 1999. There were 272 terrorist incidents, 55 suspected to be such incidents, and 130 were prevented terrorist acts. In 70% of the cases, attacks involved bombings. Assassinations and arson were the other most used methods, used in roughly 5% of the events.

What type of attacks were taking place in the United States? The FBI didn't start tracking terrorist attacks until the mid-1970s. In the 1970s and 1980s, The vast majority of attacks were committed by left-wing and anti-war groups, such as the Weather Underground, the Black Liberation Army, the Symbionese Liberation Army, the Jewish Defense League, and the Armed Forces of Puerto Rican Liberation. Many of the incidents recorded in the early 1980s took place in Puerto Rico, conducted by groups committed to the country's independence from the United States. By the mid to late 1980s, however, most of these groups had lost their influence. Many were dismantled by law enforcement officials. Some left-wing groups subscribed to largely socialist views. The fall of Communism in Eastern bloc made the irrelevant.

Other organizations began to make attacks in the late 1980s. Animal rights and environmental organizations began a series of arson, sabotage, and bombing incidents. One of the first appears to be Earth First!, an organization thought to have been formed in the late 1970s. Other groups formed in the 1980s as concerns rose about the logging industry and the plight of endangered species. The Earth First Organization was first accused of sabotage in 1986. The first attack of the Animal Liberation Front took place in 1983 with the theft of 12 research dogs in California. These groups have been charged with malicious destruction and theft through the 1990s. The Earth Liberation Front has conducted a series of arson campaigns in recent years. Its attack on a ski resort in Vail, Colorado in 1998 — one of its more high profile efforts — did more than $12 million in damage.

The 1980s also saw the rise of right-wing extremist groups. Such organizations have existed for some time in the country, of course, the Ku Klux Klan being one of the most visible. These groups tend to have white supremacist, anti-government philosophies. Aryan Nation is suspected of attacks as early as 1984. American Front Skinheads conducted bombings in 1993. There are numerous anti-government fringe groups, although perhaps none so colorfully named as Up the IRS Inc. (yes, *Inc.*). UII that conducted bombings in California in the late 1980s and early 1990s. Some attacks have been conducted by individuals with strong anti-government attitudes but no affiliation with a particular group. Timothy McVeigh and Terry Nichols were convicted of the 1995 bombing of the Alfred P. Murrah federal building in Oklahoma City. Eric Robert Rudolph has been charged with a series of bombings, including the bombing of Millennial park during the 1996 Olympics. He remains at large. We'll look more closely at militias, patriot groups, and common-law courts in an upcoming panel.

One difficulties in measuring the number of incidents is finding the fine line between vandalism and terrorism. Is releasing animals from a testing lab a terrorist attack? Or is it just vandalism? Is such an attack intended to "coerce," as the terrorism definition suggests? Should animal rights and environmental groups be included in our nation's "War on Terrorism"? Another problem of classification is the distinction between personal and political motivations. The FBI does not classify Ted Kaczynski (the Unabomber) as a terrorist: they're not certain of the motivation behind his exploding letters. In 1993, Amil Kanzai killed two CIA employees and wounded two others outside the organization's Langley headquarters. He killed government workers, true, but he was determined to be acting for personal rather than ideological reasons. He is not a terrorist either. A series of bombings of black churches took places in the South in the 1990s. Was that terrorism? A hate crime?

There have been fewer terrorist incidents since the 1970s. From 1971 to June 1975, 641 terrorist activities took place, including 166 bombings, 120 fire bombings, and 118 shootings. Between 1980 and 1985, the number of incidents was just 184. Indeed, from 1980 to 1999, fewer terrorist (and suspected) incidents took place than in the earlier five year period in the 1970s.

But the growing threat of terrorism can be seen in the pre-September 11, 2001 numbers. Law enforcement prevented 64 attacks in the 1990s (about the same number as in the 1980s). The bulk of thwarted incidents took place in just the last three years of the decade. This certainly speaks to the activity-level of terrorist organizations, as well as the attention such groups are receiving from law enforcement officials.

Source: Federal Bureau of Investigations, *Terrorism in the United States, 1999.*

The United States As Terrorist Target

Global Terrorist Attacks, 1992-2000

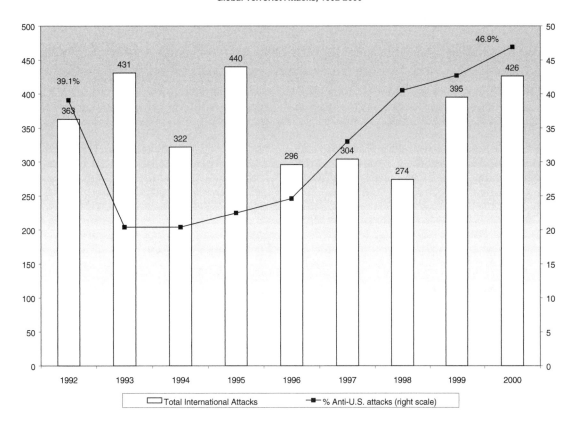

International terrorism, according to the State Department, "involves groups or individuals whose terrorist acts happen outside the US and/or are directed by groups outside the US, or whose activities transcend national boundaries."

The number of terrorist incidents in 1992 was a 35% drop from the previous year. Indeed, the 361 acts of terrorism that occurred that year were the lowest level recorded since 1985.

There was an increase in events in 1993. The State Department reports that the source of the increase was 150 attacks launched by the Kurdistan Workers Party (PKK) against Turkish interests. Without such attacks, the number of total incidents would have continued to fall. The year also saw the World Trade Center bombing in February, in which six were killed and more than 1,000 injured. The incident is considered international because of the political motivations of the attack and because the perpetrators were foreign nationals.

The number of attacks increased from 1994 to 1995, driven by attacks in Germany and by the PKK. Anti-U.S. attacks increased from 66 to 99. What might have sparked the increase? Several significant arrests and convictions of terrorists might have spurred their "brethren" on. Pakistan arrested and extradited Ramzi Usef to the United States. Ramzi was a key figure in the 1993 World Trade Center bombing. Jordan handed an accomplice of his, Eyad Mahmoud Ismail Najim, over to the U.S. Several important convictions took place that year as well, most notably of a group planning a series of bombings at the United Nations on Manhattan — and of Abd al-Rahman, a leader of an organization that had declared a "holy war" on America because it saw the U.S. as a threat to Islam.

What else? America's very presence in the Middle East has been a source of rage among some Arabs. U.S. military bases in Saudi Arabia — on Islamic holy ground — is repeatedly cited as a source of the militants' anger. Some in the Middle East view the U.S.-Saudi relationship with very jaundiced eyes. The Saudi princes are thought to be venal and corrupt in many Arab circles. The United States' repeated backing of Israel in the Israeli-Palestinian "relationship" is another source of conflict. Some people see their culture threatened by spreading American capitalism, culture, brands. In 1999, a farmer vandalized a McDonalds in France. He happened to be protesting high American taxes on Roquefort cheese, but that such an identifiable American brand as McDonalds should have been his target is something revealing in itself.

But Anti-American interests are elsewhere as well. Attacks against the U.S. surged 52% between 1998 and 1999. They were concentrated in Colombia, Greece, Nigeria, and Yemen, and were largely aimed at commercial interests and an oil pipeline.

In the year 2000, nearly half of all terrorist attacks were directed at the United States. The year 2001 would, of course, see a devastating attack upon our nation. As the world's last superpower, is this unavoidable?

Source: *Patterns of Global Terrorism, 1989-2000*. Retrieved September 10, 2002 from the World Wide Web: http://www.fas.org.

Fighting Terrorism: Security vs. Privacy

What Price Security? Americans' Feelings on Governmental Scrutiny

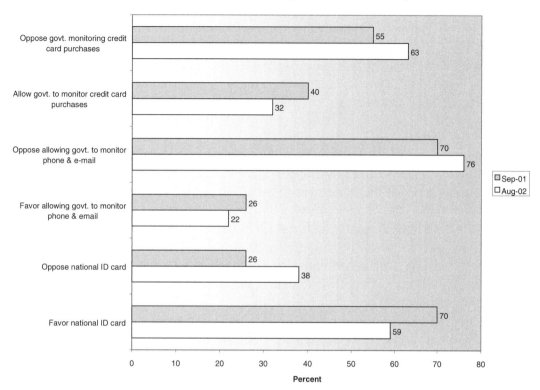

As the War on Terror continues, Americans are less willing to sacrifice their civil liberties in the interest of national security.

In a survey by the Pew Research Center, Americans expressed more of an unwillingness to allow the government into their private lives than at the beginning of the war. Fewer people in the survey supported ID cards and more people were unwilling to have the government examining e-mail or credit card purchases. Not too surprisingly, respondents were less willing to have the government examining their personal lives. In other words, the government reading e-mail is one thing; the government reading *my* e-mail is quite another. Thirty-three percent favored the government examining phone calls or e-mail; when it is their own communications, support dropped to 22%.

People were more willing to support other — but equally controversial — security issues. In the August 2002 survey, 68% favored letting pilots to carry handguns. Fifty-nine percent had no problem with racial profiling at airports.

How do we feel about our freedom? In a survey conducted in 1996, 65% of those polled agreed that civil liberties should not be curbed to fight terrorism (what must have seemed like a very distant threat, indeed). Even now, Americans seem to hold the same feelings: 62% expressed the same view. So, what do some people have to say about the new anti-terrorist legislation passed in October 2001?

Shortly after the September attacks, the PATRIOT Act was passed. It has made it easier for law enforcement groups to conduct surveillance and investigations. What are some of the powers granted by the new legislation? It is now easier for law enforcement to conduct secret search and seizures. The FBI has broader powers to conduct wiretaps. It is now easier to designate any group, foreign or domestic, a terrorist organization. The CIA now has access to testimony conducted by federal grand juries. Some of these new laws have already been put into practice: According to Justice Department statistics, more than 600 immigrants nationwide have been subjected to immigration hearings that were closed to the public and press. Two U.S. citizens were labeled "enemy combatants" to deny them legal protections. Other plans call for monitoring confidential attorney-client conversations.

Those on the other side of the fence immediately sounded the alarm. Several groups have also taken issue with the broad definitions in the legislation and the possible chilling outcomes of these new powers. Is the government headed back to the 1960s and 1970s, for example, when under Operation CHAOS, the CIA spied on anti-war and left-wing groups? Has "Big Brother" finally arrived? Or will these new powers be "checked and balanced"? It appears they will be. In August 2002, a Cincinnati Court of Appeals struck down a policy ordering that all immigration trials have to be conducted in secret when told to do so by the Justice Department. The court declared in its decision "democracies die behind closed doors." There was intense criticism of The Justice Department's Terrorism Information and Prevention System, known as Operation TIPS, a "national reporting system that allows American workers, whose routines position them well to observe unusual events, to report suspicious activity." Detractors claim that system will turn neighbor against neighbor. They imagine nervous meter readers and cable installers snooping in people's homes, looking for potential terrorists. The protesters raise a good point: Just how easy would it be for someone of Middle-Eastern descent to be considered "acting suspiciously"? Justice Department officials insist the systems would gather information....not names. (The U.S. Postal Service has declined to participate in the program).

Sources: "Temporary Turnabout." Public Perspectives, September/October 2002, p. 29; "Appeals court hear arguments today in second ACLU challenge to secret immigration hearings." Retrieved from http://www.aclu.org; Walter Shapiro. "Less-Adversarial Ashcroft An Image That Has Limits." USA Today, July 25, 2002; Abraham McLaughlin. "CIA Expands its Watchful Eye to the U.S." Christian Science Monitor, December 17, 2001, p. 2; "Postal Service Snubs Operation TIPS." Retrieved from http://www.cnn.com. All Internet data retrieved September 19, 2002.

The Cost of Keeping Us Safe

Homeland Defense Spending

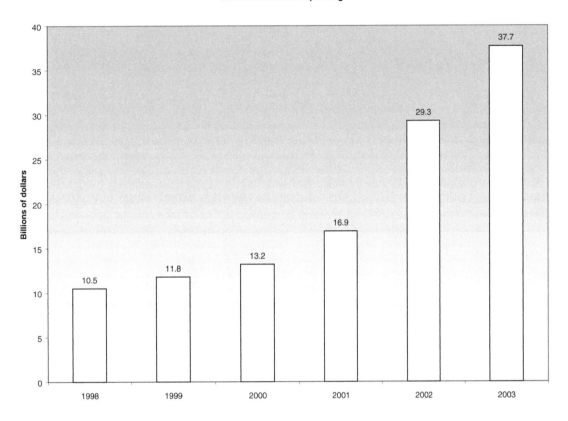

On October 8, 2001, Executive Order 13228 established the Office of Homeland Security (OHS) and the Homeland Security Council. The mission of the office would be "to develop and coordinate the implementation of a comprehensive national strategy to secure the United States from terrorist threats of attacks." It was envisioned that this would become a cabinet level department. Bush administration officials have called the creation of this new department the most dramatic change in the federal government since World War II. This new department would have a budget of $37.4 billion and pull together 169,000 employees from the federal workforce.

The table on the next page details the budget for various programs and shows the dramatic increases over the previous year's budget.[1] It is quite likely that even more funds will be devoted to security. What area will receive the most funding? Border security. Statistics from OHS point to the formidable undertaking here. The United States shares a 7,500 mile land and air border with Canada and Mexico. Every year 500 million people are admitted into this country; 330 million are non-citizens. 7,500 foreign-flagged ships make 51,000 calls in ports annually. 16 million cargo containers enter these ports annu-

---

[1] Other homeland security includes Pentagon funding for such items as jet-fighter patrols over U.S. cities.

ally. How is security handled? The Immigration and Naturalization Service has no way to track foreigners who overstay their visas. Only 2-3% of those 16 million containers are screened at ports.

The White House's Proposed Budget for Fiscal Year 2003

	($ Billions)	Increase Over 2002
First responders	0.3	1066.6%
Bioterror-related	5.9	321.4%
Information technology	0.7	250.0%
Aviation security	4.8	220.0%
Border security	10.6	20.4%
Other homeland security	12.2	64.8%

Who will receive the greatest increase in funding? "First responders," which includes state and local police, firefighters, and emergency medical professionals. They are the first on the scene, and most capable of saving lives and treating casualties. The loss of life among New York police, firefighters, and port authority officers must have played a significant role in such a dramatic increase in funding. But many cities, recognizing their need to be more prepared, are looking at ways to better train emergency personnel or provide upgraded equipment or improve communications. The level of preparedness varies by city, however.

Information technology is set to increase 250% over the 2002 budget. This category is particularly vital. Just as terrorists have exploited technology to suit their needs, so too do law enforcement officials need to upgrade their computer and communication methods to track them. The FBI in recent years came under fire for its jungle-like bureaucracy and lack of updated computer systems. Ron Kessler, who has written about both the FBI and CIA, made this recent observation: "The fact is the FBI literally had computers that no one would have taken even as a donation to a church. When they had to send a photo of a suspect to another office, they would actually send it to their home computer or to a police station because they couldn't download it at the FBI." The updates on technology are not just for investigations. Computer networks need to be protected from cyber-attacks. Money is needed for new forms of high-tech security, such as voice or face scanning technology.

Funding for aviation security is set to increase from $1.5 billion to $4.8 billion for fiscal years 2002 and 2003. Since the attacks, the airlines have been struggling to recover financially as well as implement the changes requested by the government. The plan to hire 33,000 federal airport screeners by November 19, 2002 is far behind schedule. The plan to install 1,100 new explosive screening machines and screen all checked baggage by November 2002 now appears impossible — indeed has been shoved out a year.

Who will provide this new software and technology? Big business. The security industry is booming. Companies such as 3M, Raytheon, Visionics, and Northrop Grumman are providing sensors, face scanning devices, and other high-tech equipment. When Transportation Security Norman Y. Mineta made over $92 million available to ports to improve security, *American Shipper* describes it as a "dinner gong" sounding to companies that sell, tag and track cargo containers. Even the director of homeland security, Tom Ridge, recognizes the role of corporate America when he made these comments to the

Electronic Industries Alliance: "The entrepreneurial spirit is a potent weapon against terrorism. We look to your enlightened self-interest. We want you to do well by doing good." The new technologies can make a difference. With new software and X-ray machines, New Jersey's Newark Elizabeth Seaport now scans 10% of its risky cargo, up from 2% a year ago. Work remains to be done, however. Nor is it just the government that will need to be protected; billions of dollars in security measures will be needed for private America as well.

How ultimately will the government handle the security issue? The first step in solving problems is simply to identify them, of course. Some important steps have been made. Intelligence agencies are sharing information on terrorists with law enforcement; indeed, the FBI and CIA, which once worked separately are now reportedly sharing information.

Will the OHS simply put Band-Aids on real problems? Will we have the kind of inefficiency and overlap of which the government is so often accused? While more than 40 federal entities are included in the structure of the OHS — including Border Patrol, the Immigration and Naturalization Service, Transportation Security Administration and the Secret Service — some have wondered why the FBI and CIA have been omitted. The *USA Today* reports that in 1998 the Justice Department gave grants to local and state governments to combat terrorism. As of March 2002, $243 million had yet to be spent. Nearly $1 million was spent on equipment that couldn't be used because it wasn't distributed, was missing, or because no one was able to operate it. Nor did the Justice Department develop a standard to measure if the governments were able to improve their ability to handle terrorist attacks.

Sources: "Sluggish Sept. 11 Response Leaves Holes in Security." *USA Today*, May 29, 2002, p. 12A; "Securing the Homeland Strengthening the Nation." Retrieved from http://www.whitehouse.gov; "A huge government reorganization for homeland security." Retrieved from http://www.cnn.com; Dreazen, Yochi J. "Spreading the Wealth." *Wall Street Journal*, March 28, 2002, p. R7; "High-Tech is Starting to Kick In." *BusinessWeek*, September 16, 2002, p. 30; Michel Martin. "Spy vs. Cop." Retrieved from http://www.abcnews.com; Steven Roberts. "Office of Homeland Security Facing Daunting Challenges." *National Defense*, April 2002, p. 48. "America's Biggest Job." *BusinessWeek*, June 10, 2002, p. 34; "Chasing the Security Dollar." *American Shipper*, August 2002, p. 70. Jim Drinkard. "Businesses See Bonanza in Homeland Security." *USA Today*, July 10, 2002.

Terrorism: Tracking the Deaths

Deaths of U.S. Citizens from Domestic and International Terrorism, 1981-1999

Killed internationally   Killed domestically

Shortly after the attacks of September 11, the National Center for Health Statistics designated terrorism as a new classification of death.

Categories for terrorism are not included under the two major codes used to track mortality in the United States: the World Health Organization's International Classification of Diseases and the United States Clinical Modification of the ICD. Without these new codes, it would be difficult to identify and track deaths by terrorism.

Shortly after the September attacks, the victims were categorized as homicides and the terrorists as suicides. However, a short time later the CDC began receiving requests from medical examiners and state vital statistics offices requesting a uniform method of categorizing deaths and injuries from the tragedy. The CDC put together a coding system with two dozen subcategories of death by terrorist activity. Their blueprint was this definition of a terrorism death: "Injuries resulting from the unlawful use of force or violence against persons or property to intimidate or coerce a Government, the civilian population, or any segment thereof, in furtherance of political or social objectives."

The CDC provides a mortality classification for terrorism involving the explosion of marine weapons, the destruction of aircraft, "fires, conflagration, and hot substances," nuclear weapons, and biological or chemical weapons. "What we hope is that these codes never get used again," said Dr. Robert Anderson, lead statistician in the mortality statistics branch of the National Center for Health Statistics.

The designation of homicides will remain for the victims of September 11. The additional terrorism categories serves as an additional layer to provide explanation for the large number of deaths in the country. The nearly 3,000 deaths will represent a significant increase in the homicide rate for 2001. By subtracting the terrorism casualties, CDC officials will have a more accurate picture of the homicide rate (which has been declining over recent years). Final statistics have not been released, but some expect homicide to jump from perhaps the 14th leading cause of death to the 12th. The new category will not be applied to earlier terrorism deaths, such as the victims of the Oklahoma City bombing in 1995. If it were, more than 700 more deaths would receive such a classification.

There have been other recent additions to mortality statistics. HIV was included in 1987. Sudden Infant Death Syndrome was included in 1973.

Source: Chart data comes from http://www.albany.edu/sourcebook/1995/pdf/t3201.pfd; Hostetler, A.J. "U.S. Focus: Understanding Homicide Rate." *Times-Dispatch*, September 110, 2002; "Classification of Death and Injury Resulting from Terrorism." Retrieved September 12, 2002 from http://www.cdc.gov; Elizabeth Weinstein. "Tracking Terror's Rising Toll." *Wall Street Journal*, January 25, 2002, P. A13.

September 11, 2001: By the Numbers

Number killed in the attack on America: **3,025**

Number of New York firefighters killed: **343**

Number of New York Police officers: **60**

Time it took to build the World Trade Center: **6 years, 8 months** (from 1966 to 1973)

Time it took to destroy the Towers, from first impact to second collapse: **1 hour, 42 minutes**.

Number of days to remove debris from the World Trade site: **261**

Square feet of leased office space destroyed in the World Trade Center: **14 million**

Estimated number of employers who had to relocate at least temporarily after the attacks: **100,000**

Number of people who lost their jobs directly or indirectly from the attacks: almost **129,000**

Starting salary of New York City police officer: **$31,304**

Starting salary of a New York Port Authority police officer: **$32,361**

Starting salary of an airport security baggage screener: **$35,000**

Spending on homeland defense in 1998: **$10.5 billion**

Spending on homeland defense budgeted for 2003: **$37.7 billion**

Number of detainees being held at the U.S. Navy base in Guantanamo Bay, Cuba, accused of belonging to Al-Qaeda or the Taliban (as of September 2002): **564**

Number of FBI agents devoted to the investigation of terrorist activities: **2,600**

Number of air marshals thought to have been hired since September 11, 2001: as many as **6,000** (the exact number of air marshals is classified)

Number of air marshals thought to have quit: fewer than **80**

Number of books published about the attacks as of September 2002: over **150** (and counting)

Number of applications to trademark the phrase "Let's Roll" (stated by Todd Beamer on Flight 93 before passengers seized control of the hijacked plane): **14**

Number of people who requested Peace Corps applications after President Bush's State of the Union speech in 2002 (encouraging people to become more involved in their communities): over **76,000**; number requesting Citizen Corps program applications: **48,000**

Number of items confiscated by airport security from February 17, 2002 to March 26, 2002: **449,417**

Cost of the attack on New York City: **$83-95 billion**

Amount lost on Broadway on September 12-13, 2001: **$3 million**

Cost of the attack on the Pentagon: **$700 million**

Insurance payments from the Sept. 11 attacks: **$40.2 billion**

Estimated cost of 1993 World Trade Center bombing: **$9 million**

Estimated cost of Oklahoma City bombing: **$250 million**

Amount raised by *America: A Tribute to Heroes* telethon: **$112 million**

Amount raised by the 36 largest charities related to September 11: **$2.4 billion**

Amount of money stolen from a Red Cross relief fund by 12 Port Authority employees who claimed, falsely, to have lost their jobs: **$14,065**

Looting arrests in New York City on September 11: **6**; By October 11: **60**

Number of bomb threats phoned into police on September 11: **92**

Sales increase of Fisher-Price's "Rescue Heroes" (fire fighter, paramedic, and police officer action figures) in one year: **70%**

Sales increase for G.I. Joe: **56%**

Sales of flags at Wal-Mart on September 11, 2000: **6,400**; Sales on September 11, 2001: **116,000**

Sales increase of survival gear (like gas masks) at CheaperthanDirt.com: **500%**

New York City's annual revenue from tourism: **$25 billion**

Number of domestic tourists to New York City in 2000: **29.4 million**; in 2001: **29.5 million**

Number of estimated visitors to ground zero by the end of 2002: **3.6 million**

Those who said they are "more loving" to family members in a recent survey: **80%**

Sources: "September 11: For the Record." *USA Today*, September 10, 2002, p. 6D; "Remains of a Day." *Time*, September 9, 2002, p. 59; Grant, Peter and Motoko Rich. "How Damaged Is Downtown?" *Wall Street Journal*, September 11, 2002, p. B1; Kim Campbell. "The New Normal: Gas Masks, Insomnia and Civility." *Christian Science Monitor*, September 27, 2001, p. 2; "9/11 Charities: Where the Money Went." *Kiplinger Magazine*, September 2002; Michael Okwu. "Flight 93 charity seeks 'let's roll' trademark." Retrieved from http://www.cnn.com; Blake Morrison. "Air Marshals' Resignations Flood TSA, Managers Say." *USA Today*, August 29, 2002; "U.S. toy trends break with the past after 11th september attacks." Retrieved from http://www.tdctrade.com; Chrisena Coleman. "Fresh faces for PA." Retrieved from http://www.nycpba.org; David Broder. "No Service?" *Detroit Free Press*, September 5, 2002, p. 15A; "Airport Breaches Challenge Security Agency." *USA Today*, April 10, 2002, p. 5A; Michael Freedman. "Compensatory Damages." *Forbes*, September 16, 2002, p. 50; Barbara Hagenbaugh. "U.S. Economy's Resilience Could be Greatest Story." *USA Today*, September 11, 2002, p. B1; Bob Minzesheimer. "Sept. 11, 2001: A Date That Lives on the Best Seller List." p. D1; Jayson Blair. "Americans Visit More but Spend Less." *New York Times*, September 5, 2001, p. A19; "New York City police officer." Retrieved from http://www.learnatest.com; "House, Senate pass aviation security bill," "NYC officials predict uneven hotel occupancy for 9/11," "FBI unveils reorganization to focus on terror." Retrieved from http://www.cnn.com; Jennifer Harper." Poll Shows Effects of Terrorism Fading." *Washington Times*, July 28, 2002. "For the Record." November 19, 2001, p. 27; Kate Carillo. "Even theater can't escape." Retrieved from http://www.freshangles.com/diversionz/theatre/articles/26.html; All Internet sources retrieved September 18, 2002.

Chapter 8

Law Enforcement

Less than 1 million men and women are sworn law enforcement officers — carry a firearm and have the ability to make arrests. People depend on them to protect property, save lives, and to uphold the law. This chapter will examine law enforcement officers and the issues surrounding this profession.

As stated through this book, the crime rate fell dramatically over the last two decades. In earlier chapters we've seen the murder rate fall and areas enjoy lower incidents of property crime. There are complex reasons for these decreases, of course. But what role has the police played in this development?

Some agencies are now better equipped. Many now have computers and other forms of technology to help them do their work, something they did not have pre-1990. Many departments have boosted training and requirements of their new cadets. A smarter, more mature, better trained cadet has a better chance of being a more effective law enforcer.

In the 1990s, many departments adopted a policy of "zero tolerance" — most notably the New York Police Department (the nation's largest police force). Law enforcement would vigorously go after smaller crimes just like the big ones — the belief being that behavioral crimes like loitering and drunkenness may lead to more violent crimes. The police also refined crime prevention programs, or instituted new ones, aided by the 1994 Crime Act. Police could now really target the ills that plague the population: gangs, drugs, missing children, drunk driving, and bias-related assaults.

It's difficult to argue with such efforts. Cities saw their murder rate plunge and many areas in cities were suddenly deemed "safe" again. But some people, often from minority communities, have found law enforcement's efforts simply too aggressive. Many people of color have charged police with racism and brutality. Several panels in this chapter will examine these issues. What is "use of force"? How present is it in police departments? Racial profiling is another contentious issue making headlines. Does it exist? Is so, what are its origins?

The chapter's focus will shift slightly and examine federal law officers. How large are their law enforcement departments? We'll pay special attention to the rise of women and minorities in its ranks, and how the agencies have been shaped by the threat of terrorism. The chapter also examines how terrorism has shaped common law enforcement practices.

Indeed, 70 law enforcement officers were killed in the terrorist attacks on the World Trade Center. The police — and all who provide public service — found themselves receiving a new level of respect from the nation. One can only hope that such respect will endure.

Significant Dates in Law Enforcement

1712 – The first full-time paid law enforcement officials are hired in the United States by the city of Boston.

1784 – First officer in United States history, U.S. Marshal Robert Forsyth, is killed in the line of duty.

1823 – Stephen F. Austin (regarded as the father of Texas) obtains permission from the Mexican government to employ ten men to protect the new Texas frontier. This marks the beginning of the Texas Rangers.

1858 – Boston and Chicago are the first police departments to issue uniforms to their officers.

1878-1881 – "Billy the Kid" kills six law enforcement officers in New Mexico.

1902 – Fingerprinting is first used in the United States.

1916 – The first female member of law enforcement is killed.

1924 – J. Edgar Hoover is appointed director of the FBI.

1932 – Bonnie and Clyde and their gang murder 10 law enforcement people, more than any other individual criminal — or pair.

1932 – After the Lindbergh kidnapping case, the Federal Kidnapping Act is passed, giving the FBI (then the Bureau of Investigation) the right to investigate kidnappings that involve crossing state borders.

1933 – Gangster "Machine Gun" Kelly reportedly coins the name "G-Men" for FBI agents (G-men stands for government men).

1935 – The New York Police Department's Commissioner orders policewomen to adopt a uniform and to learn how to shoot.

1935 – The Department of Investigations becomes the Federal Bureau of Investigations.

1937 – Two-way communication between patrol cars and precincts is introduced in New York City.

1950 – The FBI initiates the Ten Most Wanted Fugitives Program as a way to capture elusive criminals.

1951 – *Dragnet* airs on December 16 on NBC with Jack Webb as its star, the TV version of the 1949 radio show of the same name.

1965 – The case Miranda vs. Arizona makes its way to the Supreme Court. The justices rule that the accused have the right to remain silent and that prosecutors may not use statements made by defendants while in police custody unless police have advised defendants of their rights, now known as Miranda Rights. (In the case, Miranda's lawyers argued that his signed confession should have been thrown out because Miranda did not know he had the right not to incriminate himself).

1965 – The TV show, *The FBI*, begins to air on ABC starring Efrem Zimbalist, Jr. Each show had to be cleared by the FBI and FBI's J. Edgar Hoover.

1966 – President Johnson signs the Freedom of Information Act.

1969 – The 911 system and computer-aided dispatch are instituted, which allow for a quicker response to emergency calls.

1972 – The FBI opens a new training facility at Quantico, Virginia.

1973 – The film *Serpico* is released, starring Al Pacino as the real life New York undercover policeman who exposed undercover corruption on the force.

1975 – Kevlar body armor begins field testing in 15 urban police departments.

1985 – The year is christened the "Year of the Spy" after a number of high profile espionage cases.

1988 – 50% of the killings in New York City are drug related.

1988 – The Fox network premiers *America's Most Wanted*, a show that profiles wanted fugitives.

1992 – Police protest the song *Cop Killer* by Rap music star Ice T.

1993 – A bomb explodes under the World Trade Center in New York City, killing six persons and injuring over 1,000 others; the Bureau of Alcohol and Tobacco raids the compound of David Koresh in Waco, Texas; Louis Freeh is sworn in as the new director of the FBI.

1999 – Osama bin Laden is added to the FBI's list of most wanted fugitives.

2001 – The FBI and the Joint Terrorist Task Force investigate the September 11 attacks on the World Trade Center and Pentagon.

Sources: "Ernest Miranda, Miranda vs. Arizona" available online at http://www.thecapras.org; "A Historical Look at the Texas Rangers." Available online at http://destinynet.com/texasrangers/history.htm; "Remember When?" available at http://www.cleat.org; "Important Dates in Police History." Available at http://www.nleomf.com; and FBI timeline from http://www.fbi.gov. Data retrieved November 5, 2002.

Law Enforcement Personnel

Number of Sworn Law Enforcement Employees in the United States

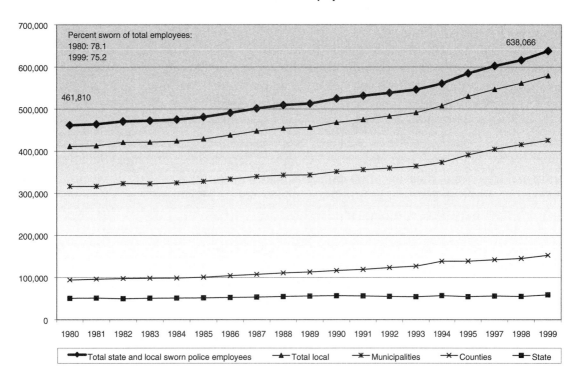

In 2000, there were 796,518 full-time sworn law enforcement officers in the United States. This figure includes people at 12,666 local police stations, in 3,070 sheriff departments, at 1,376 special jurisdiction police agencies, in 49 primary state offices, and in 623 Texas constable offices.[1] These agencies provides employment for 1,019,496 individuals, including non-sworn (civilian) personnel. The panel above analyzes only sworn employees who make up roughly three quarters of law enforcement personnel. The remaining employees are civilians.

Employment in law enforcement is on the increase. Between June of 1996 and 2000, the number of full time employees increased by about 97,500; this translates into 44,500 new sworn employees (a jump of 6.7%) and 53,000 for civilians (a jump of about 20%). This increase in employment means the number of state and local law enforcement employees has increased almost 10% since 1992, from 330 to 362 per 100,000 residents. The Northeast had the highest ratio of sworn officers to the population, 2.8 per 1,000.

---

[1] Of the roughly 760 county constable offices in Texas, 623 operated on a full-time basis and employed sworn personnel with general arrest powers as of June 2000. Texas constables are elected officials who are responsible for providing services for the justice, county, and district courts. Nearly half of the sworn personnel employed by constable offices primarily performed court-related duties. Nearly half of constable offices had sworn personnel regularly assigned to respond to calls for service.

The New York City Police Department is the largest, and the largest law enforcement agency of any kind in the country, with 53,029 full-time employees and 40,435 officers. The largest sheriff's office is in Los Angeles County, with 8,468 officers. The California Highway Patrol is the largest state agency, with 6,678 officers.

What does it take to be a police officer? According to the Department of Labor, candidates must be U.S. citizens and usually be at least 20 years of age. Candidates may expect to complete a number of physical tests, including vision, hearing, and strength. They will also have to complete written and oral exams. Candidates will also undergo psychological testing. Does the potential recruit possess the morals that all police officers should possess? Is he or she honest, in possession of good judgment, integrity and a sense of responsibility? Does he or she have basic "people skills" — respect, patience and ability to listen? Most candidates will undergo a lie detector test. In state and local departments, recruits get training in their agency's police academy, which lasts 12 to 14 weeks, although many are closer to 20 weeks. Employment for police and detectives is growing faster than the national average through the year 2010.

The term "men in blue" to describe police officers is still quite accurate; men constitute 89% of all sworn officers nationally. They represent 89.1% of the sworn officers in cities, 91.9% of those in rural counties, and 87.2% in suburban counties. Women were 11% of all sworn officers nationally; they were about 63% of all civilian employees.

Civilians constituted 29.4% of the total law enforcement workforce in 2000, up slightly from 28% in 1996. They were 22.7% of the law enforcement employees in cities, but 39.4% in suburban counties and 38.5% in rural counties, figures that have changed little since 1996.

The image of the police officer in society seems dominated by two stereotypes. One is a noble enforcer of the law. We turn to them in a crisis; we teach our children to seek them out when in trouble. Shows such as *COPS* and *NYPD Blue* have been on television for nearly a decade and have devoted followings. There's also an uglier image of law enforcement. A number of films in recent decades show cops beating up suspects, addicted to drugs, and "on the take" from organized crime. News reports of police misconduct make the news on a regular basis. Law enforcement arguably received its blackest eye in recent years during the O.J. Simpson trial with reports of cops being racists, planting evidence, and mishandling crime scenes.

The rest of this chapter will look at those in charge of upholding the law. Is the police force changing along with our society?

Sources: Chart data comes from Department of Justice Sourcebook and *Bureau of State and Local Law Enforcement Agencies, 2000.* Job information comes from *Occupational Outlook Handbook* available online from http://stats.bls.gov/oco/ocos160.htm.

The Few Who Serve Many

Areas of Duty for Full-Time Personnel, 1996 and 2000

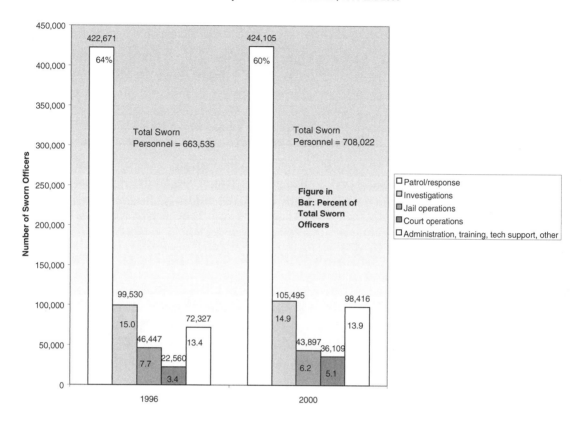

Roughly 424,000, or 60%, of full-time state and local sworn employees were patrol officers or other uniformed officers whose regularly assigned duties included responding to calls for service. Uniformed officers are assigned a specific area to patrol, such as a section of a downtown area or a residential neighborhood. They may work alone, but in large cities they frequently have a partner. During their shift they observe and resolve problems in the community, pursue and arrest suspects, identify potential hazards, and enforce traffic laws. State patrol officers (sometimes called state troopers or highway patrol officers) arrest criminals statewide and are best known for issuing tickets to motorists.

Less than half a million officers are available to answer calls for service — for a nation of 275 million people. What is the ratio to population? The per capita ratio of uniformed officers, whose regular duties include responding to calls for service, is just 151 per 100,000 people nationally.

For most local law enforcement agencies, roughly half of the force is devoted to responding to service calls. The New York City Police Department has 39,099 sworn officers; 21,142 of them (or 54%) respond to calls for service from the 9.3 million residents of the city. The Los Angeles Department has 9,573 officers; 5,000 of them (or 52%) respond to calls for aid from the 9.5 million residents. How many calls for service do agencies receive? It varies, of course, but even large departments and cities may find themselves devoting considerable time and resources to dealing with the public. For the year ended June 1999, the California Highway Patrol received more than 4 million 911 and non-emergency calls. Chicago operators, by one count, must field 15 million emergency requests every year.

Approximately 1 in 9 officers perform duties related to jail or court operations. Nearly 44,000 officers had duties primarily related to jails, a figure down about 5.5% from 1996. The number of officers whose primary duties involved administrative or training work increased 36% between 1996 and 2000.

The personnel whose primary duties were in court operations increased 60% between 1996 and 2000, from 22,560 to 36,109 officers.[2] More officers were needed to provide security at the nation's overburdened court system. The 1980s and 1990s saw the rise of night, family, drug and even mental health courts to address citizens' needs. Indeed, many of the 300 plus drug courts in the country came into existence just in the early 1990s (see Chapter 10 for more information on the court system). Law enforcement personnel were needed to serve papers and documents, to provide security at entrances and throughout the building, to protect judges, and to provide escort services.

What about those who really actively work to solve the cases? Only 15% of sworn personnel (about 105,000) are devoted primarily to investigations. The number of officers represents a 6% increase over the figure for 1996. Some investigators, according to the Department of Labor, may work on special programs to combat specific crimes. Most of the others spend time doing what one sees on numerous police shows: interviewing suspects, reviewing documents, observing suspects, conducting raids, and making arrests.

Between 1996 and 2000, there was a 36% increase in officers performing administrative or training work. More personnel are involved in helping the legal system to run. This is important, to be sure. But when one considers how few crimes are actually cleared by arrest (about 20%), one wonders: should the police be better funded? Should more officers be on the street?

Sources: U.S. Department of Justice, Bureau of Justice Statistics, *Census of State and Local Law Enforcement Agencies, 1996 and 2000; Law Enforcement Management and Statistics, 1999*; court data comes from U.S. Department of Justice and job data from the Department of Labor.

---

[2] Of the roughly 760 country constable offices in Texas, 623 operated on a full-time basis and employed sworn personnel with general arrest powers as of June 2000. Texas constables are elected officials who are responsible for providing services for the justice, county and district courts. Nearly half of the sworn personnel employed by constable offices primarily performed court related duties. Nearly half of constable offices had sworn personnel regularly assigned to respond to calls for service.

A Changing Police Force

Minorities in Large Police Departments

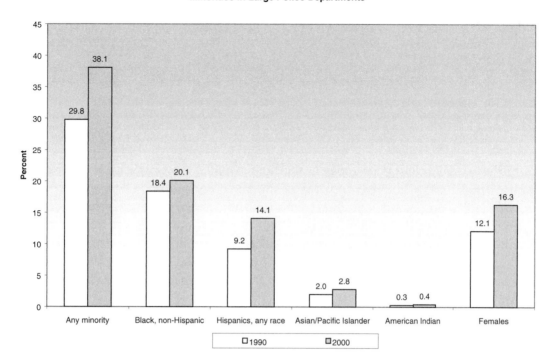

Many police departments have made a concerted effort to hire more minority officers. Are police forces starting to resemble the diverse population they serve?

The graphic shows that more women and minorities appear among the ranks of law enforcement personnel in large cities in 2000 than in 1990. Roughly 38% of officers were a member of a minority, up from about 30% in 1990. Just over 16% of the force were women, up from 12% in 1990. The shifts represent some significant growth rates. In the 1990s, the percentage of the force that belonged to a minority climbed 28% and the percentage that were females climbed 35%.

The Department of Justice uses a ratio to calculate the racial composition of police forces in relation to city residents.[3] From 1990 to 2000, the average ratio increased from .59 to .63 for minorities overall. Police departments had 63 minority police officers for every 100 minority residents in 2000, up from 59 officers from 1990. In other words, the racial and ethnic makeup of police departments were slightly more representative of the cities they served.

But there is still much work to be done. Large cities such as New York, Los Angeles, and Chicago tend to be ethnic and racial melting pots. As the table shows, the largest police

---

[3] The ratio is based on the percentage of sworn personnel who were members of a racial or ethnic minority relative to the percentage of city residents who were members of that minority group.

forces in the nation do have more officers of African American and Hispanic descent. Their ranks do not yet represent the diverse population of their cities.

Blacks and Hispanics in the Largest Police Forces

	% of Blacks, Sworn Person-nel, 1990	% of Blacks, Sworn Person-nel, 2000	% of City Population that are Black, 2000	% of His-panics, Sworn Personnel, 1990	% of His-panics, Sworn Personnel, 2000	% of City Population that are Hispanic, 2000
New York	12.6	13.3	27.0	12.1	17.8	27.0
Los Angeles	13.4	13.6	11,2	21.0	33.1	47.0
Chicago	23.6	25.9	37.0	6.0	12.7	26.0
Houston	14.4	19.4	25.0	11.4	17.9	37.0
Philadelphia	23.2	34.5	43.0	2.8	5.6	9.0

Some of the most striking gaps occur in the higher ranks. According to a 1999 study by the *New York Times*, of the 499 captains in the New York Police Department, 94% are white. Of the 237 inspectors and chiefs who run the force, 92% are white. Decisions to hire officers, sergeants, lieutenants, and captains are based on test scores. Some minority recruits contend they just don't perform as well as their white counterparts on promotion exams, making it difficult for them to rise through the ranks. In a study of 4,706 officers who passed the entrance exam and entered the Police Academy from 1997 to 1999, 65% were white, 20% Hispanic, and 11% black.

One study suggests a real benefit associated with more minority officers. John J. Dono-hue III of the Stanford Law School and Steven D. Levitt of the University of Chicago analyzed data from 134 large cities from 1977 to 1993. They discovered that when mi-nority officers patrolled neighborhoods largely composed of their own race, fewer arrests were made of people of that race. Also, while own-race policing had little effect on vio-lent crime arrests, it appears to have significantly reduced property crime arrests. Could black or Hispanic officers be real deterrents to crime in their neighborhoods? Could they even be held up as role models and boost the image of the police department in general?

Law enforcement has always had a strained relationship with minority communities. In a recent Harris Poll, 56% of both blacks and Hispanics thought police treat one or more of the races unfairly, while only 27% of whites claimed to feel this way. In a Henry J. Kai-ser, Harvard University, and Washington Post poll, 37% of blacks and 20% of Hispanics and Asians claim to have been stopped by police because of their race. In a five year study of the Cincinnati, Ohio police department, police confirm drawing their weapons 39 times during traffic stops, drug sweeps, the interrogation of suspects, and the detaining of people on the street; in all but one case they involved African-American citizens.

Highly publicized cases of white cops and black victims in recent years have only served to fan charges of corruption and bigotry. In 1991, Rodney King was beaten by four offi-cers of the Los Angeles Police Department. In 1997, Haitian immigrant Abner Louima was brutalized by Officer Justin Volpe with a toilet plunger in a New York police station bathroom. In February 1999, four white police officers approached Amadou Diallo out-side his South Bronx apartment and, in the confusion that followed, shot him 41 times, sparking public protests (and a song by Bruce Springsteen). In April 2001, a white police officer shot and killed unarmed Timothy Thomas in a Cincinnati alley. It was the fifth shooting of an African American male in six months by Cincinnati police, and the fifteenth since 1995. Three days of riots followed, prompting the mayor to impose a curfew.

In recent years the relationship between law enforcement and minorities has become even more strained through the practice of racial profiling. The next panel will examine this issue.

Sources: Chart data from U.S. Department of Justice, Bureau of Justice Statistics, *Police Departments in Large Cities, 1990-2000*, available online at http://www.ojp.usdoj.gov; Other data from the Sourcebook of Criminal Justice Statistics Online, located at http://albany.edu/sourcebook/1995/pdf/110015.pdf; "New York Police Department Among Least Racially Diverse." *Jet*, March 29, 1999, p. 40; Anglen, Robert. "Police Draw Guns on Blacks." *Cincinnati Enquirer*, April 21, 2002. "Justice Isn't Color Blind." *Business Week*, May 3, 1999, p. 27. "Most New Yorkers See Police Bias, Poll Finds." Available online from http://mbhs.bergtraum.k12.ny.us/cybereng/nyt/polls.htm. Data retrieved October 25, 2002.

Fighting Crime

Percent of Large Police Departments with Full-Time Special Units of Part-Time Personnel

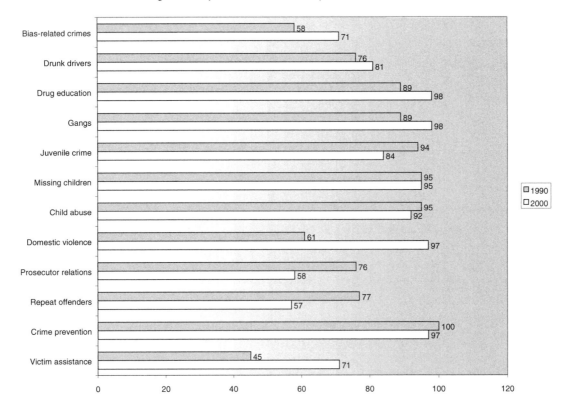

	1990	2000
Bias-related crimes	58	71
Drunk drivers	76	81
Drug education	89	98
Gangs	89	98
Juvenile crime	94	84
Missing children	95	95
Child abuse	95	92
Domestic violence	61	97
Prosecutor relations	76	58
Repeat offenders	77	57
Crime prevention	100	97
Victim assistance	45	71

Police departments in large cities (250,000 or higher) operate special units to target certain types of crime. The 1994 Crime Act played a vital role in this fight. The legislation, regarded as the most comprehensive piece of crime fighting legislation in history, authorized $8.8 billion in grants in community policing efforts. It also helped put an extra 100,000 police officers on the street.

In 1990, all large departments reported having personnel devoted full or part-time to crime prevention. That figure fell to 97% in 2000, perhaps in response to a decrease in the number of crimes being reported to law enforcement. Perhaps departments decided their efforts would be better served in targeting specific crimes. Crime prevention programs have obvious value: target problem areas and educate the public on how to protect themselves. When crimes do occur, more departments seem ready to help the victims: Agencies with units devoted to victim assistance increased from 45% to 71%.

Some of these special units specifically target young people — who are both perpetrators and victims of many types of crime. Ninety-eight percent of departments now have either part-time or full-time personnel addressing gangs. Gangs have traditionally been a thorny issue for law enforcement. The Department of Justice argues that government and police have often turned a blind eye to gangs, while citizens' groups and social agencies were more likely to acknowledge the problems created by these young people. In the 1970s, youth gangs were reported in 19 states; in 1995, all 50 states and the District of Columbia reported gang problems in at least one of their cities. Assuming the Department of Justice's belief is true, more departments appear willing to address this issue. Drug education in schools slipped only slightly during the 1990s; 95% of agencies have some sort of unit devoted to this (perhaps futile) task.

Many of these departments address behavior; they try to change attitudes and actions before a crime actually occurs. What about those who have had a "few too many"? Over 80% of police departments now have special units devoted to drunk driving, up from 76% in 1990. Alcohol played a role in 38% of all traffic fatalities in 2000, down from 50% in 1990. But more than 17,000 people died from alcohol-related accidents in 2001, about one every half hour, according to Mothers Against Drunk Driving. More than 70% of police departments now have units devoted to bias-related crimes, up sharply from 1990. Over 8,000 such crimes were reported in 2000. The issue of hate crime legislation became energized by several high profile murders of gays and blacks during the decade. Indeed, the government only began to track the number of bias-related incidents in the mid-1990s. Police efforts are important in tracking a crime that may be vastly underreported.

The percent of departments with personnel devoted to domestic violence increased during the 1990s. Roughly 1 million reported actions of violence by an intimate partner (current or former spouse, current of former boyfriend/girlfriend) are reported annually. But how many occur behind closed doors? The programs provide information to victims about where to go for help.

The percent of agencies with some sort of missing children's program remained steady during the decade. Most of these are part-time departments, in existence for when the unthinkable happens. How many children vanish each year? Justice Department officials and missing children groups estimate that between 2,400 and 3,600 kids are taken each year. These numbers include those children found very quickly after their disappearance.

Sources: U.S. Department of Justice, Bureau of Justice Statistics, *Police Departments in Large Cities, 1990-2000*; Leinwand, Donna. "Kidnapping Problem Impossible to Quantify." *USA Today*, August 15, 2002, p. 3A; community policing data comes from http://www.usdoj.gov; "Gang Cities." available from http://www.ncjrs.org; Mothers Against Drunk Driving website located at http://www.mad.org.

How the Police Do Their Jobs

Departments With Selected Policies

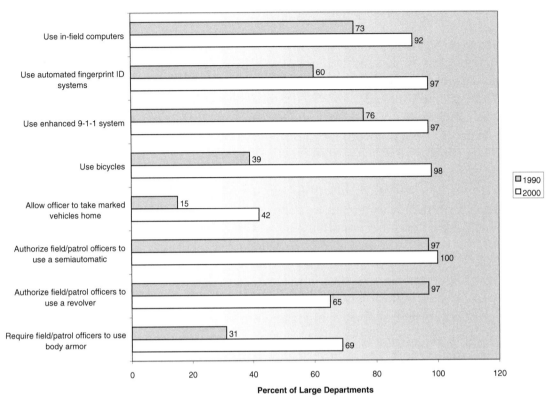

Many large police departments saw significant changes in the 1990s.[4]

Are more police agencies seeing new forms of crime fighting technology? The percent with enhanced 9-1-1 capabilities, which allow the caller's location to be electronically pinpointed, grew from 76% in 1990 to 97% in 2000. Those using in-field computers grew from 73% to 92% and those with automated fingerprint ID systems with 60% to 97%.

Some departments have recognized the value of getting back to basics. Nearly all departments have officers on bicycles, up significantly from 1990. Law enforcement has come to recognize the value of making police officers visible to the public. Many of these cops are now "walking their beat" as they did a century ago, integrating into the community that they protect. In some cases, bikes are simply a more cost- and time-effective way to patrol the city.

What of an officer's personal protection? The percent of agencies authorizing the use of a revolver fell from 97% to 65%. But all agencies now authorize the use of semi-automatic weapons. Thirty-one percent of agencies required officers to wear at least some body ar-

---

[4] Large departments serve a population of 250,000 citizens or more.

mor in 1990; ten years later, 69% of agencies make this requirement. Perhaps this requirement was seen as just "sound policy." More officers died by firearms in the 1990s then at any other time in this century.

A most interesting point is the change in police officer training. The median number of training hours increased 16% during the decade, from 760 to 880 hours. The median hours of field training increased 15%, from 520 to 600 hours. The minimum educational requirement for new officers has increased. Nearly 10% of departments require a 2 year degree; nearly 5% require a four year degree.

The typical officer is getting more training. More crime fighting tools are at his disposal. Salaries remained stubbornly flat during the 1990s. The average starting base salary for a police chief (in a city of more than 250,000 residents) rose by about 2% from $95,393 to $97,215. The average starting salary for a sergeant increased 3%, from $49,081 to $50,541. An entry-level patrol officer fell 1%, from $35,002 to $34,556.

Minimum Starting Salaries in Departments

Serving More than 250,000 Residents

Position	1990	2000
Chief	$95,393	$97,215
Sergeant	$49,081	$50,541
Entry-level Patrol Officer	$35,002	$34,556

More agencies reported offering shift differential pay in 2000 than 1990 (76% vs. 66%). But fewer agencies reported offering hazardous duty pay (56% to 50%) and merit pay (35% to 34%).

Source: Reaves, Brian Ph.D. and Matthew J. Hickman. Bureau of Justice Statistics. *Police Departments in Large Cities, 1990-2000.*

The Deaths of Police Officers

Police Officers Killed in the Line of Duty, 1900-2000

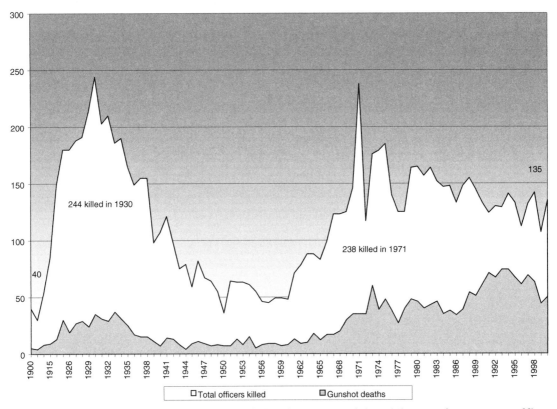

244 killed in 1930

238 killed in 1971

40

135

☐ Total officers killed   ☐ Gunshot deaths

From 1900 to 2000 more than 14,000 federal, state and local law enforcement officers were killed in the line of duty.

The number of police officer deaths roughly tripled from 1900 to 1920, from 40 to 150. Prohibition began in January 1920 — and with it came an organized network of crime to distribute alcohol illegally to the thirsty population. The rise of organized crime proved deadly for police. There were over 1,800 officers killed in the 1920s, the most of any decade in this century. In 1929, more than 200 police officers were killed for the first time. A year later, 244 officers were killed. This remains as the largest number of deaths of police officers in a single year. By 1933, the year Prohibition was repealed, the number of police officer deaths began to decline.

The number of police officer deaths began to climb in the 1960s and 1970s, coinciding with a jump in the violent crime rate (see Chapter 2). A complex combination of social and economic factors were at work during these decades. A generation of young people were experimenting with rock music and drugs. They were protesting the Vietnam War. Labor and civil rights groups were actively staging protests. Encounters between police and blacks were often tense and increasingly violent; blacks rioted in Detroit and other cities. Some leftist political groups were pursuing violence as a way to address some political cause (Chapter 13, Terrorism, focuses on some of these groups). Law enforcement

— seen as oppressors and/or traditional authority — were invariably targets. Police officer deaths climbed from 125 in 1965 to 150 in 1966 to 180 in 1967. In 1971, a total of 238 officers were killed, the second highest total in the 100 year period.

The police recognized the need to protect themselves through new programs and better training. SWAT (Special Weapons and Tactics) teams originated with the Los Angeles Police Department in the 1960s when it became obvious, as the National Tactical Officers Association puts it, that "the average police officer, equipped only with a revolver and a basic training, had become especially vulnerable to the kind of organized and vicious criminal and terrorist activity that existed more frequently at that time in America." Training was indeed a critical issue. Training policies varied from state to state and even within the state itself. California was the first state to standardize the way it trained its law enforcement personnel with the creation of the Peace Officer Standards and Training Commission in 1959. Other states soon followed California's lead. There was also better protection available. After several years of testing, Kevlar body armor (light-weight bulletproof vests that an officer could wear full-time) was subjected to its first field test in 1975 when it went into use in 15 urban police departments.

What has been the single largest cause of police deaths over the century? Guns. Firearms were implicated in about half of all deaths of police officers. Since the 1970s, guns are claiming more lives: 405 officers were killed in the 1970s, 426 in the 1980s, and 651 in the 1990s. Do we need stricter gun control laws in this country? Could such legislation help control police deaths? Guns claimed the lives of 6,846 officers over the last century, according to the National Law Enforcement Officers Memorial Fund (NLEOMF). The next highest category, auto accidents, claimed only a third of this number: 2,090.

Leading Causes of Deaths

for Law Enforcement, 1900-1998

Cause	Percent of All Deaths
Firearms	49%
Automobile accidents	15%
Motorcycle accidents	7%
Struck by vehicle	7%
Job-related illness	4%

The vast majority of these officers have been male. From 1900 to 2000, only 156 of officers killed in the line of duty have been females. The first was a jail matron in Ohio named Anna Hart killed during a July 1916 escape attempt. According to the NLEOMF, over the last 100 years the average age of officers killed was 38. The average length of service was about eight years. Recent statistics from the FBI and Department of Justice show that from 1980 to 1999, between 80-90% of those feloniously killed have been white. Black officers constitute most of the remaining deaths. Also, a growing percentage of these officers were in uniform at the time (52% in 1982, 63% in 1990 and 80% in 2000).

In the 1970s the government began to make a distinction between accidental and felonious deaths (those committed by a felon). The leading accidental cause of death, as stated above, were automobile accidents. In recent years, accidents have claimed more lives

Accidental and Felonious Police Deaths

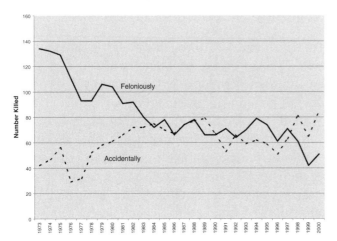

than felonious actions. Automobile deaths were responsible for about half of the 1,423 police officers who died accidentally from 1980 to 2000. The number of auto accident fatalities is up slightly: 33 deaths in 1997, 48 in 1998, 41 in 1999 and 42 in 2000. Some of these vehicle accidents involved a certain type of police car: the Crown Victoria. The vehicle had been involved in a series of crashes across the country; a dozen officers have died since 1983. In October 2002, the National Highway Traffic Safety Administration concluded that the Crown Victoria Police Interceptor meets federal standards that require a vehicle to withstand a rear crash at 30 mph without leaking fuel. While the vehicles are not defective, they will be made safer with the installation of gas tank shields. The shields will reduce the chances of a fire if the vehicle is struck.

An additional 279 officers were struck by other vehicles at traffic stops, directing traffic or assisting motorists. The next leading causes of death were airplane accidents and being struck by a vehicle while directing traffic or assisting a motorist, each with about 11% of the total.

More than 230 police officers were killed in the line of duty in 2001, making it the deadliest year since 1974. Included in the total are the 70 officers killed at the World Trade Center.

Sources: Chart data from 1900-1944 comes from the National Law Enforcement Officers Memorial Fund; 1945-2000 comes from *Historical Statistics of the United States* and *Statistical Abstract of the United States, 2001*; Gunshot data from http://www.odmp.org/index.php. Figures are all estimates. Data on accidental and felonious killings come from Sourcebook of Criminal Justices Online, table 3.175 and 3.179 from http://www.albany.edu/sourcebook/1995/pdf/t3179.pdf; "About the NTOA." Available online from http://www.ntoa.org/about/ntoa.html; "A History of Body Armor." Available from http://www.investors.about.com/library/investors/blforensic2.htm; "Police Training in a Democracy." Available online from http://usinfo.state.gov/journals/itdhr/1197/ijde/marinen.htm; Othon, Nancy. "Ford to Install Gas Tank Shields on Police Cars Nationwide." *Knight-Ridder/Tribune Business News*, October 8, 2002.

Use of Force

Reported Incidents of Force Used in City Departments, 1991

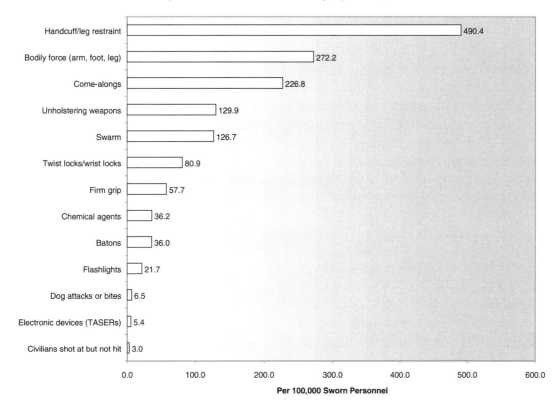

Category	Per 100,000 Sworn Personnel
Handcuff/leg restraint	490.4
Bodily force (arm, foot, leg)	272.2
Come-alongs	226.8
Unholstering weapons	129.9
Swarm	126.7
Twist locks/wrist locks	80.9
Firm grip	57.7
Chemical agents	36.2
Batons	36.0
Flashlights	21.7
Dog attacks or bites	6.5
Electronic devices (TASERs)	5.4
Civilians shot at but not hit	3.0

Per 100,000 Sworn Personnel

An estimated 43.8 million people 16 years or older had some contact with the police during 1999, according to the Justice Department. Roughly 422,000 of these contacts (or less than 1%) resulted in police force or threat of force. Force is given a very broad definition by the Department of Justice. It includes pushing a person, firm grips on the arm, the use of chemical agents, the use of a baton or a revolver. Officers are trained to use only the force necessary to diffuse a situation.

Of all contacts with the police, 2% of both blacks and Hispanics reported force or the threat of force. Just under 1% of whites reported force or threat of force. Significantly, 57% of those involved in a police force situation reported that they had argued, disobeyed or resisted, or had been using drugs or alcohol at the time of the encounter.

In the 1960s and 1970s, citizens frequently came into contact with the police during labor, anti-war, and civil rights demonstrations. In these situations, the police did use what would be called excessive force. As the name suggests, this means force in excess of what is appropriate for the situation. But there is no definition of what is "reasonable" or "appropriate" force in a particular situation; an officer must decide on a case-by-case basis, a situation that can potentially lead to charges of police brutality.

Deadly or excessive force is difficult to analyze because of a dearth of statistics on the subject. The government does not collect comprehensive statistics. Police departments are, for obvious reasons, unwilling to release data on the misconduct of officers. Also, to address the issue of excessive force, some critics have argued data must be collected on all use of force.

Anthony Pate and Lorie Fridell conducted a study on the use of force by police in 1994. They used a representative sample of 1,697 law enforcement agencies that covered four population categories (below 10,000; 10,000 to 24,999; 25,000 to 49,999; and 50,000 or more). Their results, included in the government report *National Data Collection - Police Use of Force*, are shown in the graph above. The most common types of force used were those least likely to result in injury: handcuffs, restraints, or verbal threats. The methods that are more likely to hurt a civilian happen less frequently: chemical agents (Mace, for example), batons, flashlights, or police dogs. Not included in the panel are the most lethal forms: vehicle rammings (at a rate of 1 per 100,000 sworn officers), civilians shot and killed (0.9), or those shot and wounded (0.2).

It's intriguing data and frustrating to analyze: it only offers a single year's examination of officers' behavior. As with many surveys, there is a catch: not all departments require reporting the use of force. (Nearly all require reporting the use of deadly force, however.) Pate and Fridell report that 82% of departments require reporting the use of a baton, 72% require the use of chemical agents, and only 29% require reporting the use of handcuffs. The Bureau of Justice also notes that force data are easy to misrepresent by reason of overlapping terminology: *police use of force*, *excessive use of force* and *use of excessive force* represent three different types of conduct. The definitions become even more problematic because no standard definition of "force" exists.

Again, force is to be used as a last resort. Officers are trained to consider their presence in a situation as a potential deterrent to a crime, claims Lt. Colonel Richard Janke of the Cincinnati police, interviewed for a recent Cincinnati Enquirer article. Their presence can certainly help diffuse a situation. Step two is a verbal warning. Step three is a chemical irritant. Most experts agree that situations are generally resolved at this point. But what happens when they aren't? What about the worst-case scenario?

When police are asked to control public situations, charges of brutality inevitably follow. The 1999 World Trade Organization meeting in Seattle found police overwhelmed by groups of people who had come to protest the WTO's policies. In the American Civil Liberty Union's analysis of the event (a report called *Out of Control: Seattle's Flawed Response to Protests Against the World Trade Organization*) they cite the police's many abuses against peaceful protestors and bystanders, including the use of rubber bullets and tear gas and civil rights violations. Law enforcement out of control? Maybe. But police also observed protestors who were, according to a FAIR report, "at times playing to the television cameras by feigning injury." Activists were also supposedly trained to "fall down and start screaming and yelling whether you hit them or not." A small number in the crowd smashed windows and were responsible for $3 million in property damage. Certainly, many political activists know how to advance their agendas. But is it possible for an undertrained officer, in a threatening situation, to cross into the shadowy region called "excessive force"?

A look at individual police departments offers an interesting view of how individual agencies are handling this issue:

In 2001, a two-year federal investigation concluded that there was a pattern of excessive force in the **Washington D.C.** police department in the 1990s. An independent monitor will oversee the police force for the next five years. D.C. officers reportedly killed more people per resident in the 1990s than any other large city police force. Fifteen percent of the time force was used by police, it was determined to be excessive. The D.C. police were also found to be misusing police dogs. In analyzing data from 1996 to 1999, investigators found police dogs bit someone 70% of the time they were used (the rate should actually be 10% of the time). The police implemented a number of new programs during the investigation, and their efforts appear to be paying off: the number of people killed by police fell 82% from 1998 to 2000.

The **Cincinnati** police force faced a federal investigation after a series of excessive force incidents. The city faced a curfew when protestors rioted after a police officer was cleared in the shooting of black teenager Timothy Thomas. According to statistics, Cincinnati officers have more than 1 million contacts with citizens annually. Force complaints resulted from less than 1% of these cases. There had been 48 reported incidents in 2000, down from 54 in 1999 and 77 in 1998. The use of chemical sprays increased during this period, however, from 752 incidents in 1998 to 1,000 in 2000.

A September 2000 analysis of FBI data by the *Detroit Free Press* placed **Detroit** as the leader in deadly shootings by police. Detroit averaged 0.92 fatal shooting per resident, compared to 0.39 in New York, 0.56 in Los Angeles, and 0.68 in Houston (cities with larger forces and populations). Lawsuits against cops cost Detroit taxpayers $124 million in judgments from 1987 to 1999. New policies include department cadets getting 26 hours of training on when and how to use deadly force, up from the current 16 hours. Officer Eugene Brown grabbed headlines when he sued the Detroit Police department in 2001. He claimed lost wages and emotional duress when the Detroit Board of Police Commissioners reopened an investigation into his history of police shootings. Brown had killed three people and wounded a forth in nine separate shooting incidents since joining the force in 1993. He has been involved in more shootings than any other officer.

The **New York** Police Department is the largest in the country. The mostly white force has had a deeply troubled relationship with segments of the city's population. In the 1970s, there were reports of some officers regularly abusing their power — using their nightsticks on citizens with little or no provocation, for example. In the 1990s, Mayor Giuliani adopted a policy of "zero tolerance" to quality of life crimes (public drinking, vagrancy, etc.) saying that such crimes led to the more violent variety. The efforts paid off, to be sure; homicides fell 50% from 1990 to 1996. Businesses began to return to Times Square, and people felt safe walking the streets. But some have argued that zero tolerance policing was simply too aggressive. According to Charles Williams, 80 people died in confrontations with police in Mayor Giuliani's first term. The city paid $100 million to settle police misconduct complaints.

In 2001, there were 4,260 complaints filed against officers with the New York City Civilian Complaint Review Board, a 4% increase over complaints in 2000. (An interesting fact considering the events of 2001.) Complaints include force, abuse of authority, discourtesy, and offensive language. The complaints are down 11% from 1997 and 1999 however. Half of the filers are African Americans. The NYPD has made an effort to better integrate its force. Police Commissioner Safir has acknowledged that excessive force dipped 23% since he raised the age and educational requirements of new officers.

Sources: U.S. Department of Justice, Bureau of Justice Statistics, *National Data Collection on Police Use of Force*, April 1996; "Force or Threatened Force Used in Less than 1% of All Police-Public Interactions." available online from http://www.ojp.usdoj.gov; Andersen, Peggy. "Seattle Police Admit They Weren't Ready for WTO Violence." *Seattle Post Intelligencier*, April 4, 2000; "Pre-Convention Coverage Whitewashes Police Violence, Distorts Activists Agenda." Fairness and Accuracy in Reporting release available online at http://www.fair.org; David A. Fahrenthold. "U.S. Faults D.C. Police Use of Force in the 90s." *Washington Post*, June 14, 2001, p. B1; Charles Williams. "A Brief Look at the Historical Routs of Racism Towards Blacks." available online from http://kalumumagazine.com/police_brutality.htm; *New York City Civilian Complaint Review Board Status Report*, January-December 2001, available online at http://nyc.gov/html/ccrb/home.html; "A Bruised Thin Blue Line." *U.S. News & World Report*, March 29, 1999, p. 35; Jane Prendergast. "Police Use of Force Less than in Past." *Cincinnati Enquirer*, January 7, 2001; Ashenfelter, David and Joe Swickard. "Detroit Cops are Deadliest in the U.S." *Detroit Free Press*, May 15, 2000; "Detroit Cop Charged." Available online from http://www.abcnews.go.com.

Police Shootings

Justifiable Homicides by Police and Police Officers Killed

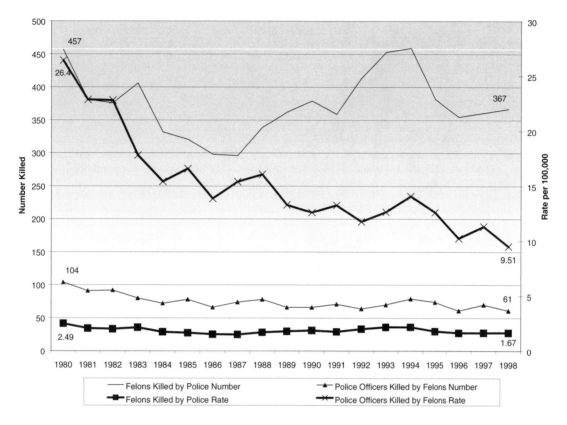

According to the Bureau of Justice Statistics, the killing of a felon is considered justified when it is done to "prevent the imminent death or serious bodily injury to the officer or another person."[5]

More than 7,000 felons were killed by police in justifiable homicides from 1980 to 1998. The rate fell from 2.49 per 100,000 people in 1980 (when 457 felons were killed) to 1.69 people in 1998 (when 367 felons were killed). These felons were almost always men. For the period shown, men have consistently made up at least 95% of such homicides. In 1998, the most recent year for statistics, 97.5% of felons killed were men and 2.5% were women.

These felons are usually white as well. At least half of the felons killed by police over the two decades shown have been white. The percent of felons that were African-Americans fell from a high of 48% in 1980 to 35% in 1998. Those of other races represent 2-3% of

---

[5] Data excludes negligent homicides, justifiable homicides by private citizens and murders in which the victim is someone other than a police officer slain in the line of duty.

---

felons killed by police. The racial distribution of felons is shown for selected years in the chart below.

Justifiable Homicides: The Race of Felons Killed by Police

	1980	1985	1990	1993	1994	1995	1996	1997	1998
White	51	61	62	55	57	59	61	63	62
Black	48	35	36	42	40	38	37	35	35
Other	1	4	2	3	3	3	2	2	3

What of police killed by felons? About 1,400 police officers were killed by felons. The rate fell from 26.44 to 9.51 per 100,000 sworn officers from 1980 to 1998. It is important to note that this rate is far higher than the rate for police shootings of felons.

Roughly 85% of officers killed during this period were white. As more African Americans join the force, they will potentially represent a growing share of police officer deaths. In 1998, 9% of police officer deaths were blacks. Just two years later, they represented 18.5% of officer deaths. Through the early 1990s they represented 15-16% of deaths. In 1998, 86.9% of officers killed by felons were white, 11.5% were black and 1.2% were of other races.

The current rate of justifiable homicides and police killings has been dramatically reduced over the rate of the 1980s. Crime overall is down, of course; this is a major factor. As well, training has improved in many departments — both training on dealing with suspects and on gun use.

Source: U.S. Bureau of Justice Statistics, *Policing and Homicide, 1976-1998: Justifiable Homicides by Police, Police Officers Murdered by Felons*, Series NCJ 180987, March 2001.

High-Speed Pursuits: To Protect and to Swerve

Number of Reported Pursuits by the Los Angeles Police Department

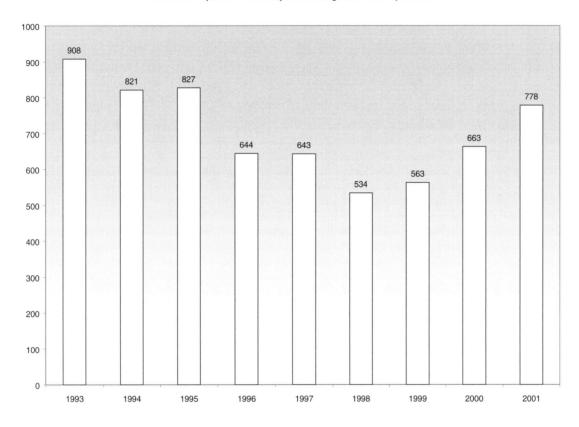

Before a pursuit is initiated, a patrol officer must make a split-second decision: do the benefits of apprehending a suspect outweigh the potential risks to the public and police?

Police pursuits have begun to be examined by the media and law enforcement studies after a number of high profile cases in large cities. No major study of high-speed chases has been done, and many police departments have only recently begun to track the number of incidents in their own jurisdictions.

Some of the figures cited by organizations are as alarming as they are contradictory. A National Highway Traffic Safety Administration report estimates that 350 deaths per year are the results of police pursuits. Over 5,300 pursuit-related deaths were reported to the federal government from 1980 to 1996, although most critics suspect this number is low. Other data places the figure far higher: 2,500 people die and 55,000 people are injured annually as a result of high speed chases. One out of four chase-fatalities are bystanders.

No one is certain how many police chases occur each year. The organization Solutions to Tragedies of Police Pursuits (STOP) claims 250,000 high-speed chases occur annually. California is thought to lead the nation, but once again no one seems certain how commanding its lead to be. The panel shows the number of pursuits recorded by the Los Angeles department. Roughly 500 to 800 have been occurring in recent years. However,

Geoffrey Alpert, a University of South Carolina professor of criminal justice and expert on police pursuits, claims the number is actually closer to 10,000. (Using STOP's 250,000 estimate, could 240,000 chases occur in the rest of the state each year?) Only 1% of police chases are thought to result in fatalities, although somewhere between 17% and 45% are thought to end in some form of property damage.

More than half of police chases are initiated over traffic violations. Why? Erik Beckman, a criminal justice professor at Michigan State University argues that it's panic. "They run because they have Uncle Freddie's car, when Uncle Freddie told them not to. Or they have a six pack of beer in the car and they're underage. Or they have an expired license. Or they have an outstanding warrant." In other words, the typical runner tends to be a young male.

A recent study was conducted of 146 jailed suspects who were drivers in high-speed chases. Seventy percent said they would have slowed down if the police had slowed down or given up the chase. Fifty-three percent said they would run at all costs from the police. Sixty-two percent said they were concerned for the safety of others. Clearly, law enforcement has a crucial decision to make: to give chase or to abandon the pursuit.

Many people have argued that police should only chase suspects involved in a rape or a murder. Geoffrey Alpert argues that it isn't just a legal issue, but a moral one as well. "Police are not only sworn to uphold the law, but also sworn to protect the public." But Spike Helmick, Commissioner of the California Highway Patrol, points out that the law is clear; it is a crime to flee. "If you no longer pursue people, what do you think your bank robbers and auto thieves are going to do?"

In 1998, the issue came before the Supreme Court. The parents of Sacramento teenager Philip Lewis claimed Sacramento Sheriff's deputy James E. Smith violated their son's rights to due process under the law. The teenager was accidentally struck and killed by a police car during a chase in which speeds approached 100 mph. The court ruled unanimously that police can only be held liable in such situations when their actions would "shock the conscience" — such as deliberately trying to kill someone.

The ruling was no doubt watched by police departments across the nation. Curiously, in Los Angeles — not far from the Sacramento incident — the reported number of chases increased after 1998. Was law enforcement feeling emboldened by the court's ruling? What about other states? Many departments' pursuit policies were formulated in the 1970s and are now being updated. In a National Institute of Justice (NIJ) survey of 436 law enforcement agencies, 87% had made the laws more restrictive. Many departments have also recognized officers need to know not just "when to pursue but *how* to pursue," as one report puts it. Again, from the NIJ report: 60% of agencies reported providing entry-level driving training at their academies (meaning 40% do not). The average time devoted to this training was less than 14 hours. Once the officer is in service, he averaged slightly less than 3 hours a year in such training. The officer receives training in actual driving tactics, but little on when to pursue, why to pursue, or how to terminate a chase with minimal risk to himself and to the public.

America seems to have a certain affection for police pursuits — the ultimate in "reality television." Stations in Los Angeles frequently interrupt broadcasts to televise the chases, sometimes with disastrous results (one cornered criminal pulled a shotgun out of his truck and committed suicide on a live broadcast in 1998). Roughly 90 million people are thought to have watched O.J. Simpson flee the police in a white Ford Bronco. The Fox network's broadcast of *World's Scariest Police Chases* attracted 73 million viewers during its first broadcast and two repeated airings.

Sources: Chart data comes from the Los Angeles Police Department, located online at http://www.lacp.org; Alpert, Geoffrey. "Police Pursuit: Policies and Training, National Institute of Justice Research in Brief, May 1997; Rick Van Sant. "In Police Chases, Cars Can be Deadly Weapons." *Cincinnati Post*, August 11, 1998; "Dangerous Pursuits: the thrill and price of police chases." Available online from http://www.abcnews.com; Aaron Epstein. "Supreme Court to Hear Arguments in High-Speed Police Chase Case*." Knight-Ridder/Tribune News Service*, December 5, 1997; "High-Speed Police Pursuits." Available online from http://www.fbi.gov/publica tions/leb/2002/july2002; Jane Prendergast. "Cops Pursuit Rules Vary." *Cincinnati Enquirer*, June 17, 1997; Andrea Fine, "In a Pursuit, Should Cops Let Bonnie and Clyde Go?" *Christian Science Monitor*, August 24, 1999; "Real Entertainment Releases the Action-Packed World's Scariest Police Chases on Home Video." *PR Newswire*, June 30, 1998.

Racial Profiling

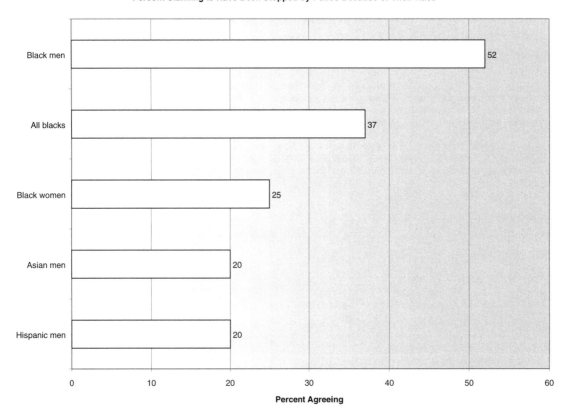

Percent Agreeing

The Institute on Race and Poverty defines racial profiling as "the practice of targeting people for police or security stops based on their race or ethnicity in the belief that certain ethnic groups may be more likely to commit a particular crime."

How often do minorities feel they are singled out by their race? The panel shows that over half of all black men, a quarter of black women, and 20% of Hispanic and Asian men claim to have been stopped by the police by virtue of their race or ethnicity. The figures come from a survey of 1,709 adults in a poll conducted by the *Washington Post*, Henry J. Kaiser Foundation, and Harvard University.

There are two sides to the racial profiling issue. Many people argue that singling out people by virtue of race or ethnicity is a very real practice of law enforcement. Others claim that racial profiling is a myth; there is little credible evidence to suggest this practice exists. They may also feel race is just a factor in identifying potential criminals. Those on either side of the issue seem to agree on one thing: that the practice of profiling began during the nation's war on drugs that began in the 1970s. A special agent with the Drug Enforcement Administration developed a typical profile for a drug courier while assigned to the Detroit Metropolitan Airport. Agents were encouraged to consider all aspects of a suspect's behavior: did the suspect carry new luggage or no bags at all? Did he seem nervous? Had he recently visited a country that had been flagged as a producer of heroin or cocaine?

The war on drugs intensified in the 1980s. In 1985, the Drug Enforcement Administration launched Operation Pipeline, a program designed to dismantle the networks that aided in the transporting of drugs to large drug markets. In the program police were trained to recognize evidence of concealment in the vehicle as well as to identify suspicious behavior by the driver. Race began to be unfairly emphasized in the profiling efforts, some activists feel, and black and Hispanic male drivers began to be stopped and detained by police.

Gary Webb points out that the California Highway Patrol described the traffic stops as "intensified enforcement" of traffic laws, or "generating a very high volume of legal traffic enforcement to screen for criminal activity, which may include drug trafficking." As the officer writes tickets or issues warnings, he may determine if the motorist fits a drug courier profile. The driver may then face a search of his vehicle. The stops became so commonplace among people of color that terms "Driving while Black" or "Driving while Brown" were coined to address them.

The "intensified enforcement" policy had an additional benefit for law enforcement. Recently implemented legislation allowed law enforcement to seize the property of suspected drug dealers. According to the Department of Justice, local police departments received $490 million worth of cash, goods, and property from drug asset forfeiture programs during fiscal 1997 (Callahan, Anderson).

In 1998, the Operation Pipeline program came under increasing scrutiny. The Joint Legislative Task Force on Government Oversight began to investigate the Operation Pipeline program in California. It determined that the program's success rate was overstated and that 80 to 90% of arrests since 1991 involved minorities. Roughly 66% of those pulled over were Latino. Motorists were reportedly questioned about their employment, family members, immigration status, criminal histories and use of drugs or alcohol.

The Department of Justice launched an investigation into the Operation Pipeline program in New Jersey. Black motorists told stories similar to those of minority motorists in California: repeatedly being questioned by the police and made to feel like a criminal (particularly if they were driving through predominantly white areas). One example: Dr. Elmo Randolph, a 42 year-old black dentist, who claimed to have been stopped in his gold BMW by the police 50 times between 1991 and 1999. He claims to not drive at excessive speeds and has never been issued a ticket. Police check his license and registration and then quiz him about drugs or weapons in the car.

When New Jersey officials handed over documents, the data on traffic stops was as troubling as the California data. Over a 10 year period, 80% of state highway searches involved black or Latino drivers. In June 1998, 11 black motorists in Maryland filed a federal lawsuit, claiming black drivers were being unfairly targeted along Interstate 95 (a favored route for weapon and drug smuggling). State police claimed to have pulled over twice as many whites as blacks. The plaintiffs countered with numbers of their own: 17%

of Maryland drivers are black, yet they comprised 70% of those pulled over. Whites represent 75% of all drivers, yet only 23% of those stopped by the police.

Operation Pipeline — and, presumably, the policy of targeting certain groups of people — has been taught to 27,000 police officers in 48 states, according to law professor David Harris. The media attention brought by these (and other) cases prompted changes in law enforcement policies. More than 20 states now have laws on the books that specifically forbid such practices. As well, many states are now required to collect data on traffic stops to determine if racial profiling is taking place. (Rhode Island police were charged with contempt of court in October 2002 with failing to gather such figures). Law enforcement opposes the push to keep more detailed records of traffic and police stops. Robert Scully, the executive director of the National Association of Police Organizations, fears that record keeping will take "valuable time away from police work to do more administrative work."

The attacks of September 11 have added a new dimension to the debate over racial profiling. Some American Muslims reported being verbally or physically intimidated immediately after the attacks, or, at the very least, viewed with hostility. "Just having a Muslim name like Omar or Ali raises suspicions," stated Shaheen Ahmed, a pathologist in Kansas who was born in India. Suddenly all Muslims or anyone of Arab descent was a potential terrorist. A young man of Lebanese background was asked to leave a Delta Airlines flight in the summer of 2002. The pilot reportedly did not like his looks and told him "I'm not comfortable with you on this flight." The teenager was from Ohio, an honor student and, according to relatives, was so totally American he could barely speak Arabic. Air marshals subdued an unruly passenger at gunpoint on a flight from Atlanta to Philadelphia and told the nervous passengers to remain seated for the rest of the flight. Dr. Bob Rajcoomar was later arrested and questioned because he had reportedly "watched the event too closely." In perhaps the most embarrassing incident, Secret Service agent Walied Shater was kicked off an American Airlines flight on his way to guard the president.

How do the races feel about this method of profiling? In a 1999 Gallup poll, more than half of Americans surveyed believed police actively engage in racial profiling. Eighty-one percent of respondents disapproved of the practice. Not too surprisingly, far more Blacks than whites saw it as pervasive. Has 9/11 changed people's attitudes? In one Atlanta study, 74% of whites and 32% of blacks favored racial profiling in the war against terror.

The *Washington Post* poll in the graphic above asks minorities if they have been stopped by the police because of their race. This is a question of perception, of course; those who see racial profiling as a myth might argue they could have stopped for some other reason. In a Department of Justice study, 74% of blacks and 82% of Hispanics felt that police had stopped them for legitimate reasons (meaning, of course, that 26% and 18%, respectively, did not). The most common challenge to the idea of racial profiling is that race is just one characteristic used in identifying a potential criminal, not the only one. A report released in April 2002 found that black drivers were more likely to speed on the New Jersey turnpike than their white counterparts. A few critics have pointed to this controversial report as if to say: could this somehow explain why black drivers found themselves stopped so frequently by the police?

The strangest charge of racial profiling? A Pennsylvania councilwoman has accused her borough's police dog of racial profiling and claims that the canine should be destroyed. The charge came after K-9 officer Schawn Berger was wrestling with a suspect. The dog lunged and ended up biting a 9-year African American boy instead of the suspect. Berger claims the dog simply became confused in the commotion of the struggle. Councilwoman Dixon claims to have received a half dozen complaints against the dog. Three of these people had problems with drugs; the other three were blacks who claimed they were attacked by the dog because of their race. While dogs can certainly be trained to differentiate between the smell of heroin and cocaine, for example, canine experts remain divided as to whether or not the dog would be able to make distinctions between the races.

Sources: Chart data taken from "Racial Profiling Rampant" at *State Government News*, August 2001, p. 8; U.S. Department of Justice, Bureau of Justice Statistics, *Characteristics of Drivers Stopped by Police, 1999*; Webb, Gary. California Legislature's Task Force on Government Oversight report on Operation Pipeline retrieved from http://www.aclunc.org/discrimiantion/webb-report.html; Gene Callahan and William Anderson. "The Roots of Racial Profiling." *Reason*, August 2001, p. 37; "Police Dog Accused of racial profiling." available online at http://www.foxnews.com; "New Jersey releases controversial racial speeding study," available online from http://www.cnn.com; Cynthia Cotts, "New Jersey Cops to Racism." *Village Voice*, December 6, 2000. "Airline security run amok: terrorism prevention or racial profiling?" available online from http://www.counterpunch.org; Pat Morrison. "American Muslims are Determined Not to Let Hostility Win." *National Catholic Reporter*, September 6, 2002, p. 9;, p. C1.Alex Tizon. "Black Belt Wrestles with enigma of profiling." Knight Ridder/Tribune News Service, September 10, 2002; "Minorities Targeted for Traffic Stops." Available online from http://www.ndsn.org; "Racial Profiling Data Collection Status Report." Available online from http://www1.ymn.edu/irp/publications/ARB/ARB%20.html; "Opposing Views on Racial Profiling." *Insight on the News*, July 1999; John Lamberth. "Driving While Black." *Washington Post*, August 16, 1998, p. C1.

Federal Law Enforcement

Number of Full-Time Officers Authorized to Carry Firearms and Make Arrests, 2000

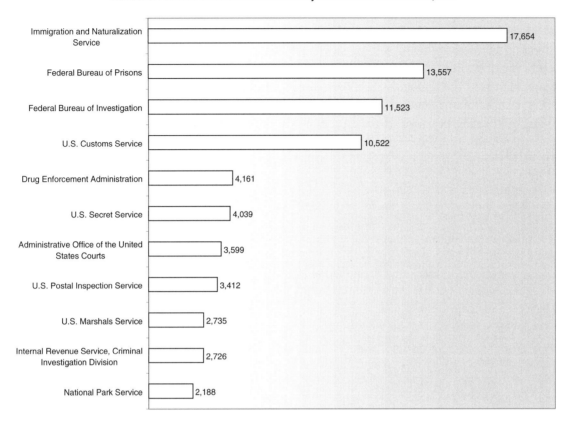

As of June 2000, there are more than 88,000 personnel authorized to make arrests and carry firearms in federal agencies.

The Immigration and Naturalization Service has the largest number of officers with firearm authority (17,654), followed by the Federal Bureau of Prisons (13,557) and the Federal Bureau of Investigation (11,523). Has the war against drugs shaped employment in any way? From 1998 to 2000, the Drug Enforcement Administration saw a 26% increase in officers, the largest of all the agencies.

Women accounted for 14.4% of Federal officers in 2000, or 1 in 7 of all officers with arrest and firearm authority. Their presence varies by agency. The highest percentages of women were found in the Internal Revenue Service (27.3%), the U.S. Customs Service (19.1%), the U.S. Capitol Police (17.8%), and the Federal Bureau of Investigation (17.1%). The 17.1% of women in the FBI is up 21% from the 14.5% they represented in 1996. It's the largest increase in female enrollment among federal agencies. Is this by chance? Did the FBI recruit women more aggressively? Or did the agency reap some benefit from fans of FBI Agent Clarice Starling of *Silence of the Lambs* or Agent Dana Scully of the *X-Files*? It's difficult to say. (But the truth is out there!)

Minority representation has increased also, from 28% in 1996 to 29.5% in 1998 to 30.5% in 2000. Hispanics and Latino officers comprised 15% of the force in 2000. Non-Hispanic blacks followed with 11.7%, Asians and Pacific Islanders with 2.2% and American Indians with 1.2%.

Percent of Federal Officers by Race

	1996	2000
Whites	72.0	69.5
Hispanics or Latinos (any race)	13.0	15.2
Blacks, non-Hispanic	12.0	11.7
Asians/Pacific Islanders	2.0	2.2
American Indians	1.0	1.2

Among the leading agencies, the Federal Protective Service has the largest share of minority workers (44.4%), an organization that provides security to government buildings. Other agencies with a sizeable minority presence included the INS (41.4%), the Bureau of Prisons (39.2%), and the Postal Inspection Service (35.7%). The highest percentage of black officers were at the Federal Protective Service (32.4%) and the U.S. Capitol Police (28.8%). The INS (33.2%) and U.S. Customs (23.8%) had the most Hispanic officers. The U.S. Forest Service employed the highest percentage of American Indians (8%). The Postal Inspection Service had the highest percentage of Asians (3.6%).

Where are minorities least visible? The Bureau of Diplomatic Security (7.1%) and the National Park Service, Ranger Division (10.6%). Where are female officers least likely to be found? The Drug Enforcement Administration. Their agents are 91.6% male.

What effect has terrorism had on government agencies? As of November 2002, the final effect remains to be seen, of course. The INS received negative attention after the September 11 attacks for its inability to track foreigners who enter the country. Six months after the September 11 attacks, the organization approved student visas for two of the hijackers. After the incident, an INS spokesman pointed to the current INS systems for tracking non-immigrants as "antiquated, outdated, inaccurate and untimely." New plans call for all foreign visitors to the country to be photographed and fingerprinted — a policy that has already stirred protests in some circles. Keeping America's borders safe is a critical issue; the INS Border Patrol is now more than double in size compared to its 1993 level.

The FBI and CIA had to share blame for the intelligence failures that led to the September attacks. The two organizations are reportedly sharing information with each other, although some members of these groups say the territoriality that plagued these agencies before the attacks is returning. In January 2002, the FBI put out a call for 900 new special agents to bolster its ranks.

The number of officers of the Bureau of Alcohol, Tobacco and Firearms grew 14% from 1998 to 2000. The group assisted in investigating the 1993 World Trade Center bombing case and the 1995 Oklahoma bombing. Since September 11, it has tightened laws around foreigners' ability to purchase guns.

The Secret Service has roughly 4,000 officers. The number of those with Secret Service protection increased from 17 to 38 after September 11, according to *U.S. News & World Report*. The number currently stands at 22. Not only has the organization been asked to guard more people, but the levels of security that surround these people are being reduced. The Secret Service has cut the number of posts where agents and officers stand guard, eliminated technical assistance such as ballistic glass and armored plating, and withdrawn counter sniper and surveillance squads. One veteran agent offered this analysis for the article: "Basically, what we are doing now and what we were trained to do are at different ends of the spectrum." Many agents are being overworked. They average 81 overtime hours a month. More than 250 uniformed agents have left the Secret Service from October 2001 to September 2002. The loss of manpower is disturbing; equally unsettling, the article points out, is the experience that leaves with them.

Sources: U.S. Department of Justice, Bureau of Justice Statistics, *Federal Law Enforcement Officers, 1996 and 2000*, published January 1998 and July 2001. Potter, Mark and Rich Philipps. "Six months after Sept. 11 hijackers' visa approval letters received." Available from http://www.cnn.com; Chitra Ragavan. "Safety First." *U.S. News & World Report*, September 9, 2002, p. 16.

Listening In

Number of Court Authorized Wiretaps, 1969-2001

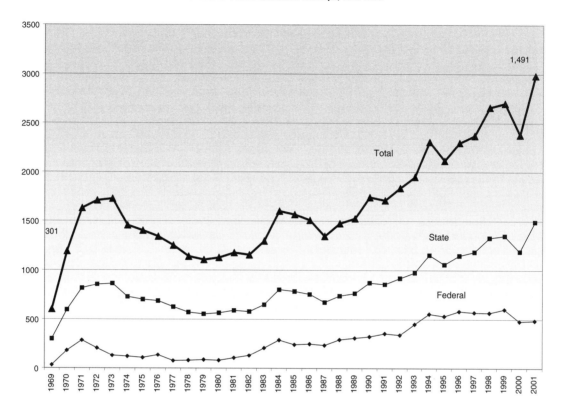

The number of court-ordered intercepts of wire, oral, and electronic communications has risen 395% over the last three decades — but the total number in 2001 was just 1,491 people. If Big Brother was listening, he was listening only to 0.0007% of all adults..

Most wiretaps are ordered by the state. According to the *Report on Applications for Orders Authorizing or Approving the Interception of Wire, Oral or Electronic Communications*, the typical wiretap was authorized to last 27 days in 2001, a figure that has changed little in the last decade. The number of extensions, however, has increased. There were 601 extensions in 1991, a figure that rose almost steadily to a high of 1,367 in 1999. In 2001, a total of 1,008 extensions on wiretaps were granted.

Perhaps the most striking thing to be found in the statistics is that 68% of intercepts were placed on portable devices.[6] Law enforcement has clearly recognized the way cellular phones and pagers have changed the way we communicate. Now, thanks to the Electronic Communications Privacy Act of 1986, "roving" wiretaps are used to target a specific *per-*

---

[6] Before 2000, requests for intercepting communications from mobile telephones, electronic pagers, and cellular telephones were categorized as "other." The government has recently changed the way it categorizes requests to reduce the number in the other category.

---

son instead of a specific telephone or location. The next leading category was for personal residences, which had about 14% of all intercepts.

Location of Authorized Intercepts, 1998-2001

	1998	1999	2000	2001
Portable devices	NA	NA	719	1,007
Personal residence	436	341	244	206
Business	87	59	56	60
Other	584	663	62	101

The influence of the war on drugs, frequently noted in this book, is present in connection with this issue as well. Narcotics is the most specified offense in wiretap reports. Through the 1990s it represented more than half of all cited offenses in wiretap applications. It increased in the final years of the decade and in 2001 represented roughly 80% of all charges cited in applications. Drug offenders were targeted in 978 of the interceptions concluded in 1999, up from 471 in 1989, a 108% increase. Gambling and racketeering were the second and third most common offenses cited in applications.

Franklin D. Roosevelt was the first president formally to assign the FBI the task of wiretapping and eavesdropping on potential enemies of the United States. In the 1960s and 1970s, the government continued to bug political and social activists they perceived as threats to security — Martin Luther King Jr. being perhaps the most infamous example. This surveillance was made public in the 1970s. As a way to strike a balance between security and individual rights, the CIA was banned from most domestic investigations and the FBI implemented a more restrictive policy around its investigations. The Foreign Intelligence Surveillance Act (FISA) was adopted in 1978, which drew a line between law enforcement practices aimed at criminals and those directed at monitoring foreign powers. Wiretaps on foreign powers had less restrictive guidelines than those on domestic taps. All FISA wiretap orders went to the Foreign Intelligence Surveillance Court, composed of federal judges. These wiretaps stay secret forever.

Terrorism complicated this matter. Can we really make a distinction between foreign powers and domestic law enforcement when terrorists may walk on American soil? Part of the Patriot Act — anti-terrorism legislation passed after the September attacks — loosened the requirements on FISA wiretaps, encouraged law enforcement bodies to share information, and allowed for roving wiretaps.

In May 2002, the Foreign Intelligence Surveillance Court criticized the government for a number of problems found in FISA applications. The government admits to making 75 errors on applications in September 2000, which is just one example cited. Other problems: the FBI's e-mail intercept program formerly known as Carnivore captured correspondence from people not under investigation. The FBI also recorded cellular phone conversations of people not under investigation. The court claimed the government had violated demands for information sharing between investigators and prosecutors in terror cases. The FBI has stated that new procedures have dramatically reduced the number of mistakes they make.

Just how effective is electronic surveillance? In a 1995 study, only 17% of intercepted conversations were deemed incriminating by prosecutors. (Is this perhaps the reason for the increasing number of time extensions — investigators wishing to listen long enough until somebody *finally* says something?) Electronic surveillance is also expensive. The average cost is $48,198 per order, down from $61,436 in 1996.

Sources: Chart data comes from U.S. Department of Justice, Bureau of Justice Statistics, *Sourcebook of Criminal Justice Statistics, 2000*; Administrative Office of the U.S Courts, *Report on Applications for Orders Authorizing or Approving the Interception of Electronic Communication*, annual; Eggen, Dan. "FBI Misused Secret Wiretaps, According to Memo." *Washington Post*, October 10, 2002, p. A14; "Electronic Surveillance Increases Sharply in 1994, Efficiency Falls." available from the Electronic Privacy Information Center (EPIC) at http://www.epic.org/alert/epic_alert_2.07.html; historical data comes from Podesta, John and Peter Swire, "Speaking about wiretaps." available online at http://foi.missouri.edu/foiintelligence/speakingout.html; data available as of November 5, 2002.

Flying the Friendly Skies?

Airline Passenger Screening, 1977-1999

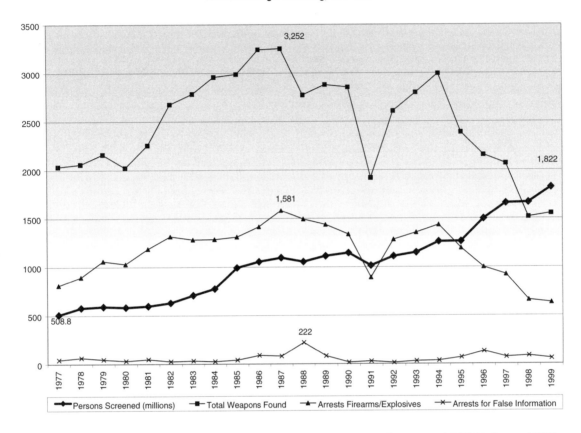

The number of people moving through our nation's airports increased 258% from 1977 to 1999. Roughly 1.8 million people are thought to travel by air daily. Airline travel boomed in the late 1990s. The economy was healthy, businesses were willing to send workers on trips, and bargain airline seats were available on Internet ticket sites.

The number of weapons seized increased steadily through the 1980s, most of them handguns. The number of people arrested on firearms or explosives charges increased during the same period, peaked at 1,581, and then decreased steadily in the 1990s. Less than 100 people are arrested for providing false information each year. There was a sudden jump in 1988; when airports might have briefly stepped up security after the bombing of a Pan Am flight over Lockerbie, Scotland.

Airline security was an issue even before the events of September 11. There has been talk of federalizing airport security since 1973 when federal law first dictated that all passengers and carry-on luggage must be searched. (The legislation was intended to stop a string of hijackings — which it did.) A Government Accounting Office Report found that in 1978 screeners failed to detect 13% of potentially dangerous objects carried by Federal Aviation Administration officials. In 1987, screeners missed 20% of the objects. The percentage increased in the 1990s, but the figures are deemed too sensitive to reveal. Perhaps the most unsettling information: In the 1990s, FAA agents got 243 fake guns, hand grenades, and bombs past screeners at Logan International Airport in Boston — the same airport where terrorists hijacked two Boeing 767s on September 11.

But who actually provides the security? The government or the airport? The airlines technically provide it, but what they actually do is bid the work out to private security firms. Senator Max Cleland of the Senate Commerce, Science and Transportation Committee nicely summarizes the problem with this issue: "So, if you have the airlines responsible for $1.8 billion worth of security at 700 checkpoints in America, they're dumbing down the system. They go to the lowest cost per person out there — minimum wage people — so they can make a little money."

What *about* those screeners?[7] According to a General Accounting Report, the starting salary of security screeners at the largest 18 airports was $6 or less before 2001. Average screener turnover rate in a one year period was 126%. Certain cities saw far greater turnover: St. Louis' rate was 416%, Atlanta's 375%, and Boston's 200%. Some screeners were found not to be U.S. citizens or to have criminal records. They were also poorly trained. How poorly trained? A security expert Ed Brigeman made this statement in an interview with a Cincinnati television station: "We know for a fact that people who work at Starbucks got more training than people who were doing the bulk of the screening."

It might have been tempting to ask the nation's largest chain of coffee shops to take over screening passengers for weapons and explosives. However, the Transportation Security Administration took over security of the nation's airports on February 17, 2002. What happened? In the month following the takeover, there were nearly 1,700 security delays and over 200 security related arrests. A total of 449,417 items were confiscated in this 30 day period, a total that dwarfs the number of items confiscated in the 20 years shown in the chart. Security personnel seized 236,204 cutting instruments, 119,948 knives, 5,312 box cutters and an assortment of pepper sprays, tear gas, fireworks, clubs, bats, and bludgeons (as well as 72 firearms). To be fair, the terrorists of September 11 proved that anything could be used as a weapon. Pre-2001, screeners need only look for guns, knives, and explosives; now nail clippers and hat pins suddenly could be used as weapons and had to be confiscated.

There are now more than 300 airports with federal screeners. Screeners now receive 44 hours of classroom and 60 hours of on-the-job training. They now must be U.S. citizens, have a high school degree or GED equivalent or have at least one year screening experience.

Airports are struggling to meet deadlines imposed by the government, some of which, as of November 2002, are widely viewed as impossibly tight. Travelers are slowly returning

---

[7] Screening consists of "the systematic examination of persons and property using weapons-detecting procedures or facilities (electronic or physical search) for the purpose detecting weapons and dangerous articles and to prevent their unauthorized introduction into sterile areas or aboard aircraft." (See Source, 1993, p. 42.)

to the nation's airports after September 2001 and often still wait in lines at checkpoints or are delayed by security breeches.

Sources: Chart data comes from U.S. Department of Justice, Bureau of Justice Statistics, *Sourcebook of Criminal Justice Statistics, 2000*, table 3.203; "Many local airport screeners may lose their jobs soon." available online at http://wepo.com; Umhoefer, Dave and Mike Johnson. "Weapons get past Mitchell screening." *Milwaukee Journal Sentinel*, September 27, 2001; Cleland quote comes from Mike Fish. "Airport security: a system driven by the minimum wage." available online at http://www.cnn.com; information on screener requirements comes from http://www.tsa.gov; "airport breeches challenge security agency." *USA Today*, April 10, 2002, p. 5A. Data available online as of November 5, 2002.

Chapter 9

Prisons

Nearly two million people (one out of every 142 Americans) welcomed the millennium in the confines of an American correctional institution, ending the most punishing decade in American history. With about 5% of the world's population, America has the distinction of housing about one-quarter of the world's prisoners in what may well be the world's largest prison system.

This chapter begins by delineating who resides in prisons and what brought them there. We will see (again) how the lives of disproportionate numbers of African-American men and women are affected by new mandatory minimum prison terms, sometimes for relatively minor crimes. Today, fewer convicts are paroled and more convicts are spending more time behind bars, thanks to federal legislation that rewards states for being punitive.

We then take a look at the perception and the reality of prison conditions to answer the question: Are prisoners being coddled at taxpayers' expense?

Next we look at the high costs associated with imprisoning so many people and some of the solutions we have tried. Today we spend more money on corrections than we spend on higher education. We've built and filled new prisons but we can't keep up with the demand. So we privatized prisons, and by the mid-1990s private prisons were one of the nation's leading growth industries. We've contracted convict labor to private companies and used the proceeds to offset prison costs. These decisions raise troubling questions. Is punishment the proper realm of big business? What are the implications of handing over responsibility for punishment to people who have an interest in keeping people locked up? Is convict labor exploitation? Have we created a slave labor force for corporate America? Or is it true that meaningful jobs created by private companies can turn a convict's life around?

Studies show that prison work programs reduce recidivism rates. So do rehabilitation programs. Have we given up on rehabilitation in favor of punishment? What happens to the "graduates" of our penal institutions? Our last panels look at these issues.

Who's in Prison?

Adults in State Prison by Most Serious Offense

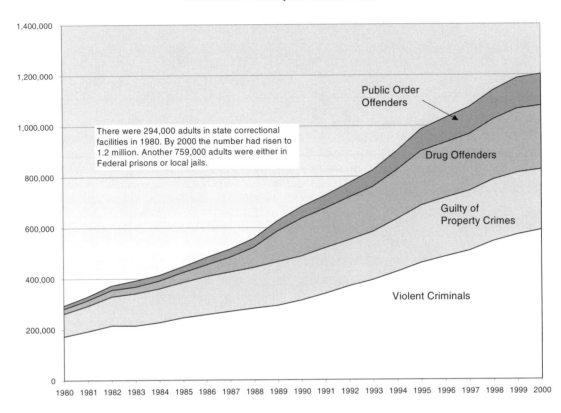

There were 294,000 adults in state correctional facilities in 1980. By 2000 the number had risen to 1.2 million. Another 759,000 adults were either in Federal prisons or local jails.

Public Order Offenders

Drug Offenders

Guilty of Property Crimes

Violent Criminals

Who's in prison these days? Violent criminals, drug offenders, persons who committed property crimes, and public order offenders.[1] More than 90% of state prisoners have either committed one or more serious violent crimes or have served a previous jail term or been on probation. The chart shows state imprisonment trends from 1980 through 2000. Two things are strikingly different about the prison population in 2000 compared to that of 1980. The population was much larger — the number of adults in state prisons grew 309% between 1980 and 2000. And as both the chart and table show, the distribution of offenses that sent adults to prison changed in the 20-year period.

Total and Percentage Distribution of State Prison Population by Most Serious Offense

Year	Total	Violent Crime	Property Crimes	Drug Offenses	Public Order
1980	294,000	58.9	30.4	6.5	4.2
1985	448,200	54.9	31.3	8.7	5.1
1990	681,400	46.0	25.5	21.8	6.7
1995	985,500	46.6	23.0	21.6	8.8
2000	1,203,300	49.0	19.8	20.9	10.4

---

[1] Public-order offenses include weapons, drunk driving, escape/flight to avoid prosecution, court offenses, obstruction, commercialized vice, morals and decency charges, liquor law violations, and other public-order offenses.

Drug offenders made up only 6.5% of the state prison population in 1980, which then numbered about 300,000, but drug offenders grew to 21% of a prison population of 1.2 million by 2000. Offenders against the public order comprised 10.4% of the prison population in 2000, up from 4.2% in 1980. Violent criminals, who were 59% of the prison population in 1980, made up 49% in 2000, which means that in 2000, a scant majority of the population in state prisons (51%) was there for nonviolent crimes.

According to the Justice Policy Institute (JPI), the 1990s was "the most punishing decade on record in American History.... As the doors to new cellblocks opened, the number of prisoners and jail inmates soared, in good times and bad times, independent of whether the crime rate rose or fell." During the 1990s, prisons added 275,500 violent offenders and 102,500 drug offenders to their rosters. As a percentage of the total growth in the 1990s, violent offenders accounted for 51%, drug offenders 20%, property offenders 14%, and public-order offenders 15%.

**Prisoners Under Sentence of Death:
1953-2000**

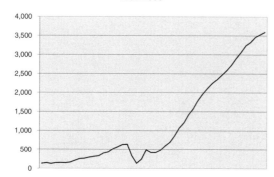

Also in prison are people sentenced to death. The small chart shows the trend over the period 1953 to 2000. The number rose 2,643%, from 131 to 3,593.

Is there a connection between falling crime rates and rising rates of incarceration? Can we sleep more soundly, knowing that America has more of its citizens behind bars than any other country in the world? JPI calls the connection between crime rates and incarceration "elusive." Comparing violent crime rates and rates of imprisonment in New York and California in the 1990s, JPI says: "New York experienced a percentage drop in homicides which was half again as great as the percentage drop in California's homicide rate, despite the fact that California added 9 times as many inmates per week to its prisons as New York."

Getting tough on crime, states have adopted measures like mandatory minimum sentencing, tighter parole policies, and longer prison sentences. Under the popular "3 strikes and you're out" policy, lesser criminals can find themselves behind bars for life if convicted of a felony for a third time. In November 2002 the constitutionality of California's "3 strikes" law, the toughest in the country, was under consideration by the U.S. Supreme Court.

To accommodate growing numbers of prisoners, more prisons must be built. The number of state prisons grew 14% between 1990 and 1995, from 1,207 to 1,375. Federal prisons grew 56%, from 80 to 125.

Sources: Bureau of Justice Statistics, Correctional Populations in the United States, 1997, and Prisoners in 2000, http://www.ojp. us-doj.gov/bjs/glance/corrtyp.htm, and Prisoners on death row, Capital Punishment 2000, December 2001, NCJ 190598, http://www.ojp.usdoj.gov/bjs/glance/tables/drtab.htm. Justice Policy Institute, The Punishing Decade: Prison and Jail Estimates at the Millennium, May 2000, www.cjcj.org/punishingdecade/.

Prisoner Demographics: Men

Number of Sentenced Male Prisoners by Age Group

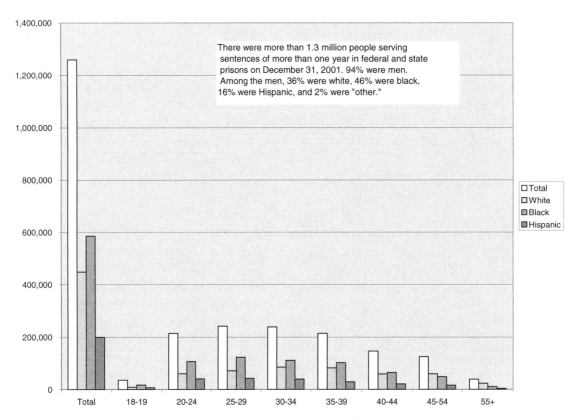

There were more than 1.3 million people serving sentences of more than one year in federal and state prisons on December 31, 2001. 94% were men. Among the men, 36% were white, 46% were black, 16% were Hispanic, and 2% were "other."

Prison is very much the domain of men. At the end of 2001, there were more than 1.3 million people serving sentences of longer than one year in federal or state prisons; 94% of them were men.[2] The chart shows the distribution of these male prisoners by age, race, and Hispanic origin.

Obviously, African American males have high rates of incarceration. As the chart and table show, black men sentenced to more than one year in prison (585,800) outnumbered both white men (449,200) and Hispanic men (199,700). What is particularly shocking is that in percentage terms, on New Year's Eve 2001, 10% of *all* black non-Hispanic males between the ages of 25 and 29 were in prison. In the same age group, 1.2% of white males and 2.9% of Hispanic males welcomed the New Year in prison.

Loss of the right to vote is an often overlooked consequence of imprisonment. Mauer estimated that 14% of the black male population is either currently or permanently disen-

---

[2] The total includes American Indians, Alaska Natives, Asians, Native Hawaiians, and other Pacific Islanders. Black excludes Hispanics. If all types of institutions are taken into account, including territorial prisons, local jails, Immigration and Naturalization Service incarceration facilities, military facilities, jails in Indian country, and juvenile facilities, the United States incarcerated 2.1 million people at the end of 2001.

franchised because of felony convictions. The high rate of incarceration of black males is usually attributed to the war on drugs and the police focus on law enforcement in inner cities.

What about youthful offenders in adult prisons? Rising rates of violence among young people in the 1980s and early 1990s led to a call to try the worst offenders as adults (see Chapter 5). In a three-year period in the early 1990s, 29 states passed laws to deal with youthful offenders. Some lowered the age at which they could be tried in adult court, for example. Data on juveniles in the adult correctional system are sketchy. A report from the U.S. Department of Justice contains data from 36 states where 81% of the 1996 population aged 10 to 17 resided. The data showed 5,599 new commitments of youths to adult prison systems in 1996, a 6% decrease from 1992.

Number of Sentenced Male Prisoners in State and Federal Institutions: 2001

Age	Total Men	White Men	Black Men	Hispanic Men
Total	1,259,481	449,200	585,800	199,700
18-19	35,600	8,900	17,400	7,000
20-24	214,600	60,000	106,500	40,600
25-29	241,800	71,000	122,500	42,100
30-34	238,600	85,100	110,700	39,100
35-39	214,500	81,900	102,000	28,900
40-44	145,900	58,400	64,300	21,200
45-54	124,800	59,500	48,400	16,100
55+	38,400	23,300	10,800	4,100

The aging of the population and new laws requiring prisoners to serve all or most of their sentences are reflected in prison demographics. We look at the topic of older men in prison next.

Sources: Chart and table: Bureau of Justice Statistics, "Prisoners in 2001," NCJ 195189, tables 15 and 16, http://www.ojp.usdoj.gov. Marc Mauer, *Intended and Unintended Consequences: State Racial Disparities in Imprisonment,* www.sentencingproject.org/policy/9050smy.pdf. Howard N. Snyder et al., Juvenile Offenders and Victims: 1999 National Report, U.S. Dept. of Justice, http://www.ncjrs.org/html/ojjdp/nationalreport99/index.html. Information retrieved November 13, 2002.

Prisoner Demographics: Older Men

Growth in the Age 45+ Population in Federal and State Prisons: 1991 and 1997

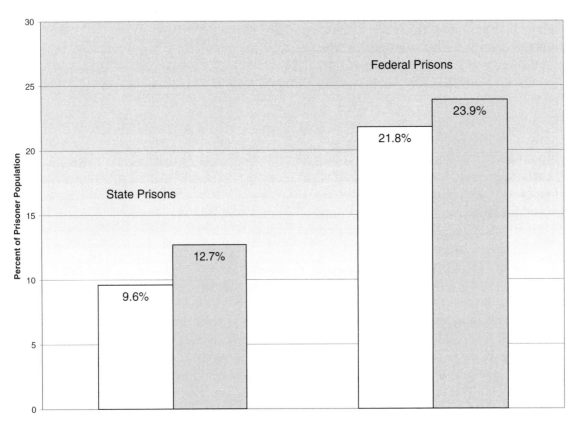

"Grant Cooper knows he lives in prison, but there are days when he can't remember why." — Rick Bragg, from his Pulitzer-Prizewinning feature

The 1990s saw a dramatic increase in the number of incarcerated older persons. In 2001, a scant majority (52%) of the prisoners aged 50 and up were doing time for non-violent offenses. The chart shows the percentage of the prisoners in state and federal prisons who were aged 45 and up in 1991 and 1997. The percentage increases are not as dramatic as the numbers. In 1979 there were 6,500 federal and state prisoners over age 55. In 1990 there were 19,160, a figure that more than doubled by 2001 to 38,400.

Combine the pre-incarceration lifestyle of the typical elderly prisoner with what the U.S. Administration on Aging (AoA) calls the "poor living conditions in prison," and the result is an expensive drain on the prison system. AoA estimates that it costs almost three times more to maintain elderly prisoners, mostly because of the expense of health care. The nature of the problem is graphically summarized by APB News: "Corrections employees find themselves in a strange, new environment: caring for quadriplegics who can barely move, tending paralyzed stroke victims confined to wheelchairs, and monitoring schizophrenics and Alzheimer's patients who require round-the-clock medication." One proposed solution is early release of non-violent older offenders who are at low risk of reoffending — release to someplace where they can be cared for more cost-effectively.

Geriatric patients are taking up room that might be filled with younger, more dangerous prisoners. Burl Cain, warden at Louisiana's infamous Angola State Penitentiary, told Rick Bragg of *The New York Times*: "We need our prison beds for the predators who are murdering people today."

Next we look at the phenomenon of rising numbers of nonviolent women in prison.

Sources: Chart: *Sourcebook of Criminal Justice Statistics*, Table 6.38, http://www.albany.edu/sourcebook/1995/wk1/t638.wk1. Primary Source: U.S. Department of Justice, Bureau of Justice Statistics, *Correctional Populations in the United States, 1997*, NCJ 177613 (Washington, DC: U.S. Department of Justice, 2000), Table 4.1 (Table adapted by SOURCEBOOK staff). U.S. Administration on Aging, "Aging Internet Information Notes: Older Adults in Prisons," http://www.aoa.gov/naic/notes/olderadultsinprison.html. "Imprisoning Elderly Offenders: Public Safety or Maximum Security Nursing Homes, Survey Report – Executive Summary," Elderly Prisoner Initiative/Coalition For Federal Sentencing Reform, http://www.sentencing.org/exec.pdf. Jim Krane, "Demographic Revolution Rocks U.S. Prisons," April 12, 1999, http://www.apbnews.com/cjsystem/behind_bars/oldprisoners/mainpris0412.html. Rick Bragg, "Where Alabama Inmates Fade Into Old Age," http://www.pulitzer.org/year/1996/feature-writing/works/prison.html. Information retrieved November 13, 2002.

Prisoner Demographics: Women

Number of Sentenced Prisoners Per 100,000 in Age Group

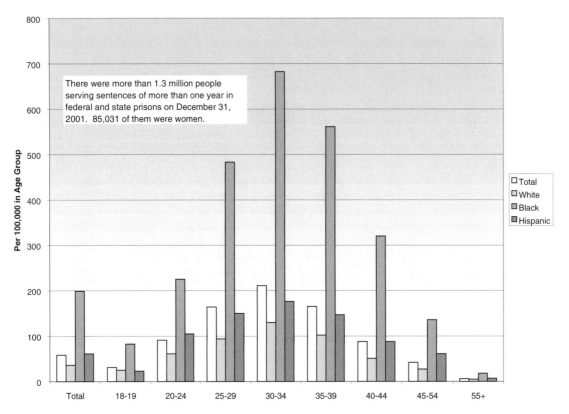

There were more than 1.3 million people serving sentences of more than one year in federal and state prisons on December 31, 2001. 85,031 of them were women.

Far fewer women are incarcerated than men. At the end of 2001, there were more than 1.4 million people serving sentences of more than one year in federal and state prisons. Of that number, 85,031 were women (called "sentenced inmates"; an additional 8,000 women had sentences of less than one year). More women are going to prison now; back in 1980, there were only 13,269 women in prison. The chart shows the distribution of female prisoners per 100,000 in their age group by age, race, and Hispanic origin.

African American women represent a disproportionate share of female prisoners. Their 43% share of the prison population is just about equal to white women's share. Hispanic women comprise 12%. The table shows the number of women incarcerated as of Decem-

Number of Sentenced Female Prisoners in State and Federal Institutions: 2001

Age	Total Women	White Women	Black Women	Hispanic Women
Total	85,031	36,200	36,400	10,200
18-19	1,300	700	500	100
20-24	8,500	3,700	3,200	1,500
25-29	15,200	5,600	6,600	2,000
30-34	21,100	8,700	9,400	2,400
35-39	18,600	8,000	8,400	2,000
40-44	10,100	4,200	4,700	1,000
45-54	8,000	3,900	3,000	1,000
55+	1,800	1,300	500	100

ber 31, 2001: 36,200 white, 36,400 black, 10,200 Hispanic, and 2,231 other women.[3]

In 1994 the Bureau of Justice Statistics (BJS) released a special report on women in state prisons (but not federal), the most recent report of its kind. It summarized characteristics of the female state prison population in 1991 (their number had grown 75% since 1986, to 39,917). Among the BJS findings: Women were far less likely than men to be imprisoned for a violent crime and far more likely to be serving time for a drug offense. Most of the women were over age 30 and at least high school graduates or holders of a GED. Most were unmarried, mothers of children under age 18, and had grown up in homes without both parents present. Before entering prison, 34% of the women had experienced physical or sexual abuse. With regard to criminal history, 28% of the women reported no prior imprisonment or probation compared to 19% of male prisoners.

Five years after the BJS report, *Nightline* aired a six-part television series entitled *Crime and Punishment: Women in Prison*. Ted Koppel and the show's producers spent a week in California's Valley State Prison, "home" to 3,600 women and said to be the largest women's prison in the world. They reported on what they called the unique problems of women in prison: "Most women are there for non-violent crimes. Most [80%] are there for drugs or drug-related crimes. Most [more than 85%] have children. Most [about 80%] were abused, physically and/or sexually before they got to prison. Most women have few family members or friends who visit them. Many have no visitors" (which might be due to the relatively small number and remote locations of women's correctional facilities). The producers of the *Nightline* series got feedback. Viewers wondered why anyone should care about the plight of female prisoners. The show's producer responded to the effect that in our "get tough on crime" climate, with more and more money being spent on prison construction and personnel, it might make sense to consider alternatives like the drug rehabilitation program offered at Valley State. Participants in the program had a recidivism rate of 20%, compared to 80% for nonparticipants.

In a report presented to the American Society of Criminology in 2001, the authors contended that "growing incarceration rates have resulted in nearly 1.5 million children (or 2 percent of the entire population under age 18) having a parent incarcerated." What will be the long-term effects on American society?

Next we look at the distribution of prisoners on death row by state.

Sources: Chart and table: "Prisoners in 2001," Bureau of Justice Statistics, NCJ 195189, tables 15 and 16, http://www.ojp.usdoj.gov. AOA, "Aging Internet Information Notes: Older Adults in Prisons," http://www.aoa.gov/naic/notes/olderadultsinprison.html. *Crime and Punishment: Women in Prison*, ABCNews.com, http://abcnews.go.com/onair/Nightline/nl991029.html.. James Austin et all, "The Use of Incarceration in the United States A Policy Paper Presented by the National Policy Committee to the American Society of Criminology," February 2001, http://www.asc41.com/policypaper1.html. Information retrieved November 15, 2002.

---

[3] The total includes American Indians, Alaska Natives, Asians, Native Hawaiians, and other Pacific Islanders. Black excludes Hispanics. If all types of institutions are taken into account, including territorial prisons, local jails, Immigration and Naturalization Service incarceration facilities, military facilities, jails in Indian country, and juvenile facilities, the United States incarcerated 2.1 million people at the end of 2001.

Death Row Demographics and Issues
Prisoners on Death Row by State: 2002

"We know to a moral certainty that the single most important factor in whether a defendant receives a death sentence is the quality of his lawyer." — Edward Lazarus

Death row is the area of a prison where prisoners sentenced to death reside, sometimes for decades, as appeals of their convictions wend their way through the justice system. The map shows the nationwide distribution of the 3,718 death row inmates known to the NAACP Legal Defense Fund on July 1, 2002. The top 5 states (and their population rank) are California (1), Texas (2), Florida (4), Pennsylvania (6), and North Carolina (11).

The table shows the demographic breakdown of inmates on death row in July 2002 by race, gender, and juvenile status. Whites and blacks are represented in nearly equal numbers, but blacks make up 46% of the federal and state prison population, while whites make up 36%. Whether racial disparities exist in the application of the death penalty has been the subject of much discussion and study. In a summary of two of the studies, Richard C. Dieter, Executive Director of the Death Penalty Information

Inmates on Death Row: 2002

Characteristic	Number	% Death Row Pop	% 2001 Prison Pop
Race			
White	1,683	45.27	36.10
Black	1,605	43.17	46.27
Latino/Latina	348	9.36	15.61*
Native American	41	1.10	NA
Asian	40	1.08	NA
Unknown	1	0.03	NA
Gender			
Male	3,666	98.60	93.67
Female	52	1.40	6.32
Juveniles			
Male	83	2.20	NA
Total	3,718		0.23

*Hispanic. NA Not available. Prison population includes state and federal.

Center, stated that in Philadelphia, the odds of receiving the death penalty were nearly 4 times higher if the defendant was black, and the disparity nationwide, he wrote, may be partially explained by the fact that the key decision makers are "almost exclusively white men." A 2000 U.S. Department of Justice study of the federal death penalty found that minorities made up 74% of 183 defendants in federal cases who were recommended for capital punishment between 1995 and 2000. That study found geographic differences in the application of the federal death penalty. Nine of 94 U.S. attorney districts accounted for 43% of all death penalty recommendations. Two were in the New York region, the rest in Missouri, Tennessee, Texas, New Mexico, Virginia, Maryland, and Puerto Rico.

In nearly every case, murder is the offense for which the death penalty is applied. All states that have the death penalty list murder as a punishable (capital) offense. Some states include treason, kidnapping, train robbery, perjury causing execution, drug trafficking, sexual battery, aircraft hijacking, child rape, and solicitation by command or threat in furtherance of a narcotics conspiracy.[4] Twelve states do not have the death penalty (Alaska, Iowa, Hawaii, Maine, Minnesota, Vermont, Massachusetts, North Dakota, West Virginia, Michigan, Rhode Island, Wisconsin, and the District of Columbia).

The application of the death penalty in Texas (where 457 people were on death row in 2002) came under national scrutiny during the 2000 presidential campaign. Texas has executed more people, including juveniles, the mentally ill, and the mentally retarded, than any other state. Of 218 people executed between 1982 and 2000; 131 died between the time George W. Bush was elected governor in 1995 and June 2000, when Bush told reporters: "I know there are some in the country who don't care for the death penalty, but I've said once and I've said a lot, that in every case, we've adequately answered innocence or guilt." Casting doubt on the adequacy of the Texas system was a June 2002 U.S. Supreme Court decision refusing to grant the state's appeal in the case of Calvin Burdine. Burdine sought to overturn his 1983 conviction on the grounds that his court-appointed attorney had slept through much of the trial. In March 2000 U.S. District Judge David Hittner ordered Texas to either release or retry Burdine because it had been well established that his attorney slept and "a sleeping counsel is equivalent to no counsel at all."

In 2000 Illinois Governor George Ryan imposed a moratorium on the death penalty in the face of evidence that it was not being fairly applied. Two years later, the Governor's Commission on Capital Punishment issued a report concluding: "The Commission was unanimous in its belief that no system, given human nature and frailties, could ever be devised or constructed that would work perfectly and guarantee absolutely that no innocent person is ever again sentenced to death." Supporting that contention is this posting on the Web site of the Innocence Project at the Benjamin N. Cardozo School of Law: As of November 14, 2002, 115 wrongfully convicted people were exonerated after DNA testing sponsored by the Project proved their innocence.

---

[4] See http://www.deathpenaltyinfo.org/capitaloffenses.html for a complete breakdown.

The Supreme Court has been in the headlines with several decisions, among them a June 2002 ruling that executing mentally retarded prisoners violates the 14th Amendment provision against cruel and unusual punishment. In October 2002 the Supreme Court refused by a 5-4 vote to reconsider the constitutionality of the death penalty for juveniles (or those who committed their crime as juveniles). However, in dissenting, Justice John Paul Stevens opined: "The practice of executing such offenders is a relic of the past and is inconsistent with evolving standards of decency in a civilized society." To get back to statistics, Justice Sandra Day O'Connor had this to say in July 2001: "If statistics are any indication, the system may well be allowing some innocent defendants to be executed."

The graphic shows how occupancy on death row grew since 1968 and how the violent crime victimization rate started to trend down in 1995. A majority of the public (70%) favors the death penalty, according to a Gallup Poll (October 29, 2002). Those in favor contend that even if there is no deterrent effect, we are well rid of the murderers who are executed. The United States has been criticized in the international community for its imposition of the death penalty. The *Columbia Encyclopedia* reports that as of 2001, the United States and China imposed the penalty more frequently than any country that allows it.

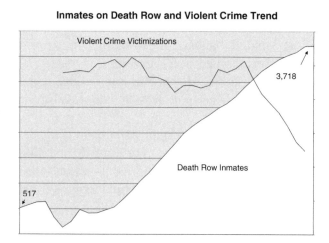

Inmates on Death Row and Violent Crime Trend

In recent years, Pope John Paul II has interceded on behalf of American death row inmates, but the death row inmate's chance of being granted clemency for humanitarian reasons is not very good. According to the Death Penalty Information Center, only 48 inmates were granted clemency between 1976 and 2002. Reasons ranged from doubt about the prisoner's guilt, contention that the sentence was out of proportion to the crime, and questions about the prisoner's mental capacity. The center also reports that between 1973 and August 2002, 102 people were released from death row with evidence of their innocence.

Sources: Graphic and table: Deborah Fins, *Death Row USA,*, Criminal Justice Project of the NAACP Legal Defense and Educational Fund (LDEF), Summer 2002, http://www.deathpenaltyinfo.org/DEATHROWUSArecent.pdf. Small graphic: "Size of Death Row by Year (1968-Present)," Death Penalty Information Center, http://www.deathpenaltyinfo.org/DRowInfo.html#year; Primary sources: BJS, *Sourcebook of Criminal Justice Statistics 1999, Capital Punishment 1999*; LDEF. Richard C. Dieter, "The Death Penalty in Black & White: Who Lives, Who Dies, Who Decides," Death Penalty Information Center, June 1998, http://www.deathpenalty info.org/racerpt.html#Executive Summary. District Court's decision in Burdine v Johnson, http://www5.law.com/tx/today/burdine. htm. Innocence Project, http://www.innocenceproject.org/. Robert L. Jackson, "Study Finds Racial Gap on Death Row, *Los Angeles Times*, September 13, 2000, http://www.commondreams.org/headlines/091300-02.htm. Edward Lazarus, "A Basic Death Penalty Paradox That Is Tearing the Supreme Court Apart," October 31, 2002, http://writ.findlaw.com/lazarus/20021031.html

The Good Life of Hard Time?

Population Housed in Federal and State Prisons as a Percent of Highest Capacity

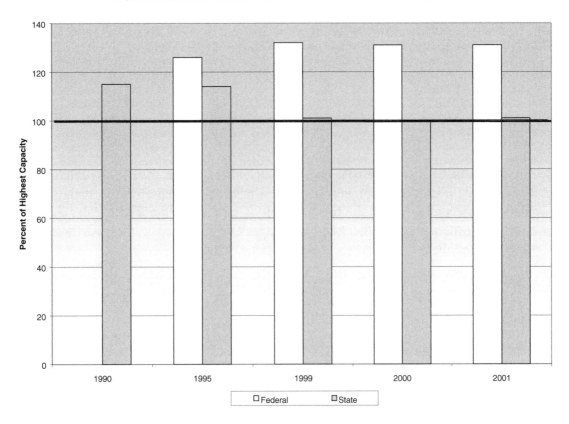

"If they only knew how much fun I was having in here, they would turn me loose." — Richard Speck, mass murderer, from a videotape made in a maximum-security prison cell

Is the corrections system too lenient? Many people seem to think so. When the ACLU recently asked: "From what you know, do you think life in prison is too harsh, not harsh enough, or about right?" 42% of respondents answered "Not harsh enough" and 35% said "About right."[5] The nation has gotten tough on crime. One result? By 1995, our prisons were bursting at the seams, as the chart shows (federal data for 1990 are not available). That year, 40 states, two territories, and the District of Columbia were under court orders to deal with the issue of overcrowding in their prison systems.[6] How did they do it? In

---

[5] Attitudes may be changing, according to a report prepared by Peter D. Hart Research Associates, Inc. for The Open Society Institute ("Changing Public Attitudes Toward the Criminal Justice System"; http://www.welfareinfo.org/polling.asp). That report states that "the public now favors dealing with the roots of crime over strict sentencing by a two to one margin, 65% to 32%.

[6] David B. Kopel, "Sentencing Policies Endanger Public Safety," *USA Today Magazine*, November 1995, 65 (cited in McCormick, see Source notes).

many cases, they let violent repeat offenders go early while retaining nonviolent drug "criminals," many of them first offenders.

Are prisoners enjoying themselves at taxpayers' expense? Consider the typical prison, overfilled with a 50/50 mix of violent/nonviolent men, 36% of them white, 46% of them black, 16% Hispanic, about half of them under the age of 30. This seems more likely to be a recipe for trouble than a paid vacation. And so the research shows.

A 1996 report from Human Rights Watch documented "pervasive sexual harassment, sexual abuse and privacy violations by guards and other corrections department employees in state prisons in California, the District of Columbia, Georgia, Illinois, Michigan, and New York." Amnesty International reported in 1999 that physical and sexual abuse of women in American prisons was widespread, adding that 12 states had no law prohibiting sexual contact between female prisoners and their jailers. A 2001 Human Rights Watch report documents widespread prisoner-on-prisoner sexual abuse in male prisons. Compounding the problems are the transmission of HIV, the abandonment of rehabilitation efforts, and the lack of medical and corrections personnel. The Congressional Institute calls the conditions in America's prison system "deplorable."

But things might not be so bad all over. For the benefit of disgraced CEOs, *Forbes* magazine recently published a list of "The Best Places to Go to Prison." The table shows where these federal prisons ("Club Fed") are. According to *Forbes*, convicts don't get to choose their prison, but they can always make requests. However, according to Herb Hoelter, the director of the National Center on Institutions and Alternatives, a program that tries to improve the lot of inmates: "My experience with white-collar criminals is that the guards treat them much more harshly … It's a power issue. They now have control over someone who once made $15 million a year." And even these posh places are not immune to the growing trend of "no frills" for prisoners. Coffee, weightlifting equipment, and hot meals are out in some jurisdictions; chain gangs are back in others. Legislation was introduced in Congress in 2001 to eliminate cable television and other frills from federal prison cells. Whether such punitive measures will have any effect on recidivism remains to be seen.

Forbes "Best Places to Go to Prison"

Institution	Location
Federal Correctional Institute Morgantown	Morgantown, W. Va.
Federal Prison Camp Eglin	Fort Walton Beach, Fla.
Federal Prison Camp Otisville	Otisville, NY
Federal Prison Camp Nellis	North Las Vegas, Nev.
Federal Prison Camp Allenwood	Montgomery, Pa.

Sources: Graphic: Bureau of Justice Statistics, "Prisoners in 2001," NCJ 195189, Table #15. "Nary a speck of decency," *Time*, May 27, 1996, v147, n22, p34. Amnesty International, "Not Part of My Sentence: Violations of the Human Rights of Women in Custody," http://www.amnestyusa.org/rightsforall/women/report/index.html. Human Rights Watch, http://www.hrw.org/reports98/women/Mich. htm#P37_769. "Optimism, Pessimism, and Jailhouse Redemption: American Attitudes on Crime, Punishment, and Over-incarceration, Findings from a National Survey Conducted for the ACLU by Belden Russonello & Stewart," www.aclu.org/issues/criminal/overin carceration_report.pdf. Patrick T. McCormick, "Just Punishment and America's Prison Experiment," *Theological Studies* 61 (2000), p508+. Human Rights Watch, "No Escape: Male Rape in U.S. Prisons," http://www.hrw.org/reports/2001/prison/ report.html. The Congressional Institute, "Prisons," http://www.conginst.org/OurLibrary/C/prisons.html. Jennifer Senior, "You've Got Jail," NewYork Metro.com, http://www.newyorkmetro.com/nymetro/news/crimelaw/features/6228/index2.html. Peter Finn, "No-frills prisons and jails: a movement in flux," Federal Probation, Vol.60 No.3 (Sept. 1996), http://www.strengthtech.com/correct/issues/mediais/2000/ flux.htm. Information retrieved November 26, 2002.

Prison Dollars

Corrections Expenditures and Reported Robberies, Burglaries, and Larcenies/Thefts

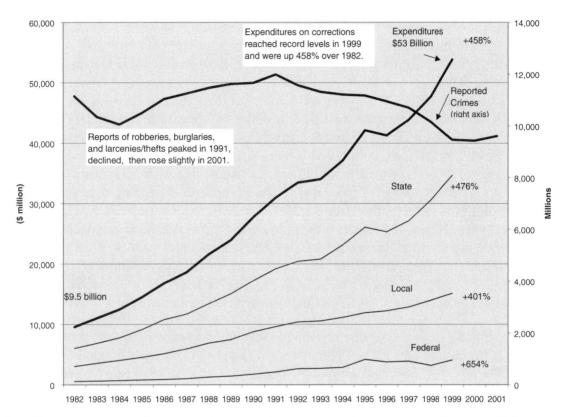

"…this most recent prison experiment … has generated a corrections boom which is extraordinary even by U.S. standards and has led to the construction of the largest prison system in human history aimed at controlling crime." — Patrick C. McCormick

At the end of 2001, 1,962,220 people (one out of every 142 residents) were in America's jails and prison. With about 5% of the world's population, America houses about one-quarter of the world's prisoners, according to McCormick, who contends that between 1980 and 2000, about 1,000 new jails/prisons were built to accommodate the growing number of incarcerated. If the prisoner population keeps growing, he writes, about one new, 1,000-bed facility per week will have to be added to the system through 2010. McCormick and other analysts cite annual costs of $25,000 to $70,000 to house each adult prisoner and $100,000 to construct each new cell.

The chart shows that expenditures on the corrections system grew 458% between 1982 and 1999, from $9.5 billion to $53 billion, with state governments picking up the lion's share; it came to $34.6 billion (64%) in 1999. Local governments picked up 28% and the federal government contributed 8%. As part of the Violent Crime Control and Law Enforcement Act of 1994, the federal government increased appropriations to state and local governments in return for imposing longer sentences for violent crimes or requiring criminals to serve at least 85% of their sentences before parole (the violent offender incarceration and truth-in-sentencing incentive grant [VOITIS] program).

In 1999, the year state governments spent $34.6 billion on corrections, they spent $36 billion on highways, $22 billion on health, and $20 billion on higher education. Are they getting their money's worth? The chart shows a decline in the 1990s in robberies, burglaries, and larcenies/thefts reported to law enforcement agencies. According to a 1998 report from the National Center for Policy Analysis, crime goes down when crime becomes costly to perpetrators; that is, when their likelihood of going to prison increases. The report cites numerous studies to support the contention that while the cost of building and maintaining prisons is high, "the cost of not doing so appears to be higher." When a crook is in jail, the theory goes, even if it costs $25,000 to maintain him, a dozen or more nondrug crimes are not being committed, saving society upwards of $53,900 a year. The report does note: "Prisons, however, do not pay for themselves with many drug offenders, who have grown to 30 percent of new state prisoners, up from 7 percent in 1980. There is no social benefit for incarcerating drug dealers ... because they are readily replaced in the drug marketplace. Hence, the researchers calculate that prisons cannot pass a cost-benefit test for about one in four prisoners." Mark Cohen, economics professor at Vanderbilt University, told *The New York Times* that longer prison terms, the modern solution to crime, would be economical in terms of reducing rape, assault, and automobile theft, but they would not be economical when it comes to burglars and larcenists.

Might prevention be more cost-effective? Peter Greenwood examined four programs for the Rand Corporation: Head Start, parent training, and two program aimed at high-risk juveniles. He reported that these programs "would be twice or three times as cost effective as just putting people in prison."

These days, it seems, we hear more about profit than prevention. We look at for-profit prisons next.

Sources: Chart: Bureau of Justice Statistics, "Justice Expenditure and Employment in the United States, 1999," February 2002, NCJ 191746, Table 2, http://www.ojp.usdoj.gov/bjs/pub/pdf/jeeus99.pdf, and FBI, *Sourcebook of Criminal Justice Statistics, 2001*, Table 1. Patrick T. McCormick, "Just Punishment and America's Prison Experiment," *Theological Studies* 61 (2000), p508+. National Center for Policy Analysis, "Crime and Punishment in America: 1998," NCPA Policy Report No. 219, September 1998, http://www.ncpa.org/~ncpa/studies/s219.html. Butterfield, Fox, "Prison: Where the Money Is," *The New York Times*, June 2, 1996, pE16.

Punishment for Profit

Growth of Private Prisons: Openings by CCA and Wackenhut

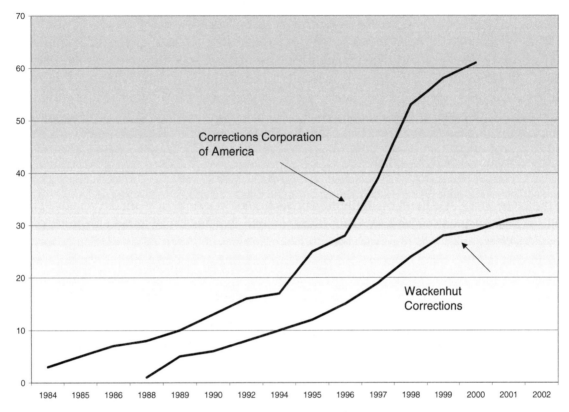

"It may not be the most tasteful way to make a buck, but it is an honest investment nonetheless." — Betsy Schiffman, on investing in the prison industry (see Source notes)

Motivated by the public's demand to imprison more criminals for longer periods of time at the lowest possible cost, cash-strapped states have turned to the private sector for help. Private-sector, for-profit prisons, first proposed in the early 1980s, are a growth industry whose revenues came to about $1 billion in 1997, up from about $650 million in 1996. The two largest providers are Corrections Corporation of America (CCA) and Wackenhut Corrections. Sometimes these companies simply take over the management of an existing correctional facility, or they build new ones. The chart shows the growth trend in facilities opened by CCA and Wackenhut since 1984, when CCA first signed a contract with the Immigration and Naturalization Service to run detention centers for illegal aliens. By 1997, about 64,000 people were confined in about 140 privately run U.S. facilities (prisons, jails, and illegal immigrant detention centers). By 1998, the number had risen to 85,000 .

In 2002, with more than 55,000 inmates under its care in about 60 facilities in 20 states and the District of Columbia, CCA was the sixth-largest corrections system in the country, behind Texas, California, the Federal Bureau of Prisons, New York, and Florida (New York Stock Exchange symbol: CXW; 2001 1-year sales growth: 214.3%). That same year, its chief rival, Wackenhut Corrections, operated more than 50 facilities with more than 40,000 beds, mostly in the United States but also in Australia, New Zealand, Puerto Rico, South Africa, and the United Kingdom (NYSE: WHC; 2001 1-year sales growth, 12.1%). Some of the country's biggest corporations are investing in the private prison business, including American Express and Goldman Sachs & Co.

On its Web site, CCA promises to try to "return a better person to our communities through programs geared to the inmate population. These programs range from substance abuse to behavior modification to life skills to education and job training." Wackenhut supplies design, security, food, health care, education, rehabilitation, and management services. Both companies (and their rivals) claim they can do all of these things cheaper than government can do them. Typically, a private company signs a contract with a state, agreeing to house and care for prisoners at a daily rate that is lower than what the state pays. In Florida, for example, each contract requires at least a 7% savings.

Studies of the cost efficiency of public versus private prisons show mixed results. The issue is complicated; costs vary from state to state and no broad generalizations can be made. After looking at the available studies, the General Accounting Office reported to Congress in 1996 that "comparisons of operational costs indicated little difference and/or mixed results," and "comparisons of quality are unclear." One looming issue: rapidly rising health care costs. As we saw earlier, this is a growing part of correctional costs.

The private prison industry has been plagued by problems, but we don't seem to hear much about them. According to Project Censored of the Sonoma State University in California, private prison expansion and the abuses associated with it were one of the top 25 neglected news stories of 1998, suggesting that prison reform is not a high national priority. The abuses mentioned included low wages for non-union, poorly trained staff; bad food; and overcrowding.[7] CCA made the news on April 20, 1999, when it agreed to pay $1.65 million to settle a class action lawsuit brought by inmates of an Ohio facility; they complained of abusive guards and inadequate medical care, among other things. A report on the facility commissioned by the U.S. Department of Justice noted a "destructive pattern of extensive inmate idleness," a "lack of correctional experience on the part of almost all staff," and, after the second homicide in three weeks, the institution of a search procedure that "could fairly be described as a reign of humiliation directed indiscriminately at the entire inmate population." A bill was introduced in Congress the day after CCA agreed to pay. Known as the Public Safety Act, it provides that no applicant for funds under the violent offender incarceration and truth-in-sentencing incentive grant program (VOITIS) will be granted such funds unless the applicant agrees not to use private prison contractors. The measure was still wending its way through the legislative process at the time of writing (November 2002).

In 1999 the London *Observer* reported that the state of Texas terminated Wackenhut's contract to run a prison "pending the expected criminal indictment of several staff for

---

[7] Private correctional facilities are concentrated in Sunbelt states (Texas, Florida, California, Tennessee), where labor unions tend to be weaker.

sexually abusing inmates"; the inmates were delinquent girls. Judith Greene reported that a class action lawsuit filed against Wackenhut in Dallas alleged that the girls were "degraded, humiliated, assaulted, harassed, and emotionally abused." One of the girls, who had been raped, committed suicide. It should be noted that this type of abuse is not limited to private prisons; we emphasize, as well, that there are many well-run private and public prisons.

In order to turn a profit, private prison companies must build prisons and fill them. Silverstein writes that corners are cut in every possible way and drug rehabilitation, counseling, and literacy programs often fall by the wayside. State Senator Cal Hobson of Oklahoma told George M. Anderson that lobbyists from four private prison firms are regularly to be found in the state capitol, "and all are after the same resource: additional incarcerants to put into their systems." Anderson writes that private prison companies profit more when an inmate's status is upgraded from minimum to medium security.

It is not just private prison companies who are looking for a piece of the prison pie. Telephone companies, for example, contract with states to supply phone service to prisons in exchange for a share of the profits. When a prisoner makes a telephone call, it must be paid for by the recipient, often at extremely high rates. States and private prisons collect millions of dollars each year through this scheme.

Our next panel looks at the issue of profits from prison labor.

Sources: Chart: Corrections Corporation of America, http://www.correctionscorp.com/index.html., and Wackenhut Corrections Corp., http://www-2.hoovers.com/co/capsule/5/0,2163,42155,00.html. Betsy Schiffman, "Profits Behind Bars," Forbes.com, http://www.forbes.com/2002. Project Censored, http://www.projectcensored.org. Blackstone, Erwin, "Privately managed prisons go before the review board," *American City & County*, April 1996 v111 n4 p40(7). "Report to the Attorney General: Inspection and Review of the Northeast Ohio Correctional Center, November 25, 1998, http://www.usdoj.gov/ag/youngstown.htm. Smalley, Suzanne, "A Stir Over Private Pens," *National Journal*, May 1, 1999 v3 i18 p1168(1). "Oregon's Inmate Work Crews," http://www.doc.state.or.us/publicaffairs/pubs/pdf/work_crews.pdf. "Government Profits From Family Misery," http://www.progress.org/prison05.htm. Gregory Palast, "Wackenhut's Free Market in Human Misery," *The Observer (London)*, September 26, 1999, http://www.corpwatch.org/. Judith Greene, "Prison Privatization: Recent Developments in the United States," paper presented at the International Conference on Penal Abolition, May 12, 2000, http://www.oregonafscme.com/corrections/private/prison_privatization.htm. General Accounting Office, "Private and Public Prisons," GAO/GGD-96-158, http://www.gao.gov. Anderson, George M., Prisons for Profit: Some ethical and practical problems," *America*, Nov 18, 2000 v183 i16 p12. Ken Silverstein, "America's Private Gulag," *Prison Legal News*, June 1, 1997 http://www.corpwatch.org/issues/PID.jsp?articleid=867. Information retrieved November 25, 2002.

Prison Industries: Excellent Idea or Exploitation?

Well-Known Companies That Use Convict Labor

3Com	Microsoft
AT&T	Motorola
Boeing	Nordstrom
Compaq	Nortel
Dell	Prison Blues® ("Made to Do Hard Time")
Eddie Bauer	Pierre Cardin
Honeywell	Revlon
IBM	TWA
Jostens	Texas Instruments
Kaiser Steel	Toys R Us
MCI	UNICOR (Federal Prison Industries)
McDonald's	Victoria's Secret

"Whereas the people of the state of Oregon find and declare that inmates who are confined in corrections institutions should work as hard as the taxpayers who provide for their upkeep ... now, therefore, the people declare ... All inmates of state corrections institutions shall be actively engaged fulltime in work or on-the-job training." — 1994 amendment to Oregon's constitution

Who would argue with the logic of Oregon's constitutional amendment? This is the trend of the 1980s and 1990s: States mandating that all prisoners work. The rationale behind the mandate? There is no reason why prisoners should be allowed to sit idly by, at taxpayers' expense, when they can learn a useful trade that will (1) offset the cost of their incarceration, (2) pay court-ordered fines, (3) give something back to their victims, (4) help support the estimated 2.2 million children and the 1 million mostly low-income women they left on the outside, and (5) set them on the straight and narrow path once they get out. Considering that the prison population is made up mostly of "poorly educated and low skilled men who experienced high unemployment before incarceration" (Pigeon and Wray), is society not doing them a favor by forcing prisoners to work?

The concept is not new and it's not illegal: The 13th Amendment states: "Neither slavery nor involuntary servitude, *except as a punishment for crime whereof the party shall have been duly convicted,* shall exist within the United States..." (emphasis added). At the end of the 19th century, an estimated 90% of prisoners worked. But labor unions opposed prison industries, laws were passed forbidding the use of prison labor for interstate commerce, a 1928 report to Congress decried the "ruinous and unfair competition between prison-made products and free industry and labor," and the practice fell out of favor.

The pendulum began to swing the other way in the 1980s. We got tough on criminals, the prison population started to grow, at least 30 states passed laws allowing the use of convict labor by private companies, and prison industries expanded. The term actually describes several types of working arrangements. Federal and state prisons put inmates to work producing goods for sale to government and on the open market. Private companies (like those shown on the chart above) contract with prisons to use convict labor, and private prisons employ their own inmates for private profit, either for themselves or for outside companies. Prisoners who work may have time subtracted from their sentences. Prisoners who refuse get longer sentences and lose privileges (Erlich).

Of the total 160,193 inmates in federal prisons in 2002, about 25% worked for the factories of Federal Prison Industries (FPI), earning 23 cents to $1.15 per hour making furniture, electronics, textiles, metal objects, or graphic arts. FPI (better known as UNICOR) is a government corporation created in 1934 to provide workplace experience to federal inmates. In fiscal year 2000, FPI produced nearly $600 million in goods and services for the federal government in accordance with 1950s-era agreements that prisoner-produced goods would not compete with private businesses or labor.[8]

In 2000 an estimated 6% of state prison inmates worked in prison industry programs. What do other prisoners do? In 1999 about 600,000 prisoners in all types of penal institutions did some type of prison support work (food service, plumbing, painting, and so on). Federal prisoners are paid 12 to 40 cents per hour. State rates vary and may be zero (as was voted in Oregon). Too many prisoners remain idle, according to analysts, for reasons that include the fact that prisons were not designed to be factories. Some prisoners work on chain gangs, a solution reintroduced in the 1990s in a few states.

Proponents of prison industries say that by using prison labor, companies are keeping jobs at home that might otherwise have been sent overseas. Prison industries of all kinds employed an estimated .00056% of the national civilian work force in 1996 (Smith), but the complaints against them are loud. Critics charge that working prisoners are paid Third-World wages, do not get the same kind of benefits that workers on the outside enjoy, and are putting some small businesses out of business. The loudest complaints come from the apparel and furniture industries, which claim to be disproportionately harmed by prison industries.

As for the prisoners involved, some are glad of the work, while some liken the conditions to sweatshops. There could be more jobs on the horizon. The Prison Industries Reform Act, introduced in Congress several times in the 1990s and still awaiting action by the Subcommittee on Crime at the time of writing (November 2002), is designed to encourage the use of low-wage prison labor as a way of competing with imports from low-wage countries. Some goods produced by prisoners are now being exported, a tactic we call a human rights violation when used by China.

James A. Gondles Jr. sums up the contradictions inherent in our expectations of prisons: "During the past half century, we have been faced with seemingly incompatible goals. Prisons were urged to keep inmates as busy as possible in meaningful work while, at the same time, not competing with outside industries and displacing jobs." Does prison work

---

[8] It has been alleged that FPI's competitive practices are unfair to small businesses looking to expand into the federal procurement arena. The Federal Prison Industries Competition in Contracting Act of 2001, approved by the House Judiciary Committee on April 25, 2002, would require FPI to compete for federal contracts.

reduce recidivism? Data are sketchy, but estimates range from a 3% to 20% reduction in recidivism among prisoners who worked. We look at recidivism next.

Sources: Chart: "Slavery With a New Name," *Oregon's Inmate Work Crews,* http://www.doc.state.or.us/publicaffairs/pubs/. Gondles, James A. Jr., "Prison Industries: A New Look at an Old Idea, *Corrections Today,* Oct 1999 v61 i6 p6. Pigeon, Marc-Andre, and L. Randall Wray, "Can Penal Keynesianism Replace Military Keynesianism? An Analysis of Society's Newest 'Solution' for the Hard to Employ and a Proposal for a More Humane Alternative," *Social Justice,* V27, No.2 (2000). Reese Erlich, "Prison Labor: Workin' for the Man," http://www-unix.oit.umass.edu/~kastor/private/prison-labor.html. Ingley, Gwyn Smith, and Maureen E. Cochran, "Ruinous or Fair Competition?" *Corrections Today,* Oct 1999 v61 i6 p82 "Slavery With a New Name," http://www.prisonactivist.org/prison-labor/. Information retrieved November 25, 2002.

Rehabilitation or Punishment?

Rates of Recidivism for State Prisoners Released in 1983 and 1994

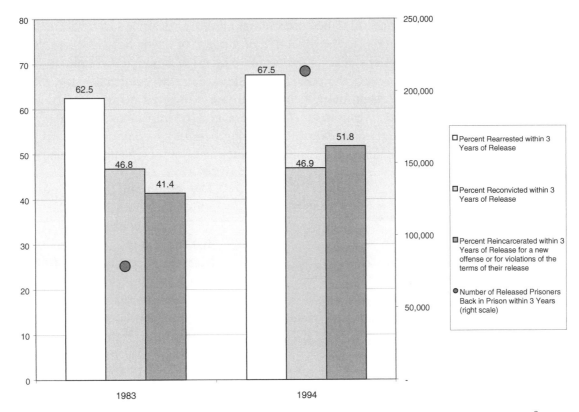

□ Percent Rearrested within 3 Years of Release

□ Percent Reconvicted within 3 Years of Release

■ Percent Reincarcerated within 3 Years of Release for a new offense or for violations of the terms of their release

● Number of Released Prisoners Back in Prison within 3 Years (right scale)

In 2001 there were just over 2 million people incarcerated in the United States.[9] Approximately 635,000 people were released from state and federal correctional facilities in that year alone. This is equal to 1,700 prisoners reentering society each day.

With this fact before us, a question naturally arises: Have those reentering society after a period of incarceration been rehabilitated? From a look at available data on recidivism rates, the answer is no. Prisoners released from state prisons in 1983 and in 1994[10] were *re*arrested, *re*convicted, and *re*incarcerated at very high rates.

If recidivism rates from the 1994 study are applied to all prisoners released in 2001, then we can expect the following: (1) to see 279,400 of the total 635,000 rearrested before the end of 2002; (2) to see 136,525 of these ex-convicts reconvicted by the end of 2002; and (3) to see 66,040 back in prison by New Year's Day 2003. Those are just the predictions

---

[9] At the end of 2001 there were 2,100,146 persons incarcerated in the U.S. They were in federal and state prisons, territorial prisons, local jails, facilities handling illegal migrants, military facilities, jails in Indian country, and juvenile facilities.

[10] The 1983 data are for 11 states and represent 57% of all state prisoners released that year. The 1994 data are for 15 states and represent 66% of all state prisoners released in 1994.

---

for the first year. By New Year's Day 2005, more than half of those released from prison in 2001 (328,930) can be expected to have been returned to prison for either a new offense or a violation of the terms of their 2001 release. Most systems with a 50% failure rate would be judged harshly.

However, this statement implies that the correctional system is designed to rehabilitate. In fact, there is legitimate debate as to the objective of a penal or correctional system. Some will argue that the penal system is responsible for punishing convicted criminals. They further assert that the more severe the punishment, the greater its deterrent value. Others believe that a penal system must attempt to rehabilitate convicted criminals. The argument here is that a rehabilitative system will have a greater impact on reducing crime than a strictly punitive system. With ever growing numbers of ex-convicts reentering society and persistently high recidivism rates, this debate takes on increasing poignancy.

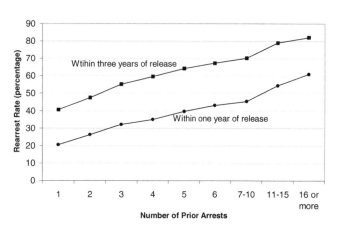

The graph on the left presents additional data from the 1994 study on recidivism. It shows that the number of times a prisoner has been arrested prior to incarceration can be used as a gauge for predicting whether that prisoner will continue to commit crimes after being released from prison. As the number of prior arrests rises, the likelihood of being rearrested rises, as does the likelihood of being reconvicted and reincarcerated. The more "hard core" the criminal, the more likely he or she is to get back into the criminal life upon reentry into society.

Another predictor of recidivism rates is age. If we look at rearrest rates by age we get a clear pattern. The younger a person is upon release from prison, the more likely he or she is to be rearrested within three years. This result is fairly predictable since criminal activity decreases with age. It's also a result that suggests that efforts at rehabilitating youthful offenders may have a greater impact on recidivism and crime rates than would similar programs for older offenders.

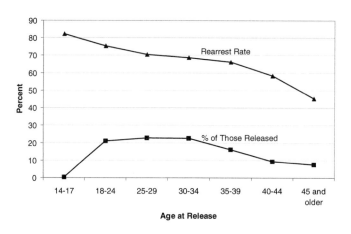

What are the results of studies done to try and ascertain the effectiveness of criminal rehabilitation programs? Are there characteristics of the prison population that make certain types of rehabilitation programs more effective than others? These are the questions we will attempt to answer in the next panel.

Source: U.S. Department of Justice, Bureau of Justice Statistics, *Recidivism of Prisoners Released in 1983*, April 1989, pp. 1 and 3. *Recidivism of Prisoners Released in 1994*, June 2002, pp. 1, 3, 7. *Prisons in 2001*, July 2002, p. 1. *Probation and Parole in the United States, 2001*, August 2002, p. 1.

Likelihood of Re-offense by Type of Crime Committed

Recidivism Rates by Criminal Offense for Which Imprisoned, 1994.

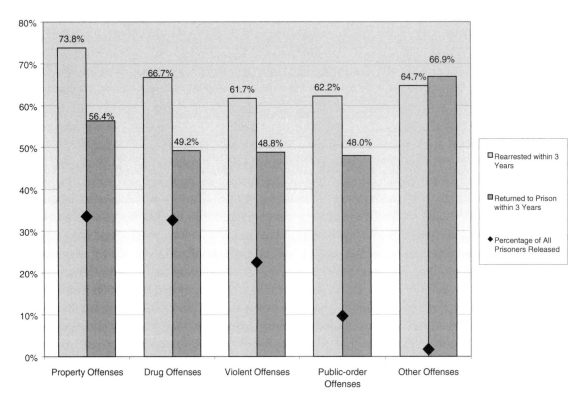

Recidivism rates vary a bit by the type of crime for which a prisoner is serving time. In 1994 a total of 272,111 state prison inmates were released. On average, 68% of them were rearrested within three years of their release and just over half (52%) were back in prison. Although recidivism rates are high across all criminal categories, they are marginally lower for those serving time for the most violent crimes[11].

For the category that covers all violent crimes — homicide, rape, kidnapping, sexual assault, robbery, and aggravated assault — the rearrest rate was 62% and the rate at which prisoners were returned to prison within three years was 49%. However, within this category it was the lesser violent crimes that had the highest rates of recidivism. Robbery and assault had high rearrest rates, 70% and 65% respectively. Of murderers released, a smaller percentage was rearrested, although still alarmingly high at 41%.

Burglars, check kiters, car thieves and swindlers, were all offenders for whom the highest rates of recidivism were seen in 1994. The property crime category overall saw a rearrest rate of 74%. Within three years more than half of all prisoners released after doing time

[11] The new crime types committed by recidivating ex-convicts are not necessarily the same crimes for which they are listed here, namely the crimes for which they have serviced time in prison.

for a property crime were back in prison[12] (56.4%). The offense category with the highest rearrest rate was motor vehicle theft (78.8%) and the offense category with the highest rate of return to prison was "other unspecified drug offenses" (71.8%), not possession or trafficking in other words.

These recidivism rates are simply high and little of a positive nature can be said about them other than the fact that the most violent offenders are recidivating at slightly lesser rates. We appear to be cultivating a segment of the population that is in a revolving door relationship with the law. They "do time" and then are released to wreak a bit more havoc before being sent back to prison for more of the same. This is an unpleasant cycle, and it suggest strongly that we should do everything possible to keep young people from entering this cycle, or "system," in the first place.

What do studies on the effectiveness of criminal rehabilitation programs say? Are there characteristics of the prison population that make certain types of rehabilitation programs more effective than others? These are the questions we will attempt to answer in our last panel.

Source: U.S. Bureau of Justice Statistics, *Recidivism of Prisoners Released in 1994*, June 2002, p. 8.

---

[12] Please note that "return to prison" rates listed here include all those returned for committing and being convicted of a new crime *as well* as all those who failed to meet the terms of their release.

The Basic Skills Needed in the Modern Society

Select Characteristics of the Adult Population and the State Prison Population

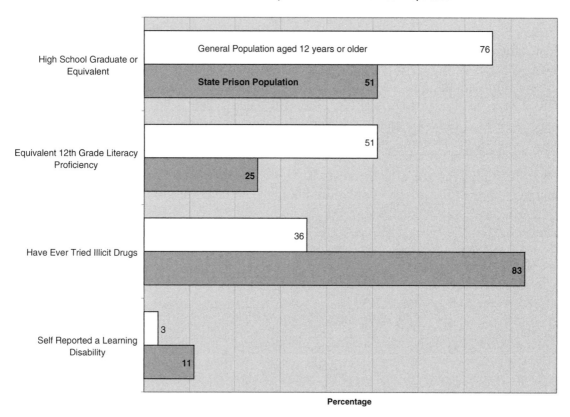

High School Graduate or Equivalent
- General Population aged 12 years or older: 76
- State Prison Population: 51

Equivalent 12th Grade Literacy Proficiency
- 51
- 25

Have Ever Tried Illicit Drugs
- 36
- 83

Self Reported a Learning Disability
- 3
- 11

Percentage

"By failing to prepare, you are preparing to fail." - Benjamin Franklin

The same may be said of society. The graph presents data on four selected characteristics of the general adult population and of the state correctional population. It would appear that we are failing to prepare a large part of our society and it is, in turn, failing us. The lower levels of educational attainment and functional literacy seen in prison populations are two indicators of this failure. Is the justice system in America having to pick up the slack for a failing education system? Should the correctional system focus on rehabilitating offenders or merely punishing them?

Following an era of experimentation in criminal rehabilitation programs, an influential study was published in 1974 entitled *What Works? Questions and Answers About Prison Reform.* The study debunked the idea that it is possible to rehabilitate prison inmates or, in fact, to reform any criminal at all. It soon became known as "Nothing Works." It was received warmly by a justice system reeling under the strain of sharply rising crime rates. The late 1970s ushered in a new correctional philosophy, one based on getting tough on offenders.

In the late 1980s a new study was published which concluded that "successful rehabilitation of offenders had been accomplished, and continued to be accomplished quite well…

Reductions in recidivism, sometimes as substantial as 80%, had been achieved in a considerable number of well-controlled studies." (Gendreau and Ross) The new report was not picked up with the same alacrity as the first study mentioned, but as the years went by, it began to acquire adherents. As incarceration rates continued to rise and recidivism rates remained high, a new look at rehabilitation seemed in order.

The literacy demands of the modern workplace leave anyone without a functional literacy level at a disadvantage. And a high school degree has become an entry-level requirement for many jobs. Yet only half of prison inmates have a high school degree or equivalent and only one quarter are literate at the 12th grade level.

It seems reasonable to assume that delivering literacy skills to inmates might be one proactive way to try and reduce recidivism rates. It is also more cost-effective to teach an inmate to read than to receive him back into the system for another extended stay. According to a Federal Bureau of Prisons report, "Results of this analysis provide substantial evidence that prison education program participation reduces the likelihood of recidivating irrespective of post-release employment."

Another type of rehabilitation program that has shown itself to be useful in reducing recidivism rates and thus crime rates is drug treatment. The 1992 data on drug use by state prison inmates showed that 83% of inmates have tried illegal drugs. That is more than twice the rate for the general population. More importantly still, 70% reported having used drugs regularly and 33% claim to have used drugs during the commission of the offense for which they were incarcerated. Addressing drug addiction should be part of any criminal rehabilitation program.

According to an Office of National Drug Control Policy report, drug treatment program results were very positive, reducing both recidivism and post-release drug use. Furthermore, "this resulted in an average savings of three to one: every one dollar spent on treatment saved society three dollars. The savings resulted from reduced crime-related costs, increased earnings, and reduced health care costs that would otherwise be borne by society."

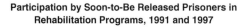

Participation by Soon-to-Be Released Prisoners in Rehabilitation Programs, 1991 and 1997

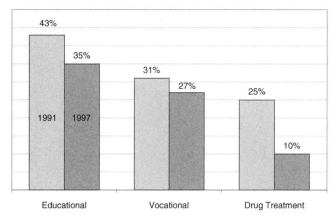

Why then are these rehabilitation programs *not* used more vigorously? Far fewer than half of all prison inmates who were within 12 months of their release date report being involved in educational programs, vocational programs or drug treatment programs. And the participation rates have dropped during the 1990s. One simple reason for the failure to use rehabilitation programs more is that, quite simply, they cost. As prison officials try and make already tight budgets cover ever larger numbers of people cuts are made. To this we add the "get tough of crime" philosophy of the 1980s and 1990s and rehabilitation programs have suffered.

More than a prison program is needed to turn a person's life around. But, the opportunity at education, drug treatment and vocational training has shown at least some impact in reducing recidivism rates. We seem to be failing to prepare prisoners for reentering society as productive members. We should, perhaps, not be surprised if so many of these prisoners fail to succeed in the reentry to civilian life.

Source: National Center for Education Statistics, *Literacy Behind Prison Walls: Profiles of the Prison Population From The National Adult Literacy Survey*, 1994, available online at http://nces.ed.gov/naal/resources/92results.asp. *Adult Literacy and Education in America*, August 2001, p. 74. Miller, Jerome G. "The Debate on Rehabilitating Criminals: Is It True that Nothing Works?," *Washington Post*, March 1989, available online at http://www.ncianet.org/rehab.html. U.S. Department of Justice, Federal Bureau of Prisons, *Prison Education Program Participation and Recidivism: A Test of the Normalization Hypothesis*, May 1995, p. 16. U.S. Office of National Drug Policy, *Drug Treatment in the Criminal Justice System*, March 2001, available online at http://www.whitehousedrupolicy.gov/publications/factsht/treatment/. Gendreau, Paul and R. Ross. "Revivification of Rehabilitation: Evidence from the 1980s," *Justice Quarterly*, Academy of Criminal Justice Sciences, September 1987, Vol. 4. Travis, Jeremoy, Amy L. Solomon and Michelle Waul. From Prison to Home: The dimensions and Consequences of Prisoner Reentry, published by the Urban Institute Justice Policy Center, June 2001, p. 17.

Chapter 10

The Legal System

The legal system is the whole apparatus that dispenses justice. Is our legal system in trouble? We will try to answer that question by looking at how criminal cases are handled, since crime is near the top of the list of Americans' concerns.

Our first panels address two issues: Is the criminal justice system too overburdened to guarantee a speedy trial? And: What is the likelihood of a person being convicted of a crime? The principle that justice should be meted out fairly and quickly was spelled out in the Magna Carta (1215): "Justice be to none denied or delayed." The American Constitution guarantees that "in all criminal prosecutions, the accused shall enjoy the right to a speedy and public trial." Nineteenth-century British statesman William Ewart Gladstone (1809-1898) opined: "Justice delayed is justice denied." Today, one of the most frequently voiced criticisms of the American justice system is the excessive length of time it takes for justice to be served. Is it really taking longer these days to resolve cases, and if so, why? We will see that the war on drugs has created a crisis in the nation's courtrooms. And if likelihood of conviction is supposed to be an important determinant in crime prevention, where do we stand? How many persons arrested for crimes ever come to trial?

We continue with a look at the use of the insanity defense. Arguably, no other aspect of the criminal justice system is as controversial. Are more people "getting away with murder" by pleading insanity these days? Will they soon be set free by the wonders of modern medication and come after you?

We move next to a consideration of access to justice. Are the poor getting a fair shake when it comes to representation in the nation's courtrooms? We conclude the chapter with a look at hate-crime legislation. How is the Justice System coping with violent acts directed against people, property, or organizations because of the group to which they belong or identify with?

You Are Under Arrest

Arrest Trends: 1971-2000 and Justice System Employment: 1982-1999

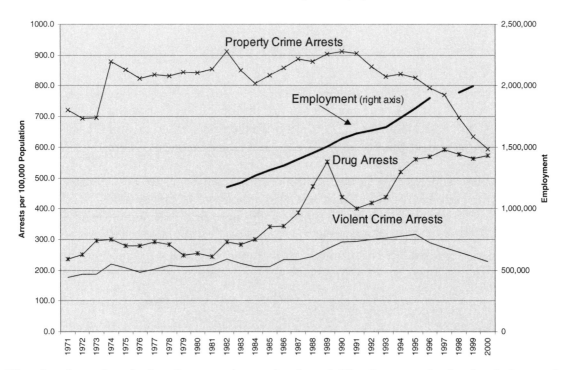

We often hear that the legal system is overburdened. The four panels that begin here address this issue — whether it is true and why, and how it manifests itself. As a way of trying to bring the issue home, over the course of these panels we will follow you as you are arrested, charged with a crime, released on bail, and finally tried and convicted.

We begin with a look at the volume of alleged scofflaws who pass through the legal system each year. This chart tracks arrests per 100,000 people over a 30-year period. Included are (1) arrests for the eight serious offenses reported to the FBI that constitute the "crime rate" and (2) drug arrests (among the top arrest offenses but not part of the "crime rate." See Chapters 1 and 6). Arrest figures do not measure the number of *persons* arrested, because industrious criminals may be arrested more than once during the course of a year.

The chart shows an 18% drop in arrests for property crimes over the 30-year period but a 60% rise in arrests for violent crimes. The War on Drugs (declared in 1970) made drug arrests climb an astounding 280%, resulting in a dramatic increase in caseloads in the nation's courts. How has the system responded? We present an excerpt from a Bureau of Justice Assistance report on Cook County, Illinois, the first system in the nation to be forced to establish night courts to handle the drug caseload:[1]

---

[1] The Bureau of Justice Assistance is part of the U.S. Department of Justice.

"The drug night court program in Cook County Circuit Court began as an emergency measure to cope with rapidly expanding caseloads. In 1975, 6,000 felony cases were filed in the court.[2] Two years later that number had more than doubled — to 14,000. In another 10 years, filings doubled again, to 28,000 — and half that 28,000 were narcotics arrests."

With arrests up, more personnel were called for. The chart shows that justice system employment at the state and local levels (where the vast majority of the nation's litigation is handled) rose 70% from 1982 to 1999.[3] Some personnel were diverted to the new types of courts that came into existence — notably drug, family, and teen courts. The Bureau of Justice Statistics reports that by 1998, there were 327 drug courts across 43 states, the District of Columbia, and Puerto Rico, the majority of which came into existence between 1992 and 1996. By 1998 all but 17 states had family courts and teen courts had grown from 50 in 1991 to somewhere between 400 and 500. In 1997 Broward County, Florida, established the nation's first mental health court to deal with the increasing numbers of nonviolent mentally ill persons who cross paths with the legal system.

Estimated Totals of Top 7 Arrest Offenses

Type of Arrest	Number
Total Arrests	13,980,300
Drug Abuse Violations	1,579,600
Driving Under the Influence	1,471,300
Simple Assaults	1,312,200
Larceny/Theft	1,166,400
Liquor Laws	683,100
Disorderly Conduct	638,700
Drunkenness	637,600

This table shows the top seven arrest offenses handled by the legal system in the year 2000 and the estimated total of persons arrested for those offenses. Persons arrested in 2000 were most likely to have been wanted for a drug abuse violation, driving under the influence, simple assault, or larceny/theft.

Let us say you were arrested for larceny/theft.[4] You were probably arrested by a police officer, who was either in possession of an arrest warrant or had reason to believe you had a connection to illegal activity. The officer who arrested you may have taken you "downtown" for booking (photographs and fingerprinting) then put you in a jail cell. Or you may have been booked at the crime scene and let go in exchange for a written promise to appear in court at a later date. So what happens next?

Sources: Chart: Sourcebook of Criminal Justice Statistics Online, Section 1, Table 1.19, and Section 4, Table 4.2, http://www.albany.edu/sourcebook/1995/tost_4.html#4_a. Table: Bureau of Justice Statistics, "Enforcement"; Primary source: FBI, *Uniform Crime Reports, Crime in the United States*, annual; http://www.ojp.usdoj.gov/bjs/dcf/enforce.htm#arrests (the arrest totals are based on all reporting agencies and estimates for unreported areas). "Criminal Law: An Overview," http://www.nolo.com. Bureau of Justice Assistance, "Drug Night Courts: The Cook County Experience," August 1994, http://www.ncjrs.org/txtfiles/dncc.txt. Bureau of Justice Statistics, "Court Organization Statistics," http://www.ojp.usdoj.gov/bjs/courts.htm#courts. Information retrieved October 29, 2002.

---

[2] Felonies involve violence, drugs, weapons, or property (motor vehicle theft, for example).

[3] Includes police protection, judicial and legal, and corrections. Data for 1996 were not reported.

[4] Larceny/theft is defined by the FBI as "the unlawful taking, carrying, leading, or riding away of property from the possession or constructive possession of another. It includes crimes such as shoplifting, pocket-picking, purse-snatching, thefts from motor vehicles, thefts of motor vehicle parts and accessories, bicycle thefts, etc., in which no use of force, violence, or fraud occurs."

You Are Charged With a Crime

Percent of Crime Index Crimes Cleared by Arrest

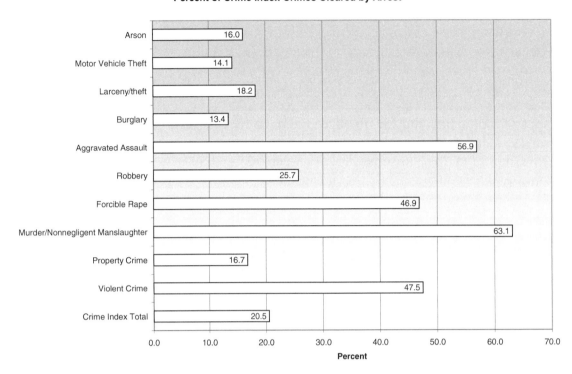

In the preceding panel, you were arrested for larceny/theft. Next you will be charged and turned over to the court for prosecution, thereby clearing one of the eight crime index offenses tracked by the FBI. This is how you fit into the FBI's definition of a cleared offense: "when at least one person is arrested, charged with the commission of an offense, and turned over to the court for prosecution." The other way an offense is cleared is when the perpetrator dies.

The chart shows the percentage of index crimes that were cleared by an arrest in the year 2000.[5] Looking at it, you can see that your luck ran out when you were arrested, since relatively few crimes are cleared by arrests. In the year 2000, only 18.2% of all larcenies/thefts reported to police were cleared. In fact, only 20.5% of the total of all crimes reported to police in the year 2000 were cleared. This low clearance pattern held true regardless of whether the offense was committed in a big city or a small town. In eight cities with a population of 1 million or more, 17.5% of reported crimes were cleared by an arrest. In 641 cities with a population of 25,000 to 49,999, 21.4% of reported crimes were cleared by an arrest. Further evidence of your bad luck — the FBI reports that less effort goes into investigating crimes against property (like yours) than crimes against persons.

---

[5] We might have had you arrested for a drug abuse violation — more people are arrested for this than for any other offense, but FBI data for crimes cleared by arrests are only available for crime index crimes.

In 2000, 47.5% of violent crimes were cleared, compared to 16.7% of property crimes (excluding arson).

According to the laws of most states, shortly after being arrested, you will be charged either with a serious crime (felony) or a misdemeanor, all depending on the value of the articles you, ah, appropriated. A felony calls for a bigger fine (if applicable) and longer imprisonment (more than a year) than a misdemeanor. Because yours is a criminal matter, not a civil case, you must make a first (initial) appearance in a trial court (or district court) for a hearing (your arraignment).[6] One of about 9,065 full-time authorized judges serving in 71 statewide trial court systems of general jurisdiction will most likely preside.[7]

Because the Constitution bans secret accusations, your appearance is public unless you request otherwise, and you must be present at this hearing (if you were a juvenile, your hearing would most likely be private). You enter a plea, and the judge determines whether there is sufficient evidence to schedule a trial. The answer is yes. You get a court-appointed lawyer (if you can't afford to pay for one). You ask to be released on little or no bail (the money or other security you leave to guarantee your presence at trial). Our next panel looks at the likelihood of your being released.

Sources: Chart: FBI, Uniform Crime Reports, 2000, Section IV, Table 25, http://www.fbi.gov/ucr/00cius.htm. "Criminal Law: An Overview," http://www.nolo.com. Bureau of Justice Statistics, Court Organization Statistics, http://www.ojp.usdog.gov/bjs/courts.htm.

---

[6] A civil case usually involves a dispute "over the rights and duties that individuals and organizations legally owe to each other" (Nolo.com).

[7] Courts of general jurisdiction have authority (granted by federal and state laws) to decide cases of many different types.

You Wait for Justice to Be Served

Percentage of Felony Defendants Released or Detained Until Case Disposition:
1992-1998

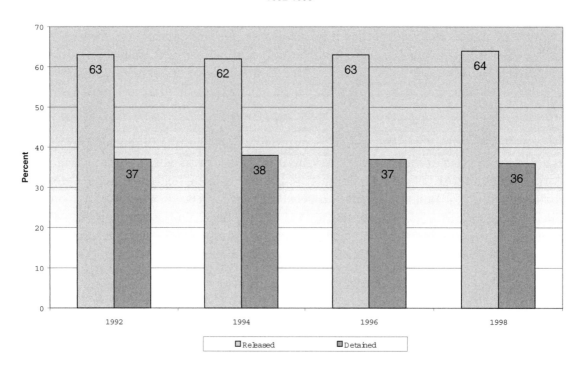

You have been charged with larceny/theft of a sufficient amount to count as a serious crime — a felony. A judge has determined there is sufficient evidence to set a trial date, and it is set. What happens to you now?

Assume you are a resident of one of the nation's 75 largest counties, where about one-half of all serious crimes occur. The chart presents U.S. Department of Justice data on what happened to defendants charged with felonies in those counties in the month of May 1992, 1994, 1996, and 1998 (total defendants in 1992, 51,002; in 1994, 50,241; in 1996, 51,234; and in 1998 54,458).[8] Nearly two-thirds of defendants were sent home while the other third sat in jail. Proving that some people never learn, in 1998, 31% of those who were released were rearrested for a new offense or did not show up for a court date or violated some other condition of their pretrial release.

As might be expected, those charged with the most violent crimes were the most likely to be held until trial. In the nation's 75 most populous counties, 409 defendants had murder charges filed against them in the month of May 1998; 87% of the 409 were detained until

---

[8] The Bureau of Justice Statistics (BJS) initiated the biennial National Pretrial Reporting Program (NPRP), from which these data came, in February 1998. NPRP collects demographic, criminal history, pretrial processing, adjudication, and sentencing information on felony defendants in state courts of the nation's 75 most populous counties. The NPRP data do not include defendants charged with federal crimes.

---

trial. These individuals may be flight risks and/or dangers to themselves or the community. (Complete data for the various arrest charges can be found at the back of this book.) In 1998, in cases like yours (larceny/theft), 5,316 defendants (73%) were released to await trial.

Assume you have been released. While you wait for trial, the person responsible for prosecuting your case will most likely do one of two things: Prepare a case against you to prove "beyond a reasonable doubt" that you committed the crime of which you are accused or strike a plea bargain with you and your attorney. A plea bargain is an agreement between you and the prosecutor in which you plead guilty or no contest to criminal charges. In exchange, the prosecutor drops some charges, reduces a charge, or recommends that the judge enter a sentence that is acceptable to you. According to Nolo.com ("Law for All"), the nation's criminal courts are so clogged that plea bargaining is the method by which most criminal cases are now settled.

But there is no plea bargain for you, and your case is readied for trial. As we shall see in the next panel, from the time of your arrest to the disposition of your case, nothing will happen quickly. What is outlined here is just a bare-bones summary of the ordeal you have already endured — from police questioning (of you and most likely your friends and family too), to searches, to finding a lawyer, and more. And you haven't even told your story to the judge yet. How long will it take from beginning to end? Let's have a look at the statistics.

Sources: U.S. Department of Justice, "Felony Defendants in Large Urban Counties," 1992, 1994, 1996, 1998, http://www.ojp.usdoj.gov/bjs/pretrial.htm. "Criminal Law," http://www.nolo.com. Information retrieved November 4, 2002.

At Long Last, Justice Is Served

Median Number of Days Between Arrest and Sentencing for Felony Cases Disposed by State Courts

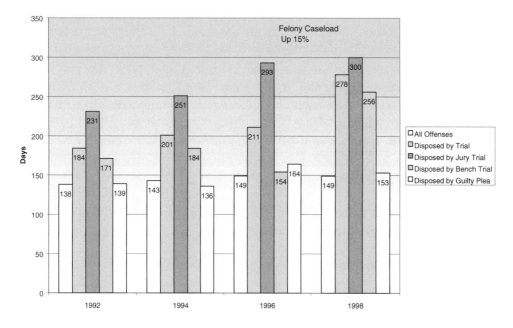

"A basic challenge confronting the contemporary justice system remains: Is it possible to resolve cases expeditiously without sacrificing the quality of justice?" — Ostrom and Hanson (see Source notes)

One might expect that in an overburdened system, cases would take longer to dispose of than they used to. To find out, we look at felony cases involving adults who were convicted and sentenced in state courts. As in the preceding panel, the data come from the nation's 75 largest counties, where half of the nation's serious crimes occur. The charted data show median elapsed time from arrest to sentencing and median elapsed time according to case disposition (jury trial, bench trial [one that is heard by a judge with no jury present], and guilty plea).

According to the FBI, there were 14.5 million arrests in 1998 for all causes. According to the Bureau of Justice Statistics, state courts convicted nearly 930,000 adults of a felony in 1998. This was up 39% over 1988 (667,366) and up 4% over 1992 (893,630). Government statistics sources do not reveal how many cases were plea bargained.

Felony cases are complicated and take longer than other types of cases to resolve. The table beginning on the next page shows the percent change from 1992 to 1998 in the median number of days to dispose of cases by type of felony offense and case disposition.

Percent Change in Median Elapsed Time

from Arrest to Sentencing: 1992 to 1998

Offense	Percent Change in Median Number of Days for Cases Disposed by:				
		Trial			Guilty
	Total	Total	Jury	Bench	Plea
All Offenses	8	51	30	50	10
Violent Offenses	10	37	24	51	15
Property Offenses	15	61	57	35	20
Drug Offenses	-7	54	31	50	2
Drug Possession	-9	58	37	51	0
Drug Trafficking	2	42	30	43	3
Weapons Offenses	-2	30	14	52	1
Other Offenses[1]	5	70	20	77	9

[1] Nonviolent offenses such as receiving stolen property and vandalism.

In 1998 the median disposition time for all felony cases was 149 days, up 8% over 1992. At a median 300 days in 1998, jury trial cases took the longest time (up 30% over the 1992 median of 231). Bench trials took 256 days (up 50% over the 1992 median of 171). Guilty plea dispositions took the least amount of time — 153 days (up 10% from 1992, 139 days). The only offenses for which median days declined were weapons offenses (down 2%) and drug offenses (down 9%). The decline for drug offenses was due to a decline in median number of days to dispose of cases of drug possession.

To return to your case: At the start of your trial for larceny/theft, you would have been given the choice of a jury trial or a bench trial. Let us say you chose a bench trial. Some 256 days after your arrest, the judge finds you guilty. As the saying goes: "The mills of the gods grind slowly but they grind exceedingly fine." The judge now hands down a sentence that you don't like. What can you do? You might consider appealing to a higher (appellate) court. What are your chances of prevailing there? Not very good, according to Nolo.com: "Appeals judges generally resist overruling trial court judgments and prefer to give trial judges wide discretion in the conduct of trials. As many appellate courts have said, defendants are not guaranteed 'perfect' trials. Normally an appellate court will overturn a guilty verdict only if the trial court made an error of law that significantly contributed to the outcome." Too bad for you. Upon reflection, and after a review of the attorney fees you have paid up to now, you choose not to appeal. Refer to Chapter 9 for a discussion of prisons.

Returning to the topic of our overburdened legal system, the independent National Center for State Courts (NCSC) provides heavily footnoted (that is, often incomplete) data on appellate and trial court caseloads in the states, District of Columbia, and Puerto Rico. Some highlights from NCSC's report for 2001: The total number of cases filed in state trial courts (both criminal and civil cases) reached an eight-year high of 92 million. Domestic violence filings were up 11% over the preceding five years. The number of felony cases filed between 1998 and 2000 remained stable.

We have seen that only a fraction of the crimes reported to the police are ever resolved by an arrest, and only a fraction of the miscreants arrested ever go to trial. For example, homicide, with the highest clearance rate of all serious crimes, had only a 69% clearance rate in 1999, down from 76% in 1976 (homicides of children are the most likely to be cleared). One might wonder what would happen to our legal system if the clearance rate were higher — if more people, in other words, were arrested and then tried?

In the 1980s, calls for court reform led to the adoption of performance standards and measures in state courts.[9] Many states now have deadlines for completing felony cases — deadlines that can't always be met. For example, the state of Florida recommends 180 days to complete a felony case. In July 2002 the *Tallahassee Democrat* reported on court costs and case delays in Leon County (Tallahassee is the seat). More than 25% of felony cases in Leon County took longer than 180 days to resolve, up from 10% of cases in 1992. The newspaper reported that the biggest factor contributing to the delays is the number of felony case filings, but "legislators, prosecutors, defendants and their attorneys all help bog down the system."[10] Why should the public care? Because "operating the [Leon County] court costs more than twice as much as it did 10 years ago, even though the crime rate has been dropping." Taxpayers foot the bill.

Ostrom and Hanson (quoted at the beginning of this panel) studied nine criminal trial courts. They suggest that overburdened courts might simply be inefficient: "Timeliness and the quality of justice are not mutually exclusive either in theory or in fact," they wrote. "The evidence suggests that well-performing courts should be expected to excel in terms of both timeliness and quality."

The American legal system is complex, confusing, sometimes infuriating, constantly evolving, and everyone has an opinion about its fairness, impartiality, and incorruptibility. With regard to its timeliness, Supreme Court Justice Warren E. Burger reminded the American Bar Association back in 1972 (when technology was being touted as the way to expedite case disposition): "Concepts of justice must have hands and feet or they remain sterile abstractions. The hands and feet we need are efficient means and methods to carry out justice in every case in the shortest possible time and at the lowest possible cost. This is the challenge to every lawyer and judge in America."

The insanity defense (next) is also a challenge to lawyers and judges. How do we reconcile the complexities of the human mind and the rigidity of the law?

Sources: Chart: U.S. Department of Justice, Bureau of Justice Statistics, *Felony Sentences in State Courts*, various years; http://www. ojp.usdoj.gov/bjs/. Brian J. Ostrom and Roger A. Hanson, *Efficiency, Timeliness, and Quality: A New Perspective From Nine State Criminal Trial Courts*, National Center for State Courts, 1999. Court Statistics Project, *State Court Caseload Statistics, 2001*, (National Center for State Courts 2001)., Table 15, and Press Release (March 28,2002), http://www.ncsconline.org/. James L. Rosica, "A slow process," July 19,2002, http://www.tallahassee.com/mld/tallahassee/news/special_packages/justice/3696380.htm. James Alan Fox and Marianne Zawitz, *Homicide Trends in the United States*, Bureau of Justice Statistics, http://www.ojp.usdoj.gov/bjs/ pub/pdf/htius.pdf. Fredric I. Lederer, "Courtroom Technology From the Judges' Perspective, http://www.courtroom21.net/About_Us/ Articles/judicial.html#N_9_. Information retrieved October 24, 2002.

[9] See Pamela Casey, "Defining Optimal Court Performance: The Trial Court Performance Standards," retrieved October 22, 2002, from

[10] According to a study by the National Center for State Courts, in 1999 Leon County had the highest number of felony filings per 1,000 population (21.8) of all major urban areas in the country.

Insanity Defense Overview

Some Landmarks in the Use of the Insanity Defense

1843	M'Naghten case establishes the first modern insanity defense.
1886	Appellate court decision in *Parsons v Alabama*.
1954	Supreme Court decision in *Durham v United States*.
1962	American Law Institute develops new insanity rule as part of Model Penal Code.
1975	Supreme Court decision in *Drope v Missouri*.
1979	Montana abolishes the insanity defense.
1981	John Hinckley not guilty by reason of insanity in attempted assassination of President Reagan.
1984	Congress passes and President Reagan signs Insanity Defense Reform Act.
1994	Supreme Court decisions in *Cowan v Montana* & *Shannon v United States*.

The insanity defense is based on the centuries-old principle that a person ought not to be punished for wrongdoing unless criminal intent can be established. A person using the defense seeks to be acquitted of a crime by reason of insanity. In the past, it seems, judges knew a "lunatic" when they saw one, and when a person was acquitted of a crime by reason of insanity, he might expect to spend years or a lifetime locked up in an institution for the criminally insane. Today, advances in psychiatric treatment and concern for the rights of the mentally ill have changed the way the legal system deals with insanity ("insane" is a legal term, not a medical diagnosis). In this panel we look at some landmark court decisions regarding the use of the insanity defense. The next panel looks at popular perceptions of this defense.

Court Cases Establish Precedents: The modern insanity defense, incorporating the concepts of "knowing right from wrong" and "temporary insanity" was inscribed in Western law books in 1843 when a British court found Daniel M'Naghten (a k a McNaughtan) not guilty by reason of insanity (NGRI) of trying to assassinate the prime minister. The defense became so popular in America that Mark Twain complained: "This country, during the last thirty or forty years, has produced some of the most remarkable cases of insanity of which there is any mention in history.... Is not this insanity plea becoming rather common?"

The M'Naghten Rule was the standard used in American courtrooms until 1962, but not everyone was happy with it. Long before 1962, some complained that the rule excused only the most profoundly mentally ill from criminal conduct. Shouldn't there be some consideration for the person who couldn't stop himself, even though he knew an act was wrong? In 1886 there appeared the first of a series of court decisions establishing new criteria for the insanity defense — *Parsons v Alabama*; it added the concept of "irresistible impulse."[11] In 1962 the American Law Institute (A.L.I.) proposed a new standard; at least half of the states use the standard now.[12] Among other things, the A.L.I. test recognized that there are varying degrees of incapacity.

Meanwhile, the field of psychiatry emerged with new theories, definitions, and treatments for the mentally ill. In 1954 the U.S. Supreme Court ruled in *Durham v United States* that a person could not be held criminally responsible if his act was the "product of a mental disease or defect." This decision eliminated any consideration of right and wrong from the insanity defense and is credited with bringing legions of psychiatrists into courtrooms to expound on the meaning of "product" and "mental disease" and "defect" and so on.

Public Perceptions: As the legal establishment struggled to clarify the appropriate use and interpretation of the insanity defense, the public seemed to think that the defense was being used too often and frivolously. Members of the psychiatric profession came to be seen as too willing to tailor their testimony to favor the side that paid them. In one particularly noteworthy case, former San Francisco policeman Dan White was tried in 1979 for the murders of Mayor Harvey Milk and an aide (to which he confessed). Medical experts testified that White was depressed when he committed the crimes, and his uncharacteristic consumption of junk food was offered as evidence of his depression. The press gleefully coined the term "Twinkie Defense." White was convicted of involuntary manslaughter and served five years in prison. Many believed that White got away with murder, and the Twinkie Defense is now part of urban legend.

In the year of the Twinkie Defense, Montana became the first state to abolish the insanity defense, a decision the U.S. Supreme Court allowed to stand in 1994 when it declined to review *Montana v Cowan*. Soon after, Utah, Idaho, and Kansas abolished the insanity plea,[13] a position that is supported by the American Medical Association. According to some analysts, what actually happens in places where the insanity defense is abolished is that an obviously insane defendant is ruled incompetent to stand trial and is immediately committed to an institution, bypassing any question of a defense.

---

[11] A person could use the insanity defense if he could prove that "by reason of duress of mental disease he had so far lost the power to choose between right and wrong, and to avoid doing the act in question, as that his free agency was at the time destroyed" (an irresistible impulse).

[12] The American Law Institute (A.L.I.) was formed in 1923 to "promote the clarification and simplification of the law." Every state has its own criminal (penal) codes. The Model Penal Code established by A.L.I. in 1962 sought to reconcile the codes into one "American criminal code" (Robinson; see Source notes). The A.L.I. language stated that a defendant is not responsible for a criminal offense if "at the time of such conduct as a result of a mental disease or defect, he lacks substantial capacity either to appreciate the criminality of his conduct or to conform his conduct to the requirements of the law."

[13] These states restrict the admission of psychiatric evidence to the issue of *mens rea* (criminal intent), thus abolishing insanity as a separate affirmative defense (that is, a defense raised by the defendant, who then carries the burden of proving it).

Another landmark in the history of the insanity defense, and one that led to widespread tinkering with policies, procedures, and standards, came on the heels of John Hinckley's 1981 assassination attempt on President Reagan. The court acquitted Hinckley, finding him "not guilty by reason of insanity." Even though Hinckley did not go free (he remains hospitalized), there was a heated public outcry, reflecting a pervasive fear that violent criminals acquitted by reason of insanity walk freely among us. Reform of the system was again called for. In 1984 Congress passed the Insanity Defense Reform Act, which created a special verdict of "not guilty *only* by reason of insanity." In federal courts, the burden was now on the defendant to prove by "clear and convincing evidence" that "as a result of a severe mental disease or defect" the defendant did not know right from wrong.

In state courts, approaches to reforming the system involved placing a heavier burden of proof on the defendant, making changes in commitment and release procedures, and/or adopting other sentencing options. Arizona and Oregon offer the option "guilty except insane." In 1975 Michigan was the first state to enact a "guilty but mentally ill" verdict after two insanity acquittees raped two women and murdered another after their release from inpatient hospitalization. About 14 states now permit this verdict; it usually requires that the defendant be hospitalized and serve a reasonable prison sentence if discharged.

More Landmark Court Cases: In 1975 the Supreme Court ruled on the issue of competence to stand trial in *Drope v Missouri*. Charged with raping his wife, Drope tried to commit suicide. His absence during trial was termed "voluntary" by the court, the trial proceeded without him, and he was found guilty. Drope appealed, claiming he had been deprived of due process of law by the trial court's failure to order a psychiatric examination with respect to his competence to stand trial. The Supreme Court ruled that his irrational behavior, demeanor at trial, and prior medical opinion should have been taken into account in determining his competence to stand trial.

In 1994 the Supreme Court ruled in *Shannon v United States* that a federal district court is not required to instruct the jury regarding the consequences to the defendant of an NGRI verdict. Shannon had requested that the jury be advised that he would face involuntary commitment if he were found NGRI.

And so the refinements and the controversy continue. According to *JAMA*, there are at least 100,000 insane people in this county.[14] If they take to lives of crime, will they get away with murder? Our next panel looks at public perceptions of the insanity defense.

Sources: Twain, Mark, "A New Crime," in *Sketches, New and Old* (Hartford, Conn.: American Publishing Company, 1875), Jim Zwick, ed., http://www.boondocksnet.com/twaintexts/new_crime.html. Flanagan, Newman, "Not Guilty Does Not Mean Innocent." http://www.massbar.org/article.php. Paul H. Robinson, *An Introduction to the Model Penal Code*, http://www.law.nwu.edu/faculty/fulltime/robinson/articles/intromodpencode.pdf. American Psychiatric Association, "The Insanity Defense Position Statement," Approved October 1982, http://www.psych.org/archives/820002.pdf. "Heredity as a social burden," *JAMA, The Journal of the American Medical Association*, August 14, 1996 v276 n6 p444B(1).

---

[14] *JAMA Journal of the American Medical Association* (see Source notes).

Getting Away With Murder?

Wyoming Citizens' Estimates of the Number of Defendants Who Entered a NGRI Defense

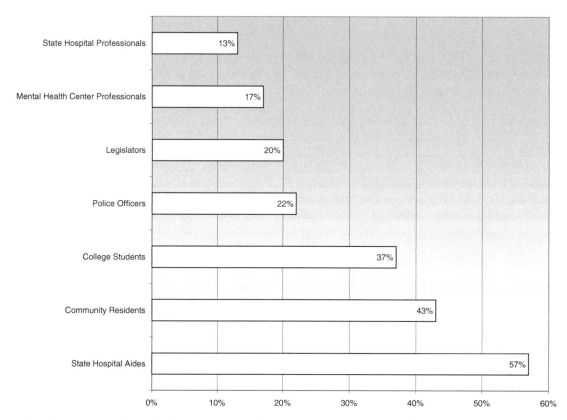

"Though vigorously criticized, the insanity defense is only rarely employed. Annual acquittals via NGI in the United States are rarer than the reported annual incidence of snake bite in New York City." — Ernest C. Miller, M.D. (see Source notes) (NGI and NGRI are abbreviations for "not guilty by reason of insanity.")

Misperceptions about the insanity defense are common, as the chart demonstrates. Wyoming residents were asked to estimate what percentage of defendants entered NGRI pleas. Their estimates ranged from 13% to 57%. When the same group was asked to estimate the percentage of persons entering the plea who were so adjudicated, the estimates ranged from 19% to 44%. The actual results: "Of the 22,012 indicted defendants, 102 (0.46%) had presented the defense. Of these 102 defendants, only one (0.0045% of the 22,012) was found NGRI."

In a 1981 poll conducted by Roper Center for Public Opinion Research for NBC News/ Associated Press, 87% of respondents said "yes" to the question: "Do you think that too many accused murderers are using the insanity defense to keep from going to prison, or don't you think so?" In a 1994 poll conducted by Roper for ABC News, 65% of men and 62% of women disagreed with the statement: "Most of the people who are found not guilty by reason of insanity really were insane when they committed the crime." In a 1993 Roper poll conducted for ABC News/Washington Post, 64% of men and 67% of women said the insanity defense should not be allowed when asked: "When people are put on trial for murder, do you think the courts should continue to allow them to plead 'not guilty by reason of insanity', or do you think the rules should be changed so that people charged with murder cannot use an 'insanity' defense?"

What is a civilized society supposed to do about mentally ill offenders who commit violent acts? In law, it is still the standard that a person who commits a crime as a result of mental illness should not be held criminally responsible because he lacks the criminal intent to commit the act. But the law, the medical establishment, and the public do not always see eye to eye. According to Christina Studebaker: "Insanity is a legal defense that is raised relatively infrequently, and rarely pleaded successfully." But a sizeable segment of the public is uneasy with the failure to assign responsibility and to punish the transgressor that seems to be part of an NGRI acquittal. This is, after all, the "get tough on crime" era. Nusbaum contends that the public does not mind quite as much when the defense is used and the trial results in a conviction, "yet if the trial results in a NGRI verdict the system has failed for allowing a 'wrong verdict' to come about. Quite possibly, as Dr. Loren Roth has suggested, 'the American public may simply be nothing more than a 'bad loser.'"

But it is also true that the American public does not want to see the perpetrator of an awful crime freely walking the streets. "One of the true ironies of our legal system is that the sicker you are, the less likely you are to be successful with the insanity defense," says attorney Roy Black, who has tried several insanity cases. "Especially with particularly horrific crimes, jurors want to know whether these people will ever get out. And the prospect of their getting out scares jurors to death" (quoted by Robinson).

Consider the horrific case of Andrea Yates. In March 2002, a panel of Texas jurors debated her fate. A devoted mother with a history of postpartum psychosis, hallucinations, and two suicide attempts, Yates admitted to drowning her five children in a bathtub. Prosecutors conceded that Yates was mentally ill but knew right from wrong and so was not legally insane at the time of the murders. In Texas, writes Timothy Roche, "the law on insanity defenses is among the most restrictive in the nation," and under the law, jurors could not be told that Yates would be hospitalized if she were found NGRI. The jury rejected her claim of mental illness, found her guilty, spared her the death penalty but sentenced her to life in prison. There, "she will be kept in protective custody because of her ongoing mental problems and possible threats from other inmates … Unless she needs intensive psychiatric care … [she] will eventually mingle with the general population at the prison known for housing some of the toughest, meanest women in Texas" (Roche).[15] Yates's symptoms are controlled by medication.

---

[15] The outcome might have been different if Yates had a bench trial (without a jury). According to Miller (see Source notes), when judges rule on the issue of insanity, they tend to reject the plea in fewer than 50% of cases, while juries reject the plea 85% of the time. Barry Wall, M.D., President of the Rhode Island Psychiatric Society, says judges are well aware that many people are in jail because society has failed to provide them with adequate mental health treatment. Juries, on the other hand, are not so knowledgeable or sympathetic.

We saw in the preceding panel how the clamor after Hinckley's NGRI acquittal brought the insanity defense under attack and how various "reforms" were enacted. Donald M. Linhorst, Ph.D., et al. evaluated three popular proposals for the disposition of mentally ill offenders: abolishing the insanity defense, substituting a guilty but mentally ill verdict, or retaining the insanity defense with a conditional-release community monitoring program (the authors favor the last option). The authors state:

"The three disposition options are influenced by the competing interests of the criminal justice and mental health systems. The criminal justice system seeks to protect public safety, while the primary goal of the mental health system is to treat and rehabilitate persons with mental illness. The balance between these competing interests is influenced by the political environment. The current conservative political environment has shaped statutory revisions and alternative policy options for mentally ill offenders and has generally promoted public safety over due process rights and treatment needs of mentally ill offenders."

Another often expressed concern is that criminals can fake insanity. How common is that? Miller says "most individuals accused of crime lack psychological sophistication" and are not likely to be able to fool the experts for long. Successful fakers may find themselves spending more time in a mental hospital than they would have spent in jail.

According to Maier: "Studies also suggest that the idea of a fraudulent resort to the insanity defense is a persistent myth. Between 70 and 90 percent of insanity cases end with the prosecutor agreeing the defendant is insane." In a 1996 study of the Baltimore Circuit Court, 8 of 60,432 indicted defendants pleaded NGRI. All eight pleas were uncontested by the state. Howard Zonana, medical director of the American Academy of Psychiatry and the Law, told the *Washington Post* that the Academy's studies have concluded that "the overwhelming majority" of defendants acquitted by reason of insanity suffer from schizophrenia or another mental illness. Such individuals are usually committed to treatment centers until it has been determined that they are no longer a danger. But can medical experts accurately predict who will commit dangerous acts in the future?

We know that state court caseloads are up. Let's see who is representing the indigent.

Sources: Chart: Data appear in a footnote in Daniel J. Nusbaum, "The craziest reform of them all: a critical analysis of the constitutional implications of 'abolishing' the insanity defense," *Cornell Law Review*, Sept 2002 v87 i6 p1509(64). Data are attributed in a footnote on page 1512 to George L. Blau and Richard A. Pasewark, *Statutory Changes and the Insanity Defense: Seeking the Perfect Insane Person*, 18 *Law & Psychol. Rev.* 679, 69 (1994. On the same page is the reference to Dr. Loren Roth, author of "Preserve but Limit the Insanity Defense," 58 *Psychiatric Q*, 91,91 (1986-87, and the quote from Christina Studebaker, *Evaluating the Insanity Defense: Identifying Empirical and Moral Questions*, 5 U. Chi. L. Sch. Roundtable 345,345 (1998). Ernest C. Miller, M.D., "The Insanity Defense: On Being Insane In Sane Places," http://www.dcmsonline.org/jax-medicine/1997journals/march97/insanitydefense.htm. Bryan Robinson, "Too Crazy to Be Insane: Horrific Crimes Are Often a Detriment to Insanity Cases," ABCNews.com, June 21, 2001, http://abcnews.go.com/sections/us/DailyNews/insanity010621.html. Timothy Maier, "One flew into the cuckoo's nest," *Insight on the News*, Sept 14, 1998 v14 n34 p10(4). Timothy Roche, "Andrea Yates: More to the Story," *Time* online, http://www.time.com/time/. Donald M. Linhorst and P. Ann Dirks-Linhorst, "A Critical Assessment of Disposition Options for Mentally Ill Offenders, *Social Service Review*, March 1999 v73 i1 p65(1). Criminal Justice/Mental Health Consensus Project, http://consensus project.org/content/stat10. John P. Martin, "The Insanity Defense: A Closer Look," washingtonpost.com, February 27, 1998, http://www.washingtonpost.com/wp-srv/local/longterm/aron/qa227.htm. Mary Jo Curtis, "Inquiring Minds: Barry Wall on the mentally ill and the legal system," *George Street Journal*, February 8, 2002, http://www.brown.edu/Administration/George_Street_Journal/vol26/26GSJ17e.html. Information retrieved November 1, 2002.

And Justice for All

Representation of Felons in State Courts in the 75 Largest Counties: 1996

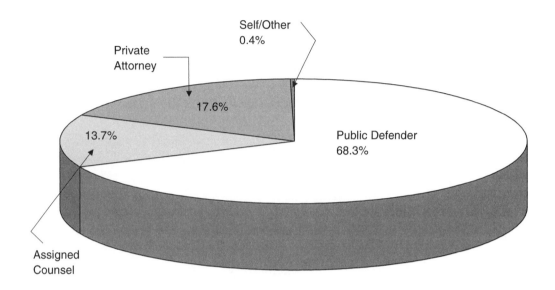

Self/Other
0.4%

Private
Attorney

17.6%

13.7%

Public Defender
68.3%

Assigned
Counsel

"There can be no equal justice where the kind of trial a man gets depends on the amount of money he has." — U.S. Supreme Court Justice Hugo Black

In this great country, it is a truth almost universally acknowledged that every poor accused person has the right to have court-appointed legal counsel. Some may be surprised to learn that this right was only recently acquired.

Back in 1791 the Sixth Amendment to the Constitution established the right of an accused person in criminal proceedings "to have the Assistance of Counsel for his defense." But for more than 140 years, the Sixth Amendment was interpreted to mean that anyone who wished counsel *and was able to pay for it* could have counsel. Our modern understanding of the right to counsel came from landmark Supreme Court decisions in the 20th century, beginning with *Powell v Alabama* (1932). In that case, the court set aside the conviction for rape of eight illiterate, indigent young black men (the "Scottsboro boys") sentenced to death in a hasty trial carried out without recourse to legal counsel. The court ruled that it was the state's responsibility to see that the defendants had adequate legal counsel.

In 1963 the Supreme Court held in *Gideon v Wainwright* "that in our adversary system of criminal justice, any person haled into court, who is too poor to hire a lawyer, cannot be assured a fair trial unless counsel is provided for him." In practice, the decision meant that accused persons in state criminal proceedings acquired the right to counsel. *Argersinger v Hamlin* (1972) extended the right to felony and criminal cases if conviction carried a sentence of imprisonment. In a further refinement of indigent defendants' rights, Justice Hugo Black incorporated the quote at the beginning of this panel in the Supreme Court's decision in *Griffin v Illinois* (1964), which ordered the state of Illinois to pay for indigent Griffin's trial transcript so he could file an appeal.

How many people are now represented by court-appointed attorneys? The chart above shows statistics from the country's 75 largest counties. In 1996, 82% of defendants charged with a violent crime in those counties had court-appointed counsel. According to Adkins, that percentage can increase to "as high as 90% in some jurisdictions in response to the war on crime and crackdown on drugs in recent government administrations."

The states have been left to their own devices to formulate systems for providing counsel for indigent defendants and to pay for such counsel. Three types of systems have emerged: Public defender programs (public or private nonprofit organizations with salaried staffs); assigned counsel systems (in which courts appoint willing private attorneys from a list of those available); and contract attorneys (who agree with governmental units to provide services for a specified period and fee). According to the National Prosecutors Survey of the nation's 75 largest counties, in 1992, 41% of jurisdictions used a combination of methods. Public defenders were used exclusively in 28% of jurisdictions and 23% of jurisdictions used the assigned counsel system exclusively.

Providing legal counsel to the poor is a noble concept. How does it play out in the real world? Our next panel looks at funding for indigent defense services.

Sources: Chart: Harlow, Caroline Wolf, Ph.D., "Defense Counsel in Criminal Cases," Bureau of Justice Statistics Special Report, NCJ 179023, November 2000. Steven K. Smith et al., "Indigent Defense," BJS Selected Findings, NCJ-158909, February 1996. "The Greatest Trials of All Time: The Scottsboro Boys," Court TV Online, http://www.courttv.com/greatesttrials/scottsboro/trials.html.

The Price of Defending the Criminal Poor

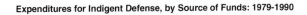

Expenditures for Indigent Defense, by Source of Funds: 1979-1990

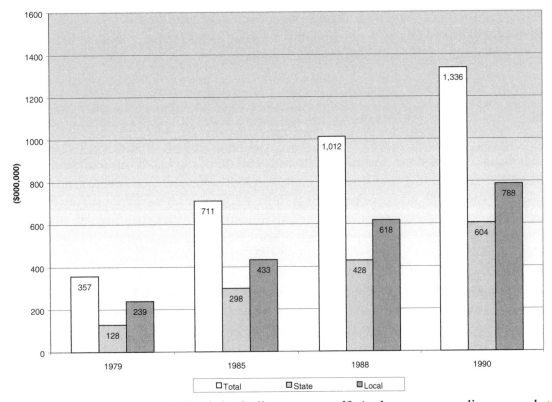

How much does it cost to defend the indigent accused? And are we spending enough to give them a proper defense? The graphic shows total expenditures and the breakdown by source of money for legal counsel for indigent defendants in civil and criminal suits.[16] As might be expected in a legal system in which caseloads continue to rise, expenditures went up, from $357 million in 1979 to $1.3 billion in 1990. In constant 1990 dollars, expenditures doubled from 1979 to 1990. In 1979 expenditures at the state level were 36% of spending. By 1990 state contributions accounted for 45% of spending.

The Bureau of Justice Statistics (BJS) provides more recent data on criminal cases only, from what it calls the only two systematic studies of indigent defense that have been done. The first study in the early 1980s included 50 counties. The second, in 1999, included 100 of the nation's most populous counties. Expenditures for indigent criminal defense services in 1982 in 50 counties totaled about $464 million (inflation-adjusted). Expenditures in 1999 in the same 50 counties totaled about $877 million, a 47% increase. Expenditures in 1999 for the 100 counties were an estimated $1.2 billion.

---

[16] Expenditures presented are not adjusted for inflation. Expenditures are for public defense, which includes legal counsel and representation in either criminal or civil proceedings as provided by public defenders and other government programs.

How big a bite does indigent defense take out of state court prosecutors' budgets? Using 1996 budget data for 81 of the 100 most populous counties, BJS is able to inform us that state court prosecutors in those 81 counties had budgets of $1.9 billion in 1999 (inflation-adjusted) and they spent $1.1 billion of that on indigent criminal defense services.

What do these figures mean? If the defense of indigent criminals is consuming 61% of state prosecutors' budgets, is that enough for a good defense? Let's look at some reports from the states regarding indigent defense spending.

According to the local newspapers, Georgia is facing an indigent defense crisis. The *Augusta Chronicle* (September 2002) advises: "About 80 percent of criminal defendants in Georgia are too poor to hire a lawyer. Last year, Georgia spent $55.4 million on indigent defense, 5 percent more than in 2000." Georgia ranks at or near the bottom in the states for indigent defense spending. The state's share of the $55.4 million spent in 2001 was 12%. Critics of Georgia's system complain that because local government picks up the lion's share of the tab, poor defendants in wealthy counties are better represented than poor defendants in poor counties. One proposed solution? More state money. Is there the political will? Georgia state representative Tom Bordeaux forthrightly explained: "Nobody ever gets a lot of votes by campaigning for the rights of criminals.... [The slogan] 'We Provided Accused Criminals With a Better Defense' just doesn't fit on a bumper sticker." In Georgia and elsewhere, the impetus for reform comes from a judge's bench. According to Georgia Supreme Court Justice Robert Benham: "This is an issue that does not have a natural constituency; there is no hue and cry out there."

In New York, lawyers refuse to take any more indigent cases, citing pay rates — unchanged for 16 years — that do not cover expenses ($40 an hour in court, $25 an hour for work out of court). In North Carolina, a reduction in hourly fees from $74 to $65 prompted some court-appointed lawyers to say they would no longer accept indigent clients. In New Jersey, public defenders in death penalty cases are paid $50 an hour. In Cameron County, Texas, court-appointed attorneys earned a maximum of $100 per misdemeanor case and $350 per felony in 1999, no matter how much time they put into a case. According to a 1997 study by the American Bar Association, Alabama had a $1,000 cap in death penalty cases to cover the entire investigation and trial (Hand).

This suggests two questions: Are publicly-financed lawyers as zealous on behalf of their clients as private attorneys are, and are lawyers overpaid? There is plenty of anecdotal evidence about stereotypically incompetent publicly-financed defenders. If they were doing an inadequate job, one might expect to see more of their clients convicted. BJS reports that in the late 1990s, conviction rates in both federal and large state courts were the same regardless of the type of attorney a defendant had. However, defendants with publicly financed attorneys who were found guilty were more likely to go to prison (71% compared to 54% in large state courts, and 88% compared to 77% in federal courts). BJS does not speculate on why this is so. When it comes to length of sentence, a study of 19,000 misdemeanor, felony, and capital murder cases in the state of Virginia found disparities depending on what type of publicly-financed attorney a person had. Defendants represented by court-appointed lawyers could expect to spend two more years in prison than defendants represented by salaried public defenders — or by a private attorney. As

**Operating Expenditures and Cases Handled by
Indigent Criminal Defense Programs, 100 Most Populous Counties: 1999**

| Expenditures and Cases (000) | Total | Type of Indigent Defense Service | | |
		Public Defender	Assigned Counsel	Contract
Number of counties	100	90	89	42
Total expenditures	$1,205,136	$880,920	$247,204	$70,012
Median per county	6,941	5,689	2,450	517
Total cases	4,174	3,413	618	143
Median per county	24	20	4	2
Number of programs	314	123	126	65

the table shows, and luckily for indigent criminals, public defender programs handle far more cases than do court-assigned attorneys.

What is the effect of underfunding when it comes to capital cases, where a convicted defendant faces the ultimate penalty? Professor James E. Coleman Jr. of Duke University School of Law told *The Star-Ledger* (Newark): "Poor compensation almost inevitably means that virtually the only lawyers who are available to handle capital cases for indigent defendants are inexperienced, ill-prepared and under-funded."

Do lawyers charge too much? Consider the state's murder case against accused Oklahoma City bombing conspirator, Terry Nichols, who is indigent.[17] When defense attorneys submitted a bill for $1.7 million for trial preparation, the judge asked for expense reports containing enough detail to determine if they were reasonable. When more justification of expenses was ordered, defense lawyers called the judge "hostile," the trial was stalled, and the matter went to the Oklahoma Supreme Court, which in October 2002 issued a decision placing a new judge in charge of overseeing payments. Defense attorneys estimated they would need an additional $2.7 million to continue the case.

More than $4 million in attorney fees — that sounds like a lot of money. But Adkins points out that the money paid to public defenders must cover not only attorney fees but also expenses including legal research and the compensation of expert witnesses and investigators. In this "get tough on crime age," funding has increased for law enforcement and prosecutors' offices, Adkins contends, but there has been no corresponding increase for public defenders, who may find themselves handling caseloads 5 to 10 times larger than the loads of their prosecutorial opponents. He wonders which voices lawmakers listen to at appropriations time: the ones that want our streets made safer or the ones that want to "ensure that poor Americans accused of crimes have a fair defense."

Sources: Chart, Table: DeFrances, Carol J., Ph.D., et al., "Indigent Defense Services in Large Counties, 1999, BJS, NCJ 184932, November 2000. "Atlanta Law Firm Assists Indigent," *Augusta Chronicle*, September 1, 2002 , pB06. David C. Adkins, "The Silent Repeal of the Sixth Amendment: The Indigent Defense Crisis in the United States," *The Prelaw Society Journal* (Towson University), Spring 2002, Vol. 15, No. 2, http://www.towson.edu/polsci/polsci.html. Doug Gross, "Providing lawyers for poor no easy job, but some say it's just matter of political will," *The Florida Times Union*, July 1, 2002, pB1. Frank Green, "Court-appointed lawyers criticized," *Times-Dispatch*, Dec 18, 2001, http://www.criminaljustice.org/. "Crisis in the court," The JournalNews.com, March 10, 2002, http://www.thejournalnews.com/newsroom/031002/10edlawyerpay.html. Viveca Novak, "The cost of poor advice," CNN.com, June 28, 1999, http://www.cnn.com/. Judson Hand, "In capital cases, poor defendants get what they pay for," *The Star Ledger*, August 13, 2000, p002. Information retrieved November 6, 2002.

---

[17] The bombing occurred in 1995. Nichols was tried in Federal court and found guilty of involuntary manslaughter and conspiracy. The Oklahoma City district attorney is prosecuting Nichols on state murder charges that could bring the death penalty.

Hate-Crime Overview

Significant Events in the Hate-Crime Legislation Movement

1968 —	Civil Rights Act of 1968 is enacted.
1979 —	Massachusetts enacts first state law aimed at hate crime.
1981 —	Anti-Defamation League drafts model hate crime legislation.
1982 —	Vincent Chin, a Chinese-American, is attacked and beaten to death with a baseball bat (Michigan).
1983 —	U.S. Civil Rights Commission issues a report calling for study of bias-motivated crimes.
1985 —	First Congressional hearing on hate crime is held.
1990 —	Hate Crime Statistics Act of 1990 is enacted.
1991 —	Rodney King, an African American, is beaten by Los Angeles police.
1994 —	Hate Crime Sentencing Enhancement Act is enacted.
1996 —	Church Arson Prevention Act is passed after a rash of arsons in Southern churches.
1998 —	James Byrd, Jr., a black man, is chained alive to the back of a pickup truck and dragged for several miles until his body is ripped apart (Texas). Matthew Sheppard, a homosexual, is pistol-whipped, tied to a fence and left to die (Wyoming).
1998-2000 —	Hate Crime Prevention Act is introduced in Congress three times but fails to come to a vote in the House.
1999 —	Forty-seven states have some type of hate-crime law. Benjamin Nathaniel Smith, a white supremacist, kills one African American, one Korean-American, wounds 6 orthodox Jews and 3 blacks before committing suicide.
2002 —	The Local Law Enforcement Enhancement Act fails to pass.

Ignoble acts associated with intolerance and bigotry — the worst of which constitute what we now call hate crimes — have always been with us, but the anti-hate-crime movement is a recent phenomenon. It grew out of the Civil Rights movement of the 1950s and 1960s, which was a reaction to hate violence in the South. Congress responded with a flurry of antidiscrimination legislation, including the Civil Rights Act of 1964. After three young men working to register black voters in Mississippi were turned over by police to the Ku Klux Klan and were subsequently found murdered, the Civil Rights Act of 1968 was passed. It included language that criminalized acts committed against someone because of his or her race, religion, or nationality.

That legislation and highly publicized atrocities (just a few of which appear in the timeline) gave momentum to advocates for other groups, including religious, women, ethnics, lesbian/gay/bisexual/transgendered individuals (LGBT), and the disabled, who sought the passage of federal, state, and local laws affording special punishments for crimes committed because of a person's affiliation with the group. At the federal level, though, as of the time of writing (November 2002), the 1968 criminal statute covering crimes based on race, religion, and national origin remained the standard.

The meaning of hate crime, how it differs from "ordinary crime," what types of people and institutions should be protected by hate-crime legislation, whether we need such legislation at all — these are topics of passionate debate. The numerous pieces of hate-crime legislation proposed at the federal and state levels have met with varying degrees of success. Supporters frequently mention the symbolic importance of passing hate-crime legislation, regardless of what such laws may actually do. In an address to Congress at the first hate-crime hearing in 1985, Representative John Conyers, Jr. said that hate-crime legislation "will carry to offenders, to victims, and to society at large an important message, that the Nation is committed to battling the violent manifestations of bigotry."

At the state level, Massachusetts passed the nation's first hate crime law in 1979 after riots broke out over court-ordered busing. The Massachusetts Civil Rights Act protected civil rights without regard to status characteristics (e.g., race, ethnicity, gender, sexual orientation). In 1981 the Anti-Defamation League drafted model hate-crime legislation (1) to address vandalism against churches, cemeteries, and public institutions, and (2) to enhance penalties for crimes based on a victim's perceived or actual religion, race, or national origin. Sexual orientation and gender were later added to the model.[18] By 1999, 47 states had adopted some type of hate-crime legislation. Most states used the ADL model but did not adopt it wholesale. For example, New Jersey's law includes gender (and disability), but Pennsylvania's does not. About 20 states do not protect individuals based on sexual orientation.[19] This issue is controversial, which is not surprising considering that some of those states still have anti-sodomy laws on the books.

At the federal level, four hate-crime bills have been introduced in Congress since 1990. Three passed. The winners: The Hate Crime Statistics Act, which mandated the collection of information about hate crimes (see the next panel for some examples); the Church Arsons Prevention Act, which makes it easier to prosecute church arsons as federal offenses; and the Hate Crime Sentencing Enhancement Act, providing for longer sentences in certain federal cases.

The Hate Crimes Prevention Act was introduced by Congressman Conyers in 1998, 1999, and 2000, and by Congressman Sheila Jackson-Lee in 2001, but it did not come to a vote in the House. It sought to add sexual orientation and disability to the list of characteristics protected by federal law. Arguing for passage on behalf of the American Civil Liberties Union, Christopher E. Anders, Legislative Counsel, pointed out that federal legislation is needed because state and local governments are often unwilling or unable to prosecute hate crimes. Anders contends that law enforcement agencies are often hostile to gay men and lesbians. The Act was revised (to add gender) and renamed the Local Law Enforcement Enhancement Act. If passed, it would provide support for criminal investigations and prosecutions by state and local law enforcement officials.

Critics of hate-crime laws say they violate the equal-protection provisions of the 14th Amendment. They ask: Are crimes against African Americans or homosexuals more se-

---

[18] The Anti-Defamation League was formed in 1913 "to expose and combat the purveyors of hatred in our midst." The ADL and groups such as the National Asian Pacific American Legal Consortium and the National Gay and Lesbian Task Force collect hate crime data. Their data typically show a higher prevalence of hate crime than do the federal statistics mandated by 1990 legislation, some of which are presented in our next panel.

[19] As of September 2001, according to http://www.religioustolerance.org.

rious, worthy of a more severe punishment, than crimes against, say, white males? Some contend that hate crimes are best dealt with at the community level. But former Michigan Supreme Court judge and former Detroit mayor Dennis Archer explained the importance of having recourse to justice under local or state and federal laws when prosecuting hate crimes by pointing out what happened to the attackers of Vincent Chin (see timeline). The state district court granted them probation, but a subsequent trial in federal court led to conviction of one of the attackers. In the Rodney King beating case, state prosecutors failed to get assault convictions but a federal jury convicted two of the four police officers charged with violating King's civil rights. And the U.S. Department of Justice points out that hate crimes victimize more than the immediate target and have a ripple effect. "A bias-motivated offense can cause a broad ripple of discomfiture among members of a targeted group, and a violent hate crime can act like a virus, quickly spreading feelings of terror and loathing across an entire community. Apart from their psychological impacts, violent hate crimes can create tides of retaliation and counterretaliation. Therefore, criminal acts motivated by bias may carry far more weight than other types of criminal acts."

While the debate rages, intolerance is still with us. In the year 2000 the Southern Poverty Law Center of Montgomery, Alabama, a non-profit organization that tracks hate crimes, reported that in the one-year period following college student Benjamin Smith's rampage through Illinois (timeline), the World Church of the Creator, of which he was a member, expanded from 41 to 76 chapters in 25 states and 5 foreign countries. Its two special groups for women grew from 5 to 10 chapters. The church is "Dedicated to the Survival, Expansion, and Advancement of the White Race."

The next panel presents FBI statistics on hate crimes.

Sources: Randy Amdt, "Panel discusses hate crimes, solutions," *Nation's Cities Weekly*, March 15, 1999, v22 i11 p3 (1). Brian Levin, "From Slavery to Hate Crime Laws: The Emergence of Race and Status-Based Protection in American Criminal Law," *Journal of Social Issues*, Vol 58, No. 2, 2002, pp. 227-245. Testimony of Legislative Counsel Christopher Anders on S. 622, the "Hate Crimes Prevention Act of 1999" Before the Senate Judiciary Committee, May 11, 1999, http://www.aclu.org/. US Department of Justice — A Policymaker's Guide to Hate Crimes," March 1997, http://usinfo.state.gov/usa/race/hate/bjahate.htm. Information retrieved November 8, 2002.

Reporting Hate Crimes

Number of Law-Enforcement Agencies Participating in Hate-Crime Data Collection and Number of Hate Crimes Reported

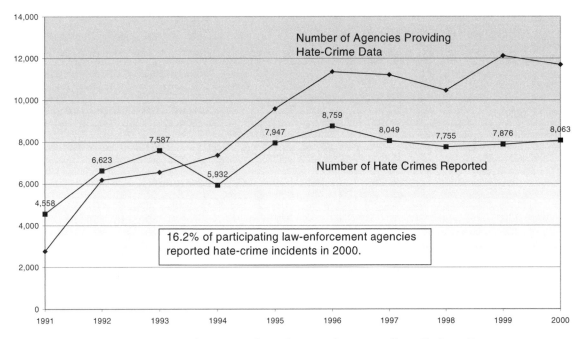

"Man's inhumanity to man Makes countless thousands mourn." — Robert Burns

We have no way of knowing how many hate crimes are perpetrated. The FBI has collected and published statistics on hate crimes reported to it since 1991. Some FBI data are shown on the charts above and on the next page. We see on the first chart the number of law enforcement agencies that provided hate-crime data and the number of hate crimes reported. More of the 16,000 agencies that participate in the FBI's Uniform Crime Reports voluntarily submitted data to the Hate Crime Data Collection Program in 2000 than in 1991 (11,690, up from 2,771 in 1991). Of the 11,690 agencies reporting in 2000, 16.2% reported at least one hate crime in their jurisdictions. The number of hate crimes reported ranged from a low of 4,558 to a high of 8,759. The FBI cautions that hate crimes are underreported by both victims and police.

The FBI gives reasons for requesting the data: "The statistics may assist law enforcement agencies in addressing potentially problematic issues for their particular locales or provide lawmakers with justification for certain legislation. The data may supply the media with credible information or simply show hate crime victims that they are not alone." Law enforcement agencies providing hate-crime data to the FBI must investigate crimes with sufficient zeal to be able to state with certainty the perpetrator's motivation. How does this play out in the real world? Consider Florida, one of 19 states that mandate the reporting of hate crimes. Many of the state's 400 police agencies do not report hate crimes, for reasons ranging from failure to recognize hate motivation to ignorance of the law to unwillingness to besmirch their community's image.

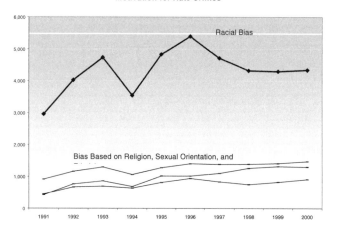

Motivation for Hate Crimes

Racial Bias

Bias Based on Religion, Sexual Orientation, and

The chart shows what motivated the hate crimes reported to the FBI. Racial bias was the major motivator, followed in order by religious, sexual orientation, and ethnicity biases. The FBI defines hate crimes as "those offenses motivated in part or singularly by personal prejudice against others because of a diversity — race, sexual orientation, religion, ethnicity/national origin, or disability." If women were included, the incidence of hate crimes would be higher.

Most hate crimes are directed against individuals (about 30% involve property crimes). In 2001 the U.S. Department of Justice released an analysis of 3,000 of the nearly 24,000 hate crimes reported from 1997-1999. The report reveals that hate crimes are much more likely than other crimes to be violent, that a disproportionately high percentage of both victims and perpetrators are under age 25, and that only 20% of crimes result in an arrest.

Hate crimes are not necessarily born of ignorance. Since 1992 the Department of Education has collected data on hate crimes on college campuses, the third most common venue. According to the American Psychological Association, most perpetrators of hate crimes are "otherwise law-abiding young people" sometimes emboldened by alcohol and drugs and convinced that attacks on certain groups of people are sanctioned by our society. Both the federal and state governments have brought suit against college students for hate crimes involving threats, bombings, assaults, and derogatory e-mail.

Events like recessions or terrorist attacks can cause spikes in hate crimes. At the time this was written, FBI data on hate crimes in 2001 were not ready, but one must wonder what effect September 11 had on hate crimes motivated by ethnicity. Research revealed that in Montana, reported hate crimes declined to 13 in 2001 from 20 the year before, but California reported a 15.5% rise in hate crimes over 2000, sparked by anti-Arab sentiment and reversing a downward trend. According to Congressman John Conyers, Jr., Illinois had five times more hates crimes against people of Arab descent in 2001 than in 2000. The Council on American-Islamic Relations received more than 300 reports of harassment and abuse against Muslims and southeast Asians in the two-day period September 12-14.

Sources: Charts: FBI, Hate Crime Statistics, *Uniform Crime Reports*, 1992-2000. Andres Viglucci, "Despite drop in numbers, authorities still concerned about hate crime," *Knight Ridder/Tribune News Service*, November 23, 2001, pK1315. "ADL Calls New Justice Department Report on Hate Crimes 'A Valuable Look at Bias,'" Anti-Defamation League Press Release, October 1, 2001, http://www.adl.org/. "Anti-Arab Sentiment Fuels Hate-Crime Rise," *Los Angeles Times*, September 19, 2002, pB-10. "Hate Crimes Today: An Age-Old Foe In Modern Dress," American Psychological Association, http://www.apa.org/pubinfo/hate/. Conyers Urges Republican Leadership to Bring Hate Crimes Bill to the Floor, Congressman John Conyers, Jr., press release, September 25, 2002, http://www.house.gov/judiciary_democrats/hatecrimesdischargepr92502.pdf. U.S. Department of Justice, Bureau of Justice Assistance, *Hate Crimes on Campus,* NCJ 187249, October 2001, http://www.campussafety.org/schools/187249.pdf.

Part II

Data Presentation

Data used to create graphics in the first part of this book are present in Part II in tabular format. The tables are arranged by chapter and follow the same sequence as the panels in the chapters. Locating the appropriate table should, therefore, be easy.

In most instances, the data shown are the same as those used to generate the graphics. From time to time, however, additional time series are presented or data are presented for more years. For an explanation of the data, please consult the panel in which they are used. The tables carry some explanatory notes, but the relevance of the data — and the reasons they were selected — are not spelled out.

Tables carry source notes. However, for more information on the subject, including other sources of information, please consult the source notes and (if present), the footnotes shown in the relevant panel in Part I of this volume.

Chapter 1
CRIME OVERVIEW

Official FBI Crime Index, 1973 to 2000

| Year | Per 100,000 Population | | |
	Total Crime	Violent Crime	Property Crime
1973	4,154	417	3,737
1974	4,850	461	4,369
1975	5,282	482	4,800
1976	5,266	460	4,807
1977	5,055	467	4,588
1978	5,109	487	4,622
1979	5,566	549	5,017
1980	5,950	597	5,353
1981	5,858	594	5,264
1982	5,604	571	5,033
1983	5,175	538	4,637
1984	5,031	539	4,492
1985	5,207	557	4,651
1986	5,480	618	4,863
1987	5,555	610	4,940
1988	5,664	637	5,027
1989	5,741	663	5,078
1990	5,820	732	5,089
1991	5,898	758	5,140
1992	5,660	758	4,903
1993	5,484	747	4,738
1994	5,374	714	4,660
1995	5,278	685	4,593
1996	5,087	637	4,450
1997	4,930	611	4,319
1998	4,619	568	4,052
1999	4,267	525	3,742
2000	4,124	506	3,618

Source: U.S. Department of Justice, Federal Bureau of Investigation, *Uniform Crime Reports*, multiple years.

National Criminal Victimization Survey

Victimizations reported to the Justice Department's survey by individuals in 49,000 households expressed as a ratio per 100,000 population.

Year	Victimizations per 100,000 population		
	Total	Violent	Property
1973	18,924.9	2,181.4	16,743.5
1974	20,289.8	2,272.8	18,017.0
1975	20,345.0	2,115.6	18,229.4
1976	20,286.5	2,099.8	18,186.7
1977	20,417.2	2,101.8	18,315.4
1978	20,248.8	2,055.0	18,193.8
1979	20,420.9	2,148.7	18,272.2
1980	19,693.5	2,056.2	17,637.3
1981	20,044.6	2,198.8	17,845.8
1982	18,966.8	2,081.1	16,885.7
1983	17,189.1	1,812.3	15,376.8
1984	16,375.5	1,916.9	14,458.6
1985	15,786.4	1,727.9	14,058.5
1986	15,401.5	1,671.6	13,729.9
1987	15,750.3	1,730.3	14,020.0
1988	15,888.2	1,785.4	14,102.8
1989	15,794.6	1,752.7	14,041.9
1990	14,775.1	1,720.4	13,054.7
1991	15,042.6	1,814.8	13,227.8
1992	14,105.1	1,903.3	12,201.8
1993	13,898.3	1,969.5	11,928.8
1994	13,540.1	1,969.0	11,571.1
1995	12,560.5	1,618.2	10,942.3
1996	11,504.1	1,497.4	10,006.7
1997	10,753.6	1,386.8	9,366.8
1998	9,494.0	1,246.2	8,247.8
1999	8,668.0	1,125.7	7,542.3
2000	7,710.6	955.5	6,755.1

Source: U.S. Department of Justice, National Criminal Victimization Survey, multiple years.

Total Estimated Arrests for Indexed and Other Offenses in 1995 and 2000

Indexed crimes are made part of the official "crime index" or "crime rate." Details may not add to totals because of rounding.

	1995	2000	Change 95 to 00
TOTAL ARRESTS	15,119,800	13,980,297	-1,139,503
Indexed Crime Arrests			
Murder and nonnegligent manslaughter	21,230	13,277	-7,953
Forcible rape	34,650	27,469	-7,181
Robbery	171,870	106,960	-64,910

[Continued]

Total Estimated Arrests for Indexed and Other Offenses in 1995 and 2000
[Continued]

	1995	2000	Change 95 to 00
Aggravated assault	568,480	478,417	-90,063
Burglary	386,500	289,844	-96,656
Larceny-theft	1,530,200	1,166,362	-363,838
Motor vehicle theft	191,900	148,225	-43,675
Arson	20,000	16,530	-3,470
Violent crime	796,250	625,132	-171,118
Property crime	2,128,600	1,620,928	-507,672
Crime Index total	2,924,800	2,246,054	-678,746
Non-Indexed Crime Arrests			
Other assaults (simple)	1,290,400	1,312,169	21,769
Forgery and counterfeiting	122,300	108,654	-13,646
Fraud	436,400	345,732	-90,668
Embezzlement	15,200	18,952	3,752
Stolen property; buying, receiving, possessing	166,500	118,641	-47,859
Vandalism	311,100	281,305	-29,795
Weapons; carrying, possessing, etc.	243,900	159,181	-84,719
Prostitution and commercialized vice	97,700	87,620	-10,080
Sex offenses (except forcible rape and prostitution)	94,500	93,399	-1,101
Drug abuse violations	1,476,100	1,579,566	103,466
Gambling	19,500	10,842	-8,658
Offenses against family and children	142,900	147,663	4,763
Driving under the influence	1,436,000	1,471,289	35,289
Liquor laws	594,900	683,124	88,224
Drunkenness	708,100	637,554	-70,546
Disorderly conduct	748,600	638,740	-109,860
Vagrancy	25,900	32,542	6,642
All other offenses (except traffic)	3,865,400	3,710,434	-154,966
Curfew and loitering law violations	149,800	154,711	4,911
Runaways	249,500	141,975	-107,525
NonIndex % of total	80.7	83.9	3.3

Source: U.S. Department of Justice, Federal Bureau of Investigation, *Uniform Crime Reports*, 1995 and 2000, accessible at http://www.fbi.gov/ucr/00cius.htm.

Estimated Non-Indexed Offense Arrests Summarized by Major Category for 2000

Non-specified, non-traffic offenses are specific violations of state and local laws and ordinances not included in the above.

Category	Non-Indexed Offense Arrests (Number)
Violent crime arrests	625,132
Property crime rate arrests	1,620,928
Simple assault, weapons offenses	1,471,350
Money-related and gambling	884,126
Sex-offenses, prostitution (non-rape)	181,019
Drug related	1,579,566
Alcohol-related and DWI	2,791,967
Conduct, vagrancy, etc.	967,968
Spousal, child, elder abuse	147,663
Non specified, non-traffic	3,710,434

Source: U.S. Department of Justice, Federal Bureau of Investigation, *Uniform Crime Reports*, 1995 and 2000, accessible at http://www.fbi.gov/ucr/00cius.htm.

Total Estimated Drug Violation Arrests in the United States, 1980 to 2000

Year	Total Estimated Drug Arrests	Arrests for Sale/ Manufacturing	Arrests for Possession	Possession as % of Total
1980	580,900	-	-	-
1981	559,900	-	-	-
1982	676,000	135,200	540,800	80.0
1983	661,400	145,500	515,900	78.0
1984	708,400	155,800	552,600	78.0
1985	811,400	194,700	616,700	76.0
1986	824,100	206,000	618,100	75.0
1987	937,400	243,700	693,700	74.0
1988	1,155,200	311,900	843,300	73.0
1989	1,361,700	435,700	926,000	68.0
1990	1,089,500	348,600	740,900	68.0
1991	1,010,000	333,300	676,700	67.0
1992	1,066,400	341,200	725,200	68.0
1993	1,126,300	337,900	788,400	70.0
1994	1,351,400	364,900	986,500	73.0
1995	1,476,100	369,000	1,107,100	75.0
1996	1,506,200	376,500	1,129,700	75.0
1997	1,583,600	324,600	1,259,000	79.5
1998	1,559,100	330,500	1,228,600	78.8

[Continued]

Total Estimated Drug Violation Arrests in the United States, 1980 to 2000

[Continued]

Year	Total Estimated Drug Arrests	Arrests for Sale/ Manufacturing	Arrests for Possession	Possession as % of Total
1999	1,532,200	300,300	1,231,900	80.4
2000	1,579,600	301,700	1,277,900	81.0

Source: U.S. Department of Justice, Federal Bureau of Investigation, *Crime in the United States*, annual, *Uniform Crime Reports*.

Number of Persons in Custody of State Correctional Authorities and Federal Drug Offenders, 1980 to 2000

Year	State Prisoners incarcerated for:					Federal Drug Prisoners	Per 100,000 Population				
	Violent Crime	Property Crime	Drug Offenses	Public Order Violations	Total		Violent Crime	Property Crime	Drug Offense	Public Order Violations	Federal Drug Prisoners
1980	173,300	89,300	19,000	12,400	294,000	4,749	76.3	39.3	8.4	5.5	2.1
1981	193,300	100,500	21,700	14,600	330,100	5,076	84.2	43.8	9.5	6.4	2.2
1982	215,300	114,400	25,300	17,800	372,800	5,518	92.9	49.4	10.9	7.7	2.4
1983	214,600	127,100	26,600	24,400	392,700	7,201	91.8	54.4	11.4	10.4	3.1
1984	227,300	133,100	31,700	21,900	414,000	8,152	96.4	56.4	13.4	9.3	3.5
1985	246,200	140,100	38,900	23,000	448,200	9,491	103.5	58.9	16.3	9.7	4.0
1986	258,600	150,200	45,400	28,800	483,000	11,344	107.7	62.5	18.9	12.0	4.7
1987	271,300	155,500	57,900	31,300	516,000	13,897	112.0	64.2	23.9	12.9	5.7
1988	282,700	161,600	79,100	35,000	558,400	15,087	115.6	66.1	32.4	14.3	6.2
1989	293,900	172,700	120,100	39,500	626,200	18,852	119.1	70.0	48.7	16.0	7.6
1990	313,600	173,700	148,600	45,500	681,400	24,297	125.7	69.6	59.6	18.2	9.7
1991	339,500	180,700	155,200	49,500	724,900	29,667	134.6	71.7	61.5	19.6	11.8
1992	369,100	181,600	168,100	56,300	775,100	35,398	144.7	71.2	65.9	22.1	13.9
1993	393,500	189,600	177,000	64,000	824,100	41,393	152.6	73.6	68.7	24.8	16.1
1994	425,700	207,000	193,500	74,400	900,600	45,347	163.5	79.5	74.3	28.6	17.4
1995	459,600	226,600	212,300	86,500	985,500	46,669	174.9	86.2	81.0	32.9	17.8
1996	484,800	231,700	216,900	96,000	1,029,400	49,096	182.8	87.4	81.8	36.2	18.5
1997	507,800	236,400	222,100	106,200	1,072,500	52,059	189.6	88.3	82.9	39.7	19.4
1998	545,200	242,900	236,800	113,900	1,138,800	55,984	201.7	89.9	87.6	42.1	20.7
1999	570,000	245,000	251,200	120,600	1,186,800	60,399	209.0	89.8	92.1	44.2	22.1
2000	589,100	238,500	251,100	124,600	1,203,300	63,898	213.4	86.4	91.0	45.1	23.1

Source: U.S. Department of Justice, *Correctional Populations in the United States*, 1997, and *Prisoners in 2001*.

Correctional Population Trends

| Year | Per 100,000 Population | |
	Federal and State Prison Population	Combined Prison and Jail Population
1957	114.0	-
1958	118.0	-
1959	117.2	-
1960	118.6	-
1961	119.8	-
1962	117.3	-
1963	114.8	-
1964	111.7	-
1965	109.5	-
1966	101.6	-
1967	98.1	-
1968	93.6	-
1969	96.7	-
1970	96.7	-
1971	100.0	-
1972	103.3	-
1973	106.7	-
1974	110.0	-
1975	113.3	-
1976	122.9	-
1977	132.4	-
1978	135.4	-
1979	137.3	-
1980	139.2	222.5
1981	154.9	243.7
1982	170.6	265.6
1983	178.5	278.2
1984	188.0	290.8
1985	200.6	314.2
1986	216.0	335.1
1987	229.0	356.0
1988	244.0	390.7
1989	271.0	438.9
1990	294.5	460.5
1991	309.6	483.4
1992	331.8	507.8
1993	359.4	531.1
1994	388.6	567.2
1995	411.1	603.3
1996	427.0	620.6
1997	445.0	651.1

[Continued]

Correctional Population Trends
[Continued]

Year	Per 100,000 Population	
	Federal and State Prison Population	Combined Prison and Jail Population
1998	461.0	672.3
1999	476.0	694.2
2000	476.8	701.8

Source: U.S. Bureau of the Census, *Historical Statistics of the United States*, September 1995 and *Statistical Abstract of the United States*, 1980, 1990, 1995, 2001. The primary data source cited by these sources are data from the FBI s *Uniform Crime Reports* (for crime rate) and the U.S. Bureau of Justice Statistic s *Prisoners in State and Federal Institutions* and *Correctional Populations in the United States.*

Percent of Individuals Reporting Victimization to Police - 2000

Victimization Category	% Reported to Police
Rape/sexual assault	48.1
Robbery	56.3
Aggravated assault	56.7
Simple assault	43.6
Personal theft	35.0
Burglary	50.7
Motor vehicle theft	80.4
Theft	29.5

Source: U.S. Department of Justice, National Criminal Victimization Survey, 2000, accessible at http://www/ojp/usdoj.gov/bjs/welcome.html.

Persons Under Correctional Supervision by Sex, 1986 to 2001

Correctional supervision includes probation, parole, jail, and prison supervision.

Year	Persons Under Correctional Supervision			% Female
	Male	Female	Total	
1986	2,829,100	410,300	3,239,400	12.7
1987	3,021,000	438,600	3,459,600	12.7
1988	3,223,000	491,100	3,714,100	13.2
1989	3,501,600	554,000	4,055,600	13.7
1990	3,746,300	601,700	4,348,000	13.8
1991	3,913,000	622,600	4,535,600	13.7

[Continued]

Persons Under Correctional Supervision by Sex, 1986 to 2001

[Continued]

Year	Persons Under Correctional Supervision			% Female
	Male	Female	Total	
1992	4,050,300	712,300	4,762,600	15.0
1993	4,215,800	728,200	4,944,000	14.7
1994	4,377,400	763,900	5,141,300	14.9
1995	4,513,000	822,100	5,335,100	15.4
1996	4,630,100	852,800	5,482,900	15.6
1997	4,797,200	895,300	5,692,500	15.7
1998	5,215,598	968,159	6,183,757	15.7
1999	5,288,236	1,099,258	6,387,494	17.2
2000	5,369,711	1,117,878	6,487,589	17.2
2001	5,484,370	1,141,748	6,626,118	17.2

Source: U.S. Department of Justice, Bureau of Justice Statistics Correctional Surveys, File CPGEND.WK1, http://www.ojp.usdoj.gov/bjs/welcome.html.

Correctional Populations in the United States

Year	Number of Persons Supervised				
	Probation	Jail	Prison	Parole	Total
1980	1,118,097	183,988	319,598	220,438	1,842,121
1981	1,225,934	196,785	360,029	225,539	2,008,287
1982	1,357,264	209,582	402,914	224,604	2,194,364
1983	1,582,947	223,551	423,898	246,440	2,476,836
1984	1,740,948	234,500	448,264	266,992	2,690,704
1985	1,968,712	256,615	487,593	300,203	3,013,123
1986	2,114,621	274,444	526,436	325,638	3,241,139
1987	2,247,158	295,873	562,814	355,505	3,461,350
1988	2,356,483	343,569	607,766	407,977	3,715,795
1989	2,522,125	395,553	683,367	456,803	4,057,848
1990	2,670,234	403,019	743,382	531,407	4,348,042
1991	2,728,472	424,129	792,535	590,442	4,535,578
1992	2,811,611	441,781	850,566	658,601	4,762,559
1993	2,903,061	455,500	909,381	676,100	4,944,042
1994	2,981,022	479,800	990,147	690,371	5,141,340
1995	3,077,861	499,300	1,078,542	679,421	5,335,124
1996	3,164,996	510,400	1,127,764	679,733	5,482,893
1997	3,266,837	557,974	1,176,922	690,752	5,692,485
1998	3,670,441	592,462	1,224,469	696,385	6,183,757
1999	3,779,922	605,943	1,287,172	714,457	6,387,494
2000	3,826,209	621,149	1,316,333	723,898	6,487,589
2001	3,932,751	631,240	1,330,980	731,147	6,626,118

Source: Bureau of Justice Statistics Correctional Surveys (*The Annual Probation Survey, National Prisoner Statistics, Survey of Jails,* and *The Annual Parole Survey.*) Totals for 1998 through 2001 exclude probationers in jail or prison.

Persons Under Correctional Supervision by Race, 1985 to 2000

Correctional supervision includes probation, parole, jail, and prison supervision. Totals do not agree with previous table due to rounding and a different method of developing the subtotals.

Year	Number of People Supervised				Per 100,000 Population 18 + Over			
	White	Black	Other	Total	White	Black	Other	Total
1985	1,867,300	998,800	38,900	2,905,000	1,243	5,275	772	1,668
1986	2,090,100	1,117,200	32,100	3,239,400	1,379	5,809	600	1,840
1987	2,192,200	1,231,100	36,300	3,459,600	1,434	6,300	639	1,943
1988	2,348,075	1,325,300	39,800	3,713,175	1,522	6,676	662	2,061
1989	2,520,100	1,488,500	45,400	4,054,000	1,619	7,376	712	2,224
1990	2,665,500	1,632,700	49,800	4,348,000	1,685	7,834	736	2,340
1991	2,742,400	1,743,400	49,900	4,535,700	1,721	8,227	707	2,418
1992	2,835,900	1,873,200	53,500	4,762,600	1,766	8,693	725	2,514
1993	2,872,200	2,011,600	60,200	4,944,000	1,776	9,195	784	2,585
1994	3,058,000	2,018,000	65,300	5,141,300	1,878	9,090	823	2,665
1995	3,220,900	2,024,000	90,200	5,335,100	1,963	8,971	1,098	2,738
1996	3,294,800	2,083,600	104,500	5,482,900	1,993	9,088	1,230	2,787
1997	3,429,000	2,149,900	113,600	5,692,500	2,057	9,214	1,291	2,863
1998	3,496,378	2,436,997	161,241	6,094,616	2,079	10,260	1,775	3,032
1999	3,910,725	2,448,066	139,625	6,498,416	2,305	10,138	1,490	3,199
2000	3,893,294	2,477,013	126,077	6,496,384	2,275	10,085	1,305	3,163

Source: Bureau of Justice Statistics Correctional Surveys (*The Annual Probation Survey, National Prisoner Statistics, Survey of Jails,* and *The Annual Parole Survey.*) Totals for 1998 through 2001 exclude probationers in jail or prison.

Persons Under Correctional Supervision by Race and Type of Correction, 1985 to 2000

Data on Hispanics not reported for probation or parole separately. Most Hispanics are white.

Race/Origin	Prison or Jail		Probation or Parole	
	Number	Percent	Number	Percent
Whites	727,400	37.7	2,856,341	62.6
Blacks	861,100	44.6	1,624,673	35.6
Hispanics	310,400	16.1	-	-
Asians, Indians, Pacific Islanders	33,000	1.7	84,046	1.8

Source: Bureau of Justice Statistics Correctional Surveys (*The Annual Probation Survey, National Prisoner Statistics, Survey of Jails,* and *The Annual Parole Survey*).

Justice System Employment, All Levels of Government, 1982 to 1999

Year	Total Employees				Percent of Total		
	Total Justice System	Police Protection	Judicial and Legal	Corrections	Police Protection	Judicial and Legal	Corrections
1982	1,270,342	723,923	247,697	298,722	57.0	19.5	23.5
1983	1,313,831	733,070	261,436	319,325	55.8	19.9	24.3
1984	1,373,354	746,974	277,578	348,802	54.4	20.2	25.4
1985	1,422,718	757,000	293,025	372,693	53.2	20.6	26.2
1986	1,464,070	771,917	300,126	392,027	52.7	20.5	26.8
1987	1,524,976	792,831	312,331	419,814	52.0	20.5	27.5
1988	1,583,713	804,658	323,641	455,414	50.8	20.4	28.8
1989	1,636,895	811,528	336,872	488,495	49.6	20.6	29.8
1990	1,710,413	825,417	350,761	534,235	48.3	20.5	31.2
1991	1,760,563	837,038	362,178	561,347	47.5	20.6	31.9
1992	1,797,704	857,593	373,611	566,500	47.7	20.8	31.5
1993	1,825,953	865,002	375,266	585,685	47.4	20.6	32.1
1994	1,901,773	890,384	390,731	620,658	46.8	20.5	32.6
1995	1,983,747	926,086	401,444	656,217	46.7	20.2	33.1
1997	2,078,192	950,877	419,072	708,243	45.8	20.2	34.1
1998	2,133,240	976,394	433,493	723,353	45.8	20.3	33.9
1999	2,189,477	1,017,922	454,982	716,573	46.5	20.8	32.7

Source: U.S. Department of Justice, *Sourcebook of Criminal Justice Statistics*, 2000, downloaded from http://www.albany.edu/sourcebook/.

Justice System Employment in 1999 by Level of Government

Level of Government	Total Employment				% of Total Justice System Employment	Percent of Sector		
	Total Justice System	Police Protection	Judicial and Legal	Corrections		Police Protection	Judicial and Legal	Corrections
Federal	191,169	104,096	56,099	30,974	8.7	54.5	29.3	16.2
State	704,902	99,686	148,463	456,753	32.2	14.1	21.1	64.8
County	606,645	223,281	190,418	192,946	27.7	36.8	31.4	31.8
Municipal	686,761	590,859	60,002	35,900	31.4	86.0	8.7	5.2

Source: U.S. Department of Justice, *Sourcebook of Criminal Justice Statistics*, 2000, downloaded from http://www.albany.edu/sourcebook/.

Justice System Expenditures, All Levels of Government, 1982 to 1999

Year	In Millions of Actual Dollars				In Millions of 2000 Constant Dollars			
	Total Justice System	Police Protection	Judicial and Legal	Correc-tions	Total Justice System	Police Protection	Judicial and Legal	Correc-tions
1982	35,841.9	19,022.2	7,770.8	9,048.9	63,958.3	33,944.2	13,866.6	16,147.4
1983	39,680.2	20,648.2	8,620.6	10,411.4	68,603.7	35,699.0	14,904.3	18,000.4
1984	43,942.7	22,685.8	9,463.2	11,793.7	72,829.0	37,598.5	15,683.9	19,546.5
1985	48,563.1	24,399.4	10,628.8	13,534.9	77,719.0	39,048.0	17,010.1	21,660.9
1986	53,499.8	26,255.0	11,485.4	15,759.4	84,057.2	41,251.0	18,045.6	24,760.6
1987	58,871.3	28,767.6	12,555.0	17,548.8	89,239.8	43,607.2	19,031.5	26,601.2
1988	65,230.5	30,960.8	13,970.6	20,299.2	94,951.0	45,067.2	20,335.8	29,547.9
1989	70,949.5	32,794.2	15,588.7	22,566.6	98,528.2	45,541.6	21,648.1	31,338.5
1990	79,434.0	35,923.5	17,356.8	26,153.7	104,655.9	47,329.9	22,868.0	34,458.0
1991	87,566.8	38,971.2	19,298.4	29,297.2	110,712.2	49,272.0	24,399.3	37,041.0
1992	93,776.9	41,326.5	20,988.9	31,461.4	115,098.9	50,722.9	25,761.1	38,614.8
1993	97,541.8	44,036.8	21,558.4	31,946.7	116,240.2	52,478.4	25,691.1	38,070.7
1994	103,470.6	46,004.5	22,601.7	34,864.3	120,226.9	53,454.7	26,261.9	40,510.4
1995	112,868.4	48,644.5	24,471.7	39,752.2	127,532.5	54,964.5	27,651.1	44,916.9
1996	120,194.2	53,007.4	26,157.9	41,028.8	131,914.8	58,176.4	28,708.7	45,029.7
1997	129,793.5	57,753.5	28,528.8	43,511.1	139,255.0	61,963.6	30,608.4	46,683.0
1998	135,899.5	60,828.2	29,901.4	45,169.9	143,569.9	64,261.5	31,589.1	47,719.3
1999	146,555.5	65,364.1	32,184.6	49,006.9	151,481.7	67,561.2	33,266.4	50,654.2

Source: U.S. Department of Justice, *Sourcebook of Criminal Justice Statistics*, 2000, downloaded from http://www.albany.edu/sourcebook/.

Per Capital Expenditures on Justice System Activities, 1982 to 1999 in Actual and Constant Dollars

Fiscal Year	July 1 population (000)	In Actual Dollars				In 2000 Constant Dollars			
		Total Justice System	Police Protection	Judicial and Legal	Correc-tions	Total Justice System	Police Protection	Judicial and Legal	Correc-tions
1982	231,664	154.72	82.11	33.54	39.06	276.09	146.52	59.85	69.70
1983	233,792	169.72	88.32	36.87	44.53	293.43	152.70	63.75	76.99
1984	235,825	186.34	96.20	40.13	50.01	308.83	159.44	66.51	82.88
1985	237,924	204.11	102.55	44.67	56.89	326.65	164.12	71.49	91.05
1986	240,133	222.79	109.34	47.83	65.63	350.04	171.79	75.15	103.12
1987	242,289	242.98	118.73	51.82	72.43	368.32	179.98	78.55	109.79
1988	244,499	266.79	126.63	57.14	83.02	388.35	184.33	83.17	120.85
1989	246,819	287.46	132.87	63.16	91.43	399.20	184.52	87.71	126.97
1990	249,402	318.50	144.04	69.59	104.87	419.63	189.78	91.69	138.17
1991	252,131	347.31	154.57	76.54	116.20	439.11	195.43	96.77	146.91
1992	255,028	367.71	162.05	82.30	123.36	451.32	198.90	101.01	151.41
1993	257,783	378.39	170.83	83.63	123.93	450.93	203.58	99.66	147.69
1994	260,341	397.44	176.71	86.82	133.92	461.80	205.33	100.88	155.61
1995	262,755	429.56	185.13	93.14	151.29	485.37	209.18	105.24	170.95

[Continued]

Per Capital Expenditures on Justice System Activities, 1982 to 1999 in Actual and Constant Dollars

[Continued]

Fiscal Year	July 1 population (000)	In Actual Dollars				In 2000 Constant Dollars			
		Total Justice System	Police Protec-tion	Judicial and Legal	Correc-tions	Total Justice System	Police Protec-tion	Judicial and Legal	Correc-tions
1996	264,741	454.01	200.22	98.81	154.98	498.28	219.74	108.45	170.09
1997	267,252	485.66	216.10	106.75	162.81	521.06	231.85	114.53	174.68
1998	269,773	503.75	225.48	110.84	167.44	532.18	238.21	117.10	176.89
1999	281,375	520.85	232.30	114.38	174.17	538.36	240.11	118.22	180.02

Source: U.S. Department of Justice, *Sourcebook of Criminal Justice Statistics*, 2000, downloaded from http://www.albany.edu/sourcebook/.

Justice System Expenditures in 1999 by Level of Government

Level of Government	Total Expenditures (Millions)				% of Total Justice System Employment	Percent of Sector		
	Total Justice System	Police Protec-tion	Judicial and Legal	Correc-tions		Police Protec-tion	Judicial and Legal	Correc-tions
Actual Dollars								
Federal	28,312.7	15,294.1	8,801.4	4,217.3	17.2	54.0	31.1	14.9
State	59,108.7	9,955.3	13,307.6	35,845.8	36.0	16.8	22.5	60.6
County	36,298.7	12,875.7	10,894.8	12,528.2	22.1	35.5	30.0	34.5
Municipal	40,646.1	34,246.9	3,487.2	2,912.0	24.7	84.3	8.6	7.2
Constant 2000 Dollars								
Federal	29,264.4	15,808.2	9,097.2	4,359.0				
State	61,095.6	10,290.0	13,754.9	37,050.7				
County	37,518.9	13,308.5	11,261.0	12,949.3				
Municipal	42,012.4	35,398.1	3,604.4	3,009.9				

Source: U.S. Department of Justice, *Sourcebook of Criminal Justice Statistics*, 2000, downloaded from http://www.albany.edu/sourcebook/.

Chapter 2
VIOLENT CRIME

Adjusted Violent Victimization Rates

| | Number of Victimizations per 1,000 Population Age 12 and Over | | | | | |
	Total Violent Crime	Murder	Rape	Robbery	Aggra-vated Assault	Simple Assault
1973	47.71	0.09	2.49	6.74	12.49	25.90
1974	48.00	0.10	2.57	7.18	12.88	25.27
1975	48.40	0.10	2.38	6.76	11.92	27.24
1976	47.96	0.09	2.22	6.46	12.23	26.96
1977	50.43	0.09	2.33	6.22	12.38	29.41
1978	50.56	0.09	2.55	5.89	12.02	30.01
1979	51.75	0.10	2.83	6.26	12.30	30.26
1980	49.37	0.10	2.48	6.56	11.42	28.81
1981	52.27	0.10	2.51	7.41	11.97	30.28
1982	50.65	0.09	2.10	7.09	11.53	29.84
1983	46.45	0.08	2.13	6.03	9.88	28.33
1984	46.37	0.08	2.46	5.82	10.81	27.20
1985	45.18	0.08	1.88	5.07	10.25	27.90
1986	42.00	0.09	1.74	5.14	9.75	25.28
1987	43.98	0.08	1.97	5.29	9.96	26.68
1988	44.11	0.08	1.68	5.26	10.83	26.26
1989	43.33	0.09	1.77	5.42	10.25	25.80
1990	44.13	0.09	1.69	5.66	9.76	26.93
1991	48.78	0.10	2.24	5.89	9.92	30.63
1992	47.94	0.09	1.79	6.08	11.07	28.91
1993	49.10	0.10	1.60	6.00	12.00	29.40
1994	51.19	0.09	1.40	6.30	11.90	31.50
1995	46.08	0.08	1.20	5.40	9.50	29.90
1996	41.57	0.07	0.90	5.20	8.80	26.60
1997	38.77	0.07	0.90	4.30	8.60	24.90
1998	35.96	0.06	0.90	4.00	7.50	23.50
1999	32.06	0.06	0.90	3.60	6.70	20.80
2000	27.36	0.06	0.60	3.20	5.70	17.80
% Change 1973 to 2000	-42.67	-41.49	-75.90	-52.52	-54.36	-31.27

Source: U.S. Bureau of Justice Statistics, National Criminal Victimization Survey, *Violent Crime Trends, 1973-2001,* August 2002, available on-line at http://www/ojp/usdoj.gov/glance/tables/viortrdtab.htm.

Homicide Rate and Other Indicators

The dash (-) indicates that data for the year were not available. Homicide data for the period before 1933 are incomplete. In 1900 only 10 states reported (26% of the population). By 1910, coverage had increased to 50%. From 1933 on, 100% of the population is represented.

Year	Homicide Rate per 100,000 Population	Males 20-34 as % of Population	Incarceration Rate per 1,000 Population
1900	1.2	25.56	-
1901	1.2	-	-
1902	1.2	-	-
1903	1.1	-	-
1904	1.3	-	-
1905	2.1	-	-
1906	3.9	-	-
1907	4.9	-	-
1908	4.8	-	-
1909	4.2	-	-
1910	4.6	26.32	-
1911	5.5	-	-
1912	5.4	-	-
1913	6.1	-	-
1914	6.2	-	-
1915	5.9	-	-
1916	6.3	-	-
1917	6.9	-	-
1918	6.5	-	-
1919	7.2	-	-
1920	6.8	25.01	-
1921	8.1	-	-
1922	8.0	-	-
1923	7.8	-	-
1924	8.1	-	-
1925	8.3	-	-
1926	8.4	-	-
1927	8.4	-	-
1928	8.6	-	-
1929	8.4	-	-
1930	8.8	24.29	1.04
1931	9.2	-	-
1932	9.0	-	-
1933	9.7	-	-
1934	9.5	-	-
1935	8.3	-	-
1936	8.0	-	-
1937	7.6	-	-
1938	6.8	-	-
1939	6.4	-	-
1940	6.3	25.01	1.32

[Continued]

Homicide Rate and Other Indicators

[Continued]

Year	Homicide Rate per 100,000 Population	Males 20-34 as % of Population	Incarceration Rate per 1,000 Population
1941	6.0	-	-
1942	5.9	-	-
1943	5.1	-	-
1944	5.0	-	-
1945	5.7	-	-
1946	6.4	-	-
1947	6.1	-	-
1948	5.9	-	-
1949	5.4	-	-
1950	5.3	23.39	1.10
1951	4.9	-	-
1952	5.2	-	-
1953	4.8	-	-
1954	4.8	-	-
1955	4.5	-	-
1956	4.6	-	-
1957	4.5	-	-
1958	4.5	-	-
1959	4.6	-	-
1960	4.7	18.75	1.19
1961	4.7	-	-
1962	4.8	-	-
1963	4.9	-	-
1964	5.1	-	-
1965	5.5	-	-
1966	5.9	-	-
1967	6.8	-	-
1968	7.3	-	-
1969	7.7	-	-
1970	8.3	20.31	0.97
1971	9.1	-	-
1972	9.4	-	-
1973	9.7	-	-
1974	10.1	-	-
1975	9.9	-	-
1976	9.0	-	-
1977	9.1	-	-
1978	9.2	-	-
1979	10.0	-	-
1980	10.7	25.71	1.40
1981	10.3	-	-
1982	9.6	-	-
1983	8.6	-	-

[Continued]

Homicide Rate and Other Indicators
[Continued]

Year	Homicide Rate per 100,000 Population	Males 20-34 as % of Population	Incarceration Rate per 1,000 Population
1984	8.4	-	-
1985	8.4	-	-
1986	9.0	-	-
1987	8.7	-	-
1988	9.0	-	-
1989	9.3	-	-
1990	10.0	24.97	2.97
1991	10.5	-	-
1992	10.0	-	-
1993	10.1	-	-
1994	9.6	-	-
1995	8.7	-	-
1996	7.9	-	-
1997	7.4	-	-
1998	6.8	-	-
1999	6.2	20.24	4.77

Source: U.S. Centers for Disease Control, National Center for Health Statistics, Vital Statistics, *Homicide rate per 100,000 population, 1900- 1999*, October 2001, available online at http://www.cdc.gov.

Homicide Rates by Age Groups, 1976-1999

Year	Rates per 100,000 population					Number of Offenders						
	14-17	18-24	25-34	35-49	50+	Under 14	14-17	18-24	25-34	35-49	50+	All ages
1976	10.6	22.4	19.4	11.1	4.0	103	1,775	6,244	6,192	3,855	2,184	20,353
1977	10.0	22.1	18.7	11.4	4.0	101	1,660	6,265	6,186	3,978	2,199	20,389
1978	10.1	23.1	19.0	11.4	3.7	120	1,645	6,630	6,425	4,058	2,105	20,983
1979	11.7	26.2	20.3	11.6	4.1	98	1,894	7,578	7,086	4,205	2,324	23,185
1980	12.9	29.5	22.2	13.3	3.8	112	2,083	8,705	8,200	4,901	2,199	26,200
1981	11.2	25.7	20.3	12.8	3.8	77	1,793	7,674	7,883	4,765	2,283	24,475
1982	10.4	24.2	19.0	11.3	3.5	98	1,616	7,179	7,500	4,408	2,079	22,880
1983	9.4	22.1	17.5	10.2	3.0	77	1,437	6,512	7,022	4,150	1,809	21,007
1984	8.5	21.5	16.9	9.5	3.0	72	1,266	6,268	6,933	3,982	1,815	20,336
1985	9.8	21.4	16.0	9.4	3.0	93	1,437	6,162	6,706	4,104	1,871	20,373
1986	11.7	23.4	17.6	9.9	2.9	94	1,718	6,634	7,476	4,448	1,810	22,180
1987	12.3	24.1	16.2	9.2	2.9	111	1,793	6,696	6,989	4,318	1,796	21,703
1988	15.5	26.9	16.5	8.9	2.7	101	2,240	7,325	7,158	4,300	1,708	22,832
1989	18.1	30.2	16.4	8.4	2.5	129	2,594	8,055	7,114	4,222	1,592	23,706
1990	23.7	34.4	17.6	9.5	2.5	103	3,143	9,187	7,552	4,906	1,573	26,464
1991	26.6	40.8	18.6	8.2	2.3	131	3,576	10,734	7,984	4,356	1,487	28,268
1992	26.3	38.4	16.8	7.7	2.3	140	3,596	9,964	7,125	4,235	1,488	26,548
1993	30.2	41.3	15.9	7.4	2.4	158	4,172	10,798	6,816	4,126	1,566	27,636

[Continued]

Homicide Rates by Age Groups, 1976-1999

[Continued]

Year	Rates per 100,000 population					Number of Offenders						
	14-17	18-24	25-34	35-49	50+	Under 14	14-17	18-24	25-34	35-49	50+	All ages
1994	29.3	39.6	15.2	7.4	2.0	180	4,115	10,227	6,413	4,238	1,316	26,489
1995	23.6	36.7	14.4	6.7	2.0	139	3,432	9,318	5,978	3,945	1,376	24,188
1996	19.6	35.7	13.4	6.2	1.8	97	2,914	8,929	5,483	3,749	1,242	22,414
1997	16.7	33.1	12.6	5.5	1.8	92	2,548	8,174	5,120	3,429	1,238	20,601
1998	12.9	31.0	12.3	5.4	1.6	98	2,005	7,684	4,903	3,395	1,167	19,252
1999	10.7	27.7	11.0	5.0	1.5	89	1,674	7,009	4,285	3,197	1,133	17,387

Source: U.S. Department of Justice, Federal Bureau of Investigation, Supplementary Homicide Reports, 1976-1999, accessible at www.ojp.usdoj.gov/bjs/homicide.

Criminal Victimization by Gender, Race and Income, 1993-2001

	Number of Violent Crimes per 1,000 Persons Age 12 or Older								
	1993	1994	1995	1996	1997	1998	1999	2000	2001
Gender									
Male	59.8	61.1	55.7	49.9	45.8	43.1	37.0	32.9	27.3
Female	40.7	43.0	38.1	34.6	33.0	30.4	28.8	23.2	23.0
Race									
White	47.9	50.5	44.7	40.9	38.3	36.3	31.9	27.1	24.5
Black	67.4	61.3	61.1	52.3	49.0	41.7	41.6	35.3	31.2
Other	39.8	49.9	41.9	33.2	28.0	27.6	24.5	20.7	18.2
Annual Household Income									
Less than $7,500	84.7	86.0	77.8	65.3	71.0	63.8	57.5	60.3	46.6
$7,500-$14,999	56.4	60.7	49.8	52.1	51.2	49.3	44.5	37.8	36.9
$15,000-$24,999	49.0	50.7	48.9	44.1	40.1	39.4	35.3	31.8	31.8
$25,000-$34,999	51.0	47.3	47.1	43.0	40.2	42.0	37.9	29.8	29.1
$35,000-$49,999	45.6	47.0	45.8	43.0	38.7	31.7	30.3	28.5	26.3
$50,000-$74,999	44.0	48.0	44.6	37.5	33.9	32.0	33.3	23.7	21.0
$75,000 or more	41.3	39.5	37.3	30.5	30.7	33.1	22.9	22.3	18.5

Source: U.S. Department of Justice, *Criminal Victimization 2001: Changes 2000-01 and Trends, 1993-2001,* accessible at http://www.ojp.usdoj.gov/bjs/pub/pdf/cv01.pdf.

Homicide Offending Rates by Gender

Year	Rates per 100,000 Population	
	Male	Female
1976	16.30	3.10
1977	16.20	3.00
1978	16.80	2.80
1979	18.60	2.90
1980	20.60	3.10
1981	18.90	2.90
1982	17.40	2.80

[Continued]

Homicide Offending Rates by Gender

[Continued]

Year	Rates per 100,000 Population	
	Male	Female
1983	15.80	2.60
1984	15.20	2.30
1985	15.20	2.20
1986	16.50	2.30
1987	16.00	2.20
1988	16.80	2.20
1989	17.40	2.10
1990	19.60	2.20
1991	20.70	2.20
1992	19.30	1.90
1993	19.90	2.00
1994	18.80	1.90
1995	17.20	1.60
1996	15.50	1.70
1997	14.20	1.50
1998	13.00	1.50
1999	11.70	1.27
% Change		
1976-99	-28.22	-59.03
1993-99	-41.21	-36.50

Source: U.S. Department of Justice, Bureau of Justice Statistics, *Homicide Trends in the United States*, accessible at www.ojp.usdoj.gov/bjs/homicide.

Violent Victimization Rates by Gender, 1973-2001

Year	Victimization Rate per 1,000 Persons 12 and Older		
	Total	Males	Females
1973	48.5	68.0	31.4
1974	49.1	69.4	31.3
1975	48.9	66.8	33.1
1976	48.5	65.8	33.3
1977	50.5	71.1	32.4
1978	50.2	70.0	32.8
1979	51.5	69.7	35.3
1980	49.4	68.1	33.0
1981	52.6	70.9	36.5
1982	51.0	66.9	36.9
1983	46.2	61.7	32.4
1984	46.2	60.6	33.4
1985	44.7	59.5	31.6
1986	41.9	54.3	30.9

[Continued]

Violent Victimization Rates by Gender, 1973-2001

[Continued]

Year	Victimization Rate per 1,000 Persons 12 and Older		
	Total	Males	Females
1987	43.7	56.8	32.0
1988	44.2	55.0	34.4
1989	43.4	56.8	31.4
1990	44.0	57.6	32.0
1991	48.0	64.5	33.4
1992	47.8	59.3	37.2
1993	49.9	59.8	40.7
1994	51.8	61.1	43.0
1995	46.6	55.7	38.1
1996	42.0	49.9	34.6
1997	39.2	45.8	33.0
1998	36.6	43.1	30.4
1999	32.8	37.0	28.8
2000	27.9	32.9	23.2
2001	25.1	27.3	23.0
% Change			
73 to 01	-48.3	-59.8	-26.7
93 to 01	-49.7	-54.3	-43.5
2000 to 01	-10.0	-17.0	-0.9

Source: U.S. Department of Justice, Bureau of Justice Statistics, National Crime Victimization Survery and *Uniform Crime Reports*, accessible at http://www.ojp.usdoj.gov/bjs/glance/tables.

Gun and Non-Gun Homicide Arrest Rates by Age, 1976-1999

Year	Homicide Arrest Rates per 100,000 Population							All Violent Crime with Gun
	Under 18		18-24		Under 25		All Murders With Gun	
	Gun	Non-Gun	Gun	Non-Gun	Gun	Non-Gun		
1976	5.71	4.79	12.63	9.36	7.79	6.16	5.58	143.10
1977	5.91	3.99	12.06	9.60	7.79	5.71	5.52	139.40
1978	5.31	4.56	13.39	9.19	7.83	6.00	5.70	141.10
1979	6.34	5.30	15.12	10.31	9.13	6.89	6.17	154.60
1980	7.29	5.53	16.94	12.06	10.39	7.63	6.38	174.00
1981	6.62	4.86	14.29	11.09	9.10	6.87	6.13	172.90
1982	5.73	5.00	12.66	11.14	7.97	6.98	5.46	160.90
1983	5.06	4.68	11.24	10.52	7.06	6.57	4.81	141.20
1984	4.83	3.77	11.32	9.96	6.89	5.73	4.65	139.40
1985	5.74	3.90	11.67	9.65	7.59	5.69	4.67	142.80
1986	6.77	4.81	13.29	10.21	8.76	6.46	5.05	156.00
1987	7.71	4.65	13.89	10.29	9.56	6.34	4.88	150.30
1988	10.75	5.23	16.37	10.41	12.41	6.76	5.11	157.00
1989	14.50	4.66	19.55	10.11	15.97	6.25	5.40	165.20
1990	17.45	6.13	23.03	11.21	19.10	7.63	6.04	198.10

[Continued]

Gun and Non-Gun Homicide Arrest Rates by Age, 1976-1999

[Continued]

Year	Homicide Arrest Rates per 100,000 Population							All Violent Crime with Gun
	Under 18		18-24		Under 25		All Murders With Gun	
	Gun	Non-Gun	Gun	Non-Gun	Gun	Non-Gun		
1991	20.35	6.24	29.13	11.60	22.88	7.78	6.49	217.60
1992	20.94	5.31	28.84	9.52	23.17	6.50	6.35	221.70
1993	24.10	5.73	31.74	10.21	26.21	6.97	6.61	225.50
1994	23.03	5.37	30.81	9.46	25.14	6.48	6.27	208.40
1995	18.15	5.00	28.07	9.04	20.79	6.08	5.59	192.00
1996	14.03	5.12	26.79	9.15	17.37	6.18	5.02	172.80
1997	12.81	3.63	24.21	8.51	15.82	4.92	4.61	154.90
1998	9.25	3.67	21.09	9.07	12.41	5.11	4.06	135.00
1999	7.44	3.25	18.98	7.83	10.56	4.49	3.71	124.10

Source: U.S. Bureau of Justice Statistics, Key Facts at a Glance, *Crimes Committed with Firearms, 1973-2000,* table available online at http://www.ojp.usdoj.gov/glance/tables/guncrimetab.htm.

Murders With and Without Guns

Data show actual numbers and percentages.

	All Murders	Murders w/ Firearms	Non-Gun Murders	% With Firearms	% Without Firearms
1973	19,510	13,072	6,438	67.0	33.0
1974	20,600	13,987	6,613	67.9	32.1
1975	20,510	13,496	7,014	65.8	34.2
1976	18,780	11,982	6,798	63.8	36.2
1977	19,120	11,950	7,170	62.5	37.5
1978	19,555	12,437	7,118	63.6	36.4
1979	21,456	13,582	7,874	63.3	36.7
1980	23,040	14,377	8,663	62.4	37.6
1981	22,520	14,052	8,468	62.4	37.6
1982	21,010	12,648	8,362	60.2	39.8
1983	19,310	11,258	8,052	58.3	41.7
1984	18,690	10,990	7,700	58.8	41.2
1985	18,980	11,141	7,839	58.7	41.3
1986	20,610	12,181	8,429	59.1	40.9
1987	20,100	11,879	8,221	59.1	40.9
1988	20,680	12,553	8,127	60.7	39.3
1989	21,500	13,416	8,084	62.4	37.6
1990	23,440	15,025	8,415	64.1	35.9
1991	24,700	16,376	8,324	66.3	33.7
1992	23,760	16,204	7,556	68.2	31.8
1993	24,530	17,048	7,482	69.5	30.5
1994	23,305	16,314	6,992	70.0	30.0
1995	21,597	14,686	6,911	68.0	32.0
1996	19,645	13,319	6,326	67.8	32.2

[Continued]

Murders With and Without Guns
[Continued]

	All Murders	Murders w/ Firearms	Non-Gun Murders	% With Firearms	% Without Firearms
1997	18,208	12,346	5,862	67.8	32.2
1998	16,914	10,977	5,937	64.9	35.1
1999	15,533	10,128	5,405	65.2	34.8
2000	15,517	10,179	5,338	65.6	34.4

Source: U.S. Bureau of Justice Statistics, Key Facts at a Glance, *Crimes Committed with Firearms, 1973-2000,* table available online at http://www.ojp.usdoj.gov/glance/tables/guncrimetab.htm.

Percent of Students Ages 12 Through 19 Who Report That Street Gangs Were Present at School, by Place of Residence

Percent of total population indicates the percentage living in central cities, suburban areas, and non-metropolitan areas respectively.

	1989	1995	% Change	% of Total Population
Central City	24.8	40.7	64.1	30.0
Suburban Area	14.0	26.3	87.9	48.0
Non-Metropolitan Area	7.8	19.9	155.1	22.0

Source: U.S. Department of Justice, National Crime Victimization Survey, School Crime Supplement, available online at http://www.ojp/usdoj.gov/bjs/abstrat/srsc/htm.

Presence of Gangs in Schools by Race and Ethnicity, 1989 and 1995

Data show percent reporting the presence of gangs.

	1989	1995	% Change
All Students	15.3	28.4	85.6
White	11.7	23.0	96.6
Black	19.8	34.7	75.3
Hispanic	31.6	49.5	56.6
Other	25.4	31.2	22.8

Source: U.S. Department of Justice, National Crime Victimization Survey, School Crime Supplement, available online at http://www.ojp/usdoj.gov/bjs/abstrat/srsc/htm.

Number and Percent of Murders, Robberies, and Aggravated Assaults in Which Firearms Were Used, 1973 to 2000

Year	All Violent Victimizations (Number)	Percent with firearms (%)	Murders (Number)	Percent with firearms (%)	Robberies (Number)	Percent with firearms (%)	Aggravated Assaults (Number)	Percent with firearms (%)	Source of Firearm Possessed During Current Offense Purchase or Trade (%)	Family or Friend (%)	Street or Illegal (%)
1973	818,460	44.1	19,510	67.0	382,680	63.0	416,270	25.7	-	-	-
1974	914,610	35.7	20,600	67.9	441,290	44.7	452,720	25.4	-	-	-
1975	970,190	35.3	20,510	65.8	464,970	44.8	484,710	24.9	-	-	-
1976	929,840	33.0	18,780	63.8	420,210	42.7	490,850	23.6	-	-	-
1977	946,480	31.9	19,120	62.5	404,850	41.6	522,510	23.2	-	-	-
1978	994,695	30.9	19,555	63.6	417,038	40.8	558,102	22.4	-	-	-
1979	1,102,550	30.9	21,456	63.3	466,881	39.7	614,213	23.0	-	-	-
1980	1,226,810	32.0	23,040	62.4	548,810	40.3	654,960	23.9	-	-	-
1981	1,240,370	31.9	22,520	62.4	574,130	40.1	643,720	23.6	-	-	-
1982	1,207,942	30.8	21,010	60.2	536,890	39.9	650,042	22.4	-	-	-
1983	1,159,060	28.5	19,310	58.3	500,220	36.7	639,530	21.2	-	-	-
1984	1,189,050	27.7	18,690	58.8	485,010	35.8	685,350	21.1	-	-	-
1985	1,240,100	27.5	18,980	58.7	497,870	35.3	723,250	21.3	-	-	-
1986	1,397,710	26.9	20,610	59.1	542,780	34.3	834,320	21.3	-	-	-
1987	1,392,890	26.3	20,100	59.1	517,700	33.0	855,090	21.4	-	-	-
1988	1,473,740	26.2	20,680	60.7	542,970	33.4	910,090	21.1	-	-	-
1989	1,551,540	26.4	21,500	62.4	578,330	33.2	951,710	21.5	-	-	-
1990	1,717,570	28.7	23,440	64.1	639,270	36.6	1,054,860	23.1	-	-	-
1991	1,805,170	30.4	24,700	66.3	687,730	39.9	1,092,740	23.6	20.8	33.8	40.8
1992	1,823,210	31.0	23,760	68.2	672,480	40.3	1,126,970	24.7	-	-	-
1993	1,819,390	32.0	24,530	69.5	659,760	42.4	1,135,100	25.1	-	-	-
1994	1,762,072	30.8	23,305	70.0	618,817	41.6	1,119,950	24.0	-	-	-
1995	1,701,321	29.6	21,597	68.0	580,545	41.0	1,099,179	22.9	-	-	-
1996	1,586,509	28.9	19,645	67.8	537,050	40.7	1,029,814	22.0	-	-	-
1997	1,539,943	26.9	18,208	67.8	498,534	39.7	1,023,201	20.0	13.9	39.6	39.2
1998	1,437,941	25.4	16,914	64.9	446,625	38.2	974,402	18.8	-	-	-
1999	1,341,586	25.2	15,533	65.2	409,670	39.9	916,383	18.0	-	-	-
2000	1,334,103	25.6	15,517	65.6	407,842	40.9	910,744	18.1	-	-	-

Source: U.S. Bureau of Justice Statistics, *Estimated Firearm Crime*, "Murders, Robberies, and Aggravated Assaults in which a Firearm were Used, 1973-2000," available online at http://www.ojp.usdoj.gov/bjs/glance/tables/guncrimetab.htm.

All Females Murdered and Those Murdered by An Intimate Partner, 1976-1999

	All Female Victims of Homicide	Female Victims Murdered by an Intimate Partner White	Black	Other	Total	% of Female Victims Killed by a Partner
1976	4,590	849	714	37	1,600	34.86
1977	4,710	831	570	34	1,435	30.47
1978	4,642	868	583	30	1,481	31.90
1979	5,017	883	594	29	1,506	30.02
1980	5,232	913	588	34	1,535	29.34
1981	5,096	952	591	27	1,570	30.81
1982	5,093	946	504	29	1,479	29.04
1983	4,703	910	513	37	1,460	31.04

[Continued]

All Females Murdered and Those Murdered by An Intimate Partner, 1976-1999

[Continued]

	All Female Victims of Homicide	Female Victims Murdered by an Intimate Partner				% of Female Victims Killed by a Partner
		White	Black	Other	Total	
1984	4,741	938	467	34	1,439	30.35
1985	4,881	1,005	492	48	1,545	31.65
1986	5,109	1,000	532	52	1,584	31.00
1987	5,268	968	486	35	1,489	28.26
1988	5,238	1,007	527	36	1,570	29.97
1989	5,085	883	474	42	1,399	27.51
1990	5,115	952	490	45	1,487	29.07
1991	5,394	931	520	55	1,506	27.92
1992	5,217	890	509	48	1,447	27.74
1993	5,550	989	542	43	1,574	28.36
1994	5,007	900	463	35	1,398	27.92
1995	5,023	874	387	50	1,311	26.10
1996	4,470	862	422	28	1,312	29.35
1997	4,124	761	401	40	1,202	29.15
1998	4,125	878	393	38	1,309	31.73
1999	3,800	812	338	62	1,212	31.89

Source: U.S. Department of Justice, Bureau of Justice Statistics, *Homicide Trends in the United States*, "Intimate Homicides," January 4, 2001, available online at http://www.ojp.usdoj.gov/bjs/homicide/intimates.htm.

Intimate Homicide Rate by Victim's Race, Sex and Relationship with Offender

Rate per 100,000 population ages 20-44 by marial satus. The number of married or divorced persons is the population base used to calculate spouse and ex-spouse rates and the number of never married or widowed persons is the population base used to calculate boyfriend/girlfriend rates.

Year	White				Black			
	Husband or ex-husband	Boyfriend	Wife or ex-wife	Girlfriend	Husband or ex-husband	Boyfriend	Wife or ex-wife	Girlfriend
1976	0.97	0.68	1.73	1.70	18.42	12.96	12.61	10.69
1977	1.01	0.72	1.62	1.53	16.92	11.68	10.26	7.83
1978	0.98	0.61	1.73	1.64	14.98	10.63	11.21	7.46
1979	1.11	0.63	1.73	1.72	15.88	9.63	9.74	8.66
1980	0.99	0.72	1.69	2.33	14.35	9.62	10.05	8.01
1981	1.02	0.67	1.76	1.83	12.88	8.87	8.47	8.28
1982	0.84	0.76	1.76	1.81	10.80	8.35	7.07	7.30
1983	0.91	0.63	1.54	1.84	10.70	7.49	8.23	6.84
1984	0.65	0.79	1.56	1.97	8.37	7.11	5.90	7.25
1985	0.73	0.64	1.60	2.05	7.73	7.17	6.30	6.79
1986	0.70	0.68	1.53	2.42	7.72	7.34	6.75	7.80
1987	0.66	0.64	1.48	2.16	6.85	6.97	6.10	6.09
1988	0.55	0.68	1.51	2.22	6.69	6.53	6.21	7.06

[Continued]

Intimate Homicide Rate by Victim's Race, Sex and Relationship with Offender

[Continued]

Year	White				Black			
	Husband or ex-husband	Boyfriend	Wife or ex-wife	Girlfriend	Husband or ex-husband	Boyfriend	Wife or ex-wife	Girlfriend
1989	0.53	0.62	1.21	2.24	6.74	6.66	5.57	6.73
1990	0.54	0.66	1.39	2.03	5.77	6.40	5.84	7.06
1991	0.45	0.69	1.35	2.01	5.08	5.62	6.05	7.16
1992	0.56	0.51	1.29	1.84	4.54	4.65	6.09	5.92
1993	0.43	0.60	1.29	2.46	4.52	4.96	6.04	6.70
1994	0.46	0.48	1.39	1.89	4.75	4.36	4.13	6.09
1995	0.39	0.36	1.12	2.28	2.93	3.70	3.71	4.98
1996	0.39	0.34	1.15	1.92	2.39	3.35	4.26	5.30
1997	0.31	0.44	0.99	1.91	2.08	2.50	3.45	4.75
1998	0.28	0.45	1.20	1.96	1.83	4.36	4.41	4.71
1999	0.26	0.34	0.96	2.12	1.33	3.97	3.03	3.87

Source: U.S. Department of Justice, Bureau of Justice Statistics, *Homicide Trends in the United States*, "Intimate Homicides," January 4, 2001, available online at http://www.ojp.usdoj.gov/bjs/homicide/intimates.htm.

Homicide Offender and Victimization Rates by Race, 1976-1999

Rates are the number per 100,000 population.

Year	Homicide Offender Rates			Victimization Rates		
	White	Black	Other	White	Black	Other
1976	5.1	44.7	7.4	5.1	37.1	7.9
1977	5.3	42.3	8.3	5.4	36.2	7.6
1978	5.5	42.3	7.0	5.6	35.1	7.1
1979	6.0	45.2	9.5	6.1	37.5	8.9
1980	6.7	49.9	6.2	6.3	37.7	5.7
1981	6.1	44.8	6.2	6.2	36.4	6.1
1982	5.8	39.8	6.8	5.9	32.3	6.5
1983	5.3	35.6	6.4	5.3	29.4	6.4
1984	5.3	32.8	5.2	5.2	27.2	5.4
1985	5.1	33.3	5.6	5.2	27.5	5.4
1986	5.4	36.8	6.4	5.3	31.3	6.2
1987	5.3	35.6	4.9	5.1	30.6	5.2
1988	5.0	40.3	4.3	4.9	33.3	4.0
1989	5.1	41.9	4.3	4.9	34.9	4.2
1990	5.6	46.9	4.1	5.4	37.7	4.2
1991	5.7	50.4	5.4	5.5	39.3	6.0
1992	5.2	46.8	5.8	5.3	37.2	5.4
1993	5.2	49.3	5.6	5.3	38.7	5.5
1994	5.0	46.1	4.9	5.0	36.4	4.6
1995	4.9	39.1	5.1	4.8	31.6	4.9

[Continued]

Homicide Offender and Victimization Rates by Race, 1976-1999

[Continued]

Year	Homicide Offender Rates			Victimization Rates		
	White	Black	Other	White	Black	Other
1996	4.5	35.8	4.7	4.3	28.3	4.1
1997	4.1	32.4	4.5	3.9	26.1	4.1
1998	4.1	28.3	3.5	3.8	23.0	2.9
1999	3.5	25.6	3.9	3.5	20.6	3.2

Source: U.S. Bureau of Justice Statistics, *Homicide Trends in the United States*, based on data from the *National Crime Victimization Survey* and the *Uniform Crime Reports* series, March 2001, available online at http://www.ojp.usdoj.gov/bjs/homicide/homtrnd.htm.

Serious Violent Crime Victimization Rates by Race, 1973-2001

Rates are the number of victimizations per 1,000 people age 12 or older in the population.

Year	White	Black
1973	20.0	37.3
1974	20.9	37.3
1975	19.1	36.7
1976	18.8	38.2
1977	19.4	34.4
1978	18.8	33.2
1979	19.6	33.2
1980	18.7	34.0
1981	19.7	40.4
1982	19.0	36.9
1983	16.3	33.1
1984	17.1	32.7
1985	15.6	28.9
1986	15.6	25.2
1987	15.0	33.8
1988	16.0	31.4
1989	16.1	29.5
1990	15.4	31.8
1991	16.2	31.3
1992	16.9	33.0
1993	17.8	34.3
1994	17.1	33.5
1995	13.5	26.4
1996	13.3	26.3
1997	12.9	20.7
1998	11.6	19.2
1999	10.2	19.5

[Continued]

Serious Violent Crime Victimization Rates by Race, 1973-2001

[Continued]

Year	White	Black
2000	8.7	16.2
2001	8.4	12.7

Source: U.S. Bureau of Justice Statistics, *Violent Crime Victims by Race*, based on data from the *National Crime Victimization Survey*, August 2002, available online at http://www.ojp.usdoj.gov/bjs/cvict_v.htm#race.

Average Annual Number of Rapes, Attempted Rapes and Sexual Assaults, 1992-2000

	Total	Male Victims	Female Victims	Percent Reported to Police
Completed Rape	140,990	9,040	131,950	36%
Attempted Rape	109,230	10,270	98,970	34%
Sexual Assault	152,680	17,130	135,550	26%

Source: U.S. Department of Justice, Bureau of Justice Statistics, *Rape and Sexual Assault: Reporting to Police and Medical Attention, 1992-2000*, August 2002, p. 1.

Violent Crime Victimization Rate by Type of Residential Area, 1993-1998.

Rates are number of victimizations per 1,000 persons age 12 years or older. The crimes included are rape, sexual assault, robbery, aggravated assault and simple assault.

Year	Urban	Suburban	Rural
1993	73.75	49.70	42.14
1994	68.44	53.33	37.44
1995	59.86	45.06	35.68
1996	57.90	40.06	32.40
1997	52.47	38.77	29.40
1998	47.65	37.19	27.84

Source: U.S. Bureau of Justice Statistics, *Urban, Suburban, and Rural Victimization, 1993-1998*, October 2000, pp. 3 and 11.

Number of Homicides by Location Type, 1976-1999

Large cities refer to cities with a population of 100,000 or higher and small cities are those with fewer than 100,000 population.

Year	Large City	Small City	Suburban Area	Rural Area
1976	9,860	2,297	3,954	2,669
1977	10,398	2,203	3,836	2,683
1978	10,563	2,341	3,963	2,692
1979	11,825	2,469	4,362	2,805
1980	12,605	2,609	4,845	2,982
1981	12,615	2,413	4,866	2,626
1982	11,118	2,490	4,847	2,555
1983	10,856	2,148	4,189	2,117
1984	10,187	2,042	4,350	2,110
1985	10,160	2,141	4,480	2,198
1986	11,622	2,252	4,610	2,127
1987	11,021	2,208	4,725	2,146
1988	12,191	2,213	4,221	2,055
1989	12,913	2,300	4,214	2,073
1990	14,078	2,478	4,597	2,287
1991	15,247	2,748	4,533	2,172
1992	14,402	2,437	5,025	1,896
1993	14,989	2,632	5,030	1,879
1994	14,008	2,882	4,762	1,678
1995	13,047	2,498	4,290	1,775
1996	11,574	2,369	3,941	1,767
1997	10,849	2,123	3,556	1,682
1998	9,560	2,127	3,625	1,598
1999	9,007	1,909	3,166	1,448

Source: U.S. Bureau of Justice Statistics, *Homicide Trends in the U.S.*, "Homicides by Location Types," January 2001, available online at http://www.ojp.usdoj.gov/bjs/homicide/ tables/urbantab.htm.

Homicide Rates by Location Type

Year	Area Type		
	Urban	Suburban	Rural
1993	28.57	4.96	3.88
1994	26.67	4.68	3.45
1995	24.32	4.09	3.78
1996	21.61	3.61	3.99
1997	19.89	3.21	3.78
1998	17.84	3.22	3.59

Source: U.S. Bureau of Justice Statistics, Homicide Trends in the U.S., *Homicides by Location Types,* January 2001, available online at http://www.ojp.usdoj.gov/bjs/homicide/ tables/ urbantab.htm.

Rates of Violent Victimization in the Workplace by Occupational Field, 1993-99

Rates for the leading six occupations are reported. The rate is the number of victimizations per 1,000 people in the workforce.

Year	Medical	Mental Health	Teaching	Law Enforcement	Retail Sales	Trans-portation
1993	20.3	64.4	25.8	163.1	21.9	20.6
1994	16.7	63.7	19.3	156.4	22.8	24.1
1995	16.0	56.7	15.4	157.2	22.2	13.8
1996	11.8	63.9	16.6	125.9	20.4	12.6
1997	8.4	39.7	14.9	122.0	20.5	15.4
1998	9.2	49.3	18.9	88.5	16.2	18.3
1999	10.0	46.1	12.4	74.1	14.1	8.4

Source: U.S. Department of Justice, Bureau of Justice Statistics, *Violent Crime Victimization Survey 2000*, "Violence in the Workplace, 1993-99," December 2001, available online at http://www.ojp.usdoj.gov/bjs/abstract/cvusst.htm.

Chapter 3
PROPERTY CRIME

Property Crime Rates

Data show reported incidents per 100,000 people. 1993 data and beyond based on collection year while earlier years based on data year.

	Total Rate	Burglary	Theft	Vehicle Theft
1973	519.9	110.0	390.8	19.1
1974	551.5	111.8	421.0	18.8
1975	553.6	110.0	424.1	19.5
1976	544.2	106.7	421.0	16.5
1977	544.1	106.2	420.9	17.0
1978	532.6	103.1	412.0	17.5
1979	531.8	100.9	413.4	17.5
1980	496.1	101.4	378.0	16.7
1981	497.2	105.9	374.1	17.2
1982	468.3	94.1	358.0	16.2
1983	428.4	84.0	329.8	14.6
1984	399.2	76.9	307.1	15.2
1985	385.4	75.2	296.0	14.2
1986	372.7	73.8	284.0	15.0
1987	379.6	74.6	289.0	16.0
1988	378.4	74.3	286.7	17.5
1989	373.4	67.7	286.5	19.2
1990	348.9	64.5	263.8	20.6
1991	353.7	64.6	266.8	22.2
1992	325.3	58.6	248.2	18.5
1993	318.9	58.2	241.7	19.0
1994	310.2	56.3	235.1	18.8
1995	290.5	49.3	224.3	16.9
1996	266.4	47.2	205.7	13.5
1997	248.3	44.6	189.9	13.8
1998	217.4	38.5	168.1	10.8
1999	198.0	34.1	153.9	10.0
2000	178.1	31.8	137.7	8.6
2001	166.9	28.7	129.0	9.2

Source: U.S. Department of Justice, Bureau of Justice Statistics, National Crime Victimization Survey, *Criminal Victimization 2000.*

Property Crime Arrest Rates, 1971-2000

Rate per 100,000 inhabitants.

	Total Crime	Property Crime	Burglary	Larceny-Theft	Vehicle Theft	Arson
1971	897.1	721.4	202.9	434.2	84.2	NA
1972	881.5	695.0	196.0	423.1	76.0	NA
1973	883.4	696.1	204.1	415.6	76.4	NA
1974	1,098.0	878.3	254.1	544.2	80.0	NA
1975	1,059.6	852.9	250.7	535.1	67.1	NA
1976	1,016.8	823.7	231.8	528.8	63.1	NA
1977	1,039.4	836.7	238.1	527.8	70.9	NA
1978	1,047.6	832.2	234.6	523.6	74.0	NA
1979	1,057.2	844.7	228.8	536.8	70.2	9.0
1980	1,055.8	841.4	230.4	539.8	62.3	8.9
1981	1,070.0	853.2	228.4	558.8	57.0	9.0
1982	1,148.9	912.0	232.9	612.1	58.0	9.0
1983	1,071.9	850.8	207.1	582.5	52.6	8.6
1984	1,019.8	807.3	185.9	561.4	51.9	8.2
1985	1,046.5	834.0	188.1	580.7	56.9	8.3
1986	1,091.8	857.3	189.2	595.6	64.7	7.8
1987	1,120.1	886.4	185.3	621.0	72.5	7.5
1988	1,123.5	879.7	175.6	615.4	81.0	7.7
1989	1,173.1	904.4	178.4	627.3	91.4	7.3
1990	1,203.2	912.5	176.3	641.4	87.0	7.7
1991	1,198.8	905.8	173.1	639.8	85.1	7.9
1992	1,162.4	861.9	168.6	605.5	80.3	7.6
1993	1,131.6	828.8	158.0	584.4	78.8	7.5
1994	1,148.4	837.7	154.1	595.5	80.1	8.1
1995	1,140.3	825.0	148.8	592.7	75.9	7.6
1996	1,081.8	793.2	139.1	577.3	69.5	7.2
1997	1,042.9	769.3	134.2	564.2	63.3	7.5
1998	954.0	695.2	125.5	505.6	57.5	6.5
1999	880.0	635.5	112.1	462.2	54.9	6.3
2000	821.8	593.6	104.0	429.5	54.2	5.9

Source: U.S. Department of Justice, Bureau of Justice Statistics, *Sourcebook of Criminal Justice Statistics, 2000*, Washington D.C., USGPO, 2001, p. 353.

Percent of All Larcenies, by Type

Figures are rounded and may not add up to 100%. Thefts from vehicles does not include accessories.

	Pocket-picking	Purse Snatching	Shoplifting	From Vehicle	Vehicle Accessory	Bicycles	From Buildings	Coin Operated Machines	All Other
1973	1	2	11	17	16	17	17	1	18
1974	1	2	11	18	16	17	17	1	17
1975	1	2	11	18	19	13	17	1	18
1976	1	2	10	20	22	10	15	1	18

[Continued]

Percent of All Larcenies, by Type

[Continued]

	Pocket-picking	Purse Snatching	Shoplifting	From Vehicle	Vehicle Accessory	Bicycles	From Buildings	Coin Operated Machines	All Other
1977	1	2	11	17	20	11	16	1	20
1978	1	2	11	17	19	11	17	1	21
1979	1	1	11	17	19	11	16	1	22
1980	1	2	11	17	19	10	17	1	23
1981	1	2	11	18	19	9	17	1	22
1982	1	1	12	19	20	9	16	1	21
1983	1	1	13	19	19	8	16	1	22
1984	1	1	13	19	18	8	16	1	22
1985	1	1	14	20	17	8	16	1	23
1986	1	1	15	21	17	7	15	1	22
1987	1	1	15	21	17	6	15	1	23
1988	1	1	15	22	16	6	15	1	23
1989	1	1	16	22	16	6	15	1	24
1990	1	1	16	22	15	6	14	1	24
1991	1	1	16	22	14	6	14	1	24
1992	1	1	16	23	14	6	14	1	25
1993	1	1	15	23	14	6	13	1	26
1994	1	1	15	24	13	6	13	1	27
1995	1	1	15	24	12	6	12	1	28
1996	0.5	1	15	25	11	6	13	1	29
1997	1	1	15	26	10	6	14	1	28
1998	1	1	15	26	10	5	13	1	29
1999	1	1	14	26	10	5	14	1	29
2000	1	1	14	25	10	4	13	1	32

Source: U.S. Department of Justice, Bureau of Justice Statistics, *Sourcebook of Criminal Justice Statistics, 2000.*

Number of Larcenies, 1980-1999

Year	Larcenies
1980	7,136,900
1981	7,194,400
1982	7,142,500
1983	6,712,800
1984	6,591,900
1985	6,926,400
1986	7,257,200
1987	7,499,900
1988	7,705,900
1989	7,872,400
1990	7,945,700
1991	8,142,200
1992	7,915,200
1993	7,820,900

[Continued]

Number of Larcenies, 1980-1999

[Continued]

Year	Larcenies
1994	7,879,800
1995	7,997,700
1996	7,904,700
1997	7,743,800
1998	7,376,300
1999	6,957,400

Source: U.S. Department of Justice, Bureau of Justice Statistics, *Sourcebook of Criminal Justice Statistics, 2000.*

Auto Thefts

Number of thefts are estimated.

	Number of Motor Vehicle Thefts	Number of Motor Vehicle Registered	Thefts per 100,000 Registered	Ratio of Vehicles Stolen to Registered
1980	1,131,700	161,614,294	700	0.140972222
1981	1,087,800	164,287,643	662	0.146527778
1982	1,062,400	165,298,024	643	0.150000000
1983	1,007,900	167,718,000	601	0.156944444
1984	1,032,200	169,446,281	609	0.155555556
1985	1,102,900	175,709,000	628	0.152083333
1986	1,224,100	181,890,000	673	0.145138889
1987	1,288,700	186,137,000	692	0.141666667
1988	1,432,900	183,930,000	779	0.130555556
1989	1,564,800	188,981,016	828	0.125694444
1990	1,635,900	194,502,000	841	0.124305556
1991	1,661,700	194,897,000	853	0.122916667
1992	1,610,800	193,775,000	831	0.125000000
1993	1,563,100	198,041,338	789	0.129861111
1994	1,539,300	201,763,492	763	0.132638889
1995	1,472,400	205,297,050	717	0.138194444
1996	1,394,200	210,236,393	663	0.146527778
1997	1,354,200	211,580,033	640	0.150000000
1998	1,242,800	215,496,003	577	0.161805556
1999	1,152,100	220,461,056	523	0.174305556
2000	1,165,600	225,821,241	516	0.176388889

Source: U.S. Department of Justice, Bureau of Justice Statistics, *Sourcebook of Criminal Justice Statistics, 2000.*

Burglaries by Time of Day

Distribution is shown in percent. Non-residences refer to stores, offices, etc.

	Residence			Non-residence		
	Night	Day	Unknown	Night	Day	Unknown
1976	22	25	16	23	5	9
1977	23	26	16	21	5	9
1978	22	26	16	20	6	10
1979	21	26	16	21	6	10
1980	21	28	17	18	5	10
1981	22	29	17	18	5	9
1982	22	27	16	19	6	10
1983	23	26	18	18	6	10
1984	22	27	18	17	6	10
1985	21	27	18	17	6	10
1986	22	28	18	17	6	10
1987	21	28	18	16	6	10
1988	21	29	18	16	7	10
1989	20	28	17	16	8	10
1990	21	29	16	16	8	9
1991	21	28	17	16	8	10
1992	21	29	16	16	9	9
1993	21	29	16	16	8	10
1994	20	30	17	15	9	9
1995	20	29	17	14	9	10
1996	20	28	19	15	8	11
1997	19	28	19	15	8	11
1998	19	29	19	14	8	11
1999	19	29	18	14	9	11
2000	19	30	16	15	11	10

Source: U.S. Department of Justice, Bureau of Justice Statistics, *Sourcebook of Criminal Justice Statistics, 2000.*

Items Stolen from 12-17 Year Olds, 1996-97

Data show percent of teenagers that have experienced a particular type of theft. Figures from a survey.

	Percent
Motor vehicle or parts	2
Purse	3
Toys, recreation equipment	4
Wallet	8
Bicycle or parts	9
Jewelry, watch, keys	9
Only cash	10

[Continued]

Items Stolen from 12-17 Year Olds, 1996-97

[Continued]

	Percent
Clothing, luggage	17
Electronics, photo gear	18

Source: "The Property Taken." available from http://www.ncjrs.org.

Items Stolen from Adults, 1996-97

Data show percent of adults that have experienced a particular form of theft. Figures from a survey.

	Percent
Wallet	6
Credit cards	6
Jewelry, watch, keys	6
Only cash	6
Clothing, luggage	7
Tools, machines	9
Electronics, photo gear	10
Motor vehicle or parts	19

Source: "The Property Taken." available from http://www.ncjrs.org.

Reporting Property Crime

Figures show rate per 100,000 people. Violent crime rate is included for comparison.

	1993	1994	1995	1996	1997	1998	1999	2000
Property crime	33.5	33.2	33.6	34.8	35.1	35.3	33.8	35.7
Burglary	50.2	48.5	51.4	50.6	51.8	49.4	49.3	50.7
Motor vehicle theft	74.7	79.0	76.2	76.5	79.8	79.7	83.7	80.4
Theft	26.2	25.9	26.4	28.4	27.9	29.2	27.1	29.5
Personal theft	25.8	29.9	35.0	37.6	30.5	34.0	25.9	35.0
Violent crime	43.2	40.4	42.0	42.8	44.5	45.9	43.9	47.9

Source: U.S. Department of Justice, Bureau of Justice Statistics, *Sourcebook of Criminal Justice Statistics, 2000*, p. 209.

Arson: Number of Fires, Value of Damage and Loss of Life

Figures do not include fires with cause unknown or unreported. Includes deaths occuring in incendiary or suspicious structure fires only. Number of fires and dollar losses are estimated. Losses do not include Oakland Fire storm.

	Structure Fires Number	Dollar Losses (mil.)	Vehicle Fires Number	Estimated Dollar Losses (mil.)
1978	160,000	1,111	48,000	55
1979	148,500	1,328	63,500	167
1980	146,000	1,706	45,000	75
1981	154,500	1,658	44,500	107
1982	129,000	1,604	48,000	138
1983	122,000	1,421	48,000	122
1984	110,500	1,417	50,500	138
1985	117,000	1,670	45,500	134
1986	111,000	1,677	57,000	151
1987	105,000	1,590	51,000	135
1988	99,500	1,594	53,000	151
1989	97,000	1,558	46,000	139
1990	97,000	1,394	51,000	167
1991	98,000	1,531	49,000	182
1992	94,000	1,999	44,000	158
1993	84,500	2,351	41,500	137
1994	86,000	1,447	43,500	156
1995	90,500	1,647	47,000	175
1996	85,500	1,405	47,000	202
1997	78,500	1,309	46,500	214
1998	76,000	1,249	45,000	215
1999	72,000	1,281	45,000	195
2000	75,000	1,340	46,500	186

Source: John R. Hall, Jr., *U.S. Arson Trends and Patterns* (Quincy, MA: National Fire Protection Association, 2001), pp. 12-14, 16, 17; and Michael J. Karter, Jr., *Fire Loss in the United States During 2000* (Quincy, MA: National Fire Protection Association, 2001), p. 13. Table constructed by Sourcebook of Criminal Justice Statistics staff. Reprinted with permission from NFPA, Fire Analysis Research. Copyright 2001 National Fire Protection Association, Quincy, MA 02269.

Counterfeit Money Production

Figures show share of counterfeit money produced on laser printers and the value of the currrency, in thousands of dollars.

	Share	Value
1995	0.5	175
1996	3.0	760
1997	19.0	6,121
1998	43.0	17,050

Source: United States Treasury Department, *The Use and Counterfeiting of United States Currency Abroad*, p. 63.

Estimated Cases of identity Theft

	Cases
1998	250,000
1999	400,000
2000	500,000
2001	750,000
2002	1,000,000
2003	1,400,000
2004	1,600,000

Source: Gillin, Eric. "Protecting Yourself Against Identity Theft" available from http://www.thestreet.com and Celent Corp. estimates.

Who Commits Health Care Fraud

	Percent
Medical professionals	72
Laboratories, med. equipment suppliers, others	10
Consumers	10
Hospitals, clinics and psychiatric hospitals	8

Source: Health Insurance Association of America, based on a 1999 survey conducted with the assistance of the Blue Cross and Blue Shield Association and the National Health Care Anti-Fraud Association.

U.S. Copyright Losses to Trade Piracy

Figures are estimates in millions of dollars.

	1997	1998	1999	2000	2001
Books	665.30	685.20	685.40	671.80	650.80
Records & music	1,250.30	1,732.50	1,723.50	2,065.40	2,339.10
Motion pictures	1,776.00	1,768.50	1,268.00	1,264.50	1,323.00
Entertainment software	3,223.60	3,400.50	2,906.80	1,582.80	1,888.70
Business applications	4,779.10	4,652.90	2,761.90	2,926.50	3,207.40

Source: International Intellectual Property Association, available at http://www.iipa.org.

U.S. Customs Seizures

Figures show the value of counterfeit goods seized by Customs in millions of dollars. Number of seizures also shown.

	Value	Number
1997	54.1	1,943
1998	75.8	3,409
1999	98.5	3,691
2000	45.3	3,244
2001	57.4	3,586

Source: the U.S. Customs Service, available at http://www.customs.ustreas.gov.

Chapter 4
LESSER CRIMES & OFFENSES

Total Estimated Arrests - United States - 1984 to 2000 - Part I

All data are actual arrests.

	Grand Total	Crime Index Arrests								Crime Index Summary		
		Murder/Non-negl. Man-slaughter	Forcible Rape	Robbery	Aggravated Assault	Burglary	Larceny-Theft	Motor Vehicle Theft	Arson	Violent Crime	Property Crime	Total Crime Index
1984	11,564,000	17,770	36,700	138,630	300,860	433,600	1,291,700	121,200	19,000	493,960	1,865,600	2,359,500
1985	11,945,000	18,330	36,970	166,870	350,390	443,300	1,348,400	133,900	19,500	497,560	1,945,100	2,422,700
1986	12,487,500	19,190	37,140	145,800	351,770	450,600	1,400,200	153,600	18,700	553,900	2,023,200	2,577,100
1987	12,711,600	19,200	36,310	138,290	352,450	443,400	1,469,200	169,300	18,000	546,300	2,099,900	2,646,200
1988	13,812,300	21,890	38,610	149,100	416,300	463,400	1,571,200	208,400	19,700	625,900	2,262,700	2,888,600
1989	14,340,900	22,300	39,110	165,060	459,000	468,900	1,604,400	228,500	18,600	685,500	2,320,400	3,005,800
1990	14,195,100	22,990	39,160	167,990	475,330	432,600	1,554,800	211,300	19,100	705,500	2,217,800	2,923,300
1991	14,211,900	24,050	40,120	173,820	480,000	436,500	1,588,300	207,700	20,000	718,890	2,252,500	2,971,400
1992	14,075,100	22,510	39,100	174,310	507,210	197,600	1,729,970	197,600	19,900	742,130	2,146,000	2,888,200
1993	14,036,300	23,400	38,420	173,620	518,670	402,700	1,476,300	195,900	19,400	754,110	2,094,300	2,848,400
1994	14,648,700	22,100	36,610	172,290	547,760	396,100	1,514,500	200,200	20,900	778,730	2,131,700	2,910,400
1995	15,119,800	21,230	34,650	171,870	568,480	386,500	1,530,200	191,900	20,000	796,250	2,128,600	2,924,800
1996	15,158,100	19,020	33,050	156,270	521,570	364,800	1,486,300	175,400	19,000	729,900	2,045,600	2,775,500
1997	15,284,300	18,290	32,060	132,480	534,920	356,000	1,472,600	167,000	20,000	717,750	2,015,600	2,733,400
1998	14,528,300	17,450	31,070	120,870	506,630	330,700	1,307,100	150,700	17,200	675,900	1,805,600	2,481,500
1999	14,355,600	14,920	29,200	109,840	490,790	301,500	1,213,300	144,200	17,100	644,700	1,676,200	2,320,900
2000	13,980,297	13,277	27,469	106,960	478,417	289,844	1,166,362	148,225	16,530	625,132	1,620,928	2,246,054
2001	13,699,254	13,653	27,270	108,400	477,809	291,444	1,160,821	147,451	18,749	627,132	1,618,465	2,245,597

Source: U.S. Department of Justice, Federal Bureau of Investigation, *Uniform Crime Reports*, 1984 through 2001. Most recent issues are accessible at http://www.fbi.gov/ucr/00cius.htm.

Total Estimated Arrests - United States - 1984 to 2000 - Part II

All data are actual arrests.

	Assault/Weapons		Forgery, Fraud, Money-Related						Sex-Related Offenses		Conduct Offenses	
	Simple Assault	Weapons: Carrying, Possessing	Forgery and Counter-feiting	Fraud	Embez-zlement	Stolen Property Offenses	Vandal-ism	Gambling Offenses	Prostitution/ Commerc. Vice	Non-Rape Sex Offenses	Disorderly Conduct	Vagrancy
1984	527,000	177,500	82,400	270,700	8,100	123,100	245,900	34,700	112,200	97,800	665,900	29,100
1985	637,600	180,900	87,600	342,600	11,400	127,100	259,600	32,100	113,800	100,600	671,700	33,800
1986	711,000	190,500	92,200	349,300	12,600	135,800	259,600	30,500	112,600	100,600	676,400	38,700
1987	787,200	191,700	93,900	341,900	12,700	139,300	273,500	25,400	110,100	100,100	698,700	36,100
1988	901,800	221,800	101,700	366,300	15,500	166,300	295,300	23,600	104,100	106,300	760,500	36,500
1989	978,900	225,200	105,400	376,600	18,200	176,800	307,800	20,600	107,400	104,800	776,600	33,800
1990	1,014,100	221,200	94,800	291,600	15,300	165,200	326,000	19,300	111,400	107,600	733,000	38,500
1991	1,041,200	232,300	103,700	427,800	14,000	170,000	335,000	16,600	98,900	108,000	757,700	38,500
1992	1,074,700	239,300	105,400	424,200	13,700	161,500	323,100	17,100	96,200	108,400	753,100	34,300

[Continued]

Total Estimated Arrests - United States - 1984 to 2000 - Part II

[Continued]

| | Assault/Weapons | | Forgery, Fraud, Money-Related | | | | | | Sex-Related Offenses | | Conduct Offenses | |
	Simple Assault	Weapons: Carrying, Possessing	Forgery and Counter-feiting	Fraud	Embez-zlement	Stolen Property Offenses	Vandal-ism	Gambling Offenses	Prostitution/ Commerc. Vice	Non-Rape Sex Offenses	Disorderly Conduct	Vagrancy
1993	1,144,900	262,300	106,900	410,700	12,900	158,100	313,000	17,300	97,800	104,100	727,000	28,200
1994	1,223,600	259,400	115,300	419,800	14,300	164,700	323,300	18,500	98,800	100,700	746,200	25,300
1995	1,290,400	243,900	122,300	436,400	15,200	166,500	311,100	19,500	97,700	94,500	748,600	25,900
1996	1,329,000	216,200	121,600	465,000	15,700	151,100	320,900	21,000	99,000	95,800	842,600	27,800
1997	1,395,800	218,900	120,100	414,600	17,400	155,300	318,400	15,900	101,600	101,900	811,100	28,800
1998	1,338,800	190,600	114,600	394,600	17,100	137,900	300,200	12,800	94,000	93,600	696,100	30,400
1999	1,322,100	175,000	109,300	371,800	17,300	124,100	285,000	10,400	92,200	93,800	655,600	30,800
2000	1,312,169	159,181	108,654	345,732	18,952	118,641	281,305	10,842	87,620	93,399	638,740	32,542
2001	1,315,807	165,896	113,741	323,308	20,157	121,972	270,645	11,112	80,854	91,828	621,394	27,935

Source: U.S. Department of Justice, Federal Bureau of Investigation, *Uniform Crime Reports*, 1984 through 2001. Most recent issues are accessible at http:// www.fbi.gov/ucr/00cius.htm.

Total Estimated Arrests - United States - 1984 to 2000 - Part III

Data are actual arrests and national population data in thousands.

| | Arrests | | | | | | |
	Drug Abuse Violations	DWI	Liquor Law Violations	Drunken-ness	Offenses Against Family/Child	Run-aways	All Other Except Traffic[1]
1984	708,400	1,779,400	505,500	1,152,300	44,300	147,000	2,406,900
1985	811,400	1,788,400	548,600	964,800	58,800	161,200	2,489,200
1986	824,100	1,793,300	600,200	933,900	58,400	165,200	2,730,500
1987	937,400	1,727,200	616,700	828,300	58,700	160,400	2,836,700
1988	1,155,200	1,792,500	669,600	818,600	69,900	166,900	3,078,900
1989	1,361,700	1,736,200	657,300	822,500	74,200	159,200	3,214,700
1990	1,089,500	1,810,800	714,700	910,100	85,800	174,200	3,267,800
1991	1,010,000	1,771,400	624,100	881,100	99,400	177,300	3,240,000
1992	1,066,400	1,624,500	541,700	832,300	109,200	181,300	3,389,500
1993	1,126,300	1,524,800	518,500	726,600	109,100	180,500	3,518,700
1994	1,351,400	1,384,600	541,800	713,200	117,200	248,800	3,743,200
1995	1,476,100	1,436,000	594,900	708,100	142,900	249,500	3,865,400
1996	1,506,200	1,467,300	677,400	817,700	149,800	195,700	3,786,700
1997	1,583,600	1,477,300	636,400	734,800	155,800	196,100	3,884,600
1998	1,559,100	1,402,800	630,400	710,300	146,400	165,100	3,824,100
1999	1,557,100	1,549,500	683,600	673,400	153,500	150,700	3,809,000
2000	1,579,566	1,471,289	683,124	637,554	147,663	141,975	3,710,434
2001	1,586,902	1,434,852	610,591	618,668	143,683	133,259	3,618,164

Source: U.S. Department of Justice, Federal Bureau of Investigation, *Uniform Crime Reports*, 1984 through 2001. Most recent issues are accessible at http://www.fbi.gov/ucr/00cius.htm. *Notes:* 1. All Other includes crimes/offenses under state laws or local ordinances not included elsewhere.

Total Estimated Arrests - United States - 1984 to 2000 - Part IV

Data are arrests per 100,000 population aged 18 years old or older.

	Grand Total	Crime Index Arrests								Crime Index Summary		
		Murder/Non-negl. Man-slaughter	Forcible Rape	Robbery	Aggravated Assault	Burglary	Larceny-Theft	Motor Vehicle Theft	Arson	Violent Crime	Property Crime	Total Crime Index
1984	6,714	10	21	80	175	252	750	70	11	287	1,083	1,370
1985	6,858	11	21	96	201	254	774	77	11	286	1,117	1,391
1986	7,091	11	21	83	200	256	795	87	11	315	1,149	1,463
1987	7,138	11	20	78	198	249	825	95	10	307	1,179	1,486
1988	7,666	12	21	83	231	257	872	116	11	347	1,256	1,603
1989	7,869	12	21	91	252	257	880	125	10	376	1,273	1,649
1990	7,641	12	21	90	256	233	837	114	10	380	1,194	1,573
1991	7,576	13	21	93	256	233	847	111	11	383	1,201	1,584
1992	7,428	12	21	92	268	104	913	104	11	392	1,133	1,524
1993	7,339	12	20	91	271	211	772	102	10	394	1,095	1,489
1994	7,592	11	19	89	284	205	785	104	11	404	1,105	1,508
1995	7,761	11	18	88	292	198	785	98	10	409	1,093	1,501
1996	7,706	10	17	79	265	185	756	89	10	371	1,040	1,411
1997	7,687	9	16	67	269	179	741	84	10	361	1,014	1,375
1998	7,227	9	15	60	252	165	650	75	9	336	898	1,234
1999	7,066	7	14	54	242	148	597	71	8	317	825	1,142
2000	6,807	6	13	52	233	141	568	72	8	304	789	1,094
2001	6,612	7	13	52	231	141	560	71	9	303	781	1,084

Source: U.S. Department of Justice, Federal Bureau of Investigation, *Uniform Crime Reports*, 1984 through 2001. Most recent issues are accessible at http://www.fbi.gov/ucr/00cius.htm.

Total Estimated Arrests - United States - 1984 to 2000 - Part V

Data are arrests per 100,000 population aged 18 years old or older.

	Assault/Weapons		Forgery, Fraud, Money-Related						Sex-Related Offenses		Conduct Offenses	
	Simple Assault	Weapons: Carrying, Possessing	Forgery and Counter-feiting	Fraud	Embez-zlement	Stolen Property Offenses	Vandal-ism	Gambling Offenses	Prostitution/ Commerc. Vice	Non-Rape Sex Offenses	Disorderly Conduct	Vagrancy
1984	306	103	48	157	5	71	143	20	65	57	387	17
1985	366	104	50	197	7	73	149	18	65	58	386	19
1986	404	108	52	198	7	77	147	17	64	57	384	22
1987	442	108	53	192	7	78	154	14	62	56	392	20
1988	501	123	56	203	9	92	164	13	58	59	422	20
1989	537	124	58	207	10	97	169	11	59	58	426	19
1990	546	119	51	157	8	89	175	10	60	58	395	21
1991	555	124	55	228	7	91	179	9	53	58	404	21
1992	567	126	56	224	7	85	171	9	51	57	397	18
1993	599	137	56	215	7	83	164	9	51	54	380	15
1994	634	134	60	218	7	85	168	10	51	52	387	13
1995	662	125	63	224	8	85	160	10	50	49	384	13
1996	676	110	62	236	8	77	163	11	50	49	428	14
1997	702	110	60	209	9	78	160	8	51	51	408	14
1998	666	95	57	196	9	69	149	6	47	47	346	15
1999	651	86	54	183	9	61	140	5	45	46	323	15
2000	639	78	53	168	9	58	137	5	43	45	311	16
2001	635	80	55	156	10	59	131	5	39	44	300	13

Source: U.S. Department of Justice, Federal Bureau of Investigation, *Uniform Crime Reports*, 1984 through 2001. Most recent issues are accessible at http://www.fbi.gov/ucr/00cius.htm.

Total Estimated Arrests - United States - 1984 to 2000 - Part VI

Data are arrests per 100,000 population aged 18 years old or older.

	\multicolumn{7}{c}{Arrests}						
	Drug Abuse Violations	Driving While Intoxicated	Liquor Law Violations	Drunken-ness	Offenses Against Family/Child	Run-aways	All Other Except Traffic[1]
1984	411	1,033	293	669	26	85	1,397
1985	466	1,027	315	554	34	93	1,429
1986	468	1,018	341	530	33	94	1,551
1987	526	970	346	465	33	90	1,593
1988	641	995	372	454	39	93	1,709
1989	747	953	361	451	41	87	1,764
1990	586	975	385	490	46	94	1,759
1991	538	944	333	470	53	95	1,727
1992	563	857	286	439	58	96	1,789
1993	589	797	271	380	57	94	1,840
1994	700	718	281	370	61	129	1,940
1995	758	737	305	363	73	128	1,984
1996	766	746	344	416	76	99	1,925
1997	796	743	320	370	78	99	1,954
1998	776	698	314	353	73	82	1,902
1999	766	763	336	331	76	74	1,875
2000	769	716	333	310	72	69	1,807
2001	766	693	295	299	69	64	1,746

Source: U.S. Department of Justice, Federal Bureau of Investigation, *Uniform Crime Reports*, 1984 through 2001. Most recent issues are accessible at http://www.fbi.gov/ucr/00cius.htm. *Notes:* 1. All Other includes crimes/offenses under state laws or local ordinances not included elsewhere.

Sentencing for Drugs and Public Order Crimes

Figures show average sentence in months. Data comes from analysis by the U.S. Sentencing Commission. Number of cases in the analysis for each year have been included.

	1996	1997	1998	1999	2000	2001
Environmental/wildlife	4.7	3.7	4.1	4.7	5.6	5.2
Antitrust	2.4	4.8	6.1	6.7	6.6	6.0
Embezzlement	6.2	5.8	5.5	6.4	7.2	6.3
Gambling/lottery	5.8	6.0	7.2	5.0	5.3	6.8
Drugs - simple possession	6.0	4.5	6.4	6.6	7.0	7.1
Bribery	13.1	14.0	12.7	11.9	10.2	8.0
Tax	8.6	8.6	8.5	10.4	10.8	10.7
Forgery/counterfeiting	10.3	11.1	10.7	11.0	11.4	11.7
Civil rights	37.2	21.2	33.0	27.1	24.8	13.3
Administration of Justice	15.4	14.5	13.8	17.4	16.7	15.6
National Defense	14.1	42.2	11.7	61.0	19.7	25.8
Immigration	18.4	18.8	22.6	26.1	26.1	26.2
Money Laundering	33.5	33.7	31.6	35.8	38.4	37.8
Drugs - Communication Facility	35.2	38.6	39.3	41.3	40.6	40.3

[Continued]

Sentencing for Drugs and Public Order Crimes

[Continued]

	1996	1997	1998	1999	2000	2001
Pornography/prostitution	29.1	27.1	39.6	41.6	43.3	52.8
Drugs - Trafficking	82.8	78.6	76.2	73.3	72.3	69.4
Racketeering/Extortion	90.5	107.1	88.8	92.0	91.1	94.1
Number of cases	42,436.0	48,848.0	50,754.0	55,557.0	59,846.0	59,897.0

Source: U.S. Sentencing Commission, available online at http://www.ussc.gov.

Alcohol and Crime, 1996

Figures show the number of convicted offenders. It includes the estimated number of offenders for whom alcohol was a factor in their crime.

	Offenders	Alcohol Related
Federal prison	105,544	11,610
Local jail	215,136	84,979
Parole	704,709	206,480
State prison	1,074,976	347,217
Probation	3,180,363	1,268,965

Source: U.S. Department of Justice, Bureau of Justice Statistics, *Alcohol and Crime,* April 1998.

DUI Arrests, 1986-1997

Figures show number of licensed drivers in thousands, number of arrests and the rate per 100,000 drivers.

	Licensed Drivers	Arrests for DUI	Rate
1986	159,486	1,793,300	1,124
1987	161,816	1,727,200	1,067
1988	162,854	1,792,500	1,101
1989	165,554	1,736,200	1,049
1990	167,015	1,810,800	1,084
1991	168,995	1,771,400	1,048
1992	173,125	1,624,500	938
1993	173,149	1,524,800	881
1994	175,403	1,384,600	789
1995	176,628	1,436,000	813
1996	179,539	1,467,300	817
1997	182,709	1,477,300	809

Source: U.S. Department of Justice, Bureau of Justice Statistics, Bureau of Justice Statistics, *DWI Offenders Under Correctional Supervision*, June 1999.

Alcohol Related Fatalities

| | Fatalities Vehicle Crashes | Fatalities Alcohol Crashes | Percent Alcohol | Blood Alcohol Concentration Level | | | | | |
| | | | | 0 | | 0.01 to 0.09 | | 0.10 or more | |
				Number	Percent	Number	Percent	Number	Percent
1982	43,945	25,165	57	18,780	43	4,809	11	20,356	46
1983	42,589	23,646	56	18,943	44	4,472	10	19,174	45
1984	44,257	23,758	54	20,499	46	4,766	11	18,992	43
1985	43,825	22,716	52	21,109	48	4,604	11	18,111	41
1986	46,087	24,045	52	22,042	48	5,109	11	18,936	41
1987	46,390	23,641	51	22,749	49	5,112	11	18,529	40
1988	47,087	23,626	50	23,461	50	4,895	10	18,731	40
1989	45,582	22,404	49	23,178	51	4,541	10	17,863	39
1990	44,599	22,084	50	22,515	50	4,434	10	17,650	40
1991	41,508	19,887	48	21,621	52	3,957	10	15,930	38
1992	39,250	17,858	45	21,392	55	3,625	9	14,234	36
1993	40,150	17,473	44	22,677	56	3,496	9	13,977	35
1994	40,716	16,580	41	24,136	59	3,480	9	13,100	32
1995	41,817	17,247	41	24,570	59	3,746	9	13,501	32
1996	42,065	17,218	41	24,847	59	3,774	9	13,444	32
1997	42,013	16,189	39	25,824	61	3,480	8	12,710	30
1998	41,501	16,020	39	25,481	61	3,526	8	12,494	30
1999	41,717	15,976	38	25,741	62	3,523	8	12,453	30
2000	41,821	16,653	40	25,168	60	3,761	9	12,892	31

Source: U.S. Department of Transportation, National Highway Traffic Safety Administration, *Traffic Safety Facts 2000* (Washington, DC: U.S. Department of Transportation, 2001), p. 32. and *Sourcebook of Criminal Justice Statistics.* Notes: *1. These data are based on information from two of the National Highway Traffic Safety Administration's data systems: the Fatality Analysis Reporting System (FARS) and the National Automotive Sampling System/General Estimates System (GES). FARS contains data from a census of fatal traffic crashes occurring in the 50 States, the District of Columbia, and Puerto Rico. FARS data include crashes involving motor vehicles traveling on a trafficway customarily open to the public and resulting in the death of a vehicle occupant or a nonmotorist within 30 days of the crash. GES data are obtained from a nationally representative probability sample selected from all police-reported crashes. To be eligible for the GES sample, a police accident report must be completed and the crash must involve at least one motor vehicle traveling on a trafficway, and result in property damage, injury, or death. 2. A fatal crash is defined as alcohol-related or alcohol-involved if either a driver or a nonmotorist (usually a pedestrian) had a measurable or estimated blood alcohol concentration (BAC) of 0.01 or more grams per deciliter. BAC values are estimated by the source when alcohol test results are unknown.*

Online Gambling

Figures show estimated online profits in billions of dollars.

	Billions
2000	2.2
2001	3.0
2002	4.1
2003	6.0
2004	8.3
2005	10.2

Source: McCoy, Kevin. "Online Gamble Pays Off for Internet Sports Books." *USA Today,* March 29, 2002, p. B1 and estimates from Christiansen/Cummins Advisors.

Stalking

Data show the relationship between stalker and victim. For example, 36% of men were stalked by a stranger and 23% of women were.

	Men	Women
Relative other than spouse	2	4
Cohabiting partner/ex-partner	9	10
Date/former date	10	14
Acquaintance	34	19
Stranger	36	23
Spouse/ex-spouse	13	38

Source: Tjaden, Patricia and Nancy Thoennes. U.S. Department of Justice, National Institute of Justice Centers for Disease Control and Prevention Research in Brief, *Stalking in America: Findings from the National Violence Against Women Survey,* April 1998.

New York Sex Offenders

Data show the number of sex offenders registered in New York state.

	Number
1998	7,756
1999	9,336
2000	10,930
2001	12,206
2002	14,444

Source: Mahoney, Joe. "Pervert List Growing." available from http://www.nydailynews.com.

Chapter 5
KIDS

Crime at School

Number of nonfatal crimes against students ages 12 through 18 occurring at school or on the way to or from school per 1,000 students, by type of crime and selected student characteristics: 1992 to 1994. NA Not reported. Serious violent crimes include rape, sexual assault, robbery, and aggravated assault. Violent crimes include serious violent crimes and simple assault. Total crimes include violent crimes and theft. At school includes inside the school building, on school property, or on the way to or from school. Population sizes are 23,740,295 students ages 12 through 18 in 1992 and 25,326,989 in 1994. Because of rounding or missing data, detail may not add to totals.

	1992				1994			
	Total	Theft	Violent	Serious Violent[1]	Total	Theft	Violent	Serious Violent[1]
Student characteristics								
Total	144	95	48	10	150	94	56	13
Gender								
Male	168	105	64	15	162	97	65	15
Female	117	85	32	5	137	90	47	10
Age								
12-14	172	105	67	16	187	109	78	18
15-18	120	87	33	6	119	81	38	9
Race/ethnicity								
White, non-Hispanic	156	105	52	9	156	101	55	11
Black, non-Hispanic	114	67	46	18	140	81	59	15
Hispanic	113	72	41	10	137	74	63	22
Other, non-Hispanic	129	110	19	NA	109	71	39	13
Urbanicity								
Urban	141	92	50	15	143	78	65	21
Suburban	155	105	50	10	169	107	62	13
Rural	124	80	44	6	121	84	37	4
Household income								
Less than $7,500	123	65	57	14	96	47	49	21
$7,500-14,999	111	65	46	13	119	75	44	6
$15,000-24,999	125	60	65	16	134	85	50	12
$25,000-34,999	137	94	43	5	162	89	73	16
$35,000-49,999	180	133	47	9	164	105	59	11
$50,000-74,999	150	119	31	4	166	105	61	13
$75,000 or more	206	136	70	17	179	129	51	8

Source: U.S. Departments of Education and Justice, *Indicators of School Crime and Safety, 2001,* http://nces.ed.gov/pubs2002/crime2001/. Primary Source: Bureau of Justice Statistics, National Crime Victimization Survey, 1992 to 1999. *Note:* 1. Serious violent crimes are also included in violent crimes.

Crime at School

Number of nonfatal crimes against students ages 12 through 18 occurring at school or on the way to or from school per 1,000 students, by type of crime and selected student characteristics: 1996 to 1998. NA Not reported. Serious violent crimes include rape, sexual assault, robbery, and aggravated assault. Violent crimes include serious violent crimes and simple assault. Total crimes include violent crimes and theft. At school includes inside the school building, on school property, or on the way to or from school. Population sizes are 26,151,364 in 1996 and 26,806,268 in 1998. Because of rounding or missing data, detail may not add to totals.

	1996				1998			
	Total	Theft	Violent	Serious Violent[1]	Total	Theft	Violent	Serious Violent[1]
Student characteristics								
Total	121	78	43	9	101	58	43	9
Gender								
Male	134	78	56	11	111	59	52	10
Female	107	77	30	6	91	58	33	8
Age								
12-14	151	91	60	9	125	65	60	14
15-18	97	67	30	8	83	53	30	6
Race/ethnicity								
White, non-Hispanic	129	83	45	7	105	60	45	9
Black, non-Hispanic	105	73	32	12	111	64	48	12
Hispanic	109	58	51	15	82	48	34	11
Other, non-Hispanic	108	72	36	11	89	57	32	4[2]
Urbanicity								
Urban	126	76	50	14	117	68	49	13
Suburban	130	82	48	8	97	56	40	7
Rural	95	71	24	4	93	50	43	11
Household income								
Less than $7,500	86	55	31	8	110	56	53	17[2]
$7,500-14,999	92	54	38	9	97	38	59	12[2]
$15,000-24,999	120	68	52	15	126	64	62	10
$25,000-34,999	130	78	52	10	102	50	52	15
$35,000-49,999	131	84	48	9	86	57	29	6
$50,000-74,999	138	95	43	7	110	68	42	10
$75,000 or more	139	104	35	5	112	75	37	6[2]

Source: U.S. Departments of Education and Justice, *Indicators of School Crime and Safety, 2001,* http://nces.ed.gov/pubs2002/crime2001/. Primary Source: Bureau of Justice Statistics, National Crime Victimization Survey, 1992 to 1999. *Notes:* 1. Serious violent crimes are also included in violent crimes. 2. Estimate based on fewer than 10 cases.

Reports of Violent Incidents at School

Percentage of public schools that reported one or more serious violent incidents to police, by seriousness of the incident, urbanicity, and selected school charactersitics: 1996-97. - Fewer than 30 sample cases. Serious violent crimes include murder, rape or other type of sexual battery, suicide, physical attack or fight with a weapon, or robbery. Less serious violent or nonviolent crimes include physical attack or fight without a weapon, theft/larceny, and vandalism. Any incidents refers to any of the crimes listed. Not included are any crimes not listed here and any crimes not reported to police. Schools were asked to report crimes that took place in school buildings or on school buses, on school grounds, and at places holding school-sponsored events. Population size is 78,000 public schools.

	Serious Violent Incidents				
	Total	City	Urban Fringe	Town	Rural
Total	10.1	16.8	11.2	5.4	7.8
Instructional level					
Elementary school	4.2	6.1	3.3	2.0	5.1
Middle school	18.7	35.8	21.7	7.0	15.0
High school	20.6	48.0	33.0	12.7	9.4
Region					
Northeast	6.8	9.5	6.9	2.6	11.0
Southeast	9.2	17.3	13.2	4.9	4.9
Central	11.1	16.4	12.4	6.4	10.2
West	11.9	20.2	13.3	7.2	5.7
School enrollment					
Less than 300	3.9	-	-	8.8	2.5
300-999	9.3	12.5	9.0	3.2	13.9
1000 or more	32.9	44.2	29.8	15.9	-
Minority enrollment					
Less than 5 percent	5.8	-	5.9	3.3	7.3
5-19 percent	10.9	14.5	11.3	10.6	6.8
20-49 percent	11.1	19.1	10.1	5.0	8.0
50 percent or more	14.7	17.6	17.8	4.4	11.6
Free/reduced-price lunch					
Less than 20 percent	8.6	12.2	9.9	7.1	5.6
21-34 percent	11.7	18.4	13.3	7.1	11.6
35-49 percent	11.6	34.2	8.6	3.0	8.6
50-74 percent	8.9	22.9	10.3	2.0	2.3
75 percent or more	10.2	8.4	-	-	-

Source: National Center for Education Statistics, *Indicators of School Crime and Safety, 2000*, Table 8.1. Primary source: U.S. Department of Education, National Center for Education Statistics, Fast Response Survey System, Principal/School, http://nces.ed.gov/pubs2001/crime2000/.

Juvenile Arrests for Violent Crimes: 1970 to 1999

Juveniles in 1970 and 1975 were persons between the ages of 10 and 17. For later years, juveniles were persons under 18 years of age. Arrest statistics report the number of arrests made by law enforcement agencies in a particular year, not the number of individuals arrested nor the number of crimes committed. The number of arrests is not equivalent to the number of people arrested because an unknown number of individuals are arrested more than once in the year. Population (000) is the total number of people covered by the law enforcement agencies reporting arrests.

Offense	1970	1975	1980	1990	1992	1993	1994	1995	1996	1997	1998	1999
Population (000)	145,014	156,854	169,439	204,543	217,754	213,705	208,035	206,762	195,805	194,925	194,612	195,324
Number												
Violent crime, total	54,860	76,131	77,220	97,103	118,358	122,434	125,141	123,131	104,455	100,273	90,201	81,715
Murder	1,350	1,373	1,475	2,661	3,025	3,473	3,114	2,812	2,184	1,887	1,587	1,131
Forcible rape	3,233	3,457	3,668	4,971	5,451	5,490	4,873	4,556	4,228	4,127	3,988	3,544
Robbery	29,363	39,388	38,529	34,944	42,639	44,598	47,046	47,240	39,788	36,419	29,989	26,125
Aggravated assault	20,914	31,913	33,548	54,527	67,243	68,873	70,108	68,523	58,255	57,840	54,637	50,915

Source: U.S. Bureau of the Census, *Statistical Abstract of the United States: 1995*, Table 323, and *Statistical Abstract of the United States: 2001*, Table 309. Primary source: U.S. Federal Bureau of Investigation, *Crime in the United States*, annual.

Juvenile Female Violent Crime Arrest Rate

Rate by age (per 100,000).

Year	Age of Juvenile Females				
	12 and under	13-14 years	15 years	16 years	17 years
1967	3.4	43.0	52.2	44.2	38.6
1968	2.9	39.8	48.8	49.9	49.7
1969	2.9	50.5	62.8	61.7	62.6
1970	3.5	57.1	73.2	67.2	65.7
1971	4.0	64.7	90.4	86.7	82.1
1972	4.5	75.6	94.4	92.8	78.2
1973	4.4	71.3	88.8	94.7	86.1
1974	5.0	78.6	111.5	112.3	104.5
1975	4.7	72.3	119.1	113.7	104.5
1976	4.0	71.0	103.4	117.3	105.4
1977	4.1	65.2	94.1	113.7	107.6
1978	3.7	69.1	103.5	115.2	115.2
1979	3.1	72.6	107.9	118.2	111.3
1980	2.9	69.9	117.1	124.5	129.6
1981	3.1	72.0	120.3	129.1	115.8
1982	3.1	70.2	113.7	123.3	129.7
1983	3.4	65.5	110.5	119.5	114.8
1984	3.3	69.5	110.8	118.3	116.5
1985	3.0	70.9	107.6	117.5	117.6
1986	3.2	73.9	110.2	130.4	124.4
1987	3.3	79.1	118.7	121.1	121.7
1988	3.7	86.6	135.5	134.9	122.8
1989	4.6	106.4	151.0	158.5	155.7
1990	4.9	123.2	176.8	193.0	178.7
1991	5.2	129.9	191.6	203.5	188.0
1992	5.8	144.8	214.1	217.4	195.3
1993	6.4	167.4	249.3	253.3	232.5
1994	6.9	184.2	272.7	274.8	246.7

[Continued]

Juvenile Female Violent Crime Arrest Rate

[Continued]

Year	Age of Juvenile Females				
	12 and under	13-14 years	15 years	16 years	17 years
1995	7.3	180.5	279.4	287.6	258.2
1996	6.7	159.0	248.8	255.3	255.1

Source: FBI, *Crime in the United States: 1997*, Section V: "Juvenile Female Crime: A Special Study," Table 5.1, http://www.fbi.gov/. *Crime in the United States: 1998*.

Juvenile Arrests for Violent Crimes by Race: 1980-1990

Arrests of youths ages 10 to 17 per 100,000 youths ages 10 to 17 in racial group. Violent crime index includes murder and nonnegligent manslaughter, forcible rape, robbery, and aggravated assault. Hispanics may be of any race; arrests of Hispanics are not counted separately.

	Violent Crime Index										
	1980	1981	1982	1983	1984	1985	1986	1987	1988	1989	1990
White	334.1	322.6	314.5	296.0	297.5	303.0	316.7	310.6	326.5	381.6	428.5
Black	1,190.4	1,193.1	1,146.7	1,102.7	1,110.4	1,096.3	1,150.0	1,142.4	1,160.6	1,360.9	1,435.3
American Indian	211.8	169.1	200.5	161.1	153.9	183.3	175.7	181.8	205.3	204.1	217.0
Asian	134.0	106.7	118.0	98.2	90.2	86.5	86.8	91.9	113.7	109.1	133.5

Source: U.S. Department of Justice, Office of Juvenile Justice and Delinquency Prevention, http://ojjdp.ncjrs.org/ojstatbb/asp/. Primary Source: Arrest data for 1980-1990 from unpublished data from the Federal Bureau of Investigation. Population data from the U.S. Bureau of the Census, *U.S. Population Estimates, by Age, Sex, Race, and Hispanic Origin: 1980-1990* [machine-readable data files available online, released April 11, 2000].

Juvenile Arrests for Violent Crimes by Race: 1991-2000

Arrests of youths ages 10 to 17 per 100,000 youths ages 10 to 17 in racial group. Violent crime index includes murder and nonnegligent manslaughter, forcible rape, robbery, and aggravated assault. Hispanics may be of any race; arrests of Hispanics are not counted separately.

	Violent Crime Index									
	1991	1992	1993	1994	1995	1996	1997	1998	1999	2000
White	284.0	293.8	301.4	318.9	312.7	297.5	276.6	261.2	247.6	239.2
Black	1,512.2	1,595.9	1,689.1	1,730.9	1,708.6	1,439.4	1,175.9	1,021.6	893.3	909.4
American Indian	227.7	249.5	285.3	332.1	333.4	307.4	275.2	277.8	269.6	243.5
Asian	156.1	156.8	170.8	191.7	188.0	200.0	151.5	131.8	126.7	122.1

Source: Office of Juvenile Justice and Delinquency Prevention, http://ojjdp.ncjrs.org/ojstatbb/asp/. Primary Source: Arrest data for 1990- 1997 from unpublished data from the Federal Bureau of Investigation and for 1998, 1999, and 2000 from *Crime in the United States* reports. Washington, DC: U.S. Government Printing Office, 1999, 2000, and 2001, respectively. Population data from the U.S. Bureau of the Census, *U.S. Population Estimates, by Age, Sex, Race, and Hispanic Origin: 1991- 1999* (With Short-term Projection to Dates in 2000) [machine-readable data files available online, released April 11, 2000].

Child Victimization Rates: 1990-2000

Data are from the National Child Abuse and Neglect Data System (NCANDS), the primary source of national information on abused and neglected children known to state child protective services agencies.

Reporting Year	Child Population	Victim Rate per 1,000	Estimated Victims
1990	64,163,192	13.4	861,000
1991	65,069,507	14.0	912,000
1992	66,073,841	15.1	995,000
1993	66,961,573	15.3	1,026,000
1994	67,803,294	15.2	1,032,000
1995	68,437,378	14.7	1,006,000
1996	69,022,127	14.7	1,012,000
1997	69,527,944	13.8	957,000
1998	69,872,059	12.9	904,000
1999	70,199,435	11.8	829,000
2000	72,293,812	12.2	879,000

Source: U.S. Department of Health and Human Services, Administration on Children, Youth and Families, *Child Maltreatment 2000* (Washington, DC: U.S. Government Printing Office, 2002).

Reasons Children Went Missing: 1999

Data from a study conducted by the U.S. Department of Justice, Office of Juvenile Justice and Delinquency Prevention. Thrownaway children have been forced out of the home or refused permission to return.

Reason	Percent	Number
Nonfamily abduction	0.03	33,000
Family abduction	0.09	117,200
Runaway/thrownaway	0.48	628,900
Missing involuntary, lost, or injured	0.15	198,300
Missing benign explanation	0.28	374,700

Source: U.S. Department of Justice, *National Incidence Studies of Missing, Abducted, Runaway, and Thrownaway Children,* http://www.ojjdp.ncjrs.org.

Some Statistics About Video Games and Violence

Item	Number
Video game revenues 1999	$6.3 billion
Percentage of households w/children that have rented/owned video/computer game	90.0
Average minutes per day young people spend playing video games	20.0
Percentage of youngsters' favorite games w/violent/aggressive content	80.0
Percentage of youngsters surveyed who played video games 7-30 hours a week	25.0

[Continued]

Some Statistics About Video Games and Violence
[Continued]

Item	Number
Percentage polled who favor regulating violence in video games	67.0
Percentage polled who blame video game violence for juvenile crime	56.0

Source: Video Game Violence, Mediascope Issue Briefs, http://www.mediascope.org; Arlene Moscovitch, *Electronic Media and the Family,* http://www.vifamily.ca/cft/media/media.htm.; *USA Weekend' s Third Annual America s Poll*, http://www.usaweekend.com/; *Media Violence: Its Effect on Children*, www.marymount.k12.ny.us.

Chapter 6
DRUGS

Total Estimated Drug Law Violation Arrests in the United States

	Total	Adult	Juvenile
1970	415,600	322,300	93,300
1971	492,000	383,900	108,100
1972	527,400	407,300	120,100
1973	628,900	463,600	165,300
1974	642,100	474,900	167,200
1975	601,400	456,000	145,400
1976	609,500	464,100	145,400
1977	642,700	493,300	149,400
1978	628,700	480,000	148,700
1979	558,600	435,600	123,000
1980	580,900	471,200	109,700
1981	559,900	468,100	91,800
1982	676,000	584,900	91,200
1983	661,400	583,500	77,900
1984	708,400	623,700	84,700
1985	811,400	718,600	92,800
1986	824,100	742,700	81,400
1987	937,400	849,500	87,900
1988	1,155,200	1,050,600	104,600
1989	1,361,700	1,247,800	113,900
1990	1,089,500	1,008,300	81,200
1991	1,010,000	931,900	78,100
1992	1,066,400	980,700	85,700
1993	1,126,300	1,017,800	108,500
1994	1,351,400	1,192,800	158,600
1995	1,476,100	1,285,700	190,400
1996	1,506,200	1,295,100	211,100
1997	1,583,600	1,370,400	213,200
1998	1,559,100	1,360,600	198,500
1999	1,532,200	1,365,100	192,000
2000	1,579,600	1,375,600	203,900

Source: U.S. Department of Justice, Bureau of Justice Statistics, from *Crime in the United States*, available from http://www.ojp.usdoj.gov as arrtot.wk1, prepared April 8, 2002.

Drug-Using Population in 1999 and 2000

Subtotals may not add to totals because individuals may report multiple uses of drugs.

| | Data in Thousands | | | | | |
| | Lifetime | | Past Year | | Past Month | |
	1999	2000	1999	2000	1999	2000
Any Illicit Drug	87,734	86,931	25,402	24,535	13,829	14,027
Marijuana and Hashish	76,428	76,321	19,102	18,589	10,458	10,714
Cocaine (All Forms)	25,406	24,896	3,742	3,328	1,552	1,213
Crack	5,910	5,307	1,045	721	418	265
Heroin	3,054	2,779	353	308	154	130
Hallucinogens (All)	25,061	26,125	3,191	3,483	922	971
PCP	5,693	5,804	245	264	55	54
LSD	19,215	19,642	1,905	1,749	482	403
Inhalants	17,138	16,702	1,937	1,918	570	622
Nonmedical Use of Medical Substances	34,076	32,443	9,220	8,761	3,952	3,849
Pain Relievers	19,888	19,210	6,582	6,466	2,621	2,782
Tranquilizers	13,860	13,007	2,728	2,731	1,097	1,000
Stimulants	15,922	14,661	2,291	2,112	950	788
Methamphetamine	9,442	8,843	1,140	1,031	435	387
Sedatives	7,747	7,142	631	611	229	175

Source: U.S. Department of Health and Human Services, SAMHSA, accessible at http://www.samhsa.gov/oas/WebOnly.htm.

Drug Arrests per 100,000 Population

	Drug Arrests	U.S. Population	Drug Arrests per 100,000 Population
1970	415,600	205,052,174	203
1971	492,000	207,660,677	237
1972	527,400	209,896,021	251
1973	628,900	211,908,788	297
1974	642,100	213,853,928	300
1975	601,400	215,973,199	278
1976	609,500	218,035,164	280
1977	642,700	220,239,425	292
1978	628,700	222,584,545	282
1979	558,600	225,055,487	248
1980	580,900	227,224,681	256
1981	559,900	229,465,714	244
1982	676,000	231,664,458	292
1983	661,400	233,791,994	283
1984	708,400	235,824,902	300
1985	811,400	237,923,795	341
1986	824,100	240,132,887	343
1987	937,400	242,288,918	387

[Continued]

Drug Arrests per 100,000 Population

[Continued]

	Drug Arrests	U.S. Population	Drug Arrests per 100,000 Population
1988	1,155,200	244,498,982	472
1989	1,361,700	246,819,230	552
1990	1,089,500	249,464,396	437
1991	1,010,000	252,153,092	401
1992	1,066,400	255,029,699	418
1993	1,126,300	257,782,608	437
1994	1,351,400	260,327,021	519
1995	1,476,100	262,803,276	562
1996	1,506,200	265,228,572	568
1997	1,583,600	267,783,607	591
1998	1,559,100	270,248,003	577
1999	1,532,200	272,690,813	562
2000	1,579,600	276,059,000	572

Source: U.S. Department of Justice, Bureau of Justice Statistics, from *Crime in the United States*, available from http://www.ojp.usdoj.gov as arrtot.wk1, prepared April 8, 2002. Population data from U.S. Bureau of the Census.

Users of Illicit Drugs in Lifetime and in the Past Year and Drug Arrests

Data for users for 1980-1984 and 1986-1990 are extrapolations. All data are in thousands.

| Year | In Thousands | | |
	Lifetime Users	Past Year Users	Drug Arrests
1979	56,414	31,485	559
1980	58,040	31,486	581
1981	59,667	31,486	560
1982	61,293	31,487	676
1983	62,919	31,487	661
1984	64,546	31,488	708
1985	66,172	31,488	811
1986	66,686	30,009	824
1987	67,200	28,529	937
1988	67,714	27,050	1,155
1989	68,228	25,571	1,362
1990	68,742	24,091	1,090
1991	69,256	22,612	1,010
1992	68,528	20,046	1,066
1993	70,776	21,402	1,126
1994	71,935	22,663	1,351
1995	72,426	22,662	1,476

[Continued]

Users of Illicit Drugs in Lifetime and in the Past Year and Drug Arrests

[Continued]

Year	In Thousands		
	Lifetime Users	Past Year Users	Drug Arrests
1996	74,390	23,182	1,506
1997	76,960	24,189	1,584
1998	78,123	23,115	1,559
1999	87,734	25,402	1,532
2000	86,931	24,535	1,580

Source: Substance Abuse and Mental Health Administration (SAMHSA), National Household Survey on Drug Abuse. Arrest data from *Uniform Crime Reports*.

Drug Arrests by Race, Per 100,000 Population of Those Aged 18 or Older

	White	African American	Asian/ Pacific Islander	American Indian Alask. Native
1993	358	1,739	82	275
1994	416	1,935	95	321
1995	433	1,868	101	360
1996	412	1,890	102	375
1997	409	1,735	108	394
1998	404	1,734	93	385
1999	377	1,465	88	342
2000	390	1,460	93	342

Source: U.S. Department of Justice, Bureau of Justice Statistics, from *Crime in the United States*, available from http://www.ojp.usdoj.gov as arrtot.wk1, prepared April 8, 2002. Population data by race and age group from U.S. Bureau of the Census.

Percentage of Population (12 and Older) Reporting Having Ever Used Drugs

Race/Ethnicity	Annual Average of 1999 and 2000 Data					
	Data in Thousands, Age 12 or Older Ever Used Any Illicit Drug			% of 12 and Older Population		
	Lifetime	Past Year	Past Month	Lifetime	Past Year	Past Month
White	67,807	18,411	10,231	37.9	10.3	5.7
Black	9,186	3,028	1,734	33.6	11.1	6.3
American Indian or Alaska Native	587	213	129	30.5	11.1	6.7
Asian/Pacific Islander	1,273	366	192	14.3	4.1	2.2
Hispanics	6,791	2,335	1,266	25.5	8.8	4.8
Total	85,644	24,353	13,552	35.1	10.0	5.6

Source: U.S. Department of Health and Human Services, SAMHSA, Office of Applied Studies, National Household Survey on Drug Abuse, 1999 and 2000.

Percent of Those Arrested and Percent of Those Convicted of All Drug Offenses

Year	White		Black	
	Arrested	Convicted	Arrested	Convicted
1992	59.8	39.3	42.0	55.0
1994	60.6	41.0	38.4	59.0
1996	60.4	45.0	38.4	53.0
1998	61.5	46.0	37.3	53.0

Source: Sourcebook of Criminal Justice Statistics, 1994-2000, downloaded from http://www.albany.edu/ sourcebook/ or obtained from the Sourcebook CD- ROM.

Drug Arrests per 100,000 Population by Age Groups and Race

Year	Under 18 Years of Age			18 and Older		
	Total[1]	White	Black	Total[1]	White	Black
1965	9.5	7.9	17.9	36.4	23.4	154.5
1966	16.1	13.5	30.1	49.6	33.9	193.6
1967	41.8	39.2	55.4	78.3	59.4	248.9
1968	88.1	89.1	80.4	120.2	99.0	310.5
1969	115.9	116.1	112.2	175.2	143.9	458.5
1970	156.4	161.2	121.3	258.0	217.6	628.7
1971	166.0	172.9	120.9	301.7	251.6	757.3
1972	195.0	204.6	139.7	315.3	265.0	767.0
1973	272.5	284.9	205.9	361.3	312.4	805.4
1974	317.3	328.7	255.4	406.8	349.5	906.8
1975	250.9	262.9	191.3	342.1	299.5	714.5
1976	246.6	252.1	219.5	342.7	283.0	854.1
1977	237.4	245.6	199.6	334.8	277.3	829.5
1978	241.7	249.5	203.5	318.9	264.2	765.6
1979	201.3	207.5	176.6	287.7	242.0	681.0
1980	183.6	188.3	179.2	308.6	256.1	780.3
1981	172.4	173.2	187.3	333.3	275.3	851.5
1982	148.6	145.0	185.2	358.6	288.7	974.8
1983	133.9	128.5	178.3	370.9	289.1	1,079.4
1984	137.8	130.9	192.5	381.3	294.8	1,129.2
1985	152.2	142.1	226.5	423.5	327.6	1,246.0
1986	134.4	115.6	256.2	440.6	328.9	1,393.6
1987	142.8	113.0	323.9	492.5	361.8	1,601.4
1988	157.2	109.6	433.9	552.5	383.8	1,959.7
1989	174.7	109.9	542.9	665.5	449.1	2,463.8
1990	129.1	80.0	413.4	549.8	378.9	1,992.7
1991	120.8	74.0	390.0	509.4	352.9	1,821.4
1992	147.3	88.5	483.9	554.7	381.3	1,999.9

Source: U.S. Department of Justice, Bureau of Justice Statistics, from *Crime in the United States*, available from http://www.ojp.usdoj.gov as arrtot.wk1, prepared April 8, 2002. *Note:* 1. Includes races not classified as white or black.

Drug Arrests by Type of Drug, 1982 to 2000

	Total Arrests					Percent of Arrests			
	Heroin/ Cocaine	Mari- juana	Synthetic Narcotics	Other Dan- gerous Non- narcotic Drugs, e.g., Barbiturates	Total	Heroin/ Cocaine	Mari- juana	Synthetic Narcotics	Other Dan- gerous Non- narcotic Drugs, e.g., Barbiturates
1982	87,900	486,700	27,000	81,100	682,700	12.9	71.3	4.0	11.9
1983	152,100	403,500	19,800	86,000	661,400	23.0	61.0	3.0	13.0
1984	184,200	418,000	21,300	85,000	708,500	26.0	59.0	3.0	12.0
1985	243,400	446,300	24,300	97,400	811,400	30.0	55.0	3.0	12.0
1986	337,900	362,600	24,700	107,100	832,300	40.6	43.6	3.0	12.9
1987	431,200	375,000	28,100	112,500	946,800	45.5	39.6	3.0	11.9
1988	600,700	392,800	34,700	127,100	1,155,300	52.0	34.0	3.0	11.0
1989	735,300	394,900	27,200	204,300	1,361,700	54.0	29.0	2.0	15.0
1990	588,300	326,900	21,800	152,500	1,089,500	54.0	30.0	2.0	14.0
1991	555,500	282,800	20,200	141,400	999,900	55.6	28.3	2.0	14.1
1992	565,200	341,200	21,300	138,600	1,066,300	53.0	32.0	2.0	13.0
1993	563,200	382,900	22,500	157,700	1,126,300	50.0	34.0	2.0	14.0
1994	635,200	486,500	27,000	216,200	1,364,900	46.5	35.6	2.0	15.8
1995	620,000	590,400	29,500	236,200	1,476,100	42.0	40.0	2.0	16.0
1996	602,500	647,700	30,100	241,000	1,521,300	39.6	42.6	2.0	15.8
1997	565,300	695,200	41,200	283,500	1,585,200	35.7	43.9	2.6	17.9
1998	570,600	682,900	45,200	260,400	1,559,100	36.6	43.8	2.9	16.7
1999	528,600	704,800	47,500	251,300	1,532,200	34.5	46.0	3.1	16.4
2000	529,200	734,500	52,100	262,200	1,578,000	33.5	46.5	3.3	16.6

Source: U.S. Department of Justice, Bureau of Justice Statistics, from *Crime in the United States*, available from http://www.ojp.usdoj.gov.

Views of the Drug Market: Expenditures and Tonnages Distributed, 1988 to 2000

Meth stands for Methamphetamine. Tonnage data on "other drugs" is not available. Dollar data are in constant 1998 dollars.

Year	Billions of 1998 Dollars					Other Drugs	Metric Tons			
	Total	Marijuana	Cocaine	Heroin	Meth		Marijuana	Cocaine	Heroin	Meth
1988	116.5	11.3	76.9	21.8	3.2	3.3	894.0	401.0	8.5	NA
1989	108.8	11.1	70.8	20.9	3.2	2.8	866.0	394.0	10.5	15.3
1990	97.3	13.5	61.3	17.6	2.6	2.2	837.0	271.0	8.8	11.6
1991	86.1	12.8	55.0	13.8	2.2	2.3	793.0	299.0	6.8	11.2
1992	76.5	12.5	49.4	10.9	2.3	1.5	761.0	273.0	6.5	9.9
1993	71.5	11.2	45.9	10.2	2.7	1.5	791.0	296.0	7.9	12.7
1994	70.0	11.4	42.2	10.5	3.3	2.6	874.0	305.0	10.5	17.1
1995	68.9	9.3	43.0	11.2	2.8	2.7	848.0	304.0	11.4	15.0
1996	67.2	9.0	41.3	11.7	2.4	2.7	874.0	288.0	12.4	14.3
1997	68.6	10.1	41.8	12.2	2.0	2.6	960.0	312.0	13.1	11.8
1998	65.6	10.7	39.0	11.6	2.2	2.5	952.0	291.0	12.5	15.9

[Continued]

Views of the Drug Market: Expenditures and Tonnages Distributed, 1988 to 2000

[Continued]

Year	Billions of 1998 Dollars					Other Drugs	Metric Tons			
	Total	Marijuana	Cocaine	Heroin	Meth		Marijuana	Cocaine	Heroin	Meth
1999	63.7	10.2	37.1	12.0	2.2	2.3	982.0	276.0	12.9	15.4
2000	62.9	10.4	36.1	11.9	2.2	2.3	1,009.0	269.0	12.9	15.4

Source: Office of National Drug Control Policy, the White House, *What America s Users Spend on Illegal Drugs*, 1988-1998, Abt Associates, available at http://www.whitehousedrugpolicy.gov/publications/pdf/spending_drugs_1988_1998.pdf.

Illicit Drug Users by Drug, 1989 to 2000

	Illicit Drug Users in Thousands					
	Total	Cocaine	Heroin	Marijuana	Metham-phetamine	All Other Drugs
1989	38,846	8,815	1,036	10,900	386	17,709
1990	34,496	7,786	937	10,200	339	15,234
1991	35,517	7,648	1,076	10,400	290	16,103
1992	31,249	6,762	934	9,700	314	13,539
1993	31,430	6,682	924	9,600	389	13,835
1994	31,697	6,297	1,076	10,100	479	13,745
1995	32,492	6,637	1,283	9,800	414	14,358
1996	34,226	6,835	1,372	10,100	376	15,543
1997	34,981	6,990	1,532	11,100	310	15,049
1998	31,325	6,559	1,233	11,000	356	12,177
1999	31,153	5,759	1,461	11,400	356	12,177
2000	31,204	5,480	1,491	11,700	356	12,177
Change, 1989 to 2000 - %	-19.7	-37.8	43.9	7.3	-7.8	-31.2

Source: Office of National Drug Control Policy, the White House, *What America s Users Spend on Illegal Drugs*, 1988-1998, Abt Associates, available at http://www.whitehousedrugpolicy.gov/publications/pdf/spending_drugs_1988_1998.pdf.

Federal Drug Control Budget and Expenditures by People on Illegal Drugs

Year	Actual Federal Drug Control Budget (billions)	Federal Budget (in 98 $ - billions)	People's Spending on Drugs (in 98 $ - billions)
1989	6.7	8.8	108.8
1990	9.8	12.2	97.3
1991	11.0	13.1	86.1
1992	11.6	13.4	76.5

[Continued]

Federal Drug Control Budget and Expenditures by People on Illegal Drugs

[Continued]

Year	Actual Federal Drug Control Budget (billions)	Federal Budget (in 98 $ - billions)	People's Spending on Drugs (in 98 $ - billions)
1993	11.9	13.5	71.5
1994	12.0	13.2	70.0
1995	13.0	13.9	68.9
1996	13.0	13.5	67.2
1997	14.4	14.6	68.6
1998	15.2	15.2	65.6
1999	17.1	16.8	63.7
2000	17.8	16.9	62.9

Source: Office of National Drug Control Policy, the White House, *What America s Users Spend on Illegal Drugs*, 1988-1998, Abt Associates, available at http://www.whitehousedrugpolicy.gov/publications/pdf/spending_drugs_1988_1998.pdf.

U.S. Drug Control Budget for FY 2001 and 2002

	2001 (millions)	2002 (millions)
Drug abuse treatment	2,837.8	3,023.2
Drug abuse prevention	2,226.1	2,146.3
Prevention research	352.6	402.4
Treatment research	497.2	564.2
Domestic law enforcement	9,463.8	9,513.1
International	663.2	1,098.8
Interdiction	2,054.9	2,074.8
Total	18,095.6	18,822.8

Source: Office of National Drug Control Policy, the White House, FY 2003 National Drug Control Budget, February 2002, from http://www.ojp.usdoj.gov/bjs/dcf/dcb/htm.

Alcohol and Tobacco Consumption per Capita in the United States, 1934 to 1998

Alcohol consumption, up to 1969, based on population 15 and older; from 1970 to 1998, based on population 14 and older. Cigarette consumption is measured based on population 18 and older and does not imply that each adult smoked.

	Per Capital Alcohol Consumption Population 14 and Older (gallons)				Cigarettes Per Capita 18 and Older (Number)
	Beer	Wine	Spirits	All Beverages	
1934	0.61	0.07	0.29	0.97	1,483
1935	0.68	0.09	0.43	1.20	1,564
1936	0.79	0.12	0.59	1.50	1,754
1937	0.82	0.13	0.64	1.59	1,847
1938	0.75	0.13	0.59	1.47	1,830
1939	0.75	0.14	0.62	1.51	1,900
1940	0.73	0.16	0.67	1.56	1,976
1941	0.81	0.18	0.71	1.70	2,236
1942	0.90	0.22	0.85	1.97	2,585
1943	1.00	0.17	0.66	1.83	2,956
1944	1.13	0.18	0.76	2.07	3,039
1945	1.17	0.20	0.88	2.25	3,449
1946	1.07	0.24	0.99	2.30	3,446
1947	1.11	0.16	0.76	2.03	3,416
1948	1.07	0.20	0.70	1.97	3,505
1949	1.06	0.22	0.70	1.98	3,480
1950	1.04	0.23	0.77	2.04	3,552
1951	1.03	0.20	0.78	2.01	3,744
1952	1.04	0.21	0.73	1.98	3,886
1953	1.04	0.20	0.77	2.01	3,778
1954	1.01	0.21	0.74	1.96	3,546
1955	1.01	0.22	0.77	2.00	3,597
1956	1.00	0.22	0.81	2.03	3,650
1957	0.97	0.22	0.80	1.99	3,755
1958	0.96	0.22	0.80	1.98	3,953
1959	1.00	0.22	0.84	2.06	4,073
1960	0.99	0.22	0.86	2.07	4,171
1961	0.97	0.23	0.86	2.06	4,266
1962	0.99	0.22	0.90	2.11	4,266
1963	1.01	0.23	0.91	2.15	4,345
1964	1.04	0.24	0.95	2.23	4,194
1965	1.04	0.24	0.99	2.27	4,258
1966	1.06	0.24	1.02	2.32	4,287
1967	1.07	0.25	1.05	2.37	4,280
1968	1.09	0.26	1.10	2.45	4,186
1969	1.12	0.26	1.13	2.51	3,993
1970	1.14	0.27	1.11	2.52	3,985
1971	1.15	0.31	1.12	2.59	4,037
1972	1.17	0.30	1.09	2.56	4,043
1973	1.20	0.31	1.10	2.62	4,148

[Continued]

Alcohol and Tobacco Consumption per Capita in the United States, 1934 to 1998

[Continued]

	Per Capital Alcohol Consumption Population 14 and Older (gallons)				Cigarettes Per Capita 18 and Older (Number)
	Beer	Wine	Spirits	All Beverages	
1974	1.25	0.31	1.11	2.67	4,141
1975	1.26	0.32	1.11	2.69	4,122
1976	1.27	0.32	1.10	2.69	4,091
1977	1.29	0.29	1.06	2.64	4,043
1978	1.33	0.31	1.07	2.71	3,970
1979	1.37	0.32	1.06	2.75	3,861
1980	1.38	0.34	1.04	2.76	3,849
1981	1.39	0.35	1.02	2.76	3,836
1982	1.38	0.36	0.98	2.72	3,739
1983	1.37	0.36	0.96	2.69	3,488
1984	1.35	0.37	0.94	2.65	3,446
1985	1.33	0.38	0.90	2.62	3,370
1986	1.34	0.39	0.84	2.58	3,274
1987	1.34	0.38	0.82	2.54	3,197
1988	1.33	0.36	0.79	2.48	3,096
1989	1.31	0.34	0.77	2.42	2,926
1990	1.34	0.33	0.78	2.45	2,826
1991	1.29	0.30	0.71	2.30	2,720
1992	1.29	0.30	0.71	2.31	2,641
1993	1.28	0.29	0.68	2.25	2,538
1994	1.26	0.29	0.66	2.21	2,522
1995	1.25	0.29	0.64	2.17	2,515
1996	1.25	0.30	0.64	2.19	2,443
1997	1.24	0.31	0.63	2.18	2,372
1998	1.25	0.31	0.63	2.19	2,300

Source: National Institute on Alcohol Abuse and Alcoholism, U.S. Department of Health and Human Services, *Apparent Per Capita Alcohol Consumption*, December 2000; U.S. Department of Agriculture (tobacco figures).

Alcohol- and Drug-Related Arrests, 1984 to 2000

	Alcohol-Related Arrests				Total Drug-Related	All Arrests	Drug As % of Total
	Driving Under the Influence	Liquor Law Violations	Drunken-ness	Total Alcohol-Related			
1984	1,779,400	505,500	1,152,300	3,437,200	708,400	11,564,000	6.1
1985	1,788,400	548,600	964,800	3,301,800	811,400	11,945,000	6.8
1986	1,793,300	600,200	933,900	3,327,400	824,100	12,487,500	6.6
1987	1,727,200	616,700	828,300	3,172,200	937,400	12,711,600	7.4
1988	1,792,500	669,600	818,600	3,280,700	1,155,200	13,812,300	8.4
1989	1,736,200	657,300	822,500	3,216,000	1,361,700	14,340,900	9.5
1990	1,810,800	714,700	910,100	3,435,600	1,089,500	14,195,100	7.7

[Continued]

Alcohol- and Drug-Related Arrests, 1984 to 2000

[Continued]

	Alcohol-Related Arrests				Total Drug-Related	All Arrests	Drug As % of Total
	Driving Under the Influence	Liquor Law Violations	Drunken-ness	Total Alcohol-Related			
1991	1,771,400	624,100	881,100	3,276,600	1,010,000	14,211,900	7.1
1992	1,624,500	541,700	832,300	2,998,500	1,066,400	14,075,100	7.6
1993	1,524,800	518,500	726,600	2,769,900	1,126,300	14,036,300	8.0
1994	1,384,600	541,800	713,200	2,639,600	1,351,400	14,648,700	9.2
1995	1,436,000	594,900	708,100	2,739,000	1,476,100	15,119,800	9.8
1996	1,467,300	677,400	817,700	2,962,400	1,506,200	15,158,100	9.9
1997	1,477,300	636,400	734,800	2,848,500	1,583,600	15,284,300	10.4
1998	1,402,800	630,400	710,300	2,743,500	1,559,100	14,528,300	10.7
1999	1,549,500	683,600	673,400	2,906,500	1,557,100	14,355,600	10.8
2000	1,471,289	683,124	637,554	2,791,967	1,579,566	13,980,297	11.3
Change, 1984 to 2000 - %	-17.3	35.1	-44.7	-18.8	123.0	20.9	84.4

Source: U.S. Department of Justice, Federal Bureau of Investigation, *Crime in the United States*, annual, *Uniform Crime Reports*, downloaded from http://www.ojp.usdoj.gov/bjs/dcf/enforce.htm.

Official Crime Rate in the Context of Drug Arrests and Corrections

	Total, Official Crime Rate Rate Arrests	Drug Abuse Violation Arrests	Crime Rate and Drug Arrests Combined	State Corrections Total, With Drug Offenders	State Corrections Without Drug Offenders
1984	2,359,500	708,400	3,067,900	414,000	382,300
1985	2,422,700	811,400	3,234,100	448,200	409,300
1986	2,577,100	824,100	3,401,200	483,000	437,600
1987	2,646,200	937,400	3,583,600	516,000	458,100
1988	2,888,600	1,155,200	4,043,800	558,400	479,300
1989	3,005,800	1,361,700	4,367,500	626,200	506,100
1990	2,923,300	1,089,500	4,012,800	681,400	532,800
1991	2,971,400	1,010,000	3,981,400	724,900	569,700
1992	2,888,200	1,066,400	3,954,600	775,100	607,000
1993	2,848,400	1,126,300	3,974,700	824,100	647,100
1994	2,910,400	1,351,400	4,261,800	900,600	707,100
1995	2,924,800	1,476,100	4,400,900	985,500	772,700
1996	2,775,500	1,506,200	4,281,700	1,029,400	812,500
1997	2,733,400	1,583,600	4,317,000	1,072,500	850,400
1998	2,481,500	1,559,100	4,040,600	1,138,800	902,000
1999	2,320,900	1,557,100	3,878,000	1,186,800	935,600

[Continued]

Official Crime Rate in the Context of Drug Arrests and Corrections

[Continued]

	Total, Official Crime Rate Rate Arrests	Drug Abuse Violation Arrests	Crime Rate and Drug Arrests Combined	State Corrections Total, With Drug Offenders	State Corrections Without Drug Offenders
2000	2,246,054	1,579,566	3,825,620	1,203,300	952,200
Change, 1984 to 2000 - %	-4.8	123.0	24.7	190.7	149.1

Source: Arrest data: U.S. Department of Justice, Federal Bureau of Investigation, *Crime in the United States*, annual, *Uniform Crime Reports*, downloaded from http://www.ojp.usdoj.gov/bjs/dcf/enforce.htm.

Chapter 7
TERRORISM

Number of Terrorist Incidents in the United States

	Terrorist Incidents	Suspected Incidents	Terrorist Preventions
1980	29	0	1
1981	42	4	0
1982	51	1	3
1983	31	2	6
1984	13	3	9
1985	7	6	23
1986	25	2	9
1987	9	8	5
1988	9	5	3
1989	4	16	7
1990	7	1	5
1991	5	1	5
1992	4	0	0
1993	12	2	7
1994	1	1	0
1995	1	1	2
1996	3	0	5
1997	4	0	21
1998	5	0	12
1999	10	2	7

Source: Federal Bureau of Investigations, *Terrorism in the United States, 1999.*

International Terrorism Attacks Against the United States

	Total International	% of Anti-U.S. Attacks
1992	363	39.1
1993	431	20.4
1994	322	20.4
1995	440	22.5
1996	296	24.6

[Continued]

International Terrorism Attacks Against the United States
[Continued]

	Total International	% of Anti-U.S. Attacks
1997	304	33.0
1998	274	40.5
1999	395	42.7
2000	426	46.9

Source: Patterns of Global Terrorism, 1989-2000 available from: http://www.fas.org.

Americans and Privacy

Figures are in percent based on a survey. Respondents were asked what types of privacy intrusions they would find acceptable to fight terrorism.

	Jul-01	Aug-02
Favor national ID card	70	59
Oppose national ID card	26	38
Favor allowing govt. to monitor phone & email	26	22
Oppose allowing govt. to monitor phone & e-mail	70	76
Allow govt. to monitor credit card purchases	40	32
Oppose govt. monitoring credit card purchases	55	63

Source: "Temporary Turnabout." *Public Perspectives,* September/October 2002, p. 29.

Homeland Defense Spending

Figures are in billions of dollars.

	Billions
1998	10.5
1999	11.8
2000	13.2
2001	16.9
2002	29.3
2003	37.7

Source: "Sluggish Sept. 11 Response Leaves Holes in Security." *USA Today,* May 29, 2002, p. 12A.

Deaths of U.S. Citizens by Terrorism

	International	Domestic	Wounded intl.
1981	7	4	40
1982	8	8	11
1983	271	6	115
1984	11	1	31
1985	38	2	157
1986	12	1	100
1987	7	0	47
1988	192	0	39
1989	16	0	18
1990	9	0	34
1991	7	0	16
1992	2	0	1
1993	7	6	1,004
1994	6	1	5
1995	10	169	60
1996	25	2	510
1997	6	0	21
1998	12	1	11
1999	5	3	6

Source: U.S. Department of Justice, Bureau of Justice Statistics, *Sourcebook of Criminal Justice Statistics, 2000.*

Chapter 8
LAW ENFORCEMENT

State and Local Sworn Police Full-Time Employment

Sworn police officers carry firearms and may make arrests. Figures are by level of government for October 1980-95 and March 1997-99. The formula for computing full-time equivalent employment changed in 1986; see source for more information. Some data have been revised by the source. Data for local governments are estimates subject to sampling variation.

| Total | Sworn Police | | | | | Percent Sworn |
	State	Local	Counties	Municipal	Employees	
1980	461,810	50,672	411,138	94,533	316,605	78.1
1981	464,141	51,177	412,964	96,326	316,638	78.0
1982	470,909	49,865	421,044	97,829	323,215	77.8
1983	472,459	50,965	421,494	98,695	322,799	78.1
1984	475,124	51,155	423,969	99,045	324,924	77.7
1985	481,146	51,761	429,385	100,916	328,469	77.6
1986	491,276	52,754	438,522	104,643	333,879	76.3
1987	501,440	53,542	447,898	107,811	340,087	76.0
1988	509,619	54,978	454,641	111,306	343,335	76.0
1989	513,242	56,084	457,158	113,479	343,679	75.8
1990	525,075	56,729	468,346	116,836	351,510	75.6
1991	531,706	56,294	475,412	119,383	356,029	75.7
1992	538,510	55,104	483,406	123,851	359,555	75.3
1993	546,047	54,283	491,764	127,234	364,530	75.3
1994	560,509	56,981	507,783	138,817	373,221	74.9
1995	584,925	54,704	530,221	139,078	391,143	75.1
1997	602,718	56,023	546,695	142,330	404,365	75.5
1998	616,377	55,224	561,153	145,472	415,681	75.4
1999	638,066	58,917	578,909	153,075	425,834	75.2

Source: U.S. Department of Justice, Bureau of Justice Statistics, *Trends in Justice Expenditure and Employment*, NCJ 178276, Table 9 [Online]. available: http://www.ojp.usdoj.gov/bjs/data/eetrnd09.wk1 [Mar. 27, 2002].

Areas of Duty for Law Enforcement

	1996	Percent	2000	Percent
Patrol/response	422,671	63.7	424,105	59.9
Investigations	99,530	15.0	105,495	14.9
Jail operations	46,447	7.7	43,897	6.2
Court operations	22,560	3.4	36,109	5.1
Administration	72,327	10.2	98,416	13.9

Source: U.S. Department of Justice, Bureau of Justice Statistics, *Census of State and Local Law Enforcement Agencies, 1996 and 2000.*

Minority Law Enforcement

Figures are in percent.

	1990	2000
Any minority	29.8	38.1
Black, non-Hispanic	18.4	20.1
Hispanics, any race	9.2	14.1
Asian/Pacific Islander	2.0	2.8
American Indian	0.3	0.4
Females	12.1	16.3

Source: Chart data from U.S. Department of Justice, Bureau of Justice Statistics, *Police Departments in Large Cities, 1990-2000.*

Law Enforcement Programs

Figures show percent of large city departments (cities with residents over 250,000) that have part-time or full-time staff or deparments devoted to each crime.

	1990	2000
Victim assistance	45	71
Crime prevention	100	97
Repeat offenders	77	57
Prosecutor relations	76	58
Domestic violence	61	97
Child abuse	95	92
Missing children	95	95
Juvenile crime	94	84
Gangs	89	98
Drug education	89	98
Drunk drivers	76	81
Bias-related crimes	58	71

Source: U.S. Department of Justice, Bureau of Justice Statistics, *Police Departments in Large Cities, 1990-2000.*

Law Enforcement Methods

Figures show the percent of large city departments (cities with residents over 250,000) that use each method.

	1990	2000
Require field/patrol officers to use body armor	31	69
Authorize field/patrol officers to use a revolver	97	65
Authorize field/patrol officers to use a semiautomatic	97	100
Allow officer to take marked vehicles home	15	42
Use bicycles	39	98
Use enhanced 9-1-1 system	76	97
Use automated fingerprint ID systems	60	97
Use in-field computers	73	92

Source: U.S. Department of Justice, Bureau of Justice Statistics, *Police Departments in Large Cities, 1990-2000.*

Law Enforcement Officers Killed, 1900-2000

1945-2000 data are from the Federal Bureau of Investigation's (FBI) Uniform Crime Reporting Program. Federal, State, and local law enforcement agencies participating in the UCR Program submit data on any sworn officer killed feloniously or accidentally in the line of duty within their jurisdictions. FBI field divisions and legal attache offices also report such incidents occurring in the United States and its territories, as well as those in which a United States law enforcement officer dies while assigned to duties in another country (Source, 2000, p. 3).

	Total Killed	Feloniously	Accidentally	Gun Deaths
1900	40	NA	NA	5
1905	30	NA	NA	4
1910	54	NA	NA	8
1915	85	NA	NA	9
1920	149	NA	NA	13
1925	180	NA	NA	30
1926	180	NA	NA	19
1927	188	NA	NA	27
1928	191	NA	NA	29
1929	214	NA	NA	24
1930	244	NA	NA	35
1931	203	NA	NA	31
1932	210	NA	NA	29
1933	186	NA	NA	37
1934	190	NA	NA	31
1935	165	NA	NA	25
1936	149	NA	NA	17
1937	155	NA	NA	15
1938	155	NA	NA	15
1939	98	NA	NA	11
1940	107	NA	NA	7
1941	121	NA	NA	14

[Continued]

Law Enforcement Officers Killed, 1900-2000

[Continued]

	Total Killed	Feloniously	Accidentally	Gun Deaths
1942	98	NA	NA	13
1943	75	NA	NA	8
1944	79	NA	NA	4
1945	59	NA	NA	9
1946	82	NA	NA	11
1947	67	NA	NA	9
1948	64	NA	NA	7
1949	55	NA	NA	8
1950	36	NA	NA	7
1951	64	NA	NA	7
1952	63	NA	NA	13
1953	63	NA	NA	8
1954	61	NA	NA	15
1955	55	NA	NA	5
1956	46	NA	NA	8
1957	45	NA	NA	9
1958	49	NA	NA	9
1959	49	NA	NA	7
1960	48	NA	NA	8
1961	71	37	34	13
1962	78	48	30	9
1963	88	55	33	10
1964	88	57	31	18
1965	83	53	30	12
1966	99	57	42	17
1967	123	76	47	17
1968	123	64	59	20
1969	125	86	39	30
1970	146	100	46	35
1971	238	238	NA	35
1972	117	117	NA	35
1973	176	134	42	60
1974	179	132	47	39
1975	185	129	56	48
1976	140	111	29	38
1977	125	93	32	27
1978	125	93	52	40
1979	164	106	58	48
1980	165	104	61	46
1981	157	91	66	40
1982	164	92	72	43
1983	152	80	72	46
1984	147	72	75	35
1985	148	78	70	38
1986	133	66	67	34
1987	148	74	74	39
1988	155	78	77	54
1989	145	66	79	51

[Continued]

Law Enforcement Officers Killed, 1900-2000

[Continued]

	Total Killed	Feloniously	Accidentally	Gun Deaths
1990	133	66	67	61
1991	124	71	53	71
1992	130	64	66	67
1993	129	70	59	74
1994	141	79	62	74
1995	133	74	59	67
1996	112	61	51	61
1997	132	71	63	69
1998	142	61	81	63
1999	107	42	65	44
2000	135	51	84	50

Source: U.S. Department of Justice, Federal Bureau of Investigation, *Law Enforcement Officers Killed*, 1981, *FBI Uniform Crime Reports* (Washington, DC: USGPO, 1982), p. 12; *Law Enforcement Officers Killed and Assaulted*, 1982, pp. 10, 40; 1992, pp. 23, 57; 2000, pp. 23, 69; *FBI Uniform Crime Reports* (Washington, DC: U.S. Department of Justice). Data also from National Law Enforcement Memorial Fund.

Use of Force in City Departments, 1991

Figures are per 100,000 people.

	Rate
Civilians shot at but not hit	3.0
Electronic devices (TASERs)	5.4
Dog attacks or bites	6.5
Flashlights	21.7
Batons	36.0
Chemical agents	36.2
Firm grip	57.7
Twist locks/wrist locks	80.9
Swarm	126.7
Unholstering weapons	129.9
Come-alongs	226.8
Bodily force (arm, foot, leg)	272.2
Handcuff/leg restraint	490.4

Source: U.S. Department of Justice, Bureau of Justice Statistics, *National Data Collection on Police Use of Force*, April 1996.

Justifiable Homicides and Police Shootings

Figues show number of deaths and rate per 100,000 people.

	Felons Killed by Police		Officers Killed by Felons	
	Number	Rate	Number	Rate
1980	457	2.49	104	26.44
1981	381	2.06	91	22.86
1982	376	2.00	92	22.81

[Continued]

Justifiable Homicides and Police Shootings

[Continued]

	Felons Killed by Police		Officers Killed by Felons	
	Number	Rate	Number	Rate
1983	406	2.14	80	17.80
1984	332	1.73	72	15.41
1985	321	1.65	78	16.57
1986	298	1.52	66	13.87
1987	296	1.50	74	15.40
1988	339	1.70	78	16.06
1989	362	1.80	66	13.30
1990	379	1.88	66	12.61
1991	359	1.76	71	13.26
1992	414	2.01	64	11.76
1993	453	2.17	70	12.64
1994	459	2.18	79	14.07
1995	382	1.80	74	12.61
1996	355	1.65	61	10.25
1997	361	1.66	70	11.32
1998	367	1.67	61	9.51

Source: U.S. Bureau of Justice Statistics, *Policing and Homicide, 1976-1998: Justifiable Homicides by Police, Police Officers Murdered by Felons*, Series NCJ 180987, March 2001.

High-Speed Pursuits by the Los Angeles Police Department

	Pursuits
1993	908
1994	821
1995	827
1996	644
1997	643
1998	534
1999	563
2000	663
2001	778

Source: Los Angeles Police Department, located online at http://www.lacp.org.

Racial Profiling

Percent of each group claiming to have been stopped because of their race, based on a survey.

	Percent
Hispanic men	20
Asian men	20
Black women	25
All blacks	37
Black men	52

Source: "Racial Profiling Rampant" *State Government News,* August 2001, p. 8.

Federal Officers

Federal agencies employing 100 or more full-time officers authorized to carry firearms and make arrests as of June 2000. Data were provided by federal agencies in response to a survey conducted by the U.S. Department of Justice, Bureau of Justice Statistics. The data include all supervisory and nonsupervisory personnel with federal arrest authority who were authorized (but not necessarily required) to carry firearms in the performance of their official duties. The data presented exclude law enforcement personnel in the U.S. armed forces and those serving in foreign countries. Excludes employees in U.S. territories. Includes all Federal probation officers employed in Federal judicial districts that allow officers to carry firearms. Includes 1,544 Park Rangers commissioned as law enforcement officers and 644 U.S. Park Police officers.

Agency	Number of Full-Time Officers
Immigration and Naturalization Service	17,654
Federal Bureau of Prisons	13,557
Federal Bureau of Investigation	11,523
U.S. Customs Service	10,522
Drug Enforcement Administration	4,161
U.S. Secret Service	4,039
Administrative Office of the United States Courts	3,599
U.S. Postal Inspection Service	3,412
U.S. Marshals Service	2,735
Internal Revenue Service, Criminal Investigation Division	2,726
National Park Service	2,188
Bureau of Alcohol, Tobacco and Firearms	1,967
U.S. Capitol Police	1,199
U.S. Fish and Wildlife Service	888
General Services Administration, Federal Protective Service	803
Bureau of Diplomatic Security, Diplomatic Security Service	617
U.S. Forest Service, Law Enforcement and Investigations	586
U.S. Mint	354
Veterans Health Administration	342
Amtrak	316

Source: U.S. Department of Justice, Bureau of Justice Statistics, *Federal Law Enforcement Officers, 2000,* Bulletin NCJ 187231 (Washington, DC: U.S. Department of Justice, July 2001), pp. 2, 5. Table adapted by SOURCEBOOK staff.

Wiretap Orders

Figures show the number of court-authorized intercepts authorized of wire, oral, or electronic communications.

	Federal	State	Total
1969	33	268	301
1970	182	414	596
1971	285	531	816
1972	206	649	855
1973	130	734	864
1974	121	607	728
1975	108	593	701
1976	137	549	657
1977	77	549	626
1978	81	489	570
1979	87	466	553
1980	81	483	564
1981	106	483	589
1982	130	448	578
1983	208	440	648
1984	289	512	801
1985	243	541	784
1986	250	504	754
1987	236	437	673
1988	293	445	738
1989	310	453	763
1990	324	548	872
1991	356	500	856
1992	340	579	919
1993	450	526	976
1994	554	600	1,154
1995	532	526	1,058
1996	581	568	1,150
1997	569	617	1,186
1998	566	763	1,331
1999	601	749	1,350

[Continued]

Wiretap Orders

[Continued]

	Federal	State	Total
2000	479	711	1,190
2001	486	1,005	1,491

Source: Administrative Office of the United States Courts, Report on Applications for Orders Authorizing or Approving the Interception of Wire or Oral Communications for the Period January 1, 1977 to December 31, 1977 (Washington, DC: Administrative Office of the United States Courts, 1978), p. xvi; *Administrative Office of the United States Courts Report on Applications for Orders Authorizing or Approving the Interception of Wire Oral, or Electronic Communications for the Period January 1, 1988 to December 31, 1988* (Washington, DC: USGPO, 1989), p. 19; and *Administrative Office of the United States Courts, 1999 Wiretap Report*, p. 32; 2001, p. 32 (Washington, DC: Administrative Office of the United States Courts). *Notes:* The Director of the Administrative Office of the United States Courts is required, in accordance with provisions of 18 S.C. 2519(1), to transmit to Congress a report regarding applications for orders authorizing or approving the interception of wire, or oral, or electronic communications. This report is required to contain information about the number of such orders and any extensions granted. Every state and federal judge is required to file a written report on each application made. This report is required to contain information on the grants and denials, name of applicant, offense involved, type and location of device, and duration of authorized intercept. Prosecuting officials who have applied for intercept orders are required to file reports containing information on the cost of the intercepts; the number of days the device was in operation; the total number of intercepts; the number of incriminating intercepts recorded; whether encryption was encountered in the course of the intercept; and the results of the intercepts in terms of the number of arrests, trials, convictions, and motions to suppress evidence obtained through the use of intercepts. Forty-six jurisdictions (the Federal Government, the District of Columbia, the Virgin Islands, and 43 States) had statutes authorizing the interception of wire, oral, or electronic communications during 2001; 25 of these jurisdictions had court-authorized orders for interception during 2001 (Source, 2001, pp. 6, 7).

Airline Passenger Screening

Screening consists of "the systematic examination of persons and property using weapons-detecting procedures or facilities (electronic or physical search) for the purpose of detecting weapons and dangerous articles and to prevent their unauthorized introduction into sterile areas or aboard aircraft."(Source, 1993, p. 42.) Prior to 1992, the firearm category of other included items such as starter pistols, flare pistols, and BB guns. Beginning in 1992, this category was expanded and now also includes stunning devices, chemical agents, martial arts equipment, knives, bludgeons, and certain other designated items. From 1992 to 1994, the method of counting explosive/incendiary devices was revised. Individual items were counted rather than packages (i.e., one box of firecrackers counted as 20 firecrackers; one box of ammunition counted as 50 cartridges).

	Persons Screened (mil.)	Total Weapons Found	Arrests Firearms/Expl.	Arrests False Inform.	Handguns	Long guns	Other	devices
1977	508.8	2,034	810	44	1,827	64	240	5
1978	579.7	2,058	896	64	1,962	67	164	3
1979	592.5	2,161	1,060	47	1,878	55	144	3
1980	585.0	2,022	1,031	32	2,124	36	108	8
1981	598.5	2,255	1,187	49	2,559	44	87	11
1982	630.2	2,676	1,314	27	2,634	57	60	1
1983	709.1	2,784	1,282	34	2,766	67	83	4
1984	775.6	2,957	1,285	27	2,823	100	91	6
1985	992.9	2,987	1,310	42	2,981	90	74	12
1986	1,055.3	3,241	1,415	89	3,012	146	114	11
1987	1,095.6	3,252	1,581	81	2,591	99	141	14
1988	1,054.9	2,773	1,493	222	2,397	74	108	11
1989	1,113.3	2,879	1,436	83	2,490	92	390	26
1990	1,145.1	2,853	1,337	18	1,597	59	304	15
1991	1,015.1	1,919	893	28	2,503	47	275	94

[Continued]

Airline Passenger Screening
[Continued]

	Persons Screened (mil.)	Total Weapons Found	Arrests Firearms/Expl.	Arrests False Inform.	Handguns	Long guns	Other	devices
1992	1,110.8	2,608	1,282	13	2,707	105	NA	167
1993	1,150.0	2,798	1,354	31	2,860	91	NA	251
1994	1,261.3	2,994	1,433	35	2,230	134	NA	505
1995	1,263.0	2,390	1,194	68	1,999	160	NA	631
1996	1,496.9	2,155	999	131	1,905	156	NA	NA
1997	1,659.7	2,067	924	72	1,401	162	NA	NA
1998	1,666.5	1,515	660	86	1,421	114	NA	NA
1999	1,822.0	1,552	633	58		131	NA	NA

Source: U.S. Department of Transportation, Federal Aviation Administration, *Semiannual Report to Congress on the Effectiveness of the Civil Aviation Security Program,* July 1 to December 31, 1978, Exhibit 10; July 1 to December 31, 1982, Exhibit 10; July 1 to December 31, 1984, Exhibit 7; July 1 to December 31, 1989, p. 11 Washington, DC: U.S. Department of Transportation; U.S. Department of Transportation, Federal Aviation Administration, *Annual Report to Congress on Civil Aviation Security,* January 1, 1993-December 31, 1993, p. 9; January 1, 1995-December 31, 1995, p. 11 (Washington, DC: U.S. Department of Transportation); and data provided by the U.S. Department of Transportation, Federal Aviation Administration.

Chapter 9
PRISONS

People in State Prisons

Number of persons in custody of state correctional authorities by most serious offense, 1980-2000.

Year	Most Serious Offense				
	Violent	Property	Drug	Public Order	Total
1980	173,300	89,300	19,000	12,400	294,000
1981	193,300	100,500	21,700	14,600	330,100
1982	215,300	114,400	25,300	17,800	372,800
1983	214,600	127,100	26,600	24,400	392,700
1984	227,300	133,100	31,700	21,900	414,000
1985	246,200	140,100	38,900	23,000	448,200
1986	258,600	150,200	45,400	28,800	483,000
1987	271,300	155,500	57,900	31,300	516,000
1988	282,700	161,600	79,100	35,000	558,400
1989	293,900	172,700	120,100	39,500	626,200
1990	313,600	173,700	148,600	45,500	681,400
1991	339,500	180,700	155,200	49,500	724,900
1992	369,100	181,600	168,100	56,300	775,100
1993	393,500	189,600	177,000	64,000	824,100
1994	425,700	207,000	193,500	74,400	900,600
1995	459,600	226,600	212,800	86,500	985,500
1996	484,800	231,700	216,900	96,000	1,029,400
1997	507,800	236,400	222,100	106,200	1,072,500
1998	545,200	242,900	236,800	113,900	1,138,800
1999	570,000	245,000	251,200	120,600	1,186,800
2000	589,100	238,500	251,100	124,600	1,203,300

Source: Bureau of Justice Statistics, *Correctional Populations in the United States, 1997,* and *Prisoners in 2000,* http://www.ojp.usdoj.gov/bjs/glance/corrtyp.htm.

Men in State Prisons by Race

Sentenced prisoners are those who are serving sentences of longer than one year. Based on custody counts from National Prisoner Statistics (NPS-1A) and updated from jurisdiction counts by gender at yearend. Estimates by age derived from the Survey of Inmates in State and Federal Correctional Facilities, 1997.

Age	Number of Sentenced Prisoners			
	Total[1]	White[2]	Black[2]	Hispanic
Total	1,259,481	449,200	585,800	199,700
Percent of Total	100	36	47	16
18-19	35,600	8,900	17,400	7,000
20-24	214,600	60,000	106,500	40,600
25-29	241,800	71,000	122,500	42,100
30-34	238,600	85,100	110,700	39,100
35-39	214,500	81,900	102,000	28,900
40-44	145,900	58,400	64,300	21,200
45-54	124,800	59,500	48,400	16,100
55+	38,400	23,300	10,800	4,100

Source: Bureau of Justice Statistics, *Prisoners in 2001*, NCJ 195189, tables15 and 16, http://www.ojp.usdoj.gov. *Notes:* 1. Includes American Indians, Alaska Natives, Asians, Native Hawaiians, and other Pacific Islanders. 2. Excludes Hispanics.

Older Prisoners

Prisoners aged 45 and older in state and federal prisons, 1991 and 1997. Percent of prisoners. Median age in years of all prisoners.

Age	State		Federal	
	1991	1997	1991	1997
45 to 54 years	6.5	9.8	15.0	16.3
55 to 64 years	2.4	2.2	5.7	6.2
65 years and older	0.7	0.7	1.1	1.4
Total	9.6	12.7	21.8	23.9
Median age	30.0	32.0	36.0	36.0

Source: Sourcebook of Criminal Justice Statistics, Table 6.38. Primary Source: U.S. Department of Justice, Bureau of Justice Statistics, *Correctional Populations in the United States, 1997*, NCJ 177613 (Washington, DC: U.S. Department of Justice, "2000), Table 4.1.

Women in State Prisons by Race

Sentenced prisoners are those who are serving sentences of longer than one year. Based on custody counts from National Prisoner Statistics (NPS-1A) and updated from jurisdiction counts by gender at yearend. Estimates by age derived from the Survey of Inmates in State and Federal Correctional Facilities, 1997.

Age	Number of Sentenced Prisoners			
	Total[1]	White[2]	Black[2]	Hispanic
Total	85,031	36,200	36,400	10,200
Percent of total	100	43	43	11
18-19	1,300	700	500	100
20-24	8,500	3,700	3,200	1,500
25-29	15,200	5,600	6,600	2,000
30-34	21,100	8,700	9,400	2,400
35-39	18,600	8,000	8,400	2,000
40-44	10,100	4,200	4,700	1,000
45-54	8,000	3,900	3,000	1,000
55+	1,800	1,300	500	100

Source: Bureau of Justice Statistics, *Prisoners in 2001*, NCJ 195189, tables 15 and 16, http://www.ojp.usdoj.gov. *Notes:* 1. Includes American Indians, Alaska Natives, Asians, Native Hawaiians, and other Pacific Islanders. 2. Excludes Hispanics.

Inmates on Death Row by State

Inmates known to NAACP Legal Defense Fund on July 21, 2002. Eight prisoners were sentenced to death in more than one state. They are included in the table for each state in which they were sentenced to death.

State	Total	Black		White		Latino/a		Native American		Asian	
		Number	Percent	Number	Percent	Number	Percent	Number	Percent	Number	Percent
AL	189	86	0.46	100	0.53	2	0.01	0	-	1	0.005
AZ	127	16	0.13	89	0.70	18	0.14	3	0.02	1	0.008
AR	42	25	0.60	16	0.38	1	0.02	0	-	0	-
CA	611	219	0.36	241	0.39	120	0.20	14	0.02	17	0.030
CO	5	2	0.40	1	0.20	1	0.20	0	-	1	0.200
CT	7	3	0.43	3	0.43	1	0.14	0	-	0	-
DE	20	9	0.45	9	0.45	2	0.10	0	-	0	-
FL	388	136	0.35	216	0.56	34	0.09	1	0.003	1	0.003
GA	121	58	0.48	60	0.50	2	0.02	0	-	1	0.008
ID	22	0	-	22	1.00	0	-	0	-	0	-
IL	175	110	0.63	55	0.31	10	0.06	0	-	0	-
IN	39	12	0.31	27	0.69	0	-	0	-	0	-
KS	4	0	-	4	1.00	0	-	0	-	0	-
KY	41	9	0.22	31	0.76	1	0.02	0	-	0	-
LA	96	66	0.69	27	0.28	2	0.02	0	-	1	0.010
MD	17	11	0.65	6	0.35	0	-	0	-	0	-
MS	69	38	0.55	31	0.45	0	-	0	-	0	-
MO	71	30	0.42	41	0.58	0	-	0	-	0	-
MT	6	0	-	6	1.00	0	-	0	-	0	-
NE	7	1	0.14	5	0.71	1	0.14	0	-	0	-
NV	88	37	0.42	41	0.47	9	0.10	0	-	1	0.010
NJ	17	7	0.41	10	0.59	0	-	0	-	0	-

[Continued]

Inmates on Death Row by State

[Continued]

State	Total	Black		White		Latino/a		Native American		Asian	
		Number	Percent	Number	Percent	Number	Percent	Number	Percent	Number	Percent
NM	4	0	-	3	0.75	1	0.25	0	-	0	-
NY	6	2	0.33	3	0.50	1	0.17	0	-	0	-
NC	223	124	0.56	84	0.38	4	0.02	9	0.04	2	0.009
OH	204	101	0.50	97	0.48	2	0.01	2	0.01	2	0.010
OK	121	42	0.35	65	0.54	4	0.03	9	0.07	1	0.008
OR	30	1	0.03	25	0.83	2	0.07	1	0.03	0	-
PA	247	156	0.63	75	0.30	14	0.06	0	-	2	0.008
SC	77	36	0.47	41	0.53	0	-	0	-	0	-
SD	5	0	-	5	1.00	0	-	0	-	0	-
TN	106	41	0.39	59	0.56	2	0.02	2	0.02	2	0.020
TX	457	189	0.41	153	0.33	110	0.24	0	-	5	0.010
UT	11	2	0.18	6	0.55	2	0.18	1	0.09	0	-
VA	26	10	0.38	15	0.58	0	-	0	-	1	0.040
WA	12	5	0.42	7	0.58	0	-	0	-	0	-
WY	2	0	-	2	1.00	0	-	0	-	0	-
US Gov.	26	18	0.69	6	0.23	2	0.08	0	-	0	-
Military	7	5	0.71	1	0.14	0	-	0	-	1	0.140
TOTAL	3,726	1,607	0.43	1,688	0.45	348	0.09	42	0.01	40	0.010

Source: Deborah Fins, *Death Row USA, Criminal Justice Project of the NAACP Legal Defense and Educational Fund*, Summer 2002, http://www.deathpenaltyinfo.org/DEATHROWUSArecent.pdf.

Prisoners and Prison Capacity

NA Not reported. Sentenced prisoners are prisoners with sentences of more than one year.

December 31	Number of Inmates		Sentenced Prisoners Per 100,000 Resident Pop		Population Housed as a % of Highest Capacity	
	Federal	State	Federal	State	Federal	State
1990	65,526	708,393	20	272	NA	115
1995	100,250	1,025,624	32	379	126	114
1999	135,246	1,228,455	42	434	132	101
2000	145,416	1,245,845	44	425	131	100
2001	156,993	1,249,038	48	422	131	101

Source: Bureau of Justice Statistics, *Prisoners in 2001*, NCJ 195189, Table #15.

Corrections Expenditures

In millions of dollars.

Year	Federal				State				Local			
	Total	Police Protection	Judicial and Legal	Correc- tions	Total	Police Protection	Judicial and Legal	Correc- tions	Total	Police Protection	Judicial and Legal	Correc- tions
1982	4,458	2,527	1,390	541	11,602	2,833	2,748	6,020	20,968	14,172	3,784	3,011
1983	4,844	2,815	1,523	606	12,785	2,963	2,950	6,873	23,186	15,276	4,361	3,548
1984	5,868	3,396	1,785	687	14,213	3,173	3,271	7,768	25,154	16,516	4,627	4,011
1985	6,416	3,495	2,129	792	16,252	3,469	3,636	9,148	27,462	17,847	5,090	4,524
1986	6,595	3,643	2,090	862	18,556	3,749	4,005	10,802	30,178	19,356	5,691	5,132
1987	7,496	4,231	2,271	994	20,157	4,067	4,339	11,691	33,265	21,089	6,230	5,947
1988	8,851	4,954	2,639	1,258	22,837	4,531	4,886	13,420	36,098	22,371	6,826	6,901
1989	9,674	5,307	2,949	1,418	25,269	4,780	5,442	15,047	38,825	23,672	7,682	7,471
1990	12,798	5,666	5,398	1,734	28,345	5,163	5,971	17,211	43,559	26,097	8,676	8,786
1991	15,231	6,725	6,384	2,122	31,484	5,507	6,754	19,223	47,075	28,017	9,418	9,640
1992	17,423	7,400	7,377	2,646	33,755	5,593	7,723	20,439	50,115	29,659	10,052	10,404
1993	18,591	8,069	7,832	2,690	34,227	5,603	7,820	20,803	52,562	31,733	10,283	10,546
1994	19,084	8,059	8,184	2,841	37,161	6,000	8,026	23,135	55,517	33,365	11,023	11,130
1995	22,651	9,298	9,184	4,169	41,196	6,451	8,676	26,069	58,933	35,364	11,674	11,895
1996	23,344	10,115	9,459	3,766	39,903	6,499	8,110	25,294	62,811	38,227	12,355	12,229
1997	27,065	12,518	10,651	3,896	42,353	6,670	8,567	27,117	66,916	40,974	13,079	12,863
1998	22,834	12,208	7,462	3,165	49,454	7,996	10,858	30,599	70,831	43,312	13,559	13,960
1999	27,392	14,797	8,515	4,080	57,186	9,632	12,875	34,680	74,830	45,593	14,142	15,096

Source: Bureau of Justice Statistics, *Justice Expenditure and Employment in the United States, 1999*, February 2002, NCJ 191746, Table 2, http:// www.ojp.usdoj.gov/bjs/pub/pdf/jeeus99.pdf.

Robberies, Burglaries, Larcenies/Thefts

Crimes reported to law-enforcement agencies.

Year	Population	Crime Index Total	Rate Per 100,000	Robbery	Rate Per 100,000	Burglary	Rate Per 100,000	Larceny/ Theft	Rate Per 100,000	Total Rob/ Burg/LT
1982	231,664,458	12,974,400	5,601	553,130	238.8	3,447,100	1,488.0	7,142,500	3,083.1	11,142,730
1983	233,791,994	12,108,630	5,179	506,567	216.7	3,129,851	1,338.7	6,712,759	2,871.3	10,349,177
1984	235,824,902	11,881,755	5,038	485,008	205.7	2,984,434	1,265.5	6,591,874	2,795.2	10,061,316
1985	237,923,795	12,430,357	5,225	497,874	209.3	3,073,348	1,291.7	6,926,380	2,911.2	10,497,602
1986	240,132,887	13,211,869	5,502	542,775	226.0	3,241,410	1,349.8	7,257,153	3,022.1	11,041,338
1987	242,288,918	13,508,708	5,575	517,704	213.7	3,236,184	1,335.7	7,499,851	3,095.4	11,253,739
1988	244,498,982	13,923,086	5,695	542,968	222.1	3,218,077	1,316.2	7,705,872	3,151.7	11,466,917
1989	246,819,230	14,251,449	5,774	578,326	234.3	3,168,170	1,283.6	7,872,442	3,189.6	11,618,938
1990	249,464,396	14,475,613	5,803	639,271	256.3	3,073,909	1,232.2	7,945,670	3,185.1	11,658,850
1991	252,153,092	14,872,883	5,898	687,732	272.7	3,157,150	1,252.1	8,142,228	3,229.1	11,987,110
1992	255,029,699	14,438,191	5,661	672,478	263.7	2,979,884	1,168.4	7,915,199	3,103.6	11,567,561
1993	257,782,608	14,144,794	5,487	659,870	256.0	2,834,808	1,099.7	7,820,909	3,033.9	11,315,587
1994	260,327,021	13,989,543	5,374	618,949	237.8	2,712,774	1,042.1	7,879,812	3,026.9	11,211,535
1995	262,803,276	13,862,727	5,275	580,509	220.9	2,593,784	987.0	7,997,710	3,043.2	11,172,003
1996	265,228,572	13,493,863	5,088	535,594	201.9	2,506,400	945.0	7,904,685	2,980.3	10,946,679
1997	267,783,607	13,194,571	4,927	498,534	186.2	2,460,526	918.8	7,743,760	2,891.8	10,702,820
1998	270,248,003	12,485,714	4,620	447,186	165.5	2,332,735	863.2	7,376,311	2,729.5	10,156,232
1999	272,690,813	11,634,378	4,267	409,371	150.1	2,100,739	770.4	6,955,520	2,550.7	9,465,630
2000	281,421,906	11,608,070	4,125	408,016	145.0	2,050,992	728.8	6,971,590	2,477.3	9,430,598
2001	284,796,887	11,849,006	4,161	422,921	148.5	2,109,767	740.8	7,076,171	2,484.6	9,608,859

Source: Chart: Bureau of Justice Statistics, *Justice Expenditure and Employment in the United States, 1999*, February 2002, NCJ 191746, Table 2, http://www.ojp.usdoj.gov/bjs/pub/pdf/jeeus99.pdf, and FBI, *Sourcebook of Criminal Justice Statistics, 2001*, Table 1.

Growth of Private Prisons

Cumulative total of private prisons owned by Corrections Corporation of America and Wackenhut, the two largest private prison operators. Years are approximate and are for the purpose of showing the trend.

Year	CCA	Wackenhut
1984	3	-
1985	5	-
1986	7	-
1988	8	1
1989	10	5
1990	13	6
1992	16	8
1994	17	10
1995	25	12
1996	28	15
1997	39	19
1998	53	24
1999	58	28
2000	61	29
2001	-	31
2002	-	32

Source: Corrections Corporation of America, http://www.correctionscorp.com/index.html., and Wackenhut Corrections Corp., http://www.hoovers.com.

Recidivism Rates for State Prisoners Released in 1993 and 1994

Data for 1983 are from 11 reporting states and represent 57% of all state prisoners. Data for 1994 are for 15 reporting states and represent 66% of all state prisoners. Numbers are percentages.

	1983	1994
Rates of Rearrest		
All released prisoners	62.5	67.5
Violent	59.6	61.7
Property	68.1	73.8
Drug	50.4	66.7
Public-order	54.6	62.2
Percent Reconvicted	46.8	46.9
Percent Returned to Prison	41.4	51.8

Source: U.S. Department of Justice, Bureau of Justice Statistics, *Recidivism of Prisoners Released in 1983*, April 1989, pp. 1 and 3. *Recidivism of Prisoners Released in 1994*, June 2002, pp. 1, 3, 7.

Recidivism Rates of State Prisoners by Number of Arrests Prior to Incarceration, 1983 and 1994

Number of Arrests Prior to Release	Percent of all Released Prisoners	% of Released Prisoners Who Were Rearrested Within	
		1 Year	3 Years
Total	100.0	44.2	67.5
1 prior arrest	6.9	20.6	40.6
2 prior arrests	7.4	26.2	47.5
3 prior arrests	7.8	32.2	55.2
4 prior arrests	7.7	35.1	59.6
5 prior arrests	7.7	39.7	64.2
6 prior arrests	7.4	43.2	67.4
7-10 prior arrests	20.9	45.5	70.3
11-15 prior arrests	16.2	54.5	79.1
16 or more prior arrests	18.0	61.0	82.1

Source: U.S. Department of Justice, Bureau of Justice Statistics, *Recidivism of Prisoners Released in 1983*, April 1989, pp. 1 and 3. *Recidivism of Prisoners Released in 1994*, June 2002, pp. 1, 3, 7.

Recidivism Rates by Age of Prisoner Upon Release, 1994

Age at Release	% of Released Prisoners	Percent of Released Prisoners Who, Within 3 Years, Were:		
		Rearrested	Reconvicted	Returned to Prison
14-17	0.3	82.1	55.7	56.6
18-24	21.0	75.4	52.0	52.0
25-29	22.8	70.5	50.1	52.5
30-34	22.7	68.8	48.8	54.8
35-39	16.2	66.2	46.3	52.0
40-44	9.4	58.4	38.0	50.0
45 and older	7.6	45.3	29.7	40.9

Source: U.S. Department of Justice, Bureau of Justice Statistics, *Recidivism of Prisoners Released in 1994*, June 2002, pp. 1 and 7.

Recidivism Rates by Offense for Which a Prison Sentence Was Served, 1994

	% of All Released Prisoners	Percent of Released Prisoners Who, Within 3 Years, Were:		
		Rearrest	Reconvicted	Return to Prison
All Released Prisoners	100.0	67.5	46.9	51.8
Property Offenses	33.5	73.8	53.4	56.4
Drug Offenses	32.6	66.7	47.0	49.2
Violent Offenses	22.5	61.7	39.9	48.8
Public-order Offenses	9.7	62.2	42.0	48.0
Other Offenses	1.7	64.7	42.1	66.9

Source: U.S. Department of Justice, Bureau of Justice Statistics, *Recidivism of Prisoners Released in 1994*, June 2002, pp. 8.

Recidivism Rates of State Prisoners by Criminal Offense for Which Prisoner Has Served Time, 1994

Offense	% of All Released Prisoners	Percent of Released Prisoners Who, Within 3 Years, Were:		
		Rearrest	Reconviction	Return to Prison
All Released Prisoners	100	67.5	46.9	51.8
Violent Offenses	22.5	61.7	39.9	48.8
Homicide	1.7	40.7	20.5	31.4
Kidnapping	0.4	59.4	37.8	29.5
Rape	1.2	46.0	27.4	43.5
Other sexual assaults	2.4	41.4	22.3	36.0
Robbery	9.9	70.2	46.5	54.7
Assault	6.5	65.1	44.2	51.2
Other violent	0.4	51.7	29.8	40.9
Property Offenses	33.5	73.8	53.4	56.4
Burglary	15.2	74.0	54.2	56.1
Larceny/theft	9.7	74.6	55.7	60.0
Motor vehicle theft	3.5	78.8	54.3	59.1
Arson	0.5	57.7	41.0	38.7
Fraud	2.9	66.3	42.1	45.4
Stolen property	1.4	77.4	57.2	62.1
Other property	0.3	71.1	47.6	40.0
Drug Offenses	32.6	66.7	47.0	49.2
Possession	7.5	67.5	46.6	42.6
Trafficking	20.2	64.2	44.0	46.1
Other/unspecified	4.9	75.5	60.5	71.8
Public-order Offenses	9.7	62.2	42.0	48.0
Weapons	3.1	70.2	46.6	55.5
Driving under the influence	3.3	51.5	31.7	43.7

[Continued]

Recidivism Rates of State Prisoners by Criminal Offense for Which Prisoner Has Served Time, 1994

[Continued]

Offense	% of All Released Prisoners	Percent of Released Prisoners Who, Within 3 Years, Were:		
		Rearrest	Recon-viction	Return to Prison
Other public-order	3.3	65.1	48.0	43.6
Other Offenses	1.7	64.7	42.1	66.9

Source: U.S. Bureau of Justice Statistics, *Recidivism of risoners Released in 1994*, June 2002, p. 8.

Chapter 10
THE LEGAL SYSTEM

Justice System Employment and Arrest Trends

Arrests per 100,000 inhabitants. NA Not reported.

Year	State and Local Justice System Empl.	Total Crime Index[1]	Violent Crime[2]	Property Crime[3]	Drug Arrests
1971		897.1	175.8	721.4	236.9
1972		881.5	186.5	695.0	251.2
1973		883.4	187.3	696.1	296.7
1974		1,098.0	219.7	878.3	300.2
1975		1,059.6	206.7	852.9	278.4
1976		1,016.8	193.1	823.7	279.5
1977		1,039.4	202.7	836.7	291.8
1978		1,047.6	215.5	832.2	282.4
1979		1,057.2	212.5	844.7	248.2
1980		1,055.8	214.4	841.4	255.6
1981		1,070.0	216.8	853.2	244.0
1982	1,175,787	1,148.9	236.9	912.0	291.8
1983	1,209,989	1,071.9	221.1	850.8	282.9
1984	1,266,428	1,019.8	212.5	807.3	300.3
1985	1,312,065	1,046.5	212.4	834.0	341.0
1986	1,351,695	1,091.8	234.5	857.3	343.1
1987	1,403,655	1,120.1	233.8	886.4	386.8
1988	1,453,267	1,123.5	243.8	879.7	472.4
1989	1,502,349	1,173.1	268.6	904.4	551.6
1990	1,570,614	1,203.2	290.7	912.5	436.7
1991	1,610,465	1,198.8	293.0	905.8	400.5
1992	1,635,502	1,162.4	300.5	861.9	418.1
1993	1,664,167	1,131.6	302.9	828.8	436.9
1994	1,740,715	1,148.4	310.7	837.7	519.1
1995	1,816,632	1,140.3	315.2	825.0	561.6
1996	1,901,453	1,081.8	288.6	793.2	567.8
1997	NA	1,042.9	273.6	769.3	591.3
1998	1,948,100	954.0	258.8	695.2	576.9

[Continued]

Justice System Employment and Arrest Trends
[Continued]

Year	State and Local Justice System Empl.	Total Crime Index[1]	Violent Crime[2]	Property Crime[3]	Drug Arrests
1999	1,998,308	880.0	244.5	635.5	561.8
2000		821.8	228.2	593.6	572.1

Source: Sourcebook of Criminal Justice Statistics Online, Section 1, Table 1.19, and Section 4, Table 4.2, http://www.albany.edu/sourcebook/1995/tost_4.html#4_a. *Notes:* 1. Includes arson beginning in 1979. 2. Violent crimes are offenses of murder and nonnegligent manslaughter, forcible rape, robbery, and aggravated assault. 3. Property crimes are offenses of burglary, larceny/theft, motor vehicle theft, and arson.

Crimes Cleared by Arrest

Percent of Crime Index offenses cleared by an arrest in 2000. 11,369 agencies reported.

	Crime Index Total	Violent Crime	Property Crime	Murder/Non-Negligent Manslaughter	Forcible Rape	Robbery	Aggravated Assault	Burglary	Larceny/ Theft	Motor Vehicle Theft	Arson
Total	9,366,936	1,131,923	8,235,013	12,291	72,453	319,078	728,101	1,669,364	5,598,789	966,860	73,172
% Cleared by Arrest	20.5	47.5	16.7	63.1	46.9	25.7	56.9	13.4	18.2	14.1	16

Source: FBI, *Uniform Crime Reports, 2000*, Section IV, Table 25, http://www.fbi.gov/ucr/00cius.htm.

Between Arrest and Case Disposition

Felony defendants released before or detained until case disposition (large urban counties): 1992-1998.

Year	Number of Defendants	Percent Released	Percent Detained
1992	51,002	63	37
1994	50,241	62	38
1996	51,234	63	37
1998	54,458	64	36

Source: U.S. Department of Justice, *Felony Defendants in Large Urban Counties, 1992, 1994, 1996, 1998*, http://www.ojp.usdoj.gov/bjs/pretrial.htm.

Waiting for Justice to Be Served

Median number of days between arrest and sentencing for felony cases disposed by state courts: 1992-1998. Grand total includes all cases, whether or not conviction type was known.

| Most Serious Conviction Offense | Total | Number of Days Between Arrest and Sentencing for Cases Disposed by | | | |
| | | Trial | | | Guilty Plea |
		Total	Jury	Bench	
All Offenses					
1992	138	184	231	171	139
1994	143	201	251	184	136
1996	149	211	293	154	164
1998	149	278	300	256	153
Percent Change	8	51	30	50	10
Violent Offenses					
1992	172	234	268	192	160
1994	174	228	260	207	163
1996	184	263	315	181	188
1998	189	320	333	290	184
Percent Change	10	37	24	51	15
Property Offenses					
1992	125	152	167	164	123
1994	132	177	239	173	128
1996	142	182	281	154	156
1998	144	245	263	222	148
Percent Change	15	61	57	35	20
Drug Offenses					
1992	146	171	214	173	141
1994	138	189	232	183	133
1996	136	202	264	155	159
1998	136	264	281	259	144
Percent Change	-7	54	31	50	2
Drug Possession					
1992	134	155	169	172	142
1994	123	167	278	169	118
1996	129	170	262	142	163
1998	122	245	231	259	142
Percent Change	-9	58	37	51	0
Drug Trafficking					
1992	140	192	220	182	141
1994	149	206	232	196	142
1996	139	227	264	168	157
1998	143	273	287	261	145
Percent Change	2	42	30	43	3
Weapons Offenses					
1992	148	192	232	164	151
1994	143	202	207	173	136
1996	148	232	300	163	161
1998	145	249	265	249	152

[Continued]

Waiting for Justice to Be Served

[Continued]

Most Serious Conviction Offense	Total	Number of Days Between Arrest and Sentencing for Cases Disposed by			Guilty Plea
		Trial			
		Total	Jury	Bench	
Percent Change	-2	30	14	52	0.7
Other Offenses[1]					
1992	138	147	230	128	140
1994	132	208	240	212	127
1996	157	162	255	128	167
1998	145	250	276	227	152
Percent Change	5	70	20	77	9

Source: U.S. Department of Justice, Bureau of Justice Statistics, *Felony Sentences in State Courts*, various years; http://www.ojp.usdoj.gov/bjs/. *Notes:* 1. Composed of nonviolent offenses such as receiving stolen property and vandalism.

Public Perceptions of Insanity Defense

Wyoming citizens' estimates of the percentage of defendants who entered a Not Guilty by Reason of Insanity (NGRI) defense, by occupation.

Occupation	Estimate
State Hospital Aides	57%
Community Residents	43%
College Students	37%
Police Officers	22%
Legislators	20%
Mental Health Center Professionals	17%
State Hospital Professionals	13%

Source: Data appear in a footnote in Daniel J. Nusbaum, "The craziest reform of them all: a critical analysis of the constitutional implications of abolishing the insanity defense," *Cornell Law Review*, Sept 2002 v87 i6 p1509(64). Data are attributed in the footnote (page 1512) to George L. Blau and Richard A. Pasewark, "Statutory Changes and the Insanity Defense: Seeking the Perfect Insane Person," 18 *Law & Psychol. Rev.* 679, 69 (1994).

Indigent Defense

Representation of felons in 75 largest counties in 1996. Public defender programs are public or private nonprofit organizations with salaried staffs. In assigned counsel systems, courts appoint willing private attorneys from a list of those available. Contract attorneys agree with governmental units to provide services for a specified period and fee.

Type of Counsel	% of Felons
Public Defender	68.3%
Assigned Counsel	13.7%
Private Attorney	17.6%
Self/Other	0.4%

Source: Harlow, Caroline Wolf, Ph.D., *Defense Counsel in Criminal Cases*, Bureau of Justice Statistics Special Report, NCJ 179023, November 2000.

The Cost of Defending the Indigent

Expenditures for indigent defense: 1979-1990. In thousands of dollars, for public defense. Public defense includes legal counsel and representation in either criminal or civil proceedings as provided by public defenders and other government programs. Detail may not add to total because of rounding. Expenditures presented are not adjusted for inflation.

	1979	1985	1988	1990
Total	357,030	711,243	1,012,831	1,336,266
State	127,892	297,555	427,788	603,674
Local	239,159	433,068	617,910	788,437
Counties	196,296	350,603	480,515	605,708
Municipalities	44,638	85,782	142,946	189,362

Source: DeFrances, Carol J., Ph.D., et al., *Indigent Defense Services in Large Counties, 1999,* BJS, NCJ 184932, November 2000.

Hate Crimes

Number of hate crimes and the motivations for them, as reported to the FBI: 1991-2000. NA Not available. % of pop represented is the percentage of the population that reporting law-enforcement agencies represent.

	1991	1992	1993	1994	1995	1996	1997	1998	1999	2000
Participating Agencies	2,771	6,181	6,551	7,356	9,584	11,355	11,211	10,730	12,122	11,690
Total Incidents Reported	4,558	6,623	7,587	5,932	7,947	8,759	8,049	7,755	7,876	8,063
Motivation										
Racial Bias	2,963	4,025	4,732	3,545	4,831	5,396	4,710	4,321	4,295	4,337
Religious Bias	917	1,162	1,298	1,062	1,277	1,401	1,385	1,390	1,411	1,472
Ethnicity	450	669	697	638	814	940	836	754	829	911
Sexual Orientation	425	767	860	685	1,019	1,016	1,102	1,260	1,317	1,299
Number of States (including D.C.)	32	42	47	44	46	50	49	47	49	49
% of Pop. Represented	NA	51	58	58	75	84	85	79	85	84.2

Source: FBI, "Hate Crime Statistics," *Uniform Crime Reports,* 1992-2000.

KEYWORD INDEX

This index allows users to locate all subjects, issues, government agencies, companies, programs, associations, schools, educational institutions, books, reports, personal names, and locations cited in *Social Trends & Indicators USA: Crime & Justice*. Page references do not necessarily identify the page on which a topic begins. In the cases where the topic spans two or more pages, page numbers point to where the index term appears-which may be the second or subsequent page on the topic. Cross-references have been added to index citations for ease in locating related topics.

CUMULATIVE KEYWORD INDEX

This index allows users to locate all subjects, issues, government agencies, companies, programs, associations, schools, educational institutions, books, reports, personal names, and locations cited in *Social Trends & Indicators USA: Work & Leisure*; *Social Trends & Indicators USA: Community & Education*; *Social Trends & Indicators USA: Health & Sickness*; and *Social Trends & Indicators USA: Crime & Justice*. Page references do not necessarily identify the page on which a topic begins. In cases where the topic spans two or more pages, page numbers point to where the index term appears-which may be the second or subsequent page on the topic. Cross-references have been added to index citations for ease in locating related topics.

African-Americans continued:
— *See also:* Blacks
— arrests, p. IV:53
— births, pp. II:6, II:321*t*
— causes of death, pp. III:8, III:31, III:33, III:35-36, III:43
— diseases, pp. III:14, III:97
— employment, p. I:16
— families, pp. II:53, II:62
— homicides, pp. IV:217-218
— hospital closings, p. III:370
— income, p. II:21
— infant mortality, pp. II:21, III:313
— law enforcement personnel, p. IV:204
— life expectancy, p. II:20
— population, pp. II:24, II:70-71, II:345*t*
— population mobility, p. II:39
— risk behaviors, p. III:17
— single-parent households, p. II:61
— specialized museums, p. I:229
— Total Fertility Rates, p. II:8
African wastewater treatment, p. III:326
Age-based discrimination, pp. I:161, I:163, I:167
Age groups
— abortion rates, p. III:307
— book purchases, p. I:220
— death rates, 1917-1918, p. II:17
— depression, p. III:64
— disabled population, p. III:226
— employment, pp. I:20, III:296
— first marriages, p. II:338*t*
— high-school completion rates, p. I:39
— illegal labor, pp. I:43, I:301*t*
— Internet use, pp. I:272-273, I:378*t*
— mathematics proficiency, p. II:161
— population, p. I:345*t*
— psychiatric treatment, p. III:262
— reading proficiency, p. II:159
— retirement, pp. I:139, I:344*t*
— sexual activity, p. III:270
— suicides, p. III:261
— volunteering, pp. I:239-240, I:370*t*
— voter turnout, p. II:104
— work hours, p. I:44
Agency for Healthcare Research and Quality, p. III:361
Aggravated assaults, p. IV:135
— by sex, pp. IV:36, IV:38
— juveniles arrested, pp. IV:133, IV:137-138
— recidivism, p. IV:260
— reported, p. IV:5
— victimization, p. IV:31
Aging population, p. III:485*t*
— *See also:* Elderly population
— *See also:* Senior citizens
— causes of disability, p. III:228
— health problems, pp. III:203-204
— living arrangements, pp. III:191-192
— Medicaid, p. III:386
— perceptions of quality of life, pp. III:205-206
Agoraphobia, pp. III:252-253

Agriculture, pp. II:256-257, II:262
— child labor, p. I:46
— employment, pp. I:3-4, I:291*t*
— workplace injuries, p. I:156
The AGS Foundation for Health in Aging, p. III:344
Aides
— *See:* personal home care aides
AIDS
— attendant diseases, pp. III:3, III:61, III:333
— by race/ethnicity, pp. III:52, III:54
— causes of death, pp. III:53, III:131, III:440*t*
— Centers for Disease Control and Prevention (CDC), p. III:287
— cyclical patterns, p. III:51
— disability benefits, p. III:243
— funding, pp. III:400-402
— new cases, p. III:506*t*
— origins, pp. III:62, III:95
— total occurrences reported, pp. III:444*t*
— treatment, p. III:286
AIDS Coalition to Unleash Power
— *See:* ACT UP
Air pollution, pp. III:316-320, III:518*t*
Air Rage: Crisis in the Skies, p. III:140
Aircraft hijacking, p. IV:245
Aircraft pilots and flight engineers, pp. I:27-28
— *See also:* airline pilots
Airline passenger screening, pp. IV:232-234, IV:367*t*
Airline pilots, pp. I:22, I:296*t*
— *See also:* aircraft pilots and flight engineers
Airplane crashes, p. III:4
al-Rahman, Abd, p. IV:184
Alabama, pp. II:246, IV:284, III:370
Alaska, pp. IV:121, II:217, III:409
Alaska Natives, pp. IV:159-160
— diseases, pp. III:288-289
— educational attainment, pp. II:258-259, II:287-290
— low birth weight, p. III:40
— physicians, p. III:337
— population, pp. II:70-72
— risk behaviors, p. III:136
Albuterol, p. III:167
Alcohol
— adults, p. III:121
— cirrhosis, pp. III:6, III:108
— mouth cancer, p. III:161
— North America, p. III:64
— teenagers, pp. III:117-118
Alcohol consumption, pp. III:108, IV:173, IV:352*t*
Alcohol-related arrests, pp. IV:112, IV:334*t*
Alcohol-related crimes, p. IV:334*t*
— crime rate, p. IV:10
— Prohibition era, p. IV:29
— public-order crimes, pp. IV:101, IV:104, IV:111-112
— rate fluctuation, p. IV:174
Alcohol-related deaths, pp. IV:115-116, III:125, III:131, IV:174, IV:335*t*
Aleuts, p. II:24
All Handicapped Children Act, p. II:299
Allegra, p. III:178

Baby Boom generation continued:
— causes of death, pp. III:69-70
— dependency ratio, p. I:141
— elderly population, p. I:53
— employment, p. I:19
— fertility rates, pp. III:293-294
— home purchases, p. I:195
— income, p. I:77
— Medicare, pp. III:380, III:382
— psychiatric treatment, p. III:262
— reproduction, p. III:291
— retirement, pp. I:21-23, I:24, I:27
— television programs, p. III:222
Bach, Robert, p. I:50
Bachelor's degrees, pp. III:42, I:264-265, II:401*t*
— by race/ethnicity and residency, pp. II:287-288
— by sex, p. II:283
— by specialization, p. II:284
— earnings, p. II:295
— income, p. I:94
— job openings, p. I:61
— student loans, p. II:275
Back problems, pp. III:227-228
Back to Basics Movement, pp. II:167, II:204-205
Bacteria, pp. III:315, III:323
— antibiotics, pp. III:329-330
— causes of death, p. III:2
— food-borne illnesses, pp. III:111-112
— sepsis, p. III:10
— VRE, p. III:330
Baggage screeners, pp. IV:232-233
Baha'i, pp. II:134-135, II:140-141, I:252-253
Balanced Budget Act, p. III:382
Balanced Budget Refinement Act, p. III:383
Ballet, p. I:216
Balloon angioplasty, pp. III:25, III:151
Bangladesh, p. III:332
Banking, p. I:273
Bankruptcy, p. IV:85
Baptists, pp. II:130-132, II:135
Barbers, p. I:54
Barbiturates, p. IV:11
Baseball, p. I:202
Basketball, pp. I:202, I:208-209
Bates, Brian, p. IV:125
Baxter, Clifford, p. IV:85
Bayer Corporation, pp. III:392-393
Beginning to Read, p. II:201
Behavioral Risk Factor Surveillance System, p. III:205
Belarus, p. II:163
Belgium, pp. II:163-165
Benefits, pp. I:127, I:242, I:341*t*
Bergen, Candice, p. II:62
Best Practices for Comprehensive Tobacco Control Programs, p. III:408
Bethesda Oak (OH), pp. III:370-371
Bias-related crimes, p. IV:206
— *See also:* Hate crimes
Bicycling, p. I:200

Bilingual education, p. II:307
Binge eating, pp. III:249, III:251, III:256
Biological sciences, p. II:284
Bioterrorism, pp. III:88, III:392-393
Bipolar disorder, pp. III:247-248, III:251-252, III:254
Birth control, pp. III:102, III:104, III:294
Birth defects, pp. III:310-311
Birth weight, low
— *See:* Low birth weight
Births, pp. II:315*t*
— Baby Boom generation, p. II:2
— by age group, pp. III:292, II:322*t*
— by race/ethnicity, pp. II:6, II:10, II:319*t*
— selected years, p. III:306
Black Liberation Army, p. IV:181
Black-white death rate ratio, p. II:327*t*
Black, Roy, p. IV:279
Blacks
— *See also:* African-Americans
— abortions, pp. II:10, II:12-13, II:321*t*
— activities of daily living, p. III:204
— births, pp. II:10, III:39, I:40, II:319*t*
— breastfeeding, p. III:41
— cancer survival rates, pp. III:156-158
— causes of death, pp. III:8-9, II:21
— childbirth, p. III:23
— computer learning opportunities, p. II:263
— crib death, pp. III:45-46
— deaths, pp. III:15, III:18, II:21
— diseases, pp. III:14, III:18, III:28, III:52, III:54, II:70-71, III:288-289
— drug arrests, pp. IV:161, IV:164
— drug convictions, p. IV:164
— drug sentences, pp. IV:165-166
— drug use, pp. IV:53, III:126-127, IV:159-160
— earnings, p. I:71
— educational attainment - college, pp. II:151-153, II:287-290
— educational attainment - high school, p. I:39
— educational attainment - high school and more, pp. I:112, I:118-119
— educational attainment - murders, p. IV:53
— educational attainment - vocational education, pp. II:258-259
— employment, pp. I:16, I:35-37, I:41, I:67-68
— families, p. I:38
— homicides, pp. IV:52-53
— housing, p. II:35
— immunizations, p. III:99
— income, pp. I:82-83
— Internet use, pp. I:270-271
— interracial marriages, pp. II:54-55
— juveniles arrested, pp. IV:137-138
— law enforcement personnel, p. IV:203
— learning disabilities, p. III:66
— life expectancy, pp. III:47-48, III:403-404
— literacy, pp. II:154, II:159
— low birth weight, pp. III:44, III:308-309
— mammograms, p. III:18
— marriages, pp. II:52-53
— maternal mortality, pp. II:21, III:22-23, II:24, II:25-27, III:30,

California *continued:*
— nursing legislation, p. III:349
— prison population, p. IV:248
— racial profiling, p. IV:223
— sex offender registry, p. IV:122
— vacation time, p. I:190
— youth gangs, p. IV:138
California Business Roundtable, p. II:262
California Department of Developmental Services, p. III:258
California Highway Patrol, pp. IV:200, IV:202, IV:223
California Institute of Technology, p. II:280
California Obesity Prevention Initiative, p. III:407
Calorie Control Council, p. III:115
Calories, pp. III:89-90
CAM
— *See:* Complementary and alternative medicine
Cambodia, p. III:332
Cambodian population, p. II:74
Camel cigarettes, p. III:138
Campylobacter infections, p. III:111
Canada, pp. I:47, IV:125, II:254, III:334
— literacy, p. II:163
— mathematics class characteristics, p. II:165
— mathematics proficiency, p. II:164
— mathematics scores, TIMSS, p. II:254
Cancer, pp. III:3, III:5, II:18
— *See also:* Malignancies
— *See also:* Melanomas
— *See also:* Neoplasms
— *See also:* Specific cancers
— by race/ethnicity, p. III:18
— causes of death, pp. III:2-4, III:8-9, III:67, III:69-70, III:401
— causes of disability, p. III:227
— contributing factors, pp. III:68, III:160-161, III:328
— deaths, pp. III:446*t*
— detection, p. III:156
— digestive organs, p. III:3
— elderly population, p. III:210
— funding, pp. III:400-401
— hospice care, p. III:376
— survival rates, pp. III:19, III:156-158, III:478*t*
— treatment, p. III:159
Cannabis sativa, p. IV:153
— *See:* Marijuana
Capital punishment
— *See:* Death penalty
Capitol Police, pp. IV:226-227
Car-rental firms, p. I:196
Carbon monoxide (CO), pp. III:316, III:318
Cardiac catheterization, p. III:151
Cardiovascular disease, pp. III:2, III:150, III:168, III:210, III:310, III:341, III:405
— *See also:* heart disease
Caribbean wastewater treatment, p. III:326
Carpal Tunnel Syndrome, pp. I:155, III:236
Carrots, p. III:87
Cars, p. I:190
Case resolutions, pp. I:163, I:167-168, I:353*t*
Cashiers, pp. I:61-62

CAT
— *See:* Computerized axial tomography
Catheterization, cardiac
— *See:* Cardiac catheterization
Catholic Church, p. IV:56
Catholic Family and Human Rights Institute, p. IV:125
Catholic hospitals, pp. III:366-367
Catholics, pp. II:110, II:130-133, II:135
Catholics for a Free Choice, pp. III:366-367
Cats, p. I:191
Caucasians, pp. II:24-25
Causes of death
— accidents, pp. III:1-2, III:4, III:32
— alcohol, pp. III:125, III:131
— Baby Boom generation, pp. III:69-70
— black-white death ratio, p. II:21
— by race/ethnicity, pp. III:8-9, III:31
— by sex, pp. III:6-7, III:12, III:32-34, III:43
— diseases, pp. III:3, III:53, III:67-72, III:475*t*
— elderly population, p. III:448*t*
— government health funding, p. III:401
— heart failure, pp. III:3, III:12
— homicides, pp. III:4, III:8-9, III:36-38, III:131
— immunizations, p. III:99
— leading causes by year, pp. III:421*t*
— leading causes, by sex, pp. III:6-7, III:13, III:24-30
— perinatal conditions, p. III:9
— research funding, p. III:401
— risk behaviors, pp. III:4, III:125, III:131
— shootings, p. III:4
— suicides, pp. III:4, III:6, III:8, III:34-36, III:131
Causes of disability, pp. III:227-228
CD4 lymphocyte, p. III:53
CDC
— *See:* Centers for Disease Control
Celebrex, pp. III:178, III:275
Celera Genomics, p. III:105
Cendant Corp., p. IV:84
Center for Budget and Policy Priorities, p. III:387
Center for Nutrition Policy and Promotion, pp. II:66-67
Centers for Disease Control, pp. III:16, III:36, III:43, III:49, III:66, III:95, III:97-99, IV:190
— abortions, p. III:306
— active community environments, pp. III:405-406
— antibiotics, pp. III:329, III:331
— *Best Practices for Comprehensive Tobacco Control, Programs*, p. III:408
— bioterrorism, pp. III:392-393
— birth defects, p. III:310
— diseases, pp. III:109, III:161, III:287-288
— food poisoning, pp. III:111-112
— infant mortality, p. III:310
— maternal mortality, p. III:23
— risk behaviors, pp. III:135, III:147
— sexual activity of teenagers, p. III:284
Centers for Medicare and Medicaid Services, p. III:382
Central America, p. I:47
Central cities, pp. II:27-28
Central Intelligence Agency (CIA), pp. IV:186, IV:188-189,

Cisco Systems Inc., p. I:59
Cities, central, p. II:27
Citizens for Safe Drinking Water, p. III:328
Citizenship, p. II:349*t*
Civil liberties, p. IV:185
Civil Rights Act, p. IV:284
Civil Rights movement, p. IV:286
Civil rights violations, pp. IV:108-110
Civil Unions Law, p. II:65
Civilian employment, p. I:13
Claritin, pp. III:167, III:178, III:276
Class Size Reduction Program, pp. II:195-197
Classical music, p. I:218
Clean Air Act, p. III:316
Clean Water Act, pp. III:315, III:321
Clergy, p. II:143
Cleveland Scholarship and Tutoring Program, p. II:240
Clinical laboratory technologists, pp. III:359-360
Clinical nurse specialists, p. III:351
Clinton administration, pp. IV:95, III:106, IV:128, I:166
A Clockwork Orange, p. I:231
Clothing, pp. II:66-67
Club drugs, pp. III:120, IV:154
Clubs, p. I:185
CO
— *See:* Carbon Monoxide
— *See:* Carbon monoxide (CO)
Coaches' salaries, pp. I:206-207
Coalition Against Insurance Fraud, p. IV:94
Coalition for the Prevention of Economic Crime, p. IV:91
Coast Guard Law Enforcement Detachments, p. IV:24
Coca-Cola, p. II:310
Cocaine, p. IV:147
— arrests, p. IV:11
— emergency room visits, p. III:124
— illicit substance use, adults, p. III:121
— lifetime use reported, pp. IV:151-152
— school-based health centers, p. III:104
— trafficking, pp. IV:167-168
— use by race/ethnicity, pp. III:126-127
— use by teenagers, pp. III:117-119
— youth gangs, p. IV:34
Code Red, p. I:280
Coffee consumption, p. III:139
Cohabitation, pp. II:51, II:57-58, II:338*t*
Collagen injections, pp. III:277-279
Collectibles, p. I:286
College, p. II:151
College affordability, pp. II:275-276
College athletics, p. I:363*t*
College Board, pp. II:172, II:293, II:295
College completion rates, p. I:300*t*
College costs, pp. II:271-273, II:275, II:395*t*
College degrees, pp. I:24, I:57, I:61, I:114-116
College education, pp. I:51, I:67, I:94, I:264-265
College enrollment, pp. II:150-151
College preparatory curricula, pp. II:261-262
College sports, pp. I:199, I:206, I:208
Colonoscopy, p. III:31

Colorado, pp. II:63-64
Colorectal cancer, pp. III:67-68, III:430*t*
— causes of death, p. III:30
— obesity, p. III:405
— screening, pp. III:31, III:211
— survival rates, pp. III:156, III:158
Columbia University, p. II:294
Columbine High School, p. II:243
Commerce, p. I:280
Commercial Alert, p. II:265
Commercial participant amusements, p. I:185
Commercialized vice, p. IV:136
Commission on Pornography, p. III:280
Common Good Fear of Litigation Study, p. III:417
Communications, p. II:284
Communications Industry Forecast, p. I:268
Community foundations, pp. I:242, I:245-246
Community health centers, pp. III:100-101, III:436*t*
Community Learning Centers, pp. II:226-227
Community Protection Act (Washington state), p. IV:121
Community water systems, pp. III:326-327, III:519*t*
Commuting, pp. I:135, III:140
Complementary and alternative medicine (CAM), pp. III:74, III:82
Compliance officers, p. I:45
Comprehensive Drug Abuse and Control Act, pp. IV:12, IV:149
Computed tomography, p. III:355
Computer cracker, p. I:281
Computer hacking, pp. IV:92, I:280-281, I:379*t*
Computer learning opportunities, pp. II:263, II:393*t*
Computer products, p. I:185
Computer-related occupations, pp. I:32, I:52, I:54-55, I:58-59, I:61-62, II:296
Computer systems administrators
— *See:* Network and computer systems administrators
Computer use, p. II:264
Computer viruses, p. I:280
Computer worms, p. I:280
Computerized axial tomography, p. III:152
— *See also:* CAT scans
Computerized axial tomography (CAT) scans, p. III:152
Computerized Axial Tomography (CAT) scans, p. III:155
Computers, p. I:286
Concerts, p. I:216
The Condition of America's Schools: 1999, p. II:199
Condoms, pp. II:15, III:104, III:304-305
Congenital malformations, pp. III:10, III:236, III:312
Congregationals, pp. II:132-135, II:144
Congressional Budget Office, p. III:387
Connecticut, pp. II:217, III:338, III:373-374
Conservatives, p. II:114
Construction, p. II:32
— employment, p. I:34
— injuries in the workplace, p. I:156
— occupational fatalities, p. I:151
— productivity, pp. I:104-107, I:329*t*
Consumer Research Study on Book Purchasing, p. I:220
ConsumerSentinel, p. IV:82
Continuing care retirement communities, p. III:194

Contraceptive practices, pp. II:14-15, III:161, III:304-305, II:323*t*

Contracts, p. I:14

Contusions, p. I:155

Convict labor, pp. IV:254-255

Conyers, Jr., John, p. IV:287

Cook County (IL), pp. IV:266-267

Copyright infringement, pp. IV:95-97, IV:328*t*

Cornell University, pp. III:195, II:294

Coronary bypass, p. III:25

Corporate profits, pp. I:122, I:124, I:339*t*

Correctional population, pp. IV:19-20, IV:299*t*

Corrections Corporation of America (CCA), pp. IV:251-252

Corrections system employment, pp. IV:21-22

Corrections system expenditures, pp. IV:249-250, IV:373*t*

Cosmetic surgery, pp. III:179, III:277-279, III:504*t*

Cough syrup, p. III:130

Coughlin, Lt. Paula, p. I:166

Council on Graduate Medical Education, p. III:344

Counterfeiting, pp. IV:88-89, IV:99-100, IV:105, IV:108, IV:327*t*

County mental hospitals, p. III:264

Court trials, pp. IV:273-274

Crack cocaine, pp. IV:151, IV:162

Cream products, p. III:83

Creatine, p. III:130

Creative writing, pp. I:218-219

Creditcards.com, p. IV:91

Creek Indian tribe, pp. II:72-73

Creole, French
— *See:* French Creole

Crib death, pp. III:45-46
— *See also:* Sudden Infant Death Syndrome (SIDS)

Crime Act, p. IV:206

Crime and Punishment: Women in Prison, p. IV:243

Crime control costs, pp. IV:23-24

Crime Index, pp. IV:3, IV:6, IV:14

Crime prevention, p. IV:206

Crime rate
— arrests, pp. IV:102, IV:149, IV:175-176, IV:354*t*
— history, p. IV:15
— justice system employment, p. IV:21

Crimes Against Children, p. IV:139

Crimes against the family, p. IV:136

Crimes cleared by arrest, p. IV:379*t*

Crimes in schools, pp. II:245, II:387*t*

Croatia, p. II:163

Crocheting, p. I:218

Cross-country sports, pp. I:208-209

Cruises, p. I:196

Crystal Cathedral, p. II:145

Cuba, p. II:163

Culture and humanities
— *See also:* arts, culture, and humanities p. I:242

Curfew violations, pp. IV:106-107, IV:136

Curriculum specialization, p. II:261

Cuts, p. I:155

Cyberchurches, p. II:145

Cyberstalking, p. IV:120

Czech Republic, pp. II:163-165, I:187

Dance, pp. I:218-219

Danish, pp. II:76-77

D.A.R.E.
— *See:* Drug Abuse Resistance Education

Database administrators, p. I:52

Date-rape drugs, pp. IV:56, IV:154
— *See also:* Rohypnol

Dating online, pp. I:284-285

DAWN
— *See:* Drug Abuse Warning Network

DCBE
— *See:* Double-Contrast Barium Enema
— *See:* Double-contrast barium enema (DCBE)

DDT, p. III:323

Deaconess-Waltham Hospital (MA), p. III:370

Dead Rabbits, p. IV:43

Deafness, pp. III:227, III:229, II:298

Death penalty, pp. IV:245-246

Death row inmates, pp. IV:244, IV:246, IV:371*t*

Death With Dignity Law, p. III:216

Deaths
— by cause, pp. III:1-2
— by race/ethnicity, p. II:21
— diseases, pp. III:15, III:18, III:423*t*
— influenza epidemic, p. II:17
— life expectancy, pp. II:324*t*
— police officers, pp. IV:210-212, IV:217-218, IV:361*t*
— schools, p. II:243
— terrorism, pp. IV:190-191, IV:358*t*

Defense Department, pp. I:13, I:293*t*

Defense research and development, p. III:398

Degree completion, pp. I:260-262, I:265

Degrees conferred, pp. I:58, II:283, I:296*t* II:399*t*

Degrees conferred, professional
— *See:* professional degrees conferred

Deism, pp. II:134-135, I:252-253

Delaware, pp. II:64, II:187, II:217

Dementia, pp. III:71, III:198, III:204, III:243

Democratic Republic of the Congo, pp. III:332, III:334

Democrats, p. II:98

Denmark, p. IV:125

Dental care benefits, pp. III:103, I:131, I:133, III:210

Dentists, pp. III:79, IV:93, II:286, II:290

Department of Education, pp. IV:290, II:304

Department of Health and Human Services, p. III:63

Department of Justice, pp. IV:203, IV:207, IV:270, IV:290

Department of Labor, p. I:45

Dependency ratio, pp. II:22, I:141

Depressants, p. IV:153

Depression, pp. III:445*t*
— age groups, p. III:262
— cases, pp. III:247-248
— senior citizens, p. III:204
— treatment, pp. III:63-64, III:169
— treatments, pp. III:75-76

Dermabrasion, pp. III:277-278

Desktop publishers, p. I:52

Detective supervisors
— *See:* police and detective supervisors
Detroit (MI), pp. IV:72, IV:124, IV:215
Detroit Receiving Hospital (MI), p. III:265
Developmental delay, p. II:298
Dewey, John, p. II:203
Dexedrine, p. II:303
Diabetes
— Baby Boom generation, pp. III:69-70
— cause of death, pp. III:4-5, III:8-9
— elderly population, p. III:203
— funding, p. III:401
— obesity, p. III:405
— prevalence, pp. III:426t
— women, pp. III:12-14, III:21
Diagnostic and Statistical Manual of Mental Disorders, p. III:115, III:170, III:236, III:251, III:254-255
Diagnostic procedures, pp. III:152-154, III:341
Diallo, Amadou, p. IV:204
Diaphragms, pp. II:15, III:304-305
Diet, pp. III:108, III:115
— Atkins, Dr., p. III:90
— cancers, p. III:161
— causes of disability, p. III:228
— pills, p. III:130
— recommended intake, pp. III:20-21, III:29
— supplements, p. III:75
Dietary Guidelines for Americans, p. III:114
Dietary Supplement Health and Education Act, p. III:76
Dieter, Richard C., p. IV:244
Digestive system diseases, pp. III:3, III:150, III:155, III:236, III:310
Digital rectal exam (DRE), p. III:31
Digital television sets, p. I:227
Dining at home, p. I:180
Dining out, pp. III:109, I:187, I:358t
Diphtheria, pp. III:55-56, III:94-95
Diptheria, Tetanus, and Pertussis (DTP), p. III:96
Direct Instruction Movement, p. II:202
Disability-based discrimination, pp. I:161, I:167
Disability benefits, pp. III:235-239, III:241, III:243, III:495t
Disability insurance, p. I:128
Disability payments, p. I:29
Disabled population, pp. III:224-227, III:492t
— Americans with Disabilities Act, p. III:223
— children, pp. III:229, II:298
— educational attainment, pp. III:240-242
— Medicaid, p. III:386
— special education programs, pp. III:230-231
— workforce population, pp. III:233-234, III:244-245
Discrimination cases
— by category, pp. I:161, I:163
— merit resolutions, pp. I:167-169, I:352t
— workplace, pp. I:149, I:159
Diseases, p. III:49
— *See also:* Infectious diseases
Disorderly conduct, pp. IV:105, IV:112
Disposable income, pp. I:347t
Distance education, pp. II:291-292, II:404t

District of Columbia, pp. II:217, IV:248, III:338, III:369-370
Dividend income
— *See:* interest and dividend income
Diving, pp. I:208-209
Divorced parents, p. II:59
Divorces, pp. II:48-49, II:335t
DNA testing, p. IV:245
Doctoral degrees conferred, pp. I:94, II:285, II:289-290, II:403t 404t
Doctors of Medicine, pp. IV:93, III:210, II:277-278, III:336, III:340-341
— *See also:* Physicians
Doctors, virtual
— *See:* Telemedicine
Dogs, p. I:191
Domestic abuse, pp. IV:106-107
Domestic partners, pp. II:120, I:136, II:357t
Domestic violence, pp. IV:10, IV:47-49, IV:206
Dominican Republic, pp. III:42, I:47
Double-contrast barium enema (DCBE), p. III:31
Down's Syndrome, p. III:328
Dragonball, p. I:283
Drawing, p. I:218
DRE
— *See:* Digital Rectal Exam
— *See:* Digital rectal exam (DRE)
Drinking (alcohol), p. III:104
Drinking water, pp. III:326-328
Drion, Hulb, p. III:218
Driving under the influence (DUI), pp. IV:112-114
Drope v Missouri, p. IV:277
Drownings, pp. III:4, II:18
Drug abuse, pp. IV:12, III:108, III:128-131
Drug Abuse Resistance Education
— *See:* D.A.R.E.
Drug Abuse Resistance Education (D.A.R.E.), pp. III:133-134
Drug Abuse Warning Network (DAWN), p. III:124
Drug-control legislation timeline, p. IV:195
Drug education, p. IV:206
Drug Enforcement Administration (DEA), pp. III:130, IV:155-156, IV:223, IV:226-227, II:303
Drug expenditures, pp. IV:349t
Drug Free Schools and Communities Act, p. IV:129
Drug-Induced Rape Prevention and Punishment Act, p. IV:56
Drug Information Service, p. III:390
Drug Price Competition and Patent Term Restoration Act, p. III:176
Drug-related arrests, pp. IV:296t 354t
— by presidential administration, pp. IV:149-150
— by race/ethnicity, pp. IV:161-163, IV:165-166
— convictions and sentencing, pp. IV:158, IV:164, IV:348t
— crime rate, pp. IV:14, IV:175-176
— effect on drug use, pp. IV:157-158
— incarcerations, p. IV:13
— juveniles, p. IV:149
— not included in crime rate, p. IV:10
— possession, p. IV:11
— sentencing, p. IV:108

Drug-related arrests continued:
— trafficking, p. IV:245
Drug-related crimes, pp. IV:101-104
— Baby Boom generation, p. IV:29
— firearms-related crimes, p. IV:40
— not included in crime rate, p. IV:10
— possession and trafficking, p. IV:109
— recidivism, p. IV:260
— state prisons population, pp. IV:236-237
Drug-resistant bacteria, p. III:329
Drug shortages, pp. III:389-391, III:530*t*
Drug treatment programs, p. IV:263
Drug use, pp. IV:157-158, IV:345*t*
— by race/ethnicity, pp. IV:159, IV:162
— by type of drug, pp. IV:169-170
DrugFreeTeenagers.com, p. III:133
Drugs distributed, pp. IV:349*t*
Drunk driving, pp. IV:101, IV:104, IV:206
— *See also:* Driving under the influence
DTP, p. III:96
— *See:* Diphtheria, Tetanus, and Pertussis (DTP)
DUI
— *See:* Driving under the influence
— *See:* Driving under the influence (DUI)
DUKE NUKEM, p. IV:145
Duke University, pp. III:81, I:171, III:237, II:294, III:345
Durable goods, p. I:102
Durex [company], pp. III:271, III:273
Durham versus United States, p. IV:276
Durkheim, Emile, p. III:35
Dutch, p. II:77
DVD players, p. I:227
Dyslexia, p. III:243
E-learning, p. II:292
E-mail, pp. I:273, I:278
E-tailers, p. I:284
Ear infections, p. III:229
Ear surgery, pp. III:150, III:277-279
Earnhardt, Dale, p. I:211
Earnings, p. III:498*t*
— by educational attainment and sex, p. II:295
— by race/ethnicity and sex, p. I:71
— by sex, pp. I:318*t*
— college degrees, pp. I:114-116
— disabilities, pp. III:244-245
— doctoral degrees, p. II:404*t*
— householders, pp. I:322*t*
— independent contractors, pp. I:71, I:307*t*
— workforce, p. I:342*t*
Earth First!, pp. IV:177, IV:181
Earth Liberation Front, p. IV:181
Eastern equine encephalitis, p. III:392
Eating habits, pp. II:211, III:466*t*
— disease prevention, p. III:90
— eating disorders, pp. III:256-257
— mental health, p. III:247
— stress, pp. III:139-140
— U.S. Surgeon General's recommendations, p. III:83
— weight, pp. III:89, III:115-116

eBay, pp. IV:100, I:282, I:380*t*
Ebola virus, pp. III:62, III:95
Echinacea, p. III:75
Eckankar, pp. II:134-135, I:252-253
Economic Growth and Tax Relief Reconciliation Act of 2001, p. II:278
Economic sectors, pp. I:3, I:104, I:291*t*
Ecstasy, pp. III:119-120, III:124, IV:147, IV:153
Ectopic pregnancy, p. III:23
Edison project, p. II:233
Education
— accountability, p. II:166
— adults, p. I:233
— attainment, pp. II:284-285
— charitable giving, pp. I:242-244
— college preparatory, p. II:262
— costs of universities, p. II:281
— elementary and secondary, pp. II:189-190
— employment, pp. I:1, I:10-12
— enrollment, p. I:292*t*
— expenditures, p. II:399*t*
— funding, pp. II:377*t*
— grants, p. II:273
— job advancement, pp. I:260-262
— volunteering, pp. I:245-246
Education administrators, pp. I:22, I:24-25, I:58-59
Education assistance, p. I:135
Education budget, p. II:384*t*
Education for All Handicapped Children Act, p. III:232
Education of the Handicapped Act, p. III:232
Education revenues, pp. II:212, II:279, II:397*t*
Educational achievements, pp. II:293, II:369*t*
Educational attainment, pp. IV:53, I:56, IV:264, I:335*t*
— adults, pp. I:264-265, I:332*t*
— Asians, pp. I:118-119
— blacks, pp. I:112, I:118-119
— breastfeeding mothers, p. III:42
— disabled population, p. III:497*t*
— earnings, pp. I:114-116, II:295, I:318*t* 405*t*
— exercise habits, p. III:92
— Hispanics, pp. I:112, I:118-119
— householders, pp. I:322*t*
— income, pp. I:94-95, II:177
— labor force, p. I:304*t*
— literacy, p. II:155
— men, p. I:94
— productivity, pp. I:110-111
— race/ethnicity, pp. II:152-153
— smoking, p. III:136
— teachers, pp. II:184-185
— volunteering, pp. I:238, I:370*t*
— whites, pp. I:112, I:118-119
— women, p. I:94
— workforce, p. I:56
Educational services, pp. I:104-105
EEOC
— *See:* Equal Employment Opportunity Commission (EEOC)
Eggs, p. III:83

Egoistic suicides, p. III:35
Eight-ball chicks, p. IV:134
El Salvador, p. I:47
E.L.A., p. II:169
Elder abuse, pp. IV:10, III:198, III:486t
— Adult Protective Services, p. III:199
— American Medical Association, p. III:197
— nursing homes, pp. III:201-202
— perpetrators, p. III:200
Elderly population, pp. II:22, II:35, IV:83, III:189, III:196, IV:241
— causes of death, p. III:448t
— diseases, p. III:210
— geographic distribution, pp. III:189-190
— health care, p. III:379
— health problems, pp. III:210-211
— immunizations, p. III:463t
— living arrangements, p. III:195
— living wills, p. III:211
— Medicare benefits, p. III:207
— prisoners, pp. I:141, IV:240
Elders, Jocelyn, p. III:107
Electrical and electronics engineers, p. I:58
Electronic commerce, pp. I:196, I:280
Electronic Communications Privacy Act, p. IV:229
Electronic fetal monitoring, p. III:302
Electronic surveillance
— See: wiretapping
Electronics, pp. I:286, I:367t
Electronics engineers
— See: electrical and electronics engineers
Electronics purchases, p. I:227
Elementary and Secondary Education Act, p. II:199
Elementary education, pp. I:11, II:189-190, I:292t
Elementary school principals, p. II:308
Elementary school teachers
— job openings, pp. I:24-25, I:58, I:61-62
— retirement, pp. I:22-23
— worker shortages, p. I:59
Eli Lilly & Co., p. III:170
Eligibility clerks, p. I:27
Elliptical motion trainers, p. I:200
Embezzlement, pp. IV:105, IV:108, IV:136
Eme Edict, p. IV:40
Emergency medical technicians (EMTs), pp. III:357-358
Emergency medicine physicians, p. III:341
Emergency room visits, pp. III:124-125, III:130, III:471t
Emory University, p. II:280
Emotional abuse of elderly, p. III:199
Emotional problems, pp. III:227, III:229-231, III:264
Emotionally disturbed children, pp. II:298-299
Emphysema, pp. III:3, III:5-6
Employee benefits, pp. I:127-130, I:133, I:135-138
Employee contributions, p. I:132
Employees, pp. I:127, I:296t
Employer costs, pp. I:127-128, I:131
Employment, pp. I:1, I:16, IV:22
— administrative support occupations (including clerical), pp. I:20, I:296t
— by industry, pp. I:1, I:3-7, I:9-14, I:20, I:34, III:141-143, III:234,

Employment continued:
    III:244-245, I:291t
— by race/ethnicity and sex, p. I:16
— disabled workers, p. III:233
— Fair Labor Standards Act, p. II:146
— high school diplomas, p. II:177
— high school education, pp. I:11-12
— justice system, p. IV:21
— literacy, pp. II:157-158
Employment-practice liability cases, p. I:170
EMTs
— See: Emergency medical technicians
— See: Emergency medical technicians (EMTs)
End-stage renal disease, p. III:380
Endocrine system, pp. III:150-151, III:236
Endometrial cancer
— See: Uterine cancer
Endoscopy, p. III:151
Endotracheal tube insertion, p. III:152
Endowments, p. II:279
Engineering occupations, pp. II:284-285, II:296
Engineering services, p. I:7
Engineers, p. I:32
— See also: computer engineers
Engineers (industrial), pp. I:22-25, I:296t
England, pp. IV:125, II:165
English language, p. II:284
English Language Arts test
— See: E.L.A.
English literature, p. II:284
English, honors
— See: Honors English
Enrollment, pp. II:222-223, II:231
— elementary education, p. I:292t
— high school sports, pp. I:204-205
— Medicaid, p. III:386
— Medicare, pp. III:490t
Enron Corp., pp. IV:85, IV:109
Entertainment, p. I:268
— See also: arts and entertainment
Environment, pp. I:242-246, III:315
Environmental crimes and sentencing, p. IV:108
Environmental interest organizations, p. IV:181
Environmental Protection Agency, pp. III:322, III:327
Epidemic-related deaths, p. III:463t
Epilepsy, pp. III:229, III:231
Episcopalians, pp. II:130-133, II:135-138
Episiotomy, p. III:151
Equal Employment Opportunity Commission (EEOC), p. I:159, I:163, I:165, I:167, I:169, I:353t
Equipment and software, p. I:102
Equipment cleaners and laborers
— See: handlers, equipment cleaners, and laborers
Erectile dysfunction treatments, pp. III:275-276
Escherichia coli infections, p. III:111
Eskimos, p. II:24
Esophageal cancer, pp. III:156, III:161
Estonia, p. II:163
Estrogen, p. II:18

Estuaries, pp. III:323, III:325
Ether, p. III:120
Ethical and Religious Directives for Catholic Health Education, p. III:367
Ethiopia, p. III:332
Ethnicity, pp. II:10, II:12-13
— See also: Race/ethnicity
— abortions, pp. II:10, II:12-13, II:321*t*
— advanced classes, p. II:259
— Bachelor's Degree recipients, pp. II:287-288
— births, pp. II:10, II:321*t*
— college enrollment, p. II:151
— computer learning opportunities, p. II:263
— doctoral degrees conferred, pp. II:289-290
— educational attainment, pp. II:152-153
— fertility rates, p. II:321*t*
— home ownership, p. II:35
— honors English classes, p. II:259
— population, pp. II:24, II:70, II:343*t*
— Population Replacement Rate, p. II:8
— reading proficiency, p. II:159
— single-parent households, p. II:61
— Total Fertility Rates, pp. II:6-8
— vocational education credits accumulated, p. II:258
Euro RSCG [company], pp. III:271, III:273
Europe, pp. II:5, II:24, I:41, III:326
Euthanasia, pp. III:214-215, III:218
— See also: Physician-assisted suicide
Evaluation and the Academy: Are We Doing the Right Thing?, pp. II:293-294
Evangelicals, pp. II:132-133, II:136-138
Excessive force, pp. IV:213-214, IV:363*t*
Executive, administrative, managerial occupations, pp. I:20, I:69-70, I:296*t*
Exercise habits, pp. III:20-21, III:92, III:161, I:203
Expenditures, pp. II:215-217
— defense of the indigent, pp. IV:283-284
— drug control, pp. IV:171-172
— fast food, p. III:109
— health care, pp. I:130, III:484*t*
— Medicare, pp. III:490*t*
— prescription drugs, p. III:484*t*
— psychotherapy, p. III:263
— restaurant, p. III:109
— worker's compensation claims, p. I:153
Expulsions from school, pp. II:245-246
Extortion and sentencing, p. IV:108
Eye treatments, pp. III:150, III:277-279
Fabricators and laborers
— See: Operators, fabricators, and laborers
Fair Labor Standards Act (FLSA), pp. I:43, II:146
Families
— income, pp. I:92, II:264
— leisure time, p. I:173
— mealtimes, p. I:180
— poverty rates, pp. I:92-93, I:315*t*
Family and Medical Leave Act (FMLA), pp. I:137-138, I:344*t*
Family entertainment concerns, p. I:231
Family households, pp. II:42, II:44, II:53, II:333*t*

Family leave, pp. I:135, I:137
Family Violence Prevention and Services Act of 1992, p. III:199
Fanning, Shawn, p. IV:95
Farmers and ranchers, p. I:54
Farmers' markets, p. III:87
Farming, forestry, and fishing occupations, pp. I:20, I:31, I:69-70, I:200, I:296*t*
Farmlands, p. III:458*t*
Fast-food expenditures, pp. III:109-110
Fast Food Nation, pp. III:110, III:112, II:310-311
Fast-pitch softball, p. I:200
Fat injections, p. III:279
Fatalistic suicides, p. III:35
Fatalities, pp. I:149, I:151, I:156
Fathers, pp. II:53, II:62, I:183
Fats, pp. III:20-21, III:83
Fecal occult blood test (FOBT), p. III:31
Federal appropriations, p. II:279
Federal Aviation Administration, p. IV:232
Federal Bureau of Investigation (FBI)
— arrests, p. IV:272
— arson, p. IV:81
— burglaries, pp. IV:73-74
— crime index, pp. IV:9-10, IV:14, IV:293*t*
— curfew violations, p. IV:107
— federal law enforcement, pp. IV:226-227
— hate crimes, pp. IV:289-290
— property crime index, p. IV:8
— terrorism, pp. IV:180-181, IV:186, IV:188-189
— *Uniform Crime Report*, pp. IV:3, IV:5
Federal Bureau of Prisons, p. IV:226
Federal Correctional Institute Morgantown, p. IV:248
Federal financial aid, pp. II:211, II:226-227, II:273-274
Federal Firearms Act, p. IV:46
Federal government employment, pp. I:1, I:9-10, I:13, I:292*t* 293*t*
Federal government funding, p. I:256
Federal government grants and contracts, pp. III:100, II:279
Federal Interstate Anti-Stalking Law, p. IV:120
Federal law enforcement personnel, pp. IV:226-227, IV:365*t*
Federal Prison Industries, p. IV:255
Federal prisons, pp. IV:237, IV:245, IV:248, IV:370*t*
Federal Protective Service, p. IV:227
Federal Trade Commission, pp. IV:82, IV:90-91
Federal Wire Act, p. IV:118
Felony defendants
— released or detained until case disposition, pp. IV:379*t*
— trial dates, pp. IV:270-274
Female-male teacher ratio, pp. II:182-183
Females, pp. III:137, III:150, III:154, III:304, II:322*t*
— See also: Women
— athletes, p. I:204
— childbearing years, p. II:21
— gangsters, p. IV:135
— larcenies, p. IV:136
— law enforcement personnel, p. IV:203
— murdered, pp. IV:314*t*
— prisoners, p. IV:17

Females continued:
— violent crimes, pp. IV:135-136
— vocational education, pp. II:258-259
Fertility rates
— birth rate, pp. III:507*t*
— by decade, pp. II:2, II:4
— by race/ethnicity, p. I:40
— European community, p. II:5
— live births, pp. II:315*t*
— population replacement rates, p. II:4
— reproductive patterns, pp. III:292-295
Fibril injections, pp. III:277-278
Fiction, p. I:220
Filipinos, pp. III:40, II:74
Finance, insurance, and real estate, pp. I:6, I:104-105, I:292*t*
Financial aid, p. II:273
Financial Executives International, pp. IV:84, I:171
Financial exploitation of elderly, p. III:199
Financial managers, pp. I:22, I:24-25, I:58
Financial restatements, p. IV:84
Finland, p. II:163
Finnish, p. II:76
Firearms, p. II:245
Firearms-related crimes, pp. IV:45, IV:47-48, IV:314*t*
Fires, p. III:4
First Church of Cyberspace, p. II:145
First-line supervisors and managers, pp. I:61-62
First marriages, p. II:338*t*
Fishing occupations
— *See:* farming, forestry, and fishing occupations
Fitness centers, p. I:135
Fitness trainers and aerobics instructors, p. I:52
Five Point Gang, p. IV:43
The Fix, p. IV:30
Flexible spending accounts, p. I:136
Flexible workplace, p. I:135
Flight engineers
— *See:* aircraft pilots and flight engineers
Florida
— gay-couple households, pp. II:63-64
— geographic distribution of elderly population, p. III:190
— hate crimes, p. IV:289
— hospital beds, p. III:369
— malpractice litigation, pp. III:415, III:417
— sex offender registries, pp. IV:121-122
— smoking prevalence, p. III:409
— vacation travel, p. I:190
— youth gangs, p. IV:138
Florida State Department of Health, p. III:392
Flour, p. III:83
Flowers, pp. I:185, I:284
FLSA
— *See:* Fair Labor Standards Act
— *See:* Fair Labor Standards Act (FLSA)
Flu epidemic
— *See:* influenza epidemic
Fluid cream products, p. III:83
Fluoride, pp. III:315, III:327-328

FOBT
— *See:* Fecal occult blood test
— *See:* Fecal occult blood test (FOBT)
Food and Drug Administration, pp. III:176, III:330, III:389-391
Food Guide Pyramid, p. III:83
Food poisoning, pp. III:111-112
Food preparation workers, pp. I:61-62
Food services, p. II:262
— *See:* accommodations and food services
FoodNet, p. III:111
Foods, pp. II:66-67
— bioterrorism, p. III:88
— consumption of major commodities, pp. III:451*t*
— nutrient levels, pp. III:459*t*
— pesticide use, pp. III:87-88
— phytochemicals, p. III:90
Foods, organic
— *See:* organic foods
Fools Gold: A Critical Look at Computers in Childhood, p. II:265
Football, p. I:209
Foreign-born physicians, p. III:337
Foreign-born population, pp. I:301*t*
Foreign-educated physicians
— *See:* IMGs
Foreign Intelligence Surveillance Act (FISA), p. IV:230
Foreign languages used in the United States, pp. II:76-77, II:344*t*
Forensic pathology physicians, p. III:341
Forestry and fishing occupation
— *See:* farming, forestry, and fishing occupations
Forestry and fishing occupations
— *See:* farming, forestry, and fishing occupations
Forgery, pp. IV:105, IV:108
Fortune 500 firms, p. II:120
Foundations, pp. I:242, I:245-246
Fourth graders, p. II:200
Fractures, p. I:155
France
— breastfeeding, p. III:42
— duration of school year, p. II:254
— entertainment, p. I:187
— literacy, pp. II:163-165
— prostitution, p. IV:125
— terrorism, p. IV:184
— tuberculosis, p. III:334
— vacation time, p. I:192
Franklin W. Olin College of Engineering, p. II:280
Fraternal organizations, p. I:185
Fraud, pp. IV:64, IV:82, IV:85, IV:101, IV:104-105, III:376
Fred Hutchinson Cancer Research Center, p. III:144
Free weights, p. I:202
French, p. II:76
French (language), p. II:77
French Creole, p. II:77
Fresno (CA), p. IV:72
Friends Don't Let Friends Drive Drunk, p. IV:113
Frost & Sullivan, p. IV:117
Fruits, p. III:83
Funding, pp. II:211, II:224-225, I:256, II:377*t*

Hashish, pp. III:118, III:121, III:124, IV:152
— illicit substance use, teenagers, p. III:117
Hate crimes, pp. IV:286-290, IV:382t
— *See also:* Bias-related crimes
Hawaii, p. II:64
Hawaiian Natives, p. II:72
Hay fever, p. III:229
Hayflick Limit, p. III:48
Hazelden Foundation, p. III:123
HBV immunizations, p. III:97
HDL
— *See:* High-Denisty Lipoprotein (HDL)
Head injuries, pp. III:227, III:243
Head Start, pp. II:222-225, II:383t
Heaemophilus influenzae type b
— *See:* Hib
Health assessments, pp. III:488t
Health care, pp. I:242-244, III:484t
— costs for children, pp. II:66-67
— employment, pp. I:7, I:34
— expenditures, p. I:342t
— fraud, pp. IV:93-94, IV:328t
— Medicare enrollment, p. III:379
— productivity, pp. I:104-105
— vocational education, pp. II:256-257, II:262
— volunteering, pp. I:245-246
Health Care Financing Administration, p. III:374
Health clubs, pp. I:200-201
Health information technicians
— *See:* medical records and health information technicians
Health insurance, p. I:131
— employee benefits, pp. I:128-130, I:132
— independent contractors, p. I:72
— same-sex partners, p. I:136
Health Maintenance Organizations (HMOs), pp. III:345, III:382-383
Health Professional Shortage Areas, p. III:338
Health professions, p. II:284
Health sciences, p. II:284
Health services, pp. III:394-395, III:531t
Health violations in community water systems, p. III:326
Healthy Eating Index, p. III:84
Healthy People, pp. III:73, III:303, III:403-404, III:408
Hearing impairments, pp. III:203, III:227, III:229, II:298, III:487t
Hearing screenings, p. III:103
Heart attacks, pp. III:3, III:275-276
Heart disease, pp. III:5, III:14, II:18
— *See also:* Cardiovascular disease
— aging population, p. III:203
— Baby Boom generation, p. III:69
— causes of death, pp. III:4, III:6, III:8-9, III:12, III:24-25, III:69, III:401
— causes of disability, p. III:227
— funding, pp. III:400-401
— risk behaviors, p. III:136
— risk factors, pp. III:12, III:328
— treatments, pp. III:25, III:155
Heat burns, p. I:155

Hebrew, p. II:77
Helpers and laborers, p. I:43
Hemic system surgical procedures, pp. III:150-151
Hemorrhages in maternal mortality, p. III:23
Henderson, Charles, p. II:145
Hepatitis, pp. III:6, III:61, III:96, III:148, III:444t
Herbal therapies, pp. III:75, III:77, III:82, III:450t
Herbs, medicinal
— *See:* medicinal herbs
Hero Syndrome, p. IV:81
Heroin, p. IV:147
— control legislation, p. IV:11
— description, pp. IV:151-152
— emergency room visits, pp. III:124-125
— trafficking, pp. IV:12, IV:167-168
Herpes, genital
— *See:* Genital herpes
Heterosexuals, pp. III:53, III:289
Hib vaccinations for children, pp. III:96-97
High blood pressure
— *See also:* Hypertension
— causes of disability, pp. III:227-228
— obesity, p. III:405
High-Density Lipoprotein (HDL), pp. III:20-21
High school
— diplomas, pp. I:39, II:148, II:177, I:300t
— dropouts, pp. II:148-149
— sports, pp. I:199, I:204-205, I:362
— students, pp. I:250-251
— vocational education, pp. II:256-257, II:260-262, II:363t
High school education
— adults, p. I:264
— earnings, pp. I:114-116
— employment, pp. I:11-12
— enrollment, pp. I:292t
— income, p. I:94
— staff, p. I:292t
— workforce, p. I:57
High-speed pursuits, pp. IV:219, IV:364t
Highly Active Anti-Retroviral Therapy, p. III:54
Hill, Anita, pp. I:162, I:165
Hinckley, John, pp. IV:277, IV:280
Hindi (language), p. II:76
Hinduism, pp. II:134-135, II:140-141, I:252-253
Hispanics, p. I:47
— abortions, pp. II:12-13
— births, pp. II:10, I:40, II:321t
— breastfeeding, p. III:41
— causes of infant mortality, pp. III:44, III:313
— computer learning opportunities, p. II:263
— deaths, pp. III:8-9, III:15
— diseases, pp. III:97, III:289
— drug use, pp. IV:159-160
— earnings, p. I:71
— education, pp. II:161-162, II:259
— educational attainment, pp. I:39, I:112, I:118-119, II:151-153, II:258, II:287-290
— employment, pp. I:16, I:30, I:37, I:67-68
— families, p. I:38

Infant mortality continued:
517*t*
— rates, pp. III:43, III:312-313
— selected years, pp. III:44-45
Infants, pp. III:10-11, III:41
— *See also:* Children
— *See also:* Juveniles
— *See also:* Teenagers
— *See also:* Youth
Infectious diseases, pp. III:94, III:236, III:462*t*
— *See also:* Diseases
Infertility, p. III:299
Influenza, p. III:5
— causes of death, pp. III:2, III:4, III:8-9, III:69-70, III:99, III:401
— epidemic of 1918, pp. III:2, II:17, II:20, III:94
— immunizations, pp. III:96, III:98-99
Information clerks
— *See:* receptionists and information clerks
Information scientists (research)
— *See also:* computer and information scientists p. I:52
Information services, pp. I:104-105
Information systems managers
— *See:* computer and information systems managers
Information technology, p. IV:188
Inglewood Unified School District (CA), p. IV:131
Inhalants, pp. III:119-120, IV:151
Injectables, p. II:15
Injuries, pp. I:153, III:228, III:235, III:238
Ink jet printers and counterfeiting, p. IV:88
Inpatient hospitals, pp. III:207-209
INS
— *See:* Immigration and Naturalization Service
Insanity defense, pp. IV:275, IV:277-280, IV:381*t*
Insanity Defense Reform Act, p. IV:277
Inspectors
— *See:* machine operators, assemblers, and inspectors
Instant messaging, p. I:278
Institute on Race and Poverty, p. IV:222
Instrumental activities of daily living, pp. III:203-204
Insurance
— *See:* finance and insurance
Insurance claims and policy processing clerks, p. I:54
Insurance companies, p. III:416
Insurance fraud, p. IV:80
Insurance Information Institute, p. IV:79
Integrative medicine, p. III:82
Integumentary system, pp. III:150-151
Intellectual property, p. IV:97
Interest and dividend income, pp. I:145-146
Internal Revenue Service (IRS), pp. IV:91, IV:226, I:283
International Anti-Counterfeiting Coalition, p. IV:100
International Chamber of Commerce, p. IV:100
International Classification of Diseases, p. III:22
International Intellectual Property Association, p. IV:97
International Parental Kidnapping Crime Act, p. IV:141
International Task Force on Euthanasia and Assisted Suicide, p. III:217
Internet
— *See also:* Worldwide Web

Internet continued:
— charitable giving, p. I:235
— computer hacking, p. I:280
— counterfeiting, p. IV:100
— dating, pp. I:284-285
— entertainment, pp. I:226, I:233, I:268
— missing children, p. IV:143
— online travel spending, p. I:196
— productivity, p. I:97
— religion, pp. II:142-143, II:145
— schools, p. II:264
— search terms, pp. I:282-283, I:379*t*
— volunteering, p. I:246
Internet copyright piracy, pp. IV:95, IV:98
Internet fraud, pp. IV:82, IV:91
Internet gambling, pp. IV:101, IV:117-118
Internet Public Library, pp. I:257-258
Internet use, pp. I:276, I:377*t*
— age groups, p. I:378*t*
— by race/ethnicity and sex, pp. I:270-276, I:377*t*
— children, pp. I:278, I:379*t*
— household income, p. I:378*t*
Internists' medical malpractice premiums, p. III:415
Interracial marriages, pp. II:54-55, II:339*t*
Interuterine devices (IUDs), pp. II:15, III:304-305
Interviewers and clerks
— *See:* loan interviewers and clerks
Intrauterine Devices
— *See:* IUDs
Iowa, p. II:218
Ireland, pp. III:42, II:163-165
Irish gangs, p. IV:43
Iron lung, p. III:95
Iroquois, pp. II:72-73
Irradiation, p. III:112
IRS, p. I:283
Is Love Colorblind?, p. II:55
Is Single Gender Schooling Viable in the Public Sector?, p. II:309
Ischemic heart disease (IHD), pp. III:4, III:8, III:424*t*
Islam, pp. II:140-141
— fastest-growing religions, pp. I:252-253
— increase/decrease in membership, pp. II:132-135
— terrorism, p. IV:184
Israel, pp. II:164, IV:184
Italian (language), p. II:76
Italian gangs, p. IV:43
Italy, pp. II:163, I:187, I:192, III:334
Items stolen, p. IV:326*t*
Jackson-Lee, Sheila, p. IV:287
Jacob Wetterling Act, p. IV:121
Jails, pp. III:265-266
Japan, pp. II:5, II:163-165, I:187, II:254
Japanese, pp. III:43, II:74, II:76-77
Jazz concerts, p. I:216
Jehovah's Witnesses, pp. II:132-133, II:136-138
Jenkins, Henry, p. IV:145
Jewelry making, p. I:218
Jewish Defense League, p. IV:181

Jewish gangs, p. IV:43
Jews, pp. II:110, II:145
Jobs, pp. I:52-53
— advancement, pp. I:260-262, I:265
— college education, pp. I:51, I:58, I:61-62
— entrants, p. I:37
— gains, pp. I:32-33, I:299t
— leavers, p. I:37
— losses, pp. I:33, I:299t
— openings, pp. II:189-190, I:296t
— satisfaction, p. II:295
— training, pp. I:260-262
— worker supply, pp. I:24-25, I:27-28
Joe Camel, p. III:138
Jogging, p. I:202
Johns Hopkins University, p. II:294
Joint Legislative Task Force on Government Oversight, p. IV:223
Jones, Paula, p. I:166
Jonesboro (AR), p. IV:129
Jordan, Michael, p. I:211
Journal of the American Medical Association, pp. III:81, III:168, III:273-274, III:405
Judaism, pp. II:130-133, II:135, II:140-141
Judges, p. I:32
Jupiter Communications, p. I:196
Jury awards, p. I:170
Justice Policy Institute, pp. IV:129, IV:134, IV:237
Justice system employment
— arrests, pp. IV:266, IV:378t
— by government level, p. IV:302t
— crime rate, pp. IV:21-23
Justice system expenditures, pp. IV:303t
Justifiable homicides, pp. IV:217, IV:363t
Juveniles, pp. IV:39-40, IV:70, IV:101, I:221
— *See also:* Children
— *See also:* Infants
— *See also:* Teenagers
— *See also:* Youth
— arrests by race/ethnicity, pp. IV:133-137
— by sex, p. IV:340t
— drugs, p. IV:149
— poverty, p. IV:134
— special units of police departments, p. IV:206
— violent crimes, pp. IV:340t
Kaczynski, Theodore, p. IV:181
Kaiser Family Foundation, p. I:231
Kanner, Leo, p. III:259
Kansas, p. IV:276
Kanzai, Amil, p. IV:182
Kazakhstan, p. II:163
Kennedy School of Government, p. III:75
Kennedy, President John F., p. IV:46
Kennedy, Robert F., p. IV:46
Kentucky, pp. II:187, III:409
Kenya, p. III:332
Kerr-Mills Act, p. III:384
Ketamine, p. IV:154
Kevorkian, Dr. Jack, p. III:216

Kidnapping, pp. IV:142, IV:245, IV:260
Kidney diseases, pp. III:8, III:40, III:161
— *See also:* Nephritis, nephrosis, and nephrotic syndrome
Kids Walk-to-School Program, p. III:406
Kilpatrick, William Heard, p. II:204
King, Jr., Dr. Martin Luther, p. IV:46
King, Rodney, pp. IV:204, IV:288
KKK
— *See:* Ku Klux Klan
Klaas, Polly, p. IV:142
Koppel, Ted, p. IV:243
Korea, pp. II:164-165, II:195, II:254
Korean population, pp. II:74, II:76-77
Kozol, Jonathan, p. II:221
Kru, p. II:77
Ku Klux Klan (KKK), pp. IV:181, IV:286
Kubler-Ross, Elisabeth, pp. III:212, III:374
Kurdistan Workers Party, p. IV:183
Kyrgyzstan, p. II:163
Labor force distribution, pp. I:299t
Labor law violations, p. I:45
Labor relations managers
— *See:* personnel and labor relations managers
Laboratory animal caretakers
— *See:* veterinary assistants and laboratory animal caretakers
Laboratory technologists
— *See:* Clinical laboratory technologists
Lacerations, p. I:155
Lakes and water pollution, pp. III:323, III:325
Landscaping and groundskeeping laborers, pp. I:61-62
Language-impaired children, pp. II:298-299
Lanoxin, p. III:167
Laotian population, p. II:74
Larcenies
— arrests, pp. IV:68-69
— by type, pp. IV:322t
— corrections system expenditures, p. IV:249
— females, p. IV:136
— property crime, pp. IV:7-8
— reported to police, p. IV:373t
Larsen, Elena, p. II:142
Las Vegas (NV), p. IV:124
Laser skin resurfacing, pp. III:277-279
Last Tango in Paris, p. I:231
Latin America, pp. II:25, I:47, III:326
Latinos, pp. I:41, II:70-71
Latter-Day Saints, pp. II:130-131
Latvia, pp. II:5, II:163-164
Law, pp. II:286, II:290
Law enforcement, pp. IV:30, I:157-158, IV:201-202, IV:205
— by race/ethnicity and sex, pp. IV:203-204, IV:360t
— deaths, pp. IV:361t
— departments, p. IV:199
— employment, p. IV:359t
— salaries, p. IV:209
— timeline, pp. IV:197-198
Lawyers, pp. I:22-25, I:32, I:58
LDP
— *See:* Low-Density Lipoprotein

Lead, pp. III:316-317, III:324

Learning disabilities in children

— Attention Deficit/Hyperactivity Disorder, p. III:65

— by cause, pp. III:229-231

— demographics, p. III:446*t*

— special education programs, pp. II:298-303

Leavenworth (KS), p. IV:24

Legal occupations, pp. I:7, IV:281-282, II:296

Legionnaire's Disease, pp. III:61, III:95, III:444*t*

Leisure activities, pp. I:176-177, I:356*t*

— by type, pp. I:216-218, I:365*t*

— families, p. I:173

— sports, p. I:199

— travel, p. I:191

Leon County (FL), p. IV:274

LEP, pp. II:306-307

Leprosy, pp. III:58, III:60, III:442*t*

Lesbians, pp. III:54, II:63-64, I:191

— *See also:* Gays

— *See also:* Homosexuals

— *See also:* Same-sex partners

Lettuce, p. III:87

Leukemia, pp. III:3, III:67-68, III:156

Liberal arts, p. II:194

Liberals, p. II:114

Libraries, pp. I:233, I:254, I:256-259, I:374*t*

Licensed practical nurses (LPNs), pp. I:58-59, I:62, III:353-354

Life expectancy

— Baby Boom generation, p. III:187

— births and deaths, pp. II:324*t*

— by decade, pp. II:16-20

— by race/ethnicity and sex, pp. III:47-48

— Hayflick Limit, p. III:48

— *Healthy People*, pp. III:403-404, III:437*t*

— Social Security, pp. I:143-144

Life insurance, pp. I:128, I:133

Life sciences, pp. II:284-285

Lightner, Candy, p. IV:113

Limited English Proficiency, pp. II:306-307, II:407*t*

— *See also:* LEP

Lindbergh Law, p. IV:142

Lipitor, pp. III:167, III:176, III:276

Liquid Candy, p. II:311

Liquor-law violations, pp. IV:112, IV:136

Listening to Prozac, p. III:64

Listeria infections, p. III:111

Literacy

— adults, p. II:156

— by educational attainment, pp. IV:263, II:365*t*

— by race/ethnicity, pp. II:154-155

— employment, pp. II:157-158

— international comparisons, p. II:163

Literacy surveys, p. I:221

Literature, p. I:216

Lithium, pp. III:64, III:251

Lithuania, p. II:163

Littleton (CO), pp. IV:129, II:243

Live births, pp. II:10, II:315*t*

Liver disease, pp. III:8-9, III:161

Liver disease continued:

— *See also:* Cirrhosis

Lives on the Boundary, p. II:155

Livestock, p. III:458*t*

Living arrangements, pp. II:46, II:58, II:61, III:192, II:341*t*

Living to 100, p. III:73

Living wills, pp. III:211, III:215

La Leche League, pp. III:41-42

Loan interviewers and clerks, p. I:54

Local Education Foundations, p. II:212

Local government, pp. I:1, I:9, II:211, I:256, I:292*t*

Lodging

— *See:* Hotels and lodging

Logan International Airport, p. IV:232

Loitering, pp. IV:106-107, IV:136

LoJack Corporation, p. IV:71

Long-term-care insurance, p. I:135

Look-say method, pp. II:200-201

Looking Fit Tanning Book 2002-2003, p. III:147

Los Angeles, pp. II:30, II:75

Los Angeles (CA), pp. IV:40-41, IV:203

Los Angeles County Sheriff's Department, p. IV:200

Los Angeles Police Department, pp. IV:201, IV:211

Los Angeles Unified School District, p. IV:131

Lost work time, p. I:350*t*

Louima, Abner, p. IV:204

Louisiana, pp. III:370, III:409

The Love Bug, p. I:280

Low birth weight

— by race/ethnicity, pp. III:308-310, III:515*t*

— causes of death, pp. III:10, III:312

— hypertension, pp. III:11, III:40

— kidney diseases, p. III:40

— live births, p. III:435*t*

— sexually transmitted diseases, pp. III:40, III:52

— singletons, pp. III:39-40

— smoking, p. III:40

Low-Density Lipoprotein (LDP), p. III:20

Low-fat milk, p. III:83

Lower respiratory diseases, pp. III:3-5, III:401

LPNs

— *See:* Licensed practical nurses

— *See:* Licensed practical nurses (LPNs)

Lucky Strike cigarettes, p. III:136

Lumbee Indian tribe, pp. II:72-73

Lung cancer, p. III:160

— by sex, pp. III:13, III:26-28

— death rates, pp. III:67, III:428*t*

— risk behaviors, pp. III:3-4, III:26, III:136, III:160

— survival rates, pp. III:19, III:156, III:158

Lung diseases, pp. III:227-228

Lutherans, pp. II:130-133, II:135

Lyme Disease, pp. III:61-62, III:95, III:444*t*

Lymphatic system diseases, pp. III:67-68, III:150-151, III:156

Lysergic acid diethylamide (LSD), pp. III:119, IV:151, IV:153, IV:162

Macao, p. II:30

Machine feeders and offbearers, p. I:54

Machine operators, assemblers, and inspectors, pp. I:20, I:32,

Machine operators, assemblers, and inspectors continued:
   I:296t
MADD
— *See:* Mothers Against Drunk Driving (MADD)
Mail and message distributing occupations, p. I:32
Maine, pp. II:64, II:218
Major League Baseball (MLB), pp. I:210-211
Making Weight, p. III:116
Malaria, pp. III:58-59, III:442t
Malaysia, pp. II:5, I:187
Malcolm X, p. IV:46
Male-female teacher ratio, pp. II:182-183
Males, pp. IV:17, IV:136, III:137, III:150-151, I:204
— *See also:* Men
Malignancies, pp. III:2-4
— *See also:* Cancer
— *See also:* Neoplasms
Mammograms, pp. III:18, III:156, III:210, III:425t
Managed care, pp. III:207-209, III:344
Management analysts, pp. I:22-25, I:296t
Managerial and professional specialty occupations, pp. I:31-32
Managerial occupations
— *See:* executive, administrative, managerial occupations
Manhattan Project, p. III:105
Manic depression
— *See:* Bipolar disorder
Manslaughter, p. IV:135
Manufacturing
— compensation, p. I:326t
— employees, pp. I:329t
— employment, p. I:34
— income, p. I:120
— injuries in the workplace, p. I:156
— productivity output, pp. I:98-99, I:104-105
Maps, p. I:185
Marihuana Tax Act, p. IV:12
Marijuana, pp. III:126, III:133, IV:173
— adults, p. III:121
— consumption, p. III:104
— drug-related arrests, pp. IV:11, IV:147, IV:175
— emergency room visits, p. III:124
— lifetime drug use reported, pp. IV:151-153
— teenagers, pp. III:117-118, III:132
— trafficking, pp. IV:167-168
Marital status, pp. I:65-68
Marketing, pp. II:256-257, II:262
Marketing, advertising, public relations managers, p. I:58
Marriage, pp. II:48-49, II:335t
— age at first marriage, p. II:50
— Baby Boom generation, p. II:51
— by race/ethnicity, pp. II:52-54
Married-couple households, pp. II:45-47, I:92, III:269-270, I:315t
Maryland, pp. II:63-64, IV:223, III:338
The Maryland Report, p. II:304
Massachusetts, pp. II:63-64, IV:121, II:217, IV:287, II:305, III:338, III:370, III:409
Massachusetts Institute of Technology, p. IV:145
— *See:* MIT

Massachusetts Institute of Technology (MIT)
— grade inflation, p. II:293
— honor graduates, p. II:294
— private gifts, p. II:280
— tuition costs, p. II:268
Massage therapy, pp. III:78-79, III:162
Master's degrees, pp. II:94, II:283
Match.com, p. I:284
Matchmaker.com, p. I:284
Material exploitation of elderly population, p. III:199
Material moving occupations
— *See also:* transportation and material moving occupations
Maternal age at conception, p. III:40
Maternal complications of pregnancy, p. III:10
Maternal mortality, pp. II:21, III:22-23, IV:53, III:427t
Maternity leave, p. I:137
Mathematics, p. II:392t
— achievement, pp. II:390t
— class characteristics, pp. II:165, II:195
— doctoral degrees conferred, p. II:285
— proficiency, pp. II:161-162, II:164, II:203, II:237, II:366t II:386t
— salaries, p. II:194
— scores, p. II:254
Mathematics-related occupations, p. II:296
Mayhem: Violence as Public Entertainment, p. IV:145
MBA, p. I:212
McDonald's restaurants, pp. III:110, IV:184
McNaughtan, Daniel
— *See:* M'Naghten, Daniel
McVeigh, Timothy, pp. IV:179-181
Mealtimes, p. I:180
Measles, pp. III:55, III:94-95, III:97
Measles, German
— *See:* German measles
Meat cutters
— *See:* butchers and meat cutters
Meats, p. III:83
Media images, p. III:221
Medicaid
— elderly population, pp. III:220, III:363
— enrollment, pp. III:529t
— fraud, p. IV:94
— health care expenditures, p. I:131
— nonelderly population, pp. III:384-388
Medical assistants, pp. I:52-53
Medical care, p. I:133
Medical ethics, p. III:188
Medical hospitals, pp. III:364-365
Medical Injury Compensation Reform Act (CA), p. III:418
Medical liability reform legislation, p. III:418
Medical malpractice, pp. III:303, III:415-417, III:540t
Medical procedures, pp. III:477t
Medical professionals, pp. IV:93, I:157-158, III:520t
Medical records and health information technicians, pp. I:52-53
Medical review boards, p. III:418
Medical schools, pp. III:82, II:277, II:396t
Medical technologists
— *See:* Clinical laboratory technologists

Michigan continued:
— litigation for school funding, pp. II:220-221
— medical liability insurance premiums, pp. III:415-417
— NAEP rankings, p. II:217
— physician-assisted suicide, p. III:216
— prison population, p. IV:248
— sex offender registries, p. IV:121
— uncertified teachers, p. II:187
Michigan Department of Community Health, p. III:407
Michigan Educational Assessment Program test, p. II:169
Microsoft Corporation, p. I:59
MIDCAB
— *See:* Minimally Invasive Direct Coronary Artery Bypass
Midwestern United States, p. III:189
Migrant workers, p. I:46
Military, pp. II:122, II:357*t*
Militia, p. IV:181
Milk, low-fat, p. III:83
Milk, Mayor Harvey, p. IV:276
Milk, whole, p. III:83
Million Man March, p. II:61
Minimally Invasive Direct Coronary Artery Bypass (MIDCAB), p. III:25
Minimum wage, pp. I:90-91, I:316*t*
Mining, pp. I:104-106, I:156
Minnesota, pp. II:187, II:218
Missing children, pp. IV:141-143, IV:206, IV:342*t*
Mississippi, pp. IV:286, III:369-370, III:418
Missouri, pp. II:63, II:246, III:387, III:409
MMR, pp. III:57, III:96
— *See:* Measles, Mumps, and Rubella vaccine
M'Naghten, Daniel, p. IV:275
Moderates, p. II:114
Modern dance, pp. I:218-219
Moldova, p. II:163
Mon-Khmer (language), p. II:77
Monaco, p. II:30
Monetary damages, pp. I:165-166, I:169
Money-related crimes, pp. IV:10, IV:105, IV:108
Mongolia, p. II:30
Monitoring the Future, pp. III:118-119, III:132, III:137
Monk Eastman Gang, p. IV:43
Monoamine oxidase inhibitors, p. III:64
Montana, pp. II:75, II:218, IV:276, IV:290, III:369, III:387
Montana v Cowan, p. IV:276
Mood disorders, pp. III:251-252, III:499*t*
Morehouse College, pp. II:53, II:61
Mormons, pp. IV:12, II:130-133
Morning-after pill, p. II:15
Morphine, p. III:124
Mortality, maternal
— *See:* maternal mortality
Mothers, p. I:183
Mothers Against Drunk Driving (MADD), pp. IV:113, IV:207
Motor vehicle accidents, pp. III:4, II:21, III:32, III:131
Motor vehicle thefts, pp. IV:7, IV:65, IV:67, IV:76-77
Mouth cancer, pp. III:150, III:161
Movie admissions, pp. I:185, I:222
Movie ratings, pp. I:230-231, I:368*t*

Movie releases, p. I:230
Movie rentals, pp. I:187-188, I:358*t*
Movies, pp. I:222, I:286, I:366*t*
Mozambique, p. III:332
MP3, pp. I:227, I:282
MSAs, p. II:29
Multifactor Productivity, pp. I:108-109
Multinational Monitor, p. III:138
Multiple births, pp. III:39, III:299-300, III:512*t*
Multiple jobs, pp. I:63-64, I:306*t*
Multiple sclerosis, p. III:225
Multipurpose Arcade Combat Simulator (MACS), p. IV:145
Mumps, pp. III:55-56, III:94-95
Municipal government, p. I:9
Murders, pp. III:36-38
— *See also:* Homicides p. IV:5
— by age group, p. IV:33
— by race/ethnicity, p. IV:52
— by race/ethnicity, sex, and marital status, pp. IV:50-51
— crime index, p. IV:6
— death penalty, p. IV:245
— firearms-related, pp. IV:39, IV:312*t*
— juveniles, pp. IV:33, IV:133, IV:135, IV:137-138
— rate fluctuation, pp. IV:25-26
— victimization, p. IV:38
Murphy Brown, p. II:62
Murray, John, p. IV:144
Musculoskeletal system diseases, pp. III:150, III:155, III:235, III:238, III:310
Museums, pp. I:7, I:216, I:228-229, I:368*t*
Music, pp. I:218, I:268, I:286
Musical plays, p. I:216
Muslims, pp. II:132-135, II:145, IV:224
NAACP Legal Defense Fund, p. IV:244
Najim, Eyad Mahmoud Ismail, p. IV:184
Nandrolone, p. IV:153
Napster, pp. IV:95, I:283
Narcotics, pp. IV:12, IV:153
NASCAR, pp. I:211, I:283
— *See:* National Association for Stock Car Auto Racing
A Nation At Risk, pp. II:162, II:167, III:174, II:176, II:199, II:204
A Nation Online, pp. I:273, I:278
National Academy of Science, pp. III:21, III:327
National Adult Literacy Survey, pp. II:156-157
National Alliance for the Mentally Ill, p. III:251
National Ambulatory Medical Care Survey, p. III:63
National Assembly on School-Based Health Care, p. III:102
National Assessment of Educational Progress (NAEP), p. II:159, II:162, II:203, II:235-236
National Assessment of Educational Progress (NAEP) rankings, pp. II:217-218, II:376*t*
National Association for Stock Car Auto Racing (NASCAR), p. I:211, I:283
National Association of Anorexia Nervosa and Associated Disorders, p. III:257
National Association of Bilingual Education, p. II:307
National Association of Gifted Children, p. II:304
National Association of Police Organizations, p. IV:224

National Association of Realtors, p. I:194

National Association of School Nurses, p. II:303

National Basketball Association (NBA), p. I:210

National Burglar and Fire Alarm Association, p. IV:73

National Cancer Institute, pp. III:31, III:400-401

National Center for Chronic Disease Prevention & Health Promotion, p. III:90

National Center for Complementary and Alternative Medicine, pp. III:76, III:80-81, III:162-163, III:451*t*

National Center for Education Statistics, pp. II:234-235, II:269

National Center for Missing and Exploited Children, p. IV:141

National Center for Policy Analysis, p. IV:250

National Center for State Courts, p. IV:273

National Center on Addiction and Substance Abuse (CASA), p. IV:155

National Center on Institutions and Alternatives, p. IV:248

National Child Abuse and Neglect Data System, p. IV:139

National Cholesterol Education Program, p. III:167

National Coalition for Parent Involvement in Education, p. II:198

National Collegiate Athletic Association (NCAA), p. IV:118

National Commission on Excellence in Education, p. II:257

National Conference of Catholic Bishops, p. III:367

National Consumer League, p. IV:83

National Council of Teachers of Mathematics, p. II:205

National Crime Victimization Survey
— actual crimes reported, pp. IV:4, IV:6-9
— crimes reported, p. IV:294*t*
— gangs in schools, p. IV:42
— property crime, p. IV:65
— rate fluctuation, p. IV:26
— victimization of children, p. IV:139

National Data Collection - Police Use of Force, p. IV:214

National Defense Act, p. II:204

National Education Association, p. I:221

National Elder Abuse Incidence Study, pp. III:199-200

National Electronic Injury Surveillance System, p. I:205

National Endowment for the Arts, p. I:218

National Firearms Act, p. IV:46

National Football League (NFL), pp. I:210-212

National Fraud Information Center, p. IV:83

National Gambling Impact Study Commission, p. IV:117

National Governors Association, p. III:387

National Health and Nutrition Examination Survey, p. III:16

National Health Care Anti-Fraud Association, p. IV:93

National health care expenditures, p. I:342*t*

National Health Service Corps, p. II:278

National Heart, Lung, and Blood Institute, pp. III:400-401

National Highway Traffic Safety Administration, pp. IV:115, IV:219

National Hockey League (NHL), p. I:210

National Home Builders Association, p. IV:63

National Hospital Discharge Survey, p. III:152

National Instant Criminal Background Check System, p. IV:46-47

National Institute for Occupational Safety and Health, p. III:141-142

National Institute of Allergies and Infectious Diseases
— *See:* NIAID

National Institute of Child Health and Human Development, p. III:45, II:201

National Institute of Diabetes & Digestive & Kidney Diseases
— *See:* NIDDK

National Institute of General Medical Sciences, pp. III:400-401

National Institute of Justice, pp. IV:132, IV:220

National Institute of Mental Health, pp. III:116, III:172, III:248, III:255-256, II:302

National Institute on Aging, pp. III:148, III:204

National Institute on Drug Abuse, p. III:128

National Institutes of Health, pp. III:3, III:28, III:76, III:105, III:143, III:163, III:167, III:400-402, III:535*t*

National Insurance Crime Bureau, p. IV:71

National Literacy Act, p. II:191

National Long-Term Care Surveys, p. III:204

National Longitudinal Study on Adolescent Health, p. IV:136

National Longitudinal Survey of Youth, p. IV:134

National Medical Care [company], p. IV:94

National Office of Drug Policy, p. IV:168

National origin-based discrimination, pp. I:161, I:163, I:167

National Park Service, p. IV:227

National Pharmaceutical Stockpile, p. III:392

National Prosecutors Survey, p. IV:282

National Public Radio, p. III:75

National Reading Panel, pp. II:201-202

National Registry of Emergency Medical Technicians, p. III:357

National School Lunch Program, pp. III:113-114, III:468*t*

National School Safety Center, pp. II:247-248

National Sleep Foundation, pp. III:140, III:143

National Survey on Drug Abuse, p. IV:157

National Tactical Officers Association, p. IV:211

National Vaccine Injury Compensation Program, p. III:97

National Water Quality Inventory, p. III:322

Native American religion, pp. II:134-135

Native Americans, pp. II:55, I:252-253, III:337

Native Hawaiians, pp. II:70-71

Native North Americans, pp. II:6-7, II:24

Natural history museums, p. I:229

Naturopathy, pp. III:78, III:80

Navajo Indian tribe, pp. II:72-73

Navigators, pp. I:22, I:296*t*

NBA, pp. I:211-212
— *See also:* National Basketball Association
— *See:* National Basketball Association (NBA)

NC-17, p. I:231

NCAA, p. I:363*t*
— *See:* National Collegiate Athletic Association (NCAA)

NCCAM
— *See:* National Center for Complementary and Alternative

Nebraska, pp. II:218, III:369

Needle use, pp. III:54, III:101

Neglect of elderly, p. III:199

Neonatal deaths, pp. III:10, III:312

Neoplasms, pp. III:3-4, III:235-236, III:238
— *See also:* Cancer
— *See also:* Malignancies

Nephritis, nephrosis, and nephrotic syndrome, pp. III:4-5
— *See also:* Kidney diseases

Obesity continued:
— eating habits, p. III:90
— elderly population, p. III:210
— *Journal of the American Medical Association*, p. III:405
— prevention programs, p. III:407
— risky behaviors, pp. III:20-21, III:107, III:109, III:115, III:425*t*
— women's health, pp. III:16-17, III:21

Obsessive-compulsive disorder, pp. III:247, III:250, III:252-253

Obstetricians, pp. III:150, III:303, III:341, III:415

Occupational fatalities, pp. I:149, I:151, I:156, I:349*t*

Occupational Safety and Health Administration, pp. I:153-154

Occupational therapy aides, p. I:53

Occupations, p. II:296
— decline, pp. I:51, I:54-55, I:303*t*
— degrees conferred, pp. I:296*t*
— growth rate, p. I:303*t*
— illegal labor, p. I:43
— independent contractors, pp. I:69, I:307*t*
— job declines, p. I:303*t*
— job openings, pp. I:296*t*
— retirement, p. I:296*t*
— workplace violence, pp. IV:60-61, I:351*t*

O'Connor, Justice Sandra Day, pp. IV:96, IV:246

Offbearers
— *See also:* machine feeders and offbearers p. I:54

Office clerks (general), pp. I:61-62

Office machine operators, pp. I:54-55

Office of Alternative Medicine, p. III:81

Office of Homeland Security, pp. IV:187-189

Office of Juvenile Justice and Delinquency Prevention, p. IV:136, IV:142

Office of National Drug Control Policy, pp. IV:174, IV:263

Ohio, pp. II:63, IV:138, III:190, III:367, III:409, III:417

Oils, p. III:83

Oklahoma City, pp. I:229, IV:285

Older Americans Act, p. IV:107

On Death and Dying, pp. III:212, III:374

On Killing: The Psychological Cost of Learning to Kill in War and Society, p. IV:145

Oneandonly.com, p. I:284

Online auctions, p. I:286

Online banking, p. I:273

Online churches, pp. II:144, II:362*t*

Online dating services, pp. I:284, I:380*t*

Online gambling, p. IV:335*t*

Online search terms, pp. I:282-283, I:379*t*

Online shopping, pp. I:273, I:277, I:279

Online travel spending, pp. I:196-197, I:360*t*

Opera, pp. I:185, I:216, I:224-225

Operation Child Watch, p. I:45

Operation Pipeline, pp. IV:223-224

Operators, p. I:54

Operators, fabricators, and laborers, pp. I:31-32, I:43, I:69-70

Ophthalmologists, p. III:341

Opium Poppy Control Act, p. IV:12

Optometry degrees conferred, pp. II:286, II:290

Oral cavity cancers, p. III:156

Oral contraceptives, p. III:161

Order Clerks, pp. I:54-55

Orderlies and attendants
— *See:* nursing aides, orderlies, and attendants

Oregon, pp. II:64, III:216, IV:277

Organic foods, pp. III:87-88, III:458*t*

Oriental medicine (traditional), pp. III:78, III:80

Orthopedic surgeons, p. III:341

Osama bin Laden, p. I:283

Osteopaths, pp. III:78-79, II:286, II:290, III:336

Osteoporosis, pp. III:168, III:328

Out of Control: Seattle's Flawed Response to Protests Against the World Trade Organization
— 214,

Outdoor track, p. I:208

Ovarian cancer, pp. III:19, III:67-68, III:158

Ovarian surgeries, p. III:151

Over-the-counter medications, pp. III:128, III:474*t*

Overweight, pp. III:17, III:90, III:107, III:210

Oxycodone, p. III:130

Oxycontin, pp. III:129-130

Oxygen-depleting substances, pp. III:323-325

Oxymetholone, p. IV:153

Oxytocin, p. III:23

P-notes, p. IV:88

Pacific Islanders
— *See also:* Asians and Pacific Islanders
— abortions, pp. II:10, II:12-13
— advanced classes, p. II:259
— Bachelor's Degrees conferred, pp. II:287-288
— causes of death, pp. III:8, III:43
— doctoral degrees conferred, pp. II:289-290
— drug arrests, p. IV:161
— drug use, pp. IV:159-160
— educational attainment, pp. II:152-153
— fertility rates, p. II:321*t*
— HIV, p. III:289
— income, pp. I:75, I:82
— Internet use, pp. I:270-271
— interracial marriages, p. II:55
— law enforcement personnel, p. IV:203
— live births, pp. II:10, II:321*t*
— low birth weight, p. III:40
— population, pp. II:24, II:71, II:347*t*
— population mobility, p. II:38
— salaries, p. I:38
— single-parent households, p. II:61
— Total Fertility Rates, pp. II:6, II:8
— vocational education credits accumulated, p. II:258

Packagers
— *See:* hand packers and packagers

Paid leave, pp. I:129, I:133

Pain, p. I:155

Pain control, pp. III:213-214

Paintball, pp. I:200-201

Painting, p. I:218

Pakistani population, p. II:74

Palliative care
— *See:* Hospice care

Palm Beach County Health Department (FL), p. III:392

Pancreas surgeries, p. III:151

Pancreatic cancer
— causes of death, pp. III:67-68
— obesity, p. III:161
— survival rates, pp. III:156, III:158
Panic disorders, pp. III:252-253
Pap smears, p. III:156
Paraguay, p. III:42
Paralysis, pp. III:227, III:229
Paramedics
— *See:* Emergency medical technicians
Parathyroid gland surgeries, p. III:151
Parents, pp. I:183-184
Parents, divorced
— *See:* Divorced parents
Parents, never married
— *See:* Never-married parents
Parents, widowed
— *See:* Widowed parents
Parkinson's Disease, pp. III:225, III:243
Parks, p. I:216
Parolees, pp. IV:18, IV:20
Part-time employment, pp. I:65-66, I:68, I:306t
Particulate matter (PM-10), pp. III:316-317
Partnership for A Drug-Free America, p. III:132
Paternity leave, p. I:137
Pathogens, pp. III:323, III:325, III:467t
Pathologists, p. III:341
Patients' Rights Movement, p. III:215
Patrick Henry College, p. II:235
PATRIOT Act, p. IV:186
Patriot groups, p. IV:181
Paxil, p. III:76
Payzant, Thomas, pp. IV:131-132
Pb
— *See:* Lead
PCBs, p. III:323
PCP, pp. IV:151-154
PCs
— *See:* Personal computers
Peace Officer Standards and Training Commission, p. IV:211
Pearl (MS), p. IV:129
Pell Grants, p. II:273
Pennsylvania
— expulsions from school, p. II:246
— gay-couple households, p. II:63
— geographic distribution of elderly population, p. III:190
— NAEP rankings, pp. II:217, IV:287, III:338, III:370
— population, p. II:36
Pennsylvania Medical Society, p. III:416
Pensions, p. I:145
Pentecostals, pp. II:130-135
Pepsi, p. II:310
Per-pupil expenditures, pp. II:217, II:281-282, II:367t
   382t
Percodan, p. III:129
Performing arts, pp. I:216-217, I:224, II:284, I:367t
Perinatal conditions, p. III:9
Perjury causing execution, p. IV:245
Perls, Dr. Thomas, p. III:73

Personal computers
— *See:* PCs
Personal computers (PCs), pp. I:226-227
Personal home care aides, p. I:52
Personal leave, p. I:133
Personal relationships, p. I:284
Personal Responsibility Work Opportunities Reconciliation Act, p. II:60
Personal savings rate, pp. I:147-148
Personal services, p. I:7
Personnel and labor relations managers, pp. I:24-25
Pertussis, pp. III:55-56, III:94-95
— *See also:* Whooping Cough
Pervasive Developmental Disorder, p. III:255
Pesticide use, pp. III:87-88
Pets, p. I:191
Pew Internet & American Life Project, p. II:142
Pew Research Center, p. IV:185
Pfizer, pp. III:167, III:276
Pharmaceutical Research and Manufacturers of America
— *See:* PhRMA
Pharmaceutical Research and Manufacturers of America (PhRMA), pp. III:175, III:179
Pharmacy degrees, pp. II:286, II:290
Pharmacy Today, p. III:140
Pharynx cancer, p. III:156
Pharynx surgeries, pp. III:150-151
Philip Morris cigarettes, p. III:136
Philippines, pp. I:47, III:332
Phobias, pp. III:252-253
Phoenix (AZ), p. IV:72
Phonics, systematic
— *See:* Systematic phonics
Photography, pp. I:22, I:24-25, I:218, I:296t
PhRMA
— *See:* Pharmaceutical Research and Manufacturers of
Physical abuse of elderly, p. III:199
Physical activity, pp. III:405, III:461t
Physical Activity and Health, p. III:93
Physical deformities, p. III:229
Physical education classes, pp. III:104, I:203
Physical sciences degrees, p. II:285
Physical therapist assistants, pp. I:52-53
Physician assistants, pp. I:52-53, III:345
Physician-assisted suicide, pp. III:215-216
— *See also:* Euthanasia
Physicians
— *See also:* Doctors of Medicine
— by race/ethnicity, p. III:337
— by specialty, pp. III:341, III:522t
— by state, p. III:338
— geographic maldistribution, p. III:344
— office staff, p. III:394
— place of medical education, pp. III:342, III:523t
— specialization, p. III:341
— supply, p. III:520t
— workplace discrimination, p. I:59
— workplace violence, p. I:58
Physicians for Reproductive Choice and Health, p. III:366

Public schools continued:
— college enrollment, p. II:150
— funding, pp. II:211, II:213
— graduates, p. II:148
— mathematics proficiency, p. II:237
Public universities, pp. II:269, II:279, II:281
Public utilities
— *See:* transportation and public utilities
Publishers (desktop), p. I:52
Pueblo Indian tribe, pp. II:72-73
Pulmonary diseases, pp. III:69-70
Punctures, p. I:155
Pupil-teacher ratio, pp. II:180, II:371*t*
Purse-snatching, pp. IV:69-70
Q fever, p. III:392
Quadruplets, p. III:39
Quayle, Dan, p. II:62
Quilting, p. I:218
Quinlan, Karen Ann, p. III:188
R-rated movies, p. I:230
Race-based discrimination, pp. I:161, I:167
Race/ethnicity
— abortions, pp. II:12-13, II:321*t*
— births, pp. II:10, I:40, II:319*t*
— cancer survival rates, pp. III:156, III:158
— causes of death, pp. III:8, II:21, III:28, III:30, III:32, III:34, III:43, III:422*t*
— computer learning opportunities, p. II:263
— correctional population, pp. IV:19-20
— crib death, p. III:45
— death row inmates, p. IV:244
— deaths, pp. III:15, II:21
— diseases, pp. III:26, III:52
— domestic homicides, pp. IV:48-49
— drug arrests, pp. IV:161-162
— drug use, p. IV:162
— earnings, p. I:71
— educational attainment, pp. I:39, I:112, I:118, II:151-152, II:258-259, II:287-290, I:300*t*
— employment, pp. I:35, I:37, I:299*t*
— exercise habits, p. III:92
— federal law enforcement officers, p. IV:227
— hate crimes, p. IV:290
— health problems, p. III:20
— housing, p. II:35
— illicit substance use, p. III:126
— income, pp. I:82, I:311*t*
— infant mortality, pp. III:313, III:517*t*
— Internet use, pp. I:270-272, I:377*t*
— law enforcement, pp. IV:203, IV:360*t*
— life expectancy, pp. II:20, III:47
— literacy, pp. II:154, II:159
— live births, pp. II:10, II:321*t*
— low birth weight, pp. III:308-309, III:516*t*
— mammograms, p. III:18
— marriage, pp. II:52-53
— maternal mortality, p. III:22
— mathematics proficiency, p. II:161
— mobility, p. II:38

Race/ethnicity continued:
— murder, p. IV:52
— physicians, p. III:337
— political-party affiliation, p. II:108
— population, pp. II:24, II:70, II:343*t*
— Population Replacement Rate, pp. II:6, II:8
— poverty, p. IV:53
— prisoners, pp. IV:238-239, IV:242
— single-parent households, p. II:61
— Total Fertility Rates, pp. II:6, II:8
— volunteering, pp. I:241, I:370*t*
— voter turnout, p. II:106
— youth gangs, pp. IV:43-44
Racial discrimination, p. IV:162
Racial profiling, pp. IV:222-225, IV:365*t*
Racketeering and sentencing, p. IV:108
Radiation, pp. III:105, III:159
Radioisotope scans, p. III:152
Radiologic technologists, p. III:355
Railroad brake, signal, and switch operators, pp. I:54-55
Railroad conductors and yardmasters, p. I:54
Ranchers
— *See:* farmers and ranchers
Rape, pp. IV:55-56, IV:58, IV:318*t*
— actual crimes reported, p. IV:5
— household income, pp. IV:31, IV:38
— juveniles arrested, pp. IV:133, IV:135, IV:137-138
— rate fluctuation, pp. IV:25-26
— recidivism, p. IV:260
Reading proficiency, pp. II:159-160, II:163, II:200-202, II:366*t*
Reagan, President Ronald, pp. IV:46, IV:277
Real estate, p. I:292*t*
Real estate, rental, and leasing services, pp. I:104-105
Reality Check, pp. II:170, II:177
Receptionists and information clerks, pp. I:61-62
Recidivism
— by race, p. IV:166
— by type of crime committed, pp. IV:260-261, IV:263
— prison industries, pp. IV:256-259
— state prisoners, pp. IV:374*t*
Recommended Energy Allowance, p. III:89
Recreation, pp. I:185, I:242, I:244-246, I:357*t*
Recreational time
— *See:* leisure time
Recreational vehicles (RVs), p. I:190
Rectal cancers, pp. III:156, III:161
Red meat, p. III:83
Registered nurses, p. III:523*t*
— growing occupations, p. I:58
— job openings, pp. I:24-25, I:61-62
— nursing school graduates, pp. III:347-348
— retirement, pp. I:22-23
— supply, p. III:349
— worker shortages, p. I:59
Rehabilitation Act, p. III:232
Rehabilitation programs, p. IV:263
Relationship Web sites, pp. I:284, I:380*t*
Religion-based discrimination, pp. I:161, I:167
Religion surfers, pp. II:142, II:361*t*

Satellite television receivers, p. I:227
SATs, pp. II:166, II:171, II:217, II:293, II:368t
Saudi Arabia, p. IV:184
Saum, William, p. IV:118
Saunders, Dr. Cicely, pp. III:376, III:378
Savage Inequalities: Children in America's Schools, p. II:221
Savings, pp. I:347t
Savings & loans fraud, p. IV:109
Saw palmetto, p. III:75
Schistosomiasis, p. III:326
Schizophrenia, pp. III:247-249
Schlafly, Phyllis, p. II:223
Schlosser, Eric, p. III:110
Scholastic Aptitude Test
— *See:* SATs
Scholastic Assessment Test
— *See:* SATs
School-based health centers, pp. III:102-104, III:464t
School choice, pp. II:239-240
School finances, pp. II:220-221, II:379t
School performance, p. II:385t
School-to-Work Opportunities Act, p. II:262
School vending machines, p. II:310
School vouchers, pp. II:241-242
School-year duration, p. II:254
Schools, p. I:34
— bullying, pp. II:249-250
— by type, pp. II:211, II:222-223, II:231, II:233, II:237
— crime, pp. IV:128, IV:130, II:245
— expulsions, pp. IV:131-132
— problems perceived by teachers, p. II:198
— problems perceived by the general public, p. II:199
— youth gangs, pp. IV:42-43
Schools and Staffing Survey, pp. II:191, II:198
Science museums, p. I:229
Sciences, advanced
— *See:* Advanced sciences
Scientific and technical services
— *See:* professional, scientific, and technical services
Scientology, pp. II:134-135, I:252-253
Scofflaws, p. IV:266
Search engines, p. I:278
Seasonal workers, p. I:46
Seconal, p. III:129
Second homes, p. I:194
Secondary education, pp. I:11, II:189-190
Secondary school teachers, pp. I:58-59, I:61-62
Secret Service, p. IV:228
Secretaries, stenographers, and typists, pp. I:32, I:61-62
Secularism, pp. I:252-253
Securities and Exchange Commission, pp. IV:84-85, IV:109
Security measures, p. I:281
Sedatives, pp. III:119, III:128
Seeds, p. I:185
Segregation, p. II:345t
Seizure disorders, pp. III:229, III:231
Self-employment income, p. I:145
Senior citizens, pp. III:187-188

Senior citizens continued:
— *See also:* Aging population
— *See also:* Elderly population
— living arrangements, pp. III:193-194
— media images, pp. III:221-222
— Medicaid expenditures, p. III:220
— Medicare expenditures, p. III:219
— quality of life, p. III:210
— risk behaviors, pp. III:489t
— suicides, p. III:260
Sentencing, pp. IV:108-110, IV:333t
SEOG, p. II:273
Sepsis, bacterial
— *See:* Bacterial sepsis
September 11, 2001
— airline passenger screening, p. IV:232
— corporate responses, p. I:171
— deaths, p. IV:190
— food-borne terrorism, p. III:112
— genetic engineering, p. III:106
— Immigration and Naturalization Service, p. IV:227
— racial profiling, p. IV:224
— terrorism, pp. IV:177, IV:182
— timeline, pp. IV:192-194
— workplace safety, p. I:150
Septicemia, pp. III:4-5, III:7-8
Service occupations
— employment, pp. I:31-32, I:291t
— independent contractors, pp. I:69-70
— injuries in the workplace, p. I:156
Serviceman's Readjustment Act, pp. II:150, II:273
— *See also:* GI Bill
Services industry, pp. II:256-257, II:262
— employment, pp. I:1, I:3-4, I:6
— productivity, p. I:102
Seventh Day Adventists, p. II:132
Severance pay, p. I:134
Sewing, p. I:218
Sewing machine operators, p. I:54
Sex-based crimes, pp. IV:10, IV:101
Sex-based discrimination
— case resolutions, pp. I:163, I:167
— charges filed with the EEOC, p. I:161
Sex education, p. III:103
Sex information, pp. III:282-283, III:505t
Sex offenders, pp. IV:121, IV:336t
Sex on TV, p. I:231
Sexes
— *See also:* Females
— *See also:* Males
— *See also:* Men
— *See also:* Women
— deaths, pp. II:17, II:21
— earnings, pp. I:71, II:295
— educational attainment, pp. II:258-259, I:262, II:283, II:285, I:318t
— employment, pp. I:65-67, I:69, I:174, I:298t I:355t
— high school athletes, p. I:362t

Special education programs continued:
  407*t*
Special education teachers, pp. I:22, I:24-25, I:58
Special units of police departments, pp. IV:206-207
Special weapons and tactics (SWAT), p. IV:211
Specialized museums, p. I:229
Specialty hospitals, p. III:365
Speech impairments, pp. III:229-231, II:298-299
Speed, p. III:124
The Spice Channel, p. III:280
Spinal problems, pp. III:227-228
Sponges, p. II:15
Sports, pp. I:199-200
— high school athletes, p. I:204
— injuries, p. I:205
— marketing, p. I:213
— online auctions, p. I:286
— professional, p. I:210
— scholarships, p. I:206
— supplies, p. I:185
— teenagers, pp. I:201-202, I:361*t*
— television, p. I:211
Sports Illustrated, p. I:213
Spouse abuse, p. IV:10
Sprains, p. I:155
Springfield (OR), p. IV:129
Stalking, pp. IV:119-120, IV:336*t*
Standardized tests, pp. II:168, II:170, II:218, II:367*t*
Stanford Sleep Disorders Clinic, p. III:144
Stanford University, pp. II:268, II:280, II:294
Starter pistols, p. II:245
State and local grants, p. II:279
State Department, p. IV:183
State government, pp. I:1, I:9-10, II:211, I:256, I:292*t*
State mental hospitals, p. III:264
State prisoners, pp. IV:236, IV:369*t*
State University of New York at Buffalo, p. II:292
STDs
— *See:* Sexually transmitted diseases
Steamfitters
— *See:* plumbers, pipefitters, and steamfitters
Stenographers and typists
— *See:* Secretaries, stenographers, and typists
Stents, pp. III:25, III:151
Sterility, p. II:14
Sterilization, pp. III:304-305
Steroid use, p. III:104
Stimulants, pp. IV:11, III:119, III:128, IV:151-152, III:173
Stock performance, p. I:103
Stomach cancer, pp. III:67-68, III:156
Streams, pp. III:323, III:325
Street gangs, p. IV:44
Street, Picabo, p. I:209
Stress
— cancer, p. III:161
— morning habits, pp. III:139-140
— nighttime habits, pp. III:143-144
— noonday habits, pp. III:141-142

Stress continued:
— risk behaviors, p. III:108
— vacations, p. III:145
Strikes, p. I:210
Strokes, p. II:18
— *See also:* Cerebrovascular disease
— Baby Boom generation, p. III:69
— causes of death, pp. III:2-5, III:8-9
— disabilities, pp. III:227, III:243, III:401
— women, pp. III:12-13
Students
— *See also:* Children
— *See also:* Juveniles
— *See also:* Teenagers
— *See also:* Youth
— deaths in school, pp. II:243-244
— disabilities, p. II:258
— financial assistance, pp. II:395*t*
— indebtedness, pp. II:275, II:277-278, III:414
— LEP, pp. II:306-307
— limited English proficiency, p. II:306
Students Against Drunk Driving, p. IV:113
Subsidized commuting, p. I:135
Substance abuse, pp. IV:53, III:102, III:411, III:471*t*
Substance Abuse and Mental Health Services Administration (SAMHSA), pp. IV:157, IV:159, III:412
Substance use, pp. III:121-123
Suburbs, pp. II:27-28, II:30, II:329*t*
Sudden Infant Death Syndrome, pp. III:10, III:437*t*
— *See also:* Crib death
— *See also:* SIDS
Sudden Sniffing Death Syndrome, p. III:120
Sugars, pp. III:20-21
Suicide, p. III:35
Suicides, pp. III:431*t*
— aging population, pp. III:204, III:261
— causes of death, pp. III:4, III:8, II:21, III:131
— Columbine High School, p. II:243
— firearms-related, p. IV:39
— men, pp. II:18, III:34-36, III:260
— mental health, pp. III:248-249
— school-based health centers, p. III:103
— terrorists, p. IV:190
Suicides, altruistic
— *See:* Altruistic suicides
Suicides, anomic
— *See:* Anomic suicides
Suicides, egoistic
— *See:* Egoistic suicides
Suicides, fatalistic
— *See:* Fatalistic suicides
Sulfa drugs, pp. III:2, II:22
Sulfur dioxide, pp. III:316-317
Sunbeam Corp., p. IV:84
Super Nintendo, p. IV:145
Supplemental Educational Opportunity Grants
— *See:* SEOG
Supplemental income, p. II:183
Supplemental pay, p. I:129

Texas continued:
— standardized tests, p. II:218
— vacation spending, p. I:190
— youth gangs, p. IV:138
Thai population, p. II:74
Thailand, p. III:42
Theatres, pp. I:185, I:217, I:224-225
Theft, p. II:245
— arrests, pp. IV:68-70
— by property stolen, p. IV:76
— correction expenditures, p. IV:249
— crimes reported to the police, p. IV:373*t*
— juveniles, p. IV:136
— property crime, pp. IV:4, IV:7-8
Theology degrees conferred, pp. II:286, II:290
Therapeutic procedures, pp. III:152-154
They Say You're Crazy, p. III:170
Third International Mathematics and Science Study
— *See:* TIMSS
Third National Incidence Study of Child Abuse and Neglect, p. IV:107
Thomas, Clarence, pp. I:162, I:165
Thomas, Timothy, p. IV:204
Thompson, Tommy, pp. III:73, III:112
Thyroid gland surgeries, p. III:151
Ticket prices, pp. I:212-213, I:222, I:364*t*
Time for Kids, p. II:249
Time for Life: Surprising Ways Americans Use Their Time, p. I:181
Timelines
— drug-control legislation, p. IV:12
— hate crimes, p. IV:286
— law enforcement, pp. IV:197-198
— September 11, 2001, pp. IV:192-194
— terrorism, pp. IV:178-179
TIMSS, pp. II:188, II:195, II:253-254
Title IX, pp. I:204, II:308
Tobacco advertising, p. III:138
Tobacco consumption, pp. IV:12, IV:148, IV:352*t*
Tobacco control programs, pp. III:102, III:408-409
Tomatoes, p. III:87
Tonsillitis, p. III:229
Tort reform, p. III:417
Total Fertility Rate, p. III:295
Total Fertility Rates, pp. II:5-8
Touch football, p. I:202
Toxemia, p. III:23
Toxic Shock Syndrome, pp. III:61-62, III:444*t*
Toyota Camry, p. IV:71
Toys, pp. II:66, I:286
Toys and sports supplies, p. I:185
Tracheal cancer, p. III:67
Track and field, p. I:209
Trade, pp. I:6, II:256-257, II:262
Traditional workers, pp. I:71-72
Traffic deaths, pp. II:18, IV:115-116
Train robbery, p. IV:245
Tranquilizers, pp. III:119, III:128, IV:151
Trans fat, p. III:109

Transportation
— assaults in the workplace, pp. I:157-158
— child rearing costs, pp. II:66-67
— college costs, p. II:271
— injuries in the workplace, p. I:156
— occupational fatalities, p. I:151
Transportation and material moving occupations, pp. I:20, I:43, I:296*t*
— *See also:* material moving occupations
Transportation and public utilities, pp. I:6, I:292*t*
Transportation and warehousing, pp. I:104-105
Transportation Security Administration, p. IV:233
Traumatic brain injury, p. II:298
Travel, pp. I:190-192
Travel agencies, pp. I:194, I:196-197, I:360*t*
Treadmill exercise, p. I:200
Treason, p. IV:245
Tricyclic antidepressants, p. III:64
Trigonometry, p. II:259
Trimox, pp. III:166-167
Trinidad and Tobago, p. II:163
Triplets, pp. III:39, III:299-300
Truancy, p. IV:101
The Truly Disadvantaged, p. II:53
Trust fund assets of Medicare, p. III:528*t*
Tuberculosis, pp. III:2-3, III:58-59
— cases and rates, pp. III:442*t*
— foreign countries, pp. III:332-334
Tufts University, pp. III:175, II:294
Tuition and fees, pp. II:151, II:269-270, II:272, II:394*t* III:539*t*
— Consumer Price Index, p. II:268
— medical school, p. II:277
— public universities, p. II:279
Tularemia, p. III:392
Turkey, p. I:187
Turkmenistan, p. II:163
Turning the Corner on Father Absence in Black America, p. II:53
Twinkie Defense, p. IV:276
Twins, pp. III:39, III:299-300
Two-parent households, pp. II:46, II:67
Typhoid fever, pp. III:58-59, III:442*t*
Typists
— *See also:* word processors and typists p. I:54
U. S. Customs Service, p. IV:329*t*
Uganda, p. III:332
Ukraine, p. II:163
Ultrasound, p. III:152
Umbilical cord complications, p. III:10
Uncertified teachers, p. II:187
Underemployment, p. I:57
Unemployment, pp. IV:53, I:145
UNESCO, p. II:250
UNICOR, p. IV:255
Uniform Crime Report, pp. IV:3-5, IV:7, IV:9, IV:14, IV:139
Uninsured population, pp. III:384-385
Unions, pp. I:1, I:14, I:16, I:294*t*
Unitarian Universalism, pp. II:134-135, I:252-253

United Church of Christ, pp. II:132-135

United Government Services, pp. III:377-378

United Kingdom, pp. II:163, III:334

United Methodist Church, pp. II:136-138

United Nations building, p. IV:184

United Nations Human Rights Committee, p. III:218

United Republic of Tanzania, p. III:332

U.S. Administration on Aging, p. III:199

U.S. Army, p. II:292

U.S. Army Reserves, p. II:278

U.S. Customs Service, pp. IV:99, IV:226-227

U.S. Department of Education, p. I:61

U.S. Department of Energy, p. III:105

U.S. Department of Justice, p. IV:3

U.S. Navy, p. II:278

U.S. Office of Dietary Supplements, p. III:75

U.S. Surgeon General, p. III:107

University of Colorado system, p. II:280

University of Michigan, pp. II:57, I:183, III:257

University of Utah Drug Information Service, p. III:389

Unsafe School Choice Option, p. IV:129

Up the IRS, Inc., p. IV:181

Urban Policy Institute, p. IV:134

Urban population, pp. II:27, II:329t

Urdu, p. II:76

Urinary tract cancer, pp. III:3, III:156

Urinary tract surgeries, p. III:150

Urologists, p. III:275

Uruguay, p. II:163

USDA, pp. III:84, III:87-90, III:109, III:113

Usef, Ramzi, p. IV:183

Utah, p. IV:276

Uterine cancer, pp. III:19, III:68, III:158, III:161, III:168

Utilities, pp. I:104-105

Uzbekistan, p. II:163

Vacation homes, pp. I:194, I:359t

Vacation spending, p. I:190

Vacation time, pp. I:128, I:133, I:187, I:189, I:191-192, I:359t

Vacations, pp. III:145-146

Vaccinations, pp. III:94-95

Vaccines, pp. III:389-392, III:463t

Vaccinia (cell culture), p. III:392

Vagrancy, pp. IV:101, IV:106-107, IV:112

Valium, p. III:129

Valley State Prison, p. IV:243

Vancomycin-Resistant Enterococci
— See: VRE

Vandalism, pp. IV:80, IV:105

Vanderbilt University, p. II:280

Varicella, p. III:96

Vasotec, p. III:167

VCRs, p. I:226

Vegetables, p. III:83

Venezuelan encephalitis, p. III:392

Vermont, pp. II:64-65, III:338

Very-low birth weight, p. III:310

Veterans, p. II:150

Veterans Administration, pp. I:131, III:264

Veterinary assistants and laboratory animal caretakers, p. I:52

Veterinary medicine degrees conferred, pp. II:286, II:290

Viagra, pp. III:267, III:275-276, III:504t

Victim assistance, p. IV:206

Victimization
— by race/ethnicity, pp. IV:316t
— by sex, race/ethnicity, and income, pp. IV:309t
— children, pp. IV:136, IV:139-140, IV:337t
— homicides, p. IV:35
— household income, pp. IV:31-32
— workplace, p. IV:320t

Video games, pp. IV:144-145, I:227, I:231, I:268, IV:342t

Video products, p. I:185

Video rentals, pp. I:222, I:366t

Video Vigilante, p. IV:125

Videocassette recorders
— See: VCRs

Vietnam, p. III:332

Vietnamese (language), pp. II:76-77

Vietnamese population, p. II:74

Violence in schools, pp. IV:128, II:245

Violent crime, pp. I:151-152, I:351t
— actual crimes reported, pp. IV:4-6
— arrests, pp. IV:16, IV:266, IV:273
— by race/ethnicity, p. IV:52
— by sex, pp. IV:35, IV:135
— crimes reported to the police, p. IV:77
— drug-related, p. IV:13
— firearms-related, p. IV:39
— household income, p. IV:31
— juveniles, p. IV:133
— not included in crime index, pp. IV:9-10
— prisoners, pp. IV:236-237
— rate fluctuation, pp. IV:26-27
— recidivism, p. IV:260
— victimization rates, p. IV:305t

Violent Crime Control and Law Enforcement Act, p. IV:47

Violent Offender Incarceration and Truth-in-Sentencing Incentive Grant (VOITIS) program, pp. IV:250, IV:252

Vioxx, p. III:178

Viral hepatitis, p. III:61

Virginia, pp. II:63, II:187, II:246

Virginia Slims cigarettes, p. III:136

Virtual doctors
— See: Telemedicine

Virtual libraries, p. I:257

Virtual volunteering, p. I:246

Viruses, pp. I:280, III:323

Vision care, p. I:133

Vision impairments, pp. III:203, III:227, III:229, III:231, II:298, III:487t

Vision screenings, p. III:103

Visual arts, p. II:284

Vitamins, p. III:75

VOC
— See: Volatile Organic Chemicals

Vocational education, pp. IV:264, II:392t
— adult education, pp. II:256-257, I:264-265
— by specialization, pp. II:261-262
— credits accumulated, p. II:258

Volatile organic chemicals, pp. III:316, III:318
Volleyball, pp. I:202, I:208-209
Volpe, Justin, p. IV:204
Volunteering, pp. I:233-234, I:369t
— age group, pp. I:239-240, I:370t
— by organization type, pp. I:245-246, I:370t
— by sex, pp. I:236-237
— educational attainment, p. I:238
— race/ethnicity, pp. I:241, I:370t
— work-related organizations, pp. I:245-246
Voter registration, p. II:352t
Voter turnout, pp. II:112, II:355t
— age, pp. II:104, II:353t
— presidential elections, pp. II:96, II:350t
— race/ethnicity, pp. II:106, II:353t
— religion, pp. II:110, II:354t
— women, p. II:102
Vouchers, school, pp. II:241-242
VRE, p. III:330
Wackenhut Corrections, pp. IV:251-253
Wages, pp. I:16, I:120, I:122, I:128, I:295t
— by occupational group, p. II:296
— manufacturing, pp. I:336t
Waiters and waitresses, pp. I:61-62
Wakeboarding, pp. I:200-201
Walking
— 200,
The Wall.org, p. II:145
Walsh, Adam, p. IV:142
War on Drugs
— arrests by race/ethnicity, p. IV:163
— murders, pp. IV:28, IV:30
— Nixon, President Richard, p. IV:147
— timeline, p. IV:12
— wiretapping, p. IV:230
— youth, p. III:118
Washington (DC), pp. II:64, IV:124, IV:132, IV:215
Washington (State), pp. II:63-64, II:246
Waste Management Inc., pp. IV:84, IV:109
Wastewater treatment in selected countries, p. III:326
Watch guards
— See also: guards and watch guards p. I:61
Water pollution, pp. III:315, III:321-325, III:518t
Waterways, pp. III:321-322
Weapons crimes, pp. IV:10, IV:101, IV:104
Weather Underground, p. IV:181
Weaving, pp. I:218-219
Weekend travel, p. I:192
Weight-control habits, p. III:115
Weight machines, pp. I:200, I:202
Welfare clerks, p. I:296t
Welfare Reform Act, p. II:47
Wellness programs, p. I:135
Wesleyans, pp. II:130-131, II:135
West Germany (former), p. II:254
West Paducah (KY), p. IV:129
West Virginia, pp. II:75, II:187, III:369-370, III:409, III:417
Western equine encephalitis, p. III:392
Western Sahara, p. II:30

Western United States, p. III:189
What Works? Questions and Answers About Prison Reform, p. IV:262
White-black death rate ratio, p. II:327t
White collar crime, pp. IV:108-109
White families, p. I:38
White House budget, p. IV:188
White, Dan, p. IV:276
Whites, p. III:28
— abortions, pp. II:12-13, III:321t
— activities of daily living, p. III:204
— arrests, p. IV:53
— births, pp. II:10, III:23, I:40, II:319t
— breastfeeding, p. III:41
— cancer survival rates, pp. III:156-158
— causes of death, pp. III:8-9, II:21, III:24-27, III:32, III:34, III:36, III:43-44
— computer learning opportunities, p. II:263
— correctional population, p. IV:19
— crib death, pp. III:45-46
— deaths, pp. III:15, III:18, II:21
— diseases, pp. III:14, III:18, III:28, III:52, III:54, III:64, III:288-290
— drug arrests, pp. IV:161, IV:163-164
— drug convictions, pp. IV:164-166
— drug use, pp. III:126-127, IV:159-160
— earnings, p. I:71
— educational attainment, pp. I:39, I:112, I:118-119, II:151-153, II:258-259, II:287-290
— employment, pp. I:16, I:30, I:37, I:67-68
— family net worth, p. I:38
— gender distribution, p. II:339t
— homicides, pp. IV:52, IV:217-218
— housing, p. II:35
— income, pp. II:21, I:82-83
— infant mortality, pp. II:21, III:313
— Internet use, pp. I:270-271
— interracial marriages, pp. II:54-55
— juveniles arrested, p. IV:137
— learning disabilities, p. III:66
— life expectancy, pp. II:20, III:47-48, III:403-404
— literacy, pp. II:154, II:159
— low birth weight, pp. III:40, III:308-309
— mammograms, p. III:18
— marriage, pp. II:52-53
— maternal mortality, pp. II:21, III:22
— mathematics proficiency, pp. II:161-162
— Medicare, p. III:380
— physicians, p. III:337
— political-party affiliation, p. II:108
— population, pp. II:24-25
— population mobility, p. II:39
— Population Replacement Rate, p. II:6
— risk behaviors, pp. III:16-17, III:135-136
— risk factors, p. III:20
— single-parent households, p. II:61
— suicides, pp. III:260, III:434t
— Total Fertility Rates, pp. II:6-8
— volunteering, p. I:241

Whites continued:
— voter turnout, p. II:106
Whole language movement, p. II:201
Whole Math Movement, p. II:205
Whole milk, p. III:83
Wholesale and retail buyers (except farm products), p. I:54
Wholesale trade, pp. I:6, I:104-105, I:156, I:292*t*
Whooping Cough, p. III:56
Whyos, p. IV:43
Wiccan, pp. II:134-135
Widowed parents, p. II:59
Willett, Dr. Walter C., pp. III:90, III:109-110
Wilson, Dr. James Q., pp. IV:52, IV:137-138
Wilson, Dr. William Julius, p. II:53
Wiretapping, pp. IV:229-231, IV:366*t*
Wisconsin, pp. IV:122, II:218
Women, p. I:298*t*
— *See also:* Females
— activities of daily living, p. III:204
— age at first marriage, p. II:50
— art purchases, p. I:219
— births, p. III:295
— cancer survival rates, p. III:158
— causes of death, pp. III:6-7, III:12, III:24, III:26, III:30, III:32, III:34, III:36, III:53, III:422*t*
— contraceptive practices, pp. II:14-15, III:514*t*
— cosmetic surgery, pp. III:277, III:279
— creative writing, p. I:219
— deaths, pp. III:15, III:424*t*
— disabled population, pp. III:225, III:236
— diseases, pp. III:13-14, III:18, III:54, III:64, III:116, III:147, III:154, III:160, III:247, III:249, III:262, III:289-290, III:366
— domestic homicides, pp. IV:48-49
— earnings, p. I:71
— educational attainment, pp. I:94, I:262, II:283, II:285
— elderly population, p. III:196
— employment, pp. I:16, I:29-33, I:36, I:65-67, I:69, I:156, I:174-175, II:182, I:262, III:296, III:509*t*
— estrogen, p. II:18
— federal law enforcement personnel, p. IV:226
— household activities, pp. I:181-182
— housing, p. III:195
— income, pp. I:84, I:94
— injuries in the workplace, pp. I:155-156
— Internet use, p. I:276
— life expectancy, pp. II:18-19, III:47
— living arrangements, p. III:192
— mammograms, p. III:18
— Medicare, p. III:380
— modern dance, p. I:219
— occupational fatalities, p. I:156
— online shopping, p. I:277
— physicians, p. III:337
— police officers, p. IV:200
— political-party affiliation, pp. II:100-101
— poverty, pp. I:92-93
— prisoners, pp. IV:18, IV:242
— risk behaviors, pp. III:16-17, III:135-136

Women continued:
— risk factors, p. III:20
— sexual activity, pp. III:269-270
— single-parent households, pp. II:46-47
— specialized museums, p. I:229
— sports, pp. I:206-209, I:363*t*
— state prisons, p. IV:371*t*
— sterility, p. II:14
— suicides, pp. III:260, III:434*t*
— Total Fertility Rate, p. III:295
— violent crime, pp. IV:35-38
— volunteering, pp. I:236-237
— voting in presidential elections, pp. II:102-103
— weaving, p. I:219
Women's Rights Movement, p. I:30
Women's Sports Foundation, p. I:207
Woods, Tiger, p. I:211
Word processors and typists, pp. I:54-55
Work activities, p. I:358*t*
Work hours, pp. I:176-177, I:356*t*
— age groups, p. I:43
— by sex, pp. I:174-175, I:355*t*
— foreign countries, p. I:187
— illegal labor, p. I:43
Work-related injuries and illnesses, p. I:350*t*
Work-related organizations, pp. I:245-246
Work-study programs, p. II:273
Worker shortages, p. I:59
Worker's compensation, pp. I:145, I:153
Workforce participation, pp. III:295-296, I:298*t*
Workforce population
— age groups, p. I:20
— Baby Boomers, p. I:21
— by sex, pp. I:29-30
— earnings, p. I:342*t*
— educational attainment, p. I:56
— fertility rates, p. I:40
— foreign-born, p. I:41
— high school education, p. I:57
— national health care expenditures, p. I:342*t*
— race/ethnicity, pp. I:29-30, I:35, I:41
— unions, p. I:294
Working for Children and Families, p. II:226
Working parents, p. I:183
Workplace assaults, pp. I:157-158
Workplace discrimination, pp. I:158-159
Workplace harassment, p. I:159
Workplace illnesses, pp. I:153, I:349*t*
Workplace injuries, pp. I:153, I:155-156, I:349*t*
Workplace issues, pp. I:164-165, I:351*t*
Workplace safety, pp. I:151-152, I:351*t*
World Church of the Creator, p. IV:288
World Health Organization, pp. III:316, III:332
World Sports Exchange, p. IV:118
World Trade Center, pp. IV:179, IV:183-184, IV:195, I:283
World Trade Organization, p. I:192
WorldCom, p. IV:85
Worldwide Web, pp. I:97, I:233, I:280
Worms, p. I:280